BEAUTIFUL LAND OF THE SKY

Beautiful Land of the Sky

John Muir's Forgotten Eastern Counterpart,
Harlan P. Kelsey

Pioneering Our Native Plants
and Eastern National Parks

Loren M. Wood

iUniverse LLC
Bloomington

Beautiful Land of the Sky
John Muir's Forgotten Eastern Counterpart, Harlan P. Kelsey

Copyright © 2013 Loren M. Wood

All rights reserved. No part of this book may be used or reproduced by any means, graphic, electronic, or mechanical, including photocopying, recording, taping or by any information storage retrieval system without the written permission of the publisher except in the case of brief quotations embodied in critical articles and reviews.

iUniverse books may be ordered through booksellers or by contacting:

iUniverse
1663 Liberty Drive
Bloomington, IN 47403
www.iuniverse.com
1-800-Authors (1-800-288-4677)

Because of the dynamic nature of the Internet, any web addresses or links contained in this book may have changed since publication and may no longer be valid. The views expressed in this work are solely those of the author and do not necessarily reflect the views of the publisher, and the publisher hereby disclaims any responsibility for them.

Any people depicted in stock imagery provided by Thinkstock are models, and such images are being used for illustrative purposes only.

Certain stock imagery © Thinkstock

ISBN: 978-1-4759-9445-2 (sc)
ISBN: 978-1-4759-9446-9 (hc)
ISBN: 978-1-4759-9447-6 (e)

Library of Congress Control Number: 2013910820

Printed in the United States of America.

iUniverse rev. date: 9/26/2013

"I feel that I have come to know Harlan Kelsey as though he had told me his story in person; indeed, when I reached the inevitable end of his life I was brought to tears, and at the end of the manuscript I felt somewhat bereft for having stepped back out of Kelsey's world."
Erin Perry, MFA in creative writing

Mount Mitchell. Southern Appalachian National Park Committee. July 30, 1924. Standing from left, Kelsey (pointing), Welsh, Temple, Smith. Seated, Gregg. Photo courtesy of Clarke Haywood.

Contents

Provocation 1

Part I—Horticulturalist: Native Plants

Chapter 1: Even as a Child (1872–89) 7
Soak in the environment that shaped the man-to-be.

>A Home in the Wilderness; Childhood and Horticulture; Building a Town; Surrounded by Mountain Folk; Moonshine Wars; Poor but Rich: Prairie Life; City Folk Arrive; Harbison Arrives; Moving On

Chapter 2: Emerging Entrepreneur (1890–96) 61
Witness the birth of his tireless crusade for native plants.

>Cranberry; Linville; Battle Lines; Kelsey Highlands Nursery; Native Plant Promotion; Plant Introductions; Lumbermen; Nagging Issues

Chapter 3: Broadening Scope (1897–1911) 99
Behold the leap from primitive settings to elite society, and the beginnings of insatiable desire to fill unmet civic needs.

>Tremont Street; The Appalachian Mountain Club; The North Shore and Florence Low; Salem and the "Gold Coast"; City Planning; Conservation; Nursery Business; Landscape Architecture; Family Distress

Chapter 4: Gaining Stature (1912–20) 143
Follow the ladder of ascension to horticultural preeminence.

> Historic Boxford; The Boxford Nursery; More City Planning; The Salem Fire; Rebuilding the City; New Holland; Nurseryman; War Clouds; Family Matters; *Standardized Plant Names*; American Association of Nurserymen; Tipping Point

Part II—Preservationist: National Parks

Chapter 5: National Stage (1921–28) 213
Observe the immediate transition from horticultural preeminence to preservation hero.

> Appalachian Mountain Club; The Appalachian Trail; National Parks; Southern Appalachian National Park Committee; Race with the Lumbermen; Yellowstone; Cosmos Club; Nursery Matters

Chapter 6: Trials and Triumphs (1929–40). 297
Switch back and forth from national park successes, to economic failures, to universal praise.

> The Spofford Barnes House; Winding Up the Commission; Collaborator; Depression; Ongoing Horticultural Issues; Why Not a White Mountains National Park; Tension in the Parks; National Parkways; Presidential Range Skyline Road; Old Derby Wharf; Bankruptcy; Horticultural Matters; Destruction; Recognition

Chapter 7: Unfinished Business (1941–58) 429
Feel the pain of unfulfilled objectives that remain unfulfilled to this day.

> *Standardized Plant Names*; Mount Cammerer; Wartime; Grandfather Mountain; Grandfather Mountain—The MacRae Years; Grandfather Mountain—The Hugh Morton Years; Moving On; Roadside Horticulture; Mississippi River Parkway Survey; Final Strokes

Chapter 8: Legacy 553
Confront comparison with John Muir. Hear a call to action for permanent recognition.

      Obligation; Remedy

Epilogue (1959–present) 573
Step back out of the first half of the twentieth century to developments of the second half.

      Changing Times; End Times

Author's Note 581

Selected Bibliography 585

References 589

Index 599

Provocation

The subtitle, *John Muir's Forgotten Eastern Counterpart, Harlan P. Kelsey,* is purposely provocative. It suggests that Harlan P. Kelsey is in the same league with the supreme icon of western wilderness and preservation—John Muir.

This is the John Muir who helped father four national parks, whose name adorns three mountains, a glacier, three trails, a section of a state highway, a woodland, a wilderness area, a beach, countless schools (including a college), numerous buildings and parks, a national historic site, a US postage stamp, and the 2005 California state quarter.

He was awarded three honorary doctoral degrees: from Harvard, Yale, and Cal/Berkeley. Even this impressive list is incomplete, but you get the idea. Muir's name and at least some of his accomplishments as the preservation hero of the West are widely acclaimed.

In contrast, Harlan P. Kelsey is an obscure, forgotten figure. Ask anyone, "Who is the preservation hero of the East?" One person in ten thousand might give you a name and would probably be wrong. I contend it is Kelsey and have the evidence to demonstrate it.

Muir helped found four national parks in the West. Kelsey helped birth four national parks in the East. Kelsey's forte was horticulture, which is what sets apart the eastern national parks. In the West the emphasis is on geological marvels (e.g., Yosemite National Park, which has three million visitors per year). In the East the marvels are horticultural (e.g., Great Smoky Mountains National Park, which has nine million visitors per year).

Kelsey's preeminence as a horticulturalist made him a natural leader in the push for national parks east of the Mississippi. This pioneering work spanned thirty years, during which he served as both a commissioner and collaborator, under four different directors of the National Park Service.

Consider Secretary of the Interior Wilbur's words to Kelsey in January 1932:

> Director Albright of the National Park Service has told me of your work ... over a period of years in connection with the establishment of the eastern national parks ... carrying with it the realization of the importance of saving, while they still could be saved, such great primitive areas as the Everglades, the Great Smokies, Isle Royale, and the like. ... None of these projects, I am confident, would have come to their present satisfying status had you not stepped in at critical moments and cheerfully given of the best that was in you. The fact that we could rely on your ripe experience, judgment, and enthusiastic interest at such critical points has contributed more to their success than you probably will realize, and for this I want to give you my most cordial thanks.

A half century ago he was nationally acclaimed by a veritable avalanche of the preeminent horticultural and conservation associations in America. They extolled, "Horticulture and all related fields will forever be indebted to him for his contributions to their advancement."

Kelsey was the trailblazer and for a half century the leader in pioneering native plants for the American landscape. The aristocrats of today's gardens are the plants he promoted from the high southern Appalachian Mountains. Back then, imported exotics were everywhere. Today, some say exotics need an excuse to be in the American garden. Additionally, he was a leading participant in bringing all of America to our native plants in their finest original setting—the Smokies—the zenith of horticultural biomass and diversity in America.

The Mountain Flora District of western North Carolina, regionally known as the "Land of the Sky," was called *On-tee-o-o-rah*, or "hills of the sky," by the early Cherokee Indians. The land envelops you with its horticultural marvels: massive old trees, deep forest smells, waterfalls saturating the adjacent flora, and riotous color with the spring bloom. When you reach the occasional overlook, only then does the sky become a presence, as you gaze out and down across seemingly endless undulating mountains. This is the setting that nourished Kelsey's start as America's youngest nurseryman at age twelve. It impelled his lifelong drive to elevate native plants to preeminence in America, and his crowning finish as "Dean of American Nurserymen."

Beautiful Land of the Sky chronicles Kelsey's journey from the humblest of beginnings to a national prominence that bordered on near adulation. Step by step, we find remarkable parallels in the odysseys of Muir and Kelsey. While this is a biography of Kelsey, not Muir, we will take every opportunity to drop in as the chronology allows, comparing the similarities, differences, and accomplishments of the two men.

In the end, the findings provide a thesis on why history has treated these two men so differently, and unjustly—one still a national hero, and the other now forgotten. It need not remain this way, and I offer remedies. And a call to action.

Part I—Horticulturalist: Native Plants

SHORTIA GALACIFOLIA. (See page 22.)

Chapter 1

Even as a Child

A Home in the Wilderness

March 1875. The three men had left behind them the Franklin–Walhalla wagon road to the Short Off community. They hiked southerly to drop into the gorge of the Sugartown River, which now climbed steeply in a southeasterly direction to gain the heights of the Sugartown Highlands. They were on the old Cherokee trail. It was known only to the local mountain people, rarely traveled, and the path was torturous and difficult. Anyone not familiar with it would easily lose the trail and struggle upward through the tangle of the deep surrounding woods.

In the lead was Charlie Jenks, a nineteen-year-old local. For the last three years he had been living, fishing, hunting deer, and trapping bear all across the Sugartown Highlands, and knew it intimately. Behind him were two men, recently from Kansas, both vigorous and hardened by life outdoors on the western prairies. They were Samuel Truman Kelsey and Clinton Carter Hutchinson, close friends looking for a site to establish a new town. They had left their families out in Kansas until provision could be made for them to come east. S. T. Kelsey and his wife, Katy, had five children: three boys and two girls.

One of the boys was two-year-old Harlan Page Kelsey. This is his story, but at age two little can be written about him personally. However, no one can understand him in later life without a detailed knowledge of the early forces that shaped him, starting at age two. For now we must focus on his father, S. T. Kelsey, who will simply be called STK for brevity, which in fact he preferred and usually used as his name. His son, Harlan, will be Kelsey, always, where Kelsey is used.

Why Jenks had chosen to guide them up the Cherokee trail instead of by the wagon road remains a mystery. It wasn't any shorter, but it certainly exposed the climbers to more dramatic scenery. Edward King, a Massachusetts journalist exploring the reconstructed South for *Scribner's Monthly*, had been guided up this trail two years earlier. His description talks of dropping down into the river gorge, hanging onto tree branches, swinging down to reach ledges, and being drawn through the dense laurel and trees by the roar of the Lower Sugar Fork Falls. When finally looking up at the hundred-foot cascade of the falls, King was awed by the blinding clouds of spray that saturated the tall trees and foliage covering the canyon walls for hundreds of feet up both sides. Climbing the falls, the trail traced up the river course, crossing the thundering torrent again and again, with the woods occasionally offering an easier grade through the massive trees of the primeval forest. Reaching a pass in the mountains, the trail opened onto the edge of cliffs where the river plunged over the upper falls of the Sugar Fork River. The falls were then and are still called "Dry Falls" because the cliff angles inward behind the massive curtain of water, allowing "dry" passage behind the falls to the other side of the river. This was even more dramatic than the earlier lower falls. From Dry Falls it is only three more miles to the Highlands plateau, after which the trail was only obstructed by swampy holes and gnarled tree roots. Now bearing northeasterly, the trail crossed the plateau ending at James Wright's farmhouse underneath Short Off Mountain.

King's account of the climb up the Cherokee trail emphasizes the river and the spectacular waterfalls. It is quite probable that STK's eyes were riveted not on the show of the river, but on the deep virgin forest through which they passed. He grew up in the forests of western New York state, became a nurseryman in Illinois, and went to Kansas to plant trees on the windswept prairies. He knew trees. But these trees defied even his imagination. "Tree-like Rhododendrons, Flame Azaleas and Mountain Laurels, six feet diameter Tulip Trees and eight feet diameter Hemlocks."[1] Never had he laid eyes on anything like this.

Jenks had called Wright's house home during his three years on the plateau, and there the three men found refuge as night fell after the long, exhausting day on the Cherokee trail. From this "headquarters," STK and Hutchinson explored the plateau with Jenks as their companion. This turned out to be the end of their long journey from Kansas. They had reached North Carolina on February 18, 1875. By wagon, mule, and on foot they had explored some six hundred miles along the Blue Ridge Mountains of western North Carolina in late February and early March 1875, looking for the perfect location to found a new town.[2]

STK and Hutchinson were no strangers to the process of founding new towns.

Shortly before the Civil War, C. C. Hutchinson had cofounded the town of Ottawa, Kansas, and built Ottawa University on twenty thousand acres of deeded Indian land. In June 1865 the university called in STK as a horticultural expert and professor and asked him to lay out and improve their lands. He had no sooner started planting and caring for forests, orchards, and hedges than he had to stop. Through an unfortunate mismanagement of Indian affairs, much of the university land that had been donated by the Ottawa Indians was returned to the donors, and the improvement project was necessarily abandoned. There had been time, however, for him to court Katy Ricksecker, a Baptist minister's daughter. They were married on October 1, 1866.

Now with family and no job, STK partnered with J. H. Whetstone in the purchase of the Pomona Project—12,000 acres of unimproved upland prairie about fifteen miles west of Ottawa. Quoting STK, "The improvement work devolved upon me and I took it up with high hopes and expectations. Selecting a section adjoining the town site on the East for a home, I built a house and became the first citizen of Pomona and Mrs. K. truly 'the first Lady of the land' ... Roads were located on all section lines, and Osage orange hedges were planted, except on the town site, around every quarter section, as soon as the ground could be prepared and the plants grown. This required about 100 miles of hedge and over 500,000 plants." And again the unexpected happened. The "Gold Panic" of 1869 brought the economy crashing down, halted the settling of Pomona, and bankrupted Kelsey. His land was gone, and he was deeply in debt, but he must have kept his house in Pomona. We have no record of the family's domestic life during this period leading to the birth of the twins, Harlan and Harry, in 1872, except that they were born in Pomona. He did, however, get a job working for the Atchison, Topeka & Santa Fe Railroad for two years (the exact dates are unclear), at a salary of $200 per month, so he could pay off his residual debt.

STK was active with C. C. Hutchinson in the founding of Hutchinson, Kansas, in 1871. Hutchinson rode a Santa Fe train to Newton, Kansas, in the fall of 1871. A. F. Homer, STK, and Hutchinson rode west on horseback to find Section 13, Township 23, Range 6, West: the site picked by Hutchinson for his town. The original town site, near the Arkansas River and bisected by Cow Creek, was roughly one square mile, bounded today by Avenue G north to Fourth Avenue, and from Plum to Monroe. Legend tells it that, lacking wooden stakes on the treeless prairie, the lots were marked with buffalo bones. For a time, the community was called "Temperance City," a reflection of Mr. Hutchinson's Baptist beliefs. By the next year, Hutchinson was incorporated as a third-class city with six hundred residents and became the Reno county seat.[3] They certainly wasted no time with this smashing success of a new town.

Now, shift back to North Carolina and the Sugartown Highlands. On March 6, 1875, STK and Hutchinson stood with Jenks on the summit of Satulah Mountain at the south side of the plateau. Jenks pointed out far below the best location for their dream of a town, surrounded by peaks, a mile and a half wide and reaching three miles north toward Short Off. In short order Hutchinson put up $1,678 of borrowed money to purchase 839 acres, about one and one-third square miles, from William Dobson. The deed to Hutchinson was dated March 1, 1875. The new town would be called Highlands, and they commenced work on it March 29, 1875.

Why? With the town of Hutchinson, Kansas, such a success, and hordes of homesteaders streaming westward, why would STK and Hutchinson pull up stakes and move east to start all over again in North Carolina? The answer is mosquitoes. Malaria was pervasive with the Kansas settlers who naturally lived near water, streams, and rivers containing backwaters and stagnant pools even during dry spells. Harlan Kelsey explains: "In the spring of 1875 when both my twin brother and I were nearly three years old, we left Kansas (having been born Jay-Hawkers) to escape 'chills and fever,' as malaria was then called, to regain our health and that of our families in the high ozone laden southern-most plateau of the Blue Ridge range, in Macon County, North Carolina."[4] Founding of the earlier Kansas towns was predicated on inducing the stream of westward-bound homesteaders to stop and settle on the land STK and Hutchinson would sell them. Highlands was different—it was to be a health-and-pleasure resort, where people could escape the summer heat and enjoy the healthfulness of the atmosphere at four thousand feet of altitude. People were not streaming in. They would have to be persuaded to come and, of course, settle on the land STK and Hutchinson would sell them.

Speculation on the motivation of STK and Hutchinson has produced a number of theories. They are neatly summarized in Gertrude Vogt McIntosh's book, *Highlands, North Carolina: A Walk into the Past.*[5]

Three different stories are told: (1) they believed the plateau could become a health resort because of the high altitude and clean, cool air, and eventually many people did come here as a result of the promotion of that idea; (2) STK had read an article by Colonel Silas McDowell about a thermal belt near the plateau, where frost is slight. As a horticulturist, STK was very interested in that report and believed he could develop a nursery business in the area; and (3) probably the most commonly held story is that STK and Hutchinson drew two lines across a map of the United States—one from Chicago, Illinois, to Savannah, Georgia, the other from New York, New York, to New Orleans, Louisiana. They believed that where the two lines intersected, a geographical center of the eastern United States was indicated and could be developed into a great population center, if commerce and travel were promoted.

Certainly reason number one aligns best with Harlan Kelsey's recollection of coming to escape malaria in Kansas. As for reason two, one wonders why STK didn't use Colonel McDowell's article among the voluminous testimonials he crammed into the promotional brochures he sent throughout the country. His brochure did use an 1867 letter from a General Clingman, writing to the president of the American Agricultural and Mineral Land Company in New York. It gave a long and very favorable account of the physical attributes of the area. As for the third reason, the intersecting lines on the map, it is the most popular one in current use in Highlands, but at this point in the author's research, no source documents have been found to support it.

It had been STK's habit in Ottawa, Kansas, to keep a daily diary, "Record of Weather and Work." This was interrupted for many years but commenced again in the same ledger book in Highlands on September 10, 1875. He prefaced the diary with a general summary of activities for the period from his February arrival to September 9.

> I came to the State of North Carolina Feb. 18, 1875 in company with C.C. Hutchinson. About the last of March we bought 830

acres of land on the Sugartown Highlands for $2.00 an acre and commenced work on it March 29th. Before purchasing we traveled about 600 miles over the mountains & along the Blue Ridge to select a location. On the land we purchased there was an old abandoned field of about 15 acres on which the brush had been cleared & trees deadened & about 50 old neglected & nearly dead apple trees from 2 to 10 inches in diameter badly covered with moss & infested with borers. During the Spring & Summer we cleared up & put into crops about 20 acres & fenced in 100 acres more for pasture. Crops all put in very late. The garden was lightly manured. The rest of the land had no manure. Apple trees have grown finely & have a fair crop and are now looking well. During the Spring I dug out & killed all the borers. Scraped off the moss & all dead bark & pruned out the dead wood & superfluous limbs. About the first of June I washed them thoroughly with soap.

The season has been very wet so that I could not give as thorough cultivation as I wished. Most of the crops were worked but twice. 4 acres of oats turned out I should judge 40 bushels. All early garden vegetables did well & late are doing well. Early cabbages, turnips, potatoes, radishes, peas, beans & have produced finely.

I have built a house costing about $350, barn costing about $100 & our families came on from Kansas in May in care of C.C. Hutchinson, I'm staying here to look after business & get ready for them. My family moved from Mr. S.W. Hills [down in Horse Cove] where they have been boarding to our new house on the Highlands June 17, 1875.

Now his daily entries start:

Sept
- 10 Clear through the day. Men at work on the road. I am crippled with a lame back, which I sprained last Monday.
- 11 Cloudy all day with East wind.
- 12 Sunday. Cloudy all day. East wind with a little drizzling rain.
- 13 Heavy fog this morning. Clear most of day East wind. Had 3 men cutting weeds in the garden & among potatoes & turnips.

And so it went day after day after day, uninterrupted for the next seven years.

Sept
- 17 Cloudy all day. Wind N.W. Heavy rain from 10 to 12 am & drizzling rain by spells during pm. Commenced cutting the Buckwheat & hauling rails. Cut some brush on C.C. Hutchinson's house sight. Cut trees and burned brush on my grounds. Finished sowing grass seed for lawn about my house.

September 18–24 are typical entries. Then a surprising entry!

- 25 Cloudy. Drizzling rain by spells. Moved the kitchen. Closed a trade with C.C. Hutchinson for his entire interest in the Highlands purchase & he goes back to Kansas.[6]

Schaffner clarifies this turn of events with Hutchinson. "During the first summer he helped [STK] clear land before departing again for Kansas in October, giving his friend power of attorney over his holdings until [STK] could afford to buy them all in July, 1878. During the fall [1878] he returned with his wife and son Reno and commenced building his home. By the spring of 1879, he had bought back half interest in the town. ... He left again with his family ... in the spring of 1879 to settle unfinished business in Kansas and never returned."[7] The burden of a successful Highlands venture now fell squarely and solely on S. T. Kelsey's shoulders.

Samuel Truman Kelsey (STK). Undated photograph, circa 1885.

In the fall of 1875, through the next winter, spring, and summer of 1876, the work was mostly agricultural in nature. STK had to establish a working farm to feed his family and to provide an infrastructure to begin the clearing of the town site and rudimentary roads. Hutchinson helped that first spring and summer but was gone after that. The diary records assistance by a Mr. Jackson, no doubt a local mountain person happy for the employment. He seems most involved making yokes and driving oxen to haul logs felled to clear roads and fields. Most of STK's help, however, came from John Teague, a local mountain resident. Teague helped build the house and the barn. After that he is periodically, and often, recorded as cutting buckwheat, mowing and bringing in hay, burning brush, hauling logs. All of these were tasks that STK himself did most of the time but handed off to others as he became more involved with the selling and surveying of land and the establishment of the town roads and clearing of lots.

The diary entries, each and every evening, were the cryptic jottings of a man exhausted by a long day's toil. Thus it is interesting to note that the only place he offered detail was for the horticultural activities. He doesn't just say he hoed "the garden" or "the garden vegetables." Rather it's "hoed the beets, carrots, parsnips and cabbage." He was more than a farmer; he talks of "putting down some magnolia and dogwood seeds" in the first October in Highlands. Ornamentals were not to be ignored even as he concentrated on food crops. He was constantly measuring the yield and quality of the various crop species he used in this new environment.

Oct 1875
- 13 Ground froze this morning ¼ inch deep in exposed places. Clear fine day. Gathered the apples about 12 bu—also the beets and onions & 16 to 18 bu of potatoes. Beets & onions did poorly.
- 14 Froze this morning harder than yesterday—Clear mild day. Dug potatoes. Brownell's Beauty Good size & handsome. Yield fair 10 bu. From ½ bu Snowflake too many small ones

> but very handsome smooth potatoes. Yield light. Western reds yield fair. Good size & good looking tubers.

STK had a special interest in his orchard crops. His entries mention trips to neighboring farmers during the winter to obtain apple scions for grafting to his own rootstock. This is not unexpected given his prior history. A revealing letter to the Kansas State Horticultural Society, written much later, December 4, 1905, flashes back to his earliest horticultural experience.

> I feel old only when I become reminiscent and recall the long ago days when a "grafted apple tree" was a rare thing. There was one in my father's orchard. It had been brought by a friend from "away down east" many years before a railroad had pierced the apparently unconquerable wilderness of South Western New York. It was, as we learned in after years, an Early Harvest, but it was known to us and our neighbors only as the "grafted apple tree." It was such an improvement over the hard unsavory seedlings that it got me to thinking. And now with the hope that it may save some ambitious boy from such disappointment as befell me, I am tempted to tell you the following true story, which has never before been written. I learned that all apple seedlings might be grafted and thought how easy for every farm to have its orchard of grafted apple trees, at little more expense than the inferior seedlings.
>
> There was my chance. I could grow and sell the trees. So after much deliberation I decided to be a nurseryman. My ambition was to get all of the best varieties, start a model orchard on the home farm, get the neighbors and all the country to planting grafted trees which they would of course buy from me, and I would become a great nurseryman, a benefactor to the country and make my fortune. It must have been 61 or 62 years ago this fall when I asked for a small piece of ground on which to

begin my nursery work. The ground was promised and my spare time was devoted to collecting apple seed. It was scarce but I succeeded in getting about a quart of bright plump seed. How beautiful it looked! I could almost see the trees loaded with choicest fruit. The ground was well prepared, the seed planted, and all ready to grow. But alas! Coming home one day I saw the field had been plowed over with the rest and my Nursery was ruined. It was a crushing blow. The old farm that had been the center of my world had no more attractions for me. Indeed I think now that if the whole state of New York had then been offered to me for 25 cents, I should have rejected the offer. I was told that they really did not mean to plow up my ground, but it was right in the way and was run over thoughtlessly. I should have more ground next fall if I wanted it, and would lose but one year, but the excuse only added weight to the blow, and when my benumbed senses were able to do a little thinking my mother was told that I would do nothing more towards starting my nursery there; but when I became 21 I would go west and be a nurseryman, and I kept my word.

STK's connection to the Kansas State Horticultural Society rises from him being one of the founders and calling its first meeting, as corresponding secretary, in Lawrence, Kansas. In 1869 the society had an exhibit at the American Pomological Society meeting in Philadelphia and took the gold medal, with Samuel T. Kelsey as one of the managers.

July 1879
    2   T 59. Clear. 2 men grubbed East of the creek. K hoed in the Nursery wrote and looked after town matters. T 60.

After four years in Highlands this is the first diary entry that mentions the word "nursery." It appears more and more frequently from here on in the diary. STK is returning to his roots. Harlan, the young observer, was seven years old at this point.

Childhood and Horticulture

S. T. Kelsey's son, Harlan, wrote:

> My earliest memories of the Carolina Mountains are clear and distinct. In the spring of 1875 when both my twin brother and I were nearly three years old, we left Kansas … to regain our health and that of our families in the high ozone laden southern-most plateau of the Blue Ridge range, in Macon County, North Carolina. Leaving the plains of Kansas for a rugged mountain home, the break in my life was of course clean-cut, with my age and the date unquestionable. I mention these incidents, otherwise trivial, as supplying positive proof of a phenomenon in child life that has greatly interested me in later years; namely, at what age does a child first retain lasting impressions of occurrences about him. A dozen incidents of happenings just before we left Kansas, and en route by railway to the East are as clear in my mind as are events of yesterday, and my memory of these events has often been confirmed by my parents.
>
> Highlands, as our new home and "town site" was named, became in time a health and pleasure resort of wide reputation, as it well deserves to be, but outside of its marvelous climate, its mountains, water-falls, flowers and other attractions which are countless, it will always mean to me the one Eden in this world which for every one of us is or should be the place of a happy childhood amidst nature's most ideal surroundings. Since then I have roamed thro the Southern Alleghenies in many states and have not seen Highlands for over twenty years, yet for me it will always be my truest and inner-most "home."

Given Harlan Kelsey's testimony above, certainly one can presume that the daily events recorded by his father in the diary were being quietly and intently observed and stored by the young Kelsey growing up. The diary entries focused solely on the "weather and work" activities of his father outside of the house. If Katy had kept a diary, we would have details of the raising of five children in the house as the house evolved with improvements over time. We would have details of the children returning from jaunts and adventures in the surrounding woods. We don't; there is no evidence that Katy ever recorded such activities.

One clue from the diary about the household environment is that on every Sunday, consistently, the family observed the Sabbath as a day of rest. The sole entries were to record the weather. Every other day saw relentless work, from dawn to dusk, rain or shine, without exception. Faithfully keeping the Sabbath should come as no surprise, given that Katy's father was a Baptist minister in Ottawa, Kansas. C. C. Hutchinson was a devout Baptist and temperance advocate. It is easy to speculate that the children were raised in a loving, though possibly strict, environment. The one exception to observing the Sabbath in over seven years came on April 16, 1882. "Sunday T 28. Built fires on smokes of old hay & rubbish among the Peach trees to save the fruit—but not till 4 AM when the Temperature was down to 30. Clear fine day but cool." It took an emergency, saving the fruit from freezing, to alter the Sabbath pattern.

Here we find two similarities between John Muir and Kelsey. Muir's family came from Scotland to the "wilderness" of a farm near Portage, Wisconsin. There Muir began his "love affair" with nature, experiencing something like Kelsey's "one Eden in this world" that was Highlands. Highlands is in plant hardiness zone 6 while Portage is in the colder zone 4, but in general the horticulture would be similar. Likewise Muir was subjected to intensive Bible study in the family's Disciples of Christ environment, while Kelsey's Baptist upbringing no doubt had similar rigidities.

An undated, unidentified newspaper clipping headlined, "Elias D. White Tells Story of First Sunday School" includes the following: "A story which may be of interest centers about that little portable melodeon which made its weekly trips from Mrs. Kelsey's home to the old 'Law House.' Mr. S. T. Kelsey first took it but from time to time others shared the task of conveying it back and forth."

We have little to go on as to details of the first few years of Harlan's childhood, other than examination of the known influences surrounding him. One solid piece of evidence does come from his 1925 reminiscences before the American Association of Nurserymen, and naturally it focuses on horticulture.[8]

> My first vivid horticultural memory, in fact the most distinctly remembered early event of my life had to do with a certain sunny Sunday, the second spring in our new Carolina home. There was great excitement when a wagon pulled by four horses, and piled high with large long boxes drove into our yard, the boxes being filled with apple, pear, cherry, plum and peach trees, and some small fruits I believe, and a few flowering shrubs.
>
> How well I remember that old fashioned Snowball, which for some reason always stayed runted, yet bloomed freely, the pink Wiegela and the yellow Harrison Rose. There were a few other things but they are dim in memory, excepting of course, a climbing fragrant honeysuckle and a Baltimore Belle Rose. These fruit trees for our future orchard and flowers for our garden, which were so laboriously hauled 34 miles in distance and 3000 feet grade up a mountain dirt road from the railroad, came from T. C. Maxwell & Son, Geneva, N. Y.
>
> Even in those halcyon days there was often difference of opinion as to whether stock was always true to name and as the apples came into bearing, I well remember how my father would have extended arguments with one Silas McDowell, a local pomologist of wide reputation whose home was in the valley

below, as to the identity of the specimens in hand. I can smell those fragrant apples today, but my memory of the taste is not nearly so clear, as we had much less opportunity to exercise the latter, as very few of those specimens were judged, or so it seemed to my brother and me, except by their flavor—and we were not considered competent judges!

Old Silas McDowell was a great tobacco chewer, and the more vigorous the argument, the more he would delay expectoration. My father often told with glee of a night in McDowell's own home, when they were seated before the open fire engaged in a particular lengthy pomological disagreement. Silas had the further custom or habit of toasting his feet, but in his excitement and getting his wires crossed, he first took off a shoe, then a sock which latter he threw forcefully into the fire, and simultaneously spit vigorously and copiously into the shoe. Probably they were discussing a Spitzenburg!

In 1885, when Harlan was twelve, three important things happened. Some of Kelsey's more notable accomplishments trace their way back to that early year. He became America's youngest nurseryman at age twelve. He had introduced to cultivation two of our most precious garden ornamentals. He met and most likely made friends with Charles Sprague Sargent, the great Boston Horticulturist. Let's hear Kelsey's 1925 reminiscences:[9]

> When I was 12 years old my father suggested that I become a nurseryman and grow and sell the beautiful native plants of the Carolina mountains. It was in the blood, and I went to it and stuck. Charles S. Sargent and many other famous botanists and horticulturists of the day visited our mountains and encouraged me by placing modest orders. Orders came also from Thomas Meehan, Hoopes Bros. & Thomas, Ellwanger & Barry, Jacob W. Manning, James and Samuel C. Moon, Samuel Parsons,

Thomas C. Thurlow, and other leading nurserymen of that time, who were quick to see the great possibilities of our native plants for use in garden and park.

From my earliest memory my father had made household words of these great men and horticulturists and also of many others including Charles Downing, A. J. Downing, Charles M. Hovey, Marshall P. Wilder, P. J. Berckmans, Norman J. Colman and H. E. Van Deman, the two later my father's lifelong personal friends.[10]

Then came Franklin Davis, Robert Douglas, Sorrs & Harrison, William Prince, F. H. Stannard, E. Y. & John C. Teas, T. V. Munson, and still others whose names I do not recall at the moment. These names are not in chronological order, but 45 years ago when I was but seven years old, I think I knew them all—names of men, every one a great horticulturist, most of them noted nurserymen, all of them mankind's benefactors.

We must give special attention to Charles Sprague Sargent. He, of course, is known as the founder and creator of the Arnold Arboretum in the Jamaica Plain area of Boston, Massachusetts. Of all the notables mentioned, young Kelsey was probably closer to Sargent personally. Certainly many years later Kelsey became quite closely involved with Sargent and the Arnold Arboretum. We will go deeper into this in later chapters. In 1925, Kelsey described Charles Sprague Sargent as follows, showing his respect for the man and his legacy:

> I would be derelict in the extreme however, not to mention here and now a few great horticulturists, not nurserymen, to whom American gardens and American nurserymen owe more than they can ever repay. First may I name that great outstanding figure, Charles Sprague Sargent, whose life work has been and happily still is the study of trees and the passing on of his wonderful knowledge and the joy it brings to his fellowmen. I

quote from Wilson's "America's Greatest Garden," which is just off the press.

Like many gardens in Europe and elsewhere the Arnold Arboretum is attached to a famous University [Harvard], but this is all it has in common with them. It is devoted solely to the acclimatization, cultivation and study of hardy trees and shrubs, for which purpose it was expressly founded in 1872. [The year of Harlan Kelsey's birth.] In this limited field the Arnold Arboretum is without a peer the world over. It is unique in that it was commenced and its work has been, and happily still is, controlled by one man over a period of more than fifty years. It has known but one director, and his energy and ability, enthusiasm and devotion have made it what it is today. It is known wherever plants are loved and studied, and of its bounty gardens in every land have shared.

Toward bringing man nearer unto man this garden is a potent force. It exists for service, which service knows no boundary of race or creed. The Arnold Arboretum is worthy of the Nation and of the Nation's pride.

In her Sargent biography, S. B. Sutton makes only a few passing references to Sargent in the North Carolina mountains. We are most interested in the first, where she says, "During the spring and summer of 1885, Sargent was busy supervising the final plans for permanent planting at the Arboretum. But in September he went off again, this time to the mountains of North Carolina." Our interest lies in a handwritten letter by Sargent under Arnold Arboretum Letterhead, dated October 6, 1885:

My Dear Mr. Kelsie,
I write to say that I got safely home last night, having been in the rain all the time since leaving Highlands and to thank you for all your kindness to us while at the interesting and beautiful place. I

have ordered a copy of a small book of lines about our trees sent to you. Please accept it from me with renewed thanks.
believe me faithfully yours
        C. S. Sargent
S. T. Kelsie Esq
    Highlands

Other than misspelling STK's name, there can be no mistake that there was a cordial relationship. We cannot pinpoint what Sargent meant by "all your kindness to us while we were at the interesting and beautiful place." It is as good a guess as any to assume Kelsey accommodated Sargent in his home. If that were the case, he would have met twelve-year-old Harlan personally at that time.

But while we are dealing with young Harlan's horticultural education, let's add that his formal education coexisted. McIntosh's book contains a chapter on schools. "The 1875 school term in Highlands was in the Old Log Law House, but by the next year that building was too small and a school building was erected in 1878 behind the present site of the town hall at the cost of $350. It boasted a splendid 350 pound bell which could be heard three miles distant. The citizens of Franklin, as well as Highlands, donated work and money to construct the building. Miss Orpha Rose, a young teacher from Chicago, taught there for six years and this school served the needs of the community for nearly 40 years."[11]

On June 8, 1941, a Mr. A. D. McKinney wrote Harlan Kelsey a letter recalling their early days in Highlands and specifically mentions Miss Rose. "Dear Bop: Before you get this I am sure you will have the Franklin Press and will note Early Highlands Days by Elias White and am sure you will be interested. Miss Rose was your first teacher, mine too. The last time you and I met I helped load a wagon of your plants to ship to Linville. Will Grant was the teamster. Lots of water has gone over the dam since then. You will remember me as a long gangling tow headed, tallow faced boy 'Dock' McKinney's oldest child. I thought lots of you; you were kind and ruled that I take my turn to bat, when some larger boys tried to kick me out."

Bit by bit, we detect in Kelsey the results of his home life, probably the values of Bible teaching from his Baptist-trained mother, stressing compassion toward the less fortunate. Here also, for the first time, we see a nickname for Harlan—"Bop." This must have been well established, because we have two letters to Harlan from his twin brother, Harry, in 1942, where in each he uses the salutation, "Dear Bop."

Samuel T. Kelsey's second brochure advertising Highlands appeared in 1887. Included were numerous testimonials, plus on pages 15 and 16, an array of twelve advertisements for local Highlands stores and services. These were apparently intended to show how well equipped the town was to meet the needs of any new settlers. The last of the ads was the one shown below for the Highlands Nursery. This would have been two years after Kelsey claims to have started his nursery at age twelve and published his first catalog.

Highlands Nursery.

Ornamental Trees and Shrubbery

native to Western N. C. including many new and rare plants such as

Rhododendron Vaseyi

and Carolina Hemlock.

FRUIT TREES

in supply for HOME TRADE. Price List sent on application. Address **KELSEY BROS.**, Highlands, Macon Co., N. C.

Highlands Nursery Advertisement. Kelsey Bros. 1887

Two things pop out of the ad. One was that he started with the first of a long string of new introductions to the nursery trade. Namely, the *Rhododendron vaseyi* (pink shell azalea) and the Carolina Hemlock, which were heretofore only botanical curiosities. The second was that Harlan wasn't alone in his venture. "Kelsey Bros." in the ad does not tell us which brother he partnered with, his older brother, Samuel Jr. (called Truman, for his middle name), or his twin, Harry. Evidently neither brother stuck with the nursery business for long. We know next to nothing at this stage about Truman. We know much more about Harry, the twin. He continued his education and ended up as a very successful dentist in Baltimore, Maryland. His 1942 letterhead shows him as president of the American Board of Orthodontics.

Harlan refers to Harry jokingly in his 1925 address to the American Association of Nurserymen. The following passage is taken from his reminiscences at the end of the address. Kelsey has just referred to hard times for his family in Kansas as "the great disaster." He then continues: "However, it was not altogether disastrous for a twin was born with me—a wiser boy—for he chose not to be a nurseryman, and consequently can go fishing or play golf pretty nearly when he feels like it, and still pay cash for his clothes, while his twin brother is hoeing the row and hoping his credit or his trousers will last until next season." Harlan and Harry were in regular correspondence with each other, and one gets the sense that they were very close in their relationship.

It matters not which of his brothers partnered with him; the nursery survived. In his later 1909 catalog, Harlan Kelsey describes his start in the business at age twelve. "From a small beginning the first season, with a price-list of four pages in which were offered seventeen species of plants occupying ground space of barely half an acre, we have gradually enlarged."

Building a Town

For STK, the whole idea of coming to North Carolina was to found a town and profit from the resulting land sales. The farming was only a necessity to provide for his family. After the first year, we find more and more entries allocating time to creating the town.

Randolph Shaffner writes: "When Richard Harding Davis arrived in the fall [1876], he marveled at the ill-fated future of the precarious venture. There was something pathetic as well as comic, he wrote, in the gravity with which Kelsey [STK] picked his way through the dense woods, frightening the squirrels as he pointed out Main Street, Laurel Avenue, and the sites for the town hall and churches."[12]

Unlike Hutchinson, Kansas, with hordes of settlers streaming west, establishing Highlands promised to be a slow grudging effort requiring dogged persistence by STK. In the early summer of 1875 the first settler arrived. "T. Baxter White, a forty-one-year-old native of Marblehead, Massachusetts, was traveling west when he happened to pass through New York and heard about the new town from Henry Stewart, associate editor of the *New York Times*. So White, a former shoemaker and farmer, came to Highlands to check it out, liked it, and stayed."[13] Next, John "Dock" McKinney moved up from the Cashiers Valley settlement, with his bride, shortly after Christmas 1875. In January George A. Jacobs moved up from near Franklin and bought land at the edge of Highlands. That's three settlers after almost a year of effort.

One of H. M. Bascom's earliest memories of his arrival from Illinois was hearing Kelsey scorned for believing that Highlands could ever exist. Bascom recalled that in 1881 he stood by "while John Houston, who had been working on Main Street with his cattle, shook the silver dollars which had just been paid him and said, 'Mr. Kelsey, I wouldn't give you that for all the town you will ever have here.'"[14]

In the late 1870s the diary entries began to show more and more effort diverted from the farm to the town work. He showed land again and again, occasionally closed a sale, surveyed the parcel, and trekked down to Franklin, the county seat, to record the deed. He worked on the town site, rolling logs, cutting brush, grubbing out laurel, improving the streets and lots. When the weather forced him inside, he wrote—possibly correspondence with potential buyers; he doesn't say. Finally he does say:

Feb 1876

2   Clear. Mercury at 4 this morning. 24 at sundown. Jackson not here. S.T.Kelsey wrote on Highlands circular.
3   Cloudy a light drizzling rain & sleet this morning 32 at sundown. No men here. S.T.K. wrote.
4   Rained a little last night and snowed a little this morning then cleared off warm and fine. No men here. S.T.K. wrote on Circular.
5   … wrote on circular.
6   Sunday …
7   [weather & work entry]
8   Clear beautiful day. Mercury 32 this morning 54 at noon. Men chopped for clearing. S.T.K. finished writing Circular.

Mar 1876

12 Went to Seneca City & Greenville to get pamphlets for Highlands advertising printed & just got home last night. Heavy rain Tuesday clear & warm rest of time. In South Carolina I found Peach trees in full bloom & the apple first coming into bloom. Warm and tried to rain a little today.

The above entries are the first to mention promotion of Highlands with circulars and pamphlets. The pamphlet was titled *The Blue Ridge Highlands of Western North Carolina* and sent to every state in the union.

Gert McIntosh writes: "Mr. Kelsey and Mr. Hutchinson were promoters, and as early as 1876 they sent pamphlets to many other states, advertising that the high altitude of Highlands was a curative for consumption, ague, yellow fever and other diseases common to the countries of the North and South. This was a popular theory of the day. The pamphlet proclaimed that there was 'no better climate in the world for health, comfort, and enjoyment' and 'superior fruit, farming, and grazing lands' were available.

The pamphlets worked, and by 1883 the village had grown to an astonishing population of 300 persons, representing 18 states and territories of the United States. Forty miles of new roads had been cut out of the forests, daily mails connected Highlands with Franklin and Walhalla, there were 6 stores, 2 saw mills, a grist mill, sash and door works, and a furniture factory. Forty-five dwellings, ranging in cost from $300 to $3,000 had been built within the town limits. ... 325 lots were laid out by Kelsey in 1875 and by 1883, there were still 181 that had not been sold."[15] Finally revenues from STK's land sales began to flow in.

STK augmented his land sale revenue by acting as brokerage agent for property sales in the county well beyond the confines of Highlands. We assume sellers came to him because of the contacts he had developed near and far with his promotional pamphlets. In 1890 he advertised the real estate agency as S. T. Kelsey & Son, Highlands, North Carolina. The son was probably Truman (STK Jr.). Ads spoke of sites for summer homes, town property of every description, even timber lands. In addition he added another source of revenue from buyers by surveying and recording their new acquisitions.

Roads were a big problem. After the Civil War, the only roads made a great "loop" around the Highlands plateau. Coming up from Georgia, a road reached Franklin west of the plateau and then bore northeast across the ridge of the Cowee Mountains via the Watauga

Gap to Webster and then bore back southerly up the Tuckasegee River east of the plateau and down into South Carolina and the town of Walhalla. A rudimentary wagon road crossed the loop from Franklin, through Short Off community on the north of the plateau, down into Horse Cove beyond which it joined the Webster–Walhalla road. This left the Highlands town site isolated below Short Off. The closest railroad terminus was in Walhalla, from which the visitor would hire wagon transit to Highlands far up on the plateau. The isolation was a constant thorn in the side of those trying to induce new settlers to come and stay.

The idea was to make Highlands a hub with spokes radiating in all directions: east down into Horse Cove; northeast down into Whiteside Cove; north down to Cashiers; west to Franklin; and south to Georgia over the top of Satulah Mountain. It was a painstaking process, with STK and the townspeople constantly nibbling away at it. STK's diary shows him repeatedly out "looking out roads" [determining the routes], doing surveys, building bridges over the river fords, and supervising groups of men doing their civic duty with road construction work. After 1879 the men in the town were required by statute to work a specified amount of time on the roads. Quoting Randolph Shaffner:

"Early Highlanders were determined … to have good roads. In May, 1879, a board of supervisors was set up for the Blue Ridge Township … with crews of men assigned to eleven districts, covering proposed roads in all four directions. At the time, all able-bodied men were required to perform road duty, no excuse permitted. Indeed it was not until 1891 that the men even had a choice."[16]

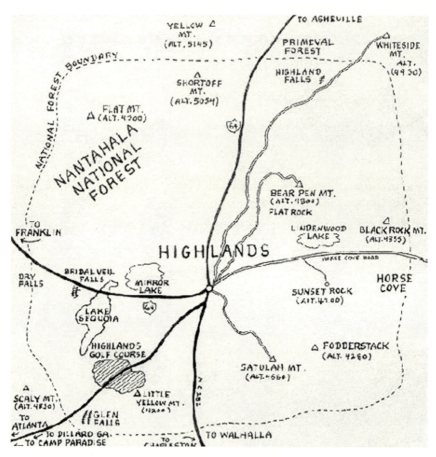

Nantahala National Forest, created in 1920. Map shows the roads radiating out from Highlands in all directions, with geological points of interest.

Surrounded by Mountain Folk

For young Harlan and his siblings there was more to observe than their father's work on the farm and the town site, more than the instruction they were receiving indoors from their mother, Katy. There was an established sinewy culture out there, readily available to the exploring youngsters.

The mountains that greeted young Harlan in 1875 contained a special breed of people of which Kelsey was apparently quite proud. While he didn't come right out and say it, after one sifts through all of his comments about these people, examining the content and the balance of his remarks, there emerges from him a deep-seated respect, perhaps even love for them. In his paper "The Carolina Mountains,"[17] he spends substantial time on the people, rather than the horticulture. He writes, "The opening of the 18th century saw a great Scotch Irish immigration to America which by 1750 had given color and tone to the entire frontier, and nowhere did they make themselves more felt than in the Carolina and Virginia borders. It was in 1772 that the real settlement of the mountains began, and later here mingled with the Scotch Irish the German and the Hugenot, the English and Welch pioneer and the Quaker. And today in the Carolina Mountains one may unerringly trace in name, speech, custom and ballad this sturdy parentage, with the Scotch Irish strongly predominating. However, I do not think these mountaineers claim descent from the prolific Mayflower passenger, as do some eighty million other Americans." Kelsey did have a sense of humor.

Much further along in his paper, Kelsey comments on the then-prospective Blue Ridge Parkway. "Many portions of the famous 'Crest of the Blue Ridge Highway' are either built or are under construction. ... Nearly the whole distance of this road will be near the crest of the Blue Ridge. Yet but a short distance away from the beaten paths you will still find the mountaineer much as he was forty or more years ago, still lacking but pleading for education, hospitable and kindly. Schools are not altogether lacking but they are all too few, and there is no people anywhere perhaps who respond quicker or more readily to opportunity when it reaches them. Margaret W. Morley in her book on the Carolina Mountains has pretty fairly described their characteristics and in a friendly manner."

> One of the pleasures of being in the North Carolina Mountains is the presence of the simple and kindly people scattered everywhere over them, this great wilderness containing some

two hundred thousand inhabitants, among whom may be found men and women who even yet have never ridden on a railway train, seen an automobile, or heard of an aeroplane. Shut up within the barriers of the mountains and isolated from contact with the rest of the world, the mountain whites, like people cast upon an island in mid-ocean, have developed customs and a dialect of their own. With their quaint speech and their primitive life they form perhaps the last link left in this country between the complex present and that simple past when man satisfied his wants from the bosom of the earth, and was content to do so. All over the mountains is a network of paths and each path leads to the door of a friend. One need not fear to walk alone from village to village, from "settlement" to "settlement" to wander at will in this vast sweet forest, where every man, woman, and child is glad to see you and ready to help you get what you want.

Kelsey writes again. "When a traveler once asked how much he owed for a night's keep he got the reply: 'What yew owe me fer entertainment? Well, sir, jes this—you owe me ter cum agen.' Yet in many places, where railroads and mills are bringing 'civilization' they quickly become sophisticated and often unpleasantly so. It is the price some will always pay for progress, and contact with the outside world, which is coming in more rapidly each year." Remember, Kelsey was writing this in the early 1920s.

In his paper, Kelsey wants to be sure his readers understand the unique dialect of the mountaineers and how it relates to their culture. He quotes Marshall K. Bonsall writing in the *Southland* magazine.

> "English as she is spoke" by the mountain folks of western North Carolina, and the adjacent mountain regions is rich in quaint and curious phrases and words. Some of these are indigenous to the soil, with others brought by the early settlers

from England and have remained unchanged, here in the land of the spinning-wheel and hand loom. The mountaineer seldom refers to so 'trifling' a unit of time as the hour. The three divisions of the day, 'morning', 'evening' and 'night' are quite exact enough for him, at least when qualified by 'soon' and 'late.'

'Soon' does not mean 'in the near future'. It entirely takes the place of 'early', and is, more rarely, used as an adjective, as: 'Do you all want to take the soon train this evenin', or 'I made a soon start this morning', but frequently also as an adverb. 'I seen him pass here soon in the evenin'. The other uses referred to are hard to connect very clearly with the ordinary meaning of 'early'.

A man may boast of owning a 'mighty soon' or a 'plumb soon' hound, or horse, or even child. In this case 'soon' evidently means intelligent, clever, quick-witted.

In the sense of 'early', 'soon' may be qualified as either 'right soon' or much more frequently 'plumb soon'.

If you 'make a plumb soon start in the morning' you will, weather permitting, have some time in which to study the stars. A 'right soon start', however, would get you out about dawn, and a merely 'soon start' not before sunrise, or even 'an hour by sun'.

If you stop at the mountain cabins you will find that their inmates have usually an uncomfortable habit of arising 'plumb soon', and will probably agree with an acquaintance of the writer who, though he has always lived in the mountains, says he can see no sense in 'getting a soon start to do nothing'.

Kelsey's paper goes on quoting Bonsall on dialect for another two pages. Then he turns to his own anecdote:

"I dew crave ter quit tippin' ther bottle, but I caint get ther consent uv my mind" probably describes the condition of many a Salemite, who would express it in quite as picturesque a way as listened to by a Carolina mountaineer. [Salemite—probably Salem, Massachusetts, Kelsey's home at the time.]

Moonshine Wars[18]

Among the Scotch Irish in colonial North Carolina, nearly every farm of any size had a distillery attached. Kelsey makes a big point of how important this was in the culture and life of the mountaineers. He writes that some three years after his coming to North Carolina, a Mrs. Rebecca Harding Davis made a trip through the Southern Alleghenies with a party of friends, starting in Virginia and ending the trip at Highlands. He recalls, "I well remember her arrival, which occurred in a pouring rain, such as one experiences only in the mountains. In 1880 Mrs. Davis described her experiences in Hayers Magazine, in narrative form. Some extracts may prove interesting, as the pictures are typical of the people anywhere in the Southern Alleghenies. I am going to let Mrs. Davis describe a mountain home of the primitive type. The party has been caught in a mountain storm with night closing in."

"How absurd this will all seem tomorrow," said Sarah, laughing, with chattering teeth, "When we are eating our breakfast in dry clothes!"

"I shall never eat breakfast again, I feel that," groaned Mrs. Mulock "Hark! Do you hear the wolves?"

A prolonged yelp broke from the thicket, and the next minute a yellow beast dashed in among them, followed by a crouching figure.

"Thank God! It is a man, and he is white," cried the Doctor. "Hello! Come back boys. My friend, is there any shelter for us in these mountains? We have lost our way."

"An wimmen?" said the man looking curiously at them. "Keep straight down the mountain, and you'll find my house. I've got a little business to attend to, but I'll be thar directly."

"Business? In this hurricane?" exclaimed Mrs. Mulock. "What on earth."

The man laughed. He was a slight young fellow with white teeth and honest eyes. "It is a powerful lively shower, that's a fact. You-uns had better keep close, single file. The trails narrer, and ef you slip, you go into the 'Lufty a quarter of a mile below. My wife 'll be glad to see you." He whistled to his dog, and they disappeared.

After perilous scrambling through swamps and along precipices they reached the cabin, which was built on the shore of the little river. It was a sample of the better class of mountain huts. The log walls gaped open in many places. Inside they were pasted over with newspapers, the ceilings hung with hanks of blue yarn, red peppers, bunches of herbs, and Indian baskets filled with family clothing. The hut was divided by an open passage into chamber and kitchen. One side of the latter was given up to a roaring fire of logs. A rosy blue-eyed young woman was on her knees baking corn bread among the ashes when they burst in on her. She stood up frightened, and laughing as if she had half a mind to cry. When she understood who they were she welcomed them in a childish, eager fashion, took the women to the chamber (which turned out to be exactly like the kitchen), and sent the men up to the loft to put on some of her husband's dry clothes, while she went to work frying chicken and baking short-cake in the hot ashes.

Mrs. Polly Leduc proved to be a most talkative hostess. Her tongue ran like a child's as they ate their supper.

"You'll excuse me, Mistress Mulock," she said, "but it's two months since I've seen the face of woman, white or red. That's what ails the mountings—the awful lonesomeness. Whar I was brought up, five miles from hyar, it used to be a year that we'd not see a livin face. But times is mendin now. We hev Sunday school and pra'r some'ars every two months. Us folks goes twenty miles to 'em. Go in the mornin', and stay all day. Exercises lasts till noon, then we have dinner, as' in the afternoon we kin see each other, and hear th' news. Last pra'r was powerful big, they was nigh onto twenty folks thar."

Miss Davidge went out with her hostess the next morning to help her milk. Mrs. Polly was mortified at her bare feet, for which she had made a covering of sheep-skin.

"Thar's some things you r'ally want money fur," she said, "an Hugh an me hes hed none fur two year, 'xept eight dollars he got fur a pint of calsum gum and some ginseng roots las' spring."

Living absolutely without money was a startling glimpse to Sarah of what life could be, reduced to its simplest conditions. She looked at Mrs. Polly, and then back to the house. "It can be done," she said thoughtfully. "You have plenty to eat, you spin and weave your own clothes, and you could barter your corn for whatever else was needed. I saw the mountaineers doing that in Asheville."

"How can we kerry the corn to barter when thar is no road? Hugh packed the ginseng on his back. Thar is a way—" She stopped, coloring hotly. "Never mind. When you come agin I hope I'll hev shoes, an' a cheer for you to set on, an' baby a frock, pore little beggar!" her soft eyes filling with tears which she tried to hide by dodging behind the cow.

They reached the foot of the mountain at night-fall, and met there three men on horseback, riding Indian file. Hixley fell back eyeing them eagerly.

"Going to Hugh Leduc's gentlemen? The trail is dangerous. Better take daylight for it."

"Who are they?" demanded Mrs. Mulock as they disappeared in the twilight of the gorge.

"Revenue officers," said the Judge anxiously. "I wish I could give Leduc warning."

"This your respect for the law, eh?" said Mr. Morley, with an unpleasant laugh.

Beautiful Land of the Sky

"Oh can't we go back and help them?" cried Sarah. "Poor Polly! When all she wanted was a decent frock for her baby."

They halted a few minutes, and then unwillingly rode on, half an hour later the sound of distant shots reverberated through the mountains.

"They've found the still," said Sarah, "Polly's chance is over," not suspecting the worse fate that had befallen the moonshiners.

The cage, which forms a part of every Carolina jail, was a square room of stout iron bars, built in the center of a larger one. It was much better ventilated and lighted than an ordinary cell. The prisoner was chained to the floor, not so closely however, but that he could stand erect. In the twilight the judge knew the white teeth and honest blue eyes. He thrust his hand through the bars.

"It is you Leduc. I was afraid of it. What are you here for?"

"Murder. Some fellers came after my still the night you left and I had a right to defend my property. I didn't mean to kill him God knows."

"Where is Mrs. Polly?"

"I look for her tomorrow" with a quick, furtive glance at the jailer. "It's a long way for her to foot it, with the baby on her back, and it's strange road to her too. Polly was never furder nor Webster. But she will come—I recon I kin see her, sir?" turning to the jailer.

"Certainly Mr. Leduc," with the Southern courteous wave of the hand. There was as much grave politeness between the murderer and the jailer as if they had been setting out to fight a duel.

When the Judge rose to go, he said, "I'll see that you are well defended, Hugh."

"I'm sartin you'll do all you kin for me," replied the prisoner, heartily, but he seemed unaccountably to have very little concern about his trial.

The next day Sarah saw poor Polly trudging down the village street, with the baby on her back, still in its wolf-skin, sucking its thumb, and laughing over her shoulder. Sarah started to run to them, but checked herself, thinking that the poor creature should go first to her husband. Polly did not return, however, having found refuge in some cabin in the village. "We will find her in the morning," said Sarah to Mrs. Mulock. Both women were full of kindly plans for her, and sat up half the night making calico dresses for the baby.

But in the morning the cage was empty, and they never saw Polly nor the poor little chap in the wolf-skin again. She had brought a spring saw and cold-chisel to her husband, with which he had easily cut the bars.

"Most murderers breaks jail in the mountings," said a philosophic cancer doctor who came that way a day or two later. "The jails is not strong, and the prejudice of the people agin the moonshiners isn't strong either. They takes to the mountings, as this young man and his wife hes done. They kin lay hid thar for years comfortable. So that's how it comes that men as kill revenue officers don't hang for it. An it isn't far they should."

Mrs. Davis's story told, Kelsey continues his paper still on the subject of moonshine and its significance to the local populace.

It was in the spring of 1875 or shortly after the close of the Civil War that we arrived at Highlands. Located but a scant six miles from the point where the North and South Carolina and Georgia boundaries meet, it was naturally a favorite region for the moonshiner, who could skip from state to state when pursued by the ubiquitous revenue officers.

Although the newcomers were careful to refrain from "informing" as it is called, or meddling with a time honored trade and custom, in the early days we naturally saw much of the revenue officer, who often chose Highlands as a base for his raids, and the consequent miniature civil war which is even waged to this day, was often staged upon the streets of our little town. The charivari was not confined as in Scotland and Ireland of old to marriage celebration, but was pulled off whenever the celebrants wanted to go on a spree. And you may well believe a drunken charivari is not a pleasant experience for a small boy. I can even now hear the crack of pistols, the snapping of pickets from our picket fence, the clamor of cowbells, and tin pans, and the wild flow of oaths as the drunken raiders tore through the streets on horses or dismounted and performed a "shindig" around our house.

How did this "miniature civil war" impact young Harlan? We don't know, of course, but it probably hardened his ability in later life to live amid conflict, especially the "wars" of conservation politics, in which he was embroiled. There can be no doubt that the entire family was affected, especially Harlan's father. As one of the town's founders, STK was singled out by any disgruntled mountaineer with a complaint. And a complaint over moonshine was something to take seriously. We have one undated, hand-scribbled letter to STK from such a mountaineer, threatening him and the whole town with "clue cluck clan" vengeance.[19] The letter is extremely difficult to read and reflects the author's difficulty with spelling, punctuation, sentence structure, and vocabulary. These niceties are almost nonexistent, but the general message is crystal clear. Excerpts are reproduced here, exactly as Kelsey had to read them.

> Mr Kelsey This is to inform you that we have been hering fer a long time that you damed yankeys has ben threating to fetch the revenew to stop us g a boys from fetching whiskey to highlands and we her that you have got them to come at last and we are a wating fer them and if tha will come will still help them and if we can her when tha are at highlands we will fetch them some some whiskey up there you dam yankeys has been tring to run

> over white folks evry sence you have been her now if you think ther is no hel gist have one man tuck from ga or N C and you dam black repubicans you have made your brags that you whiped us not us but our fathers and that is a damd lie fer tha got out of ration or tha wood of ben with you yet now if you set thinks there is no hel gis ceap on if there is any body bothered through her we as a clue cluck clan will put evry staer and mil and barn in Ashes at risk of hel but gist tend to your one buzness and we will tend to ours ... we don't want to have this to do but we can be persuade to do gist what we promes yours as ever, t c

Some details of the moonshine warfare may be instructive to further appreciate the Wild West atmosphere that surrounded the youthful Kelsey. John Parris, writing a column in the local newspaper (undated clipping), gives us a closer look.[20]

> The town of Highlands, founded in 1875 by a couple of Yankee promoters named Samuel T. Kelsey and C. C. Hutchinson, was four years old when Joseph Halleck of Minnesota erected the two-story building [now the Highlands Inn] ... It was shortly after John J. Smith took over the hotel that the only battle of the Moccasin War of 1883 was fought here, albeit the three-day battle was mostly just a squander of gunpowder and lead.
>
> Back then Highlands was a "Yankee" town, built and settled by Northerners, mostly from Massachusetts, although it drew some of the natives from the surrounding countryside—the McGuires, the Nortons, the Potts, and the Dillards.
>
> The Northern settlers were very temperate folks and were uncompromisingly opposed to the use of intoxicating liquor. Adjoining Highlands township was Moccasin Township, just down the way and across the state line in Rabun County, Georgia, where blockading flourished without fear of hindrance. It was the moonshine capital of the Southern Appalachians

and many of the blockaders found a booming market for their product among the young men of Highlands.

With the whiskey traffic threatening to make a Gomorrah of their town, and with Georgia law enforcement officers seemingly unable to stop it at its source, the town fathers called upon the federal government for help. Revenue agents swarmed into the area. They cut down whiskey stills and secured indictments. But no arrests were made. And it was several years before any attempt was made to arrest the blockaders and put them on trial.

Then, with the election of John B. Dockens as sheriff, Rabun County, Georgia, started a campaign to clean out the blockaders. Dockens was a fearless man and he arrested all blockaders or traffickers in whiskey who failed to leave the county for good.

But there was a hard core of blockaders that managed to stay out of the clutches of the law. It was headed up by four brothers named Billingsly. They have been described as "big-hearted, generous men, as fearless as lions, who really believed that they had a perfect right to make and sell whiskey, law or no law." But, be that as it may, they kept their rifles nigh and the word was that their rifles were the law.

Finally, a man by the name of Henson was arrested with a wagonload of whiskey in Moccasin by federal officers and brought to Highlands since it was the nearest town. There was no jail in Highlands and Henson was confined in a room of the Smith Hotel to await trial.

Without saying anything to the Billingsly brothers, one of Henson's friends rode into Highlands with the intention of freeing him. Henson's friend pulled his horse up in front of the hotel, dismounted, and tied the reins to the hitching post. Then he strolled into the hotel. Nobody remembers, if ever they knew, what alerted the officers. But before the would-be rescuer could use his gun or reach Henson, he was arrested and put under guard in one of the hotel rooms.

Somehow the news got back to Moccasin and to the Billingsly brothers who called a council of war and mapped out their campaign. One of the brothers took a pencil and scrawled a declaration of war on a piece of paper and sent it off to Highlands by messenger. It informed the folks of the town that an "army" was preparing to push on Highlands and set a date for the attack. On the day named, a force of 18 or 20 Moccasin men, armed with rifles and pistols, rode into Highlands and took up a position behind a building directly across the street from the Smith Hotel.

The townsfolks, taking their rifles down from the pegs on the walls of their homes, barricaded themselves behind and within the hotel where the prisoners were being held. For three days and three nights the opposing forces engaged in snap-shooting. Every time a head appeared from or behind either building it drew a shot. During the exchange, one of the federal officers got in the way of a bullet and got a leg wound. The Highlands defenders hadn't dared send a messenger into the surrounding country for reinforcements because they figured whoever tried to leave the hotel would be shot down.

Finally, a native mountain man named Tom Ford took a ladder and climbed to the roof of the hotel where he steadied his rifle where the roof peaked and got one of the Moccasins in his sights. Ford squeezed the trigger and the man, who he learned later was named Ramey, fell dead. The shooting stopped. The Georgians took Ramey's body and withdrew from the town and headed back to Moccasin. But as they withdrew, they left a letter declaring that as soon as they had buried Ramey they would come back with reinforcements and wage their war to the bitter end.

This caused the Highlands folks to put out a call for help. They sent riders into Cashiers, Whiteside Cove, Norton and Hamburg to recruit as many men as they could. Dozens of men and boys old enough to use a gun rushed to defend the town against the threatened attack. They waited two or three days, but Moccasin did not return to renew the assault.

Instead, the Moccasin folks sent a messenger with a letter in which they stated, among other things, that they knew Highlands had to transport its food and all the necessities of life from Walhalla, South Carolina. The letter pointed out the only road leading from Highlands to Walhalla passed through the center of Moccasin and that, instead of returning to renew hostilities they would kill every man from Highlands who attempted to pass over the Georgia road. Meanwhile, the larders of Highlands became empty. It was necessary that the wagon trains run without interruption in order to keep the town's needs supplied. At first, none of the teamsters would volunteer to test the blockade. Then a teamster named Joel Lovin, who had been a Confederate soldier, said he wasn't afraid to go. He hitched up his team and started out.

When Lovin reached the vicinity of where the Billingsly brothers lived, he saw them coming up the road, marching single file with their rifles. He knew this was the showdown and he worried his mind about what to do—shoot first or let them make the first move. He never had put much faith in the power of prayer, but he figured it wouldn't hurt any to do a little praying. "Oh Lord," he prayed, "if there is a Lord, save my soul, if I have a soul, from going to hell, if there is a hell." The Billingsly brothers kept coming and Lovin kept driving. "Oh Lord," he prayed, "make us thankful for what we're about to receive." Still the Billingslys came on. "Oh Lord," Lovin said, "if you won't help me, don't help the Billingslys, and I'll shoot the damnyankees like I used to endurin' of the war." The Billingslys passed by, never raising their eyes to him, and the old man went on his way, never looking back.

That ended the war between Moccasin and Highlands. The wagons rolled again, food flowed into the town, and the whiskey traffic stopped.

All these flying bullets must have been heady stuff for young Harlan, only eleven years old.

Poor but Rich: Prairie Life

The spectacular success of the Boston horticulturists, Olmsted and Sargent, was rooted in wealth, privilege, connections, and prestige (perhaps Sargent more than Olmsted). Kelsey's starting point could hardly have been more different. Before we can understand Highlands, which dominated the young Harlan's development, we need to understand the family environment in which he was raised. We also need to understand frontier Kansas, which shaped that family. "Great American Desert" was a phrase used by Zebulon Pike, among others, to describe much of what became Kansas. The Indians showed them that you could farm it.[21] The frontier first nurtured the Kelseys and Rickseckers, and then it turned harshly on them with bankruptcy, demoralization, and poverty. This hardened them but also bound them together in an abiding love and strong Christian faith.

While the bullets were flying in the Moccasin War, back in Kansas, Harlan's grandparents were coming out of "the worst winter we have seen in Kansas." Harlan's grandmother wrote a long, touching letter to her daughter, Katy, in Highlands, describing conditions back on the prairie. Things were rough. Excerpts follow:

> Home Rest, Near Ottawa, Kas. Feb. 18th, 1883. To Prof. S. T. & Katy Kelsey. Dear Children, Far, Far, Away down dar: I take up my pen to say to you, that yesterday 5 P.M. arrived safely the Highlands Enterprise Vol. 1, No. 3. Well now you may bet your last dollar that we were not a little surprised and much more pleased than surprised. Well as it was near our super time we laid it softly by. And fell to our task of discussing the merits of our home like Grub.....But you see we were awfully roused up. ... So we talked Highlands, thought Highlands, and our supper

proceeded slowly such as it would were we in Highlands. Mother finally chock full, roared out, "O let's us go to Highlands. Yes, Yes, as Paddy says, to be sure that would be foine, But, But, an where are the sheckels to carry us over there?" So we as usual blued down to our lot and finally concluded that "Soup Meagre" after all was pretty comfortable fare. Especially when the Holy Word chimed in and said "Be ye content with such things as ye have" ... Old age and poverty. Changes not our humanity and hence after reading the little Highlands Exposition we just felt and still feel after reading it sideways, upside down, all every word of it, that had we the means, God sparing our lives, we would pull right up here and go and end our days in, on, and all over the Blue Ridge at and around Highlands. Yes, that's all that prevents, especially the more so since suffering the worst winter we have seen in Kansas. Thermometer for weeks down to Zero and sometimes 20 to 30 below Zero. At present we are having some rain and thermometer at 32 degrees. The first rain we have had of any note for 6 months and over. All winter stock has suffered much for water "were it so that we could, we would pull up and leave Kansas for good and all" ... O God, while it is not disgrace to be honestly poor, it nevertheless is terrible unhandy and inconvenient. Time alone can tell what God intends to do with and for us ... Pray for us that our faith and strength fail not. Our warmest love to you, Dear children, great and small, one and all, Amen. As ever, your loving Parents, M. & L. Ricksecker.

The heritage expressed in this letter from Harlan's grandmother—love, abiding faith, toughness, determination, but humble—appeared time and again in Harlan Kelsey's climb to preeminence through the years.

City Folk Arrive

The people drawn to Highlands by STK's flowery pamphlets, and who surrounded young Harlan during his impressionable years, appear to be a cosmopolitan lot from all walks of life and all parts of the country, though mostly from the North. McIntosh gives us a good feel for their makeup in her chapter, "Early Settlers in Highlands." She gives them to us in no particular order. Excerpts follow:

> In the early 1880's, I. M. Skinner, a cheese manufacturer in New York, had come to Highlands, hoping to start a cheese factory, but he couldn't induce the country people to supply a sufficient quantity of milk for the business.
>
> About that same time, Louis Zoellner came from Germany and began to farm. For about 40 years, he was the leading beekeeper of this area......Mr. Zoellner had played chamber music in Germany at command performances for the Kaiser and he taught music in Highlands. [There is no question that young Harlan and his older brother Truman were pupils. McIntosh includes a photograph of four Highlanders sitting in chairs with their instruments, captioned, "String quartet, Kelsey boys on right. Louis Zoellner, 2nd from left, taught music in Highlands in the 1880's."]
>
> One of the first families to respond to Mr. Kelsey's enthusiastic vision of what Highlands offered was that of Mr. S. P. Ravenel of Charleston, South Carolina. He built a beautiful home on the Horse Cove Road in the 1870's and his family was very helpful to the people of the area, later building the Presbyterian Church.
>
> Mr. H. M. Bascom came from Iowa in search of health, opened a tinshop and hardware and was a leading merchant for 35 years.
>
> J. J. Smith came from Indiana and started a sawmill in Highlands.
>
> C. W. Boynton came from New Jersey and operated a planning mill and woodworking shop. T. Baxter White, a dairyman from Massachusetts, became the first postmaster and Mr. William Partridge, from Kansas, operated a grist mill.

Mr. W. B. Cleaveland, from Connecticut, operated a general store and gathered one of the finest collections of Indian relics in the state of North Carolina. [And on, and on, and on.]

McIntosh later comments on the early social life:

In the very early days of the tiny village of Highlands, a debating society was formed from which sprang the Literary Society, an active group by 1878, with aims of improving and entertaining those involved. It flourished for many years, patronized by visitors and townspeople alike.

The first piano appeared in Highlands in 1880 and informal "sings" were held in various homes. A glee club was organized around that time.

The first chamber music in Highlands was provided by a local amateur orchestra in the late 1880s. It was a valuable addition to the community musical and social life.

Harlan Kelsey. Circa 1888 (sixteen years old). Highlands String Quartet. Third violin. Courtesy Highlands Historical Society.

While young Harlan roamed the forests and mountains at will and was in constant contact with the mountaineers, he lived in the village. In the village he learned the social graces of the time, which would prove vital to him in the future.

Harbison Arrives

Teachers can have a big influence on shaping young minds. Dr. Thomas Grant Harbison, known to Highlanders always as Professor Harbison, was Harlan's teacher from ages fourteen to eighteen. His story is one of education and inspiration—especially botanical education. He was a self-made man, an eminent educator, and a noted scientist. He was another perfect role model for Kelsey. He served for Harlan Kelsey the same function that Dr. and Mrs. Carr served for John Muir at the University of Wisconsin and for years afterward.

Harbison began teaching in Pennsylvania at the age of seventeen. He attended school during vacations, and, being near Bucknell University, he continued his studies under professors there even while teaching. He never had a continuous year as a resident college student. By focusing over many years on definite courses of study as laid out by the City University of New York, the National University, and botany under Dr. Coulter of the University of Chicago, he received his BS, AM, and PhD degrees. He also completed a course in landscape architecture. By age twenty-one he had a personal library of over a thousand volumes, which he added to continually, finally donating it to the Highlands Library when he departed temporarily in 1896.[22]

To get a full picture of Kelsey's education and Harbison's role in it, we need to quote overlapping accounts from three different sources. These accounts deal with the teacher, teaching methods, and facilities from an adult's perspective. One can infer what it was like for Kelsey on the receiving end. Take note that once Kelsey left Harbison's school in Highlands, his formal education ended.

The first account will be from Harbison's associates at the Elisha Mitchell Scientific Society, celebrating him following his death in 1936.

> In 1886 young Harbison and a close friend, E. E. Magee, spent the late spring and the summer in an extended walking trip down into the south. This trip took them across Maryland and eastern Virginia to Norfolk, across North Carolina to Asheville, down to Highlands, N. C., near the Georgia line, back across North Carolina, up through the Shenandoah Valley of Virginia, across Maryland and home. From Caesar these two young men had learned that troops can march and fight on a ration of grain. They took as their equipment on this trip, in addition to their clothing, a small water-proof bag to carry their ground wheat and some brown sugar, a tin bucket for a stove, and each had a copy of Wood's *Botany*.
>
> Except for the fruits along the way, they had practically no other food than the wheat mush sweetened with brown sugar, and yet they returned in fine condition. On one day, towards the end of the trip, they walked fifty-two miles.
>
> This trip had a great influence in Dr. Harbison's future life. It proved to him his own rugged constitution, and he never had fear of hard work, long hikes, and mountains; his first hand knowledge of and love for plants were increased; and he became convinced that in our own North Carolina mountains is a most satisfying place for the abode of a lover of nature. He had great love and respect for his native part of Pennsylvania, and through correspondence with relatives and friends and through a county paper he kept in touch with it to the day of his death. However, this trip was the direct cause of his becoming a North Carolinian.
>
> On his return to his home in Pennsylvania, he found that the people of Highlands had sent a call for him to teach their school. He returned to Highlands in the fall of 1886, and though away at brief intervals, he maintained a home there until death, practically 50 years later.[23]

Harbison's thousand mile walk from Pennsylvania to the Carolinas in 1886 is reminiscent of John Muir's thousand mile walk from Indiana to the Gulf coast in 1867. Muir was felled by mosquitoes (malaria) and sought refuge in the cool of the western Sierras. The Kelseys were felled by mosquitoes in Kansas ("chills and fever") and sought refuge in the cool of the southern Appalachians.

Professor Thomas G. Harbison. Courtesy Highlands Historical Society.

Can you imagine STK's delight when a well-educated nature-loving teacher, with a strong interest in botany, wandered into town and was available to fill the vacant teacher's spot?

According to Randolph P. Shaffner, Harbison was a reluctant teacher:

> Professor Harbison had arrived on foot from Pennsylvania…. Before this year ended, he had decided to his own surprise to settle in this "kind of place" that fate had selected for him.
>
> It was never his intention to stay. Samuel Kelsey had asked him shortly after his arrival to take charge of the school at $160 for a four-month term. Professor Harbison had retorted facetiously that he'd take the job at $600 for a ten-month term. Little thinking that he'd ever see Highlands again; he then left for Pennsylvania, having completed a two-month stay.
>
> Not to be deterred, however, Mr. Kelsey raised his bluff. Informing the professor by mail that $480 had been raised through private subscription, he added that he was expecting the professor to report to school the first Monday in August. Professor Harbison's fate was sealed. He himself admitted, "This is how I happened to be initiated into the order of 'Hopeful Highlanders'."
>
> Moreover, this is how the Highlands Academy was born. In its early stages it was a cesarean birth. "I arrived," Mr. Harbison reported, "and my troubles began." He described the situation confronting him in these doleful terms: "A crowded one-room building with poor furniture was filled to overflowing with pupils and students from six to twenty years of age, un-graded in subjects from the primary to algebra— nearly 100 of them. Mr. Kelsey gave me to understand that I might have the honor and the glory, but that I might likewise take the cussing."
>
> He served as principal of the new Highlands Academy for seven years, from 1886 to 1893.[24]

Kelsey was fourteen years old when Harbison arrived, today's equivalent of the ninth grade. Reluctant though he may have been to start, once hired, Harbison went straight to work.

> Mr. Harbison attacked the problems which faced him with new books, new equipment, and new methods. The clumsy, hand-made wooden desks, dating back to 1878, gave way to new furniture. Tuition was charged to those able to pay the amount asked, others were admitted free and furnished with books. During Professor Harbison's tenure, the school was not state supported.
>
> An advertisement in an 1886 *Highlander* newspaper announced that an academy would be opened at Highlands on November 8, 1886, designed to prepare pupils for college, business, or teaching. Instruction was to be given in vocal and instrumental music. The advertisement was signed by Professor T. G. Harbison, principal. Knowledge of the new school spread, and students came from far beyond the town.[25]

Given Harbison's background and expertise, it is only natural that he would include horticulture in the school's curriculum.

> He developed there, unique and effective methods of instruction. Naturally, plants had a great part in it. Besides reading, writing and arithmetic, the usual things learned in elementary schools, his pupils learned plants, not only their common names, but their Latin names as well, and what the Latin names meant and while doing so built a foundation for a knowledge of English. Through very small prizes, a penny for the first flower of each kind for the season, five cents for the rare finds, he and they learned the flora of their region. And when funds ran low they kept their school going largely through shipping plants to northern markets. He became an advocate of an educational system that would provide a garden and work shop as a part of the elementary school.[26]

Sometimes a man's achievements in later life give clues to what it was like to associate with him at an earlier stage. For this purpose we continue with excerpts gleaned and summarized from the Elisha Mitchell Scientific Society material:

In 1893, leaving Highlands, Harbison toured Europe studying their teaching methods. Returning to North Carolina he married Jessamine Cobb, a descendant of John Cobb who had built the Saugus Iron Works in 1624. He became principal for the larger Waynesville High School, converting it from a private institution to one of the first public, graded schools in the state. He was a quiet influence in the establishment of the Western Carolina State Teacher's College. But he soon graduated from eminent educator to greater stature as a botanist.

His scientific achievements in botany were well documented and lauded by colleagues at the Mitchell Society: 1) collector for the Biltmore Herbarium on the Vanderbilt Estate in Asheville; 2) southern representative for the Arnold Arboretum, collecting for twenty-one years; 3) head of botanical work for the Geological Survey of Mississippi; 4) curator of the Ashe Herbarium; 5) a founder of the Highlands Biological Laboratory; and 6) curator of the University of North Carolina Herbarium from age seventy-two until his death in 1936.

They list his numerous botanical articles and then go on to say, "The list of publications hardly begins to measure the contributions of T. G. Harbison to the science of Botany. As a plant collector he recognized many new species and varieties of plants that he passed on to others for publication and he contributed greatly to the value of many publications through the gifts and loans of specimens and through his accurate memory as to the distribution of plants and the location of the types."

If you could pick your teachers, you could hardly do better than did young Kelsey. It is likely that Kelsey inquired about Harbison's long walk from Pennsylvania to the Georgia border at Highlands. He must have soaked in the influences Harbison received from the trials and joys of the long rigorous trip, which reminds us of John Muir's "thousand-mile walk" from Indiana to the Gulf, wherein he formed the seeds of his ideas that wild nature was filled with "divine beauty" and "harmony." Of course Harbison turned around and walked all the way back to Pennsylvania; Muir boarded a ship and sailed to San Francisco.

Moving On

Everything we have portrayed has been rather pleasant, often idyllic. Father succeeded in founding his town. The land was a horticultural marvel; it was young Harlan's personal Eden. The son enthusiastically followed his father into horticulture. He was surrounded by horticulturist role models. Kelsey's family and the range of cultures surrounding him provided everything needed for an ideal personality.

However, there is some evidence that the real world of Highlands also had its rough spots. One letter in particular shows that some things were not always so smooth.[27] The letter is filled with redundancies, questionable rhetoric, and some indecipherable words. Excerpts follow:

Webster, N. C. Aug 21st
Mr. S. T. Kelsey

> I write you for the purpose of asking you for the sake of Highlands to avoid a serious conflict which otherwise will be inevitable. I refer to the present intention of including nearly one half of my property, or more in value, in the town limits for the purposes of taxation & I know not what other purposes. Your action—& I say yours, because it was done at your instigation—in cutting out a line through my property was a trespass & was wholly unnecessary. I suppose it preludes the cutting of a street on my land. It evidently means that I shall bear half the burden of the town expenses. All this I firmly object to

& shall resist ... & I propose to go to the Legislature & have monstrously foolish charter which you got by misrepresentation annulled or amended to take me out of it. ... But you cannot drive me out, even by trying to tax me out, as I have shewn to you, because I will spend in the courts a good deal more money & you will have to do the same. I value my property because it pleases me & not because Highlands is next door to it & justly I have no right to bear your burdens when I have no vote in it. If you are willing to act reasonably in this & other matters so that I can be assured there will be no conflict between us I can honestly recommend people to make their homes in your town & neighborhood. ... Pray think of these things for the sake of the people whose welfare depends in a great measure upon the advice you give them.

Yours resp
H. Stewart

P.S. I earnestly hope to have some intimation from some person, Mayor Hill for instance that a compromise may be effected at once, because I have all the evidence collected for penal suits against the town officers, & some other persons who have violated the law & have trespassed on my rights; also to procure the injunction immediately.

Exactly when this unpleasantness unfolded we cannot say, but, while hardly the cause, it may help explain motivations for the next episode in the life of the Kelsey family.

For the most part, the Highlands venture had ultimately turned out very well. On September 11, 1884, the *Blue Ridge Enterprise* carried the following lines: "An old gentleman, who was in town the other day bartering some chickens for tobacco and calico was heard to remark: 'I'll be dogged! If Highlands don't begin to look plum like a city.'—Albert Clark, ed."[28]

In 1887 STK published and distributed his second pamphlet extolling the virtues of Highlands as "The Greatest Health and Pleasure Resort in the United States. The Most Perfect Climatic Sanitarium in the World." It was expanded from his initial pamphlet eleven years earlier in 1876 and reiterated the geography, the scenic wonders, the resources, and general infrastructure that had been developed. But primarily it included page after page of testimonials from settlers that had been cured of their ailments because of Highlands's climate, including one from STK himself, stating how Highlands had solved the problems his family had experienced with malaria in Kansas. He closes with "From my boyhood I suffered at times from weak lungs, but after living here for some time I found I had greatly improved in this respect also. I now possess remarkable power of endurance, and have traveled afoot many hundreds of miles, since coming here, looking out roads, railroads routes, etc."

The pamphlet included the *Highlands Directory*, identifying names of the mayor and three commissioners, five churches, seven cultural societies, a resident physician, three hotels, several private boarding houses, a drug store, a hardware store, four stores carrying general merchandise, the Highlands Nursery, three saw and planing mills, one flour and grain mill, and the post office, which delivered two daily mails. Certainly this was more than adequate for the three hundred or so current inhabitants plus the many new settlers the pamphlet was designed to attract. This pamphlet screamed success! *Come join us.*

By the late 1880s S. T. Kelsey's purpose had been fulfilled in the Highlands. Most of the lots had been sold; his holdings had been converted to cash. If just being a farmer was his goal, he could have found easier established sites than the Sugartown Highlands for farming in the high mountains. Transportation was too difficult to make the nursery a big revenue producer. After Pomona, Hutchinson, and Highlands, STK was a confirmed developer, and there wasn't much left to develop in Highlands. He was fifty-seven years old; whatever he did in the next few years would be his "last hurrah." It was time to seek it out.

In 1889, STK abruptly pulled up stakes and moved his family to a new mountain site on the Blue Ridge about one hundred miles to the northeast of Highlands—Linville, North Carolina. Harlan was seventeen years old at the time. STK gave half interest in all his town property, apart from the nursery, to his eldest son, S. T. "Truman" Kelsey Jr., who three years later sold out to H. M. Bascom. That year, 1893, Kelsey resigned in absentia as town councilman, and Prof. Thomas G. Harbison bought and occupied his home place.[29] Truman ended up on the West Coast, first in Seattle and later in Los Angeles. In the 1921 S. T. Kelsey obituary, his two daughters are listed as Mrs. Ansel R. Ogden of Los Angeles and Mrs. J. Clarence Hodges of Helger, Montana.

Kelsey's twin, Harry, first moved with the family to Linville. In a 1941 letter, Dr. Harry Kelsey says, "I remember once running almost all the way from the Grandfather Hotel at the head of Linville River to the top of Grandfather Mountain, just to see if I could do it."[30] He certainly had to be young to accomplish a feat like that. He was at an age to pursue higher education beyond the Blue Ridge, so in 1896 he entered the Baltimore College of Dental Surgery. Possibly because of his mother's dental problems when he was a child, he became interested in the health aspect of irregularities of the teeth, and specialized in research on that subject. In 1908 he attended the Angle School of Orthodontia in New York City and continued on to his Baltimore, Maryland, career in dentistry and later national prominence in orthodontics.[31]

Linville (Avery County) lies at about 3,800 feet in the middle section of the Blue Ridge as it traces northeast through far western North Carolina. Linville nestles just south of Grandfather Mountain. The mountain (elev. 5,964 ft.) is the highest in the Blue Ridge, if you make allowances for Mount Mitchell (elev. 6,684 ft.) being in the Black Mountains, a spur of the Blue Ridge, thirty-three miles south of Grandfather. Mitchell is the highest mountain east of the Mississippi. From Linville, the Linville river courses southward forming a shallow valley bounded on the east by some lesser mountains and the immediate drop-off to the Carolina Piedmont. On the west it is bounded by numerous lesser mountains reaching about fifteen miles to Cranberry, before dropping off into Tennessee and the lower valleys to Johnson City.

Chapter 2

Emerging Entrepreneur

Cranberry

Highlands had started in 1875 with three men climbing up the old Cherokee Trail through the gorge of the Sugartown River onto a wilderness plateau with only their dreams to urge them on, and their hands and limited funds as assets. Linville was different, very different. Its founding started with a bang by a consortium of mostly wealthy men with visions that differed from man to man. They had arrived on the train after a comfortable ride up through the Doe River Gorge to Cranberry, North Carolina. The existence of this convenient train had an odd beginning.

> Three brothers, Joshua, Ben and Jake Perkins of Crab Orchard, Tennessee had attended a "log rolling" near that township and a scuffle followed the feast. The men attempted to remove the new flax shirt of one, Wright Moreland, and in the process injured his pride. Moreland was angered sufficiently to obtain warrants for the arrest of the Perkins boys. To escape prosecution, the men fled to the nearby mountains of North Carolina, where they supported themselves by digging for and selling a rare

herb known as "ginseng." In their search for the root, they discovered a vein of magnetite iron ore, near what was later called Cranberry, North Carolina. The Perkins brothers' find was reputed to be the richest vein of magnetite known in America at that time.[32]

The iron ore from the mines that developed thereafter was used by the Confederate forces during the Civil War, including that from the Cranberry Bloomery Forge. The Cranberry Iron Company passed through various hands, under various names, always constrained by the need for a transportation system to get the ore down from the mountains. Finally Ario Pardee, one of the mine's investors from Pennsylvania, and his associates took over the East Tennessee & Western North Carolina Railroad in 1875. This narrow gauge line gradually extended eastward into the mountains toward Cranberry, through the tortuous Doe River Gorge. The line to Cranberry finally opened in the summer of 1882 and large-scale mining began at the Cranberry mine. "By 1892, the workings of the Cranberry Iron & Coal Company covered over seven acres and the daily output of the mine was about 40 tons of iron ore."[33]

This was important because Cranberry was at about the same altitude and only about fourteen miles from what would soon become the town of Linville. The "Tweetsie," as the East Tennessee & Western North Carolina Railroad would affectionately become known over the next century, was the key to opening far more than the mountain mineral resources.

The documentary book, *Linville: A Mountain Home for 100 Years,* picks up the story from there:

> At a meeting with investors in early October 1888 in rooms at the Cranberry Hotel, Kelsey's vision for a new town took form. With Donald MacRae as President, the Linville Land, Manufacturing and Mining Co. was formally organized. The

other officers included STK as V.P. and General Manager. Wallace Hahn, proprietor of the Cranberry Hotel, Thomas F. Parker of Charleston, South Carolina and H.W. Brundage of Horton, Kansas, were elected Directors. Parker, who previously had lived in Philadelphia, was a son-in-law of S.P. Ravenel of Charleston. Both men owned property in Highlands and were close to Kelsey. Incorporation Papers were filed on the 14th of the month.

The town site was named Linville, for its position astride the Linville River. The name of the company was quickly simplified to read the Linville Improvement Company.

Linville

From the Morganton Herald, based on a personal 1890 interview with STK, comes probably the best description we will get of the early activity during the founding of Linville. While it is filtered though the journalist's pen, it is vintage STK, with the flowery, exaggerated style seen in his earlier brochures about Highlands. It is so much like STK that one can imagine the reporter was working directly from a press release given to him.

AMONG THE CLOUDS

A Magic Mountain City on the Bank of a Beautiful River.

Mr. S. T. Kelsey, General Manager of the Linville Improvement Company, was in Morganton Saturday night, and in conversation with a HERALD reporter gave some very interesting information with regard to the new city his company is building on the banks of the beautiful Linville River about thirty miles North of Morganton in Mitchell county.

To begin with, the company purchased from Col. W. W. Lenoir, of Watauga county, a tract of 12,000 acres of land lying on both sides of the Linville River, some 15 miles above the falls and near the base of the Grandfather mountain. ... In this magnificent mountain domain the Linville Improvement Company has laid out a city big enough and broad enough to contain a half million people. Skilled engineers have been employed to lay off avenues and streets, hundreds of laborers have been working for twelve months in building roads and in clearing out the dense undergrowth from the forests. ... There is the beautiful river, clear as crystal, its waters splashing and tumbling over the rocks and murmuring in soft unison with the sounds of the winds among the waving branches of the overhanging hemlocks. There is an atmosphere, which in summer affects like the fruit of the lotus and in winter like draughts of rare old wine.

Improvements are made on an immense scale. ... Fifteen thousand dollars worth of city lots have been sold to parties who will build on them within the next few months, and sales are made daily. A big hotel has already been built and a $50,000 modern hotel building is in contemplation. One hundred hands are still working every day on the streets and three big saw mills are cutting lumber for building purposes. Planing mills and a sash, door and blind factory are in operation. Eight or ten other houses are being constructed. There are already two large stores, one owned by Lovin Brothers, and the other by F. P. Moore & Co., late of Caldwell county, and both of them are doing a profitable business.

These are some of the facts with regard to this magic mountain city which Mr. Kelsey gave to our reporter. It is a big, breezy enterprise and the men who are pushing it have abundant capital and don't know what failure means.

Who were these men, and what was their interest in the Linville project? Three more accounts add to our story:

(1) Gert McIntosh writes, "Mr. Kelsey was on a surveying project near Grandfather Mountain and was so impressed with the area that he (with friends) founded the resort town of Linville, North Carolina."[34] In 1914 John Preston Arthur wrote, "Kelsey ... turned his attention to the development of the Linville country. Mr. S. P. Ravenel, Sr., advanced $500 for preliminary investigations, which resulted in the formation about 1890, of the Linville Improvement Company with Messrs. Ravenel and Kelsey and the late Mr. Donald MacRae of Wilmington, N.C., as the principal stockholders. Neither Ravenel nor MacRae held a majority of the stock, thus giving Kelsey the balance of power."[35]

(2) W. W. Lenoir wrote to S. T. Kelsey from Shulls Mills, in Watauga County, North Carolina., on March 7, 1888 as follows (excerpt): "I want to see you about several business matters, & to learn about the rail road survey, etc., etc. In haste, Yours very respectfully, W. W. Lenoir." Conceivably this was the surveying project near Grandfather Mountain mentioned by McIntosh above. Shulls Mills is located between Linville and Boone, just northwest of Grandfather Mountain.

(3) The heirs of Donald MacRae, today's owners of Grandfather Mountain north of Linville, provide an account in "A Brief History of Grandfather Mountain," distributed at their visitor center: "In 1885, Hugh MacRae graduated from the Massachusetts Institute of Technology (MIT) and set off to pursue a career as a mining engineer at the mica mines on Bailey Mountain in Mitchell County near Spruce Pine. He soon found his way on horseback into Avery County, and was so overwhelmed by its beauty that he immediately wrote to his father Donald MacRae in Wilmington for the funds to purchase 15,750 acres encompassing Grandfather Mountain, parts of Sugar Mountain, Grandmother Mountain and Flattop

Mountain. Most of the tracts purchased between 1885 and 1890 by MacRae belonged to Walter Waightstill Lenoir, grandson of General William Lenoir, for whom the town of Lenoir is named."

Each of the three accounts above is fragmentary, but in combination they provide a general feeling for the situation. However, the MacRae purchase between 1885 and 1890 of 15,750 acres of land from Lenoir, appears to leave out a huge intermediate period, when the land was owned by the Linville Improvement Company, and the complicated process (soon to be described) whereby MacRae finally came into possession of all the land.

The project described above was a vastly more ambitious undertaking than was Highlands, some fifteen years earlier. Curiously, a visit to Linville today reveals a lovely sleepy little resort community, much smaller than Highlands, that bears no resemblance to the "city big enough and broad enough to contain a half million people" portrayed by STK to the reporter.

What happened? The Linville Litigation account,[36] written in 1914, provides a ready answer, describing a long, tense battle between the principals of the company:

> There were three distinct lines of policy advocated by each of these gentlemen. Mr. MacRae wanted to bond the property for the construction of a railroad from Cranberry, Mr. Kelsey wished to establish an industrial center at Linville City, and Mr. Ravenel opposed both, but wanted to establish a health and pleasure resort at Linville City, sell lots and hold the 15,000 acres of timber land the company had acquired for future development. After a while Mr. Thomas F. Parker succeeded Mr. Ravenel and Mr. Hugh MacRae succeeded his father, Mr. Donald MacRae. Disagreements in relation to the general policy

to be pursued by the officers in control, and especially in respect to the method of liquidating the outstanding indebtedness and encumbering the property of the company, were involved in an action brought against that company by T. B. Lenoir, executor of W. W. Lenoir, and decided by the Supreme Court. The press was ringing with praises of the beauty of the scenery, the healthfulness of the surroundings and the general attractiveness of the place. Visitors came in numbers from various parts of the country and wished to invest in lots and build cottages. But, as the property was in litigation, titles could not be made to the lots, and the boom subsided. However Blowing Rock, about 12 miles northeast of Linville, which before had been a mere hamlet, suddenly developed rapidly and substantially, and is today [1914] one of the finest and most attractive health and pleasure resorts in the mountains.

After a while Mr. MacRae offered to sell his interest or buy that of Mr. Ravenel at a certain price. Mr. Ravenel sold.

The above account by historian John Preston Arthur raises the serious question of how the three experienced principals could agree to the corporation, with no one having clear control, when each of them had a different and conflicting vision of what he wanted for Linville. It was an open invitation for contentious implementation and ultimate failure. The original name of the corporation certainly speaks to mixed motives—the Linville Land, Manufacturing and Mining Company. An examination of the three principals lends some support to the motives expressed above in the "Linville Litigation" account:

(1) "Mr. MacRae wanted to bond the property for the construction of a railroad from Cranberry." Ferrell's Tweetsie railroad history provides an interesting observation. "With the arrival of the East Tennessee & Western North Carolina Railroad, the timber on the Blue Ridge mountainsides was more readily available to the hungry saws of the

lumbermen. As early as 1890 there was talk of narrow gauge railroads that would connect with the ET & WNC and tap the timber resources. That year Hugh MacRae and J.R. Erwin projected the Cranberry & Linville Railroad, but the line never got beyond the planning stage. Years later MacRae would build a privately owned narrow gauge logging line out of Linville, North Carolina and power it with several Shay and Climax geared locomotives."[37] Now we have some support for John Preston Arthur's account. MacRae needed the railroad to pursue his lumbering ambitions.

(2) "Mr. Kelsey wished to establish an industrial center at Linville City." There is one clue as to STK's propensity for industry. When STK partnered with John Whetstone in the founding of Pomona, Kansas, in 1867, he didn't just develop the land for sale to farmers; he had another motivation. By his own account: "Mr. Whetstone paid his share for improvements on the company land; but I had individually promised to furnish the necessary funds to build a mill on the town site at an estimated cost of $6,000 to $7,000." STK had been responsible for the "industrial" part of a typical farming community—milling the corn before you paid the freight for rail shipment to market. Again, we have some support for John Preston Arthur's account.

(3) "Mr. Ravenel opposed both, but wanted to establish a health and pleasure resort at Linville City, sell lots and hold the 15,000 acres of timber land the company had acquired for future development." Ravenel was a plantation owner near Charleston, South Carolina. Nothing on the plantation resembled any of the objectives cited for the Linville Improvement Company. But, his early experiences do match the resort theme. As a bachelor, Ravenel had helped construct a tunnel for the proposed Blue Ridge Railroad linking Charleston, South Carolina, with Knoxville, Tennessee. "During free time he would ride horse back into the higher elevations, where the wild rugged landscape captured his heart. His jaunts through forests fragrant with hemlock and azalea ... to the tablelands at the very summit of the Blue Ridge wove into his

memory the fabric of a haunting dream."[38] The Civil War halted this activity, but much later in 1879 he returned to Highlands, bought land from Kelsey and others, and constructed the first summer residence in Highlands. He had firsthand knowledge of STK's success with developing Highlands as a resort town. It is logical to conjecture that he simply wanted to repeat the process in Linville. After selling out to MacRae, Ravenel fulfilled his Linville intentions by aggressively buying more land in Highlands and supporting its further development as a resort. Again, all this seems to support John Preston Arthur's account.

A fourth participant, young Harlan Kelsey, was quietly but busily building his nursery. Shepherd H. Dugger comments on reestablishing the Highlands Nursery, now called the Kelsey Highlands Nursery. "In 1889 Mr. S.T. Kelsey, founder of Linville, also established nurseries of native ornamentals on a beautiful tract of land one mile east of where Pineola was to be. His son, Harlan P. Kelsey, for whom the nurseries were intended, helped him."[39] Harlan had to start as his father did a decade earlier, clearing the forest and creating sun-drenched fields for his nursery stock. "The mountain people looked on with surprise, that a business could be made out of what they had had to fight all their lives with mattock, axe, and fire to clear fields for farm and garden."[40]

How were they able to get the new nursery up and running as a business so soon at Linville? They shipped the most desirable nursery stock up from Highlands. We can imagine the route by wagon to Wallhala, by train through Atlanta and up to Johnson City and then up on the ET & WNC to Cranberry, and finally to Linville by wagon. But it saved time compared to starting with seedlings and grafted scions.

Kelsey's nursery expansion soon called for more land. A mortgage deed dated February 15, 1894, to a Marguerite A. Ravenel of Philadelphia, Pennsylvania, helps explain Kelsey's adept strategy. In consideration of $500 cash in hand to Harlan P. Kelsey, he sells and conveys to her six individual tracts of land in Linville, to which he holds clear title. Five of the lots he had purchased from the Linville Improvement Company. The sixth he had purchased from a Mr. E. L. Estes. If he doesn't pay her back by February 15, 1896 (two years later), she can sell the land at public auction, retain her $500, and give the remainder of the proceeds to Kelsey. First he got clear title to the land from the company, promising payment. Then he borrowed the money from one of the Ravenels and used it to pay the company. The land was pledged as mortgage collateral. Thomas Parker assumed the role as assignee related to the safeguards needed for the ultimate discharge of the mortgage.

Following is a letter to Kelsey's Nursery patrons.

HARLAN P. KELSEY,
HIGHLANDS NURSERY
Kawana, North Carolina, U.S.A., August 24th, 1895.

PERSONAL.

To Patrons and Friends of the Highlands Nursery:

On account of present inability to meet my obligations, I have thought proper, in the interests of my creditors, to make an assignment, which, however, I trust, will be but temporary.

In the meantime you may be glad to know that my assignee, Mr. Thomas F. Parker, has retained me to actively assist in the management of the business, not only that all creditors may as speedily as possible realize amounts due them, but that the friendly and business relations of such creditors and my many customers in this country and abroad be uninterrupted.

The assignment will in no way affect my patrons, as my stock is far larger and more complete than ever before, and all orders received will have my personal supervision. The past season here has been exceptionally favorable for the vigorous growth of nursery stock, and we now have 50 acres of thriving healthy American Hardy Trees, Shrubs and Herbaceous Perennials, with which to supply the demands. The outlook is bright. We have more orders booked for the coming season than at any previous year at the same date, and our stock and facilities are so increased as to enable me to promise prospective buyers prompt, faithful fulfillment of all orders entrusted to us, with the best nursery-grown stock, and at lowest possible prices.

Your continued good will and patronage will be thoroughly appreciated by the undersigned, who will use every personal effort to make the business relations between yourself and the Highlands Nursery mutually pleasant.

Yours very truly,
HARLAN P. KELSEY

The nursery's unique asset was the trove of plant species in the high southern Appalachians that were not to be found anywhere else in America or Europe. All Kelsey had to do was walk in the woods or on the high mountain "balds," collect what he needed, and start the propagation of some new plant for introduction to the nursery trade. The weather and soils were ideal for his native plants that had been evolving in the area for eons. The science of the flora in the Land of the Sky is interesting, helping us understand the amazing collection of plants where Kelsey was raised. It starts in the Ice Age. The southern Appalachians, being high and closer to the equator, escaped the ravages of the ice sheets covering most of North America. A similar situation existed in parts of Japan, China, and India. Thus, there is a striking resemblance in the plant life of those American and Asian areas. Certain species of plants are found only in the southern Appalachians and those Asian spots. Examples of this phenomenon are the tulip tree, which grows nine thousand miles away in China, the flame azalea, and the rare *Shortia*.

Botanist Asa Gray explored this phenomenon in the mid-nineteenth century. In 1855 Charles Darwin (author of *Origin of Species*) asked Gray to help him by examining the habitats and ranges of North American plants, furthering his research on evolution. This started Gray on a statistical compilation of the geographical distribution for his massive herbarium collection at Harvard. At the time, no one in the world but Gray commanded the knowledge to pursue the issue of geographical distribution of flora. In his obituary for Gray, Charles Sprague Sargent comments on it. "Gray first pointed out the extraordinary similarity between the Floras of Eastern North America and Japan, and then explained the peculiar distribution of plants through the northern hemisphere by tracing their direct descent through geological eras from ancestors which flourished in the arctic regions down to the latest tertiary period. This paper was Professor Gray's most remarkable and interesting contribution to science."[41]

Battle Lines

While STK's utopian picture of a new town on a grand scale was meeting the hard reality of competing ownership interests, something else was happening. The deep depression of 1893–96 was engulfing the country. In 1888 Grover Cleveland was defeated for a second term by Benjamin Harrison who, as a Democrat, was able to favor the interests of farmers and labor. These blocks had suffered since the Civil War from the Gold Standard, which kept money dear and depressed all commodity prices and wage rates. They now had a champion for policies to inflate farm prices and raise wages. The principal mechanism was "free silver," whereby the government purchased the hoards of silver coming out of the western mines and increased the money supply with silver coins. The resulting inflation eased the farmers' and laborers' debt burden. The eastern big business and banking interests were appalled, claiming "the government was legalizing the robbery of any creditor who lent a gold dollar and got back a cheapened silver one."

The 1892 election saw Cleveland's return to power, but it was too late. The country was wrestling with a cyclical recession, as business and banking "pulled in their horns" in the face of inflation. Concurrently the 1893 World's Fair in Chicago closed, leaving the 100,000 men who had put up and operated the massive fair to shiver, unemployed, on the wintry street corners. In 1894 things went from bad to worse to disastrous; panic and crisis ensued. There were two to three million unemployed, more than twelve thousand business failures, and almost a fifth of the nation's railroad mileage was in receivership. It was also the year of Coxey's Army marching on Washington for unemployment relief, the bloody Pullman strike, Eugene Debs's industrial unionism, and mob violence in freight yards near Chicago, as President Cleveland was persuaded to order federal troops into the city. The aftermath could only be described as a full-blown depression.

The Linville Improvement Company, like most companies carrying debt, was seriously impacted by the credit crisis in the banking sector. As defaults multiplied, banks refused to extend loans, demanding payment as they matured, thus causing further defaults. The company found it impossible to raise funds on bank credit to meet obligations.

It was in the context of this economic backdrop that the stressful proceedings of the Regular Annual Meeting of the Linville Improvement Company took place in Linville, North Carolina, during the summer of 1896. First convened on July 15, the bulk of the meeting was devoted to considering a proposal by E. H. Camp & Company to build, equip, and operate a substantial narrow gauge railroad to the city of Linville. The problem was that Camp was asking for a $25,000 contribution from the Linville Improvement Company. There was no source for this kind of money. When the meeting reconvened on August 1, and after much auditing and railroad business, President Thomas F. Parker dropped a bombshell in the form of a resolution:

First he declared that the prior year's meetings of July, August, October, and November were irregularly held and without authority to bind the company. He proposed that they be disallowed in their entirety.

He then zeroed in on one particular preamble from the August meeting that had been recorded as follows: "Whereas the deeds from the Linville

Improvement Company bearing dates July 28th, 1893 to Harlan P. Kelsey were made while the property of the company was in the possession and control of a Receiver duly appointed by the Superior Court of N.C.—and whereas the said deed was made in fraud of the rights of the stockholders of this Company and of purchasers of property from this Company." Parker asked that this be expunged from the minutes of said so-called meeting, the facts therein stated being untrue.

Finally, he presented a formal statement, asking that it be "spread on the Minutes of this meeting," to serve as the true and proper documentation of the facts surrounding the sale of company land to Harlan Kelsey. It was long and reflected a high level of tension and emotion. The essential ingredients of the statement were twofold as follows:

1. He reminded the directors of his many entreaties for them to advance funds to help relieve the company's financial embarrassment. Only $2,000 was authorized, but even that he was unable borrow on the credit of the company because of the banking crisis. He and his friends had advanced $20,000 to keep the company solvent. Despite this, the other directors showed no willingness pay them back or to help relieve further insolvency.

2. At a much earlier date, Harlan Kelsey unexpectedly made his proposition in open meeting to buy certain tracts at prices named. After the company's maps and record books had been fully exhibited, the resolution to sell the tracts was unanimously carried. Harlan Kelsey had needed the land to expand his nursery. The company desperately needed the cash. Parker's statement closed, saying, "Except as a stockholder I was not and did not contemplate becoming directly or indirectly interested in the sale of the tracts referred to, to Harlan P. Kelsey and that any statement in so far as it reflects on my integrity and sincerity of purpose to advance the interest of the Linville Imp. Co. is without foundation in fact and false." The MacRaes saw it differently, insinuating that Parker was "attempting to depreciate the stock of the Company" by selling off company land.

The resolution to accept Thomas F. Parker's complete statement into the corporate records was carried by the following vote:

Nay.	Aye.
715	761

It shows a clear MacRae block (Nay) against a Ravenel block (Aye).

The tone of this annual meeting and its reference to earlier contentious meetings highlights what a vigorous adverse relationship had developed, pitting the MacRae interests against those of Ravenel and Parker, his son-in-law and proxy. It is no wonder that MacRae pushed for one or the other to buy out the other's interest. Ravenel elected to sell and depart.

It is interesting to note that during this "time of general panic" and company credit distress, STK owned only one share of company stock. He never put his own assets at risk in the venture. It's possible he lacked the funds to own more. It's more likely he lacked the stomach for personal participation in an indebted enterprise. His early experience in Pomona, Kansas, following the Civil War, over twenty years earlier, provides ample reason to support his aversion to personal investment in the Linville affair. As one of the few remaining "old timers," STK was contacted in 1916 by the people of Pomona, Kansas, and asked to describe the early founding years of their town. He wrote back in his "Letter to the good citizens of Pomona."[42] It tells a lot about why STK acted as he did in both Highlands and Linville.

STK had left Illinois to take a job with the Ottawa (Kansas) University to lay out and improve their grounds—about fifteen thousand acres. He was to plant and care for forests, orchards, and hedges to demonstrate the practicability of growing trees on the upland prairies. Through mismanagement of the Indian affairs, most of the university land that had been donated by the Ottawa Indians was returned to the donors, and the improvement project was necessarily abandoned.

STK then joined Mr. John H. Whetstone in the purchase of the Pomona Project—twelve thousand acres of unimproved upland prairie. They planned the two sections for town and suburban residences and the outside land for farms. The improvement work fell to STK, and he took it up with high hopes and expectations. Barbed wire had not then been invented, and he built a smooth wire fence, about twenty miles long, around the tract to protect it from intrusion until hedges could be grown. Roads were located on all section lines, and Osage orange hedges were planted around every quarter section, except on the town site, as soon as the ground could be prepared and the plants grown. This required about one hundred miles of hedge and over five hundred thousand plants.

Settlers came in; they got a post office, a school house, a separate township organization, even a bridge across the adjacent river. When they bought the Pomona land, they were assured by wise railroad promoters that a railroad would soon be built from Kansas City to Emporia, Kansas, and one from Holden, Missouri, to Salina, Kansas, both of which would run by the Pomona land. Mr. Whetstone paid his share for improvements on company land, but STK also had individually promised to furnish the necessary funds to build a mill on the town site at an estimated cost of $6,000 to $7,000.

Then disaster struck out of the blue. The gold panic suddenly overturned the conditions and so demoralized prices that property became almost worthless for sale or security. Farmers burned their corn for household fuel. Many who had mortgaged their farms were unable to pay the interest, and loan companies reluctantly took their land for the debt. The mill that was to cost not over $7,000 had cost $22,000, and the hard times and lack of transportation made its operation unprofitable. The financial depression delayed the building of the railroads.

STK had put all his worldly means into the enterprise and extended his credit to the limit, hoping for a return of better times, but the financial distress continued, and he was compelled to give up the fight. He settled with creditors, paying in land at depreciated prices, and, after giving up all, still owed over $4,000, which he later earned and paid.

This experience must have been etched deeply in STK's mind, for he never again risked all with indebtedness for his future ventures. Hutchinson, Kansas, was funded by C. C. Hutchinson, as was the Highlands land purchase. When Hutchinson left Highlands, Kelsey took power of attorney to sell Hutchinson's and his own allocation of land, which he later bought with proceeds from land sales. It appeared to be a conservative "pay-as-you-go" affair. Again it looked like his personal assets were not at risk in the Linville Improvement Company. He was working as general manager.

With Ravenel out of the picture and MacRae free to retrench at his own pace, there was no more need for a general manager. STK was out of a job. But that was okay; there was still the nursery, and he could spend full-time mentoring his son. All during the period of distress and battles surrounding the Linville Improvement Company, the nursery had quietly been established, expanded, and had started generating earnings to support the family. The family was now comfortably on its own. That being said, they were totally in the dark as to what the distant future held for Kelsey and his encounters with MacRae and his Linville Improvement Company.

Kelsey Highlands Nursery

At an early point, about 1892, a young lad of fourteen gained employment in the fields of the nursery. The payroll ledger for the week ending October 20, 1894, shows him working six days a week at a rate of seventy-five cents per day. His name was Edward Culby Robbins, known as "Ed" or "E. C." Robbins. He will be mentioned often in this narrative, as he devoted his entire life to the nursery, as did his son, Edward Page Robbins, and now his granddaughter,

Katy Robbins Fletcher. In that 1894 ledger, Robbins was only one of seven full-time employees, unlike the one-man show in Highlands. The Linville nursery business was growing rapidly. Ease of plant shipment out via the railhead fourteen miles away in Cranberry probably played a strong role in the expansion. As he gained experience, E. C. Robbins soon became the Kelseys' most trusted employee.

Edward Culby ("E. C.") Robbins in Pineola, North Carolina, Kelsey's most trusted employee.

The location of the nursery was not actually in Linville; it was a few miles to the south. Through the years, various catalogs and the business letterhead carried a variety of other names—Kawana, Cranberry, Saginaw, and Pineola, North Carolina. Harlan Kelsey never moved the nursery; it grew bigger and bigger on the original location. They kept changing the address to suit the needs of the business. Kawana was a nearby postal destination. Cranberry was the railhead from where their shipments were sent or received. In 1896 construction began on a railroad from Cranberry to a sawmill in an area called Saginaw, which also had a small hotel run by a Mrs. Penland. She had a small daughter named Ola, and when it came time to select a name for the hotel, Mr. Camp, the railroad owner, combined the words "pine" and "Ola" to form Pineola. At Camp's request, the Post Office Department (now the US Postal Service) officially changed the name of the sawmill town from Saginaw to Pineola.[43] That was where the nursery was located. E. C. Robbins's granddaughter and family still run the renamed nursery today, but on a different scale and location in Pineola just southeast of the original nursery property, and on the east side of the Blue Ridge Parkway.

Pineola nursery on both sides of US Highway 221, south of Linville.

Harlan Kelsey's theme from the beginning had been "Hardy American Plants and Carolina Mountain Flowers" for gardens. These were sold wholesale through agents to other nurseries and to large estates in distant cities. His 1892–93 catalog was lavishly illustrated with line drawings of various plants—twenty-four pages printed on 8 ½" x 11" paper. Then in March 1893 he mailed a brief notice, "To My Friends and Customers," which announced unavoidable delays in his next catalog—his "Annual Handbook of Native American Plants." Perhaps the delay was caused by cash shortages from the developing recession; he doesn't say. His order book must have been feeling the general pinch. When he finally produced the 1893–94 catalog, it was down to 5" x 7" size with far fewer illustrations.

The *Watauga Valley News* for January 1893 carried an article by the editor titled "A Unique Collection—the Highland Nursery," which read in part: "The Highland Nursery is the only one of its kind in existence, making its aim the introduction to the gardens of the world, of our magnificent variety of native trees and plants. ... The owner of the Nursery, Harlan P. Kelsey, is a young man in his twenties, and since his childhood has devoted himself with passionate eagerness to the development of the business ... which has made his name known to the Botanical societies of all Europe. He has been fitly chosen to take charge of the exhibit of our native resources in tree and flower at the world's Fair, and is now occupied in forming a valuable collection for that purpose."

In 1893 he added a new twist with introductions to the florist trade. He widely circulated a one-page flyer trumpeting "New and Unique. For the coming Winter and Holiday Trade. Every Live Florist will use KELSEY'S Beautiful New Southern GALAX LEAVES. $2 per thousand everywhere. For Florists use and all Decorative Purposes ... Positively New! KELSEY'S New Southern LEUCOTHOE SPRAYS. Beautiful deep green Sprays 1 to 2 feet long, $1 per 100 Sprays." He then listed twelve stocking agencies that florists could deal with across the entire eastern United States. He had plenty of product, but his problem was reaching the markets. Tucked up in his mountain fastness, no one would come to him; he had to reach out to them. With a payroll of seven men full-time, Harlan had a new high break-even point on volume to meet costs without draining his cash reserves. Wholesale volume now was critical.

One large potential customer was located less than one hundred miles south of Linville in Asheville, North Carolina: the massive landscape being laid out by Fredrick Law Olmsted for George Vanderbilt's Biltmore Estate. Construction had begun in 1889 and the estate was open for guests Christmas Eve 1895. Olmsted needed huge amounts of nursery stock, and one could assume Kelsey was an obvious supplier. In the 1893 *Watauga Valley News* article (above), the editor addressed this: "It is pleasant to note in this connection that one of the first men in the country to recognize the merits of Mr. Kelsey's work was Mr. George Vanderbilt, who has devoted very generous space on his great estate near Asheville, to a native garden, and whom Mr. Kelsey furnished at one order with 27,000 trees." This is certainly a gross exaggeration.

One of Olmsted's first projects was creating his own nursery to supply the millions of plants needed for the grounds. In 1890 he hired as nursery superintendent Chauncey Beadle, a Canadian horticulturist. There was one exception for Kelsey. In a letter dated March 30, 1893, from Olmsted to Mr. McNamee, Vanderbilt's general business manager, this interesting passage appeared:

> In the detailed plan of our Approach Road plantations, we have found it impossible to obtain plants with evergreen foliage, suitable for a great variety of situations, that would not eventually grow higher than would be desirable. One plant which we should otherwise have used much more freely, we have hitherto been unable to obtain, except from nurseries and at a cost which was prohibitory. ... In our first orders to Kelsey we asked him to collect a small quantity of the plant. We should have ordered much more but for apprehension that it would not succeed in the latitude of North Carolina on much lower ground than that of the highest mountain tops where I had found it. The trials that we have made of it, however, have had most satisfactory results. ... Now I wish very much that you would make arrangements under which Mr. Beadle can

ascertain in what localities of the high mountains these two plants and some others can be best obtained, and then let him have means for collecting in considerable quantities ... If for any reason what we thus advise should seem to you impracticable, we should think it best to give orders to Kelsey to make similar collections. But in that case, we should have to pay a great deal more for the plants.

The principal plant in question was the box sandmyrtle, *Leiophyllum buxifolium*.[44] It would appear that the twenty-seven thousand trees in the *Watauga Valley News* article above, were most likely twenty-seven thousand box sandmyrtle seedlings, certainly not trees.

Native Plant Promotion

The presence of the Highlands Nursery, first in Highlands and later in Linville, put Kelsey in a unique position to capitalize on the many botanical discoveries in the southern Appalachians by bringing them to market for the first time. As early as 1891, when Kelsey was only nineteen years old, he was promoting native American plants for landscape use in the trade press.

The Gardening World, published February 14, 1891, carries the following commentary:

> "We have received from Mr. Harlan P. Kelsey, Highlands Nursery, Linville ... North Carolina, his catalog of the wild flowering trees, shrubs and vines of that district. ... The catalog is printed and specially meant to call the attention of his own countrymen to the neglected condition of the American flora." To his friends and customers, the compiler says: "While the whole earth outside the United States has been searched and explored to obtain the choicest trees and plants for beautifying our American parks, lawns, cemeteries and gardens, yet the

more beautiful American plants are rarely seen in cultivation, and, as a rule, are unknown to Americans."

In the January 1893 *Watauga Valley News* article (above), the editor started with a long discussion of the various plants in the Highlands Nursery. Then he said he would finish with a quotation from an article by Mr. Kelsey:

> "It is a well-known fact that till within the last few years American parks, gardens, cemeteries, lawns and other grounds have been overflowing with importations to the almost entire exclusion of our beautiful native ornamentals—a class comprising a wealth of grand and stately trees, magnificent flowering shrubs, and a profusion of fine herbaceous plants and showy climbers; beautiful and manifold forms of terrestrial orchids and variety of delicate and graceful ferns.
>
> Nurserymen's lists have cataloged but few of these 'wild plants,' and landscape gardeners were cautious about bringing them into their plans for parks and private grounds ... It is a pleasure to note the decided reaction that is taking place, and year after year we see a rapidly growing demand for 'natives,' in fact many of the newer public and private parks and pleasure grounds have a predominance of native plants.
>
> The best horticultural journals of the country are devoting much space to the popularizing of the subject, and it is only a matter of a short time when American plants will be used and appreciated in America as they should be. We want every private pleasure ground in which our wild blooms once grew, to become familiar with their lovely presence again; we want to see them in our parks and squares, native flowers over shaded by the swaying arch of native oak and elms."

Kelsey's 1894 speech was published in its entirety by the *National Nurseryman* in October 1894. Aimed solely at nurserymen, the speech took a new and somewhat different twist. He stopped trumpeting solely the horticultural benefits of native plants but also laid out a logic for increasing long-term profits of nurserymen. It went something like this: First he took to task both the nurserymen and their customers for trapping themselves in an endless cycle of mediocrity. Neither was willing to try anything new. This lowered the standard of horticulture, when the plant buyer eventually became thoroughly discouraged. Relations between buyer and seller inevitably were jeopardized. Next he cited expert advice from botanists such as Professor Liberty Hyde Bailey, who said the tide was turning in favor of superior American flora. The appearance of this flora in new public botanic gardens and national and city parks was educating the buyer, where the traditional nurseryman had failed to do so. It was time for the nurserymen to jump aboard the emerging trend.

Alongside the promotion of native plants was Kelsey's quiet but insistent promotion of naturalistic landscapes to show the plants to best advantage. His message was to place the plants as they would naturally appear in the wild: no straight lines; always curves; plant in masses where space allows; and minimize the number of isolated single plants, as they rarely show this way in the wild. This was his practice in his own landscape architecture business. He also did not hesitate to give the message to the landscapers who used his native plants.

One of the sharp contrasts between Kelsey and Muir is their direction in horticultural activity. As youths they both searched the wild woods for interesting plants, but as adults their purposes parted ways. Muir spent seven years in the late 1870s running his aging father-in-law's fruit ranch full-time, with little or no activity writing for wilderness causes. His objective was solely commercial. Examining the broad array of fruit and grape species grown on the ranch, Muir determined that two species commanded the highest prices in the market, and quickly confined the entire ranch harvest to only Bartlett pears and Tokay grapes, with great financial success. Kelsey's objective was to promote the use of native plants in the broadest way possible. In 1903 he wrote of growing "over five hundred species of hardy American trees, shrubs, bulbs, vines, ferns, and herbaceous plants" on the acreage of the Highlands Nursery: "Our shipments extending over the civilized world … We feel justly proud of the work we have accomplished in making our Native Plants known and used." Native plant promotion always trumped concentration for commercial success.

Plant Introductions

Kelsey's first plant introductions appeared in the advertisement in his father's second Highlands brochure, back in 1887, which featured "many new and rare plants such as Rhododendron Vaseyi and Carolina Hemlock." Thus began one of Kelsey's vital contributions to America's everyday gardener. These plants had been identified by botanists preceding him. They had been collected for botanical study and display at such eminent institutions as the Arnold Arboretum. However, without their propagation and sale within the nursery trade, the American gardener would not have access to them. Kelsey brought them in from the wilds and made them available to the public at large. He happened to be the one situated in the center of North Carolina's botanical treasury. Kelsey confirms this, writing in 1910 for the *National Nurseryman*, about the history of the Highlands Nursery.[45] "The Nursery made its debut, its bow to the public, by introducing the then newly discovered and exquisitely beautiful native plant, Azalea Vaseyi, named after the great agrostologist and botanist of the US Department of Agriculture. Coupled with this plant was a harmoniously beautiful partner, one of the handsomest of our American evergreens, Carolina Hemlock Tsuga Caroliniana. These two with half a dozen or more native trees and shrubs formed the offering of this juvenile nurseryman. This half-acre has extended year by year."

Pinkshell azalea, *Rhododendron vaseyi*. Kelsey's first introduction. 1885.

Carolina hemlock, *Tsuga caroliniana*. Kelsey's second introduction. 1885.

Another signature plant Kelsey introduced to the trade was *Shortia galacifolia*, Oconee Bells. In his 1932 catalog, Kelsey describes it as "A beautiful and rare low evergreen, with galax-shaped leaves and white bell-shaped flowers in earliest Spring. A dainty ground cover thriving under Rhododendrons and Kalmias. Our introduction." *Harvard Magazine*, June–July 2002, provides a few interesting vignettes on the *Shortia*. Dr. Gray named the plant in 1842, for Charles Short, a Kentucky botanist and physician. By the time the plant was rediscovered in 1877, Short had died. Thus, the botanist M. V. O'Gorman observed, the plant was "discovered by a man who didn't name it, named for a man who didn't see it, by someone who didn't know where it was." Asa Gray judged *Shortia galacifolia* "perhaps the most interesting plant in North America" for reasons not quite clear.

Oconee Bells, *Shortia galacifolia*. Kelsey's third introduction. 1886.

Shortia was first discovered by French botanist, Andre Michaux, on December 8, 1788. He had been sent to America by the French government to find new plants that might be of value to France. Michaux found and described many new species and carried back to France pressed specimens and placed them in the Jardin des Plantes in Paris. Some were labeled "unknown" and among these was a leaf and root of this plant from the mountains of western North Carolina.

Asa Gray, as a young botanist in 1839, became intrigued with the specimen while in France and wrote a scientific description of the genus. Gray soon returned to America and began his search, high in the mountains of North Carolina and Tennessee, for *Shortia*. For thirty-eight years on every field trip high in the mountains of North Carolina, Gray hunted for the elusive *Shortia*. Then, on an April day in 1877, George Hyams went fishing in the Catawba River in McDowell County. His father was a botanist whose firm collected plants for pharmaceutical purposes. Nodding and swaying in the breeze were some charming bell-shaped, waxy white flowers. George decided to take a piece home to his father. Mr. Hyams did not know the plant, but it looked so interesting that he sent a specimen to Dr. Gray at Harvard University for identification. Dr. Gray replied, "You have stumbled on what for many years I have tried so hard to find." Instead of the mountain tops where he had always looked, it had been found along a stream in the foothills. Michaux's directions had been fairly specific, but his continual references to the "high mountains" misled Gray.[46]

The end of the story was described in a piece by Bill Sharpe, North Carolina State News Bureau, Raleigh, in 1946. He goes back over the above story and continues as follows: "It remained for Dr. Charles Sprague Sargent to rediscover the place where Michaux had grubbed out the original plants. In 1886 after a hard day's work he examined a specimen, sent it to Gray, who identified it. Sargent and his party had traveled over rough mountain country and he could not recall where he had found the plant. Nevertheless, the trail was hot, and Frank E.

Boynton, of Highlands, N. C., and his brother were sent back over the route. Boynton remembered that Sargent had crossed Bear Camp Creek, a little stream flowing into the Horse Pasture River. Here they dug up Shortia and at long last a specimen was sent to Gray from the very spot described by Michaux on December 8, 1788. The old path noted by Michaux in his clues was still discernible."

On May 17, 1946, E. J. Farrington, editor of *Horticulture*, wrote Kelsey, asking him what he thought of Sharpe's piece, so far as accuracy was concerned. Kelsey replied, "The Shortia story sent out by Bill Sharpe is substantially correct. The trip to collect Shortia was made by Frank E. Boynton and his brother Charlie Boynton *and* by Harry E. Kelsey *and* his brother Harlan P. Kelsey. This was when I collected Shortia galacifolia and introduced it to cultivation thru my Highlands Nursery. ... The common names Oconeebells for S. galacifolia and Nipponbelles for S. uniflora were proposed by me and first published in *Standardized Plant Names*, 1923 edition. Oconee County, South Carolina is the home of S. galacifolia, hence Oconee Bells." It is understandable why the Kelsey twins were omitted from accounts of Boynton's successful trip, given that they were only fourteen years old at that time.

In his 1902 catalog Kelsey highlights a long listing of plant introductions: "HIGHLANDS NURSERY has introduced and disseminated throughout this and foreign countries many new plants entirely unknown before to cultivation, including:

Aconitum reclinatum	Monkshood
Adopogon (Krigia) Montana	Mountain Dwarf Dandelion
Azalea vaseyi	Pinkshell Azalea
Carex fraseri	Fraser Sedge
Dendrium buxifolium var. *prostratum*	Dwarf Allegheny Sandmyrtle
Diervilla sessilifolia	Southern Bushhoneysuckle
Gaylussacia ursine	Buckberry

Houstonia tenuifolia	Bluets
Lacinaria (Liatris) spicata pumila	Gayfeather
Lilium grayi	Grays Lily
Polygonum cilinode	Blackfringe Knotweed
Prunus allegheniensis	Allegany Plum
Rhododenddron punctatum album	White Rhod. Minus (Piedmont R.)
Robinia hispida rosea (AKA Robinia boyntoni)	Roseacacia
Saxifraga michauxii (leucanthemifolia)	Michaux Saxifrage
Shortia galacifolia	Oconeebells
Trillium stylosum	Rose Trillium
Tsuga caroliniana	Carolina Hemlock
Vaxinium erythrocarpon	Dingleberry
Vaxinium hirsutum	Hairy Whortleberry
Viola pedata alba	White Birdsfoot Violet

and others more largely of economic interest; while it has distributed many others which formerly were but rarely seen in cultivation, including:

Abies frazeri	Fraser Fir
Amelanchier botriapium	Serviceberry
Azalea arborescens	Sweet Azalea
Azalea lutea	Flame Azalea (*R. Calendulaceum*)
Bicuculla (Dicentra) eximea	Fringed Bleedingheart
Galax aphylla	Galax
Helonias bullata	Swamppink
Ilex monticola	Mountain Winterberry
Magnolia fraseri	Fraser Magnolia
Pinus pungens	Table Mountain Pine
Stuartia pentagyna	Mountain Stewartia

We also introduced 'Galax Leaves' … to the florists' trade, which now uses them by the millions … as also the graceful 'Leucothoe Spray'."

New and Unique

For the coming Winter and Holiday Trade Every Live Florist will use

Kelsey's Beautiful New Southern
Galax Leaves

$2 per thousand everywhere. SAMPLES FREE.

For Florists' Use and all Decorative Purposes.
BRILLIANT GREEN AND RICH BRONZE.
Large and Small. Long Stems.
Keeps Indefinitely. The Cheapest Evergreen.

This, positively the finest of all new decoratives, is introduced by Harlan P. Kelsey, Highlands Nursery, Linville, N. C., and now supplied to the American Florist Trade by him and his Agents everywhere the year round.

INDISPENSABLE for all fine Designs, Especially Wreaths, Crosses, etc., being high colored and unique in shape and practically imperishable. For Winter Cemetery work Kelsey's Southern Galax Leaves are without rival. The colder and snowier the weather the brighter and fresher they look, and remain so for months without any protection whatever.

KELSEY'S
BEAUTIFUL NEW SOUTHERN
GALAX LEAVES.
Green and Bronze.
Long Stems. For Florists' Use and Holiday Trade.

SPECIAL TRIAL OFFER!

Only by trial can you learn the value of Kelsey's Southern Galax Leaves and New Leucothoe Sprays, and to induce Every Florist in America, one single sample lot of 5,000 Leaves or less will be sent at half price of $1 per 100, only by addressing the Highlands Nursery direct. Leucothoe sprays, $2 per large sample box. Positively no second lot sent under this offer!

Positively New! Leucothoe Sprays.

Beautiful deep green Sprays 1 to 2 feet long, $1 per 100 Sprays; most graceful Evergreen ever offered to Florists. Possess all the keeping qualities of Galax Leaves. They work up into Elaborate designs more easily, quickly and effectively than any Evergreen now in use. SAMPLES FREE.

Agencies for **KELSEY'S** New Southern **GALAX LEAVES**, $2 per 1,000.
New Southern **LEUCOTHOE SPRAYS**, $1 per 100.

Welch Bros., 2 Beacon St., Boston, Mass. (New England.)
Salter Bros., 42 W. Main St., Rochester, N. Y. (State.)
Marschuetz & Co., 23 N. Fourth St., Philadelphia, Pa. (General.)
Kennicott Bros. Co., 34 and 36 Randolph St., Chicago, Ill. (General.)
C. Strauss & Co., P. O. Box 422, Washington, D. C.
U. J. Virgin, 140 Canal St., New Orleans, La. (State.)
A. Klokner, 219 Grand Ave., Milwaukee, Wis. (State.)
H. Franzen, 3915 Martha St., Omaha, Neb. (State.)
Arnold Puetz, Greenland, Fla. (State.)
H. C. Beebe & Co., Middletown, Conn. (City.)
Begerow & Gerlach, 946 Broad St., Newark, N. J. (City.)
Lincoln I. Neff, 4015 Butler St., Pittsburg, Pa. (State.)

Our Agencies carry large supplies at all times, and orders sent them will be promptly filled. Special Telegraphic Code used.

Address for Orders and Samples,
LINCOLN I. NEFF, Agent,
4015 Butler St., PITTSBURGH, PA.

Galax Leaves and Leucothoe Sprays. Kelsey introduction to the florists' trade. 1893.

THE BEST HARDY AMERICAN AZALEAS

1. Azalea viscosa 2. Azalea nudiflora 3. Azalea vaseyi
4. Azalea calendulacea 5. Azalea arborescens

Azalea montage. Comparing the bloom of five different species. 1925 catalog.

In his 1930 catalog Kelsey repeats some of the plant names above and cites additional plants he introduced:

Abies fraseri 'Kelsey'	Kelsey Fraser Fir
Chrysanthemum 'Jane Kelsey'	Chrysanthemum Jane Kelsey
Chrysanthemum sibericum	Korean Chrysanthemum
Cornus stolonifera HV. (Clone)	Kelsey Pygmy Dogwood
Halesia monticola	Mountain Silverbell
Lilium carolinianum	Carolina Lily
Malus floribunda HV. (Clone)	Kelsey Crab
Rhododendron carolinianum album	White Carolina Rhododendron
Rhododendron catawbiense compactum	Kelsey Catawba Rhododendron
Robinia kelseyi	Kelsey Locust
Stenanthium robustum	Featherfleece

Scientific names are as they appeared in the catalog texts of 1909 and 1930. Common names were not cited in the 1909 listing and scientific names were omitted in 1930. These have been filled in by the author based on findings in the handbook *Standardized Plant Names* from the American Joint Committee on Horticultural Nomenclature (first edition 1923, second edition 1942). Subsequent migration of both scientific names (new findings) and common names (new trade practices) has occurred in many of the old names in Kelsey's listings.

All told, there are forty-three total introductions in the combined list, based on Kelsey's own claims.

Lumbermen

Without the railroad reaching Cranberry in the 1880s, the Linville enterprise would not have been possible, and without the railroad the new Kelsey Highlands Nursery would have been doomed to a minimal existence shipping out only wagonloads, not trainloads, of nursery stock to distant markets. But the railroad also brought in the lumbermen. They, like the miners before them, were bent on removing the natural resources as fast as their facilities and markets allowed. In contrast, the town of Linville depended on the splendid natural surroundings to attract residents and vacationers. The Kelsey Highlands Nursery planted what it "harvested" and depended on replanting for its continuing viability. Not so for the lumberman. His credo was to clear and build rail spurs up into mountain slopes, quickly remove the trees within reasonable distance, and then move on. The depletion of the surrounding beauty was irrelevant to that enterprise.

"Some small scale lumbering had been going on in the area for many years, the small circle mills producing mine timbers and lumber for the local citizens as well as acid wood and tan bark. One of these sawmills … had come to be called Saginaw. Early in 1896, the three Camp brothers of Chicago came South and acquired ownership of a large stand of white pine east of Cranberry. The Linville River Railroad was incorporated … to construct a railroad from Cranberry to the mill site at Saginaw … After initial grading had begun out of Cranberry, construction activity … ceased. The timber remained untouched until the Camp brothers sold out to William T. Ritter, a West Virginia lumber baron in 1898. As soon as the 33-pound rails of the Linville River Railroad were in place as far as Pineola, the crews began laying tracks into the mountains. Eventually the trackage was quite extensive, snaking out of Pineola in five directions."[47]

By 1906 most of the timber around Pineola had been cut and the Ritter interests moved elsewhere. Eventually MacRae Lumber built its own small spur rail due north from Linville into the adjacent mountains. Hugh MacRae was finally fulfilling his lumbering ambitions harbored since the inception of the Linville Improvement Company.

One cannot help but wonder over STK's view of this denuding of the countryside. Shepherd H. Dugger talks of the elder Kelsey's early childhood experiences with deforestation in western New York State.

Mr. Kelsey was named for his father and grandfather, and was known in childhood as Little Sammy … Throughout the youth into which Little Sammy grew, the forest up Kelsey Creek was unbroken, and the stream was crystal clear; and how in after years, he bemoaned their destruction by the lumberman is told in the following pathetic lines, copied from his reply to a letter of inquiry from a lady in Pomona, Kansas. "The forest up the stream from our place remained unbroken for several years. A beautiful perennial brook, the pride and glory of the valley, ran through our farm. I played along its flowery banks, listened to the rippling water skipping along over its clean pebbly bed and fished for the speckled trout that inhabited its crystal waters. Then the lumberman came and stripped the land of its valuable timber. And they were followed by settlers who cleared off what the lumberman had left in the valley and up the hillside."

From here on, STK's own words do a more complete job of telling his story.[48]

In place of our beautiful perennial brook there remained only a dirty uncertain arroyo, with sudden changing conditions, from a dry bed with occasional slimy pools inhabited by bull frogs, mud suckers and mosquitoes, to a swollen torrent overflowing the low lands, destroying the farmers' crops and filling the lower streams with silt. I was impressed with the significance of these changed conditions and sought information where other watersheds were stripped of their forest covering. I found that the same conditions occurred wherever the watersheds were stripped of their forests. The lands were damaged by flood and drought, water powers were too unreliable for profitable use, and stream beds were filling up with silt. I was convinced that such changed conditions were caused by the clearing, and reasoned that the unchecked destruction of the Eastern forests would finally produce conditions like unto the Western wind swept, arroyo cursed plains, and that, by raising forests to provide wind and water break, the treeless plains might be transformed into a land of beauty and productiveness, and a land of promise and fulfillment to the American home maker.

Now, over a half century later, STK looked out on a scene reminiscent of his childhood distress. For Harlan Kelsey the scene must have been the antithesis of his recollections from Highlands, a hundred or so miles to the south, "the one Eden in this world which for every one of us is or should be the place of a happy childhood amidst nature's most ideal surroundings." Fortunately for Highlands, efforts to bring a railroad up to their mountain fastness never succeeded, and the lumberman never got a foothold.

Meanwhile, in distant Boston, Massachusetts, an organization was beginning to intensify efforts to control the rampant deforestation in northern New England, especially the White Mountains of New Hampshire and in the southern Appalachians. The Appalachian Mountain Club (AMC) was comprised of wealthy Boston business and professional men who enjoyed the out-of-doors and appreciated meeting with others like themselves. These were not the ultrarich Boston "Brahmins," but rather an array of newly rich Boston leaders. Their efforts at conservation ultimately resulted in the 1911 Federal "Weeks Act" for the creation of National Forests, as well as many other subsequent conservation achievements. The Boston activities may seem like a digression until one notes that far to the south, the then-only southern member of the AMC joined in 1890. He was one S. T. Kelsey of Saginaw, North Carolina. The man who bemoaned New York's deforestation and set out to plant trees in the treeless prairies of Kansas must have had motives related to conservation. With some confidence we can assume that young Harlan was adopting the same ethic.

Nagging Issues

By the year 1896, the Kelsey family role in Linville had receded back to solely the nursery. The Linville Improvement Company was under the control of the MacRaes. Their lumbering ambitions were apparent, and all their company land was immediately adjacent to the nursery. Continued deforestation was in prospect. The nursery was encumbered by a mortgage that had to be paid off soon.

All this distress is a miniature version of his father's experience in Pomona, Kansas, one quarter-century earlier. And his response is similar to that of his father—move to a new place to make things better. In this case, move to where the markets are, to expand the selling efforts of the nursery. The catalog immediately following his receivership, 1896, is from Kawana, North Carolina. The next year, 1897–98, reads quite differently:

Highlands Nursery
Hardy American Plants
Harlan P. Kelsey
Cable Address, "Kelmont, Boston"

Tremont Building   **Boston, Mass.**

NOTICE—CHANGE OF ADDRESS

Mr. Harlan P. Kelsey begs to announce that he has removed the office of Highlands Nursery from Kawana, North Carolina, to 1123 TREMONT BUILDING, BOSTON, MASS., where he has enlarged facilities for serving his clients, and requests that all correspondence in future be sent to the new address.

This move would prove crucial for growth of the Highlands Nursery in future years. But as is so often the case in life, unintended consequences would also soon follow. As Kelsey matured, totally new developments would draw him beyond just the nursery business.

Chapter 3

Broadening Scope

Tremont Street

No such letter has been found, but one might easily imagine it would read like this:

Arnold Arboretum
Jamaica Plain
Boston, Massachusetts

June 18, 1896

My dear Mr. Kelsey,

I am writing in response to your letter of April 21. I regret it has taken this long to answer your questions about opportunities in Boston, but I only returned to my office last week. I would be delighted to help you in any way I can, if you do decide to locate here.

You asked first, whether the Boston area would be a favorable market for the many native American plants you have under cultivation at your Highlands Nursery. I would answer this with a hearty yes. Our experience at the Arboretum with your mountain specimens has been excellent. The Tsuga Caroliniana and Vaseyi Azaleas that we first obtained from you in Highlands a decade ago are doing splendidly as they mature in the arboretum.

While I am not directly involved in the business side of horticulture, I do observe an increasing demand for plantings at the many estates and residential areas springing up all around Boston. These families are well established financially, and the rail cost of transporting larger specimens from the Carolinas to Boston would be inconsequential, compared to the benefit of instantly having a mature landscape to enjoy. The local nurseries near Boston don't have the material you can supply, and the ocean passage from Europe and the Far East makes that material expensive and difficult to obtain in any quantity.

One obstacle you would face in Boston is the existing perception that formal English gardens and the varieties of imported plant material are somehow more desirable than "homegrown" plants and naturalistic settings. This, of course, is not a horticultural problem, but a landscape architecture problem. So the first thing you may wish to do, if you come to Boston, is to establish yourself as a landscape architect.

In closing, I do hope business picks up for you in Linville. If this economic depression would come to an end, we would see more confidence and hopefully more buying of landscape material everywhere. It would be a real loss to the nursery trade if you had to close down. Right now you people are the only real source of supply for many, I dare say most, of the splendid plants from the North Carolina mountains.

Faithfully yours,
C. S. Sargent

Of course, this letter was never written. It was composed by this biographer to mesh together the pieces of known circumstantial evidence that surround Harlan Kelsey's abrupt move to Boston.

We do know that Sargent was acquainted with the Kelsey family and had given Harlan some business in the late 1880s as he was starting his nursery in Highlands. The only place Sargent could have used those Kelsey introductions was at the Arnold Arboretum, which was only then being planted, and the Kelsey introductions were exactly what the arboretum was intended to feature. One of the introductions, Carolina hemlock, can be pinpointed from a statement in an early Kelsey catalog. "Some fine specimens, 12 to 15 feet high are now to be seen in the Arnold Arboretum, and are the first plants of this Hemlock ever sent out, being supplied by us to Prof. C. S. Sargent, Director, in 1884."[49]

Kelsey's catalogs and letterhead of the time indicate he had agents and correspondents in other major US cities and abroad. However, they were obviously insufficient volume generators. We do know that Harlan's father, though aging, was still capable of running the Linville operation in Harlan's absence. We do know that Harlan's business strategy of focusing on a new single large market (Boston) would make the most sense if the proprietor established residence and placed all his attention on that task. And we do know that is exactly what happened.

HARLAN P. KELSEY
* * * LANDSCAPE ARCHITECT * * *
1106 TREMONT BUILDING, BOSTON.

LONG DISTANCE TELEPHONE, HAYMARKET 1862—4

Proprietor Highlands Nursery, Western North Carolina. Hardy American Ornamentals
SPECIAL ATTENTION GIVEN TO IMPROVING LARGE and SMALL ESTATES and SUMMER COTTAGE GROUNDS

The advertisement above appeared in the *Boston Directory* for the year 1899, Kelsey's third year in Boston. It is brief, but exudes the business strategy postulated earlier. Namely, we have the skill. But we have more. We also have the plants from our North Carolina nursery. Acting as both landscape architect and nurseryman may appear at first to be a conflict of interest, but it was actually on the leading edge of an emerging trend. In describing the state of the nursery industry at the turn of the century, Richard P. White had the following to say: "The increasing interest in landscaping of large estates even before World War I provided a ready and growing market for both collected and nursery-grown ornamental plants. Large sums of money were invested by the affluent in property improvements, which called for the professional services of the landscape architect, who became the nurserymen's best salesman. Orders in carload lots were not infrequent for planting on some of the larger estates. Relations between the client, the landscape architect and the nurseryman could become very involved."[50]

By combining the two functions, Kelsey was simplifying these "involved" relations, and certainly being open and aboveboard with his clients.

Climate was another reason why Kelsey may have chosen Boston for his new base of operations. The Linville nursery plants he was promoting were hardy and quite at home in the cold of the high southern Appalachian Mountains. This lies in zone 6 of the Plant Hardiness Zone Map. Zone 6 follows a narrow band up the back of the Appalachians until it reaches Pennsylvania where it drops toward the Atlantic coastline of New Jersey, New York, and New England, ending at the New Hampshire border. Washington DC is too warm, as are all of the large southern markets (zones 7 and higher). The large markets of the Midwest, Chicago, and Cleveland, are too cold (zone 5 and lower). Boston was the biggest market that exactly matched the climate of the high southern Appalachians.

The words, "Improving large and small estates and summer cottage grounds," are simple enough, but speak volumes about his target market. Large and small estates speak for themselves, but do not be deceived by the "humble" summer cottage. The word "grounds" provides a clue. Joseph E. Garland's epic history of Boston's North Shore gives us ample perspective on these cottages.[51] "Every kind of 'cottage' was to be encountered along the North Shore in the 1870's, from the rude tent on the beach to Major Henry Lee Higginson's 'Sunset Hill' at

West Manchester, described wonderingly by one guidebook as a sort of Shonburg castle." Garland continues with a description of the Shingled Shore, covering a quarter century of cottage architectural evolution. Summer house might be a satisfactory understatement for these seaside mansions. But never underestimate the penchant for Boston's elite to carry things even further. "Cottage" works fine for a twenty-five-room, three-story extravaganza; shingled, to be sure.

Harlan P. Kelsey, 1900.

Harlan P. Kelsey. 1900. Appeared in "The Highlands Nursery," *The National Nurseryman*, February 1910.

Kelsey's address on Tremont Street placed him in the center of downtown Boston. He was close to the green expanse of the Boston Common and close to most downtown business offices, financial and legal. The State House was nearby, with its political offices. Beacon Hill and Back Bay were within walking distance, with their extensive clusters of townhouse residences for the rich and notable leaders of Boston society. All were potential customers. Where did they all go to escape the furnace of Boston's downtown summertime heat? The North Shore, of course. Also to the South Shore, but Boston's North Shore was cooler. Kelsey never restricted himself to this specific area. Ultimately his work in landscape architecture covered projects from Toronto to Florida and from Boston to Kansas City.[52] But if he had an early focus, it was surely the North Shore for summertime landscaping activity. And where did his customers go for the winter? Back to their sumptuous townhouses on Beacon Hill, near his offices. Tremont Street was a good place to be, making contacts and laying out the landscape drawings for next summer's work.

Evidence that all these contacts were paying off, at least in an enhanced reputation, can be found in a March 25, 1901, letter to Kelsey from James J. Storrow. Storrow was a Boston investment banker, along with his partner Henry Lee Higginson. He was instrumental in founding General Motors and was its third president, though only for two months in 1910–11. He and his wife were active in establishing the Boy Scouts and the Girl Scouts of America. Bostonians today know him only by their constant dependence on Storrow Drive for navigating around Boston's congested inner-city streets. This two-mile-long divided highway along the banks of the Charles River Basin, looking across toward Cambridge, is one of the more scenic vistas Boston offers.

The letter enclosed a brief brochure dealing with the arguments for and against improvement of the Charles River Basin. "The members of the Committee are anxious that you should give the matter your careful consideration, as they believe that an important public improvement is involved. If, after reading this statement, you think that the proposed water park is of sufficient importance to be investigated by a commission appointed for this purpose, will you be kind enough to send your name to Henry L. Higginson, 44 State Street, Boston?" We don't know the extent of Kelsey's involvement, but at least they respected and sought his opinion.

The Appalachian Mountain Club

There may be an another explanation for Kelsey's Tremont Street location, and possibly for his motivation to select Boston as his target market. Kelsey's love of the southern Appalachian Mountains may have drawn him to the Boston-based Appalachian Mountain Club (AMC). The 1891 register of the club listed as a member S. T. Kelsey of Kawana, North Carolina. Harlan Kelsey joined the club in 1897, immediately after arriving in Boston.

Interestingly, the club had moved its offices from the Ticknor Mansion (9 Park Street) to the tenth floor (rooms 1049–51) of the prestigious new Tremont Building in October 1896. This coincided with Kelsey's arrival in Boston and his selection of offices at 1123 Tremont Building, one floor above the club. Club membership, with its contacts, made perfect sense for a young landscape architect looking for business. Closely related to the AMC, and in the same building, was Boston's Twentieth Century Club. This group was considered part of the Boston elite but was identified with "progressivism" and conservation. Numerous well-connected officers of the AMC had also relocated their personal business offices to the new Tremont Building.

Kelsey wasted no time establishing himself within the club's management ranks, and the social contacts from all this club work must certainly have aided his business. Given his earlier exposure to the ravages of lumbering along the Blue Ridge, there can be no doubt that the club's primary emphasis on conservation was a compelling reason for active membership. This early activity was the training ground for his vital contributions to conservation in later years; it was a turning point in his life.

John P. Gerber, former AMC librarian, has concisely portrayed the club's activities, which finally produced the Weeks Act in 1911 and ultimately the White Mountain National Forest. We will borrow heavily from his material below.

From its inception in 1876, the AMC's primary concern was the White Mountains [of New Hampshire]. During the early years, AMC leaders articulated a concept of visual enjoyment of the White Mountains, which helped provide a language and ideology of beauty that later became a critical factor in mobilizing support for preservation of the White Mountains. AMC leaders, such as Charles Fay and William Niles, stressed that nature was in part an aesthetic construct that could be perceived in visual terms as the "picturesque." Fay felt that the AMC "stands as perhaps the sole representative on this continent of the interests of aesthetics as related to Nature." From the perception of the White Mountains as objects of beauty, it was only a short step to calling for their preservation.

Starting in the 1870s paper manufacturers discovered that wood fibers could be used instead of rags for paper making, and the New Hampshire forests became a major source of pulpwood. The expansion of the railroads into the White Mountains also greatly accelerated logging. From 1889 to 1899 the value of the paper and pulp industry in New Hampshire grew 565 percent. Speculators added to this cutting frenzy by buying land on credit and stripping it to pay interest.[53]

The White Mountains were constantly aflame during the turn of the nineteenth and early twentieth century. The culprits were primarily the careless slash accumulation and sparks from the steam locomotives. This period saw the Zealand Valley taken by fire. In 1903 a tenth of the White Mountains were swept away. In the towns of Kilkenny and Berlin, eighteen thousand acres were burned in the mountain ranges of the Pilot, Crescent, Pliny, and the Carters. The Franconia range slopes of Garfield, Lafayette, and the Twins Mountains were burned away. After many years of unheeded proclamations lamenting the loss of natural beauty and stressing the importance of conserving the forests through rational, efficient, scientific management of timber cutting, the club's thinking turned to bolder action.

In the early 1890s, the AMC council appointed a committee to consider ways of preserving the forests and develop "no Utopian schemes, but a business-like plan." The committee helped draft a bill passed by the New Hampshire legislature, allowing the AMC to acquire and administer real estate for preservation purposes. Others in the AMC, such as J. Rayner Edmunds, favored creating publicly owned reservations. Much of the impetus for the idea of public ownership came from the AMC's successful campaign in the Boston area to turn the Middlesex Fells into a public reservation. By the turn of the century, the problems facing the White Mountains had become the focus of national publicity.[54]

In 1901 an organization was formed with the name Society for the Preservation of New Hampshire Forests (SPNHF). They hired a professional forester, Philip Ayers, who also later became a president of the AMC. An unusually effective and dynamic organizer, Ayers immediately launched a massive publicity campaign. Within the AMC a similar train of developments was unfolding. In 1900 the AMC "Department of Exploration" was changed to the "Department of Exploration and Forestry" in order to deal directly with the preservation of the White Mountain forests.

The key figure in this transformation was the department's chairman, the journalist and future AMC president, Allen Chamberlain. In the long struggle for the creation of the White Mountain National Forest, Chamberlain played an indispensable role both as an organizer and publicist. In his role as the prestigious outdoor reporter for the *Boston Transcript*, Chamberlain served as a popularizer who brought the ideas of the conservation movement to a mass audience. Chamberlain envisioned that the Department of Exploration and Forestry would become the driving force of the White Mountain preservation movement.

Chamberlain was aided in his work by his friend and close collaborator, Harlan Kelsey. Like Chamberlain, Kelsey was an ardent conservationist and a future AMC president.[55]

Kelsey was learning from some of the masters, while at the same time applying his horticultural skills as councilor of Natural History, a sister department in the AMC, from 1901 through 1903.

The North Shore and Florence Low

For our purposes, when Kelsey arrived in Boston at the turn of the century, "the North Shore was Boston's Riviera, a settled and mature summer society whose reaches were now extending onto Cape Ann."[56] Over the next decade and a half, the building, rebuilding, and enlarging of these estates was a major growth opportunity for landscaping and horticultural businesses. Kelsey's timing was almost perfect.

Also near perfect was his providential timing in meeting his bride-to-be. Florence Low graduated with the class of 1897 from Smith College in North Hampton, Massachusetts, one of the nation's elite women's colleges. She was the daughter of Daniel Low of Salem, Massachusetts, one of that city's most prominent businessmen. The *Salem Evening News* had the following to say about him:

> The firm of Daniel Low & Co., of Salem, through its tremendous mail order business became known not only throughout this entire country, but in foreign lands as well. ... This very large business by mail made it possible for Daniel Low & Co. to carry in their retail store a very much greater and more varied stock of sterling silver or solid gold than could be found in any city of similar size in the United States. ... It closed a very important transaction by purchasing the entire business of the Nevius Company ... The Nevius Company was recognized as the most important jewelry firm in New York City ... A few years ago

the Lows purchased the large mail order business of R. Harris & Co. of Washington, D. C.

Mr. Low was elected a director of the Merchants' National Bank ... was a director of the Holyoke Mutual Fire Insurance Company ... was one of the original members of the Colonial Club, of Star King lodge, F. & A. M., was at one time an active member of the Salem Light Infantry and late of the Veterans Association, of the Salem Club, the Tedesco Country Club, and was formerly connected with the Corinthian Yacht Club ... He was a Republican in politics and served at one time on the city committee.

One thing was apparent: the locus of Kelsey's activities quickly moved toward the North Shore, Salem, and Florence Low. It was business that directed Kelsey toward Salem, a business with an excellent reputation and prospects for success. From Mr. Low's perspective, Kelsey's Boston connections were admirable. With his AMC work as councilor of Natural History, he was constantly rubbing elbows with the likes of Allen Chamberlain, the well known outdoor reporter for the *Boston Transcript,* who held a companion role heading the Department of Exploration and Forestry. Outside the AMC, it didn't hurt that Kelsey was known to such Boston notables as Charles Sprague Sargent and James J. Storrow.

He most likely met Florence Low at her home, since he did work for her mother. On November 9, 1900, he wrote:

Mrs. Daniel Low, 365 Essex St., Salem, MA.

Dear Madam:
    Regarding the plans for your place, after looking the matter over, I think that these plans can be made for $50.00. This will include an itemized list of stock to be used giving cost

of each item. [He then discusses which size Rhododendrons and other evergreens should be used for what effect, and at what cost.]

I should be pleased to carry out the plans immediately and to undertake the planting and construction in the spring if you so desire. As I buy everything at wholesale for my clients the expense would be far less than would be the cost if it was carried out in the usual manner.

On November 14, 1900, he wrote again:

Dear Mrs. Low:

Your letter is received. The plans include a study of the grounds and drawings of the beds and buildings showing the location of each plant that is to be put out. ... [Again he goes into a long discourse on the various plant options available and estimates of their cost] ... This would include the planting of the plants, and the trimming of the shrubs, putting all shrubbery in good condition for growing. It also includes staking off the beds, but I did not allow ...

$250 should make a first class job including all expenses, including plans, excepting the cost of the fertilizer on the lawn, which will really be an annual expense ...

So, if you will state the exact amount you wish to expend I will be glad to undertake the work and carry it out as fully as possible with the amount allowed. ... As to the guarantee, this is rarely done by firms ... I will overstep my fixed rule and guarantee the plants to be alive and healthy six months from date of planting.

Yours very truly,
Harlan P. Kelsey

This work in the spring of 1901 on the grounds of the Low family gave Kelsey ample time to meet and start a courtship with Florence Low.

One can find ample grounds for an attraction between the two. Physically they were a match. He was a tall man in his late twenties, hardened by a lifetime of climbing in the mountains around Highlands and working in the fields of his nursery. If his twin brother could run nonstop from the base to the top of Grandfather Mountain and return, then we can assume Kelsey could do the same. A photograph of him in his late teens shows a handsome visage. In today's slang, he was a "hunk." She, in similar terms, was a "babe." A photo in her midtwenties shows a lovely woman, slender and on the tall side, with masses of probably brown hair swept up on the top of her head in a graceful Victorian manner and dressed impeccably in turn-of-the-century style. Her height was probably a deterrent with many men, so Kelsey was a perfect suitor.

Florence, as we know, was an 1897 graduate of Smith College. We will take a long leap of faith in assuming that, as a "Smithie," she was quite assertive. This is based on your author's experience, never having met a "Smithie" that wasn't. Of course that is based on a limited sample of four, one at work, one at church, and one in the extended family. The fourth was Florence in person in her terminal years, at lunch at Salem's Hawthorne Hotel. It was arranged by her son so she could examine the people he had sold "her" house to in Boxford. (We are getting ahead of ourselves here.) But let us just assume she wasn't going to let this handsome guy get away and probably set up opportunities for him to escort her to social events at her father's Tedesco Country Club, Corinthian Yacht Club, or Colonial Club.

Kelsey's opportunities to develop a relationship lay with the AMC in Boston. He could invite her to lectures, and possibly overnight outings at the Rhododendron Cottage up in southern New Hampshire, for example. Group outings, to be sure, or maybe they weren't, if the rest of the group conveniently didn't show up. She probably had never

Florence Low Kelsey, with daughter Katherine. June 1906. Salem, Massachusetts.

met anyone like him. While she could talk knowingly about Salem society and college experiences, he could take her into the mountains of North Carolina. Imagine wild tales of moonshine violence with the Billingsley brothers, gentle tales of the mountaineers' cloistered life in some mountain glen, or even how to propagate a new azalea, one found in the wilds. It is often said that "opposites attract," and this could be a perfect example.

On the evening of November 25, 1902, Harlan Kelsey married Florence Low. The *Salem News* reported it this way:

> The most brilliant wedding of the season ... The wedding was held in the home of the Lows, formerly the old Endicott mansion in which lived Miss Mary Endicott, the wife of Hon. Joseph Chamberlain, colonial secretary of England, and is among the most beautiful types of colonial architecture in the city. ... The general theme of decoration throughout the house was carried out by the use of vari-colored chrysanthemums for the most part. The hall was resplendent in American beauty roses, asparagus boughs and palms. Pink chrysanthemums and roses were the decorations in the front drawing room. Green foliage with yellow chrysanthemums was used in striking combination for the dining hall. ... Following the ceremony there was a reception attended by some 400 guests. It was one of the most brilliant society events for years. Guests were present from the leading families in this city, Boston, Brookline, New York, Philadelphia, Baltimore, Chicago, and other places, and the costumes of the ladies were beautiful. The tables were beautifully arranged with the family plate and elegant china.

All this contrasts sharply with the primitive mountain settings that surrounded the lives of Harlan Kelsey's family and friends back in North Carolina. In six short years Harlan Kelsey had come from "uneducated" bankrupt nurseryman in the sticks of North Carolina, to become the son-in-law within one of Salem's elite families. Harlan Kelsey was now a member of a family fully on a par with the MacRaes of North Carolina and South Carolina's Ravenels.

Though newly married, Kelsey did have time to enhance his credentials as a horticultural expert. Certificate No. 70077 reads as follows: "Library of Congress, to wit: Be it remembered, that on the ninth day of October, 1903, Harlan P. Kelsey, of Boston, Mass., hath deposited in this Office the title of a Book, the title of which is in the following words, to wit: **Hardy American Rhododendrons, Kalmias, Azaleas and Other Rare Ericiceae.** Harlan P. Kelsey, Boston, Mass., the right whereof he claims as author and proprietor in conformity with the laws of the United States respecting Copyrights. Office of the Register of Copyrights, Washington, D.C."

Salem and the "Gold Coast"

Salem, Massachusetts, has an extraordinary history. Founded in 1626, Salem is first remembered for the infamous witch trials. However, shipping soon launched it toward preeminence in the coastal trade from New England to the West Indies, and then, under the guns of the British, to dominance in harassing British shipping as privateers for the Continental Congress. "Salem was adept at this combination of profit and patriotism, supplying more sailors and ships (158) than any other port. After the War, with the coastal trade destroyed by the British, hardy Salemites transformed the port into a world-class shipping center. In 1786 Elias Derby's ship reached Canton, China, opening the East to Salem. The burgeoning trade in exotic goods earned Salem its reputation as the 'Venice of the New World'. So extensive were Salem's contacts in India and the East Indies that some traders there believed 'Salem' to be a sovereign nation. The port's merchants took great risks and reaped greater rewards—[Salem was] probably the richest American city per capita in 1790." This lasted until Jefferson's 1807 embargo on shipping, and the War of 1812 again prostrated Salem's shipping, which never really recovered. There was some trade until as late as 1890, but Salem's "Glory Days" in shipping were over.[57]

By the beginning of the twentieth century the city of Salem was just that, a city. As with many cities, it had a range of activities from mixed industry to retail stores, a range of social status, and a range of fairly dense architecture. As a result it stood as an interruption to the sweep of the "landed" shoreline. Southward were the low-lying towns of Marblehead, Swampscott, and the island-like Nahant. Northward across the Danvers River was the smaller city of Beverly, a lesser interruption. Then, at last, the Gold Coast, the province of the truly wealthy "summering" Bostonians. From Beverly the shore continues northeast through Beverly Cove, Prides Crossing, Manchester-by-the-Sea, Magnolia, and at last to Gloucester and Cape Ann.

Just when Harlan Kelsey was establishing himself as a landscape architect in Boston and Salem at the turn of the century, so was another element, "the invaders," doing the same on a vastly grander scale.[58] The old Boston money was already ensconced with their shore "cottages" and inland "horsey" farms. Examples that come to mind are Boston banker Fredrick H. Prince, who helped found the Myopia Hunt Club. John Greenough, financier, had one of the first summer homes on Eastern Point. The Lorings, Meyers, Higginsons, and Evanses were established Boston icons. The new element that arrived, the invaders, were the tycoons of American industry. To name a few: Senator James McMillan, the Detroit rail and steamship magnate; William H. Moore, the fabled New York stock-waterer; Henry C. Rouse, the owner of thirteen railroads; H. J. Heinz, the Ketchup King; Richard T. Crane Jr., Chicago's Prince of Plumbing; John D. Rockefeller Jr.; and Edwin Carleton Swift of the beef-packing family who named his Prides Crossing estate "Swiftmoore."

The biggest splash, however, came with the arrival of Henry Clay Frick. Frick had partnered with Andrew Carnegie to run his steel mills, establishing the absolute dominance of the Carnegie Steel Company, but later was bought out by Carnegie for a fortune. He bought several parcels in Prides Crossing near his close friend "Judge" William H. Moore. Moore started building "Rockmarge" first in 1904, with two hundred men spreading ten thousand yards of loam around the grounds. The next year Frick started building his "Eagle Rock," with some three hundred men involved with grading and stonework. From a landscaper's perspective, it is revealing to quote Joseph E. Garland's description of this activity:

> Considerable fill was brought in to create the grand expanse on the twenty-five-acre estate from the entrances of Hale Street, along which marched the magnificent $100,000 iron fence with its handsome stone pillars. Broad avenues led up to the immense Georgian palace, which looked strikingly like the White House in Washington; at two hundred feet, however, "Eagle Rock" was thirty feet longer. Forty-eight thousand yards of fill and loam, in fact (not counting other thousands spread around neighbor Moore's yard), rolled in from West Peabody by special train onto a special spur laid for the purpose at Pride's; that amounted to two and three trains a day for two months, 1650 carloads in all. Fifty or so maple trees were set out, perhaps not all on a scale with the elm that was moved to "Rockmarge" from Hamilton; that was seventy feet high, twenty-six inches in diameter, with an earth ball sixteen feet across, and it took ten horses two hours to get it there.

This is an outsized example of what was going on all along the Gold Coast with the other "invading" tycoons, each making his name in the neighborhood. It was a field day for some landscape architects, undoubtedly those far better established than the young Harlan Kelsey, only recently arrived in Boston, and now living with his new bride in Salem. It does suggest, however, that with this much talent and material being consumed on this and so many other gargantuan projects by the landscaping and nursery establishment, there was plenty of room for Kelsey to make a name for himself and his North Carolina nursery.

Within the year following the wedding, the couple built a house at 285 Essex Street in Salem, and on November 1, 1903, Harlan Page Kelsey Jr. was born. In the ensuing years three more children were born: two girls, Katherine and Jane, and a boy, Seth Low Kelsey, born in 1906 and destined to play a major role later in this narrative. Family life was beginning in earnest. Kelsey was now a husband, a father, and a commuter to Boston. He was still listed as councilor for Natural History at the AMC. Now for the first time, Florence was listed as a member, with both of their addresses at 1114 Beacon Building, Boston.

Kelsey now took on a partner in his business, Irving T. Guild. The *Boston Directory* for 1904 displayed the company name as "Kelsey and Guild, Landscape Architects." In the November 1903 announcement of the new partnership, they explained the special contributions each partner brought to the business:

> Mr. Kelsey has had fifteen years experience in arranging and planting Estates and Parks, as well as in the actual growing of the plants used in extensive landscape work. He is, therefore, thoroughly conversant with all the practical details of such problems.
>
> Mr. Guild, formerly of the architectural publishing house of Bates & Guild Company and formerly editor of the Architectural Review, is a trained architect and designer and has devoted several years to special studies in preparation for the practice of landscape architecture.
>
> Messrs. Kelsey & Guild are prepared to consult with owners or architects and to undertake landscape work of any description.

Now, just three and a half years after Kelsey's marriage into the Lowe family, with all its exposure to Salem society, something new appeared in his life. It was civic awareness. Apparently a new family, the landscape architecture business, and remote management of the North Carolina nursery wasn't enough to deter him from taking on additional responsibilities. He looked around, saw civic needs unfilled, and took steps to change things—an attitude that would grow to outsized proportions as the years progressed—until his own business interests may well have dropped to second priority. It started on April 3, 1905, when the Civic League of Salem was organized, with Harlan P. Kelsey as president.

By 1908, with Kelsey still president, the league boasted an operating council and eight standing committees, filled with some of the more (if not most) noted men in Salem. All were welcomed without regard to political affiliation. They published a "Message to Salem Citizens" outlining their past activities and future plans. They claimed their aims were of vital interest to every citizen and taxpayer of Salem. Here are only some of them listed:

1. A clean business administration of city affairs.
2. "Special Interests" should have no favored place in American institutions.
3. Operation of public utilities as will best serve all the people.
4. Strict enforcement of laws and ordinances—No exceptions or evasions.
5. Clean well-lighted streets, good shade trees, improved water fronts, better sanitary conditions, improved parks, playgrounds for all our children, larger school-yards, better housing conditions.

There were many other aims, such as citizen involvement, but this is enough to give the general idea. By setting themselves up as a watchdog over such a broad municipal scope, they must have kept the mayor and city council awake at nights, wondering what interference might come next.

And they were immediately active. Just two months after they were organized, they brought a suit in equity court to restrain the superintendent of Shade Trees from cutting down a fine shade tree that the Board of Aldermen had illegally ordered him to do. They claimed the action was taken because the board at that time, and frequently at other times, had authorized the destruction of trees on individual request regardless of "public necessity." The next month, representatives of the league attended several hearings before the Board of Aldermen and vigorously and successfully opposed applications for permits to remove certain houses then standing on the site of the new court house, as their removal would have seriously damaged many shade trees.

They weren't just fooling around. The message noted seventeen additional actions of the league by mid-1908. Trees were perhaps a minor element. They were all over the "city fathers" like a swarm of bees. Consider just one more example they reported: "The abolition of all railroad grade crossings in Salem is a vital need of the city. The Civic League energetically worked for this reform in October and November 1905. Its committee interviewed the Mayor, the Aldermen, and the City Solicitor, and urged in every way possible that proceedings be brought in the court to abolish such crossings. Subsequently at the invitation of the City Council, members of the League conferred with a committee of the City Council for the purpose of devising a plan which might be presented to the court for carrying out the work. The petitions are now pending in the Superior Court."

At the other end of the spectrum, the league fostered city beautification, not by urging the "city fathers" to do something, but rather, by sponsoring a garden contest in 1907. They wanted broad participation, so they had numerous prizes in six categories: best garden in each ward; best in the entire city; best wall or fence in each ward; best window box in each ward; best in entire city; best school garden. They wisely encouraged participation by saying, "Note particularly that the prizes for yard gardens and wall and fence gardens are for the greatest improvement shown—not the finest gardens." They sold seed to the participants for one cent a packet.

Another civic group that counted Kelsey as a member was "The Associated Charities of Salem, Mass." Their 1908–09 yearbook listed him as a board member and a member of the Social Conditions and Cooperation Committee. Pauperism in the state was an important issue. Their work must have been effective, judging by the results, comparing Salem (population 37,000) with its much larger inland neighbor Worcester (population 147,000). Reimbursements out of Almshouses: Salem $7,295. Worcester $2,429. Amount for outdoor relief: Salem $11,047,610. Worcester $3,315,620.

City Planning

It seems inconceivable that Kelsey would not at some time follow in his father's footsteps as a city planner, if not as a city founder. Just as Kelsey had a horticultural mentor beyond his father, in Highland's Professor Harbison, he also had one in city planning. It is highly likely that J. Horace McFarland had a strong influence on him. McFarland was only thirteen years older than Kelsey but was an established national figure. He and Kelsey would become more and more entwined as future events unfolded, some friendly, some not so friendly.

Cornell Professor Emeritus John W. Reps gives us a brief glimpse of McFarland as a headnote to a 1908 McFarland article, "The Growth of City Planning in America" in the publication *Charities and the Commons*.[59]

> John Horace McFarland was an untiring advocate of urban and regional planning. By profession a master printer he became an

author and publisher. He wrote several books on gardening… He also edited *The American Rose Annual* from 1916 onwards. A prolific author, he contributed articles to such publications as *Country Homes and Gardens, Ladies Home Journal … and American Home.* At least an equally strong interest in planning led to his election as President of the American Civic Association in 1904, a post he retained for twenty years. He lived in Harrisburg, Pennsylvania.

McFarland's 1908 article provides insights on the status of city planning at the turn of the century, and the status of Harlan P. Kelsey as a planner then. Only the briefest excerpts and commentary follow:

He starts with, "The assertion is ventured that the vast majority of urban dwellers would, if asked, explain that a city plan was merely a city map, and nothing more. Indeed, most of those whose minds have been more of less awakened to a civic consciousness and who are beginning to care for the interests of all, are likely to have very hazy ideas upon the subject of real city planning, and more likely to think it of slight importance … They have had, fortunately, a body of earnest women back of them, forcing upon them a real plan and a real designer, whose services and which plan they undertook to use most reluctantly, but with most happy eventual results."

He then launches into the body of the article with a chronology of successful and not so successful American city efforts at planning. He starts with Washington, DC, and proceeds to Kansas City, Chicago, St. Louis, New York City, Baltimore, San Francisco, Boston, Philadelphia, and on and on and on. "These obstreperous civic-advance men and women who push the majority along do not always live in the larger communities. Therefore we see in a hasty and all too inadequate glance over the United States, some pleasant things doing in the smaller cities and towns." He then lists numerous such examples. Within this list, he asserts "Southern cities are waking to their needs and their possibilities. Columbia, the capital of South Carolina, has secured a report on the work necessary to enable proper advantage to be taken of the hundred-foot avenues provided in the original city plan, as well as to attain needed parks, and parkways. Mr. Kelsey, who prepared the Columbia plan, has also submitted to the local Municipal League an admirable proposition for the improvement of Greenville, South Carolina." He then closes with a few passages of commentary.

"As I have said, this survey is hasty and inadequate. It has not attempted to catalog the plans proposed for community improvement, nor to even mention half the movements for better planning. Mr. Burnam, the Olmsteds, Mr. Kessler, Mr. Manning, Mr. Kelsey, Mr. Robinson, Mr. Nolen, and other students of population and nature are at work all the time, making suggestions for better things in towns and cities."

It is interesting to note that Kelsey's name is listed above, by McFarland in 1908, with the same emphasis as provided to the Olmsteds. Subsequent biographers, of course, thrust the Olmsteds into the forefront of American consciousness. One could ask how Kelsey could have attracted McFarland's attention. The answer might be that Kelsey had an ongoing business relationship with McFarland's printing operation. When Kelsey started operating in Boston in 1896, his first subsequent nursery catalog notes on the frontispiece "J. Horace McFarland, Printers, Harrisburg, Pa." And he continued to do Kelsey's printing work for many years.

Now is a good time to provide a few capsules of the planning work Kelsey did in South Carolina. He didn't simply wait for inquiries about his services. He passionately sought audiences to hear his message on city planning. An unidentified clipping from a Salem newspaper gives us a glimpse of this missionary work (possibly from a Kelsey press release):

> LECTURED IN THE SOUTH—Harlan P. Kelsey of this City Spoke on Civic Improvements.
>
> Harlan P. Kelsey of this city, landscape gardener, with headquarters in Boston, has returned from a trip through the south, where, incidental to his business, he has done considerable lecturing on the subject of civic improvement. Through these lectures quite an active interest has been created in the different places where he spoke, and work has started under various auspices for the beautifying of the streets and settlements. In many of the places women's clubs have taken up the work.
>
> Mr. Kelsey lectured at Greenville, Columbia, Marion, Rock Hill and other places in South Carolina, and everywhere he has met with marked success. His careful study, combined with his skill as a landscape gardener, has qualified him to speak understandingly and eloquently on the subject of civic improvement.

Mrs. C. A. Woods of Marion, South Carolina, had for many years run the Civic Improvement League of Marion, encouraged the removal of hitching posts, and planted grass and shrubs. "Through the National Park Association, she obtained the help of a landscape architect, Harlan P. Kelsey, of Kelsey and Guild, Boston, Massachusetts, and in September 1904 he developed a blueprint, 'Planting a Plan of Public Square.' It was converted from a horse lot to a beautiful park."[60] A burst of activity immediately followed the Marion work.

The next year, 1905, he submitted an eighty-eight-page plan to the Civic League, Columbia, South Carolina, titled simply "The Improvement of Columbia, S. C." This was especially significant, given Columbia's stature as the capital of the state.

His work must have been well received because two years later he was engaged for a similar task by the city of Greenville, South Carolina. His report dated January 1907 was an extensive review of the city's problems and opportunities. It is worth a look at some of the detail to see what he was doing and how he went about it. It was titled "Beautifying and Improving Greenville, S. C." and opened as follows:

> GENTLEMEN:
> You have requested us to report to you the possibilities for beautifying and improving Greenville and to suggest practical ways to accomplish results.

He then minces no words in imploring them to do the job correctly:

> To mistake details for fundamentals, or in the natural desire to avoid opposition, to refrain at the outset from squarely facing the larger more essential problems of city plan and development is to risk losing all. For example a street cleaning campaign is worthy and necessary but unfortunately may be only temporary; while broad tree-lined thoroughfares well paved and drained are easier to care for, are permanent and are usually kept clean without question. It is wiser and really no more expensive in the end to provide proper and adequate sanitary conditions, than to appoint boards of health to quarantine disease.

Starting with a survey of the pluses and minuses of Greenville's current planning, he quickly moves to dealing with problems and opportunities in the usual municipal areas:

1) Greenville's streets.
2) The City's gateways.
3) The grouping of Greenville's public buildings.
4) Municipal architecture and art.
5) Sanitary matters and the abatement of nuisances.

6) Parks and playgrounds.
7) Greenville's gardens.
8) Cemeteries.
9) Redeeming Reedy River.

This was not a cosmetic treatment with landscaping the answer to everything; rather a full-blown attack on the problems. On sanitary matters he goes right at them with little restraint. For example:

> A careful examination was made of a number of slaughter pens supplying the Greenville markets and hotels with fresh meats. Some of the conditions found were disgusting and foul beyond descriptions and clouds of circling buzzards were always a sure guide to these places. A description of one will indicate the general conditions prevailing in all. This slaughter-pen is situated at the northeast limits of the city not far from north Main St. On near approach the stench was frightful, and hundreds of buzzards lazily arose to join the black cloud already in the air, while a nearer view revealed large numbers perched on rotting piles of bones, hair and offal, still gorging. The "pen" was open on all sides—a mere shell—allowing free access to man and beast, and carrion birds and hogs were at home inside reveling in and adding to the reeking putrid filth that thickly covered the floors, walls and utensils.

He goes on for two more paragraphs of even more lurid descriptive material before reaching his no-nonsense conclusion, namely, "The immediate closing of all slaughter-pens is recommended and municipal or private abattoirs, built of concrete or other like material, should take their place." No half measures here.

The bulk of the report does deal with the nicer suggested elements, punctuated with maps and diagrams plus photos of attractive bridges, waterways, parks, and such from Boston, Cleveland, Tacoma, and other sites. He closes with a clever treatment of the political difficulties of city planning:

> No plan in all its details will please every one, though all may agree on certain fundamentals, and for the common objective of making a beautiful city the sacrifice of personal views oft-times becomes necessary. This personal aspect of city betterment has aptly been described as follows: *It is impossible to make a city to suit the taste of everybody at all points; there are too many kinds of people: -- (1) The indifferent who simply don't care; (2) the Puritans who care nothing for "art," but are strong on cleanliness; (3) the Bohemians who rather prefer dirt as a picturesque setting for art, and detest orderliness; (4) the nature worshippers who think that Nature is your only guide, even in a city and would make "rus in urbe" their motto; (5) the decorators who think that nature has to be improved, if only with white-washed stones and cast-iron dogs; (6) those who like neatness and symmetry so much that they would cut down a fine tree rather than bend a nice brick sidewalk a yard; (7) those who love trees, so that they would let themselves and their houses rot rather than molest a single bough of the boscage; (8) those who appreciate beauty, but are cautious of the tax rate; (9) those who would light heartedly mortgage everything in sight for improvements; (10) those who would change everything on general principles; (11) those who would keep everything as it is on general principles.*

> The first and most important step to be taken, we believe to be the creating of a *non-political Metropolitan Improvement Commission* ... which will have ample and well defined powers to adopt and carry out a comprehensive plan ... Such Commissions have been tried and found extremely efficient in many communities ... The building of a beautiful city is a work of time, requiring patience, money and above all co-operation; we believe that none of these will be found lacking in Greenville.

Harlan P. Kelsey in 1910. Appeared in "The Highlands Nursery," *The National Nurseryman*, February 1910.

Conservation

As if all this family, nursery, and business activity were not enough, Kelsey's role in the AMC began to increase. He worked on preserving the White Mountains of New Hampshire as a close collaborator with his conservation mentor, Allen Chamberlain. Overall this was a huge undertaking. Chamberlain envisioned that his Department of Exploration and Forestry (DE&F) would become the driving force of the White Mountain preservation movement. How this played out is best told by former AMC librarian John Gerber. Previously covered was Gerber's history of earlier AMC efforts at preservation. While laudable, those efforts failed to hit the mark—effective protection from lumbering. Needed was a federally governed national forest for the White Mountains.[61]

One of Chamberlain's first acts as chairman of the DE&F in 1901 was to throw his full support behind his close friend Philip Ayers and the Society for the Preservation of New Hampshire Forests (SPNHF). In 1903 a coalition composed of the SPNHF, AMC, and the New Hampshire Forestry commission helped draft a bill calling for the creation of a forest reserve in the White Mountains. This marked the beginning of an eight-year congressional struggle to protect the White Mountains, which became the AMC's primary objective during the first decade of the twentieth century.

In 1904 club records drop Kelsey as councilor for Natural History and pick him up as councilor for DE&F, replacing Allen Chamberlain. Kelsey is now free of his prior Natural History (horticulture) duties, and Chamberlain is free to devote himself full-time to his lobbying efforts as club vice president, with the thirty-two-year-old Kelsey right behind him at DE&F. In the fall of 1905 Kelsey reported, "The most active work of the Department may this year be classed under forestry ... Exploration at the present time is not a very active function of the Department but forestry is." In 1906 Chamberlain became President of the AMC and after the traditional one-year term, reverted back to his position as councilor of DE&F. Kelsey subsequently became a trustee of Real Estate.[62]

As a means of mobilizing support for the bill, Chamberlain began corresponding with other forestry movements throughout New England and the United States. In 1904, 1,400 copies of a leaflet urging endorsement of the bill were sent to civic organizations and prominent individuals. Chamberlain also went on frequent speaking tours on behalf of the bill. When the first bill failed and a new one was reintroduced in the next congress, Chamberlain began a campaign to have AMC members exert pressure directly on Congress. Club members, he argued, had a personal duty to contact their representatives, which might provide the "weight that would turn the scales favorably." In 1906 he proposed that the AMC sponsor a forestry exhibition to educate the public on the bill. Later this was scaled back to an equipment and forestry exhibit at the Boston Sportsman's Show, which was turned into a traveling exhibit.

When the second bill failed, the AMC redoubled its efforts. A Committee on Legislation was created in 1908 in order to throw the "full weight" of the club behind the bill. The committee immediately sent Harrington Putnam to represent the AMC at the hearings. To broaden support, the bill was expanded to include another forest reserve in the southern Appalachians. When this attempt also failed, supporters of the bill tied it to protection of the navigability of rivers by arguing that forest cover was necessary at the headwaters to insure the river's flow. A December 1908 flyer from the AMC pointed out that there were 145 national forests, 12 national parks, and 17 national monuments and all these were west of the Mississippi River. All the headwaters of big rivers in this country were protected by national forests, except those in the White Mountains and southern Appalachians. *"Congress should provide for these eastern waterpowers. Write your Representative."*

Finally, on the fourth attempt, the goal was achieved with the passage of the Weeks Act in 1911. An AMC leader at the time attempted to sum up the club's long role in the struggle: "While the Club urges with others the economic necessity for the establishment of this [White Mountains] national forest, it sees its especial province to put forward the aesthetic argument in this case. This it has done consistently from the outset, until the validity of the claim has been recognized by government officers."

Specifically (in the tortured language of such instruments), "The Act of March 1, 1911 (Popularly known as the Weeks Law). *Footnote. This act provides for the acquisition of national forest system lands in the Eastern United States.* **CHAP. 186.** An Act to enable any State to cooperate with any other State or States, or with the United States, for the protection of the watersheds of navigable steams, and to appoint a commission for the acquisition of lands for the purpose of conserving the navigability of navigable rivers."

The early unsuccessful legislative attempts were constantly thwarted by the tenacious conviction of the Speaker of the House, Joseph Cannon, on federal expenditures, "not one cent for scenery." The press, including national magazines such as *Collier's*, blamed "Uncle Joe" Cannon for killing the national reserve bill in one congressional hearing after another.[63] The official reasons for rejection of the bills were primarily based either on their being a regional not a federal issue, or their being unconstitutional based on the House Judiciary Committee report that the federal government had no power to acquire lands within a state solely for forest reserves, but could purchase such lands only to protect the navigability of rivers.

The fourth and final successful bill had removed all reference to specific geographical areas and focused on the dollars-and-cents issue of watershed protection. The final version that passed provided the necessary authority and the means for accumulating new National forest reserves throughout the eastern states. In general: (1) authority for agreements between the States and Federal government for purchase of selected sites and asset swaps to allow consolidation of land areas as National Forests; (2) appropriation of moneys for acquisition with secure title to the acquired lands; and (3) rules, regulations, and provisions for a myriad of operational details. Apparently these many provisions finally satisfied the constitutional issues and quieted critics, but were not conducive to speedy implementation later by the newly appointed National Forest Reservation Commission.[64]

It seems odd that they waited until the fourth attempt to use the watershed argument for the Weeks Act, given the precedent for such reasoning. Roderick Nash gives us a framework to understanding the social climate of the time.[65] As early as 1869 William H. H. Murray, pastor of Boston's fashionable Park Street Congregational Church, wrote a book, *Adventures in the Wilderness: or, Camp-Life in the Adirondacks*, which sparked a movement in New York state for preservation of the wild Adirondack forests. Recreation was the initial motivation, but soon the rationale shifted to watershed concerns for the declining water levels of the Erie Canal and the Hudson River. This brought the politically connected business interests of New York City behind the forest preservation movement, leading to the 1885 state law establishing a "forest preserve" of 715,000 acres to remain permanently "as wild forest lands." Not satisfied with these protections based on the watershed argument, New Yorkers approved a measure in 1894 to have the principle of wilderness preservation written into the state constitution, based on the additional principle of aesthetic wilderness values.

Meanwhile, activities in the West fomented a vigorous debate over the use of natural resources—aesthetic vs. economic motivations. John Muir had been busy trying to expand the already protected Yosemite Valley into a 1,500-square-mile national park, which culminated in the 1890 Yosemite Act achieving some of Muir's ends. Worried about encroachments, Muir and others founded the Sierra Club in 1892 to act as an unofficial guardian and stimulus for more protection measures in the West, including efforts to create a park around Kings Canyon in the southern Sierras. All the publicity attending these events laid the foundation for an almost unnoticed amendment to an act revising the general land laws that passed Congress in 1891. Under its provisions, the president was empowered to create "forest reserves" by withdrawing government-owned land from the public domain. President Harrison promptly proclaimed fifteen reserves totaling more than thirteen million acres, but without specifying the function of the reserved areas.

The mere existence of the new forest reserves precipitated a struggle between opposing camps over the purpose of the reserves. Muir and friends, including Harvard's Charles Sprague Sargent, thought they comprised wilderness preserves with all the protections of a national park. Muir's earlier friend, Gifford Pinchot, assumed the reserves were set aside for the practice of scientifically managed forestry, with selective cutting and reforestation. The foresters were backed up by the grazing and mining interests. The struggle severed the friendly relationship between Muir and Pinchot, who went on to became chief forester of the US Forest Service and custodian of the reserves. Pinchot's philosophy that natural resources should be used, but wisely, led him to favor opening all the reserves to carefully managed economic development.

The struggle between the preservationist and the utilitarian factions came to a head during the first decade of the twentieth century in the United States Congress. The White Mountains issue was only a skirmish compared to the huge battle in the West over utilization of Yosemite National Park. The city of San Francisco faced a chronic fresh water shortage and city engineers wanted to dam the narrow lower end of the Hetch Hetchy Valley for a reservoir. The only problem was that the 1890 act creating Yosemite National Park designated Hetch Hetchy and its environs a wilderness preserve. The battle raged at the federal level from 1906 to 1913 when President Wilson finally signed the bill approving the Hetch Hetchy grant for a reservoir. All during this time the utilitarians, supported by the forestry/grazing/mining interests, managed to dominate the prevailing sentiment within the Congress. As long as this was going on, the easterners' early versions of the Weeks Act had little chance of success because of their total focus on the aesthetic arguments. Had they shifted earlier to the watershed argument (clearly utilitarian) they might have had quicker results.

The federal forest reserves of the late nineteenth century all involved usage allocations of federal land, not private land. The White Mountains of New Hampshire, like most eastern lumbering tracts, were privately held, and the Weeks Act provided the means for the acquisition of those holdings by the government for watershed protection and preservation. In fact, the first acquisitions were not the White Mountains, but rather in the southern Appalachians, the Pisgah National Forest.[66] Since Pisgah lies in the Blue Ridge just north east of Highlands, North Carolina, Kelsey's home territory, this must have pleased him. Gradually over the ensuing decade, the bulk of today's White Mountain National Forest area was accumulated.

There was one big problem with the forest reserves and the national forests. No one had defined exactly how they were to be used. Almost immediately the lumbering, grazing, and mining interests started gaining easements and leases to continue "business as usual" within the confines of the reserves. The resulting abuses led to President Roosevelt's 1901 creation of the Bureau of Forestry (later the Forest Service) under the Department of Agriculture, and to the entry of Gifford Pinchot, as chief forester, into the administration of usage within the forests.

Pinchot had been trained in European methods of sustained forestry—judicious cutting and reforestation for sustained yield. It was the application of these good intentions that became the problem. If grazing flocks of sheep destroyed the wildflowers of the high Sierra meadows, how and when would they be restored? Who would gather the lumbering slash to avoid forest fires? Who would replant? Pinchot had to deal with the irate senators and congressmen aroused by their supporters in the western states. This led to constant compromising, and in the eyes of Muir and Kelsey, unacceptable destruction of the wilderness they had fought so hard to preserve. Two of Pinchot's positions that were particularly galling to the preservationists were his statements that sheep grazing was not harmful, and that the Hetch Hetchy dam and reservoir would not seriously damage Yosemite National Park. He offered any assistance he could to help the city of San Francisco in gaining approval for Hetch Hetchy. There were many other similar stands, and the tone was clearly set. Over the next thirty to forty years, the National Park Service resisted all efforts to accept park propositions that were under the control of the Forest Service.

Nursery Business

All during the first decade of the twentieth century Kelsey's nursery business thrived. He was riding the crest of an evolving wave of change in the nursery industry, namely "the shift of the industry from being concerned primarily with the production and distribution of fruit-bearing plants to being concerned primarily with the production and use of ornamental plants in landscape design."[67] His niche was to be constantly trumpeting the superiority of hardy American plants. In 1903 he writes, "We have gradually enlarged until now our nursery occupies some sixty acres of land on which are grown over five hundred species of hardy native American trees, shrubs, bulbs, vines, ferns and herbaceous plants. Single species are grown by tens of thousands; for instance, this season we offer 40,000 *Rhododendron maximum,* 24,000 *Kalmia latifolia,* 20,000 Hemlock, and other things in proportion, our shipments extending over the civilized world. ... We feel justly proud of the work we have accomplished in making our Native Plants known and used, for while a few years ago they were almost entirely excluded from our American parks, lawns and gardens they are now planted by hundreds of thousands, and appreciated and enjoyed as never before. Each year sees them better known, more widely used, and more loved by the refined class, to whom natural rather than exotic effects appeal."[68]

One might ask how Harlan Kelsey could oversee such a substantial operation so far away from Boston while devoting so much time to landscape architecture and to the Appalachian Mountain Club. The answer is he didn't; his father did. Again, in 1903 he writes, "Mr. S. T. Kelsey has been in active charge of the growing and shipping of stock at Highlands Nursery in North Carolina, and to him and to faithful employees who have long been with us must be given the credit." By this time E. C. Robbins had matured into S. T. Kelsey's trusted number-one employee at the nursery.

By 1908, five years later, Kelsey wrote, "I have the largest collection of strictly Hardy American Plants—and especially Rhododendrons and Azaleas—in existence. Over 100 acres and 600 species of native plants." He also says "to save freight charges, to northern points only, I ship carload lots of *Rhododendron maximum* and *Kalmia latifolia* from special supplies in the Pennsylvania mountains, but to all southern points, shipments are made from the southern mountains, the best clumps coming from the South." He adds, "At Salem Branch, Salem, Mass., is kept a fine stock of large specimen clumps, mostly budded ... Highlands Nursery is still the only large collection of American plants exclusively in existence. Over 100,000 Rhododendrons and Azaleas actually growing in Nursery."[69]

Two years later in the February 1910 issue of the *National Nurseryman*, a feature article appeared, titled "The Highlands Nursery," seemingly ghostwritten by Harlan Kelsey. It opened as follows:

> While not discouraging the importation of the best plants which foreign countries offer, the National Nurseryman has frequently advocated and consistently stands for the relatively greater value of American plants as a whole for American conditions than any exotics that may be introduced. Critics of this statement may cite some important exceptions and point to the remarkable examples of the immediate adaptation of a

few oriental plants, to American soil and climate, and we shall accept the amendment without demur. But when the whole situation is carefully considered we cannot fail to see that these are the exceptions and that they by no means rise to the dignity and importance of the rule. We are to remember also that not all plants imported from Europe are of European origin. Many of our valuable conifers for instance are of American origin but simply propagated in Europe owing to the enabling economic conditions. For these reasons we have great pleasure in presenting a descriptive sketch of a nursery that for a quarter of a century has labored consistently and intelligently for the spread of interest in purely native plants. The story of the growth of this nursery is exceedingly interesting. It is in effect the story of the life work of a man convinced that North America has a wealth of native plants unsurpassed by that of any other country and that these as a whole are better adapted to our own soil and climatic conditions than any which can be introduced.

Later, in the same publication, Kelsey explained his Salem branch. "It was desirable to maintain an establishment from which shipments of mature plants might be made on short notice. This was done by acquiring a tract of land in the historic town of Salem and equipping it with such an assortment as were most in demand by Eastern planters. Many of the rarer rhododendron hybrids are grown at Salem, which is now also the business headquarters of the Highlands Nursery." The Salem Branch is located "on Salem—Marblehead Road."[70] It must have been adjacent to the Marblehead town line, beyond the southern tip of Salem Harbor. A 1911 letter from the state nursery inspector says, "I am also notifying the pastor of the Catholic Church of Marblehead, and asking him that the lot adjoining your nursery be cleared up."

Quarantines to control the spread of pests and plant diseases first became an issue as early as 1875 when the state of Michigan enacted a law in regard to the peach yellow disease. Gradually a proliferation of state laws of quarantine spread like a cloud over the entire industry. The first national legislation was proposed in 1892: "A Bill to Prohibit the Interstate Transportation of Trees, Plants, Vines or Other Nursery Stock Infected with … and the Importation into the United States from Any Foreign Country, of Any Thereof So Affected." The bill failed to be considered, fortunately, since its enactment would have been a transportation disaster.[71]

On June 10, 1910, the state nursery inspector informed Massachusetts nurserymen that "Each shipment of stock from a Massachusetts nursery into New York or New Jersey must be immediately reported by the shipper to the nursery inspector of the state to which it goes, giving date of shipment and name and address of consignee. Nurseries within the territory occupied by the Gypsy moth or Brown-tail moth must be inspected after September 15th, by the State Nursery Inspector … at the expense of the nursery owner." On October 31, 1911, the state nursery inspector informed the nurserymen, "The situation of Massachusetts nursery stock in relation to other states is becoming acute. In New York particularly, there is some danger of an attempt to shut out all stock from here, on the ground that in spite of our inspection, the Gypsy and Brown-tail Moths are often present. This is certainly open to dispute, but cannot be helped. We need evidence on the other side to show just the condition in which stock is sent to us. … [I]f we are to meet complaint with complaint, we must know what we are getting. Will you help?"

At this point Kelsey may have been wondering at the wisdom of having both a Massachusetts and a North Carolina nursery. The quarantine issue would only become a greater thorn in the nurseryman's side as the future unfolded. Scrapping the Massachusetts nursery and retreating to solely North Carolina would seriously hamper the growth of the business. Salem, a well built-up city, didn't provide the acreage for real expansion of the Salem branch. He must find the acreage needed at a reasonable price, somewhere else in Essex County.

On November 1, 1909, the following dissolution notice was mailed:

> "By mutual consent the firm of Kelsey & Guild is this day dissolved. Mr. Kelsey will continue to practice Landscape architecture at his offices, Empire Theatre Building, Salem, and Mr. Guild at No. 4 Joy Street, Boston."

While the dissolution notice seems abrupt and elicits speculation of a falling-out between the two men, it was probably a simple act of convenience. After all, Kelsey was in fact operating out of Salem and Guild out of Boston. Further, payroll records of ensuing years show that Guild continued to work for Kelsey periodically, under contract rather than as a partner.

Landscape Architecture

A decade after opening his Boston landscape architecture business, the scope of Kelsey's influence and reputation had increased markedly. An example of this was his retention for the design and planting of Bleak House, Mr. Marsden J. Perry's new residence in Newport, Rhode Island.

Marsden Perry was a notable force in Rhode Island. A former chairman of the board, Norfolk Southern Railroad, director of the General Electric Company, and many others, he got his start organizing the American Ring Traveler Company, a Providence manufacturing firm. He acquired two electric utilities (monopolizing the industry in Rhode Island), and railway systems that comprised practically all of Rhode Island lines.[72]

The *New York Times* for July 14, 1907, helped put all this in perspective. The headline read, "Newport Season Really On—Very Few of the Notable Residences are Closed—Coming of Marsden J. Perry Noted With Interest." Within the text is the following paragraph:

The sale of the Ross R. Winans villa to Marsden J. Perry of Providence has occasioned not a little speculation as to the intentions of the Perrys in coming to Newport. In Providence Mr. Perry has held a high position in the financial world, and Mrs. Perry has been one of the principal leaders in the social world. It is known that Mrs. Perry has higher social ambitions, and that in coming to Newport as a cottage owner she will appear in the role of a climber, and that she is seeking admission into the higher circles of the select in this city. The coming of the Marsden J. Perrys to Newport is looked upon with pleasure by Newport generally, as it means the reopening of a large villa which has been closed for a number of years, the Winanses having spent nearly the entire time since the house was completed in Europe, leaving Bleak House closed.

The house stood on the east side of Ocean Drive opposite Winans Avenue, between Castle Hill and Brenton Point.

Kelsey only dealt with Perry directly when discussing general horticultural and design aspects of the landscaping work, and even then not always. At all other times he dealt through Perry's residential architect, Mr. Sheldon, of Stone, Carpenter & Sheldon of Providence. This was a difficult circumstance for Kelsey. Scheduling of the job was tight. Things started in late 1911, with a blueprint of the lot's contours not available until January 1912, and the blueprint was obsolete, requiring anecdotal statements as to the changes. These included a new road cut through the south end of the estate and a new entrance and oval recently put in. Based on this, Kelsey had to execute the landscape design and specifications by spring when the ground thawed. That left only five months, May–September, to complete all planting work before the fall freeze. Kelsey kept impressing on Mr. Sheldon that "Mr. Perry kept insisting on this to me that it must look finished this year, and if we approximate his wishes it is going to take the very kind of material that I refer to."

Sheldon, of course, was always responding to Perry's requests for tight dollar control. Kelsey couldn't meet budget targets without using, for example, smaller Rhododendrons, confounding the need for a "finished look" by fall. Perry would suggest "this" through Mr. Sheldon. Kelsey would counter with "that" for better landscape design, again through Sheldon to Perry. As early as April 2, Kelsey told Sheldon, "Already a carload of plants from my Highlands Nursery is on the way containing presumably mostly the large Rhododendrons." Kelsey was in no way cowed in dealing with the wishes of the superwealthy. His constant position, hard for his wealthy client to resist, was quality, quality, quality.

Sheldon wrote, "Mr. Perry wants to make the principal part of his planting Rhododendrons, Rosa rugosa, Barberries and Bayberries, with the other things subordinated to these. We should like to keep the planting this year down to about Five Thousand Dollars."

On March 26, Kelsey wrote Sheldon, "It is almost impossible to make such an estimate as you call for, for reasons which are easily stated. I am looking everywhere for some of the stock I want to use, and I am very anxious to use only the right thing. For the bank on the ocean side of the estate I want to use some clumps of native material collected in the vicinity with a few other plants and vines to be sent. For the Rhododendrons I am not able to state just exactly the size of the different clumps sent by my Nursery, as I have told them to pick out the best specimens in largest sizes. The same applies to the Hybrid Rhododendrons, which I must pick up in different places, where I can find well grown specimens of the hardiest varieties only."

Special effort was expended on 150 red cedars to be transplanted along the ocean side of the property, some as large as thirty-five feet in height. On April 1 Sheldon wrote, "These trees have grown on the hills several miles inland from the sound and while they have withstood high winds, are not, of course, acclimated to the salt fog and spray. We are afraid that when these trees are first wet with the salt spray and the sun strikes them the foliage will dry up. However, this is something you know a great deal more about than we do." Kelsey immediately replied, "Regarding the Cedars standing the spray, I think the proper way to test this is to have a few trees dug up in Tiverton and plant them along with those that are coming from New Canaan. This is the only way to give a fair trial of the conditions. For my part I am satisfied there will be no difference between them, but it is a very good plan to make ourselves sure in case of future planting."[73]

Family Distress

In Dugger's unpublished memoir of Mr. S. T. Kelsey, he opens with, "The writer of this sketch is the first person to whom Mr. Kelsey revealed his plans at Linville, North Carolina, and to him he sent his last farewell, when in 1910 he boarded the train at Elk Park, North Carolina, and departed never to return." Linville must have been a weight on STK's shoulders after his grand vision for the town evaporated. The lumbermen had scarred the pristine high woodlands. His wife, Katherine, had died September 18, 1909, while visiting her daughter in Las Cruces, New Mexico. The nursery was doing quite well in the supervisory hands of E. C. Robbins. The rest of the family had all moved elsewhere. He was seventy-eight years old. Until his death, he divided his time between his sons—Truman in Los Angeles, Harry in Baltimore, and Harlan in Salem.

As STK left the nursery in Pineola and settled into a decade of quiet retirement, Florence's elderly father did the opposite, aggressively continuing his jewelry business while staying in command of "all things Salem." This couldn't last. The *Salem Evening News* reported:

> On February 3rd, 1911 Daniel Low came from his home in a carriage in the forenoon and attended to business as usual, visiting several places and attending a meeting of the directors of the Merchants Bank, as was his custom. About one o'clock in the afternoon, while dictating correspondence to his stenographer, Miss Coughlin, he

complained of not feeling well. He took a pill, which he had for such attacks, but he seemed to grow steadily worse, although he did not say very much about it. In fact he talked with his son, S. Fred Low, and Henry Mitchell, the business manager, but in a few minutes it was apparent that the attack, which up to that time was similar to those to which he had been subject, was growing worse and word was instantly dispatched by telephone and messenger for three doctors. Drs. Peirson, Sargent and Ferguson responded. Mr. Low expressed the belief to Mr. Mitchell that he guessed that this attack would be fatal, and lapsed into unconsciousness from which he never rallied in spite of the efforts of the doctors, and he breathed his last just before 2 o'clock.

When it became apparent that the unfortunate man was beyond the help of earthly agencies, the shock to the entire corps of employees was terrible. Men and women alike wept, for Mr. Low was held in the fondest regard by his entire corps of employees from managers down to the most humble errand boy. One man, in fact was so affected that he fainted, while some of the young women employees were almost prostrated. The store was at once closed for the day. … The announcement in the last edition of the News yesterday afternoon of the death of Daniel Low came to thousands of citizens as a flash of lightning out of a clear sky, and expressions of the great loss sustained by the city in the death of one of her most active business men and foremost citizens were heard on every side.[74]

Evidence of Mr. Low's importance to the city lay in the fact that the excerpts above appeared as a front page lead article that had to be continued with two long columns on page 10. The heirs included Florence, her now widowed mother who had been an invalid for some time, and two brothers, Seth F. Low and Dr. Harry Low. Seth continued operating the jewelry business, and Harry became a noted orthopedic surgeon at the Massachusetts General Hospital in Boston.

Chapter 4

Gaining Stature

Historic Boxford

As early as 1628, only eight years after the Pilgrims landed at Plymouth, Gov. John Endicott came to Salem with his company and formed the first permanent settlement in Essex County, Massachusetts. Other settlers moved gradually farther up the coast to found Ipswich and Rowley on the eastern bounds, Andover on the west, and along the Merrimack River to the north. The unsettled center territory of today's Essex County was the land of the Agawams. In 1638 their sachem, Masconomet, conveyed by deed to John Winthrop, son of the governor of Massachusetts, all his right to these lands, in consideration of twenty pounds. Settlement of this interior territory, known as Rowley Village, was slow. By 1685, with forty families, the village petitioned the general court for a town charter so they could call their own minister. It was granted and they selected the name of Boxford for the new town, after the birthplace of the beloved Rev. Mr. Phillips, the minister in Rowley at this time—Boxford, Berkshire, in England, or so the story goes.

The original Boxford Village lay in the center of a flat plain with a high water table, terrific for farming. It remained just that for two hundred and fifty years. A small settlement developed in West Boxford, and later the railroad depot was identified as East Boxford. But the township's population stabilized at roughly a thousand people. It was all that the land would support on small working farms. Strong economic and population growth took place in Boston to the south, Salem to the east, Andover to the west, and the Merrimack River mill cities to the north. Traveling in Essex County out from any of these cities, Boxford was figuratively "the last place you got to."

The Boxford Nursery

Florence Kelsey gives us a firsthand picture of Boxford, and her family's interest, in excerpts from her paper written for the Boxford Literary Society, April 1940. It was titled *Houses and Happenings on a Boxford Plain*.

> For me, the happenings on this Boxford Plain or Great Pasture are full of interest, and as I have written this record partly for my family I hope you will excuse the personal references.
>
> The surface of Boxford consists of hills and valleys with the exception of two or three quite extensive plains or pastures. The largest of these is the site of the East Parish as Boxford Village is called. The second in size is the old Camp Ground, in what now is called East Boxford; third is West Boxford center.
>
> It was in 1912 … that Mr. Kelsey began to look for land in Essex County suitable for a nursery with level fields, and on a water table where plenty of water was available—and near a railroad station, which appeared to be quite necessary at that time, but is not so important now. The East Boxford Plain seemed just the place and in 1912 he purchased his first farm of 90 acres from Miss Mary Abby Herrick, where once stood the old Aaron Wood house, which was burned in 1877.

In 1912 the barn, where our present Shipping and Sales Department are now, was still standing and became the office of the Boxford Nursery—though Mr. Kelsey was still carrying on his North Carolina Nursery and the main office for both was in Salem. … I can remember in 1912, standing in the doorway of the fine old barn and looking out over the farm. I wondered when we should see signs of a nursery instead of fields of corn and grain, and as the little seedlings were started and small trees and shrubs were planted, and propagation was begun I thought what a vision and courage it took to plan for so many years ahead.

Recordings in the Essex County Registry of Deeds actually show Kelsey's 1912 purchases consisted of three separate transactions: the Stevens Farm, the Herrick Farm, and the Hayes Farm, comprising in total just under 110 acres. That was slightly more than the entire area of the North Carolina nursery at the time.

There is no record of exactly what motivated Kelsey to suddenly double his nursery capacity. We can only speculate. Business was no doubt good and expanding. Perhaps he also felt some unease with his father's recent departure from North Carolina. STK had been in charge of all the nursery production operations—propagating, planting, growing, shipment, and quality control. Now E. C. Robbins had to step into those rather large "shoes," untested in that new important role. Perhaps the Boxford Nursery was a hedge against future problems that might develop. He wasn't to know until later what a fine job Robbins would do. Robbins's descendants say that for a brief period Robbins moved up to Boxford to help Kelsey with the massive new planting job.

Florence's description that "the little seedlings were started and small trees and shrubs were planted" is a massive understatement of the job that was accomplished. Detailed nursery records show that 1912 shipments to Boxford from the North Carolina nursery included 40,720 individual specimens spanning thirty-three species from seventeen genera. In addition, orders were placed with nurseries in Massachusetts, Wisconsin, Illinois, Maine, New Jersey, Connecticut, and Rhode Island for another 17,402 individual specimens for species not available from the North Carolina nursery. All told it amounted to 58,122 specimens requiring loading off the railroad, transportation, planting, watering, and selection for propagation—all just for starters.

The fall 1912/spring 1913 catalog carries the logo: KELSEY'S Hardy American Plants, Rhododendrons and Azaleas. Always address HARLAN P. KELSEY Owner of Highlands Nursery, and Salem and Boxford Nurseries. Salem, Mass., U.S.A.

The fall 1913/spring 1914 catalog carries the same logo for Kelsey's Hardy American Plants but no longer mentions the Salem branch, only the North Carolina and Boxford nurseries. Importantly it defines more particularly his American plant message:

What We Really Plant
70 percent European trees and shrubs and horticultural* varieties.
20 percent Chinese and Japanese.
10 percent American.

What We Ought To Plant
70 percent American trees and shrubs, i.e. native to America.
20 percent Chinese and Japanese.
10 percent European and horticultural*.

* [We assume "horticultural" refers to hybrids.]

Bringing in 58,122 specimens to Boxford was a good start, but only a start for Kelsey.

September 10, 1912

Prof. C. S. Sargent,
    Arnold Arboretum,
    Jamaica Plain, Mass.

My Dear Sir:

I am anxious to make a good collection of seeds of the plants at Arnold Arboretum, and trust you can again favor me with a permit. I am anxious to get a good start at my new Nursery at Boxford growing all the best hardy shrubs, particularly of the newer varieties that you have in the Arboretum.

Also, I am particularly anxious to get some of the new Wilson material, either plants or seeds, or both.

I am making arrangements so I can give them the very best care, and I believe I have the right kind of soil to handle them successfully, particularly the ericaceous species.

I am offering the Rhododendron carolinianum as such for the first time this fall.

                Yours truly,
                Harlan P. Kelsey[75]

July 14, 1913

Prof. C. S. Sargent,
    Arnold Arboretum,
    Jamaica Plain, Mass.

Dear Prof. Sargent:

Please accept my best thanks for the packages of Prunus Sargenti which are received. I am greatly interested in all the Prunus, particularly the American species, and those with conspicuous fruit. I am wondering what is the best way to handle these seeds. I think probably I will have them stratified and planted out early next spring.

Have I the permission to have some seeds collected this year? There are some of the earlier things, which I think ought to be collected now. Last year I missed a number of the best things, including all the Prunus family.

Yours truly,

Harlan P. Kelsey[76]

Kelsey's Boxford Nursery was only twenty-five miles north of the Arnold Arboretum, a remarkable resource for him in his horticultural activities. Today the Arnold describes itself as follows:

The Arnold Arboretum of Harvard University

The 265-acre Arnold Arboretum displays North America's premier collection of hardy trees, shrubs, and vines. The grounds were planned and designed by the Arboretum's first director, Charles Sprague Sargent, and America's first landscape architect, Frederick Law Olmsted. Begun in 1872 and named for its benefactor James Arnold, the Arboretum remains one of the best preserved of Olmsted's landscapes.

The 4,500 kinds of woody plants cultivated in the Arboretum's collections are grouped together by plant family for easy comparison ... In addition to the living collections the Arboretum maintains library and herbarium collections housed in the Hunnewell Building and the Harvard University Herbaria Building in Cambridge.

The Arboretum is a National Historic Landmark and an international center for scientific research and education. It is an integral part of the series of parklands known as the Emerald Necklace and is a functioning unit of the Boston Parks Department.

While Kelsey's Boxford Nursery was now just as important to the business as the North Carolina operation, the business headquarters remained in Salem. He and Florence still lived in Salem. However, the locus of Kelsey's attention would gradually shift to Boxford over the ensuing years. He still supplied customers from the hundred-plus acres of his North Carolina nursery, but Boxford was where all his business initiatives were to be focused. By October 17, 1914, he informed the state nursery inspector that he had "about 115 acres in my nursery tract, and perhaps of this, 45 acres [are] now planted."

His order book by 1915 shows a truly national operation spanning a broad range of customers:

1915 Nursery Orders[77]

Wholesale Orders	199 Names in 31 States & Canada
Architects Orders	10 Names
Agricultural Colleges Orders	12 Names
Botanical Gardens Orders	21 Names
Cemetery Orders	9 Names
Experimental Station Orders	6 Names
Landscape Architects Orders	60 Names in 13 States
Park Orders	42 Names

It might even be said the business was international. James Veitch & Sons, Ltd., often considered England's premier nursery at the time, wrote Kelsey as follows, February 11, 1914: "Dear Sir, We are in receipt of your letter and in reply have pleasure in saying that the plants we have received from you have at all times given us satisfaction, and the packing has been good."

There may be another factor influencing the 1912 shift in emphasis from nursery operations to Boxford from North Carolina. Any local markets for the Pineola operation were blanketed at that time by vigorous competition from the huge nursery at the Biltmore Estate in Asheville. The Biltmore nursery was started in 1890 on the banks of the French Broad River, which flowed through the estate grounds. Its purpose at first was solely to generate nursery stock for planting the massive grounds and roadways of the estate, which Frederick Law Olmsted envisioned. By 1898, with the estate fully planted, the emphasis changed to commercial operations. This was wholly in keeping with Vanderbilt's overall plan. "Mr. Vanderbilt realized his dream of a productive estate. The farms yielded fruits, vegetables, grain crops, meat and dairy products, and honey from 41 beehives. The forest produced some 3,000 cords of firewood annually, which were sold along with lumber processed at Biltmore's own mill. And the 300 acre nursery complete with greenhouses, cold frames, and seed beds, offered for sale about five million plants—one of the most complete stocks in the country."[78] Their catalogs were huge 8 ½" by 11" full-color masterpieces, with numerous specialty catalogs as well. Competitively, Vanderbilt did nothing but the best, with no expense spared.

Kelsey's one-hundred-acre nursery, one hundred miles away up in the mountains, was like a gnat, not even a factor competitively, to the Biltmore folks. If Kelsey was to expand, Boxford, thousands of miles away from the Biltmore, was the better business alternative. As a post script, Kelsey needn't have worried about the Biltmore Nursery. In 1916 there was a great flood of the French Broad River (of century proportions), which scoured the plain on which the nursery sat. The nursery was effectively eradicated and never rebuilt. Mother Nature accomplished what Kelsey could never have done competitively.

More City Planning

The 1907 Greenville Plan was followed by an extended pause before Kelsey's next planning enterprise. This time his own city was involved. On December 26, 1912, the Salem City Plans Commission published its "First Annual Report." It was written entirely by the Subcommittee on City Plan, Harlan P. Kelsey, chairman. This civic work was going on at the same time as Kelsey's huge effort in establishing the Boxford Nursery.

A year and a half earlier, April 12, 1911, an "Ordinance Creating the Salem City Plans Commission" was signed by the mayor. Beyond the secretary and ex-officio members, there were five members with staggered terms. Four of them were working members of the Sub-Committee on City Plans. Kelsey had the longest term and was appointed chairman, clearly the driving force. Unlike his three prior "for-profit" plans in South Carolina, this enterprise was a "labor of love." The ordinance specified that the five members of the commission "shall serve without compensation." In actual fact, the Sub-Committee on City Plan was a three-man effort with Kelsey in the lead.

The ordinance specified that the commission would study the entire city, resulting in a plan that best adapted the present conditions to the future needs of Salem—pretty standard fare. But it went into great detail on "areas of special consideration."

The subcommittee kept pretty close to this specification, with a few telling excursions that hint at their prior commitment to its goals. There were ten specified areas, very much like the nine specific "problems and opportunities" Kelsey delineated in his 1907 report to Greenville, South Carolina.

First they emphasized how hard they had worked, with nineteen meetings not counting other joint meetings with nine other official boards and civic organizations during the year. Before getting into specific recommendations, they pounded away at the city's shortcomings from inadequate planning in the past, with stinging phrases like "revolting and unsanitary conditions," "almost intolerable," and "bartered for private selfish gain permitted by public indifference." They pulled no punches—action was needed now.

Second, they tried to prevent the common practice of acknowledging a plan and then ignoring it in practice. They lamented the absence of "home rule," which would allow the municipalities to proceed with needed improvements without legislative approval of the State. They discussed common methods used in other states and overseas to *let improvements pay for themselves*, specifically Excess Condemnation and Zone Assessment. As they treated each "area of special consideration" they emphasized how modest current costs would be in comparison to staggering costs in the future from lost opportunities.

Of course, Kelsey couldn't avoid getting in a few licks for better horticultural practices:

"Salem's shade trees are fast disappearing. Of the noble Elms and Maples of Lafayette, Chestnut, Federal and other streets and those around the Common and on certain streets in North Salem, but few can be found that are in an entirely healthy condition." Of Salem's 3,292 street trees reported in a 1906 survey, "only 481 trees were in actually first-class condition, 1,295 trees in actually bad condition, and 1,516 only in fair condition." The report even included a diagram of how the Newark, New Jersey, Shade Tree Commission selects and plants trees "to help the tree live in the city under artificial conditions."

Two of their repetitious underlying themes were (1) congestion and (2) the commingling of housing, industrial, and commercial activities.

Regarding congestion, Kelsey's subcommittee report included a separate section on "The Housing Problem." The opening paragraph is noteworthy:

Salem's population and buildings are increasing rapidly and the congestion in parts of the city is a growing menace to the health and welfare of the community. The "Point" district in Ward 5 is closely built up with mostly three- and four-deckers, and with narrow streets. The "Three-decker Madness" is extending to other parts of this Ward, the buildings usually being of flimsy and unsanitary construction and in violation of modern rules of plumbing, ventilation and home comfort. ... The fire menace from this cause is already criminal and fast increasing, and the happiness and health of thousands of Salem's mothers and children is bartered for private *selfish gain, permitted by public indifference*. No spot is left open for playgrounds or breathing spaces.

The commingling of activities was also dealt with in a separate section titled "Manufacturing, Business and Residence Zones," as follows:

Salem is a highly concentrated city. This has produced a congestion of business as well as population. Inadequate, indirect streets or lines of travel have helped to make the conditions such that the houses of our citizens are for a large part in hopeless proximity to the noises, smells and clamor of business and factory. The time is here when the ideals of a city must rise above mere commercial supremacy to the higher ground of becoming an attractive and healthful home for all of its citizens. The profound and beneficent results of the "Zone System" as demonstrated in German cities may well be considered by us if we are to progress sanely.

The Salem Fire

Kelsey didn't confine his efforts to the work of the subcommittee. He sought to expand public awareness of Salem's problems and opportunities. "Harlan P. Kelsey, of the Civic League, has delivered many illustrated lectures on city planning, showing how we could widen our streets and beautify our city. This gentleman has made a deep study of this subject both at home and abroad. He has some fine slides of pictures he took himself, among them some showing three and four deckers with no space between them."[79]

Kelsey's subcommittee wasn't alone in predicting grave future outcomes.

Franklin H. Wentworth, a Salem councilman, introduced an order that would have required all new or replacement roof coverings to be noncombustible. After a big fire, many of the working class would have to live in tents, he warned. Wentworth was accused of serving only the interest of the insurance industry, and the amendment did not pass. Another failed attempt to increase safety in Salem was undertaken by Charles J. Collins. He had visited Philadelphia, where high-pressure wagons pumped water through 3.25 inch pipes for a range of 360 feet. The argument went that high-pressure pumps would pay for themselves with the reduction of insurance fees. Protecting the entire business and mercantile district would have cost $150,000.

On May 29, 1914, the city of Salem passed an ordinance establishing the Salem Planning Board. The state had enacted the enabling legislation the year before, giving such boards broad powers and authority, and Salem was the first to take advantage of it. It had five members, without compensation, none of whom could be a councilman, an officer, or employee of the city. The earlier 1911 City Plans Commission ordinance was repealed, ceding the prior planning functions to the new board. It went into effect June 18, becoming the first of its kind in the nation. Harlan P. Kelsey was immediately appointed and then elected as chairman. But it was too late; in a matter of days, disaster struck. Arthur B. Jones, formerly assistant chief, subsequently a member of Hose Company Number 2 of Salem, wrote *The Salem Fire*, a short book on the details of the fire and its aftermath. Editorialized excerpts follow below:

Midday June 25, 1914, the city was rocked by a quick series of explosions. At 1:37 p.m., a fire alarm box was used to report a fire in the Korn leather factory, caused by combustion of acetone, amalacitate, and celluloid. The fire started in a shed, which opened by a wooden door into a room on the street floor. Reuben Salkovich was on the first floor of the factory when he discovered the fire. He said the flames burst through the door of the shed, where the explosive mixture was stored, and spread through the building so rapidly he had to run for his life. His clothing and face were scorched.

The fire spread quickly. The Quinn block on the east caught immediately and the Creedon factories on the west; the fire, crossing Proctor Street, caught the Cunney factory and burned half of the brick block formerly occupied by the Sheridan Club. The flames swept down Boston Street, crossing the street to the Keefe factory. Soon the Carr Bros., Marrs Bros., Dane Machine Company, and Way Leather Company were going, and now everything in lower Boston Street was doomed. In the meantime help was summoned from all the immediately adjacent cities and towns, and they were at work in remarkably short time. The combined efforts of these departments were unavailing, and it was left with the police department to summon other cities and towns and also to send the military call. Fire alarm boxes were being pulled everywhere in the path of the flames.

Fowler Street to the school, and nearly to the corner of North Pine, was swept. Numerous houses were dynamited as fire breaks, to no avail. The wind took embers to Leach Street and six houses here were destroyed, over a mile from the fire. And so it went all afternoon, street after street, block after block. Some of the best homes in the city were destroyed. The "point district," whose three- and four-deckers were highlighted in the subcommittee's report, caught through the side streets, the fire going down Lagrange Street after 7:00 p.m. Police and citizens got people off the point. Pickering's coal piles and wharves were on fire now, and with Lane's wharf, thousands of tons of coal were burning. At Lane's wharf, a three-story brick building with a blind wall on the east gave the firemen the opportunity desired, and the local battle was won there. The Salem spraying machine protected Derby wharf.

At 9:06 p.m. box 613 sounded for a fire starting in Merritt's Express barn and the sorely tried firemen turned their attention to this new fire, which seriously threatened North Salem and Ward 2. On into the night it went. Jones's book cited story after story of heroism and despair, irony and pathos. A sampling follows:

Engine 4 worked first at the front of the Korn factory, Robertson Court, at the corner of Boston and Essex. Here they stayed so long that Arthur Russell and Driver Gahgen in disconnecting the hose and removing the chuck had to have the Lynn boys play the hose on them.

A woman bought a new pocket book the day before the fire. Going into her house in a hurry she snatched the new pocket book and saved it, but the money, over $50.00, was in the old one.

A retired fire captain of Boston heard of the fire and came down with his son, not stopping to tell his wife where he had gone. Over around Peabody Street, a blazing pole fell on him, knocking him unconscious. After they brought him to, he hustled for home not telling his wife then where he had been, but two days after, she discovered the bruises on his shoulder and he had to confess.

A woman gave her husband two hat boxes to take to a safe place. In one were his two best suits of clothes, in the other two fine Angora kittens. Down in the crush near the dock he made up his mind to carry the kittens no further. Overboard went one of the hat boxes. When he arrived where he was to leave the hat boxes he found he had thrown overboard his two suits and carried the kittens safely to the house.

Dan O'Brien came to Warren Street and glancing at the coping of E. J. Faben's house, saw the coping under the tin roof on fire. Going to the front door Dan rang the bell. A few words of explanation to the occupant, and these two with Dibert and Dryer of Kresge's Store reached the roof, and tearing up the tin, with tea-kettles and pans of water extinguished the fire. This large house was the possible key to the situation here, as the chances are, if it had burned, lower Warren Street and Chestnut Street would have been fire-swept.

A well known business man and his wife stood and watched their fine home burn, with all their wedding presents and things they had taken so much pleasure in, and never shed a tear. The next day on the street he passed a Polish woman nursing her baby. As she passed by him crying, the terrible reality of the disaster came to him. He sat down on the curb-stone, buried his face in his hands and burst into tears.

The conflagration burned 253 acres and 1,376 buildings, the territory covered being about 1½ miles long by ½ mile wide; it left almost 20,000 people homeless and about 10,000 out of work.

The subsequent relief work was immediate and massive. The military and the Red Cross, of course, were immediately everywhere they could help. Organizations from all the surrounding cities and towns pitched in. The next day, June 26, Governor Walsh called a meeting at the State House at 9:30 a.m. to form a general relief committee. At 10:30 a.m. a check for $25,000 (1914 dollars) arrived at city hall from H. C. Frick. The president wired to Governor Walsh as follows:

> I am sure I speak for the American people in tendering heartfelt sympathy to you and to the stricken people of Salem. Can the federal government be of service to you in the emergency?
> Signed,
> Woodrow Wilson

That same day, by noon, the Ward Baking Company had two tons of bread delivered in Salem, Mayor Scanlon of Lawrence sent two car loads of bread and provisions, and fifteen truck loads of provisions arrived from Lynn. Hood offered one thousand pints of milk a day and the Mohican Market offered one thousand rations a day, and many others in the surrounding cities and towns showed similar kindness.

In Salem, the "Committee of 100" elected officers and appointed subcommittee chairmen for the main relief fund, housing, labor, transportation, clothing, publicity, insurance, and, on general information, Harlan P. Kelsey as chair. The Salem fund by July 22 had almost reached $97,000. The state fund on the same day was $569,177. Congress voted $200,000.

Tent camps arose almost immediately in the parks and open spaces that were safe. The clothing supply took care of over one thousand people a day at first, the clothing being for the most part new. Amazingly, in the camps, with thousands of people, there was a remarkable absence of sickness.

Enough—perhaps too much—detail has been provided here. However there should be no doubt now that the language and force of Kelsey's Sub-Committee on City Plan to the city council during 1913 was understated, if anything. Repeating what they had said regarding concentration and congestion, "The fire menace from this cause is already criminal and fast increasing, and the happiness and health of thousands of Salem's mothers and children is bartered for private *selfish gain, permitted by public indifference.* No spot is left open for playgrounds or breathing spaces."

Rebuilding the City

The fire, tragic as it was, immediately launched many of the provisions of Kelsey's Sub-Committee Report on City Plan. Even if the city council had "bought" the report recommendations en masse, with a sense of urgency for their implementation, without the fire it would have taken years for even the initial steps to be accomplished. Now most of the offending buildings were gone, and laying out whole new streets and new street setbacks would meet little resistance. Tree care was not an issue. Most were gone, and replanting was the issue. Zoning for various usage areas was now only a matter of getting enabling legislation from the state legislature. It was a whole new "ball game."

On June 29, four days after the fire had started, the city council adopted an ordinance as follows: "Hereafter all roofs that shall be constructed, altered or repaired shall be covered with slate or other incombustible material, and the gutters shall be of metal or covered with metal."

The Committee of 100 discussed a rebuilding commission and drew up a petition to be presented to Governor Walsh, the substance of which was that five local men be appointed, to be called the Salem Rebuilding Commission, to serve three years without pay, to have charge and control of the construction of all public buildings, take land by right of eminent domain, grant permits to build, pass regulations as to the location, size, material to be used in construction, and the space between said buildings; also changing of parks, squares, streets, sidewalks; and discontinuing, laying out, relocating, altering, widening, and repairing of all streets. This petition passed both legislative branches July 3 and went to the governor to sign July 7. Governor Walsh appointed the commission members and shortly thereafter the commission held its first meeting. Consulting architect C. H. Blackall presented a code of building laws and recommendations governing the new structures for the burned district at the next commission meeting July 13. No time was wasted.

The next day, July 14, the commission gave a hearing to the Lafayette Street residents, who had appointed their own neighborhood committee. They wanted:

1. Wires underground or on ornamental poles.
2. Trees planted along Lafayette Street.
3. Three-deckers prohibited in this district.
4. No stores or shops on Lafayette Street from Harbor Street up.
5. Park bounded by Harbor, Lafayette, and Washington Street.
6. No courts or private ways off Lafayette Street.

On their own, the residents were going Kelsey's way on zoning and beautification, even without government rules. This must have warmed his heart.

Many of the items in the Kelsey subcommittee report were not addressed. The subcommittee wanted to partially fill in the tidal flats around Collins Cove Basin and North River Basin, dam the entrances except for sluiceways to allow the tide in and out, and beautify the basin shorelines for recreation. Also they wanted to create a Shore Drive and "Ring" Street completely around the city. Today we would call this a circumferential highway with feeder roads into the city center. They were much ahead of their time. It is understandable, given the massive rebuilding task facing them, that neither of these projects came into being. Even to the present day. And the city suffers from their lack.

The *Boston Evening Record*, Saturday, November 13, 1915, carried a feature article headlined: "State Constitution Hampers City Planning, Says Expert at Women's City Club." The reporter, Katherine Brooks, continues:

> "The great fire was the best thing that ever happened to Salem."
>
> "If Boston did what was proper and reasonable in the light of common sense, it would start out and if necessary build a 120-foot street between the North and South Stations. I can show you how this could be done without costing the city a cent."
>
> Thus speaks Harlan P. Kelsey of Salem, city planning expert and guest of the Women's City Club at a dinner given at the clubhouse last evening in honor of the Metropolitan City Planning Exhibit which opened yesterday at the State House.
>
> The meeting was highly informal, and there were frequent good natured interruptions, with some banter.
>
> Mr. Kelsey drew a picture of the marvels of city planning when he referred to a South Carolina community, which is engaged in laying out a city on what is at present a lake bed.

"It is under water," said he, "but we hope that by January it will be dry land, and they will already be building a hotel."

New Holland

The reporter was wrong in that the community was actually in North Carolina, just inland from Pamlico Sound on Cape Hatteras. The lake was Lake Mattamuskeet, the largest natural lake in North Carolina, and the community was New Holland. Since 1934, the US government has owned Lake Mattamuskeet and it makes up most of Mattamuskeet National Wildlife Refuge. There is a rich history surrounding the area, and we are indebted to Lewis C. Forrest Jr. for creating the Mattamuskeet Foundation to provide research and educational activities as a nonprofit organization. The following material borrows heavily from this work.[80]

The excavation of a seven-mile canal was completed from the lake to Pamlico Sound, using slave labor. The water above sea level flowed by gravity through this canal into the sound, reducing the size of the lake from 120,000 to 55,000 acres. The bed of Lake Mattamuskeet has long been regarded as some of the richest soil in the world, having received nutrients from thousands of surrounding acres that have drained naturally into it for years. Soil experts have compared it to the rich land in the famous Nile River delta in Egypt. By the beginning of the 20th century, farmers had been farming the rich land adjacent to the lake without fertilizer for more than 200 years with record yields. Hyde County received an average of 60 inches of rainfall each year. To take advantage of the rich soil, landowners had to devise ways to drain the land and prevent flooding of their crops. In 1909 Public Law 509 authorized establishment of the Mattamuskeet Drainage District.

Since the lake bed was below sea level, the district had to excavate canals to carry the fresh water to the Pamlico Sound, and construct a pumping plant to lift the water from the lake bed into that canal system. The parties patterned the engineering design for the drainage project after the successful 1853 drainage of Haarlam Lake in Holland. Thus, the name New Holland. Work began in 1914 to re-dredge the "Outfall Canal" from the lake to the sound, under contract to A. V. Wills & Sons of Pittsville, IL. Then the dredges moved to dredge seventy-six more miles of canals into the lake bed; this was expanded by 1919 to include 130 miles of canals. The 1915 pumping plant, built by Morris Machine Works of Baldwinsville, New York, would lift 1,800 cubic feet (13,465 gallons) of water per second into the Outfall Canal.

The project also involved three private corporations that owned the lake successively from 1911 to 1934 and were partners in the drainage project. The private companies developed a community around the pumping plant that was the center of activity during this twenty-five-year project. The first of these was the Southern Land Reclamation Company, a land development business, with no intention of farming the lake bed themselves. They saw it as a huge real estate development and quickly changed their name to New Holland Farms, Inc. The drainage project from that time forward was called the "New Holland Project." They bought the land at $2.04 per acre and planned to invest an additional $10.00 per acre for draining and property improvements. Then they would sell it for $100.00 per acre with a ten-fold return on investment. Douglas Nelson Graves was president.

Graves brought in Harlan P. Kelsey to design the new town site. D. N. Graves's name is usually found as the client on the many landscape architectural drawings of the town site.[81] The Mattamuskeet Foundation materials cited Kelsey as "one of the most renowned landscape architects in America." Finally, after so many city planning projects for already established cities, Harlan Kelsey would follow in his father's footsteps. We are reminded of S. T. Kelsey starting with raw prairie for the new towns of Pamona and Hutchinson, Kansas, and then primeval forest for the new towns of Highlands and Linville, North Carolina. Now his son would start with an elevated spot on a drained lake bed.

The town site included 850 acres and was located along the south shore of the lake. The streets extended out in a semicircle like half the spokes of a wheel, with the pumping plant as the hub. The base of the semicircle was taken by the east and west canals, which fed the input to the pumping station. Actually there were only three straight spokes leading out from the hub, dividing the site into quarters. They were to be planted on each side and the center as parkways. By and large, all the other streets were either serpentine, circular, or interrupted, so that the eye always sought to find the unknowns around the bend. This speaks to landscape artistry, rarely found in the boring grids laid out by city engineers.

Open space and trees were supplied by numerous great intersection circles, parks, and playgrounds. Provision for future town expansion was clearly evident in the terminus design of the parkways.

He named all the streets, drives, roads, and avenues with much thought. The parkway heading out northeastward was Haarlem Avenue, and the one to the northwest was Amsterdam Avenue, paying homage to the Holland roots of the whole project. Many streets carried horticultural names: Cyprus, Catawba, Holly, Myrtle, Piney, Oak, Laurel, Cranberry, and Magnolia. Many were named for people, possibly important locally. Finally came the geographical place names. Kelsey even managed to slip in the home town of his North Carolina nursery—Pineola—and the town's predecessor name—Kawana.

New Holland Farms Company started developing the site out in the northwestward quadrangle, starting with the New Holland Inn, the hotel Kelsey mentioned in his Boston address. However in 1918 New Holland Farms sold out to a group of Ohio investors who incorporated a subsidiary as the North Carolina Farms Company. They continued the development, building a railroad from the pumping plant out to an adjoining county. They added a dozen private homes for company employees, a boarding house, and automotive garage, barber shop, planning mill, community water tower, depot, wharf, several farm buildings, and other structures.

By the early 1920s around 125 people were living in New Holland. The homes had running water, indoor plumbing, electric lights, and telephones. The well-maintained New Holland Inn had blue-gray furnishings with Dutch designs. There were parties at the Inn each weekend, and residents often held private parties in their homes.[82]

By 1923, after investing about $3–4 million at the lake, the Ohio parent company declared bankruptcy, including seven subsidiaries. The bankruptcy court placed North Carolina Farms into receivership. By 1934, the US government owned Mattamuskeet and during the Depression put the Civilian Conservation Corps to work there. They completed numerous projects in developing the Mattamuskeet and Swan Quarter Migratory Waterfowl Refuges, as well as converting the old pumping plant into the Mattamuskeet Lodge. The lodge welcomed its first hotel and restaurant guests in 1937 and for thirty-seven years operated as a lodge and gained a reputation as one of the favorite hunting lodges in the country. Since 1990, thousands of volunteer hours have been donated to projects to repair and save Mattamuskeet Lodge. The building has been placed on the National Register of Historic Places.[83]

As Kelsey's New Holland work drew to an end, he also closed out another area of responsibility. At the Appalachian Mountain Club, the report of the Trustees of Real Estate for the year 1916 ended with the following paragraph by Harvey N. Shepard, chairman:

> It is with great regret we part at the close of this year with Harlan P. Kelsey, who has been a member of our Board since 1910. We have relied confidently upon his excellent judgment in the planting and improvements of our Reservations, the location and building of paths, the cutting of vistas, and general landscape work. He always has been generous of his time in the

service of the Club, and also has given to it many trees, vines, and shrubs. Unfortunately for us the pressure of other matters has compelled him to decline a re-nomination.

Nurseryman

At the annual meeting of the Massachusetts Nurserymen's Association in Boston, December 11, 1911, it was recommended that an association be formed to include nurserymen from all the states of New England. A month later, January 1912, the interested nurserymen met in Boston to approve the constitution and bylaws of the New England Nurserymen's Association. The first regular meeting was held in Horticultural Hall, Boston, on March 12, 1912, where officers for the following year were elected. Twenty firms were represented.

One year later Harlan Kelsey, at age forty-one, was elected president of the New England Nurserymen's Association for the term 1913–14.[84]

Despite the constant press of business, industry, and civic interests, Kelsey was ever the inquisitive, innovative horticulturalist. That was where the fun and glory was. Take note of the following June 23, 1914, letter from Kelsey to Prof. Charles S. Sargent, Arnold Arboretum:

> [Enclosed is] a specimen of my new Rhododendron. You will see it is a deep pink with characteristics of both maximum and catawbiense very plainly exhibited. This is the first botanical specimen I have ever sent out and if you desire I shall be very glad to have you describe and name it. As a matter of advertising of course I would prefer to have it named Rhododendron kelseyi. My belief is that it is a true natural hybrid between maximum and catawbiense. The plant was collected near my nursery at Kawana, Saginaw P.O., North Carolina, and we immediately noticed the peculiarity of the leaf, although the plant was not in flower. As you will see it is entirely different

from the so-called Rhododendron maximum roseum, and the time of blooming is almost midway between maximum and catawbiense. ... I am very anxious to hear from you in regard to the Rhododendron.

Kelsey's voluminous list of horticultural introductions to the trade is probably far more important to the American gardener than the few botanical finds he made in the wild. However the glory of having a plant named for you is dramatically more important to the horticulturalist. You can see that the sole thrust of the letter was to achieve that end— "Rhododendron kelseyi." This would require a complete description in botanical Latin to demonstrate that the specimen was truly a new botanical species. Sargent was equipped to do that. Kelsey was probably not. Alas, it was not to be.

The plant was deemed not to be a new species. Rather, it was named *Rhododendron catawbiense* forma *compactum*. Specimens today can be viewed under that name in grid locations 37-SE and 37-SW at the Arnold Arboretum. Kelsey catalogs carried it with an earlier, but similar, name:

> RHODODENDRON catawbiense compactum
> KELSEY CATAWBA RHODODENDRON 4-12 ft.
> A dense growing variety discovered and introduced by Harlan P. Kelsey.
> Very distinct from the catawbiense type.[85]

Heretofore we have focused on horticulture, the attractive aspect of being a nurseryman. One of the less glamorous aspects is the administration of a nursery—accounting, payroll, personnel, field supervision, and so forth. For this you need a good superintendent. On paper Robert C. Young was ideal. His father had owned and operated the Greensboro Nurseries in Greensboro, North Carolina, for many years with a branch in Norfolk, Virginia. Robert Young described his experience: "I have been with my father all my life. For the past 8 years have had charge of all field work, propagating, grafting, budding etc. with from 15 to 125 men in charge." With Kelsey being away so much he had to depend on Young.

On February 19, 1916, Kelsey wrote to Mr. J. L. Bennett of Bay State Nurseries, the following: "For considerable irregularities discovered I have been forced to discharge my superintendent at Boxford Nursery, and am of course looking for a good man this spring. It occurred to me that you might know of some person who would be able to fill such a position." It seems Young had been taking paychecks signed by Kelsey for the workers and then forging endorsements payable to him and cashing them. The story unfolds in a February 10 letter from Kelsey's attorney to the father, John Young, advising him of all aspects of his son's case:

> Dear Sir: I am a personal friend of Mr. H. P. Kelsey, as well as his lawyer. One evening last week he called from his home to my home by telephone saying that he wished to see me about something important. I had him come over immediately and he told me of a call from two young workmen of his Boxford nursery who had just been to see him and claimed pay for back time. He was thunderstruck and could not explain it.
>
> Ever since the nursery went into operation the weekly pay roll had been sent down by your son and checks, signed by Mr. Kelsey made payable to each of the respective workmen were sent up to your son for distribution. That evening Mr. Kelsey telephoned to your son, told him about the call of the two workmen and asked him to come down to his office in the morning. Your son then went through the checks. He said that he had written the names of payees and had then cashed them as if the endorsements were genuine. I wrote down the list of checks as he picked them out and read off to me the

date, number, payee and amount. Mr. Kelsey showed you the list, with the statement signed by your son at the conference between you and Mr. Kelsey at Washington. Since then a more careful examination of all the checks was made showing a total of about one thousand dollars, the exact amount of which was contained in a letter written to you by Mr. Kelsey, and also in a letter written to you by your son.

Mr. Kelsey is nearly broken up over the situation. He and his wife have treated your son and his wife and children with the utmost kindness, and he has trusted your son implicitly since his employment. When the facts came out he was not vindictive but his impulse was to save all concerned from the inevitable and dire effects of arrest, conviction and punishment. Hence he had you come to meet him and talk with him in Washington. He understood from you that you would make up the amount of the bad checks. But he has received your telegram and your letter of February 8th in which you say in substance "to let the law take its course."

I wonder if you appreciate what this means. The crime committed is forgery. Each particular false endorsement is a separate crime. Forgery is a felony. The punishment for forgery, that is to say, for any one count or offence, is "imprisonment in the State Prison for not more than ten years or in jail for not more than two years."

This afternoon your son has again met me at Mr. Kelsey's office. I told him what you had said about letting the law take its course, and said to him that he ought to consult a lawyer in his own interests. He did not seem to care to do so but asked <u>me</u> to write to you. That is the reason for this letter. There is not the slightest question as to the facts. If the matter is not settled an indictment is inevitable. If Mr. Kelsey should not make a criminal complaint, the banks through which the forged checks passed would do so. The very time taken in this correspondence intensifies the embarrassment and offers temptation and opportunity to get away and attempt to escape. But there would be little comfort in this for sometime, somewhere he would be found and extradited.

Mr. Kelsey does not make any appeal to you to do anything. Not one man in a thousand would take the attitude toward the case that he does. Appreciating as we do what it means to "let the law take its course" he wishes to be sure that you, too, fully appreciate it before accepting your word as final.

Be kind enough, therefore, immediately on receipt of this letter to telegraph Mr. Kelsey your conclusion. Personally I hope that you may be able, even at a sacrifice, to avert consequences of which we do not like to think.

Very respectfully yours, Mr. White

The ensuing result was succinctly announced in the *Salem News* of February 18, 1916:

FORGERY CHARGE WAS DISMISSED
Father of Robert Young Makes Good Alleged Defalcation from Kelsey Nursery
A charge of forgery against Robert C. Young of Boxford, originally brought against him a week ago, was dismissed in district court today. Young was charged with forging the name of his employer, Harlan P. Kelsey of Salem, to checks to the amount of $1,000. The police stated today Young received a check for the amount from his father in Greensboro, N. C., and full restitution was made. Young will go to his southern home with his family shortly.

On February 26 Kelsey wrote to the father, "I had hoped that my unfortunate and expensive experience with your son was over." But it wasn't. John Young had asserted that the $100 he sent to pay for his son's family to travel back to North Carolina had been taken by Kelsey, except for $25, according to Cora, his daughter-in-law. Not so, replied Kelsey. He had Cora's signed receipt for the $25 and another signed receipt for the $75 balance from her husband who was to pay for her train tickets. He had given the $75 to her husband based on a signed request from the wife. "I advised Mrs. Young to let me buy her ticket and send her home, and this she refused to do. I did everything in my power to protect her and her family and continued to do so to the end, notwithstanding Mrs. Young in her distress spread reports that I was unkind and greatly to blame for having Mr. Young arrested." Kelsey was finally getting peeved.

Kelsey again wrote to the father on February 29. "Other matters have come to light which show how I have been duped at my Boxford Nursery. On bill of expenses for a collecting trip I have just found, counting R. C. Young's time and first bill of expenses, it amounts up to nearly $100, with a result of two ounces of Hemlock seed. The particulars which have been given me fully are most discouraging and lead me to know that it is only a small part of the cash lost, that has not yet come to light." Kelsey didn't pursue this. He was worn out.

By March 31, Kelsey found Mr. Andrew H. McDonald and hired him as the new superintendent. "You have general superintendence of the place, and I hope to have someone devoted as a propagator, and also other lines, but the whole place will be in your charge. My experience in the past has led me to caution you that the place is one of some responsibility. I am away on work a great deal of the time, and I must feel that I have someone who is absolutely reliable that I can depend upon to protect my interests as though they were his own. From what I have heard of you, I believe I am safe in trusting you."

War Clouds

On June 28, 1914, Gavrilo Pricip, assassin of the heir to the Austrian throne, was arrested in Sarajevo, Bosnia (then Austria-Hungary). For reasons only a dedicated historian would love to explore, this seemingly obscure event steamrolled into general war between Germany and the Franco-Russian Alliance by the end of 1914. All this while Kelsey was just getting started on New Holland at Lake Mattamuskeet. By 1916 when Kelsey's work was done at New Holland, Great Britain was drawn into the alliance against Germany, both the eastern and western fronts were ablaze, and naval warfare was rampant all around the European continent. On the western front stalemated trench warfare was established, while on the eastern front German forces gradually pushed deeper into Russia. In the United States conflicting public opinion vacillated between anger at the Germans over the invasion of Belgium and stubborn neutralism born of conviction that US vital interests were not sufficiently involved to justify voluntary intervention.

After numerous hostilities and a rupture of diplomatic relations with Germany in February 1917, events pushed the United States inexorably along the road to war. On April 6, 1917, President Wilson signed a resolution recognizing that a state of war existed between the United States and Germany. This was followed by massive mobilization. The Selective Service Act of May 18, 1917, enabled the government to enroll some 4,800,000 men in uniform before the end of the war.

Almost overnight the army needed cantonments (camps) for training and funneling men through ports of embarkation for Europe. Kelsey was immediately called into service as a civilian "engineer" to design and build the camps on a crash basis. He was most likely recommended by Frederick Law Olmsted Jr., who ended up as his immediate superior in Washington, DC. Engineers were instructed to "depart from the usual procedure and adapt means that will insure the most expeditious results."

By June 10, less than two months after the war was declared, Kelsey and a fellow engineer, Richard Messer, submitted their preliminary report for the cantonment at Petersburg, Virginia (Camp Lee). Before work could start, they had to survey and make all the necessary arrangements for rail connections, water supply, sewerage, soil, and surface drainage electric power and complete a topographical survey of the area (here was where Kelsey's landscaping background qualified him as an "engineer").

The Petersburg report closed, saying, "One party has begun work this morning, and we expect to have four or five surveying parties on the ground tomorrow morning, enabling us to give you definite suggestions for the entire layout of the Camp inside of 3 days. From our investigations and from data in hand, it appears that the typical general plan of cantonments can be closely followed with generally straight water lines and abundant room both in front and in rear and without serious complications of any kind that we can foresee."

The Petersburg Cantonment had to accommodate thirty thousand men. We get a glimpse of this activity from a Salem newspaper clipping, April 18, 1918:

> Harlan P. Kelsey spoke on "Army cantonments." Mr. Kelsey laid out the camp ... at Petersburg, Va. He also made trips to Chillicothe, Ohio, and other places. Mr. Kelsey's talk was illustrated. He showed the wonderful speed at which the camps arose out of the wildernesses. Mr. Kelsey said he liked the work very much because he had his own way practically. His camp was about the first one finished and it was but second in cost. The amazing speed at which sites were selected, ground cleared and buildings erected, was realized last night for the first time by those who heard Mr. Kelsey.

Kelsey's contracts reveal that in addition to Camp Lee, he was an engineer for Camp Gordon, Atlanta, Georgia; Camp Zachary Taylor,

Louisville, Kentucky; Camp Sherman, Chillicothe, Ohio; Camp Wheeler, Macon, Georgia (later Camp Green was substituted for Camp Wheeler); and Camp Meade in Maryland.

Curiously, one of the camps with which Kelsey was not involved was Camp Curtis Guild in Boxford, Massachusetts. It was located directly across the road from the Kelsey Highlands Nursery, on the site of an old Civil War camp, Camp Stanton.

By September 1918, his cantonment work was completed and Kelsey was under contract with the United States Housing Corporation in the Hampton Roads district of Virginia. The contract called for him to act as town planner "for housing facilities for industrial workers engaged in industries connected with and essential to the national defense, and for employees of the United States whose services in essential war work require them to reside in certain localities." The housing developments were in (or near) the cities of Norfolk, Portsmouth, and Newport News, Virginia. As town planner, Kelsey was responsible for both the design work and the supervision of construction in the field. A sample of what all this entailed can be seen by taking excerpts from an article titled, "Government Housing for War Needs—The Story of Cradock, Virginia." The opening paragraph is a summary:

> Yesterday a quiet rural spot; today a center of hustling and systematic construction; tomorrow a model city wherein 5000 or more people will be comfortably housed. Briefly this is what is being done down in Virginia near the Portsmouth Navy Yard where the wonderful city of Cradock has sprung up almost overnight to meet the terrific demand for housing which the gigantic task of supplying the sinews of war created. The combined efforts of, and the most efficient co-operation between the United States Housing Corporation, which is in charge of the entire project, and the Hegeman-Harris Company of New York City, the contracting firm, is accomplishing the

enormous task of converting corn fields and forests into a modern city.

And the same sort of thing was going on simultaneously for Kelsey in Norfolk and Newport News.

At five in the morning on November 11, 1918, in Foch's railway carriage at Rethondes, the Armistice document was signed. At eleven in the morning on the same day World War I came to an end. American involvement had lasted less than twenty months. On February 21, 1919, Kelsey wrote to Olmsted requesting that he be relieved so that he could begin devoting time to his own office at the Nursery in Boxford. By the end of February he was gone, but not without first thanking those who had served him. He wrote to the telephone operators in the Flatiron Building, Norfolk, where his office was.

> I want to take this means of expressing to you my appreciation of the unusually efficient and courteous way in which you have handled the telephone calls of this office. It has contributed largely to the efficiency of this office, particularly as the telephone system in this vicinity has been so upset for the past few months. Your patience under trying circumstances has been out of the ordinary and it is therefore a great pleasure to me to acknowledge it in this manner.

As for thanks for his own work, the only record in reference to it came October 3, 1919, from Senator Bert Fernald of Maine, chairman of the Committee on Public Buildings and Grounds, who writes: "Dear Mr. Kelsey: The Subcommittee of the Senate Committee on Public Buildings and Grounds in investigating the U. S. Housing Corporation, is of the opinion that perhaps by submitting the following information, you may be saved the inconvenience and expense of being summoned before the Committee. Will you therefore, send us by return mail if possible, the following information: …" What followed was a long list of items he had to resurrect painstakingly from old records—all his old contracts; his employees' names, pay rates, pay changes, at all different times during the years 1917 and 1918; amounts received by himself from US Housing Corporation, or any other government department, subdivided into fee, reimbursement for expenses, and overhead.

It took him most of the month of October, but on October 27 he mailed it all in to Senator Fernald. This was some "thanks" for the extraordinary effort he had expended, along with so many others, but that's government.[86]

Without specific figures we can only suppose the manpower drain on civilian activity in general had an equally suppressing effect on activity in the nursery industry. We have no indication the war caused financial distress for the Highlands Nurseries in Pineola or in Boxford. The real effect on the nursery industry came later during the short recession following the war. Dues increases for the member growers of the American Association of Nurserymen approved in 1918 were never imposed. By 1921 dues had to be rolled back.[87]

After the brief postwar recession, the country enjoyed one of its most buoyant decades—the Roaring Twenties. The economy, the stock market, and business conditions soared, as did public sentiment. Harlan Kelsey was forty-eight years old. His reputation as a leader in the fields of conservation and horticulture also soared, as did his contributions to both fields.

It is noteworthy that city planning, which occupied so much time during the prior decade, suddenly stopped and never again assumed a significant role in Kelsey's life. During the Roaring Twenties horticulture and the nursery business remained the bedrock of his existence, but city planning was totally squeezed out by the emergence of preservation activities. Changing of career patterns is not an unusual occurrence; in Kelsey's case he didn't undertake another city planning job for twenty-five years and that one was his last.

In John Muir's case, his late teens and twenties witnessed a striking talent for "inventiveness." It started with simple mechanisms, then clocks, and no end of other "gadgetry." Examples are a thermometer so sensitive that it would indicate when a person moved only a few feet nearer to it; a student's desk that would dump one textbook and replace it with another, based on times preset by the student. Most of his machines allowed improvements in productivity wherever they were applied. Wisconsin farming was on the decline, and the machine age dawned as employment in towns and cities turned to manufacturing. Opportunities for inventive young men were almost limitless.

In Muir's twenties, he mixed university education with long periods out in the Wisconsin wilderness and jobs that could use his inventiveness. These gave him food money so he could again disappear into the wilderness. Finally an industrial accident blinded him, but over time his sight was restored. This experience terminated any further activity in manufacturing, and Muir set out on his thousand-mile trek to the Gulf of Mexico and ultimately the high Sierras. He would grasp the wilderness while he could—an abrupt midlife career change.[88] Conditions were different between Kelsey and Muir, but in both cases preservation of wilderness prevailed.

Family Matters

Harlan Kelsey's father, Samuel Truman Kelsey, had retired a decade ago and his subsequent time was spent with his three sons, variously in Salem, Massachusetts, with Harlan; Los Angeles with Truman; and Baltimore with Harry. On December 20, 1919, STK wrote an interesting letter from Baltimore to E. C. Robbins, who was still managing the North Carolina nursery for Harlan:

> My Dear E C Robins
>   And Family
> Hearty Christmas greetings to every one of you.

I have shamefully neglected to write you. ... My only unreasonable excuse is, that my head and hands have joined the "Idlers Union," and been on strike demanding big pay for little, and very poor, work. We have agreed upon a limited, compromise armistice, for the holidays, under which I am allowed to dictate a few personal letters. Our scattered folks, all around were in usual health when last heard from. ... If I have failed in writing to you, I have been thinking, a good deal, about you and your work, and wondering how you were getting on with sales and closing out the Highlands Nursery. I know from experience that it is a difficult matter to dispose of a nursery, unless you can sell out to some person or Co. to take it as stands on the ground. I wish I could help you through the coming Spring. I am hoping your health is greatly improved and that the family are all well. ... With all good wishes for your health and happiness.

Yours truly,   S T Kelsey

This is the first indication we find that Harlan Kelsey is ready to abandon the North Carolina nursery operation. The solution turned out to be just what STK proposed as the most likely avenue for disposing of the Highlands Nursery—"sell out to some person or Co. to take it as stands on the ground." That person was E. C. Robbins. One account says he bought the nursery in 1920; another says 1923. Robbins quickly asserted his prerogatives as the proprietor and changed the name to Gardens of the Blue Ridge. That name is on the letterhead of a letter from Robbins to Kelsey dated June 7, 1921, and the name stands to this day. Kelsey wanted to save the name Highlands, and by October 1921 the Massachusetts Department of Agriculture notified Kelsey that they had changed their records to identify his nursery as Boxford-Highlands Nursery.

But the question still remains: why was the North Carolina operation no longer needed by Harlan Kelsey? We find the answer years later in an October 31, 1933, letter to A. F. Sanford of the Sanford Arboretum in Knoxville, Tennessee. Kelsey said, "I have long ago given up the North Carolina end of the growing because freight rates were too stiff and we can grow everything here quite as well if not better than we could down there."

When E. C. Robbins died, the nursery passed to his son Edward Page Robbins. When he died the land was too valuable for nursery operation, commanding much higher value broken up for vacation property subdivisions. The majority of the heirs insisted on the breakup, but E. P. Robbins's daughter, Katy Fletcher, and her immediate family, saved the name and ongoing business, moving to a different location in Pineola on the east side of the Blue Ridge Parkway and "out of the high rent district." They also focused the business almost exclusively on North Carolina wildflowers. It was a good move for a small operation dependent on mail order sales. Today Gardens of the Blue Ridge advertises as "the oldest continuously operating nursery in North Carolina—since 1885," when Harlan Kelsey founded it in Highlands.

The passing of the nursery to the Robbins family also marked the end of any North Carolina connection for Harlan Kelsey. Everything was now centered in Boxford, Massachusetts, though Kelsey's home and business office remained in Salem.

The Kelsey Highlands Nursery in Boxford was now vastly larger in size compared to Pineola and totally self-sufficient. That alone may account for the exit from North Carolina, but there may have been another factor. On November 9, 1921, Harlan Kelsey sent a handwritten letter to E. C. Robbins:

> Dear Ed,
>   Father died last Saturday evening at 7:15, and we took him to Baltimore and buried him yesterday.

He did not suffer the last two weeks and just peacefully went to sleep. Am enclosing a notice of his death in the Salem News which I knew you would like to see.

He thought a great deal of you and often spoke of you. We will all miss him but it was better to pass away as he did without a long siege of suffering and he would have been 89 the 14th of this month. Among his books was the photograph album you sent him of Nursery scenes. This I will prize highly for it has many pictures of you and your family. With best regards to all your family,

Your friend,

Harlan P. Kelsey

In settling his father's estate, Kelsey wrote the Linville Improvement Company asking the value of the single share of stock his father had held since 1896. R. M. Sheppard, secretary/treasurer, replied that they couldn't value the stock for him. There was enough standing timber on the Linville tract to pay off all the company's indebtedness, which would leave the land and improvements unencumbered. In fact they had recently sold about $150,000 worth of the timber. However, "There is no market for the company stock at this time; and it has been our policy to urge the stockholders to hold onto their stock, and to forget about it for the time being, in the hope that we may yet be able to make it have a real value."[89] One share? Why not just buy it for an agreeable price? No. There was no way Hugh MacRae would go out of his way to do anything for the Kelseys.

STK's passing was a quiet termination to his gradual retirement after the Linville Company episode was finished. But he remains a huge factor in this story. With every future gathering honoring his son, Harlan, one can imagine the specter of STK circling the assembled group as a background figure—the invisible but prominent cause for his son's achievements.

"Like father, like son" fits perfectly. STK was a nurseryman in New York, Illinois, and Kansas. His son in Highlands, Linville, Salem, and Boxford.

STK was a city planner (founder) in Ottawa, Pomona, Hutchinson, Highlands, and Linville. His son in Marion, Columbia, Greenville, New Holland, and Salem. STK was a conservationist at heart. So was his son. STK sought roadside beautification along railroads. His son did the same for highway beautification nationwide. STK's persistence in overcoming obstacles was echoed in his son's character, as seen by a much later accolade: "[Kelsey was] ... possessed of unselfish devotion to causes in which he believed, enthusiasm and vitality to carry out his projects regardless of obstacles." As a father, he set his son on the path his son maintained for his entire life.

There was one difference between father and son. For Harlan Kelsey there was one overarching theme to all his activities—bringing native plants to the forefront of American horticultural practice. It was there in his nursery promotions, in his highway beautification, in his influence as a leader of nursery associations, in his steady, but ignored, insistence that the National Arboretum feature native plants. At first glance his city planning work may appear to be a diversion. But no, the Civic League of Salem concerned itself with street trees and garden contests alongside the city's other needs. Marion, his first commercial city planning job, was really a "planting plan" creating a park. Columbia and Greenville were concerned with primarily the classical municipal street, zoning, sanitation, and building problems. But overlaying the solutions were such things as proper street trees, large planted traffic circles at intersections, parks, and playgrounds. All involved his horticulture. And certainly, wherever there was horticulture, it featured native plants.

In our constant comparison of John Muir and Harlan Kelsey, we can match Muir's always present preoccupation with *wilderness* and Kelsey's with *native plants*. Both wilderness and native plants feature values drawn from our existing assets rather than overlaying man's feeble attempts at betterment. Muir publicized wilderness as a treasure, not to be displaced by civic uses such as farming, ranching, mining, and such.

Kelsey emphasized native plants in naturalistic landscape settings, not to be displaced by exotic imports arranged in stiff European-style formal gardens. Every garden has a setting. Kelsey's naturalistic emphasis pushes the garden back toward wilderness by avoiding straight lines and allowing plants to assume the shape and character they show in the wilderness setting.

Standardized Plant Names

In 1923 a new book was published: *Standardized Plant Names: A Catalogue of Approved Scientific and Common Names of Plants in American Commerce.* It was copyrighted by the American Joint Committee on Horticultural Nomenclature, J. Horace McFarland, chairman, and Harlan P. Kelsey, secretary. The reasons for the book were well enumerated in its Preface, which will be excerpted and paraphrased heavily in the material below.

"The stated purpose of the Committee was to 'make buying easy' by bringing about, so far as practicable, the consistent use of a single standardized 'scientific' name, and a single standardized 'common' name for every tree, shrub, and plant in American commerce."[90]

Why? There was a problem everywhere in the plant world. Confusion reigned. The individual gardener, the landscaper, or the nurseryman often didn't get the plant he had ordered and paid for but instead got the wrong plant. The botanists occasionally didn't speak the same language, even when they spoke in botanical Latin. They too got the wrong plants. The nomenclature was a mess; that was the problem.

Suppose the home gardener wanted to buy a plant described to her by a friend who called it a Virginia creeper. As common names go, her nurseryman could have called it any one of a number of names—woodbine, American woodbine, Virginia creeper, American ivy, common Virginia creeper, Virginian creeper, wild woodvine, and five-fingered ivy. Usually one can pin down a specific plant by using its scientific Latin name. In that case, in 1916, one could find that single plant cataloged under no less than six Latin binomials—*Ampelopsis quinquefolia, A. virginica, Parthenocissus quinquefolia, P. virginica, Vitis hederacea,* and *Psedera quinquefolia.* When buying a plant the last thing the customer wants to do is get mixed up in disagreements between botanists. Thus it was often impossible for the buyer to know whether he would get what he had in mind when placing an order, or something entirely different.

And it was even worse. "A single plant was sometimes known by twenty or more different names, some very closely localized, some very widespread. For one extreme example, Van Wijk's *Dictionary of Plant Names* credited the European White Waterlily, *Nymphaea alba,* with 15 English, 44 French, 105 German, and 81 Dutch common names, or a total of 245 vernacular appellations—a ridiculous state of affairs."[91]

"Even when there was complete and well-established agreement among botanists as to the classification and naming of any given plant, mistakes by nurserymen or dealers in identification and labeling were liable to occur, giving rise to much confusion. When a dealer, either through ignorance or accident, sent out a comparatively unknown plant labeled with the name of some other little-known plant, the misapplied name was likely to follow the first plant and become established in trade. A striking case of this sort was that of the tree so widely disseminated for street planting under the common name 'Carolina Poplar.' Experts on the poplar stated that this was probably *Populus eugenei,* a hybrid originated in Europe, and that the native Carolina Poplar practically never passed in the trade under that name. In this extreme case the transferred name was so universally accepted by the trade that an attempt to correct the original mistake was inadvisable."[92]

On arriving in a new locality, people often applied familiar old plant names to totally different plants of the new locality. First settlers in a new country were likely to fix the name "laurel" to almost anything that had handsome evergreen leaves, and any evergreen conifer was likely to be called "cedar" or "pine." There were no less than thirty-one genera in which the common name "lily," usually with a qualifying adjective, had been applied—genera other than the true lily genus, Lilium, obviously because of the resemblance of the subjects to the true lily.[93]

When it came to vegetable varieties, one observer quipped, "Perhaps one thousand distinct varieties have been honored with about ten thousand names."[94]

And so it went, on and on and on.

The problems had been around for a long time, and many attempts had been made to rectify things—most notably, work by the American Pomological Society in regard to their particular branch of horticulture. There was always Bailey's *Standard Cyclopedia of Horticulture*, which included a "finding list" covering practically all plants in American commerce. But it wasn't working to the satisfaction of many in the trade. The problems persisted. The only practical remedy seemed to be that of enlisting all of the relevant horticultural organizations, acting in concert, to agree arbitrarily upon some one name for each plant, by which name it could be designated for a definite period of time. Thus, the American Joint Committee on Horticultural Nomenclature was formed in 1915 by committees of the American Association of Nurserymen and of the Ornamental Growers Association. For simplicity we will hereafter call it just the "joint committee."

The joint committee's first task was to enlist member organizations. In addition to the Nurserymen and the Ornamental Growers, they added the Landscape Architects, the Pharmaceutical Association, the Institute of Park Executives, and the Society of Florists and Ornamental Horticulturists. This provided the mass of six major American organizations acting in concert. For added heft, they established cooperative arrangements with the Dahlia Society, the Gladiolus

Society, the Iris Society, the Peony Society, the Pomological Society, the Rose Society, the Sweet Pea Society, and the Seed Trade Association. If all these people could agree, there just might be enough mass to force compliance with the ultimate standards.

Now that they had everyone involved, how was the work going to get done? They needed a small group of dedicated, persuasive individuals to create the product and then sell it to all concerned. The product was, of course, the book published eight years later in 1923. The Joint Committee had only two officers, J. Horace McFarland, chairman, and Harlan P. Kelsey, secretary. McFarland's extensive background and reputation were covered earlier, and it helped that he was a member both of the Nurserymen's Association and chairman of the Florists and Ornamental Horticulturalists Society. Kelsey, the nurseryman, controlled much of the day-to-day operations, and the Joint Committee's only address was Kelsey's, in Salem, Massachusetts.

The small group of dedicated individuals to create the product was simply called "The Sub-Committee," with the "working members" listed as:

Frederick Law Olmsted	American Society of Landscape Architects
Frederick V. Coville	US botanist, Washington, DC
Harlan P. Kelsey	American Association of Nurserymen

McFarland, as joint committee chairman, stood as ex–officio member of the subcommittee. Kelsey acted as manager[95] as well as both secretary and treasurer[96] for the subcommittee. Olmsted was not the Olmsted famous for creating New York's Central Park. That was his father, who died just after the turn of the century. The subcommittee, like the joint committee, listed the address as Salem, Massachusetts.

As a practical matter, the Joint Committee had no active organization. Everything done for the enterprise was done by McFarland and the subcommittee. An officer for the subcommittee was also a de-facto officer for the Joint Committee. With Kelsey named as manager, secretary, and treasurer he was the prime mover for the whole enterprise. Various correspondence indicates, however, that McFarland took his chairmanship very seriously and was constantly involved in almost everything that was done.

The starting point for the subcommittee was Bailey's *Standard Cyclopedia*, which fortunately had been republished in March 1917 as the sixth and final volume. They conferred regularly that year with Dr. L. H. Bailey. The result was issuance in late 1917 of *The Official Code of Standardized Plant Names*, covering only the scientific plant names. This was distributed to all of the constituent organizations then participating under the joint committee—for comments, additions, and deletions. It was gratifying that this code was widely accepted and adopted. That was the "easy" part; there was far less disagreement existing over scientific names, especially since the code made no claim of final scientific authority.

However, there were two matters of typography and spelling on scientific names where the committee broke with the prevailing practice among botanists (though not with zoologists). It wasn't unanimous, but the majority of participating organizations wanted the break for reasons of convenience and economy.

1. Use no capitals in scientific names except for invariably beginning a genus name with a capital. That is, species names following the genus would be all lowercase. In addition, for compound names in which a name properly belonging to one genus is applied in compound to a different genus, like May-apple, failure to write them as compound words, either with a hyphen or "solid," was consistently avoided. "The committee prefers and prints Mayapple. It makes no serious objection to May-apple. It objects very positively to May Apple, which is

apt to mean, for any one not familiar with the plant, that it is a species or variety of the genus Malus."
2. End all species names having the form of a second declension genitive with a single *i* instead of with *ii*. There is just as good classic Latin authority for the *i* form as there is for the *ii* form, and it seems absurd to burden ourselves with trying to follow with precision the choice of each particular original author of a Latin plant name as to whether he would spell his genitive in *ii* or in the equally proper *i* (as *thunbergi,* not *thunbergii*).

The hard part was common names. The "world was searched" for data, and they accumulated a substantial library of common names. Then they unleashed their secret weapon, the US botanist, Frederick V. Coville, with all his resources at the US Department of Agriculture, including staff. But WWI arrived in the United States, putting the brakes on the effort, as three of the assigned staff were called into the service until after the war. The work resumed in 1919.

The first task with common names was to assemble what was out there and collate all the common names given in various published material. Most, but not all, of these sources were:

1. Over two hundred leading nursery catalogs
2. The leading American and English botanical and horticultural works and publications
3. Bailey's *Cyclopedia*
4. The *Century Dictionary*
5. Sudworth's *Trees of the United States*
6. Van Wijk's *Dictionary of Plant Names*

This alone was a huge time-consumer.

Then they had to sort out and try to fix the problems. This is where the subcommittee's judgment and reputation was vital. For example:

1. Eliminate all names clearly belonging more properly to some other genus, species, or variety
2. Where elimination wasn't possible, convert to a compound name, with rules for compounding
3. Omit needless possessive names (Schwedler maple, *not* Schwedler's maple)
4. Where equally qualifying names existed, just choose a preferred name

Many times the decisions were arbitrary, but someone had to do it, and no one else had stepped forward to improve matters.

Finally came the seemingly endless attempts to coordinate methods and choices with the collaborating organizations and individuals and then resolve differences.

In the 1920 prospectus, McFarland closed with these words:

> It should be noted that the gentlemen of the subcommittee have given freely of their time in the arduous work involved in this study and preparation. No name has been perfunctorily inserted in this official catalogue, either scientific or common. Its capacity to assist sales by such determination has constantly been considered. The work is therefore a work of self-sacrificing devotion to the interest of the horticultural trades, which it is believed will be recognized by proper acceptance and support.

That was it. Eight years' work to publish a 546-page book in 1923. Then the "fun" began. Or perhaps you should call it the "real work" of promoting and selling the book to achieve universal acceptance and use. Clearly there was no one else to do it but McFarland and the subcommittee. Of course having put in all the work creating the book, they were a determined lot when it came to promoting its use.

STANDARDIZED PLANT NAMES

A CATALOGUE OF APPROVED
SCIENTIFIC AND COMMON NAMES OF PLANTS
IN AMERICAN COMMERCE

Prepared by
FREDERICK LAW OLMSTED
FREDERICK V. COVILLE
HARLAN P. KELSEY
Sub-Committee

1923
AMERICAN JOINT COMMITTEE
ON HORTICULTURAL NOMENCLATURE
SALEM, MASS.

Standardized Plant Names title page. 1923 edition.

"Standardized Plant Names" is a cracker-jack—all that we have expected. This book will help us a lot along the way. I expect it to be about the most useful book in my office. It may not be any better than the Bible, but I will probably consult it oftener.—FRANK A. WAUGH, Amherst, Mass.

STANDARDIZED PLANT NAMES

BOLD-face, whether capitals or small letters, indicates approved scientific names.
ITALIC, whether capitals or *small letters*, indicates synonyms or unapproved names.
SMALL CAPITALS indicate approved common names.
Abbreviations: Ag = Economic Herbarium of the United States Department of Agriculture; Ar = Arnold Arboretum, Harvard University; Cy = Bailey's Standard Cyclopedia of Horticulture.
A dagger (†) indicates a horticultural variety for which the Joint Committee recommends the use of the common name alone, although recognizing that the scientific name in italics, followed by the dagger, has good botanical standing according to the authority cited.

AARONSBEARD CACTUS
    Opuntia leucotricha
ABELIA . . . . ABELIA
  chinensis (*rupestris*) . CHINESE A.
  engleriana . . . . . ENGLER A.
  floribunda . . . . . MEXICAN A.
  grandiflora . . . . . GLOSSY A.
ABELMOSCHUS . . . **HIBISCUS**
ABERIA . . . . . . **DOVYALIS**
ABIES . . . . FIR
  alba Ag-Ar . . . . . **A. pectinata**
    The name A. alba is often misapplied to Picea canadensis.
  alcockiana . . . **Picea alcockiana**
    The name A. alcockiana has often been misapplied to Picea jezoensis hondoensis.
  amabilis . . . . . CASCADE FIR
    The name A. amabilis is sometimes misapplied to A. grandis.
  apollinis . **A. cephalonica apollinis**
  arizonica (*Abies lasiocarpa arizonica* Cy) . . . . . CORK FIR
  baborensis Cy . . . . **A. numidica**
  balsamea . . . . . BALSAM FIR
  —hudsonia(*hudsonica*). HUDSON F.
  brachyphylla . . . . **A. homolepis**
  bracteata . . . . . . **A. venusta**
  canadensis . . **Tsuga canadensis**
  cephalonica . . . . GREEK FIR
  —apollinis . . . . . . APOLLO F.
  cilicica . . . . CILICIAN F.
  concolor . . . . . . WHITE F.
  —lowiana . . . PACIFIC WHITE F.
    See also hort. var. list on page 2.
  douglasi . . **Pseudotsuga douglasi**
  excelsa . . . . . . **Picea excelsa**
  firma (*momi*) . . . . . MOMI FIR
  fraseri . . . . FRASER F.
  grandis . . . GREAT SILVER F.

ABIES, continued
  holophylla . . . . . NEEDLE FIR
  homolepis (*brachyphylla*) . NIKKO F.
  —umbilicata (*umbellata*)
    DIMPLECONE F.
  hudsonica . **A. balsamea hudsonia**
  lasiocarpa (*subalpina*) . ALPINE FIR
  —*arizonica* Cy . . . . **A. arizonica**
  lowiana . . . **A. concolor lowiana**
  magnifica . . . . . . RED FIR
  —shastensis . . . . SHASTA F.
    See also hort. var. list on page 2.
  mariesi . . . . . . MARIES F.
  menziesi . . . . **Picea sitchensis**
  momi . . . . **A. firma**
  nobilis . . . . NOBLE FIR
    See also hort. var. list on page 2.
  nordmanniana . . NORDMANN F.
  numidica (*A. baborensis* Cy)
    ALGERIAN F.
  orientalis . . . . **Picea orientalis**
  pectinata (*A. picea* Cy; *A. alba* Ag-Ar) . . . . . SILVER FIR
    See also hort. var. list on page 2.
  picea Cy . . . . . **A. pectinata**
  pindrow . . . . . PINDROW FIR
  pinsapo . . . . . . SPANISH F.
    See also hort. var. list on page 2.
  pungens . . . . . **Picea pungens**
  sachalinensis . . SAKHALIN FIR
  sibirica . . . . . SIBERIAN F.
  spectabilis (*A. webbiana* Cy)
    HIMALAYAN F.
  subalpina . . . . . **A. lasiocarpa**
  umbellata . **A. homolepis umbilicata**
  venusta (*bracteata*)
    BRISTLECONE FIR
  veitchi . . . . VEITCH F.
  webbiana Cy . . . . **A. spectabilis**

"Standardized Plant Names" will be of the greatest assistance to me in editing the Bulletin of the Garden Club of America.— MRS. M. H. B. MCKNIGHT, Sewickley, Pa.

Standardized Plant Names sales flyer. Sample page. 1923 edition.

It was published by Mount Pleasant Press, J. Horace McFarland Company, and was sold in three different styles at prices advertised as barely covering the actual cost of manufacture, with no publisher's profits nor authors' royalties. Orders were received in Kelsey's Salem office, and he acted as treasurer. The sales flyer carried two laudatory endorsements:

> "*Standardized Plant Names*" is a cracker-jack—all that we have expected. This book will help us a lot along the way. I expect it to be about the most useful book in my office. It may not be any better than the Bible, but I will probably consult it oftener. (Frank A. Waugh, Amherst, Mass.)

> "*Standardized Plant Names*" will be of the greatest assistance to me in editing the Bulletin of the Garden Club of America.(Mrs. M. H. B. McKnight, Sewickley, Pa.)

Universal acceptance and use of the book being the overriding purpose of the entire enterprise, everything was now focused on getting the widest possible distribution. The subcommittee members needed to shift roles from horticulturalists to that of businessmen. This shouldn't have been too difficult, since all but one of them were already running substantial successful businesses of their own—all of them except Coville, who was a government employee. After his strong contribution in creating the plant listings, Coville appeared to move into the background.

There were some ticklish business decisions right off the bat. How best to promote sales? Charge too much and the books wouldn't sell. Charge too little and the costs would soon overwhelm the enterprise. They had already milked the constituent organizations of the joint committee for contributions during the eight years of the book's creation. There was still some milk in that cow, but not that much. Who would provide the up-front cash to cover large press runs at the publisher? They gradually worked things out, but with a great deal of personal risk taken by each of the active three.

Six months into 1924 they had completed a second printing, but McFarland reported, "Sales are proceeding, not very rapidly, and it is apparent that unless they are stimulated they will soon cease to be material in amount."[97] Selling and office expense was running about 44 percent of revenues, leaving only 56 percent for mechanical printing cost—not enough. Positive cash flow was moving further into the future. McFarland's printing accounts receivable from the subcommittee were becoming too risky. "Plan A" wasn't working. It was time for "Plan B."

In the spring of 1924 McFarland was getting nervous. Printing receivables, beyond revenues from book sales, were up to about $10,000, and keep in mind that these were 1924 dollars (worth hundreds of thousands in today's dollars). He proposed a "security blanket." He asked that each of the three active members provide security to the J. Horace McFarland Company in the form of a note to personally pay up to $1,000 for receivables not recovered from future book sales. McFarland's lawyer drafted a set of documents, which were distributed. Olmsted responded with his own lawyer's counterproposal that was simpler, but more definitive. McFarland accepted. Then by midsummer Kelsey had time to digest the agreement and accepted.

It was also agreed that no part of the receipts from the second printing would go to defraying the running expenses of the secretary's office in Salem, which had been running 44 percent of book revenues, "which left no possible means of coming out square." It would be left to Kelsey to return to the Nurserymen's Association and the other joint committee participants for added contributions if he expected to recover his costs.[98] It was now clear to the "working members" that in addition to donating eight years of pro bono time and expertise, they now might have to donate a substantial piece of their own wealth. They were dedicated to solving the problems of "name chaos."

Everything now hinged on reviving sales of the book while reducing expenses—a neat trick. McFarland was aware of a book-sales promotion company that would take over the sales promotion, order taking, and accounting for book sales. All of its expenses would be paid for by a commission on sales, with 40 percent the conventional discount. McFarland adds, however, "We cannot get out [of arrears] at forty percent, and in the back of my head is the feeling that he can be persuaded to do the thing for not over thirty percent." Kelsey was already acquainted with DeLaMare from their sales presentations to the Nurserymen's Association on similar work.[99] Kelsey then put the squeeze on DeLaMare:

> Mr. McFarland tells me that you are willing to consider a proposition to take over the selling end of *Standardized Plant Names* and I told him I was thoroughly in agreement with this idea. More than this, your representatives in Atlantic City came pretty near selling a Publicity Program to our Executive Committee. Unfortunately half or more of our members there got ptomaine poisoning, ... and I was among the victims who fell so I couldn't put in an appearance at the wind up of the Executive Committee meeting, but this matter at the present moment is entirely in my hands and I have your proposition and wish to see you at the earliest possible moment with a view to coming to some definite conclusion. Therefore, I have written Mr. McFarland that the two matters might well be considered in one trip to New York.[100]

On July 8, 1924, McFarland wrote to Kelsey: "I have just wired you to the effect that DeLaMare has proposed to handle *Standardized Plant Names*, on the basis that we give him 'the sole agency of the work so that every one requiring a copy will have to come to us for it,' for a 30 percent discount. For this he says he will 'give it a full page in our catalogue, advertise it ... and give it all the publicity in our power.'"

That did it. McFarland had his "security blanket." Kelsey's office was relieved of the time and expense of sales, orders, and accounting for the book. Sales expense was locked in at a level that assured positive cash flow with each copy sold, and they had an experienced promotion specialist to sharply increase sales. Hopefully.

Plan B did appear to work better than Plan A. By 1926, contributions from the joint committee participants were being applied to the printing account, not Kelsey's running office expense. That was an improvement. However, the biggest news was on the adoption front. People who bought the book were putting it into practice.

On January 13, 1926, Kelsey wrote to McFarland the following: "This letter … is to tell you that I have put *Standardized Plant Names* across with the Ornamental Growers Association. I found I had a majority of votes … and I carried a $250.00 appropriation, but better still, I had a vote of two to one ordering *Standardized Plant Names* to be used beginning with the next August list … including the standardized common name. This means that the leading nurserymen of the United States have adopted *Standardized Plant Names* without recall and that the 45 firms will have to come across and print their catalogs correctly. I consider it the biggest step forward in our whole program and it means that they will carry the day with all the other nurserymen."

Success! A tiny, dedicated group of people was beginning to see positive results after a decade of hard work, high risk, and no offsetting compensation.

On reflection, *Standardized Plant Names* was a huge accomplishment. It was a first. Heretofore, individual botanists could disagree and there was no effective mechanism to settle issues. Some would publish exhaustive plant lists, such as Bailey's, Sudworth's, or Van Wijk's, but who had the stature to arbitrate differences? The scientists didn't care about common names anyway. *Standardized Plant Names* was the first attempt to bring together a consortium of strong central authorities with sufficient clout to settle matters. They tried unsuccessfully to bring the British on board, but it didn't matter. It paved the way for the international community to bring the whole world together, years later, on standardized scientific names and naming procedures.

It worked quite well but never did eliminate all pockets of resistance. Seven years after *Standardized Plant Names* was published, the July 1930 issue of the *House Beautiful* carried an article titled, "The Vexed Question of Plant Names," by Helen Hart Oakes:

> "'A Rose by any other name,' the poet writes, 'would smell as sweet.' This happy sentiment seems to have been adopted by many amateur gardeners in defense of their carelessness concerning plant names, and they bestow the term 'highbrow' upon those who use standardized names with some regard to their correct spelling and pronunciation. This article is dedicated to those highbrows who have been saddened (or maddened, as their dispositions decree!) by hearing gardeners glibly inform a visitor that a certain plant is Ar´-je-mon or California-poppy', thus adding mispronunciation to misinformation; that a plant called 'kiss me over the wall' flourishes in the garden … For these careless gardeners give generously to some names the syllables they filch from others!"

It appears that the one thing the joint committee could never do, was to repeal human nature.

American Association of Nurserymen

The September 1923 issue of the AAN Booster newsletter carried a front-page article with a picture of Harlan Kelsey and the following inscription surrounding it: "Harlan P. Kelsey, President of the American Association of Nurserymen, whose work on the Standardized List of Plant Names, and on many other important tasks for the benefit of the nursery industry, have won him a high reputation throughout the nursery world." Then came the lead article as follows:

An Honor Well Earned

If any man has ever earned, by hard and self-sacrificing work, the honor of being made President of the American Association of Nurserymen, that man is Harlan P. Kelsey, of Salem, Mass., our present President.

For many years Mr. Kelsey has devoted much of his spare time—and much time that no one else in the industry would spare—to the forwarding of many matters from which he got no personal gain, but which have been of inestimable value to every man engaged in the nursery business.

In the progressive movements which he has backed, Mr. Kelsey has often found members of the Association who did not agree with him in certain things. But even those who did not agree with him, when there have been any such, have always had the greatest and most sincere respect for his energy, ability, and willingness to sacrifice his personal time and interest for the good of the industry. Every member of the Association—and every man in the business, whether a member or not—is to be congratulated upon having a man of Mr. Kelsey's caliber at the helm in American nursery affairs when there is so much constructive work to be done.

The problems of the AAN never seemed to go away. In 1876, its first year of existence, they adopted grades for fruit stock, hedge plants, and grapevines. Now, a half century later, in his final president's address, Kelsey chastised the membership: "Horticultural Standards are largely a dream and we have nothing but our negligence or complacence to thank for it." There were twenty different subjects covered in the address.[101] In most of them Kelsey took the membership to task for the situations at hand, but somehow he injected just enough humor to leave them laughing, not sighing.

For example, TRUTH IN ADVERTISING was one of the shortcomings he covered:

> Is it fair to our fellow members or other fellow nurserymen, or to the public, to advertise in our catalogs or elsewhere, that we have the biggest and finest stock in existence, of apples, peaches, plums or prunes, or anything else—a mere assumption—while secretly knowing our biggest and finest stock is probably gall [a plant parasite]? Or that we are the leading, or largest, or finest, or cleanest nursery in the universe, when we know we are following where others lead? Or, that we have at last discovered, or invented, and are introducing the most magnificent of all fruits, the Peachorino, with a color that makes a California sunset look like a cold closet; a flavor and sweetness that puts saccharine and vinegar in the same class; of such productiveness that 120 lb. railroad rails must be used as limb supporters; and of such shipping qualities that Chase U. Reed, one of our most valued customers said he took a peck of them in a potato sack on his seven months' trip around the world. He ate one in each country he visited and on his return two weeks ago had three left, all in perfect condition notwithstanding his fellow traveler Reed U. Chase's steamer trunk fell on the sack twice during a typhoon in the China Sea; last Saturday these three remaining Peachorinos were made into a Peachy Pie to the convulsive delight of the little Chase U. Reeds. Yes, maybe I've exaggerated—but *not much*. It has a sort of familiar sound, hasn't it? Again let me urge that we clean our own stables, lest the legislative Health Boards burn them up for us.

OUR SECRETARY. Here he praises Charles Sizemore.

> ... special ability, untiring effort, and an unfailing courtesy, even when extracting blood from a turnip which he is compelled to

do at times. The President of the Association and the Association would be lost without him. He comes from Louisiana, Mo., but he probably can't help that. If I leave Salem I am going to buy a lot next door to his in Louisiana, Mo. Besides, his family is even nicer than he.

NATIONAL ARBORETUM AND BOTANIC GARDEN. From the beginning, Kelsey had been a stalwart backer of this concept. The *Washington Star* of December 14, 1924, carries an article headlined "Nurserymen's Executive Lauds Project for Arboretum Here—Location at Mount Hamilton Ideal, Declares Harlan P. Kelsey—Industry Said to Need Federal Standardization." Excerpts from the newspaper article, following, clearly show Kelsey's enthusiasm:

> The proposed national arboretum is greatly needed as a "bureau of standards for the identification of plants," to protect not only the legitimate horticultural industry, but also the purchasing public, in the opinion of Harlan P. Kelsey of Salem, Mass., president of the American Association of Nurserymen. There is yet no such Federal agency in existence, Mr. Kelsey pointed out in discussing the matter here yesterday, charging that this very lack allowed the activities of some "crooks" and "fly-by-night men," alleged to be selling to the public nursery stock not true to its name. … Not only are the nurserymen in favor of a national arboretum at Washington, Mr. Kelsey said, but they are in favor of the particular site at Mount Hamilton. … The climatic conditions here, Mr. Kelsey pointed out are ideal. "Washington is peculiarly placed," he said, "in the right latitude, near water and with weather which is favorable to the growth not only of nearly all plants as far south as South Carolina, but also of plants which can grow below the frost line. … It would be a means of educating hundreds of thousands, even millions of people, in the ways of trees and plants. … And it would provide a beautiful and attractive landscape, a refuge for bird life."

But, it wasn't until March 4, 1927, that Congress approved the act establishing it, with Kelsey being one of fifteen original members of the advisory council on the planning and development of the arboretum. Over the next thirty years the progress on it would become a source of pleasure, but mostly disappointment for him. Here are his comments from the address:

> The National Arboretum in Washington is still unrealized. Every effort of this Association should be made to accomplish this project at our next term of Congress and the able committee with Mr. Pyle at its head should be given unlimited backing financially and otherwise. This country needs a National Arboretum and Botanic Garden in every distinctly different climatic section of the country. These would at once become testing stations for all plant material, reliable museums for identification and correct naming of plant varieties, as well as sources for disseminating the best new things in the horticultural field. May I urge definite and effective action at this Convention.

CROWN GALL. Kelsey had little patience with those who made snap decisions as to a solution for a problem. Crown gall (parasite) was such a problem puzzling nurserymen.

> The Association has appropriated considerable money to investigate Crown Gall and I believe we are all disposed to try and get at the truth of this and similar difficulties. We are told that each of us have millions of parasites living within us and parasites on top of them, most of them for our good so long as a proper equilibrium is maintained, and only occasionally does one of us get hit by a rogue bunch of typhoid or other bugs. Perhaps one in 500,000 of us are typhoid germ-carriers, yet that is not sufficient reason for keeping all of us out of Rochester, New York, because we may perchance give some of

you Rochesterians typhoid fever. Of course, if you kill the host the disease perishes, though I take it some of you would rather run the risk a while longer than to be electrocuted. It isn't quite the modern way of science in fighting diseases.

LEGISLATION. Here Kelsey became *steely-eyed serious*. The legislation involved federal and state quarantines and embargoes banning the shipment of plant material into the country or across state lines, presumably to prevent the transmission of pests and diseases. The year 1875 marked the first such law in Michigan. The first federal legislation was attempted in 1892. Even though it failed to pass, the idea didn't go away. Conferences, resolutions, and proposals from entomologists and nurserymen continued, until on September 20, 1912, the Federal Plant Quarantine Act was passed. Its key provision was to establish the Federal Horticultural Board with the forceful Dr. C. L. Marlatt as chairman. By 1915 the board was pushing a total embargo on all imports. The targets were white pine blister rust, cotton boll weevil, chestnut blight, citrus canker, San Jose scale, gypsy and brown tail moths, elm leaf beetle, and pine shoot moth as examples. It was alleged that the losses due to any one of these pests was greater than the value of all imports of nursery stock. On November 18, 1918, Quarantine No. 37 was enacted. Then the wars started—both the US entry into the First World War and the wars between the various parties in the horticultural world who stood to win or to lose by the quarantine process.[102] This was the legislation Kelsey was addressing in 1925. His address devotes about four times the space to this as to any other subject.

> The fundamental reason which caused the legislation bringing into being the Federal Horticultural Board was to exclude plant diseases and insect pests; today, this fundamental and good reason has gradually given way to plant exclusion. ... It is quite apparent that the effect on the nursery industry in America has been exactly that which follows high protective tariff and

embargoes. ... At the present moment probably 90 percent of the members of this Association favor the strict quarantines and embargoes, which are being imposed by the Federal Horticultural Board. ...

The fact that nurserymen today are getting $8.00 to $12.00 each for a Rhododendron which before the days of Quarantine 37 sold at $2.50 or $3.00 and that prices of ornamental nursery stock generally have jumped from 50 to many hundred percent, is of course the answer why nurserymen are in favor of this protection. Without doubt as a direct result of the Federal Board's activities beyond reasonable and necessary quarantines, there has arisen a whirlwind of State restrictive legislation, which is already seriously hampering the industry, causing great loss to nurserymen and making the conduct of the nursery business hazardous and at times almost intolerable.

The gypsy and brown tail moths have lost their virulence in this country and nature has established an equilibrium as it always does and I know of no place where these pests are causing appreciable economic damage; yet our Federal and State governments are spending hundreds of thousands of dollars of tax money waging war against an enemy which practically has become innocuous. I predict exactly the same situation with regard to the Japanese Beetle. ...

So today many nurserymen are pausing and wondering what the end will be. We may finally pay dearly for the era of an unnatural price prosperity caused by stock shortage. And what of the rapidly increasing armies of Federal and State employees marshaled to meet the foes, which only after hundreds of years of normal existence and activity have so suddenly become a raging menace to our horticulture? What of the ever-swelling millions of governmental appropriations to pay for combating the bugs and bugaboos? To paraphrase a war-time cry, "Pay Mr. Taxpayer, pay 'till it hurts.'"

OUR ATTORNEY. Our last example from the address was Kelsey's closing tribute to a man with whom he had become quite close during his prior two years as president of the association.

> We have an entirely exceptional legal adviser in Washington— Mr. M. Q. Macdonald. I believe all who know him agree with me on this, and your President is unashamed to take entire credit for this discovery. He is beyond price, yet costs us amazingly little. No National legislation affecting horticulture escapes his eye, and our nursery interests have become his own, as this year's results have proven. Don't lose him!

All during his tenure as president, Kelsey had been working with Macdonald on the quarantine problems:

Macdonald wrote Kelsey December 27, 1924. "Saturday afternoon is a good time for meditation. I can't meditate properly without a better knowledge of the nursery business. Is the Jap beetle one of the kind that can be carried in building sand, on stone, and such material? ... Has the F. H. B. [Federal Horticultural Board] ever attempted to inspect, disinfect, and otherwise purify sand, gravel and stone or similar building materials? If not, why not? Why pick on nursery stock when they admit that nurseries haven't given them any trouble?"

A week later Kelsey wrote back. "Your meditations of December 27th are received. ... The point you make is exactly the one I have written you and everybody else in creation about for a long time. The nurseryman is supposed to be 100% pure while the quarryman, the lumberman and the wood chopping farmer, who is always down-trodden, can ship their materials without ever attempting to clean up their places of business, and if gypsies are found on their shipments, the Government kindly creosotes or scrapes them off. ... White Pine Blister Rust is fortunately scattered pretty much over the East, yet each State is quarantining against the other; a beautiful state of affairs! Our legislators and inspection bureaus I think all have clonorchiasis."

The State of Georgia was particularly difficult for nurserymen outside of that state. Macdonald wrote to Kelsey February 8. "You tell Ga. That you will kill their damned national park aspirations if they don't lay offen you. I'll follow on a train with a big basket of real Jap Beetles and throw them out of the windows at each station in true German fashion. They have jaundice. Everything is yellow to the jaundiced eye. The Bible or Bobby Burns says so. They are worse than Lo-The-Poor-Indian who sees God in the Stars and hears Him in the wind. They see beetles in their sleep (and they sleep a lot there) and hear them under the bed. They suffer from Dementia Japaecox induced by too much ego in their cosmos. ... I note that you are in New York. You are as ubiquitous as the Jap Beetle is said to be. First thing you know, N. J., Pa., Md., Va., N. C., and Ga. Will lay down a quarantine against you. ... Does Mrs. Kelsey reduce your board bill while you are away? ..."

Kelsey to Macdonald, March 5: "May I ask you categorically the following question: Has the Federal Horticultural Board power to quarantine one section of a State against another Section?"

Macdonald to Kelsey, March 6: "If you want to make a lawyer mad ask him for a categorical answer. In most cases, if he is honest with himself and his client he will admit that he is no doubt an ass, but that he does not know the answer for sure. Look at all the cases that go to the Supreme Court of the United States. Both sides are cock sure they are right. The Court hands down a 5-4 decision and you are perfectly sure that the majority has the right dope—until you read the dissenting opinions. ... Answering your two questions: To the best of my knowledge and belief a Federal Quarantine, based on the exercise of the power of Congress granted in the Commerce Clause of the Constitution, can apply only to interstate commerce. However, the State often fills in the gap and makes such a quarantine effective."

Macdonald to Kelsey, March 21: "You are right about this being a Scottish building. There are three McLachlens, one Cameron, one Massie, one Robb, one Williamson, and two Macdonalds. You may not have any heather or oatmeal trees, but it looks as though you made that Carolina Hemlock and the crab picture with a Zeiss lens. Even the needles are sharp and prickly, and it probably lost something in reproduction."

One last example of the banter that went on between these two kindred souls: March 23. Kelsey to Macdonald. "Your various epistles received. If you have the right kind of land you can grow a Hemlock-Heather tree just as well as you could grow a Japanese Beetle and you needn't be terribly afraid of either one of them. If, as appears from your letter, Cammerer is your general agent and receiving clerk, I'll send it to him and save you the bother of having the material trickle up and down that Scotch building your office is in. Now I'll refer to several items: [There were seven of them.]"

> Item 4. Georgia: I have just received and I am enclosing herewith letter from Haliard De La Parelle, Entomologist, with various attachments thereto and now they ask me to execute a $1,000.00 bond which most assuredly I won't do. Now, let me have your advice because I have some shipments going into Atlanta. My nursery is inspected and I have the proper State Tags and I am willing to supply these to Georgia and I am not doing business in the State of Georgia but in Massachusetts. For Heaven's Sake, man, tell me where I'm at! If I have to come across and give bond in each State for shipping clean stock into those States or because they fear that it's going to be untrue to name or for any other cause, let me know positively and definitely. I'm a wandering lost soul and while I have my layman's view, I want

naturally to comply with the law and want my shipments to go thru to destination without being stopped but I much prefer entirely cutting out Georgia than to submit to any illegal and onerous requirements. ...

On the surface it may appear that Kelsey was getting legal advice for his own business that was paid for by the Nurserymen's Association. In fact, his problems with Georgia were the same as for every other nurseryman outside of Georgia. He was taking the time to solve them for everyone in the association. And the problems did not go away. They lasted for years and years after Kelsey stepped down as president of the association. Five months after his term was up he wrote to J. Horace McFarland, November 25, 1925:

"I do not object to protective tariff or free trade if the majority wants either one and legislates for it on a fair majority basis but this protective tariff in the garb of quarantine exclusion for insect pests and plant diseases, is ridiculous in the extreme, if one really reads the law and then knows what is being done. Unfortunately the Arnold Arboretum and our friend from the Massachusetts Horticultural Society and many others are willing to give up a fight when they get their own particular little part of the trouble rectified. In other words, they would rather hang apart than hang together. I had a long talk with Doctor Wilson the other day and I guess that they had fixed matters so that they would have little trouble in importing. Here again it is an excessively un-American or totally unfair thing, that anyone should be favored above anybody else but I don't see any use in discussing all this. There you are! There are mighty few people who are willing to stand up against pressure and fight for a moral cause where it goes against their own interests to do so. I'm going to as cheerfully as possible keep plugging away with my views on the matter and some day we may find a new F. H. B. in control."

The American Association of Nurserymen, Inc.

presents to

Harlan P. Kelsey

in recognition of the time and effort he has contributed so unselfishly
toward the welfare and progress of the Association and its members,
and with grateful and sincere appreciation for his faithful service as
President of the American Association of Nurserymen, Inc.
for the year 1923-24 and 1924-25

James G. Ilgenfritz
FOR THE BOARD OF GOVERNORS

Richard P. White
EXECUTIVE SECRETARY

Certificate of Appreciation. American Association of Nurserymen. 1925.

Tipping Point

In the twenty-five years since Harlan Kelsey's 1896 arrival in Boston, his stature had gradually grown as landscape architect, nurseryman, city planner, and conservationist. From the local Boston environs his reach became regional in New England nurserymen's affairs and the Appalachian Mountain Club's conservation battles. These activities required ever-increasing contact with comparable national organizations, such as the American Association of Nurserymen and other allied national groups in each area of endeavor.

In that same twenty-five-year period, Kelsey's drive to establish native plants in the center of American horticulture had been largely fulfilled. All his nursery industry competitors were now saying "me too." His wholesaling activities and plant introductions had supplied native plants throughout the structure of plant retailing. Other wholesalers followed suit to serve the demand for his "hardy American plants." The burden of proof now lay on the backs of nurserymen who still clung to the imported exotic species. As president of the American Association of Nurserymen, there was no place left to go for greater stature in promoting native plants in the nursery trade.

The early 1920s marked a turning point in Kelsey's life, where his energies shifted to conservation causes that were dear to his heart. His nursery business always remained as the source of income for himself and family. However, more and more of Kelsey's time was spent in hotels and trains to and from Washington, New York, and elsewhere, while his home and office remained in Salem, and his operations were at the nursery in Boxford. Preservation of the primeval native horticulture in his "beautiful land of the sky" was oozing into the forefront of his priorities, replacing his push for native plants in the nursery trade and the American garden.

In the provocation earlier, we expressed the notion that while John Muir was one of the preservation heroes of the West (if not *the* preservation hero), Kelsey was, decades later, the preservation hero of the East. His accomplishments paralleled those of Muir. We also promised that the ensuing chapters would unfold the evidence. Now would be a good time to demonstrate some of the Muir parallels in Kelsey's story through the first quarter of the twentieth century:

1. While he was still a child, Muir's family left Scotland for a homestead in the wilds of central Wisconsin. When Kelsey was a baby, his family left Kansas to found a new town in the wilds of North Carolina, in the high southern Appalachians.
2. It was malaria ("chills and fever") that motivated the Kelsey family to seek the high mosquito-free climate of the southern Appalachians. It was malaria that arrested Muir's intentions to explore the Amazon and go to mosquito-free San Francisco and the high Sierras.
3. Professor and Mrs. Ezra Slocum Carr nourished Muir's appreciation for geology, botany, and other natural sciences at the University of Wisconsin. Professor Harbison did likewise for botany and horticulture with Kelsey in Highlands.
4. Muir terminated his formal education after two university years to attend the "University of the Wilderness." Kelsey left Harbison and formal education to follow his father to Linville and the Kelsey Highlands Nursery—on-the-job training.
5. Muir abandoned a promising career using his inventiveness in manufacturing, for total immersion in publicizing wilderness. Kelsey abandoned a decades-long chain of successes in city planning, for the time to preserve wilderness in our eastern national parks.
6. Muir "took as his life's mission the education of his countrymen in the advantages of wild country."[103] Kelsey took as his life's mission the education of his countrymen about the superiority of native plants. (In the end this included their preservation in the wild habitat of the eastern national parks.)
7. Muir battled with Gifford Pinchot over "use" in forestry vs. pure "preservation." Kelsey also resisted Pinchot. Both adopted

"use" at first to quickly stop the destruction by the lumberman. In the 1890s, Muir dealt with the forest reserves set aside on government lands by President Cleveland. Kelsey's work with the AMC in the early 1900s led to the Weeks Act, setting aside purchased private lands as national forests.
8. Both men quickly recognized the incompatibility of "use" and "preservation." They both struggled against Pinchot's forest service credos, and Kelsey worked tirelessly to keep the National Park Service totally independent.
9. In the battle over the damming of Hetch Hetchy, both Muir's Sierra Club and Kelsey's AMC took the lead in preparing pamphlet literature for mass distribution.

Other parallels, in the second quarter of the twentieth century, will unfold in the chapters ahead. They chronicle the momentous battles with private interests as the eastern national parks were created. Battles similar to Muir's fights for the parks in the Sierras that had unfolded as the nineteenth century closed.

Preservation of the spectacular geological wonders in the western United States, via national parks, was a well-established movement dating back to the late 1800s. Financially, it had been relatively easy. The land involved was primarily government owned, so acquisition needed only congressional approval. Private groups like the Sierra Club sprang up to protect these western assets from the despoiling reach of mining, agricultural, and ranching interests, and to fight the political skirmishes in Congress.

But east of the Mississippi the land was, for the most part, privately owned. It was east of the Mississippi where horticultural wonders flourished. It was "Kelsey country." But conservation on private property was rare. Economic interests always overwhelmed conservation, as the lumbermen marched relentlessly across their landscape. The national forest land-acquisition program was the only mitigating force, and that was only a partial solution.

Kelsey was the nation's preeminent horticultural activist. He now needed to shift his priorities and energy toward preservation, one step beyond the "use" aspects of conservation.

Part II—Preservationist: National Parks

SHORTIA GALACIFOLIA. (See page 22.)

Chapter 5

National Stage

Appalachian Mountain Club

In December 1919 Harlan Kelsey was suddenly nominated, after years in no office, for president of the AMC. One clue to the sudden reemergence was that his old friend and mentor, Alan Chamberlain, was on the nominating committee that year. Kelsey accepted the honor and responsibility, little knowing what this presaged for his future as the decade unfolded.

In 1876, the AMC was founded in Boston by Edward Pickering and thirty-three other outdoor enthusiasts. Sixteen years later in San Francisco, the Sierra Club was founded. For some time, publicist Robert Underwood Johnson and Professor J. H. Senger had urged Muir to start a preservation association. Finally on May 28, 1892, a small group gathered with Muir in an attorney's office, and the club was launched. The westerners had followed in the footsteps of the easterners.

Charles Blood, president three years after Kelsey, gives us a taste of the Kelsey style. "The Appalachian Mountain Club has been fortunate in its selection of presidents of unusual character in important periods.

Harlan Kelsey joined the Club in 1897 and became president in 1920 in a period of transition immediately after the First World War. I found him a stimulating and agreeable man to work with. He was always looking forward, always considering whether the Club might not be of greater service to the public and of more value to its members. Many of his suggestions seemed novel at the time they were made, but they were always carefully thought out and well presented to the Council, and many of them were the foundation of later action by the Club."[104]

Listen to Kelsey's encouraging words on membership—praising, colorful, almost strident, and then humorous—after his first year as president.[105]

> We have flourished from a membership standpoint, with a net gain of 500 for the year, the greatest annual increase in the Club's history, and are now but little short of the 3,000 mark. Our duty and mission to bring the great out-of-doors into the lives of others around us is only second to bringing it into our own; and so I advocate a strong, continued campaign for members—let us double our membership and then double it again.
>
> I plead the cause and conversion of the tens of thousands of the great unwashed—that they may be shown the beauties of the lilies in the fields, the joy of being led beside still waters. I want their souls restored from the soot of the city street, the dust of counting houses, the blur of the movie, the confusion of the clanging streetcar, the sordidness of competitive business, the phantom pseudo-happiness of the herd life. It is sad but true that often only direct exposure will inoculate many people with the out-of-doors or nature bug. Happily, on the other hand, once infected it is for life!

In the same address he pleaded for new emphasis on alpinism within the club. After reminding them of the extraordinary happenings of the year—the huge Mont Blanc avalanche and the preparations by the British to attempt a climb of Mount Everest—he lauds Professor Charles E. Faye's "especial fitness for such a difficult mission; yet how many others of equal fitness by lifelong experience and training have we in the Club? Should we not gravely consider if our present day Appalachian activities are adequate to produce real mountaineers or Alpinists to follow worthily in his footsteps? Should we not have an Alpine section devoted specifically to high mountain and geographic exploration, fellowship being based on specified attainments, and at least one trip a year to be predicated on these requirements? In time, no doubt, by individual initiative, graduates would add largely to a knowledge of mountain regions yet but little known, and thus help to maintain our prestige as a real Mountain Club." This was a little late because there already was just such a club in New York City, the American Alpine Club, whose mission and charter was just what Kelsey envisioned. Today it, not the AMC, provides American leadership in world alpinism.

Another portion of his address must have warmed his heart. "The year has given our Club a lusty new chapter named the Southern Chapter, with headquarters at Asheville, North Carolina, and a membership of 33. This should mark the beginning of Hut and Trail development in the beautiful Southern Appalachians, and we promise all possible aid to our Southern brethren. We should foster the forming of local chapters wherever there are enough members to function well as an organization. When these children get big enough to paddle their own canoe, and wish to do so, let us help them to become full-fledged mountain clubs in their own name, though of course, like all good parents, we will never lose interest in our children." By 1924 the southern chapter had transformed itself into the independent Carolina Mountain Club, which thrives today.

Next year, for the first time in many years, the club elected its president to serve a second term. During the two terms, Kelsey dealt with numerous issues and offered suggestion after suggestion—increasing club dues, adding a new camp closer to Boston, seeking a paid executive secretary, establishing a large all-year-round camp, providing adequate club rooms or a real clubhouse in Boston, the need for a connected chain of camps covering the Presidential Range first, and later the entire White Mountain Region. "The management of our White Mountain Club Huts by our Trustees of Real Estate was not only entirely satisfactory to those fortunate enough to use them, but financially so successful that the new and splendid group of Log Camps at Pinkham Notch was built out of the earnings."

One last area of interest was so important to Kelsey's future that a complete excerpt from his first annual address is called for:[106]

> You all know of the recent assault by predatory irrigation and water interests on our National Parks—an assault which is still vigorously maintained. Your Council was quick to take an active part in their defense. The Club made a substantial appropriation, and authorized your President to call a general conference of New England organizations, which resulted in the formation of the New England Conference for the Protection of National Parks, with your President as Chairman and Frederick Law Olmsted as Secretary.
>
> This organization has not been idle; over 30,000 informative circulars having been distributed, while every Congressman from New England has been made aware that the people of New England hold him responsible and will be content with nothing less than an established Nation policy of HANDS ABSOLUTELY OFF OUR NATIONAL PARKS. Working with other national organizations we have tried to do our part in this great people's fight, which you will be glad to know has so far been successful.
>
> The obnoxious Smith Bill, which proposed exploiting a large corner of Yellowstone National Park for the benefit of

Idaho irrigation interests, is apparently dead, though we are assured it will soon appear again in sheep's clothing. But the fight to exclude our National Parks and Monuments from the provisions of the Federal Water Power Act is by no means won, and the passage of the Esch Bill (H. R. 14469) and the Jones Bill (S. 4554) must be ensured. The Walsh Bill (S. 4529), which proposes to dam Yellowstone Lake and make of it an irrigation pond, is still on the calendar and must be defeated. I want here to thank cordially those of our members who have contributed so liberally to the defense fund. The battle is at last fully open; but the cloven hoof of private, commercial greed and special privilege will not now be withdrawn until the people of America speak overwhelmingly their permanent decision in entirely unmistakable terms.

So, seven years after John Muir's death, the battles that he fought with private business interests continued. A new champion for preservation was needed, and Kelsey stepped into the breach.

At the National Park Service in Washington, DC, Stephen Mather and Horace Albright must have been grateful for Kelsey's vigorous activities on their behalf. Allen Chamberlain was no longer in the picture at the AMC, but his early lieutenant, Harlan Kelsey, was now the warrior there, in full command of preservation issues. The battles for national forests at the turn of the century were now being replayed on behalf of the national parks. Chamberlain's old successful tactics were again being employed by Kelsey—mass communications for public awareness.

The Appalachian Trail

Just as Harlan Kelsey was asserting leadership at the Appalachian Mountain Club, Benton MacKaye, a "mild, kindly, infinitely well-meaning visionary," was fashioning a monumental plan for a trail to continuously link the AMC's northern Appalachians with Kelsey's beloved southern ones. Volumes have been written on the origin, construction, and maintenance of the Appalachian Trail. One of the more complete accounts[107] summarized things this way:

> The Appalachian Trail is too monumental an accomplishment to lay at the feet of one man or even two, and its essence is that it was built from the ground up by the local workers all along the route; but if single names must be mentioned, that of Myron Avery deserves, though it rarely gets, equal billing with that of Benton MacKaye.

Nowhere in this mass of source material is the name of Harlan P. Kelsey mentioned even once. Yet, according to MacKaye, one of the most important planning decisions influencing today's hikers can be attributed to Kelsey. We'll get to that shortly, but first the groundwork.

In 1921 MacKaye, armed with a forestry degree from Harvard, was working for the US Forest Service in Washington, DC. "At one agency he was provided with 'an upstairs cubbyhole where he welcomed anyone in for a pow-wow.' Here he would sit, smoke his pipe, and think, except that 'once a week, he'd come downstairs to the staff meeting and pep up the others with new ideas and diagrams and imagination, and then disappear upstairs again.'"[108]

In the summer of 1921 MacKaye visited a friend, Charles Harris Whitaker, editor of the *Journal of the American Institute of Architects*, who in turn put him in touch with Clarence S. Stein, chairman of the Committee on Community Planning—AIA. This resulted in a long piece in the October 1921 issue of the journal, titled "An Appalachian Trail—A Project in Regional Planning." Excerpts from Stein's introduction to the piece show the broad sweep of MacKaye's thinking:

> Mr. Benton MacKaye offers us a new theme in regional planning. It is not a plan for more efficient labor, but a plan of escape. He

would as far as is practicable conserve the whole stretch of The Appalachian Mountains for recreation. Recreation in the biggest sense—the re-creation of the spirit that is being crushed by the machinery of the modern industrial city—the spirit of fellowship and cooperation. [These words have the same ring as Muir's of the late 1800s.]

Stein goes on to explain that many portions of the trail already existed through prior efforts of numerous local and regional outdoor organizations. But "to organize the systematic development of the vast recreational plan presented in this article will necessitate the cooperation of many minds and many talents."

The backbone of the plan, of course, was the uninterrupted Main Trail linking Mount Mitchell, the highest mountain in the south, to Mount Washington, the highest in the north. Branch trails were proposed from Mount Mitchell south to Tennessee and Georgia; also north of Mount Washington to Maine and Canada. But it wasn't just a trail. MacKaye talked of shelter camps (much as we see today along the trail), which would grow naturally into community camps where people could live in private domiciles, and also food and farm camps to "provide one definite avenue of experiment in getting 'back to the land'."

Other than publicity, nothing much happened until 1925, when the Appalachian Trail Conference was formed. "It established a vehicle for getting the Appalachian Trail out of the hands of the global thinkers and into the hands of the doers." First was Arthur Perkins, the key conference leader in the late 1920s. Next came Myron Avery, made acting chairman in 1930 and then chairman in 1931. "Against MacKaye's rambling, pipe-smoking, airy visions, Avery displayed a pragmatic, no-nonsense dedication to results." One early associate recalled, "Myron was easy to work with if you were willing to work hard and do things his way." Another said, "Myron left two trails from Maine to Georgia. One was of hurt feelings and bruised egos. The other was the A. T. ... Under

Avery the concept of the Appalachian Trail changed from a broad, vague social program, as originally envisioned by MacKaye, to a simple, single, tangible, well-cleared footpath."[109] Ultimately, section by section, volunteer by volunteer, the trail was completed.

How then did Harlan Kelsey fit into this picture? For starters, there was his friendship with MacKaye. It was clearly displayed in a June 21, 1925, handwritten letter to Kelsey:

> Dear Harlan, I have just got settled, with my sister Hazel, for a few weeks (presumably) at our old home here in Shirley Center. Where are you these days? This is just to let you know that I'm in these parts and to find out if you can't drift up this way sometime and put in a week-end with us. ... Did you get your invitation to be on the Appalachian Trail Committee? I hope so & that you've accepted. It was my suggestion.
> Let me know the prospects of seeing you.

Kelsey responded July 11:

> Dear Benton, Your letter of June 21st was duly received and I am sorry I couldn't answer sooner. You ask where I am these days but it would be better to put it, where am I not.
> Now I'd like nothing better than to come up and see you on the weekend but I have promised some real work on the ... park stuff and I've got to come across with it and later on it may be different. If it is, you may be sure that I'll drop in and see you.
> I don't recall getting any invitation to be on the Appalachian Trail Committee. I'll keep your letter and name on my desk and if I get back while you are still there I really want to come and see you.

Through this friendship, Kelsey had a telling influence on the route the trail would take through the southern Appalachians. In early 1922 there was a flurry of correspondence between Kelsey and McKaye. Thanks to David M. Sherman, US Forest Service, Lands Staff, we have copies he assembled.[110] They describe Kelsey's strong endorsement of McKaye's trail, and suggestions for its location in the southern Appalachians. Equally, if not more important, is Kelsey's introduction of McKaye to Paul M. Fink, member of the Appalachian Mountain Club, from Jonesboro, Tennessee. Fink played an important role in the trail layout from the Blue Ridge across the numerous ranges and valleys to the Great Smoky Mountains. Kelsey to McKaye, January 22: "Fink is the best man I know to give you the North Carolina-Tennessee route along the Smoky Mountains and he is greatly interested in it." Kelsey to MacKaye, February 2: "Enclosed you will find letter dated January 30th from Mr. Fink, also map made up from the U. S. Geological Survey sheets covering the section he describes; also some photos of mountain tops etc., along the way. There is no better person in the south to give advice regarding the Unaka or Smoky Mountain route."

Keep in mind that MacKaye's original proposal to terminate the main trail at Mt. Mitchell continued with two "branch trails." One continued down the Blue Ridge to Georgia; the other crossed from Virginia over to the Smokies and down to Tennessee. Kelsey (February 2) continued:

> I think some of his statements regarding the Blue Ridge route are a little bit wrong, possibly because he doesn't know that route as well as I do.
> The Blue Ridge section of the trail has the advantage of a large number of very beautiful waterfalls beginning with the Linville Falls and ending with a wonderful group of cascades and waterfalls in the vicinity of Highlands and including the Tuckaseigee and White Waterfalls near the North and South Carolina line and many others I could mention.
> In the cross over from the Highlands, North Carolina section one would get the trail in the Nantahala range, a cross range between the Blue Ridge and Unaka ranges. More than

this, while undoubtedly the Unaka route has the highest peaks and the wildest country, the Blue Ridge route has the advantage of a sudden drop off to the southeast causing such wonderful sheer mountain cliffs like White Side and Caesars Head, and a sudden drop approximating four thousand feet at the Piedmont section give the mountains the feeling of greater height than one would experience on Roan Mountain.

There is no question in my mind that there should be two sections of the trail; one the Blue Ridge and the other the Unaka and let the travelers determine which would be the main route by the use they make of them.

Kelsey provided another rationale for the southeasterly Highlands route. Kelsey to MacKaye, March 30: "Enclosed letter from Mr. Hugh MacRae, Wilmington, North Carolina, which is directly on the line of what would be the Appalachian trail." Marginal notes in Kelsey's copy said, "Letter states that the Linville Improvement Company would promote section from Blowing Rock to Asheville, & branch trails to Grandfather Mt., Roan Mt., and Black Mountains."

While Kelsey couldn't resist bringing the public down through the Highlands of his childhood, we know that ultimately this southeasterly alternate loop vs. the Smokies didn't prevail. Possibly, Myron Avery's later bull-headed push for a single main trail with no distractions was the reason. Or perhaps Fink was more persuasive in his flowery case for the Unaka route, in this January 30 letter to Kelsey:

> Speaking from the viewpoint of a Southerner, this trail is needed, for we have no routes for a long trip anywhere in our mountains, at least none marked either by signs or on the maps, and each tramper must lay his own itinerary. Personally, this suits me exactly, for like the cat in one of Kipling's Just So Stories, "I walk by my wild lone," and the wilder and more unfrequented the country is the better it suits me. But the average vacationist is not

so experienced as to follow his nose into any kind of country and would welcome a well-constructed trail, sure in the knowledge of where it would lead him and certain that shelters might be found at frequent intervals along the way.

Down through the Southern Mountains I am positive that the best route for the trail should be along the Unaka Range and so have suggested. To fully illustrate my ideas I have marked the route I think proper on the various sheets of the topographical maps of the U.S. Geological Survey covering this country and am sending them to you. With this letter are a set of notes descriptive of this route and a rough sketch map of the territory. All these you may turn over to Mr. MacKaye and Mr. Stein for their consideration.

Your suggestion of Lookout Mountain as a Southern Terminus to the trail is an excellent one. Beyond this point there are but foothills and, too, the wonderful view from Lookout will leave a glorious impression in the mind of any one tramping down the trail.

On February 21, 1922, Fink wrote MacKaye directly and finished off his case with a flourish: "Nothing gives me more pleasure than to write or talk about our mountains. In my enthusiasm about them I have evolved a theory—that East Tennessee was the last part of the world to be formed, and that if the Creator had made any mistakes while fashioning the rest of the world He profited by them when He made our mountains, hills and valleys." Kelsey was right when he told MacKaye, "You can be certain that Mr. Fink is a live wire."

Benton MacKaye fills us in on Kelsey's character as MacKaye viewed him over their long acquaintanceship. His reminiscences appeared in the Cosmos Club Bulletin for June, 1959.

I first knew Harlan Kelsey 50 years ago this winter, in Boston. I recall it was the year of the Lincoln centennial

(1909). I met him first with a little group of men who used to get together, now and then, for a lingering supper in a small downtown restaurant. They were fairly young professional men and all of them liberals. There were a few college boys since come to fame. Lincoln Steffens was in town that winter, writing his book on Boston politics, which, however, was never published. Steffens, indeed, once held a little session, wherein Kelsey, calling himself "Exhibit A," was shown and praised (and razzed) for being one of the brave boys who refused city officials their brazenly demanded rake-offs on sales of nursery stock. Had the group continued it might have become the "Cosmos Club" of the Universe's Hub.[111]

Chiefly I knew Kelsey as a fellow outdoorsman. Landscaper by profession, he was the all-around, old-school naturalist. On trail or in taproom his converse was of Freyja and not Bacchus. I saw him usually at some open-spaces confab—at Bear Mountain on Hudson, or A.M.C. Rooms, or perhaps an N.P.S. picnic-pow-wow.

Kel was a traveler—a true thorough Thoreauvian traveler— the kind that goes "far" by staying "near." If the Rajah of Walden Pond could travel "a great deal" in Concord, the Nurseryman over in Boxford could do likewise within his bailiwick. I think of Kelsey as a sportive hybrid of Anglo-Frankish stock, a cross between philosopher Thoreau and geologist Guyot; I dream of him as an ambulating antipode—an Appalachian—equally at home on Mount Guyot in the southern Smokies,[112] and on Mount Guyot in the northern Franconias. And with it all a seer on life's journey; one who refrained not but never frowned, who smiled not but never ceased silently to chuckle.

Finally we get to the important question. How did the anonymous Harlan Kelsey figure importantly in the Appalachian Trail? MacKaye supplies the answer in the fourth paragraph of his Cosmos Club reminiscence.

> Club members will remember him as "Kel." He once did me a favor, with results far-reaching. He corrected my geography. It was in the early 1920's. The Appalachian Trail was in its swaddling clothes. I had proposed a route for it—"from the highest point in the north to the highest point in the south—from Mount Washington to Mount Mitchell." I was conferring thereon, in Washington, with Kel and two other illustrious Club members—L. F. Schmeckebier and Francois Matthes. Any one of these big three could have corrected my mountainous ignorance of mountains, but it was Kelsey. He was then, along with Maj. W. A. Welch, on the job of locating the Great Smoky Mountains National Park. *"Hell," quoth Kel, "don't take your Trail to Mount Mitchell—take it through the Smokies—that's where the scenery is."* And so we did, of course.

Again, in 1969, MacKay was asked by the ATC Board of Governors to set down some words for the group's half-century celebration. He spoke of laying the foundations for the trail and cited "a unique group of founding fathers … There was Harlan Kelsey, who proposed shifting the southern terminus from Mt. Mitchell to the Great Smoky Range with a terminus in Georgia, thus becoming the author of the phrase 'From Maine to Georgia'."

There you have it, straight from MacKaye. But why the Smokies? If the trail had gone to Mount Mitchell it would probably later have continued down to Kelsey's beloved Highlands territory. Yet Kelsey proposed that, by whatever route, it had to veer westward through the Smokies.

The answer may lie in the comments by early proponents of the Great Smoky Mountains National Park.

> Their supreme beauty is their mantle of shimmering verdure—practically all that remains of the original American forest. … Comparatively few lovers of woods in this generation have ever

seen, to recognize or study it, even so much as an acre of the original deciduous forest which was once the glory of America (Robert Sterling Yard). ... The Great Smokies will introduce into the picture gallery of our National Park system a new and exquisite type of mountains.

The Smokies have other titles to distinction beside the glowing beauty of their forests. The climax of a broad scenic region, this is the most massive uplift anywhere in the East, with eighteen peaks towering 6,000 feet above sea level, while few western mountains equal them in elevation above their own base levels. ... They are softly veiled with a delicate, exquisite, dreamy blue haze that gives them a loveliness and an endearing charm which the Rockies lack.

But always it is the dim, cool, cathedral-like forest of the Smokies that most enchants the visitor—a forest densely tangled with laurel and rhododendron and fragrant with azalea.[113]

The Smokies are truly the epitome of Kelsey's Beautiful Land of the Sky. No wonder he wanted no one to miss it—especially the solitary backpacker on the Appalachian Trail.

National Parks

On March 1, 1872, the year of Harlan P. Kelsey's birth, President Ulysses S. Grant signed an act that set aside a "tract of land ... near the head-waters of the Yellowstone River ... as a public park or pleasuring-ground for the benefit and enjoyment of the people." The creation of Yellowstone National Park was the world's first attempt to preserve a large wilderness area as a national park. It was preceded in 1864 by Abraham Lincoln's signing a bill granting to the State of California control of Yosemite Valley and the Mariposa Big Tree Grove. But, it did not involve a national park. Between 1872 and August 16, 1916, when a bureau to administer them was finally established, Congress set aside fourteen additional national parks, all this during John Muir's lifetime. He did not live to see the establishment of the National Park Service.

On September 24, 1906, President Theodore Roosevelt issued a proclamation setting aside Devils Tower, a 650-foot-high volcanic shaft on the Wyoming plains, as the first national monument. Between that date and August 25, 1916, subsequent presidents set aside nineteen more national monuments to be administered by the Department of the Interior. In the words of Secretary of the Interior Walter L. Fisher, these parks and monuments had "grown up like topsy." There was no central administration, nor had there been any effort to spell out a general national administrative policy. Each park had its own politically appointed superintendent. Neither personnel nor materials could be transferred between parks. The army was running Yellowstone National Park. The General Land Office was responsible for the administration of the national monuments.

The problems arising from the lack of a central administrative organization did not go unnoticed by the friends of the national parks. As early as 1908, a small group of enthusiasts, led by J. Horace McFarland, president of the American Civic Association, began to lobby for the creation of a separate bureau to administer the parks. Kelsey was well acquainted with McFarland and received various publications from the American Civic Association in that regard. He wrote McFarland February 13, 1913, expounding some of his own ideas:

> Dear Sir: The publication on National Parks is a good one. I can't for the life of me see why, if we plan cities with a park system, we should not plan states with state park systems, locally laid out to preserve natural features, which should be preserved and to accommodate the present and future population so far as can be determined in advance, and what is true of cities and states applies with even greater force to the national government on account of the necessity for taking large tracts and then

arranging so that all communities will have easy access to at least a few large, native, natural reservations. Pres. Taft's remark that we reserve Parks and Monuments piecemeal is quite true. The result is that while desirable to get everything possible until a national policy is adopted, the national reservations are too much bunched. Just why it is necessary to reserve mountain tops or large mountain forest areas is not clear to see.

Texas, Louisiana and other comparatively flat states ought to have national reservations, and might easily be notable for other reasons than mere elevation and lack of farming possibilities. In other words with our rapidly increasing density of population large national parks must be provided and the department in charge of National Parks should make a complete study of the country from Florida and Maine to Texas and Alaska, and determine on a broad policy of planning for a system of national reservations, to be connected by good boulevards or highways. Hawaii and Philippines are none too wild to take into the scheme … Is it any too early to get a broad national planning movement started or at least get people thinking about it? It seems to me a sane proposition, although many people will think that some of us are going "Planning Mad."

This is the first indication we have of Kelsey's having an interest, with a certain level of conviction, regarding national parks. Thus, Kelsey's interest in national parks preceded Muir's death in 1914, with only a one-year overlap.

McFarland wrote back February 10, acknowledging that Kelsey "showed a broad grasp of the National Park idea," but urged him to hold his fire until the current lobbying efforts for an administrative bureau were successful. Then perhaps the new commission could be urged to do some future planning. Kelsey was not in the American Civic Association, and McFarland wasn't encouraging him to get involved.

Between 1908 and 1916, some sixteen bills that proposed a new bureau to administer the parks were introduced in Congress. Concurrently, successive secretaries of the Interior tried to organize park administration on a more coherent basis, with some modest success. The decade-long effort to secure passage of a bill creating a parks bureau in the Department of the Interior had become bogged down by congressional indifference and a bitter conflict within the ranks of the conservationists. By the summer of 1916, however, those who championed the creation of a park bureau emerged victorious, and on August 25, President Woodrow Wilson signed "An Act to Establish a National Park Service."

Success of the new bureau rested squarely in the hands of Stephen T. Mather and Horace M. Albright. Albright had arrived at the Department of Interior first—on May 31, 1913, as a clerk in the office of Assistant Secretary Miller. The twenty-five-year-old Albright had already proven himself an able administrator, and he was directed to keep Mather, who replaced Miller as assistant secretary in January 1915, "out of trouble." Stephen Mather was a self-made millionaire, whose success in the private sector rested as much on his publicity skills as it did on organizational ability. Because no money for the new bureau was provided until April 1917, the new organization could not be formed until that time, and the interim organization under Robert Marshall continued to function. By the end of 1917, Marshall returned to his old position at the Geological Survey, and the secretary appointed Mather as first director and Albright as assistant director.

With the help of Horace Albright, Mather built a small, overworked organization into one that came to enjoy a reputation for efficiency, responsiveness, and devotion to its charge unparalleled in the federal government.[114] Over the years to follow, Harlan P. Kelsey was to rub elbows frequently with these two gentlemen.

Undoubtedly, Mather and Albright were well aware of Kelsey's AMC activities in arousing public interest for protecting Yellowstone Park.

They may even have been cooperating with him, or he with them. We do know that Kelsey maintained a cordial relationship with them during the late teens and early twenties. Albright spoke of this in his obituary for Kelsey in the *National Parks* magazine of 1958. Albright says Kelsey often spoke to them on the glaring dearth of national parks east of the Rocky Mountains. He urged them to consider the beauties of the southern Appalachians, especially the Blue Ridge and the Smokies. Albright says Kelsey volunteered to work on the project if they could get something started. And get something started they did, as we will soon see.

But Kelsey wasn't the only one pushing for some eastern national parks. Reed L. Engle points out that efforts to establish a large national park in the East date to meetings held in Washington in 1901 between Virginia and Tennessee congressmen. Although a bill to establish a park was drafted, nothing came of this early effort. The concept languished until 1923.[115] The May 1902 issue of *Country Life in America* carried a feature article giving more detail on that bill, paraphrased below:

During the summer of 1899, private citizens of Asheville, North Carolina, started a movement which resulted in a well-formed and chartered organization called "The Appalachian National Park Association," with the aim of securing a national park and forest reserve in the southern Appalachian Mountains. Senator Pritchard, of North Carolina, secured passage of a bill by Congress in January 1900, appropriating $5,000 for a preliminary investigation of the southern Appalachian forests. The investigation was left in the hands of the Secretary of Agriculture, whose department, with the assistance of the Geological Survey, mapped the whole region from Virginia to South Carolina and Georgia during the summer of 1900. In early 1901, the president sent a special message to Congress, including the report from the Secretary of Agriculture, with a favorable recommendation. The report was accompanied by a map calling particular attention to the area along the North Carolina-Tennessee state line (the Smokies). Senator Pritchard then introduced a bill into the Senate requesting an appropriation of $5,000,000. More important matters crowded the question out, and a vote was not taken. Despite indications for favorable consideration, nothing was done again for over twenty years.[116]

One account of the history of the Great Smoky Mountains National Park claims the idea originated with a wealthy and influential family in Knoxville, Tennessee, Mr. and Mrs. Willis P. Davis. After returning from a visit to western national parks they asked, "Why can't we have a national park in the Smokies?" The account goes on, "From this beginning, other influential citizens of Knoxville began to echo the sentiment. Politicians, businessmen, naturalists, and others began to join the movement for their own personal reasons."[117] Mr. Davis gathered his friends around him and formed the Great Smoky Mountains Conservation Association; he was president until his death in 1931. Among the first of those friends was Col. D. C. Chapman, Knoxville businessman, who immediately took hold of the situation, and during the later years of Mr. Davis's career, gave most of his time to pushing the effort to completion.[118]

Up in Virginia, boosters for the Shenandoah Valley area called a convention on January 15, 1924, with almost one thousand delegates from thirteen valley counties, "for the purpose of rallying all the resources of the valley together in a program that would tell the world of the scenic, historical, industrial, and other values of the famous Shenandoah Valley." They created a regional chamber of commerce, with a ninety-man board of directors, and at their first board meeting passed a resolution calling for the creation of a new national park in the Shenandoah Valley. (This valley land was to the west of the future Shenandoah National Park up on the Blue Ridge.)[119]

Meanwhile, the Federation of Women's Clubs and other civic bodies had spent years working for admission of Mammoth Cave in eastern Kentucky as a National Park. Bills to create Mammoth Cave National

Park had been pending in Congress since 1912, but without a recognized method for securing it. Director Mather was favorably disposed and recommended acquisition in his annual report for 1920. In the 1921 report it was bracketed with Bryce Canyon as suitable national park material.[120]

Southern Appalachian National Park Committee

It took the National Park Service itself to get a serious effort going. In the seventh annual report of the National Park Service in 1923, Director Mather stated:

> I should like to see additional national parks established east of the Mississippi, but just how this can be accomplished is not clear. There should be a typical section of the Appalachian Range established as a national park with its native flora and fauna conserved and made accessible for public use and its development undertaken by Federal funds. As areas in public ownership in the East are at present limited to a number of forest reserves acquired under the provisions of the Weeks Act authorizing the purchase of lands for the protection of forests and the headwaters of streams, it appears that the only practicable way national park areas can be acquired would be by donation of lands from funds privately donated, as in the case of the Lafayette National Park.[121] [1919 Lafayette National Park, renamed Acadia National Park 1929.]

Early in 1924 Mather spoke with his boss, Secretary of the Interior Hubert Work, about the recommendations in his report and found him to be an enthusiastic endorser. Secretary Work immediately took steps to have an investigation made of the southern Appalachian Mountain region with a view of determining whether there were areas suitable for national park purposes. He decided that this investigation could best be accomplished by a committee of five public-spirited citizens.

Secretary Work asked Congress to authorize an unpaid committee, which resolution passed on February 24, 1924.

Work then wasted no time in identifying who should serve. Three men were immediately selected as obvious candidates. On February 16, 1924, he wrote to Major W. A. Welch, general manager and chief engineer of the Palisades Interstate Park Commission, New York, a man familiar with the actual operating issues related to parks. At the same time he wrote Representative Henry W. Temple, member of Congress from Pennsylvania, who would act as chairman of the commission and provide the necessary link to the congressional authorities. Concurrently he asked the director of the Geological Survey to assign Colonel Glen S. Smith, division engineer of the Geological Survey, as a member to represent the secretary. These three men were either government employees or professional park executives. The remaining two were to be "civilians," so to speak. Secretary Work wrote to Barrington Moore, secretary of the Council on National Parks, Forests, and Wild Life, New York, asking that the council select two of its members to serve. This council, on March 4, 1924, selected Harlan P. Kelsey and William C. Gregg.

Gregg was president of the Gregg Company, manufacturers of cars and railway equipment, of Hackensack, New Jersey. What qualified Mr. Gregg for the commission was his association with the National Arts Club, New York. Arts? Digging deeper, we find that Gregg was chairman of the National Parks Committee of the National Arts Club. He was also vice president of the American Civic Association, an organization that had been a National Parks Committee booster since its inception.[122]

Then, finally, we have Kelsey. A successful nurseryman, yes, but most of the literature cites his prior tenure as president of the Appalachian Mountain Club for his dominant qualification. Director Mather had started the whole thing off with the stated desire to "preserve native flora and fauna and make them accessible for public use." Kelsey, alone among the five commissioners, was a noted expert on native flora. He was just coming off the publishing of *Standardized Plant Names*, with its wide circulation in the horticultural world. He had also just been selected as president of the American Association of Nurserymen. No one in the country was better suited to lead the search for a park in the southern Appalachians. Unlike the western parks with their soaring geology, this eastern park would have to represent the best of the East's exquisite flora in an exquisite setting. His entire horticultural career had been preparing him for this moment.

Kelsey joked about his selection in an unrelated March 6, 1924, letter to Frederick Law Olmsted. "The other day the Council on National Parks, Forest and Wildlife met in New York and I had wished on to me membership on the National Commission to pick out the best territory in the Southern Mountains for a National Park. I pick up these eleemosynary jobs quite as easily as one does beggars, ticks in hunting quail in the autumn with a woolen suit on, and they seem even harder to get rid of than nettles." [Little did he know that 'get rid of' wouldn't come for another eight years, 1924–31.] Of course I have to get my final appointment from the Secretary of the Interior." While his humor makes light of the appointment, inwardly he had to be bursting with gratification over this opportunity to influence a matter so important to him.

All five members invited to form the committee accepted, and the initial meeting was called for March 26, 1924, in the office of Director Mather. There they selected a name, the Southern Appalachian National Park Committee, and Colonel Smith was elected secretary and treasurer. All members, as volunteers, would bear their own expenses, since there were no government funds available. For miscellaneous expenses, Mr. Gregg donated $500, and later, as this fund was exhausted, John D. Rockefeller Jr. donated an additional $500 and Director Mather $250.

At the close of the first day of the meeting, Secretary Work met with the committee in his office, issued instructions, and later gave out a statement for the press. The press release announced the committee formation and officers; it then went on with excerpts as follows:

> As the Committee already has a large number of requests for examinations of territory, it was decided to send out a questionnaire to all interested communities. The Committee wishes to have it known that it considers its scope confined to the Southern Appalachian Mountains, not extending north of the southern border of Pennsylvania. ... A copy of the questionnaire is attached. ... Communications suggesting national park sites have been received from the following localities: Knoxville, Tenn., Jonesboro, Tenn., (he goes on to list twenty-three localities in total).

Ultimately, the committee's work went well beyond merely identifying the parks; it continued until 1931, when the group agreed to dissolve itself and submit a report on all of its activities and accomplishments. The report was written in narrative form, in chronological order, setting down events as they happened. This report forms the basis for most of the material that follows.[123]

By July, with the returned questionnaires in hand and evaluated, and numerous requests by the applicants for visits to their areas also in hand, the committee decided it would be necessary for them to make a trip throughout the Appalachian region to determine, by elimination, the best areas for more detailed inspection. The idea was to go all the way south to Georgia and then make a great loop in the mountain regions to the north and west. Starting in northern Georgia, where mountains blend in with the Highlands region of southwestern North Carolina, they went to Highlands, Asheville, Mount Mitchell, the Grandfather Mountain area (from Blowing Rock to the Linville Gorge), west over Roan Mountain, ending in Knoxville, Tennessee. This would give the committee a good feel for the southern end of the Blue Ridge, the cross ranges to the west, and of course the Smokies. All this was where

Kelsey's main interest lay. The northern end of the Blue Ridge and subordinate ranges could wait next in line.

If for any reason the committee had thought they could quietly and efficiently complete the tour, they would have been quite mistaken. The party, including Secretary Work, left Washington July 24, 1924, arriving, at the request of Georgia Congressman Thomas M. Bell, in Gainesville, Georgia, where they spent the night at his residence. The next day, they were overwhelmed by the locals. As they proceeded on to Clayton, Georgia, they were accompanied by about sixty prominent Georgians, including Governor Walker, US Senator Harris, together with numerous members of the press, members of chambers of commerce, and other state organizations. After two days, ending at Tallulah Falls, they proceeded up to Highlands, North Carolina, shedding the Georgians but picking up the members of the North Carolina Committee from Asheville, North Carolina. It was headed by Colonel Pratt and comprised of representatives from all over the western part of North Carolina. Clearly, this pattern of days spent viewing the natural sights surrounded by highly biased crowds of local people, and nights spent socializing with the same crowds, promised to become a grueling affair. It was at this point that Secretary Work bailed out, returning to Washington with the excuse that he was "slightly indisposed."

After one night in Highlands, they proceeded the following day down to Brevard, visiting en route Whiteside Mountain, an old Kelsey favorite, with its huge, sheer, east-facing two-thousand-foot white cliff. Call it an eastern version of Yosemite's El Capitan. The citizens of Brevard entertained them at lunch, after which a second delegation from Asheville met the committee, including the mayor of Asheville and several county commissioners, to escort them to the Grove Park Inn in Asheville for the night.

No time to rest, however. Another delegation from Tennessee called on the committee the evening of their arrival to present their case for the location of a national park in the Great Smoky Mountains area. They couldn't wait the few weeks for the committee to reach Knoxville. They wanted to "get their oar in the water" first, before the committee had been brainwashed by those from other areas. This last delegation was headed by W. P. Davis, president of the Smoky Mountains Conservation Association, accompanied by Col. David C. Chapman, chairman of the Great Smoky Mountains Park Commission of Tennessee. Included were a congressman and a number of prominent Knoxville businessmen. This detail should be enough to illustrate the frenetic pace imposed on the committee during the entire trip. Accordingly, for the remainder of the trip such detail will be skipped.

Leaving Ashville the next morning, they lunched at the hotel atop Mount Mitchell, the highest point east of the Rockies. Descending the mountain, they proceeded on to Blowing Rock, North Carolina, for the night. The next day, July 31, 1924, the party inspected the area around Grandfather Mountain, spending the night in Linville. Again, this was Kelsey country. There was no one better to sing its praises than Kelsey himself. He knew it intimately, especially the flora, which is exceptional. Because Mount Mitchell is in a spur range called the Black Mountains, Grandfather Mountain lays claim to being the highest in the entire Blue Ridge. It was almost totally owned by the Linville Improvement Company. The next day they inspected Linville Gorge, with its famous falls, on the way to Marion for lunch at the Marion Club House. Here the party split. Dr. Temple and Major Welch had had enough. They left for home. The remaining three, Kelsey, Gregg, and Smith, were taken by automobile to Bakersville, where they addressed a gathering at the county courthouse and spent the night. A local delegation then took the party on horseback to the top of Roan Mountain, where a careful inspection was made of that area, and then back to Bakersville for a second night.

That took care of the southern Blue Ridge area. Next, and last for this trip, was the Great Smoky Mountains area, the western slopes, in eastern Tennessee. On August 3 the party went on to Johnson City, where

Colonel Smith was obliged to return to Washington. Now they were down to a party of two. Kelsey and Gregg, "in response to an urgent request from the Great Smoky Mountains Park Association," proceeded to Knoxville, Tennessee. They found that all necessary preparations had been made for taking the party to Mount LeConte and other high points lying in the center of the proposed park area. A gathering of fifty or sixty people congregated at Gatlinburg, intending to make the arduous trip into the mountains with the party. This cumbersome affair was quickly modified to allow only the members of the Park Association to accompany the party. They went on horseback for their five- or six-day trip to view the area from various high points along the Tennessee/North Carolina border that bisected the proposed park. This included one night on top of Mount LeConte. On their return to Gatlinburg, they were met by the governor of Tennessee and other state officials for further discussions. Kelsey addressed local organizations in Knoxville regarding criteria for selection of national parks. Then Kelsey departed for his home in Salem.

That left only Gregg as "the last man standing." He proceeded on horseback through Indian Gap to Bryson City on the North Carolina side, where he spent some time investigating the areas in that vicinity. The committee's inspection trip that started boisterously with six, ended quietly with one, and was over. Except for official meetings in Washington, DC, this first trip was the only one where all five members of the committee were together, at least at its beginning.

Meanwhile, up north in Virginia and West Virginia some restlessness developed over the lack of response to the questionnaires they had submitted. On September 12, 1924, Major Welch and Colonel Smith went to White Sulphur Springs, West Virginia, in response to a request from Governor Morgan to attend a conference on the eligibility of that area as a national park. In the auditorium of the hotel, a large assembly of West Virginians held forth, with Governor Morgan presiding over the presentation of the case for White Sulphur Springs, which included numerous other springs. Before leaving that evening, Welch and Smith were taken by automobile to inspect the area recommended.

Welch and Smith then proceeded on to Luray, Virginia, to inspect the Blue Ridge Mountains from Font Royal in the north to Waynesboro in the south and were met by several hundred residents headed by a band. In fact there were two delegations present, one recommending the Massanutten Mountain area, and the other the Blue Ridge, headed by George Freeman Pollock. Pollock was founder and manager of Skyland, the nineteenth-century resort high up on the spine of the northern Blue Ridge. By September 1924, Pollock's group had formed the Northern Virginia Park Association, sharing two officers with the Shenandoah Valley, Inc. Welch and Gregg decided to go immediately to Skyland. The Massanutten Mountain area delegation was invited to tag along. Under Pollock's guidance, three days were spent inspecting around the immediate vicinity of Skyland. They visited White Oak Canyon, Stony Man Mountain, and the mountain ridge south of Skyland for a distance of twelve or fifteen miles. Smith and Welch were so favorably impressed with the area they postponed further investigation until arrangements could be made for the whole committee to visit. The Massanutten delegation decided it couldn't compete with the superior Blue Ridge area, and no further efforts were expended on promoting their area, which was never visited by the committee.

The committee had been invited to inspect a two-hundred-thousand-acre area in northern Alabama, extending from Muscle Shoals Dam south to the juncture with the Alabama National Forest. Only Major Welch responded, arriving in Jasper, Alabama, on October 16, 1924. This area contained a large amount of valuable coal seams and other minerals that made it impracticable for consideration as a national park.

Attention was now focused primarily on the northern Blue Ridge. It was now Mr. Gregg's turn to visit the area. After spending several days at Skyland, Gregg detoured to Harrisburg for a Rotary Club luncheon with fifty or sixty members to thrash out the divided opinion in the Shenandoah Valley over the various options before the committee, the valley itself, the Massanutten range, or the Blue Ridge crest. Gregg soon overcame the divisions and left Harrisburg with all parties now in favor of the Blue Ridge. He continued his investigation of all areas south to Waynesboro, having missed only the region north of Skyland.

But Gregg wasn't through. At his own expense, he revisited all of the areas of the southern Blue Ridge, from Georgia through Highlands and north to Linville Gorge, Grandfather Mountain, and Blowing Rock. As for the Highlands, he concluded that despite many areas of scenic importance, the areas were too thickly settled and too highly cultivated for national park purposes. What an enormous change since forty-nine years earlier, when S. T. Kelsey started grubbing out mountain laurel to create streets in the then-deserted Sugartown Highlands for his new town.

In November Pollock got Welch and Smith back to Skyland, this time with Chairman Temple in tow, for a more thorough investigation of the Blue Ridge. This late in the fall Skyland would ordinarily be closed for lack of patronage, and it was necessary to keep its stable of horses and crew of employees together well into December, at no small expense to Mr. Pollock. It was a self-imposed delay to allow the Virginians to complete a series of wooden observation towers and trails to show the scenery to best advantage. They were piloted, on horseback, for a full week visiting high and low all the way southward to pay their respects to the Rapidan area, where in later years President Hoover's camp was located. During their stay at Skyland, from November 6 to 14, the committee members were met by the governor and many other high-ranking Virginia notables. This included Robert Sterling Yard, secretary of the National Park Association. All, of course, made strong cases for the Blue Ridge as a national park.

Kelsey had begged off this trip, citing business engagements. He had a huge workload with both his nursery business and presidency of the

American Association of Nurserymen. Strangely, the committee's draft of the final report makes no mention of Kelsey ever visiting the Virginia Blue Ridge, his efforts having been focused on the case for the Smokies. But this was an error of omission.

Years later (1938) G. Freeman Pollock recounted his memories of wooing Mr. Kelsey.[124] Pollock's anecdotes reveal a lot about Kelsey's determination to do the right thing and his flexibility in defining what is right. Also, they reveal what a physically tough man he was at age fifty-two, with detail on just what an "inspection" involved. So we will devote considerable time to tell the story.

The Virginians were well aware of Kelsey's North Carolina heritage and his strong preference for the Smokies as the site for the national park. They were now confident that the other four commissioners would select their Blue Ridge as the site. But could they count on that? How influential Kelsey would be was a hidden risk they didn't dare leave open. It was a horse race, and any stumble could be fatal for their cause. They had to get him down to at least inspect their site and listen to their case. As Pollock put it, "Our Virginia associates had put it up to me to produce Harlan P. Kelsey in Virginia." One lever was to get him to attend a testimonial dinner for Hugh Naylor in celebration of his work for the park; then he would be able to inspect the area north of Front Royal, which none of the commissioners had visited. They had left this for Kelsey to do.

> His replies to our invitation indicated his disinclination to leave his business, inasmuch as his opinion of the Blue Ridge area would differ from that of his fellow members on the Commission, and would be unnecessary. Unwilling to accept this disappointing decision, I persisted in my invitation, arguments and appeals. Finally I was assured that next day Mr. Kelsey would leave to attend the Naylor dinner. ... He requested me to meet him at Front Royal, and promised to inspect the northern area.

The news thrilled me as I had seldom been before, and I have had many thrills. ... Mr. Kelsey arrived on the morning train. That evening we all enjoyed a real banquet which I am sure inspired Brother Kelsey, if not with the beauties of Virginia scenery, certainty with the determination of Virginians to have it recognized.

The next day they started on the inspection tour. A party of at least fifteen motored to the east side of the area on the eastern slope of Mount Marshall, where the horses awaited them. Now, Pollock gives an account of the day, quoted below:

The route led by old logging roads and forest trails over Mount Marshall, thence through a primeval forest area deemed important for Mr. Kelsey to see. After that we were to go south by the trail between Marshall and the neighboring mountain known as the Peak at about 2,800 feet above sea level; thence to Gravelly Spring, and thence by a worn and very steep road down the west side of Mount Marshall to Brown's Gap, and thence to Browntown in the valley, about five miles from the railroad. The last ten miles had to be ridden in darkness. Of all the trips I made with various members of the Commission, this was the most memorable because it was the most severe, and the region was strange to me. Let the reader take my word for it that forty miles on horseback over such rough country, climbing or descending steeply most of the time, is no nursery romp. ... At the foot of the mountain we still had some three or four miles to go. I called, "Come on boys, let's get going out of here!" and led off at a lively gait, followed by the entire group. We galloped over small streams, through mud holes, across bridges, until we reached Browntown. I confess I was so sore I could hardly get out of the saddle; it had been about the worst ride I had ever experienced. We had to catch the train for Luray with scarcely a minute to lose, as there were five miles to go by automobile first. Cars were waiting for us. ... We hurried our saddlebags and equipment into the cars ... and we started on a wild drive for the railroad station. Fortunately we made it, only because the train was an hour late. ... Reaching Luray nearly paralyzed with fatigue ... it had been a pretty strenuous day.

Unknown to Kelsey, Pollock had planned to persuade Kelsey to take yet another strenuous three-day horseback trip. The next day they were to drive south to the Fisher's Gap road, up to the top of the ridge, then over the Big Meadows to a log cabin nestled atop the ridge near Double Top Mountain, where they would meet the horses and spend the night. The next day they would ride northward to Skyland for a second night. The third day they would descend to Luray for Kelsey's train. Pollock was determined "that this last member of the Southern Appalachian Park Commission should see the entire area from Fork Mountain north before leaving the Blue Ridge. He [Kelsey] was game, in fact delighted."

Reaching the Fisher's Gap road about five miles from Luray we found it in very bad shape. Recently "worked" and rained on, it was very soft; so we lurched along, every once in a while getting out to push or lift the cars out of mud holes, up to the top of the ridge some 3,000 feet above the valley; thence over equally rough road to the little log cabin. The Skyland horses and guides were waiting there, a cheerful fire burning in the open fireplace, and a delicious dinner soon ready. Mr. Kelsey is a good traveling and camping companion and I shall never forget that night at Graves' log cabin. We sat up all night playing a new brand of poker in which he was instructor, I the investor.

In spite of unfavorable promise, just the day that I wanted dawned; fog and mist in patches exposed here and there magnificent vistas of primeval forest and beautiful valleys. Double Top Mountain at our front door, old Fork visible from the south porch, hungry horses grazing in the yard, our guides saddling for the trip, and sun breaking through the clouds! ... With such a lovely morning, and the thought that the impression made by what we were about to see might possibly determine "to be or not to be" for the Shenandoah National Park, it is no wonder that I had thrills such as I would like to live over again. I knew the skeptical Commission member was becoming enthusiastic and left my guides to take him to Fork Mountain summit alone, where he could gaze out over the very center of the proposed park area from the tower my men had constructed by carrying lumber some five miles up the mountain by hand. While Mr. Kelsey made this trip I broke camp preparatory to our return to Skyland, thirteen miles north. As I had expected, he returned to the cabin inspired by the magnificent view. In wind and weather somewhat colder than we were dressed for we made the rough ride, via Weakley's Ranch, the Umbrella Rocks, Fisher's Gap, Franklin Cliffs, the "cowboy fields," Spitler's Ranch, the grand old peak of Hawksbill, and thence up the Devil's Stairway to Crescent Rock and through the Limberlost Swamp, to Skyland. The last mile was through dense hemlock forest full of slanting shadows and the music of a hidden stream.

It was comforting indeed to know we were approaching home, with its welcoming warmth and food, for we were tired and cold. The moon came out as we approached the Field Cabin, where my cousin ... had a splendid duck dinner awaiting our arrival. The heavenly aroma of that roasting duck, even of the gravy and brown potatoes, was in the air, indescribably tempting. *But that moon.* And the view from the top of Stony Man! What a magical spell would be cast over misty peaks and sleepy valleys for fifty miles around. With an effort that seemed at the moment heroic I ventured to say bravely: "Mr. Kelsey the duck surely does smell good, but it will smell even better an hour from now. It is a case of now or never for the peak, because you won't have time tomorrow if you want to see White Oak

Canyon." To my surprise and relief my guest shouted in reply: "Sure thing! Sure thing!" and waving his arm toward the peak, "Let's go! Lead the way!"

So leaving tired guides behind, up we went alone. The wind, a gale, had blown all clouds away and the atmosphere was crystal clear. Reaching the summit in no time we tied our horses and climbed the lookout tower. Its platform, supported on a structure of thirty-foot poles, rocked in a wind so strong that the skirt of my poncho was flapped up over my head as we climbed the narrow ladder. We literally had to hold on to keep from being blown away. Mr. Kelsey just hung on and gazed in silence at the inspiring spectacle for perhaps five minutes. Holding on beside him, I pointed out Old Rag Mountain to the east, clearly defined in the moonlight, and Mt. Marshall, which we had visited two days before, almost as distinct, although thirty miles away to the north. Completing the magic circle were the Piedmont Valley in mysterious mist to the east, the Shenandoah Valley with its faintly twinkling diamond and ruby lights to the west, Skyland with its roofs gleaming in the moonlight at our feet, the solid bulk of old Hawksbill looming to the south. For accompaniment to this glorious outlook we could clearly hear the booming of waterfalls in Dry Run Canyon far below us to the west. And as we gazed entranced, our fragile tower was swaying, swaying, giving us the effect of a ship at sea. It was all almost unearthly, but it was very grand.

Since our dinner had been forgotten for the time, I bethought me, "Why not take this man down the Devil's Climb to the Dry Run Cliffs?" And when I proposed this, explaining that I could send back for the horses, he only said, "I am prepared for anything now. Go ahead." So down from the treetop tower to the Stony Man Cliffs, from which we started the descent of this strange stairway, a tumbled mass of broken rocks. Its hundred and fifty feet make a spectacular descent to the so-called Raven Nest Rocks, where ravens build their nests in the spring. With the rushing wind, strange rock masses, moonlit cliffs and the view from the summit I am sure brother Kelsey will never forget that trip. ... But we finally did get back to Skyland and that duck dinner and so to bed.

Mr. Kelsey's scheduled departure by train from Luray next day still allowed an inspection of White Oak Canyon, the most beautiful ravine, I think, in the whole park area and perhaps in the eastern United States. We rode down its lovely reaches. ... I thought it best to leave him to return alone and experience some of the solitude of the woods, free to linger and get out his camera. I kept well ahead but once in a while he would catch up, shaking his head in silent wonder, his camera in hand. Thus we retraced two thousand feet to the first waterfall. I thought those two miles of wild and rugged canyon with its cascades and waterfalls, whose beauty somehow does not fit into print but must be seen to be realized, a fitting finish to the Kelsey expedition. And so it seemed as he clasped my hand in farewell. As to his conclusions he was discreetly silent, as he was to confer with Secretary Work next day. But the one remaining vote in the Commission, I felt satisfied, would make the decision unanimous for our glorious area in the Blue Ridge.

The last piece of work for the committee was to get Chairman Temple and Colonel Smith down to the Great Smoky Mountains, as they were the only two members who had not visited them so far. They were met by the key officials of the Great Smoky Mountains Park Association, who ably hosted them as they covered practically the same ground that had been visited by the other members of the committee.

With all the inspections behind them, the next obvious step was to frame a report to Secretary Work describing their efforts and the conclusions they had reached. Chairman Temple called a meeting for that purpose December 12, 1924. With all members present, they thrashed out whatever differences and details that may have still existed after the eight months of working together. On the evening of that same day, Secretary Work had invited the committee, along with Director Mather of the National Park Service, to a dinner, which he gave in his private dining room at the Wardman Park Hotel. At dinner the question arose as to what name should be given to a national park in the Blue Ridge area. That was when Kelsey suggested the name "Shenandoah," presumably because wherever you were on the Blue Ridge crest, the most dramatic aspect was the steep western slope looking directly down into the historic Shenandoah Valley. Certainly that would please all those members of the recent Shenandoah Valley, Inc. that had backed down in favor of the Blue Ridge. Kelsey's suggestion met with unanimous approval of all those present. Of course there was never any question as to the name of the mountain area between North Carolina and Tennessee. It had always been known as the Great Smoky Mountains, thus the only logical name for the national park.

The committee's report was a combination of aesthetic, practical, and political factors. The report opened with some formal remarks and then gave a condensed summary of the many inspections the committee had made during the eight months of their existence. It then got right down to the criteria used in making their recommendations.

First they talked of the process of elimination, which distilled down the many applicants. Some were eliminated because, while highly scenic, they lacked sufficient area to qualify. Some were adjacent to or contained areas of the national forests, which already were under government protection and offered public recreation facilities. They enumerated six "simple" requirements that would allow "for the possible consideration of Congress:

1. Mountain scenery with inspiring perspectives and delightful details.

2. Areas sufficiently extensive and adaptable so that annually millions of visitors might enjoy the benefits of outdoor life and communion with nature without the confusion of overcrowding.
3. A substantial part to contain forests, shrubs and flowers, and mountain streams, with picturesque cascades and waterfalls overhung with foliage, all untouched by the hand of man.
4. Abundant springs and streams available for camps and fishing.
5. Opportunities for protecting and developing the wild life of the area and the whole to be a natural museum, preserving outstanding features of the Southern Appalachians as they appeared in the early pioneer days.
6. Accessibility by rail and road.

We have found many areas which could well be chosen, but the Committee was charged with the responsibility of selecting the best, all things considered." Then they got to what everyone had been waiting for. *Who was the winner?*

"Of these several possible sites the Great Smoky Mountains easily stand first because of the height of the mountains, depth of valleys, ruggedness of the area, and unexampled variety of trees, shrubs, and plants." Hallelujah. Kelsey's dream, come true. But wait. "The Great Smokys have some handicaps which will make the development of them into a national park a matter of delay; their very ruggedness and height make road and other park development a serious undertaking … their excessive rainfall also is an element for future study" as to its impact on development, administration, and recreational use. Of course it is this very rainfall that makes the Smokies one of the world's densest areas of horticultural variety.

"The Blue Ridge of Virginia, one of the sections which had your committee's careful study, while secondary to the Great Smokys in altitude and some other features, constitute in our judgment the logical place for the creation of the first national park in the Southern Appalachians. We hope it will be made into a national park and that its success will encourage the Congress to create a second park in the Great Smoky Mountains which lie some 500 miles distant southwest." They gave three additional factors in which the Blue Ridge outranked the Smokies. First, it was a three-hour ride from the nation's capital and within a day's ride of forty million inhabitants. Second, it captured all the historic interest of the Shenandoah Valley on which it looked down. Finally, "the greatest single feature however is a possible skyline drive along the mountain top following a continuous ridge and looking down on the Shenandoah Valley some 2,500 to 3,500 feet below, and also commanding a view of the Piedmont Plain stretching easterly to the Washington Monument which landmark of our National Capital may be seen on a clear day. Few scenic drives in the world could surpass it."

They didn't overreach. They kept it simple to maximize the likelihood that Congress would act with a minimum risk of delay. They also added a final recommendation to improve the chances of early implementation if Congress did in fact approve their recommendation, namely: "We suggest that if Congress thinks favorably of this proposed park site, a commission be appointed to handle the purchase and to solicit contributions, and to arrange condemnation proceedings if the State of Virginia deems it wise. The creation of such a park may well be made contingent on a limited total land cost."

At first glance it appeared that Kelsey's dream of a national park in the Grandfather area or in the Great Smokies was sacrificed on the altar of political expediency. It also was a big disappointment to the legions of North Carolina and Tennessee boosters who had put so much effort and money toward a park in the Smokies. They almost immediately learned of their demotion to second place and delay in reaching their goal. There was also the possibility they could try to place roadblocks in the way of the park in Virginia. Kelsey moved immediately to forestall any such activity. Word may have reached Kelsey that his former allies now felt he had betrayed them.

On January 20, 1925, Kelsey wrote a letter to Dr. Joseph Pratt of Western North Carolina, Inc. explaining his position and the logic of the committee. After an opening paragraph of formalities, Kelsey dove right in with his personal viewpoint. The remainder of the letter deserves quotation in its entirety:

> As a North-Carolinian by raising, having spent all of my early days in that State and always consider it as my home, you can readily see that I should never have signed a report for the proposed Shenandoah National Park, as being, all things considered, the best thing for the first National Park, had I not been absolutely convinced that that was the proper thing to do.
>
> I had supposed I knew the Appalachian Mountains from Maine to Alabama pretty thoroughly but this area on account of its location, I have simply slipped by for all these years and really didn't know it was there. In fact, I don't think anybody else really knew it until the investigation was made for the purposes of our Committee work.
>
> As the report states, the Committee realized that the greatest thing in the Appalachian System is the Big Smoky Range and outlying cross ranges. Personally, I am firmly of the belief that if North Carolina and Tennessee will back up the Shenandoah National Park to a finish that it will mean the securing of the second Park in the Great Smokies and possibly in parts of the Blue Ridge much quicker than if the recommendation had been for a Park down there first.
>
> The Shenandoah National Park area can be made available in part almost immediately and it will be a wonderful demonstration of what a National Park service will be for the people, and will lead to an overwhelming demand for a larger National Park in the Great Smokies.

I was the last of the Committee to visit this Blue Ridge area in Northern Virginia and want to say that I went very reluctantly for I thought and stated that the Committee had "slipped a cog" but I found all and far more than any of the Committee had told me about, and I honestly believe that if your North Carolina Committee and Tennessee Committee had been with us over this area and considered the whole matter ex parte, they would have even been willing to have signed the report with us.

I have just been reading a copy of a letter from Colonel Chapman of the Knoxville group who says he is going to back up the Shenandoah National Park proposition and it fills me with pleasure for I feel that if the two States of North Carolina and Tennessee particularly, throw their whole-souled influence into this that it means several large National Parks in the East in the very near future.

Last week in Washington Colonel Smith handed me your Bill to provide "for the acquisition of lands in the Southern Appalachian Mountains for the protection of the water sheds of navigable streams, etc." and in many respects I consider it very good but I do think that the matter is rather mixed up in your own mind and in this draft of a Bill, in that you speak of a special Commission for acquiring the lands in the first paragraph and then in Section 2 it seems you are putting the burden on the National Forest Reservation Commission. This latter Commission was formed particularly for the purpose of acquiring forest lands and personally I believe that the National Park program should be carried out entirely independent of the Forest Service.

It is true they should cordially work together but the fundamental objects of each are quite different and will always be different.

I can hardly tell you how happy it made me when I was with our Southern Appalachian National Park Committee to have my own North Carolinians take such a broad and sane attitude in this matter and I have no reason to think they are going to go back on me.

Personally I shall never be satisfied until we have a great National Park in the Great Smokies and either a National Park or a State Park in the Grandfather area.

With best personal regards,

Yours truly,

Harlan P. Kelsey

Only a month had passed since the committee report was released, but that was plenty of time for the political machinery in Washington to go into high gear. Who knows what horse-trading was going on in the back rooms? What emerged was most surprising. On January 27, 1925, Representative Temple introduced a bill (Public No. 437, 68th Congress), which was passed by the House and Senate and approved by the president February 21, 1925, reading as follows:

> An Act to provide for the securing of lands in the southern Appalachian Mountains and in the Mammoth Cave regions of Kentucky for perpetual preservation as national parks.
>
> Be it enacted by the Senate and House of Representatives of the United States of America in Congress assembled, that the Secretary of the Interior is hereby authorized and directed to determine the boundaries and area of such portion of the Blue Ridge Mountains of Virginia lying east of the South Fork of the Shenandoah River and between Front Royal on the north and Waynesboro on the south as may be recommended by him to be acquired and administered as a national park, to be known as the Shenandoah National Park, and such portion of the Smoky Mountains lying in Tennessee and North Carolina as may be recommended by him to be acquired and administered as a national park, to be known as the Smoky Mountains National Park, and in the Mammoth Cave regions of Kentucky and also

such other lands in the southern Appalachian Mountains as in his judgment should be acquired and administered as national parks, and to receive definite offers of donations of lands and moneys, and to secure such options as in his judgment may be considered reasonable and just for the purchase of lands within said boundaries, and to report to Congress thereon: Provided, that the Secretary of the Interior may, for the purpose of carrying out the provisions of this Act, appoint a commission of five members, composed of a representative of the Interior Department, and four national park experts, said four members to serve without compensation.

Sec. 2. A sum sufficient to secure options and to pay the necessary expenses of the commission in carrying out the provisions of this Act, including the salary of one clerk to the commission at a rate not to exceed $2,000 per annum, necessary traveling expenses of the members of the commission, and $10 per diem in lieu of actual cost of subsistence, in all, not to exceed $20,000 is hereby authorized to be appropriated.

Whoa! Instead of following the committee's conservatism, the Congress went the opposite direction. Everybody won. No one was left out. The two big parks were approved and named concurrently—no "second-class citizens." All the other applicants were still in the running if the secretary chose to recommend them to Congress for additional legislation. The Mammoth Cave area was specifically approved in the bill, and that went partially against the six criteria cited by the Committee Report. The underground caverns failed on most of the six counts. That made no difference in the politically charged chambers of Congress. Reed Engle points out that "Kentucky legislators would not support the bill without this inclusion."[125]

It was now the secretary of the Interior who was responsible to determine the boundaries and area of the three park sites; he was also to receive offers and donations of lands and moneys, including options, for the purchase of the lands. Unlike the national parks in the west, which were established on land already owned by the federal government, it was up to the states involved to raise the money, buy the lands, and donate them to the National Park Service. Implicit in that task was the judgment as to standards of acceptability for land within the boundaries.

Obviously the secretary wasn't going to do all that, so they gave him a commission to do the work, with the same set up as used for the prior committee—one representative of the Interior Department plus four volunteers serving without compensation. But now they had a clerk and money for travel expenses. And now they were no longer just a committee, but a full-blown commission. Immediately following the passage of the bill, now called the Temple Bill, Secretary Work reappointed all the previous members, again designating Representative Temple as chairman. At the first meeting, March 5, 1925, Mr. Gregg was elected vice chairman, and Colonel Smith was again elected secretary. Two days later the Northern Virginia Park Association held a banquet at the City Club, Washington, DC, in celebration of the passage of the Temple Bill. The honor guests present were, of course, the three officers of the original committee.

Having ignored Mammoth Cave in their report earlier, the new commission decided it might well be politic to get back there quickly for a new look and development of revised criteria for its inclusion as a national park. They arrived at Louisville on May 21, en route to inspect the Mammoth Cave area. They were thronged at the train station, taken to luncheon at the Pendergrass Club before attending the races as guests of the Jockey Club. This was followed by dinner at the Brown Hotel amidst several hundred guests, including a large contingent of notable political and organizational figures. Pressure? It would certainly appear that way. The next two days were spent under luxury escort to Cave City and the entire area proposed for a national park. Then back to Washington.

One month later another event took place in Rochester, New York, June 25, 1925. It was the Fiftieth Anniversary Annual Meeting of the American Association of Nurserymen, with Harlan P. Kelsey, president. He was now stepping down after two sequential terms in that capacity that exactly overlapped his time on the SANPC. Most presidents served only one term. This raises the question: how in the world could any sane man concurrently try to operate his own business (everyone knows how demanding that is), serve as president of his national trade association, and at the same time sign on as one of a mere five-man committee for the Department of Interior, with the US Congress waiting for results? Let's call it temporary insanity, but he did it. The answer perhaps lies in the chronology of events. His business and trade association commitments preceded his call to serve on the SANPC. The chance to help create a national park in his beloved "beautiful land of the sky" had been a dream all his adult life, and here was the opportunity. There was no way he could turn that down, nor could he renege on the other two commitments. His business was his livelihood. There was no place further to go in the nursery industry than president of the AAN. Kelsey couldn't forego this opportunity to place his signature on the history of the organization.

Race with the Lumbermen

The Southern Appalachian National Park Commission's work was far from finished. In fact it would go on for many more years. The wording of the Temple Bill called for the commission to establish the boundaries of the three named park sites, and to consider any other qualifying sites in the southern Appalachians. They also were to assist the states in the land-acquisition task necessary before the secretary of the Interior could accept the areas as national parks.

While Kelsey was busy winding up his Nurserymen's Association work, Will Gregg went back down alone to the North Carolina Smokies for further investigations. His main interest was to determine the feasibility of locating a scenic drive along the backbone of the high mountain range and to determine what amount of damage the numerous lumber companies were doing in the way of timber cutting in the proposed area. Gregg later commented,[126] "I accomplished on that trip all that I expected to. It included climbing Mount Guyot and Clingman's Dome and covered much of the ridge between."

Except for Highlands, which escaped the lumberman's axe, Kelsey had been constantly confronted by lumbering. The railroads in Linville had brought lumbering right into the outskirts of Pineola and around the periphery of Grandfather Mountain. The Linville Company, after it became the exclusive property of Hugh MacRae, had been an active participant in the lumbering activity. After he moved to Boston, Kelsey's Appalachian Mountain Club work focused on saving the White Mountains of New Hampshire from the lumbermen and the fires they left in their wake. This he did by helping establish the first national forests under the Weeks Act. He certainly must have known that the lumbermen would be a major obstacle to establishing the first national parks in their domain. And now it was a domain that they actually owned. It wasn't government land, as in the West, on which they had cutting rights. It was exclusively theirs.

Almost the entire crest and flanks of the Smoky Mountains were the lumbermen's property, as were the adjoining ridges and valleys. It fell equally in North Carolina and in Tennessee. And it wasn't just one or two that would have to be dealt with. Starting from the northeast was the Unaka Tanning Company, followed by major holdings of the Champion Fiber Company. Then on the North Carolina side came the Forney Creek Lumber Company, the Ritter Lumber Company, the Montvale Lumber Company, and the Kitchen Lumber Company. Above them on the Tennessee side was the Little River Lumber Company and Morton Butler. Oddly, at the southwest toe of the proposed park area was the American Aluminum Company. That's eight companies extracting forest product resources and one extracting mineral resources.

The Battery Park Hotel in Asheville, North Carolina, was the site of the first meeting, July 7, 1925, between the commission, the North Carolina National Park advocates, and representatives of the lumber companies. State Senator Mark Squires presided, lending political credence to the issue of how to acquire the lands lying in the proposed park area. It was an issue of immediate importance because the areas were currently being heavily lumbered. The discussions lasted all day. In the end it was evident that the lumber companies weren't budging. The land was theirs and they would stop lumbering only through injunctive proceedings or condemnation by the state. Of course, in their view, the concept of a national park on their land was a bad idea from the outset.

For these lumbermen, the path ahead was perfectly clear. Given the political threat they faced, they had to convert their timber assets to monetary assets as soon as possible. That meant cutting first and fastest in the areas most likely to be included in the prospective park. Of course, they could have taken the view that it was sufficient to accept the risk that compensation from eminent domain takings was adequate, coupled with public good will for saving the precious virgin stands of timber. But that wasn't the way they thought.

For the park advocates, the path ahead was a bit murky. At the moment, their hands were tied. They had no credibility in seeking injunctive relief. The boundaries of the park were still undefined. The statute establishing the commission was explicit in defining their purpose and powers, which didn't include any takings. That would have to be done by the states. There was as yet no enabling legislation from Tennessee or North Carolina. Even if there had been, there were no funds available to provide compensation from even a successful eminent domain taking. The commission reached the conclusion that no judge would establish injunctive relief without these necessary ingredients. Any such threat by the commission would have been immediately recognized by the timber companies as pure bluff.[127] So, the only recourse was to start a crash program to define the park boundaries, to fund the Parks, and to set the needed legislative wheels in motion. Time was of the essence. Whatever thoughts Kelsey and his fellow commissioners may have had that the pace of activity would now be more relaxed, were quickly dashed.

The race was on. The lumber companies were focused on cutting as fast as their crews could work. The states were focused on raising funds as fast as they could. The commission was focused on defining the boundaries as fast as they could. The lumbermen had the clear advantage. They were only accelerating on their own land what they had already been doing. The park advocates were starting from ground zero. It was unfamiliar territory, and required coordination between the various parties. There were constant distractions. They weren't set up for a race.

Senator Mark Squires, chairman of the North Carolina Park Commission, had a problem. The people up in the Grandfather Mountain and Linville Gorge area were aware of the open-ended nature of the congressional statute allowing the secretary of the Interior great latitude in defining the parks. Much pressure was being exerted on Squires's Commission to recommend their area in preference to the Smoky Mountain area. Squires asked for Colonel Smith to join the North Carolina Commissioners in the first week of July for a further review of the Smokies. After several days visiting the high peaks on the North Carolina side, the commissioners were unanimous in confirming the Smokies as the most suitable park site. This was only the first of a number of "fires" that had to be dealt with by the Southern Appalachian National Park Commission (SANPC).

Chairman Temple called the third meeting of the SANPC on July 18, 1925. The primary cause for the meeting was "the opposition that had developed on the part of a great number of land owners in the Smoky area to the establishment of a park there." It was decided that the commission would give out a statement for release to the press. In essence it announced the possibility of modifying the boundaries to cut out most of North Carolina and confine the park primarily to the

Tennessee side. It then went on to extol the virtues of the Tennessee side, and point out that if the North Carolina timber companies continued their cutting on the virgin stands, the area would not be fit for a national park. "The spruce and balsam areas which have been cut over do not reforest themselves, and immediately become covered with an almost impenetrable thicket of blackberry and other undesirable growths peculiarly susceptible to forest fires."

The commission wanted the world to know where the blame would lie if North Carolina was denied their part of the new national park—an obvious pressure move. It may have influenced the pace of the North Carolina Park advocates, but it only pressured the lumbermen to cut faster.

Concurrently the commission passed a resolution designed to give both maximum scope and maximum flexibility in designating and securing the park area. It would "designate the outside boundaries (somewhat as the Weeks Act designated forest purchase areas) with the purpose of securing at once as much as possible of the designated territory to be established as a national park; the remainder of the designated areas to be acquired as rapidly as possible."

The Smokies people responded a month later, showing up in Washington to consult with the SANPC on a proposal for fund-raising. Virginia had already started raising funds outside of Virginia through an established relationship with the Bankers Service Corporation of New York. The North Carolinians cried "foul." This would lead to unhealthy competition between the States for "outside" money that may delay rather than accelerate the fund-raising. The proposal was for the SANPC to help establish cooperation between the Shenandoah and Smokies organizations. It was evident that there was a conflict of opinion within the Smokies delegation, so the SANPC pointed out that, as a commission, they could not be drawn into any controversy between the various parties as to their methods. That was strictly the business of the various States. However they were willing and anxious to assist them by advice or any other way to bring about harmony between the three areas. They suggested a three-way conference.

Such a conference was held on the evening of August 24, 1925, in the Evening Star Building, Washington, DC, between the representatives of the three states. The Smokies' proposal was for the states to keep 100 percent of all moneys raised from within their areas and then split the proceeds obtained from outside the various states fifty-fifty between the Smokies and Shenandoah areas. "The interests of the two parks were identical, and nothing would be gained by one area having an advantage over the other. It was better to keep on an even keel and go in together to get the two parks, for competition in the matter was unwise." No agreement was reached, but plans were made for a conference at Richmond, Virginia, on the following September 9. There, the Smokies people would present their plan in more concrete detail.

Just prior to that, the SANPC met to decide on the expedient of hiring their own people to obtain options on land within the parks, using the authority and funding from the congressional statute. They decided to give it a try and set some time and dollar limits for the test. The results were not satisfactory, and the effort was later abandoned.

The September 9 meeting was opened with speeches by Governor Bird of Virginia, and Colonel Hodges of the Virginia State Chamber of Commerce at luncheon in the Hotel Jefferson. At the joint executive meeting held immediately afterward it was decided that, while each State association should work independently within its own borders, the claims of twin national parks would be presented to the nation as one object, and every outside American would be shown the advantages of presenting twin park areas to the government at one and the same time. They further framed up a definitive resolution to establish the details, such as what to do with donor-designated pledges, which would of course go 100 percent to the designated area. The Bankers Service Corporation contract would be modified to apply solely to Virginia and the District of Columbia. The whole national effort would be implemented by a new association named "The Appalachian National Parks Association, Inc." through a committee-of-five headed by Major Welch of the SANPC, with the other four from the Smokies and Shenandoah areas. All proceeds from this nationwide fund raising "outside" of the states would be shared fifty-fifty between the Shenandoah and Smokies Parks.

On September 22 Kelsey wrote to J. Horace McFarland about the always-present plant quarantine matters McFarland was currently pushing:

> Your two letters of September 19th and copy of OUTLOOK received and I will take the article home with me and read it carefully.
>
> I have given about seven weeks time on the Southern Appalachian National Park Commission work this summer and you can see where it leaves me. I am now simply overwhelmed with business and have got to attend to it, devoting some solid time to clearing up the situation or otherwise I'll lose all my best customers and clients but I admit this quarantine matter is quite as important as most other things and I'll write you after going over your article carefully.

No rest for the weary.

On December 16, two months later, Kelsey was making a speech before the Council on National Parks Forests and Wild Life, titled "Proposed National Parks in the Southern Appalachians." He related that the campaigns were coming along very favorably, but they were meeting opposition from the Champion Fibre Company and other lumbermen. In reply to an inquiry as to the cost of these parks, he admitted that the members of the commission differed on the amount; his own figures of four to six million dollars for the Smoky Mountains and three to four million dollars for the Shenandoah, covering only the land without development, were somewhat higher than most of the other commissioners. He spoke of airplane photographs around the proposed boundaries. Speaking of the Smoky Mountains, he favored taking in the foothills for the view from above, for camp grounds and administrative purposes. The forest on them was at present, he said, of poor quality short-leaf pine and other trees that he considered of no economic value. (This "taking of the foothills" was a theme Kelsey felt compelled to emphasize, over and over again, through the years, as others settled for lower cost by leaving them in private hands.) Kelsey's speaking efforts were matched by other members of the commission visiting various cities in all three states through the end of the year 1925.

Two weeks further on, Kelsey got a letter from the Smokies' campaign headquarters in North Carolina. They were anxiously awaiting word from him as to the time he could give them, especially in the districts northeast of Asheville. That was up near Linville and the Grandfather Mountain area where he was so well known. "Senator Squires has been holding back work in that section hoping that you may be available to speak at a number of meetings where he thinks your influence alone will be adequate to overcome the disappointment due to the omission of the Linville Gorge section from the proposed park area. If you can see your way clear to come to us soon, please wire me definite dates and we will at once make plans to use your time to best advantage." A month later, Colonel Chapman in Tennessee wanted him to speak at the University of Tennessee in Knoxville. A month after that, Kelsey gave a talk at Boston's Twentieth Century Club on "Skyland, Shenandoah Valley, and the Mountains of Virginia." The pressures on Kelsey's time were mounting.

As the new year dawned, January 8, 1926, Representative Temple called a meeting in Washington to settle and submit to the secretary of the Interior their selected areas for the parks. The boundaries had to be established before the states could focus on their acquisition targets.

That purpose was preempted for a period by various state organizations reporting on the progress of their campaigns. It was preempted again by Major Welch offering a resolution to "respectfully and earnestly request Mr. Adolph S. Ochs, Publisher of the *New York Times*, to accept the Chairmanship of the Appalachian National Parks Association, Inc., for the purpose of soliciting and receiving gifts of Money and land. ... and that a committee be formed to call on Mr. Ochs and present the details of this proposed movement and urge his acceptance of this office." Arrangements were made for the secretary of the Interior and the chairman of the SANPC to write Mr. Ochs requesting his acceptance to further the national campaign. It was proposed that the various governors of the states also write Mr. Ochs. It was a "full-court press," apparently to no avail. No research material to date gives any evidence of his acceptance.

The commission resumed its session the next day at the Cosmos Club, and again they didn't discuss boundaries. Instead, the question of visiting the Mammoth Cave area was brought up, and Colonel Smith and Mr. Kelsey were designated to investigate this area and make a report and also to secure additional information regarding the amount of funds already pledged for the purchase of land therein.

It wasn't until April 5, 1926, that Chairman Temple called the commission to Washington to write their complete report to Secretary Work as required by the statute, including boundaries. In the intervening months the commissioners had been responding to the various governors and state organizations for visits and conferences to arouse enthusiasm in their campaigns for raising funds. The commissioners spent April 5–8 in drawing up their report.

First they reiterated the reasons for confirming the Shenandoah and Smokies Parks; here they simply referred the reader to their December 12, 1924, report, which had given all their reasoning for the two mountainous parks.

Then they dealt with the Mammoth Cave Park, based on Kelsey and Smith's report on the area. Kelsey was mindful of Arno Cammerer's reservations about Mammoth Cave's qualifications. On August 28, 1925, Cammerer had written Kelsey. "Dear Kel, You have got to see Carlsbad Cave and by that I mean *you*. You have no idea of the beauties and grandeur and magnitude till you see it, and I still maintain that you must have a glimpse of Carlsbad before you can render a report on the Mammoth Cave. Remember our park and monument system must not be overloaded with caves and we want only the most outstanding examples." Moreover one newspaper, dated March 19, 1926, carried the notice "Kentucky Site Disapproved By Secretary of Interior. … the acreage donated there is not sufficient to constitute an area for a national park and does not include the Mammoth Cave section. …" Kelsey was on notice; this had better be good, "or else." The report pulled no punches and read:

> Mammoth Cave is the best known and probably the largest of a remarkable group of limestone caverns, twenty or more of which have been opened up and explored to a greater or less extent. Included in this group are Colossal Cavern, Great Onyx Cave, New Entrance to Mammoth Cave, Salts Cave, Proctor Cave, Long Avenue Cave, Great Crystal Cave, Cave of the Hundred Domes, Diamond Cave, Mammoth Onyx Cave, Dixon Cave and others, all of which contain beautiful and wonderful formations. There is good evidence that many more caverns yet to be discovered exist to this immediate territory, and it seems likely that most, if not all, of this entire group of caverns eventually will be found to be connected by passageways forming a great underground labyrinth of remarkable geological and recreational interest perhaps unparalleled elsewhere. The territory, which embraces this network of caverns, consists of about 15,000 acres, or an area approximately four miles wide and six miles long. Another geological feature of much interest is found in the thousands

of curious sink holes of varying sizes through which much of the drainage is carried to underground streams, there being few surface brooks or creeks.

Next, Kelsey's horticultural hand was evident:

> The Mammoth Cave area is situated in one of the most rugged portions of the great Mississippi Valley and contains areas of apparently original forests which, though comparatively small in extent, are of prime value from an ecological and scientific standpoint and should be preserved for all time in its virgin state for study and enjoyment. Much of the proposed area is now clothed in forest through which flows the beautiful and navigable Green River and its branch, the Nolin River.

This filled in the gaps on why the caves qualified as national park material, but only if certain requirements were met, namely, the inclusion of all the caves, even those not yet opened, and the addition of the considerable forested area surrounding the caves and "sink holes."

Second, they reported on the organizational efforts and financial and acquisition results, to date, by the various states. The Shenandoah people had raised donations in excess of $1,249,154. The Smokies people had raised donations of $1,066,695. The Mammoth Cave people reported, not dollars, but two donations of property aggregating 3,629.13 acres. Interestingly, they did not yet include Mammoth Cave itself. They had a long way to go, but there were no lumbering threats on Mammoth Cave's territory.

Finally, they reported on the recommended boundaries for each of the three parks. They described the metes and bounds, much as a surveyor would, starting at point A and ending up back at point A again. Shenandoah contained 521,000 acres. The Smokies contained 704,000 acres. Mammoth Cave contained 70,618 acres.

On April 9 they submitted the report to Secretary Work, who congratulated them on their accomplishments. He in turn, on April 14, submitted the report to the Speaker of the House and president of the Senate. That same day Chairman Temple introduced the necessary legislation covering the Shenandoah and Smokies Parks, which was passed by the House and the Senate, and on May 22, 1926, was approved by the president. The Temple Legislation included, for the first time, a minimum acreage required for each park, before the National Park Service would initiate administrative and protective services—250,000 acres for the Shenandoah Park, and 150,000 acres for the Smokies Park. Moreover, no general development of either park could be undertaken until a major portion of the remainder in each area had been accepted by the secretary of the Interior.

On May 8, Representative Thatcher introduced House legislation for Mammoth Cave Park. The Senate and House passed the bill, and it was approved by the president on May 25, 1926.

Three days later Secretary Work wrote letters to each member of the commission. He was under the impression that the commission's work was completed; he expressed his appreciation of the efficient service they had rendered and stated that their services were to be terminated May 31, 1926.

On receiving his letter, Chairman Temple was astonished and immediately called on the secretary to explain the necessity for continuing the commission to assist the states until the time when the secretary of the Interior accepted the areas as national parks. He followed with a letter advising the secretary more fully of the tasks ahead for the commission. There were three state governments, plus the three incorporated associations in North Carolina, Tennessee, and Virginia, for which the commission was to serve as the coordinating agency. Furthermore, Major Welch was acting as the commission's representative on the committee-of-five engaged in the coming national campaign to raise funds outside of the states. Along with several additional reasons, Temple closed with the belief the commissioners would be called upon to advise and help with promotion by the various state organizations raising funds. This would necessitate travel and other expenses, crippling them if the unexpended funds were returned to the Treasury. On learning these facts, Secretary Work immediately reversed himself, writing to each commissioner to disregard his earlier letter. They were still very much in business.

The revived Commission met June 9 in their Washington office to review the unfinished work that lay ahead. That afternoon Arno Cammerer, acting director of the National Park Service, raised the crucial question of how to instruct the states "as to the class of land they should purchase first to insure its being accepted by the Secretary of the Interior for park purposes." This innocent little question was a bombshell. Think about it. The race was still on between the park advocates and the cutting crews of the lumber companies. But the states didn't want to spend their funds on lands that might be rejected by the secretary. Nor could they take land by condemnation without the express assurance in the courts that the land would become park land once it was acquired. Nor did they want to evict the mountain people from their homes, only to say later that it was a mistake; they could leave their new homes and move back to the old ones.

In the final analysis, only the National Park Service could give assurance, in advance, that any lands would be accepted by the secretary. The commission could only act as a funnel to direct questions and issues back into the lap of Arno Cammerer's people. The commission met with Cammerer on June 29 to make some initial easy guidelines:

1. State officials were urged to acquire low-priced land first, before speculative activity raised the asking price.
2. Purchase virgin timber tracts to ensure the preservation of these areas and to stop any further lumbering.

3. Cut-over tracts were suitable as it was brought out in the discussion that these cut-over tracts, if protected from fire, would within fifteen years or so be covered with a good growth of trees or other vegetation.

Cammerer then threw the ball back to the commission suggesting that *they* should go into the proposed park areas and select certain land to be purchased first, that the land should be of national park caliber, and such as would warrant the commission and the Park Service recommending it to the secretary of the Interior. Time being precious, the commission passed a unanimous resolution to set as their guideline for park-caliber land:

1. In the Shenandoah Park, the first 250,000 acres, with the best features, along the spine of the Blue Ridge mountain tops, including the spur ridges and canyons lying between them, from Mt. Marshall to Jarmans Gap, plus such occasional holdings elsewhere within the designated area as can be secured at low cost for the purpose of establishing reasonable values for later acquisition by purchase or condemnation.
2. A similar resolution for the first 150,000 acres along the spine of the Smokies, including ridges and canyons lying between them from Mt. Guyot to Gregory Bald.

The question of allowing small settlers to occupy their present holding for a short period of years was considered possible, but Cammerer reiterated that such occupancy could not encumber the "fee simple" deed with qualifications; all land titles had to be passed on by the attorney general before lands could be accepted; the states would have to bear all expense of acquisition and clearing titles. They left the question of settlers for future consideration.

The second day of the meeting was open to the various states, to disclose and discuss the resolutions of the previous day, and prepare a press release acceptable to all, announcing the state associations' authority to commence acquisition of lands within the designated areas above. The press release discouraged speculation, citing the intention to avoid high prices and suggesting that recourse to condemnation was a possibility the associations would employ only if forced.

It appears that the press release had little immediate effect on the speculation. On July 24, 1926, Kelsey got a letter from W. P. Davis, president of the Great Smoky Mountains Conservation Association.

> Dear Mr. Kelsey:
>
> I enclose herewith a copy of the Knoxville Journal of the 21st, containing an interview by me, on the subject of the speculation of the land that has been going on in the Park Boundary, and I believe that this will result in holding back the buying and speculating of the land in that territory.
>
> Since this article was printed, one of our afternoon papers has published an article advising against the speculation … also a splendid map.
>
> If you would care to write us something that we might publish along the same line, I would appreciate very much your doing so.
>
> We have one man in the mountains securing options, and I understand that North Carolina is doing the same thing. I trust that it will not be long before we have secured sufficient options for 150,000 acres of land.

For the SANPC all the initiative was now in the hands of the State organizations and the National Park Service. The summer wore on. On August 3 Cammerer wrote Kelsey, "We had a big delegation of Virginians here the other day, including Col. Benschoff, … and Governor Byrd, trying to persuade the Secretary that he ought to reduce the minimum area for the park, since they are finding out that 250,000 acres, plus the major portion of the remainder, is going to cost them between

$4,000,000 and $5,000,000. All their feet were icy. The Secretary stood pat, however, but he did say that your Commission, with a representative from the National Parks would go down there some time during the year to help them out. This means a more intensive survey of the boundaries. I hope it will come in October when I can get away."

Kelsey responded August 10. "I note what you say about the Virginia situation. There are also matters coming up with reference to the Great Smokies. A letter from Doctor Gregg today suggests a trip down there, and I have written him we ought to at least get to Washington, that is, as many of the Commission as can be found, and talk the matters over with the National Park Service."

On October 22 Cammerer wrote, "Dear Kel, Going up to Skyland with Mac a week from Sunday for three or four days, with old Pollock, who is as crazy as ever. He was in the office an hour ago. Can't you come down and go along? It never seems the same to go into these park areas without you. ... And Mr. Mather is planning for you and your wife to be here for the evening of either the 17th or 19th for a huge dinner he is giving, and for which invitations will go out to you, and the other members of the Commission and their wives. You know some of the superintendents. And you should know the rest, and they you. The two commissions are having trouble again, in their purchase of park land, and will want another conference with your commission."

On December 2 Kelsey wrote his thank-you letter to Stephen Mather. "Mrs. Kelsey joins me in sending you most hearty thanks for the very enjoyable time you gave us at the wonderful dinner in Washington. You pulled it off as successfully as any dinner I have ever attended. Next time, however, give me a week if you are going to call on me to say something. You don't know what a fine speech in three words I could have made if I'd had even thirty seconds notice. I am all right on my feet but not always on my tongue."

The new year broke with the lumbermen still cutting and the speculators still buying. And now some of the Shenandoah Park boosters were having second thoughts, but too late. During the commission meeting on February 7 and 8, 1927, Messrs. Judd and Evans of Skyland recommended that the park line as tentatively indicated on the existing maps be changed to exclude certain residences lying in or near Skyland settlement. It was the consensus of opinion of all the commissioners that it was not only injudicious, but practically impossible to change the line to meet the wishes of owners of land which it was necessary to include within the park. This meant that poor old Pollock, who practically broke his neck to make the park a reality, would suddenly find that the reality was that he was to be evicted from his precious Skyland. He had made the fatal assumption that the Park would bring his resort prominence and him good fortune.

The discussion then turned to whether the residents could continue to occupy their residences after the areas had been accepted by the government. The answer for now was no. Mr. Kelsey advised against bringing up the question in such manner as to force a decision from the secretary of the Interior at that time. The commission felt it would lead to numerous property owners throughout the area asking similar permission, which would result in a great number of privately held lands within the heart of the park, contrary to the policy of both the secretary and the National Park Service.

How about church property? And schools? Again, no. Without people in residence there would be no need for churches and schools. Finally the commission passed a resolution making the facts perfectly clear but slightly easing the residents' apprehensions, by saying the minimum area may surround private holdings. But these must be secured as of the major part of the remainder required to comply with the provision of the act before the park could be finally developed. It was small solace, but it bought them some time.

That afternoon, a delegation of the Virginia State Conservation and Development Commission provided a status report. They had collected

$340,000, which had been placed in the bank to be held until sufficient funds were available to purchase 385,000 acres. Their aim was to get about 400,000 acres along the main crest of the park. Mr. Gregg asked why they didn't start by acquiring the 250,000 acres needed at first to fill the requirements of the act. Kelsey added that as soon as they had acquired 250,000 acres they could offer it for acceptance by the government and the National Park Service could take charge and provide fire protection and patrolling. Kelsey was always mindful of the ever present fire danger from his early experiences with the Appalachian Mountain Club. No, it seems they had boxed themselves in with their representations to donors. If they didn't get the funds to buy 385,000 acres, they had to return all the money. They had a mess on their hands, but fortunately the Virginians didn't have the lumber companies chewing up their virgin forests each day that passed.

The commission did tell the Virginians of a bill being introduced in the North Carolina legislature for a $2,000,000 bond issue for the Great Smoky Mountains National Park. Sadly, the Virginians had to inform the commission that it was contrary to the provisions of the Virginia State constitution to bond the State for any internal improvements. Also sadly, nothing had yet started on the national campaign for funding.

The next day, February 8, the Smokies people were received. They offered the same "chicken and egg" proposition that the commission had dealt with before. They now had enough money to acquire the first 150,000 acres required by the act. However, they wanted the commission and National Park Service to indicate which lands would be acceptable by the secretary of the Interior. Only then would they proceed with the purchases. The chairman assured them that representatives of the commission would visit the area early in the spring. Mr. Cammerer provided similar assurances from the National Park Service.

The commission wasted no time. Four days later, February 12, Secretary Work wrote the governors of North Carolina and Tennessee committing the National Park Service to an investigation to begin on the ground just as soon as weather conditions permitted and that the work would probably be completed about June 1, 1927. He would then designate the acceptable 150,000 acres, the minimum required to initiate administration and protection by the National Park Service. Moreover, he would designate the "major portion" of the area of seven hundred four thousand acres without which "no general development" could be undertaken, as set forth by the act. Secretary Work wanted no foot dragging. Everyone was to crank up their engines and get the job done. The governors had asked for it and now they would have it. The "ball would then be in their court," so to speak.

Kelsey needed a vacation. The only sport about which he was passionate was fishing—trout fishing in Maine and deep-sea fishing off the coast of Florida. February 14 found him and Florence at Long Key, Florida, where he received the following letter from Arno Cammerer:

> Dear Kel: That was a wonderful evening we had with you at the house and I hope it may be repeated in the future with more of our friends present. I hope the fish are biting well and that you will exceed Zane Grey's record for tarpon, without being pulled through the Gulf of Mexico toward Tampico as a floater. I understand some of these tarpon have hauled a fishing launch clear around Cape Horn, ending up somewhere at Shanghai, China, or at least until starvation forced the man holding the rod to give it up. I have an order for plant material with you at Salem and I hope you will let go the rod long before you reach Cape Horn. ...
>
> The attached newspaper clipping regarding Smoky Mountain Park will give you all the details regarding a conference that we held last Saturday. Things are coming along fast and it looks as if we all would have to spend the month of May down there. Possibly it could be held off until the first of June.   Cam

Kelsey wasn't after tarpon. He caught two magnificent sailfish. One at seventy-one and a half pounds and seven feet six inches. The other at fifty pounds and six feet nine inches. Both were caught on a six-ounce tip and twelve-thread line. Kelsey wrote the taxidermist, July 8, 1927, and congratulated him on the fine work he had done on the two fish. "The large one has gone to the Salem Country Club and I wish you could hear the favorable comments on the fine mounting. ... I haven't had a chance to throw a fly yet, which is, of course, my greatest pleasure in life." The smaller sailfish is hanging over the large stone fireplace in Kelsey's final residence—your author's current home.

Now, back to business. Secretary Work's commitment to the governors had to be fulfilled.

Cammerer to Kelsey, March 15: "Could you start on Smoky Mountain inspection trip with me and other members Appalachian Park Commission May fifteenth. This will take three to four weeks and I consider your presence particularly important. Do what you can. Please wire me."

Kelsey to Cammerer, March 16 wire: "Almost impossible to go on trip until June first." March 16 letter: "I am enclosing copy of telegram just sent you and am trying to figure out how I could have made it different, but don't see how I could. My year's business is done in the spring and it would swamp me to make the trip, much as I regret not being able to do it. ... It would be a gorgeous trip, but the Committee can do without me and I will have to fit in on the tail end of the trip of inspection."

Cammerer to Kelsey, April 18: "You must be sure to make the Great Smokies trip about the 22nd of May, because we could not do without you."

April 20 found Cammerer penning a handwritten letter from the Hotel Pennsylvania in New York. This time it was about his immediate trip to the Shenandoah Park for delineation of their acceptable lands. The letter is personal and two things need to be explained: (1)

Cammerer's great love was plants and the grounds around his house. He was constantly placing orders from Kelsey's catalog. The deliveries invariably contained additional plants, not ordered, but gratuitously sent; and (2) their personal letters usually closed not with something like "yours truly," but with the phrase "Hearts bursting with love." This was a common practice with Kelsey's close associates in Washington. The personal letters between Frederick V. Coville, US botanist; M. Q. Macdonald, AAN attorney (Mac to his close friends); and of course Arno Cammerer invariably closed this way. It stems from the brook euonymus, a common plant in the high southern Appalachians. Its fruit in the fall is a compelling red-and-orange color formed by the red berry in the center surrounded by the exfoliating skin "bursting" out in various colors of orange. Its colloquial name in the South is "Hearts-a-bustin'," or various versions thereof. The letter says a lot about their strong personal relationship:

> Dear Kel,
>
> I'm here for the day, and have time to drop you a line without interruption. The plants came, twice duly divided between Mac and myself. You've been a veritable fairy godfather in your generosity, and your motto seems to be "It is better to give than to receive." I've often felt I was imposing on your good nature by ordering what I did, but the fact that you've got me in my weak spot—my plant hobby—and your fine response, has always overcome my scruples. I hope by this time you know how deeply and genuinely grateful I am and how futile it is to try to express it—so I won't—except I may kiss you on both cheeks as the Froggies do, when I see you next.
>
> I leave for the Shenandoah Sunday until I complete the job. I should have you, and if you possibly can make it I hope you'll join me in some time. The work has to be done now, or not at all this summer—and Carson and the Governor are urging it. So I'm helpless in choice of time. You ought to go, or decide not to kick me in the pants if I do the best I can with those

birds and the circumstances, you old sun of a gun. With hearts bursting with love,
 's ever, Cam

After Shenandoah, Cammerer's trip to the Smokies did come off, and we know Kelsey relented and did join the group. In a June 13, 1927, letter to Chairman Temple, Kelsey said, "I am just back from a trip in the Smoky Mountains with Mr. Cammerer, Verne Rhodes of the North Carolina State Park Commission, and General Maloney, representing the Smoky Mountains Conservation Association and the Tennessee Park Commission."

While the National Park Service was pushing hard to settle park boundaries and land quality issues, the states had been moving ahead on the financial front in early 1927. The North Carolina Legislature introduced a $2,000,000 bond issue for acquisition of land in the Smokies. It was passed and approved by the governor February 25, 1927. A similar act by the Tennessee Legislature for a $1,500,000 bond issue was passed and approved by the governor April 27, 1927. The next day, Gregg wrote Kelsey:

Dear Harlan,
 We are going to get that great Smoky National Park. The good news from Tennessee makes it practically certain. I don't know how it affected you, but on receipt of Colonel Smith's telegram I almost went "Wet."
 Yours truly, Doc Gregg

On April 30 Kelsey wrote back:

Dear Doc,
 Three cheers! When Colonel Smith, Major Welch, and I gather around you, certainly you will have to be "wet" with us. Our labors are probably not in vain. With best regards.
 Yours truly, Harlan

It can be assumed the comments about "wet" referred to Prohibition, at that time.

The good news on State financing had barely sunk in, when the bad news came on the race with the lumber companies. Returning to Kelsey's June 13 letter to Chairman Temple:

> We were on the eastern side of the Smokies with Bryson City as headquarters. I will not go into the details of the trip, but I feel it necessary to write you about one phase of the matter which seems to me extremely important.
>
> On Hughes Ridge, Blodgett and Latham cutting, we were told, was about complete and, apparently fearing some action that would stop their cutting, they have felled most of the timber, which I understand is largely Tulip Tree, knowing that they could remove it if they actually got it cut. This tract, as you know, is north of the Big Bald on Hughes Ridge which we were on and we could plainly see the operations from the trail. The worst cutting, however, is the Suncrest operations on both sides of the Balsam Range. We were told by several people that they had increased their force and were using every effort to clean out the big timber on the top of the Range apparently before they are stopped by injunction or otherwise. I did not learn that the Champion Fibre Company were increasing their forces, but they are steadily cutting out almost everything very high up on Mt. Collins.
>
> These operations are directly in the virgin forest and unless definite action is taken very soon, the critics of the Park will have very good arguments for saying that there is too little virgin timber left to have any park at all. The three gentlemen who were with me I feel were impressed the same way, as we had repeated conversations about it. ... The original maps showing the virgin timber must be very greatly altered at the present time and every day they are eating into this virgin timber as the sun cuts into a snow bank in the middle of summer.

Chairman Temple's June 18 reply to Kelsey states, "I have been trying to discover whether there is anything that our Commission can do about it. It is discouraging. ... If anything is to be done, it must be done by the States. The attorneys of these companies have read the statute as carefully as we have, and they would certainly recognize as pure bluff anything we might try to do."

One might think that all National Park advocates, like the Sierra Club, would have been putting their efforts and support behind the southern Appalachian cause. This joining of forces was what had happened twenty years earlier to push through the Weeks Act for national forests. Also they joined in the unsuccessful fight by the Sierra Club over the Hetch Hetchy reservoir in California. It was not to be so in the current case.

On April 13, 1927, W. L. Huber, president of the Sierra Club, wrote to his counterpart at the Appalachian Mountain Club. "It is feared by many supporters of our National Parks that, through purchases of large areas of land which are not of strictly National Park caliber for inclusion in Great Smoky National Park, a dangerous precedent may be established and the present high standards of our National Parks may be lowered. The Sierra Club has been strongly urged to join in the opposition to certain purchases now proposed." He sought some expression from the officers of the AMC before taking action. Naturally, Huber contacted Kelsey to help frame a response. Kelsey replied, "There is a certain man in Washington who apparently for bitter personal reasons is making a strenuous fight against the Southern Appalachian National Parks. It seems too bad, but give him enough rope and he is going to hang himself. I doubt if very many members, including the president of the Sierra Club, have ever been to the Southern Appalachian sections under consideration. If they are to ignore the endorsement of the National Park Service on these two areas, which have been carefully investigated, and take the word of a certain citizen, then progress in this country is certainly going to be very much held up."

Apparently that "certain citizen" was Sterling Yard, editor of the National Parks Association bulletin.

On August 8, Will Gregg wrote Kelsey, "Yes, I have read the recent bulletin of the National Parks Association. The trouble with Yard and his group of backers is, that as far as I know none of them have thoroughly penetrated the designated area of the Great Smokies. Yard thinks he has gotten 'one on us', because a considerable area of cut over land is included. This agitation, I fear, will injure the National Campaign for the balance of the money presumed to be necessary to finish the Great Smoky job. I, of course do not feel very good natured over Yard's trouble making course. ... I have advised Dr. Temple, recently, that I thought we ought to do something to get Yard, Merriam and others before our commission in a conference. He does not seem to favor this. Under the circumstances, I presume nothing will be done." Nothing was done.

Two months later Kelsey wrote Arno Cammerer, "You say 'Yard is backing us strongly on the Smokies.' Did you see his article in his September bulletin? He is writing without knowledge and bucking the acquirement of adequate lowlands to protect the central part of the Park. He would do so much more good in my humble opinion if he kept entirely quiet. Perhaps it is not worth discussing. However, keep me informed and I will do ditto."

Meanwhile the administrative wheels rolled slowly onward. The governor of Virginia asked Secretary Work to make an inspection of the proposed Shenandoah National Park area, similar to the earlier Great Smokies inspection. Cammerer wrote Kelsey, "I'll need you. First of all, the nights are cold and I need a bedfellow, and secondly I need your advice on some of the holdings. Drop me a line when you can spare the time to meet me. I also feel that if and when you are along I needn't worry about not being able to find a bit of moonshine as well as sunshine." Kelsey had to decline for both business and health reasons but said, "I am anxious to show you some wonderful native virgin growth in the Shenandoah area."

On October 31, 1927, Cammerer wrote, "Dear Kel, Am sitting in Zerkel's office in Luray to get this line to you. Am about half done in my survey of the Shenandoah area, and it is evident that I won't find more than one-half of the original 521,000 acres. Glenn Smith is with me. It is important that you come down at the earliest possible date to go over some of these things with me on the ground … As ever, Cam."

Kelsey immediately replied, November 4. The shrinking of the acreage was becoming a threat. His tone was by now urgent and he clearly wanted his views to be in the records:

> I have your letter of October 31, also telegram from Smith urging me to go down and meet you at Charlottesville. I wired him I would be there next Tuesday if that was suitable.
>
> I am a little surprised that the acreage should shrink 50%. I don't think there is a single member of the Commission who did not expect it to shrink 25% or a little more. You must remember that we made an outside boundary on the same basis that the Forestry Service makes for their purchases but that the inside boundary was very flexible. Again I want to urge the importance of having the approach carefully protected. I think a vast mistake will be made if too much of the foreground is eliminated, even if it has to be reforested and only devoting ourselves to the crest of the mountain.
>
> I don't know how strongly the other Commissioners feel but I am absolutely convinced in my own mind that the campaign our friend, Yard, has waged against protecting the outside boundaries of the park is based on fallacious premises, and if the final purchases are limited as some of those the United States Park Association ask for they will never accomplish the big purpose we hope for them. The original boundary of the

Great Smoky Mountain tract was also an outside boundary as, of course, you know.

May I again repeat what I want firmly in the records, that those who are responsible for the final boundaries of these two park areas will be criticized more than anything else for making them too small rather than including foothills which may readily be covered with verdure and protect the view from the park outwards as well as to supply recreation sites on fairly level ground and for administration purposes also.

I suppose I will hear from Glenn in due course and if so, although I am extremely busy, will drop everything and beat it for Virginia. I certainly would love to dig into that matter with you for I think it is of the deepest importance and consequence, and we must try and avoid compromising too much no matter what the present outside criticism will be. Just remember we will get it hot shot from the other direction on later days, and personally I have not the slightest objection to standing unjust, unfair, and ill-advised criticism if we can get the best thing possible across for our National Parks.

By the end of November they had finished their survey, and in December Cammerer submitted his extensive report to Secretary Work. Under the Act of 1926, Congress authorized a gross acreage of 521,000 and a minimum acreage of 250,00 for the Shenandoah Park. The minimum would allow for protection and administration by the park service. However no general *development* of the park would be undertaken until a *major portion* of the remainder above minimum was acquired. The purpose of the November survey was to define the so-called major portion. But Cammerer reminded the secretary that: "This Act contemplates, under certain conditions precedent, the establishment of a national park ... under established national park rules and principles of 385,500 plus acres within a gross area of approximately 521,000 acres specified in the Act." The 385,000 acres apparently came from the state of Virginia's prior commitment to donors that their money would be held in trust until enough was raised to purchase that specific amount of acreage. And while the act never mentioned that acreage, it did link the authorization with the Virginia subscription of $1.2 million. By implication, that meant 385,000 acres.

Cammerer explained that he, Smith, and Kelsey had set the metes and bounds for a new boundary line "aimed only at the inclusion of desirable or necessary park lands, both from a scenic and an administrative standpoint, with such a topographically outlined boundary as would, all things considered, meet those requirements." The entire boundary line had been carefully inspected either by motor, or in some instances on horseback and on foot, and with a few interruptions due to inclement weather when roads were not passable and streams leading from the hills were unfordable.

Cammerer's report then detailed the reasoning and logic for their selections. This was important because he had to preempt the inevitable critics. He starts with the park's overall characteristics—length, breadth, and general features. Quoting: "The highest elevations of the ridge are lengthwise through the center with numerous outflanking high ridges more precipitous and uncultivated on the western side and less precipitous with more sloping foothills and more cultivated on the eastern side. While within the park area itself there are many imposing peaks, rivers and streams of impressive character, ravines and valleys of great depth and cliffs of great majesty, the actual cultural conditions when measured in distance of miles are very close." He then talks about the various roads entering and crossing the park, their location and condition (usually primitive), and reminding all that Washington is only ninety miles away to the east.

Immediately he turned to Kelsey's concerns: "Especial attention was given to the inclusion of such physical features at the points where the roads enter the park area as would best preserve satisfactory, dignified entrances at these points." He pointed to thousands of acres of comparatively level places scattered here and there, some cut-over, some meadows, but dotted with springs of sufficient capacity to supply hotels and camps that would be required for the accommodation of visitors. "In my opinion this park will be popular because of the unexcelled opportunities for camping on top of the ridge in the summertime when the lowlands are sweltering in the heat, and possibly to a large extent in this it will differ from all the other national parks. ... It is cultivated valleys, coves and hillsides that have formed the chief problem in the satisfactory delineation of a boundary line. ... sufficient land has necessarily had to be taken in coves and lowland areas along the foothills of the park for their protection, or protection of entrances, to provide for large camping spaces and sites for utility groups necessary for Federal administration. ... It has seemed to me absolutely imperative to protect the main road approaches and foothills, or to protect the views from within the park outward, or the main view of the park area itself from the flanking roads."

On reviewing the draft, Kelsey had suggested many additional paragraphs extolling the horticultural features in the foothills to further blunt the expected assault by the critics. The park service staff thought it unwise and decided to stick closely to the boundary issues. "It looks too much like an apology for including some of the cut-over areas, whereas we might just as well hold the argument in reserve in case the area is ever attacked."

Cammerer then went page after page discussing why he included some areas and excluded others, various matters of jurisdiction over state and county roads, and contingent areas, Dickeys Hill, which could be accepted at a later date. In the end he said: "After having studied this park line and recorded it as the best which in my judgment and opinion could be obtained under all circumstances, it was found that, exclusive of Dickeys Hill, the planimeter measurement was only 327,000 acres. ... If additional areas within the boundary line, shown on the attached map, recommended to you as including 327,000 acres, were included it would inevitably necessitate the inclusion of some of the richest cultural lands of this vicinity without any corresponding benefit to the park itself." So he recommended that the secretary advise the governor of Virginia that the park service would seek an amendment to the act to reduce the minimum acreage accordingly.

Then, one more time, he dealt with Kelsey's concerns. On the issue of park entrances, in addition to including land for protection, "the State was willing to go even farther. If it was possible within its rights to do so, by enacting zoning legislation that would prohibit uncontrolled gasoline stations, refreshment stands, billboards and the like, possibly unsightly structures and occupations along the roads within a certain distance from the park lines, and especially along or near the main Park entrances."

Secretary Work accepted the report and by February 1928 Representative Temple introduced the Shenandoah Bill, which was passed by the House and Senate and approved by the president on February 16, 1928. This act unambiguously established the park at 327,000 acres, repealing any prior inconsistent provisions. In section 2, however it surprisingly addressed the issue of whether the original settlers had to summarily move out. No, they didn't. This had been discussed at the commission's February 7, 1926, meeting, but any action was deferred. The only thing made final was the park service's stand that no deed could be encumbered with private rights. Now, Representative Temple inserted a clause allowing temporary leaseholds—and leaseholds in both the Shenandoah and Great Smoky parks. Persons, schools, and churches were covered. If the occupant had some interest or title prior to the establishment of the park, they were allowed up to two-year leases, subject to the secretary of the Interior's discretion. It seems to infer that renewals could be authorized by the secretary. Kelsey must have been pleased, given his previously noted warm regard for the mountaineers tucked back in the coves and ridges of the Highlands and the Smokies. It also solved the embarrassment of summarily "booting out" those like

Pollock and others around Skyland, who had toiled so endlessly to make the park a reality.

One month later, March 23, 1928, Virginia's Governor Byrd signed into law the last needed provision: "Providing the form and mode of procedure, and furnishing a system of procedure for the condemnation of lands and buildings and other improvements ... for use as a public park ... with the power of eminent domain. ..." Done. Whatever race existed in the Blue Ridge of Virginia, it was over. All that was left was "mop-up" activity on funding, and by the park service and the commission. And, oh yes, there was the matter of actually developing the park and its infrastructure, which would go on for many years with the park service.

But cutting continued in Kelsey's beloved Smokies. They still needed money, and the national campaign had never gotten off of its feet. Back in January, Cammerer wrote Kelsey, "Happy New Year ... When are you coming down here again? Have you heard any thing from the Major? These Tennessee people and the North Carolinians are getting frantic." The national people were still discussing sharing arrangements, and the Virginians were talking about reorganizing the committee-of-five because of resignations by the Virginia members. Major Welch, the chairman, had written to Senator Mark Squires of North Carolina, "Will you please let me have your very frank opinion of this proposed reorganization, which Governor Byrd endorses, and talk it over with your people so that we may get some action as early as possible on this question."

On January 10, 1928, Major Welch submitted his resignation as a member of the Southern Appalachian National Park Commission to Secretary Work, who accepted it on January 14. Major Welch's resignation was due to the fact that his position as chief engineer and general manager of the Palisades Interstate Park made it impossible for him to spend the necessary time. It seemed now that Cammerer and the park service were the only ones remaining with the stature and motivation to "go national."

January and February passed. Then, in the first week of March, something happened that is still celebrated on a plaque at the crest of the road across the Smokies—an extraordinary gift from J. D. Rockefeller Jr. W. P. Davis, president of the Great Smoky Mountains Conservation Association, wrote Kelsey on March 29, 1928:

> My Dear Mr. Kelsey: I have been out of the City almost ever since the great event of three weeks ago when the Laura Spelman Rockefeller Memorial made us that most generous gift of $5,000,000, for our Great Smoky Mountains National Park and, therefore, have not had an opportunity to write you and say how happy we all are, as we know that you are sharing our joy over this wonderful accomplishment. Much credit is due Mr. Cammerer for the wonderful work he did in connection with securing this great donation.
> Now that we are sure of sufficient funds to secure lands for the Park, work will go on under direction of Col. Chapman and we believe it will not be very long until the Great Smoky Mountains National Park will be a reality, and it is a great pleasure to us to have this realized and to know that you took such a prominent part in bringing it about.
> We also hope that it will not be very long until we shall have the pleasure of seeing you in Knoxville again where we can thank you in person for the work that you have done and the help which you gave in making this Park a success. ...

On March 12 Kelsey wrote, "Dear Cam: The pipe has arrived and I have smoked it day and night. It is a pippin. Certainly you are trying to make a confirmed smoker out of me. I wish I could tell you how much I appreciate it and the thought back of it, and even more the wonderful work you have done for the Great Smoky

Mountains National Park. You are the man who, after all, finally put it across."

The commission report makes no mention of separate legislation in North Carolina and Tennessee to establish condemnation and eminent domain procedures, but they may well have been included in land acquisition acts of those two states in early 1927 for bond issuance to cover acquisition. If so, that would explain the dearth of commentary about any lumber company activity after the Rockefeller gift. It appears the cutting stopped. The race in the Smokies was over. As in the Shenandoah Park, only the "mop-up" operations and the start of development remained.

Yellowstone

The National Park Service's focus on the Eastern Parks didn't mean the Western Park problems would cease to exist. A few months earlier, April 20, Acting Director Cammerer had written to Kelsey telling him that the Idaho farming and ranching interests were amending their bill to adjust the boundaries of Yellowstone Park. They wanted to exclude from the Park the southwest corner, the Bechler Meadows, for use as an irrigation reservoir. The Idaho delegation had made its case, and the House Public Lands Committee was waiting for the response from the National Park Service. Cammerer wrote, "Mr. Albright will be here on Thursday and he has suggested it would be very valuable if you could be down to assist him in combating this newest proposal. P.S. A section of the topographic map of Yellowstone is enclosed showing the proposed reservoir, the area proposed to be eliminated and an area proposed to be added by the Smith amendment." Kelsey was then serving as chairman, New England Conference for the Protection of National Parks, which gave him standing for testimony before the House Committee.

Kelsey's April 22 response was with regrets, but very detailed, with information that could prove useful before the House Committee:

It causes me particular regret that I cannot be at the Hearing next Saturday morning for in company with Mr. F. L. Olmsted, Mr. W. T. Fitzgerald and Mr. Herbert Gleason, I made a special trip thru that section, I think, about four summers ago, to look into the very question which now arises. My business is a seasonal one and practically the year's business is done in six weeks in the Spring and the Spring is now on me. Moreover, it is three weeks late and I am at my wit's ends to get even a reasonable amount of business executed before the season is over. Nothing but the direct necessity would keep me away from this Hearing.

I would gladly show you dozens of pictures of photographs which we took in this area of wonderful waterfalls but you already have a much larger collection taken by Mr. Gregg and others. I do want to tell you that we camped over a week in the area shown North of Lilypad Lake and between that and Pitchstone Plateau where our main camp was, where the Boundary Creek and Bechler River join. We galloped practically over the entire area hunting for swamps, which did not materialize, although we had been told that the whole area was swampy. We did find it a wonderful area for fishing and a veritable garden of flowers throughout the whole basin.

My chief objection to a reservoir at this place is because the Pitchstone Plateau rises very abruptly from the flora of the basin and the proposed reservoir would hug the base of the plateau almost the entire distance around the Northerly boundary of the reservoir. ... [making access] difficult, to the marvelous waterfalls on Boundary and Bechler streams and their tributaries. The abruptness of the plateau is such that many of these waterfalls are but a very short distance above where the proposed reservoir would come. Ouzel Falls and Silver Scarf Falls are samples, which are but a very short distance from the edge of the proposed reservoir. Any of these Falls can be readily reached from the basin below but to make even a system of trails on the bluffs above would be extremely difficult, besides injuring the natural beauty of the scenery.

The view from the top of Pitchstone Plateau is very impressive and I do not think would be spoiled by the proposed reservoir if it were kept at a permanent level; in fact, the glorious view of the Teatons from this point might really be improved with a lake at the base of the Plateau, but my greatest objection to the proposed reservoir comes in at this point; namely, that at the very time when visitors were in the Park would be the time that the water would be drawn off, leaving very unsightly mud banks extending, probably for a great distance, towards the dam. It makes me shudder to think what irreparable damage would be caused to this wonderful southwestern section of Yellowstone, if these mud banks were entirely around the base of these plateaus which carry this wonderful group of waterfalls.

I have been pretty well over the United States and I know of no section with as many wonderful waterfalls in the same area as exist at this place.

The New England Conference for the Protection of National Parks long ago went on record as absolutely opposed to the ruining of this section of Yellowstone National Park by the building of a reservoir and I hope you will get on record our unalterable opposition to this proposal, made after a most careful and painstaking investigation by three of our members, Messrs. Olmsted, Fitzgerald and myself.

Further, as to the proposed addition of 64,000 acres on the western boundary as shown on the map you sent me, I express no opinion as I have not been over that territory.

William C. Gregg had been in discussions with Stephen Mather of the park service and wrote him on May 24, 1926, citing the same concerns Kelsey had, and adding many new ones of his own. He starts, "You will recall our campaign of 1920 and 1921 to prevent any irrigation reservoir in this area. You will also recall the reasons we gave." He then cites them: (1) a dangerous precedent; there are over eight other reservoir sites in the park just waiting for the first to establish a pattern; (2) it would make it almost impossible to develop a road system in that area of the park and diminish the camping possibilities, which would be sorely needed as park usage continued to grow; and (3) it would destroy the park's greatest hay meadow, which would be needed in the future for winter feeding of the elk, deer, and buffalo in the park. He then adds additional commentary. There was no real current need for more grain production since farmers were already suffering from oversupply. And finally came his lack of trust in the Idaho proponents. "The advocates of the reservoir say that they will make a lower dam than formerly proposed, only using some five or six thousand acres instead of 8,000. Those of us who know the devastation caused by the 50 foot dam at Jackson Lake know also that when that dam was authorized it was to be *16 feet* high."

Nothing had happened by the end of 1926, and Will Gregg wrote December 15, "Dear Mr. Kelsey:" to encourage him to contact his congressman or senator "protesting against the Idaho attempt to grab a part of Yellowstone Park for an irrigation reservoir." Kelsey finally wrote back January 21, 1927. "Dear Doc: In the first place I would have answered your letter of December 15 sooner, or think I should have, if you had not addressed me so formally at the head of the letter. I have written my Congressman about the Yellowstone grab but I don't think there is a single New England representative or senator who would vote, and many of them would fight against such a graft. I wish it were possible for me to reach some westerners, who are really the ones who ought to be made aware of the reasons for killing this attempt."

Cosmos Club

"In the year 1878 Clarence Dutton, soldier and geologist, was asked by his New York City friends, 'Why have you not in Washington a club like the Century?' His circle of friends met to organize one at the home of John Wesley Powell, soldier, explorer, and consummate organizer." He is best known as leader of the first expedition to navigate the Grand Canyon in 1860. "The community of scientists and intellectuals in Washington grew rapidly in the 1870's. They came to serve in various government agencies ... some to explore, survey and understand the geography and resources of the United States ... others to expand its intellectual and cultural foundations ... or build its economic, social, medical, and industrial prowess ... or set forth on expeditions to learn the world's secrets."

They called it the Cosmos Club. Its stated objective: "The advancement of its members in science, literature, and art," and also "their mutual improvement by social intercourse."

"There were other societies, but they tended toward specialization and formal meetings. Powell's vision was a center of good fellowship, a club that embraced the sciences and the arts, where members could meet socially and exchange ideas, where vitality would grow from the mixture of disciplines, and a library would provide a refuge for thought and learning. The membership over the years to the present time has been honored with 51 Pulitzer and 29 Nobel prizes, and 42 Presidential Medals of Freedom.

"The Cosmos Club stands as 'the closest thing to social headquarters for Washington's intellectual elite.' So wrote Western scholar Wallace Stegner in his acclaimed work, *Beyond the Hundredth Meridian*. His judgment echoed the oft-repeated statement of World War II days that the most significant concentration of Washington's public policy intellectuals centered at the Cosmos Club, unless it was at Union Station when the night train from Boston arrived."[128] Harlan P. Kelsey was well acquainted with that night train.

In 1925 Kelsey was invited to become a member of the Cosmos Club and remained a member until his death. Many of Kelsey's principal contacts in Washington were also members. Stephen Mather, Horace Albright, and Arno Cammerer, leaders of the National Park Service, were all members, as were his close botanical friends at the US Forest Service, with whom he worked on *Standardized Plant Names*. By 1925 it was clear that Kelsey's activities in Washington were not going away, possibly increasing, and his membership would certainly ease the trials of the lone traveler in a distant city.

Nursery Matters

Times were good on the conservation front in Washington. Times were good throughout the nation. It was the time of the Roaring Twenties with the whole economy growing and the Wall Street scene booming. As one would expect, Kelsey's nursery business was benefiting accordingly. His catalogs were getting longer, with more illustrations and much more use of color printing. His land holdings were expanding in Boxford with the 1926 acquisition of Chester Killam's 156-acre farm holding. This brought the nursery right up to the Boston and Maine railroad tracks on its east side, adding valuable capacity for expansion. Beyond the tracks the terrain became hilly and unsuitable.

On April 10, 1928, Kelsey wrote to a Mr. S. B. Detwiler, complaining about how stressed he was:

> At the present moment I am so swamped with spring shipping and my nerves are all shattered on account of the terrible scare I got from three days of August weather when buds began to pop open and it looked as though we would not have any spring season left. Today it is blowing cold again and, of course, when

I think of it I know that the seasons all average up, but when I tell you that going through the nursery Sunday I found all of our Larches coming into leaf you can see how frightened I must have become. I am not over it yet but I feel a little better and will go over the matters in your letter a little later, at least after I get over this funk I have been in.

Curiously he began to get correspondence at 19 Garden Street, Cambridge, Massachusetts. He spoke of it as "my Cambridge apartments" and as accommodating more than just himself and Florence, as there was "someone in the family" sorting and misdirecting mail. It was a long jaunt from Boxford to Boston and almost as bad from Salem to Boston. Apparently having an apartment just across the Charles River in Cambridge was a great convenience, and one that he could afford. It certainly would have made catching the train to and from Washington much easier.

Then a completely disruptive bombshell went off. He was evicted from his business office in Salem. His May 3, 1928, response to his landlord, Mr. J. Fred Hussey, shows both his astonishment and his angst:

> Tuesday I received a peremptory notice to vacate my office inside of thirty days. I understand this is the action that has been taken with all tenants in this building. Of course, I shall expect to comply as, while I have not received any official notice from you that my office has been rented to others, from the intimations to that effect you have made in the past I suppose it is quite true.
>
> My relations as your tenant in the past have been very satisfactory indeed and I have appreciated the many courtesies you have always extended. At this time, however, I cannot let the matter go without expressing some surprise that you should put out tenants on thirty days notice who have been with you since the building was built and who have always paid their rent

promptly and without question, and have willingly met any rise in price you have made.

No one questions the advantage to you of renting the whole building to one tenant on a long time lease rather than having numerous tenants on short time leases with the incident bother, and had you notified me, allowing three to six month's time to make arrangements for moving, I would have cordially complied no matter to what inconvenience it might have put me. Thirty days notice, however, makes a very great hardship to move and get suitable quarters. Would it not have been quite possible and fair to have leased the building with the understanding that your old tenants were to have the privilege of remaining at least three months, so suitable arrangements for moving could have been made, and so undisturb the very cordial relations which I know all of your tenants have always held with you.

As you know, I have been to considerable expense in fitting out these offices and I appreciate your willingness to see that I am recompensed for this, as previously stated by you. Enclosed you will find copies of four bills showing the major expense, and my office will be glad to show you the originals if you care to see them. Yours truly, Harlan P. Kelsey

Kelsey needed lots of space for his office. Because of the extensive landscape architecture business, he needed space for large drafting boards, for storage of large rolled blueprints and drawings, and for storage of over thirty years' business correspondence, all in addition to normal desk space for the office staff. This was not going to be easy.

Probably Kelsey was muttering to himself, "I'm never going to let this happen to me again." But how? The only land and buildings he controlled were those of his Salem home and the Boxford Nursery. All of the dwellings on the nursery property were occupied by his sons' families, and by the family of his superintendent. But there was one remote possibility. The recently acquired Killam property had a derelict old house and barn that had been vacant and deteriorating ever since 1911. Perhaps he could restore the house for himself and Florence to live in. At the same time, reconstruct the big old barn for the nursery business office, temporarily using the residences for office work while the barn was being rebuilt. It was a stretch, and terribly inconvenient, but totally consistent with the abrupt moves his father had made in the past, and he himself with his abrupt move to Boston in 1896. At some point, very quickly, Kelsey decided, "Let's do it!"

Chapter 6

Trials and Triumphs

The Spofford Barnes House

Earlier we noted Kelsey's land holdings had expanded in Boxford with the 1926 acquisition of Chester Killam's 156-acre farm. This brought the nursery up to the Boston and Maine railroad tracks on its east side. Right at the tracks was an old dwelling with its barn next to it. The National Register of Historic Places lists that old dwelling as the "Spofford Barnes House" because of the 120-year occupancy by this single family. Benjamin Spofford bought the house in 1789, and in the mid-1800s his daughter, Sally Spofford, married Phineas Barnes, who moved in to run the farm.

There are two reasons for the National Register listing. First is the exceptional interior paneling, and second is the historical significance of Lydia Warren Barnard Wood Spofford. The Daughters of the American Revolution have installed a brass plaque at her grave site, which credits her with having captured the first British prisoner of the Revolutionary War, as the British were retreating from the battle at Concord. She married Benjamin Spofford in 1792 after the death of her second husband, Aaron Wood, bringing with her the fine paneling from her former house. By 1911 the house was used mostly as a summer residence by the family, who had moved to California, so they sold the farm to a neighbor, Chester Killam, who then sold it to Kelsey in 1926. All this rich history and much more can be found in the National Register listing documents.

The barn was the real reason for the move from Salem to Boxford, because of its size for use as the office building. First built with the old house in 1749, it had been burned nearly to the ground by the Civil War soldiers in the nearby campground. They drove a burning hay wagon around the camp and finally through the barn, in celebration on news that the war was over. It was rebuilt shortly thereafter. Kelsey wrote to W. W. Hillenmeyer, president of AAN, May 26, "I am in a difficult position and don't know whether I can make the convention or not. I unexpectedly had to move my entire office and build a new one on my grounds during the shipping season." And on June 12, 1928, he wrote Arno Cammerer, "We are gradually getting straightened out at the office, though it has been pretty bad and I don't want to go through it again very soon. You caught us at the worst time, as I guess you found out."

Kelsey had immediately hired a noted Boston architect, Gordon Robb, to design and supervise the restoration of the house and the reconstruction of the barn as an office. He couldn't afford a moment's lost time. Almost immediately, because of the eviction, some of the office work had to be conducted in the old house until the barn was converted. The east side of the house was in bad shape, but the west side was habitable for office use during restoration, with the family still residing in Salem. The barn's first floor became the sales office. The second floor was the business office, including a large personal office for Kelsey. The third-floor loft became the landscape architecture floor, crowded with drafting boards. All the windows were large, especially in the gable ends of the drafting loft, with its beautiful eight-feet-wide Palladian style windows at both ends. For more light, the loft had a long shed dormer on the north side.

Over everything were large new cedar shingles, with white framing for the windows and fascia. It was elegant.

One of the nursery's great strengths was the moving of very large trees. This Kelsey did immediately after the construction debris was off the ground, surrounding the building with large specimen trees. The two-and-a-half-acre space in front of the building included a traffic circle and the start of his arboretum, to display all the best plants that are hardy in the New England climate, with the most favorable landscape design. Northern exposures were all protected by instant tall evergreen hedges, to blunt the force of the northeast gales. All this started from flat plowed farm fields, and two years later one would have thought the whole office and house complex had been there, fully planted, since the turn of the century. Today the arboretum still supports over eighty mature species of trees and shrubs, with a constant bloom from spring on into the summer. Recently, one woman remarked that it all gave her the feeling of being in another time and place.

On March 24, 1930, Mary Barnes Sawyer wrote Kelsey, "It is such a continual pleasure to us to see our old home, and the lands in all directions, looking so fine. I do often think how pleased my father would have been. ... That was one of the sad things in coming to California, that the old home must be sold, as there did not seem to be any one to look after it. It has been such a bright spot to think you have made such a beauty spot of it."

While the house, office building, and grounds were becoming "a beauty spot," Kelsey's administrative and shipping workload from the new facility was a tangled mess. His August 8, 1928, letter to the Fourth Assistant Postmaster General in Washington, DC, sheds light on the scope of nursery operations and the new problems:

> For some years I have had a nursery at East Boxford, Massachusetts. My general office being in Salem, Massachusetts

Spofford Barnes House as acquired by Kelsey in 1926, plus corner of barn.

Barn next to Spofford Barnes House as acquired by Kelsey in 1926.

Barn under renovation. First-floor windows being installed. 1929.

Barn under renovation. Office entrance nearing completion. 1929.

Office entrance after large specimen trees planted.

Kelsey Complex completed—house/office/arboretum. 1931.

AIRPLANE VIEW OF KELS
Over 500 acres of the finest ornamental nursery stock
Kelsey airport

Completed East Boxford Nursery Installation.

EY-HIGHLANDS NURSERY
grown. Note the well planned city-block arrangement.
in foreground.

1932 catalog centerfold.

Foto by H. P. K., Jr.

KELSEY AIRPORT
Owned by Harlan P. Kelsey, Inc.

For those who travel by air we have a new landing field right at the nursery. Many visitors have already taken advantage of this new convenience that we are offering. For the business man whose time is valuable we suggest a visit to Kelsey-Highlands Nursery by airplane.

By airplane we are less than fifteen minutes from Boston and less than three hours from New York.

Foto by H. P. K., Jr.

LARGE SPECIMEN TREES
Can now be moved safely and quickly

Foto by H. P. K., Jr.
Planting large Pine with Tree Mover

It will pay you to visit Kelsey-Highlands Nursery to see our fine selection of large specimen stock which will give you the immediate effect you desire—and our tree moving equipment gives speed, safety and efficiency.

We are always glad to quote prices or make estimates. Write for information.

Foto by S. L. K.
Tree Mover with Pine at estate of W. E. Schrafft

Our new modern equipment will solve your problem of producing that immediate effect.

The pictures on this page show one of the new and better methods we use. Trees, both evergreen and deciduous, up to thirty or more feet in hight and twelve inches in caliper, can now be safely transplanted during the spring and fall planting seasons and also during the winter months.

KELSEY-HIGHLANDS NURSERY

Modern conveniences—airport and tree moving. 1932.

Boxed trees ready to ship from East Boxford RR Depot.

Nursery Staff Photo Montage. 1931 catalog.

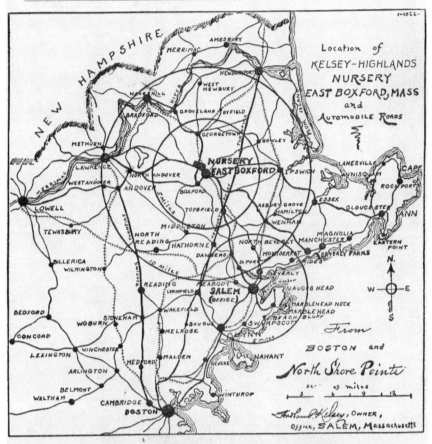

Map—Boxford Nursery and Salem. 1929.

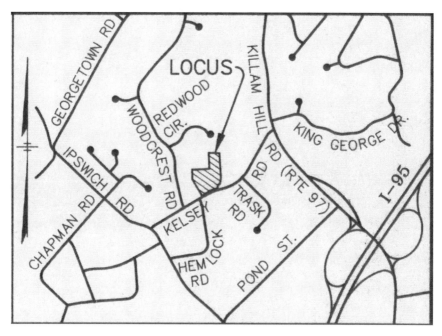

Current map—Boxford Kelsey Compound (house/office/arboretum).

until quite recently when I moved my entire office to the nursery site, I would like to have the East Boxford Post Office re-established with a postmaster and regular service direct from the Boston & Maine trains.

My mail is quite large, particularly during the Fall and Spring months and I send out perhaps fifty thousand separate pieces of printed matter per year, and the quantity is increasing all the time.

As my nursery is extremely well known, the conditions have become extremely complicated. Daily I get letters addressed as follows: East Boxford, Mass., Boxford, Mass., Salem, Mass., Georgetown, Mass., and Topsfield, Mass.

The local service is supplied by R.F.D., Route 1, from Topsfield and R.F.D. Georgetown to Boxford. Obviously such slow delivery, coming two days' late, makes it impossible for me to use it and I am still using Salem, Mass. as my Post Office.

Besides circular matter and first-class matter, throughout the year I send out quite a large number of Parcel Post packages, sometimes twenty to forty a day during the Spring season. They are too heavy and bulky to be handled by the R.F.D. carriers properly, and it makes it extremely expensive for me to send special messengers with this material to ether Georgetown or Salem.

I will be glad to get up the usual petition for the re-establishment of this office if necessary, but I believe the first proper step is for a Post Office Inspector to visit my house and let me lay the matter with all its details fully before him.

We are now preparing to send out our Fall advertising matter, and as quickly an acknowledgment as is feasible is highly desirable. ... Thanking you in advance ... Yours truly, Harlan P. Kelsey.

He quickly received permission from the town selectmen to rename the existing post office "Boxford Village" and to establish the new East Boxford post office at the railroad station adjacent to the nursery. The Boston & Maine RR also quickly agreed to change the station's name from Boxford to East Boxford, and to rent or lease space in the station for the post office and possibly an express office.

Local action was quick, but action in Washington was agonizingly slow. He wrote follow-up letters on September 18 and again on October 30. The postal inspector did finally show up on December 11, and Kelsey was left with the impression that everything was on track for approval. On January 15, 1929, he again wrote of his dismay at finding that the inspector had filed an adverse report, suggesting the nursery could simply use the post offices in surrounding towns. Digging in his heels, Kelsey found a name at the postmaster general's Washington office, pleaded his case on the phone, wrote follow-up letters to his new contact, Mr. Warner, and ultimately succeeded:

On January 30, 1929, Kelsey received a letter from the local B & M RR manager, stating, "I think it would be well to have Mr. Rollins, new postmaster, arrange to be at the station or attempt to get a key that will fit the tenement so that he can take possession and start to clean up and install his post-office."

Kelsey had "pulled the fat out of the fire" one more time. By late 1929 the nursery was humming without having missed a beat in the interim turmoil. Business was booming and Kelsey, as usual, could complain of overwork. Profits from the large and expanding nursery business provided the financial means for nearly annual fishing vacations in Florida each winter. The nursery was then dormant and frozen over. Usually he and Florence would be found at Long Key on the western gulf coast, with Kelsey fishing offshore for sailfish.

Also, by 1929 both of Kelsey's sons were out of college and deeply involved in nursery operations. This no doubt took some of the operating burden off of their father. The eldest, Harlan P. Kelsey Jr., graduated in 1922 from prep school, the Loomis Institute, Windsor, Connecticut. He went on to Harvard from 1923 to 1926, studying engineering, but did not graduate with a degree. To avoid name confusion with his father, he will hereafter be referred to as "HPK Jr." The younger son, Seth Low Kelsey, graduated from Loomis in 1923 and from Harvard in 1927 with a degree in Botany, perfect for the nursery business.

The locus of Kelsey's interests lay in East Boxford. But his heart still lay in Highlands, North Carolina. On August 2, 1929, he wrote to Miss Marguerite A. Ravenell in Highlands, "There is no other locality in the world which holds the place in my heart like Highlands and I hope before long that I can visit it every year or every two years at the least." This is the same Marguerite A. Ravenell that had taken a mortgage from him back in 1894 to fund his nursery land acquisitions from the Linville Improvement Company. She had written him earlier about the unveiling exercises for the Kelsey Memorial Tablet, commemorating

Samuel Truman Kelsey's founding of the town. The letter also told him about the reestablishment of the local Presbyterian Church "with a permanent minister the year round, as of old. ... We would be so glad to have some of the Kelsey family enrolled when we organize. ... You know the very ground on which the church stands was the gift of your mother, and I remember her saying to me once, that a church built on as earnest prayers could never fail—nor has it."

In Kelsey's August 2 response, he said "Mrs. Kelsey and my daughter Jane are now visiting my brother in Baltimore and I think they intend to make the trip to Highlands by automobile in time for the ceremony on August 10. I am going to send your letter on to my brother, who, of course, will take the greatest interest in the revival of the old Presbyterian Church at Highlands." In fact, the program for the memorial tablet ceremony featured "Unveiling of Tablet—Miss Jane Kelsey, a granddaughter." For Kelsey himself, he wrote, "It's entirely impossible for me to be down there at that time, much as I would like to."

Business everywhere was humming, especially on Wall Street. The stock market reached a new high on September 3, 1929, and then started a correction, drifting unevenly downward. On Monday, October 21, the rout began. On Wednesday, October 23, the slide began again in the final hour of trading, and the next day the bottom fell out. Trading stabilized, but only to give large holders time to capitulate, and on Tuesday, October 29, the huge volume led to the infamous Black Tuesday, normally cited as *the* day of the crash, and for many observers the beginning of the Great Depression. Nobody really foresaw the Depression at that moment, and the politicians in Washington preached confidence:

President Hoover: "I am convinced we have reestablished confidence."

Treasury Secretary Mellon: "I see nothing in the present situation that is either menacing or warrants pessimism."

Financier and presidential advisor Bernard Baruch: "The economic condition of the world seems on the verge of a great forward movement."

Yale Professor Irving Fisher: "There may be a recession in stock prices, but not anything in the nature of a crash."[129]

Other events to come, including trade and tax legislation, were more influential in pulling the rug out from under the economy, and perhaps the stock market was only anticipating them. Certainly Kelsey had no idea what was coming as far as his business was concerned.[130]

Winding Up the Commission

Vice Chairman Gregg called a meeting of the commission for January 11 and 12, 1929, with only three men present—Welch having resigned, and Temple absent for illness. Cammerer was there at the request of Mr. Gregg. It seems the North Carolina Park Commission wanted to add to the Smokies Park, an area alleged to contain about 10,729 acres involved in the Suncrest Lumber Company tract lying east of Caldwell Fork and the Cataloochee Creek. This parcel of land was a minor part of the holdings of the Suncrest Lumber Company, which otherwise lay entirely within the maximum boundary line of the proposed park. Probably in purchasing that portion of the lumber company's land lying within the boundary line, the state would be required to pay for the whole tract, which included the proposed addition. The commission was familiar with the area and approved the suggestion. An amendment to the congressional act was introduced by Representative Temple on June 30, 1929, and was approved by the president April 19, 1930.

Two more things remained for the commission's attention: finalizing the Mammoth Cave situation and cleaning up the survey work on park boundaries. The Kentucky Legislature passed a bill, approved March 22, 1930, for the conveyance of lands to the National Park Service, with a $1,000,000 appropriation to cover land cost. On October 20, 1930, Colonel Smith joined Mr. Cammerer for several days to help him locate the minimum boundary line for the proposed Mammoth Cave Park.

The commission's work of locating areas for national parks then appeared to be completed. During the past two or three years, the duties of the commission had been gradually diminishing and confined to occasional trips on the part of one or more of the commissioners to the various park areas to assist the National Park Service in finalizing park boundaries. The several state park associations that in the past had relied on the commission for advice and assistance had gradually transferred their problems to the National Park Service and looked to that service for advice and guidance. The National Park Service had also gradually assumed most of the duties of the commission, and there seemed to be very little work left for the commission to undertake.

Chairman Temple, therefore, called a meeting of the commission for December 30, 1930, with all members present except Colonel Smith, who was ill. Mr. Gregg informally moved that since the work of the commission seemed to have been completed, it should consider the advisability of making a final report and asking the secretary of the Interior to dissolve the commission. Kelsey seconded the motion. It was decided that the final report should be prepared and that Chairman Temple write the report. The report should be written in narrative form, in chronological order, setting down events as they happened. A long period of discussion established that "the functions of the Commission, viz., to select, if possible, a suitable area, or areas, for national park status, within certain limitations of territory and then devise a plan for helping the people acquire the land, without cost to the Federal Government, had been fulfilled." It was the opinion of the commission that if properly handled the funds in sight would be sufficient.

The discussion rambled along, touching on all the reasons, for the record, that the areas selected were distinct from areas already in national park status, and extolled their virtues. Mention was made that the commission had appropriations from the Federal Treasury for traveling expenses, which had been small, for surveys, and maps of certain areas. Mr. Gregg remarked, "I shouldn't be surprised if all the facts were known to find that our Commission has functioned on about as small an appropriation as any Commission ever did." Appreciation was expressed for the cooperation of the US Geological Survey in making available airplanes, airplane maps, and also to the army for furnishing airplanes for the use of the commission in survey work.

As a final shot, Kelsey called the attention of the commission to a matter that had been troubling him—that of park entrances. He stated that because of high-priced lands and the necessity of saving funds, the tendency had been to bring the line back into the park and cut out the valleys, those very spots that would provide ideal campsites.

> Exactly the opposite should be done. Those are the areas that are going to be exploited and made pest holes with their hot dog stands, etc., automobile pest holes. Take, for instance, the road going from Washington over to Luray Caverns. You know how across the Gap they have gone up with a line on both sides so far that they meet in a very narrow section of land approaching the park, just a ridge, and it is the worst possible thing that could have happened. I think it is of the greatest value to the parks to have beautiful entrances but it seems to be impossible to provide them on account of the high price of the land. The result is going to be that all the entrances to the parks will be very poor, in my opinion. The one thing I recommended on the last trip was that the States pass a law as soon as possible to control approaches to the parks. They are very much interested in it and I think they will do it. You can see how this can come about and I think it is a very unfortunate situation due very largely to the limitation of funds.

In this connection, Mr. Gregg recalled that one of the things the commission did the first time it met was to ask the question "Is it possible to create a national park in a privately-owned area," and added that this is the problem still confronting the people of the interested states.

Dr. Temple informed the commission that the current appropriation would be available until the first of July 1931. He stated that in case the commission was dissolved and Mr. Albright desired to call on them in connection with an inspection of the areas in question, it would be possible for him to detail them as *collaborators* rather than as members of the commission.

Having talked over the situation in detail, Dr. Temple put the question as to whether or not the commission should ask to be dissolved, and it was unanimously agreed that it should be dissolved. Thus ended the commission's report, and the commission, after an extraordinary seven years of work.

The finally edited version of the commission's report was submitted to Secretary of the Interior Wilbur by Chairman Temple on June 1, 1931. It was accepted and Secretary Wilbur dissolved the Southern Appalachian National Park Commission effective at the close of business on June 30, 1931.

Collaborator

While the year 1930 saw the winding down of Kelsey's work on the commission, it concurrently saw the winding up of his activities as a collaborator to the National Park Service.

In December 1929 Frederick Law Olmsted issued his annual report to the American Society of Landscape Architects. This was in his capacity as the chairman of their Committee on National Parks and Forests. The report's final paragraph read as follows:

One of the new projects for a National Park brought forward in the last Congress, whatever its merits as a truly National undertaking may prove to be, was at least initiated in a logical and thoroughly sound manner by its proponents. An act was passed calling upon the National Park Service to investigate and report on the desirability of selecting and preserving as a National Park a large area of tropical scenery and vegetation in Southern Florida, unique in the continental United States; with the expectation that, if favorably reported, such an area would be acquired by popular subscription and given to the United States for maintenance as a National Park.

Kelsey and his associates on the Southern Appalachian National Park Commission had pioneered in showing the way to create national parks on formerly private property. Recall that the prior parks were almost entirely in the west on government-owned land. The now-demonstrated success of the park advocates in Tennessee, North Carolina, Virginia, and Kentucky prompted a new wave of efforts for national parks in other states. Florida was the first to follow the lead. Ernest F. Coe was the man, as chairman of the Tropic Everglades Park Association. The lengthy description of the proposed park on their letterhead explains their aim. "An Association to promote acquaintance with the wonders of American tropics in the Cape Sable region of south Florida and adjacent areas—its scenic interests including its varied plant and animal Life; much of it unique to this section. To co-operate with measures for this Cape Sable county's preservation as a great National Park, where all forms of life will be preserved, and its varied other charms of tropic glades, jungles, azure seas, emerald isles, lakes, rivers and beaches will be forever consecrated to the benefit of all mankind."

Now the national park service needed to investigate and report. The job fell to Assistant Director Arno Cammerer, with his friend Kelsey included as one of the collaborators. On January 4, 1930, Kelsey wrote to Cammerer, "I am hoping to leave Monday night for a month in

Florida. How I wish you would run down and see me there. While I am around Miami I hope to go out and see that section which Coe and Dr. Fairchild are so much interested in making a National Park. Have you any comments to make on it. Write me at the Royal Palm Hotel, Miami, if you do it in the next few days. I am not sure that such a region should be made a national park although very possibly it is sufficiently spectacular and unique for one but certainly it should be set aside as a national monument, state park or a wild nature reservation."

On January 27, 1930, Earnest Coe wrote to Kelsey, who was again fishing off Long Key, Florida. "Dear Friend Kelsey: Letter … from Mr. A. B. Cammerer makes the following statement. We trust this is not too good to be true:

> So far as we can at this time foretell, our party will be made up of Secretary Wilbur, Director Albright, Gilbert Pearson, President of the Audubon Societies of America, Dr. Hermon C. Bumpus, who was former head of the American Museum of Natural History in New York City, and President of Tufts College, and myself. … It is possible that Harlan P. Kelsey, one of the foremost botanists of the country, who happens to be visiting in Florida, will join us; he is one of the Southern Appalachian National Park Commissioners, who did his share in the selection of the Great Smoky Mountains National Park and the Shenandoah National Park. He is most anxious to be included in the Blimp party.
>
> The enclosed is a tentative schedule for the four days this distinguished group have as scheduled for their stay here. We anticipate you are having a splendid time and getting a thorough rest-up under conditions quite to your liking. With kindest regards to Mrs. Kelsey and your good self, I am Sincerely yours, Ernest F. Coe."

On February 26 Kelsey wrote, "Dear Cam ... I cannot tell you how much I appreciate your making it possible for me to go on that historic trip. ... As soon as there is any news about the whole proposition be sure and let little Willy know. In the meantime I am having my pictures developed and if they turn out well of course you will get a full set. ... KEL"

Cammerer to Kelsey, March 3, "By all means give me the memorandum that I requested in my last letter, concerning your impressions as to whether the Everglades is or is not national park material. We think it is."

Ten months later, December 26, 1930, Cammerer to Kelsey: "Dear Kel: I am leaving tonight for the Everglades in Florida. The Senate Public Lands Committee suddenly made up their minds to go, and I have to go along. Seven senators, five of them with their wives, are going to have a personally escorted trip through the Everglades section. Both Blimp and boat have been arranged for. We are going to miss you. ... As I will not see you before the New Year, I want to tell you what might have proved embarrassing to tell you to your face, because you are such a modest fellow, and that is, that of all the friends that I have made in the past few years you are closer to me and have contributed more to my pleasure in life than anyone else. I want you to know that I treasure your friendship more than any other that I have made in my national park work, and that this is said from the bottom of my heart, old man."

Kelsey to Cammerer, January 14, "I had the nicest letter from you that I ever got from anybody and I just want you to know that the sentiments are entirely reciprocated. The friendship that overlooks all faults is the biggest thing in the world. With the best love, Old Chestnut Blight. Yours truly, Harlan P. Kelsey."

During the ten months between the two official Everglades trips Kelsey was busy on numerous park and nonpark activities. Mr. D. H. Mulloney, Assistant Secretary of Pure Oil Company in Columbus, Ohio, approached Kelsey about plant names, ordering a copy of *Standardized*

Plant Names, and asking if there was such a species as "Russian Linden." Mulloney was involved in the Dawes Arboretum in Newark, Ohio. Mr. Dawes was apparently his boss. The arboretum, located thirty miles east of Columbus, comprised three hundred acres, with over a hundred thousand specimens represented by some six hundred varieties. Kelsey replied, "Regarding ... 'Russian Linden.' Undoubtedly you have mixed this Tilia with an Ulmus. There is an Ulmus laevis, obsolete synonym effusa, obsolete synonym pedunculata. Tilia mongolica the Mongolian Linden and Tilia mandschurica the Manchurian Linden are the nearest to your inquiry that we can find. Ulmus laevis is the Russian Elm. By all means you should have the 'Manual of Cultivated Trees and Shrubs' by Rehder, the Macmillan Company, publishers. If you have any publications regarding your Arboretum I would be very glad indeed to receive them. Do you have a plan of the grounds and how large and permanent an institution are you intending to make? I am on the Advisory Council of the new National Arboretum in Washington, D. C. and of course am very much interested in state or local arboretums."

The eighteenth annual International Flower Show was held in New York, March 16–21, 1931. In 1930, the year before, the Horticultural Society of New York and the New York Florists Club, sponsors of the event, were busy organizing for it. On May 6, 1930, they wrote Kelsey, "At the last meeting of the Flower Show Committee I was instructed to convey to you their thanks and appreciation for your co-operation in acting as a Judge." Kelsey's standing and reputation in the horticultural community put him very much in demand. He had a fondness for flower shows based on his long standing work helping conduct the Boston Flower Show for the Massachusetts Horticultural Society.

In June 1930 Congress passed the infamous Smoot-Hawley Tariff Act, setting off a worldwide series of retaliatory responses in other nations. Besides tariff actions, currency devaluations were widely used to gain some trade advantages, and the phrase "beggar-thy-neighbor" was born. Rapidly declining world trade added to the deteriorating domestic economic conditions and job losses. Gradually the boom years of the 1920s began to reverse for Kelsey.

While Kelsey's business activities at his nursery were his primary obligation, his conservation interests were always lurking in the background and over the horizon, beckoning him. On July 10, Kelsey got a letter from W. P. Davis, president of the Great Smoky Mountains Conservation Association, bringing him up to date on the progress acquiring park land and telling of their plans for a "great highway" to connect Knoxville with the park entrance. "It will cost at least Five Million Dollars to build the Highway and perhaps a little more, but if carried out as planned there will be nothing like it in the world, and it and the Park will bring millions and millions of people here ... to see the beauties of this Great Park and Highway. ... We are all indebted to your Commission more than we can tell you for the wonderful work you did. ... I hope it will be our pleasure to see you in Knoxville as soon as we get our developments further along. We want to show you as soon as we can the marvelous work you have done."

Kelsey's reply, July 19, thanked Davis for the news but declined any trips south for the time being. "Just now it seems probable that I will have to go West for the Government looking over some more National Park possibilities for it seems that the whole country now wants National Parks. When I can possibly do it I am coming down that way and get up into the mountains and of course I will let you know when."

The west Kelsey spoke of turned out to be the western Great Lakes. Studying his expense account reveals an itinerary generally charged with a high level of intensity—an itinerary included to demonstrate Kelsey's willingness to endure all the rigors experienced by today's tough "road warriors" on their long business trips. At 7:05 p.m., July 31, 1930, Kelsey boarded a Pullman car on the Pennsylvania RR in Washington, DC, bound overnight for Buffalo, NY Arriving in Buffalo at 7:25 a.m., he was on board the steamship *US Juniata*, bound for Duluth, Minnesota, at 9:15

a.m. The train would have saved time, but Kelsey's targets for investigation included islands in the Great Lakes. What better way was there to become generally acquainted with the Lakes than with a four-day steamer trip across Lakes Erie, Huron, and Superior to Duluth, Minnesota?

Arriving in Duluth at 7:30 a.m., August 5, he checked into the Duluth Hotel for a day of telephone calls and arranging trip details with local and regional contacts. The first call was to Ernest C. Oberholtzer, in Minneapolis, Minnesota. Oberholtzer was the storied explorer, author, and conservationist for the Minnesota-Ontario border lakes region. No one was better equipped to advise Kelsey on what to see in that region and how to see it. Oberholtzer was later to become one of the eight founding members of the Wilderness Society. The next two calls were to Charles M. Sheridan, in Washburn, Wisconsin, on the Bayfield peninsula. He wrote for the *Washburn Times* and knew the Apostle Islands well.

Kelsey left Duluth the next day at 3:00 p.m. for Bayfield, Wisconsin, with transportation supplied by the Apostle Islands National Park Committee. After a detour to Red Cliff Bay and a view of the islands from Ole Olen Hill, he arrived in Bayfield at 6:00 p.m. This counted as the first of six days in the Bayfield area. The next day he toured the islands on board the Gary yacht *Lamora* accompanied by Congressman Peavey, the park committee, and a group of prominent local people. The day after that he flew over the islands and the Bayfield Peninsula. And so it went for six days of touring, including a dinner held in his honor, at which he gave his initial impressions from the visit. His main concern was for the extensive lumbering that had all but obliterated the original virgin forest growth.

In his report to Director Albright he lamented: "What must have been once a far more striking and characteristic landscape of dark coniferous original forest growth has been obliterated by the axe followed by fire. The ecological conditions have been so violently disturbed that probably never could they be more than remotely reproduced." On Outer Island the John Schroeder Lumber Company was still cutting, and Kelsey observed that no attempt at scientific cutting practices were evident to prevent fires or offer preservation for any future crop.

He also observed that none of his contacts during the tours had ever visited a national park and had no feeling for the extremely high standards necessary for a project endorsed by the National Park Service. At every opportunity he sought to impress them with the high level of these standards.

He cited logistical problems, such as the need for large boats for safe traffic between islands because of the violent nature of Lake Superior storms, and that access to many of the islands would be difficult, if not impossible, for several months of the year. Although he couldn't recommend them for a national park, he came out strongly for some other kind of preservation—a national monument perhaps, or a state park. "The Apostle Islands have so much inherent beauty and offer such wonderful possibilities for recreation and as a game and bird refuge, or for the production of forest products, or a combination of these, that it would be a tragic loss ... if they were further despoiled or left abandoned to individual exploitation."

On learning of Kelsey's report and rejection as national park material, the promoters were surprised and chagrined. Congressman Peavey wrote an indignant letter of rebuttal to Director Albright. Aware that Michigan's Isle Royale was also a national park candidate, and ignoring the logging issue, Peavey asserted that he was "reliably informed that the only single attraction that Isle Royale possesses not held by the Apostle Islands is the several hundred moose that live on the island." He could not resist adding "Is it not possible that your inspector got so close to one of these animals that he was unable to see anything else?" Albright's response was concise and to the point, moose or no moose:

The fact of comparative isolation of Isle Royale has resulted in the conservation of its forest cover and wild life, whereas one of the outstanding objections to the Apostle Islands project appears to be its denudation of original forest covering with consequent disappearance of wild life. Cutover areas do not make a national park.

Politically astute, Albright nonetheless offered to send an NPS employee to take a second look. It took another year to happen, and Kelsey's friend, Assistant Director Cammerer, was the elected employee.[131] Cammerer's September 1, 1931, letter to Kelsey summed things up nicely:

Dear Kel: Throughout my recent inspections of the Apostle Islands and Isle Royale National Park projects, I had occasion numerous times to refer to your individual reports on those areas and cannot resist the impulse to let you know personally what a fine job you did in your reports. They were thorough and to the point, especially the former which was the important one with me. It became my sad duty at a banquet tendered me by local enthusiasts to tell them that cut-over lands never make a national park, a job that I apparently got away with, with my hide whole and friendships intact for myself and the Service. Even the aggressive Congressman representing that Wisconsin district seemed to be satisfied. Anyway, your report was a dandy. One lesson that I think the Service gained from it, and one which you pointed out yourself, is that one collaborator should not make such investigations alone, but should have associated with him on the job one of the executives of the Service. In this particular instance I have no doubt that you are right that this matter could have been definitely settled in that way at the banquet tendered you by the same group that I had the pleasure of meeting. What a wonderful recreation area that northern Wisconsin lake section is, though! I predict it will be the playground of the United States as the years roll along.

You left a lot of good friends there who were inquiring for you, notably O'Malley, Sheridan, Burnham and Knight. When will I see you next?

> Faithfully, "with a heart bustin with love",
> Cam.   Acting Director.

Returning to the 1930 trip, on August 12 Kelsey traveled by train back to Duluth, arriving at 6:40 p.m. The next morning he took the Northland Greyhound Line headed for Isle Royale, Michigan, via Pigeon River, Minnesota, and Port Arthur, Ontario, arriving at 7:00 p.m. The morning of August 15, 1930, found him on a boat bound for Rock Harbor, Isle Royale. There he spent five, full, eventful days. Even without a detailed itinerary of those days, we can safely rely on our imaginations to fill in the blanks, helped by inspection of Kelsey's description for Arno Cammerer in July 1931, the following year.

Cammerer had written Kelsey July 13, 1931, saying he had to go out to Isle Royale, and asked, "What's the quickest way to get there?" Kelsey's July 18 response gives us a good feeling of what he experienced the prior year when he was there, and how he discovered the north's answer to the Great Smokies of the south, when it comes to exquisite flora and fauna:

> Dear Cam: Yours of July eleven is received. I just got back from a three weeks trip to try and regain my equilibrium. I was up in Northern Maine fishing and fighting black flies and mosquitoes—it's a pretty nimble insect that can escape me now.
> Now regarding Isle Royale: the immediately surrounding islands have the choicest gift of the whole proposition. It you will recall the different reports, including my own, you will see that in times past the main island, or at least, the larger portion of it long ago was devastated by a fire. But some of these smaller islands without question are primeval in the fullest sense of the term, and they are of exquisite beauty both in mass and in detail.

The black and white print you sent me of the island doesn't seem to be a very detailed one but everything shown in the area of this map should be included. Passage Island is the only one that is at all removed from the main body of the island unless it be two or three others which I think are just beyond Passage Island and not shown on this map. There could be no reason that I know of for leaving out a single island and there is every reason for taking in every single one and including it as a part of a National Park.

I am more than delighted to see that this project has a good chance of now going through in the near future. It is a hard place to get to but when you arrive at Duluth you will have two choices—one to go up to Port Arthur and go across on the rapids screen and the other is to take that little jerk water boat which stops at a number of places but goes direct to the island. You will find the Captain particularly interesting. You can read my report for details. [Kelsey had returned to Duluth on this boat after his five-day stay.]

Get in communication with Oberholtzer and if you are in a hurry, then the only way and proper way is to fly by hydroplane from Duluth, and if you can, get Dusty Rhodes for pilot. Now my real tip is coming! Wire the Department of Conservation of the State of Michigan and get permission to use their patrol boat. The boys running them know the island from one end to the other and the smaller ones are just the kind for you to go in where you ought to go and see what you ought to see. Stop at Mrs. Palmer's, Rock Harbor.

However, again I might suggest that you look at my report and you can see the dope on just how to get there and what to see. I believe in some ways, it is the most beautiful island in the world, and I only wish I could go with you, but my cue just now is to look for business. ... Yours, Kel.

On February 5, 1931, Director Albright wrote Kelsey thanking him for his reports on the Apostle Islands and Isle Royale National Park projects. He lauded the "great amount of time and careful study ... given these two projects. ... The data you present, and on which your conclusions are based, are presented in most attractive and thorough form, and the Service is indebted to you." In Kelsey's transmittal letter there was evidence that he, once again, was instrumental in naming a park. He said to Albright, "In my report I have used the original spelling Isle Royale instead of changing this name to the English form Isle Royal. It would be interesting to know what the geographic board has decided on this name. It appears, however, that both the Canadian and the American Government have used the English form, as they are confident this means that Lac la Croix becomes Lake of the Cross which, of course, is a ridiculous situation."

Events moved rapidly on Isle Royale. Director Albright's favorable recommendation was submitted to the House Committee on the Public Lands February 19, 1931. In it he waxed eloquent on all the aspects of the Islands that Kelsey had lauded, and in support wrote "It has been visited and reported on by other outstanding men of authority, notable this past summer by Harlan P. Kelsey of Salem, Mass., a botanist and conservationist, as collaborator for the service, and Dr. Frank R. Oastler, of New York City, outstanding in conservation circles and a member of the advisory board on educational problems in national parks, both of whom were high in their praise of the area from a scenic and scientific standpoint." On March 3, 1931, the House approved the act to provide for the establishment of the Isle Royale National Park (46 Stat. 1514), pending acquisition of the lands at no cost to the government. Note the French form of the name, and that it was to include acquisition of *all* of the surrounding islands as urged by Kelsey.

On March 24, 1931, Mrs. Matt Farmer of Madison, Wisconsin, wrote Kelsey on behalf of the Isle Royale Protective Association Executive Committee. "We are all very grateful to you for your share of getting the Crampton-Vanderberg bill through Congress—I am sure that your influence helped us a great deal."

Beautiful Land of the Sky

Isle Royale and the Apostle Islands were only two of the four projects Kelsey was to inspect on his August 1930 western trip. Returning to that trip, on August 20 at 11:00 a.m. Kelsey departed Rock Harbor, Isle Royale, by steamer for Duluth, arriving the next morning at 7:30 a.m. Dropping off some bags for storage at the Duluth Hotel, he quickly caught a 9:00 a.m. bus on the Northland Greyhound Line for Mineral Center, Minnesota, arriving at 4:00 p.m. Then he immediately departed by automobile for Grand Portage, arriving an hour later.

The next day, August 22, he hired a boat and engaged a guide to Pigeon River and return. On August 23 he flew out of Grand Portage via hydroplane to Lac LaCroix, arriving at 6:55 p.m. for the night at Campbell's Trading Post. The next day, with boat and guide, he spent on Lac LaCroix. On August 25 he left Lac LaCroix by hydroplane at 9:30 a.m., arriving at Rainer Island an hour later. Leaving Rainer at 5:00 p.m., he reached Duluth at 11:45 p.m., quite ready for a layover at the hotel the next day.

On August 27 he left Duluth at 11:17 p.m. on the night sleeper for Milwaukee, arriving there at 8:00 a.m. the next morning. Transferring RR Lines, he departed 11:20 a.m. for Appleton, Wisconsin, arriving there at 2:17 p.m., and booked into a hotel for two days. During those days he went to the Menominee Indian Reservation by auto (Yellow Cab Company).

On August 30 he departed Appleton at 8:15 p.m. for the return trip to Washington, DC, via Chicago and a train change. He finally reached Washington at 6:50 a.m., September 1, and took a cab to the Cosmos Club. He left on the trip July 31 and returned a month later, September 1. On his return he wrote J. Horace McFarland, "Perhaps you know that I was in the west in the interests of the National Park Service looking over four projects. … I have seen some fine things. My pay is $12.00 per annum." McFarland replied, "I am glad to know that you are so well paid for the good work you are doing for the National Park Service. A dollar a month seems excessive!"

We have covered only two of the four projects on which Kelsey was sent out to report—Apostle Islands and Isle Royale. The other two were (1) the Quetico Superior Project, and (2) the Menominee Indian Reservation. Without access to Kelsey's reports it is hard to figure how the Menominee visit figured into the National Park Service activities. We do know that as late as March 8, 1932, Director Albright was asking for Kelsey's report on the "Menominee Indian Project." Albright also asked for Kelsey's report on the Quetico Superior Project at that time; this was easily an area worthy of NPS scrutiny. At the same time Albright advised Kelsey of their need for his materials on the Grand Portage area, saying "From all indications it now appears that this proposition will be squarely before us before very long." Kelsey's itinerary started with the Pigeon River/Grand Portage visit and continued with his hydroplane flight to Lac LaCroix. While there is no evidence he recommended either area for a national park, both sites are today beneficiaries of preservation by other means, just as with the Apostle Islands.

Lac LaCroix sits at the western end of the Boundary Waters Canoe Area Wilderness [BWCAW] in the Superior National Forest and managed by the US Forest Service. This huge area of over one million acres boasts over 1,500 miles of canoe routes, nearly 2,200 designated campsites, and more than 1,000 lakes and streams, all bounded on the north by the Canadian border.[132] Immediately north of the border lies Canada's Quetico Provincial Park—thus, the NPS labeling of Kelsey's visit as being for the "Quetico Superior Project."

Mountain Lake sits at the eastern end of the BWCAW and is the headwater of the Pigeon River, which runs fifty miles east to Lake Superior. Up to the nineteenth century, the river was a primary water route for fur traders, and even earlier for Native Americans, leading through BWCAW to Lake of the Woods and thence to western Canada and Hudson Bay. As the river nears Lake Superior the gradient increases, culminating in a spectacular gorge including two notable waterfalls. This gorge is included within both Grand Portage State Park in Minnesota and Pigeon River Provincial Park across the border in Thunder Bay District, Ontario.[133] The Grand Portage was the southern land passage around this gorge, joining the Pigeon River at a westerly point above the gorge and providing water passage into the BWCAW.

For Kelsey, the Quetico Superior Project didn't qualify as national park material, most likely because the region was extensively logged for white and red pine in the early part of the twentieth century. By World War I, much of the land had either been burned away or cutover. There is definite evidence that fires were common in the area over the past several centuries. In all of the Great Lakes area, issues were determined by horticultural value, not geological. Kelsey was the ideal man to make these determinations.

While not finding national park material, Kelsey was constantly recommending preservation through other means by state and local efforts. Today's Wilderness Area, state parks, and the Grand Portage National Monument testify to the success of such efforts over time. At the time of Kelsey's visit, the boundary waters area was not part of the Superior National Forest as it is today. Kelsey didn't believe national parks and national forests should ever be intermixed, and perhaps he could foresee that for the boundary waters area. He always worried about the "working forest" aspect of Department of Agriculture management potentially interfering with the pure conservation motives of the park service. Finally, the Wilderness Act of 1964 designated the BWCAW as a unit of the National Wilderness Preservation System, putting Kelsey's worries to rest.

Depression

In retrospect it should have been easy to see the seriousness of the receding economy in late 1930. But few people did. Government officials preached "confidence" as the means to restore growth. Certainly Kelsey had no clue as to what to expect. In a letter of December 19, 1930, to Douglas Graves, his friend from New Holland days, Kelsey said, "Certainly I would be glad to be associated with you but of course you realize that I am expanding rapidly here and need every bit of money I can scrape together to put into the business." Expanding rapidly was hardly the proper strategy for facing the hard times to come. But to him times looked good. He had just received a letter from the Massachusetts Horticultural Society that at their annual meeting he had been unanimously elected a Trustee of the Society, for three years. In the December 1930 issue of *Better Homes and Gardens* he was lauded by one of their columnists:

> If I were king I should utilize Christmas to distribute honors to plantsmen who pioneer in propagating and bringing to us new and rare plants. This year I think I should single out Harlan P. Kelsey, whose nursery is near the Arnold Arboretum, in Massachusetts. For years Mr. Kelsey has been taking the new and rare shrubs and trees growing at the Arboretum and by seeds, cuttings, and grafts, has been increasing them until they exist in sufficient quantities to be offered for sale.
>
> In doing this work Mr. Kelsey is more than just a businessman. He is a public benefactor. Garden clubs and horticultural organizations in absence of any official dignitary who might do so, could well unite in paying tribute to Mr. Kelsey for his work.

With all this recognition, Kelsey had reason to believe his business would attract customers and continue to prosper. But he did take one sensible, defensive step, effective December 31, 1930. For the first time he incorporated the business. This insulated Florence's assets (the Lowe family inheritance) against claims originating from any troubles that might develop at the nursery. The new corporation started with a very healthy financial condition. Total assets were $185,139. Balanced by liabilities of only $64,603 and net worth of $120,536, with sales averaging in excess of $200,000 a year, there didn't appear to be anything to worry about.[134]

Two other Kelsey enterprises were also looking good. The January 17, 1931, issue of the *Florists Exchange* carried an article titled "*Standardized Plant Names* out of the Red." J. Horace McFarland had been totally paid back all of the funds he had advanced to publish the book, and there were modest revenues still accruing from dwindling book sales. In a side bar the editors commented as follows:

> Reading Mr. McFarland's report we are reminded of the celebrations we hear of every now and then at which some institution or community with appropriate and enthusiastic formalities burns its mortgages or other evidences of financial obligation and proclaims to the world that it has pulled itself out of debt. Those loyal and untiring individuals and groups that have been responsible for '*Standardized Plant Names*' are fully entitled to just such a party, bonfire and all; horticultural interests in America could well stage one for them and add their voices to the shouts of rejoicing over the balancing of the books of this unique and magnificent project. But more important and more needed than a celebration—and doubtless more appealing to those who have done so much already—is a decision to carry the work forward and the formulating of a plan for doing so. What will the first step be, and who is going to take it?

A second Kelsey enterprise, his management of the exhibitions at the celebrated Flower Show of the Massachusetts Horticultural Society, drew attention from the *Salem Evening News* of March 24, 1931. "Speaking of the flower show, it is interesting locally to know that the exhibition was a great financial success, more than covering all expenses, leaving in fact a nice profit to the society, because of the fact that Harlan P. Kelsey of this city was the chairman of the exhibition committee and the success was in great measure due to his management. While winning medals is a commonplace pastime for him and his Boxford nurseries, I might suggest that the Horticultural society give him one as 'champion manager.'"

While the news was good in Kelsey's immediate surroundings, it was far from good elsewhere in the nursery industry. In a February 27, 1931, letter Verne Rhoades, executive secretary of the North Carolina Park Commission, described various programs to aid the poor and unemployed in the Asheville area. For instance, they would get government wood from the Pisgah National Forest and haul it in city or county trucks to wood yards where wood choppers would split it. With the money received from the sale of the wood, they purchased groceries and supplies that were given to the wood choppers in lieu of wages. More to the point, Rhoades wanted Kelsey's opinion as to the value of the stock in a defunct nursery in which the city wanted to sell the entire stock for proceeds to fund their charitable programs. Kelsey replied:

> The nursery business itself is in the doldrums and I take it that all other businesses are equally the same. Still further, a nursery that has $23,000 worth of stock to be sold entirely would do mighty well to get even $3,000 for it as a cash proposition. In the first place there is a great expense in moving nursery stock, there is liability for damages of all kinds, both during the digging, shipping and planting out again and then the stock must be merchandised and even so it would have to be a nursery which had very special varieties that are in great demand and really of which the market would have a shortage. As a matter of fact, there are hundreds of small nurseries going out of business and this extra material is being thrown on the market to the detriment of the regular trade.

Oddly, Kelsey wasn't concerned about the business slump as it pertained to his own business. On March 26, 1931, he added to his staff Henry Rohrbach, a highly qualified propagator, for an annual salary of $3,000. He still thought his business would be the exception, and he had expansion on his mind.

In his April 11, 1931, letter to Mrs. Holden McGinley, responding to her praise for his "extraordinarily beautiful exhibit" at the Boston Flower

Show, he says, "It is a dream of mine to have some such thing as our exhibit on permanent display here at the nursery. Starting at our office I intend making a planting and border which we call an arboretum simply to designate it, extending for perhaps a mile into a most beautiful woods where a background of large Beeches and Canada Hemlocks will make a background for this very fine permanent display of the choicer plants." He did in fact start the arboretum and it still exists to this day, now functioning under a conservation restriction to restore and maintain it in perpetuity. Nonetheless, 1931 seemed like an inauspicious time to have taken on this added nursery burden.

The new nursery corporation was beginning to show some financial deterioration, a signal for more conservative operating policies, which were yet to materialize. By June 30, 1931, the nursery showed a net loss of $17,247 year to date. Three months later the loss had grown to $32,079. Net worth started the year at $120,536, dropped to $104,289 by June 30, and dropped further to $88,681 by October 31. Mortgage notes payable, which started the year at $28,000, were up to $43,000 by October 31. The trend was unmistakable.

The 1931 financial deterioration occurred despite some prestigious orders from institutions drawn to Kelsey's reputation. Notably, substantial shipments were made to the Westchester County Park Commission for the pioneering parkway projects above New York City. These might still be observed today on primarily the Saw Mill River Parkway, and also the Cross County Parkway, Central Westchester Parkway, Briarcliff Peekskill Parkway, and Bronx Parkway Extension. The order called for 32 trees mixed between fir, plum, and crabapple; 795 azaleas; 135 shrubs mixed between Kelsey locust, deerberry, and skunkbush; 17,950 ground cover plants (including 200 Scotch heather). Also noted was a huge delivery of 17,750 *Xanthorhiza simplicissima* (yellowroot), an unusual, tall ground cover. *Dirr's Manual* describes yellowroot as "a flat-topped ground cover with erect stems and celery-like leaves, filling the ground as a thicket; magnificent plant for difficult as well as normal sites especially where shade is a problem—size 2 to 3 ft. in height and spreading freely as it suckers from the roots. ... A very desirable ground cover for moist areas; little known and grown; makes a very solid mat."

In late 1931, with nursery revenues dropping faster than expenses, Kelsey obviously needed some new revenue sources if he wanted to maintain his workforce without layoffs. One avenue he chose was to add a new product—the Washington Elm. This was not just any old elm; this was a direct descendant from the great elm in Cambridge, Massachusetts, under which George Washington ceremoniously assumed command of the American army July 3, 1775. So the story goes. Each specimen from such a celebrated tree could command a price dramatically higher ($5) than the cost of growing the spliced scion for sale. The timing was good since 1932 would mark the two hundredth anniversary of Washington's birth.

Around 1908 the famous tree (*Ulmus americana*) was brought down because of the ravages of age and disease. At that time, Jackson Dawson, early superintendent of the Arnold Arboretum, grafted a branch of the old dying tree, saving it for posterity (second generation). A Mr. T. D. Hatfield took Jackson's graft and planted it on the public library grounds in Wellesley, Massachusetts. In 1925 William Judd, propagator at the Arnold Arboretum, grafted four scions (third generation) from this Wellesley elm and gave them to Harlan P. Kelsey under the auspices of Charles Sprague Sargent for the purpose of wider dissemination. One he gave back to the Arnold Arboretum; one was donated to Phillips Andover Academy; and two were planted in his own arboretum. From these two, Kelsey had grafted, certified, and sold numerous offspring (fourth generation). For example, the Boxford Grange obtained Tree No.130 on April 8, 1933.

Now enters the controversial side of the story. In December 1923, a Mr. Samuel F. Batchelder sent a letter, published by the *Cambridge*

Tribune, attempting to "debunk the myth." He followed with a thirty-six-page booklet, printed at his own expense, titled, *The Washington Elm Tradition: "Under This Tree Washington First Took Command of the American Army." Is It True? The Evidence Collected and Considered*. Paraphrasing Sheila Connor, Arnold Arboretum librarian and archivist, Batchelder argued each of his points with caustic wit and logic, only admitting that Washington "probably did do something, active or passive, beneath His elm," most likely it was simply taking shelter from the rain on his way into town.[135]

The Arnold Arboretum Bulletin, December 10, 1931, published a long adversarial discourse by Harvard's Assistant Professor J. G. Jack about "The Cambridge Washington Elm." He started out by elaborating on Samuel Batchelder's historical research seeking to debunk the traditional story. One could ask if this was appropriate material for a professor of dendrology, not a historian, publishing in a horticultural venue. He then moved closer to his field as he railed against nurserymen who "insist that the plants they offer have been propagated directly from the original tree which stood on Garden Street, bordering Cambridge Common, or were propagated from trees a generation once removed." After condemning the "glaring case" of an "extremely misleading" enterprising Chicago dealer, he moved on to "another nursery concern, with headquarters in Massachusetts … offering Washington Elms, grown by grafts from trees which are said to have been propagated from a tree which we are told was started as a scion from the old tree and was grafted at the Arnold Arboretum." This Massachusetts nurseryman could only have been Harlan P. Kelsey. Professor Jack goes on for eight paragraphs torturously trying to refute Kelsey's representations.

The *Boston Globe* immediately jumped on this juicy journalistic scoop, with an article broadcasting Professor Jack's claims. The *Boston Evening Transcript* also published an editorial on the subject. Kelsey, of course, was furious and saw the claims and the *Globe* article as slander and libel. He immediately engaged S. H. Batchelder of the eminent Boston law firm, Peabody, Arnold, Batchelder & Luther (no relation to the historian S. F. Batchelder cited earlier). While Harvard University itself was immune from prosecution, they did offer to have the Arnold Arboretum publish the following:

<u>Supplement to Bulletin #18</u>

In our Bulletin of Popular Information on December 10, 1931 we published our doubts upon the authenticity of some seedlings now being offered by nurserymen as descendants of the Washington Elm in Cambridge. It has been brought to our attention that the Arnold Arboretum itself took some part in the identification of the tree on the grounds of the Public Library at Wellesley from which these seedlings were taken and on whose descent from the original Elm their authenticity therefore depends.

For this reason, and because the Arboretum did itself once accept the identification, it does not wish to be understood as in any way impugning the good faith of the nurserymen who now rely on it.

Kelsey noted to Batchelder, "Their statement is totally inadequate and not acceptable. Moreover, it was apparently written by a lawyer (begging your pardon) and refers to the trees as 'seedlings' which of course, they are not." The trees were grafted scions, to maintain genetic purity.

The transcript said they would be very glad indeed to publish any reasonable story about the Washington Elm and Kelsey's connection with it, which Kelsey would prepare. Batchelder thought "the transcript editorial to a certain extent was really helpful … because it rather urged the authenticity of the story that Washington did take command of the troops under the Washington Elm." Batchelder advised Kelsey to accept the transcript's offer rather than to make further claims against it. The article Kelsey prepared was moot on the authenticity of the historical story but went into detail on the horticultural validity of the trees he was selling, including William Judd's August 31, 1931, letter to him:

> Gentlemen: The four plants of Ulmus americana, #18877 as given you on November 29, 1926 were grafted by me on March 10, 1925 from a tree growing in the grounds of the Public Library at Wellesley and which Mr. Hatfield told me was one given to him by Mr. Jackson Dawson. This tree was one grafted some years earlier, probably about 1908, by Mr. Dawson from the old tree at Cambridge. Very truly yours, Wm. H. Judd, Propagator

Even with this consolation, Kelsey was still blistering with anger. In a February 25, 1932, letter to Batchelder he said, "May I state in conclusion that I wish to make it just as hot and uncomfortable for Professor Jack as possible, as he has committed an unjustifiable and dirty offense—putting it in good English language." A month later Batchelder wrote Kelsey, "So far as the Boston Globe is concerned, the situation at present is that I am awaiting a reply from them to my last letter. So far as the Arnold Arboretum Bulletin is concerned, I have not as yet received a copy of what they have published or propose to publish beyond what I have already advised you. I prefer not to take any action against the Globe until the Arnold Arboretum has done what it intends to. I am now going away for a couple of weeks and when I get back, if the Arnold Arboretum Bulletin has been then published, I shall advise you whether or not I think you have a cause of action against the Globe. If you can show actual financial loss I am inclined to think that you have a cause, but I am not clear if you have a cause in the absence of financial loss."

At this point Kelsey's files go mute as to any further legal action. There was probably no demonstrable financial loss, since he continued to sell the plants. Most likely Kelsey realized that the loss from legal fees would far outweigh any modest loss in future sales, and that the real issue was "loss of face." We will close the story with a November 12, 1932, letter to Kelsey from Frank T. Garside of the American Institute of Park Executives.

> Dear Mr. Kelsey: The Washington Memorial Elm trees which you presented to the American Institute of Park Executives to be planted in the Washington park system, have been received by this office in good condition. It is planned to plant the large tree in Lafayette Park next Wednesday, November 16th. The small tree is being cared for by this office to be used in the event anything happens to the large tree. Your generosity and cooperation in presenting these trees to the Institute is greatly appreciated.

The deepening Depression was impacting Kelsey in many ways other than financial. The government public works people were unleashing numerous programs to provide work for the unemployed. An unintended consequence was laxity in administration of a road clearing program. On April 24, 1931, Harris Reynolds, secretary of the Massachusetts Forestry Association, sent his friend Kelsey a circular asking for support of a plan to save forested areas along the public highways from billboards, misplaced hot dog stands, filling stations, and dumps. Kelsey wrote back, "Have you had your attention called to the outrageous desecration of our roadsides in Massachusetts in the name of giving work to unemployed. The state has an organization trying to plant our roadsides with the very material that has been wrecked and destroyed this past winter. The Topsfield and Boxford roads have been cleaned out of the beautiful woodland growth along the sides and the trees trimmed up as a beginning toward making telegraph poles. There has been a public protest, but where is the coordinating of our towns, city and state authorities in these matters. Our roadsides are noted and have brought millions of tourists here and now we are wrecking them."

On December 14, 1931, Kelsey tried again, this time writing Dr. Gilbert, Massachusetts commissioner of agriculture, about the roadside problem, namely "the use of men (for unemployment relief) to ruin our roadsides by cutting them off to a uniform and unattractive flatness and removing the wild and natural beauty which was a very real thing along the roads of our Commonwealth. ... At the Club meeting on December 9th inst. comment was made upon the newspaper announcement that more work upon our public roads was soon to begin. Fear was expressed ... that yet more harm would result from this. It was unanimously voted that you be requested to represent the club in protesting against further such wanton destruction. ... Certain roadside work is sometimes needed, of course, but our recent experience makes us reluctant to entrust it where it was done before, and if anything further is really desirable, we are sure that the State would profit many fold in the results if it could be guided by a competent landscape architect."

As the new year dawned, the Depression expanded and the federal government began a series of steps now seen as counterproductive, if not disastrous. The federal deficit for fiscal year 1932 was the largest as a percent of federal expenditures ever experienced in peacetime, to that date. This prompted the Revenue Act of 1932. The sales tax provision was defeated, but income and other tax increases passed. This mostly affected the wealthiest 15 percent; most Americans had no tax bite. Estate taxes were 45 percent on estates greater than $10 million. To President Hoover, apparently, balancing the budget would be the key to restoring confidence. It proved to be nothing of the sort. Desperate farmers were blockading roadways. There was food looting. Workers marched on Ford's River Rouge Plant, with five dead and fifty wounded. WWI veterans made a summer encampment in Washington, DC, off of the Anacosta Flats, until they were expelled by General Douglas MacArthur's troops with fixed bayonets. The Dow Jones Industrial Average of stocks finally bottomed at 41 in 1932.

The winter of 1932–33 was the most desperate of the Depression. Twenty-five percent of the nation's workforce was unemployed. Conditions were particularly bad for farmers, who were in the second decade of their own

Depression, which had started back in the 1920s. By 1932 a bushel of wheat would fetch only thirty cents, down nearly 90 percent from the almost three dollars it had brought twelve years earlier. Hoover's chances for another term were nonexistent, and Franklin Delano Roosevelt (FDR) won the fall elections in a landslide, with his inauguration coming March 4, 1933.[136] But we are getting ahead of ourselves.

On January 5, 1932, Kelsey wrote to George F. Pollock, "It seems too bad that hard times hit the country just now and put such a drag on the Shenandoah National Park project—still, I feel that it is going to come, at least the best part of it is, and none of us have lost hope for a minute. It will seem queer to ride up to Skyland on the new road and I'm not sure that people don't enjoy things that are hard to get more than when you can sail there on flowery beds of ease. Still it ought to be a great thing for Skyland if the roadway does not come too close so as to really spoil the proposition." That same day the National Park Service wrote Kelsey that he was "appointed by the Secretary of the Interior as a Collaborator-at-large, at a new rate of compensation, i.e., $15 per diem when actually employed, together with travel expenses." This was quite a change, from twelve dollars a year to fifteen dollars a day!

Almost immediately Kelsey's continuing value as a collaborator was felt by the park service. The following letter of January 20, 1932, from Director Albright to the construction chief of the Bureau of Public Roads shows the impact Kelsey was having on shaping the Shenandoah Park as we know it today. The issue was where to locate the Skyline Drive between Thornton Gap and Front Royal:

> When our Collaborator on the Shenandoah Park, Mr. Kelsey, was at Luray in December, Mr. Austin the engineer of your Bureau, discussed this matter with him, and he gave him his reasons for the location of this road on the westerly side of Dickey's Ridge rather than on the easterly side. The fact of the matter was that in the laying out of this park boundary especial attention was given

to this particular feature by Associate Director Cammerer, who was compelled to adhere to the same views as to the park lines that Mr. Kelsey later on verified. In your letter you state that for reasons obvious, after a study of the topography involved and the scenic potentialities offered, the line on the east of Dickey's Ridge has a decided preference over the one suggested by Mr. Kelsey. Undoubtedly, from a construction standpoint alone the easterly side would be preferable, but from a scenic standpoint we cannot concede this. In the first place, the easterly side runs almost entirely though orchards and highly cultivated grass and farm lands, and the view looks out over almost unbroken landscape of such farm lands. For miles the road would have no natural protection of forests on either side. On the west of Dickey's Hill, however, the line runs through beautiful forests of pine, hemlock, mountain laurel, hardwoods, etc., with an unusually fine high view of Shenandoah Valley. Zero grade for long stretches would be easily obviated, as there is sufficient width of right of way to vary the grade to suit local conditions of scenery or engineering necessity. With careful construction this westerly line need not leave scars on the landscape that cannot be healed or attended to by proper methods.

Furthermore, the land on the westerly slope of Dickey's Hill is not only unusually beautiful park land, but is negligible in cost as compared with the high price of orchards and farm lands that would be involved if the road were located on the easterly side of Dickey's Hill.

For these various reasons I feel that we will definitely have to adhere to the line for future road locations on the westerly side of Dickey's Hill. Will you kindly make this a matter of record, advising Mr. Austin to that effect?

(Sgd.) Horace M. Albright   Director.

Albright's letter repeated, almost word for word, the letter he had received the day before from Kelsey. Skipping forward to November 17, 1932, Albright wrote Kelsey about a number of issues, one of which was the reaction to the newly completed portions of the road. "Our people down this way have gone perfectly crazy over the Shenandoah road. We only opened it to Hawks Bill Gap and about 25,000 people have already been up there and the comments ... have contained much praise for our work and more enthusiasm over park development than has ever come to us in the past. ... There is some gorgeous scenery in this region and the line through the Dickey Ridge country will give a most spectacular outlook, one of the very best in the whole park area. We followed the line of the new road and I am more than ever impressed with the magnificent job you did in revising the line. How you did it in the time at your disposal will always be a mystery to me."

Only a week later, January 27, 1932, Department of Interior Secretary Wilbur commended Kelsey with the following letter:

> My Dear Mr. Kelsey: Director Albright of the National Park Service has told me of your work in connection with the Shenandoah National Park project in its present vital stages, and of your services over a period of years in connection with the establishment of the eastern national parks and the investigation of other proposed park projects. While I know this has been a labor of love with you, carrying with it the realization of the importance of saving, while they still could be saved, such great primitive areas as the Everglades, the Great Smokies, Isle Royale, and the like, nevertheless I want you to know that the Department appreciates to the full the value of your self-denying and experienced efforts in those directions. None of these projects, I am confident, would have come to their present satisfying status had you not stepped in at critical moments and cheerfully given of the best that was in you. The fact that we could rely on your ripe experience, judgment and enthusiastic

interest at such critical points has contributed more to their success than you probably will realize, and for this I want to give you my most cordial thanks.

Sincerely yours,   Ray Lyman Wilbur   Secretary.

On March 8 Director Albright wrote Kelsey on a number of matters, closing with the good news, "I expect the Everglades bill to be up in the House on March 16. It looks as though it will pass. Several of the principal opponents have a defeatist attitude. These include Mr. Treadway, who told me not long ago that the bill will pass."

Tough times were now beginning to affect some of Kelsey's good friends from his park service activities. Ferdinand Zerkel, one of the strong Shenandoah Park activists, wrote Kelsey a heartrending letter on February 21 laying out in detail his unsuccessful efforts to find employment. The Depression had totally wiped out his real estate business in Luray, Virginia. He wrote "Dear Hardy Mountaineer: … Be assured, please, that your hope that something will come about for me in the National Park Service is deeply appreciated. It is very fine of you to hold the kindly feeling on this that you do and, with such 'friends at court', I am encouraged to believe that something will turn up." First, he thought he might be considered for the photographic concession at the Shenandoah Park but had been advised he wouldn't qualify as it would go to a photographer of outstanding artistic ability, something he couldn't demonstrate. Any regular employment within the park service was denied to him because he lacked a civil service rating, and he worried that even with his BA and MA degrees, being out of school for twenty-six years would make passing the civil service exam somewhat problematic. The civil service thing had taken away his temporary job at the Bureau of Public Roads, had taken away work as a Rodman for road construction, and left only laborer classification as a possibility. It paid only three dollars per day flat, without Sundays or holidays, too little to support a wife, three children, and an eighty-seven-year-old mother.

Kelsey explained that the government was curtailing employment in every way, and the National Park Service had not only been cut down in its appropriations, but even more rigidly under the requirement that only civil service people could be retained. Zerkel's only option was to quickly make an application to the Civil Service Commission for the examination. The basic problem was that the federal government was contracting everywhere. President Hoover was mistakenly committed to eliminating the federal budget deficit in the erroneous belief that this would restore public confidence and then business conditions would start to mend. In fact, by 1932 these budget cuts were totally counterproductive.

Ongoing Horticultural Issues

The Society of American Florists and Ornamental Horticulturalists received a report from its Committee on Nomenclature at their convention on April 7, 1932: "Why a New Edition of *Standardized Plant Names*? ... The passage of time and the tremendous growth of interest in ornamental plant life have made '*Standardized Plant Names*' become not obsolete, or indeed out of date, but incomplete. Its revision has been proposed and much controversy relating to what should be accomplished in the direction of a revision has raged through the horticultural press." The report cited the case of many disputants who were seeking a work where the name of the plant was accompanied by a description of the plant, as in "Bailey's Cyclopedia" and as in "Hortus." It continued, "But Hortus is not complete in the sense that *SPN* was complete. It has in it no list of horticultural varieties, and indeed in its preface it frankly refers readers to *SPN* for the nomenclature on the horticultural trades." The report goes on to present a series of supporting arguments in favor of an *SPN* revision.

One vigorous detractor was P. J. Van Melle, a nurseryman out of Poughkeepsie, who had opposed Kelsey on many past occasions. He wrote in the November 1931 issue of the *American Nurseryman*, "*SPN* sails under a boastful, pretentious and misleading title; is wrongly understood to represent an important step toward the standardization of trade practice pertaining to plant names; is no more and cannot be more than a spelling aid; as such there is no need of it, since we have a better handbook available in Hortus." Van Melle's criticism didn't stop with this article. Two years later, August 25, 1933, Kelsey wrote to Dr. C. G. Bowers, Maine, Broome County, New York. "Your most excellent article in the last Florists Exchange in regard to *Standardized Plant Names* and other matters was read by me with greatest pleasure. It seems to me you have answered Van Melle and others like him well, and that they will now shut up, although they have done a great good by having this book kept before the public, even with their criticisms."

None of this opposition shook the resolve of Kelsey and his compatriots. In a letter dated November 6, 1929, he remarked to Dr. Coville, "The other day I picked up A. J. Downing's old magazine 'Horticulture' and saw a plate in it of 'Norway Spruce Fir.' You see we have made some progress since 1847. … I am going to take up with the American Association of Nurserymen the entire question of financing '*Standardized Plant Names*' next edition."

Coville, in turn, outlined to Olmsted the scope of the proposed 1933 edition—ten years after the initial publication. He pointed to the large amount of additional material that had been accumulated, and that Kelsey estimated there would be 15,000–20,000 new items. This would mean a 50 percent increase in the size of the publication. Many of the new items were increases in horticultural varieties since 1923, but the main cause of the larger size was the plan to dramatically increase the scope of coverage. Coville continued with Olmsted:

> I have been accumulating a large amount of new material in the way of the names of forage plants, range plants, weeds, wild flowers, poisonous plants, drug plants, and other groups that we did not include, or included only in part, in the 1923 edition. It is probably advisable to include practically all the names given in Rehder's Manual of Cultivated Trees and Shrubs and

> Bailey's Manual of Cultivated Plants, as large numbers of these are coming into wider cultivation and into the horticultural trade. Also, as you know, the 1923 edition was deficient in tropical and subtropical plants actually in cultivation, especially in California, Texas, and Florida. We should take steps to get special lists of cultivated plants from those regions.

There was an ulterior motive in Coville's writing to Olmsted at this time. They wanted Olmsted to take over the chairmanship of the joint committee. J. Horace MacFarland had been a terrible thorn in the side of Coville and Kelsey as they were finishing the work in 1923. While he wanted to be an active chairman, MacFarland's only real contribution to the work was in compiling the rose list and managing the book printing task through his private publishing company. Perhaps because he was a decade older than the others and enjoyed broad recognition for his earlier conservation work and in founding the American Civic Association, he wanted to be in charge. He was constantly badgering them, particularly Coville, to accelerate the work to meet MacFarland's printing deadlines. But he had no leverage and resorted to a blustery style which only created frustration for everyone. MacFarland revered Olmsted and was constantly trying to get Olmsted to influence Kelsey and Coville, to no avail. In his letter, Coville continued:

> The chairmanship of the 1933 Joint Committee is of the utmost importance. Both Kelsey and I are of the opinion that the work will proceed much more effectively with a new chairman and the absence of the unnecessary and exasperating friction under which we labored before. If the present chairmanship continues it is very doubtful whether I shall continue to serve on the compilation committee and it is certain, I believe, that Kelsey would not.
>
> Both Kelsey and I are of the opinion that you are the logical chairman and that under your chairmanship the work could be conducted on a highly effective basis both so far as the compilation

is concerned and so far as the supporting organizations and the users of *Standardized Plant Names* are concerned. Even if you are not able to attend very many of our meetings we are willing to do the work of compilation. It is probable that we would employ more outside help in the compilation than we did for the last edition.

If they were to ease MacFarland out of the picture, they had to find someone else to finance and print the final edition. That was the primary problem they faced as the years progressed. Kelsey had asked the American Association of Nurserymen at their 1929 convention to finance the new edition in advance. The AAN skirted the issue by leaving the matter in the hands of the executive committee with full power to act, which they did not do. Instead they came back with the suggestion that possibly the US Department of Agriculture would undertake the publishing, making it a national publication. Coville thought it was possible but then cited numerous reasons for keeping it out of the hands of the government. It would be more influential if issued by the joint committee, sponsored by all of the using organizations, and have wider distribution. He also thought the government would impose numerous restrictions in the makeup, the paper, and the conditions of sale in a government publication. Kelsey agreed.

Obstacles to the new edition of *SPN* continued to mount. On March 7, 1933, Kelsey remarked to J. Horace MacFarland, "I haven't heard a word about Olmsted recently but I understand he is not in very good health and I begin to fear that he is out of the picture which will be a disaster."

Years would pass before the chairmanship, financing and publishing questions would be resolved. On June 13, 1933, Kelsey wrote to Dr. Heber W. Youngken, Massachusetts College of Pharmacy, "It had been hoped to get *Standardized Plant Names* new edition out by 1933 but I doubt if it will be ready before 1934 or possibly 1935." Given the economic stress of the Depression, no one was willing to allocate precious resources to updating an existing book.

As the Depression deepened, nurserymen, florists, horticulturalists, and landscapers were far more interested in preserving their businesses than with the niceties of proper nomenclature. One example was L. C. Bobbink of Bobbink & Atkins, Rutherford, New Jersey. He wrote Mr. Hillborn, President of the AAN, July 8, 1932. Hillborn had asked him to continue as a member of the AAN's Nomenclature Committee. Bobbink replied, "I have to ask you to relieve me of this work. I prefer to decline being a member of this Committee for the reason that if one is a member of such a Committee it is necessary to give one hundred percent help, like our friend Mr. Kelsey does and I am not in a position to do this, having so much other work and so many details to attend to."

Nurserymen make a "big deal" out of introducing new plants as a matter of pride and competitive distinction. It is one thing to introduce a plant to cultivation in the trade, but that is often not the end of the story. Often Kelsey had to defend his representations of plants he introduced. One was the mountain silverbell—*Halesia monticola*. On August 30, 1932, he wrote to C. C. Laney, Department of Parks, Rochester, New York, "As we all know, Halesia monticola was discovered and named in the Rochester Parks. Several times when I was there you told me that these were from material I had sent you. I have just noticed in an early Bulletin of the Arnold Arboretum that they state 'from Biltmore it was sent to the Parks of Rochester, New York.' I also notice that I had noted in lead pencil that this was incorrect and that we had sent you this material which I believe is a fact. I wish you would let me know what your record is on this matter and greatly oblige." Laney replied, "We got Halesia monticola from you before we got any from another nurseryman. The Arnold Arboretum may have furnished us plants later, but the first plants came from you."

Only one week later, Hardy Evergreen Gardens out of Marion, North Carolina, wrote him asking that Kelsey surrender his 1932 catalog claim to introducing the Rhododendron carolinianum album. They claimed to have all the correspondence from Professor Sargent and the Arnold

Arboretum, and from Kelsey himself, when they first sold stock of it from Hicks in New England and other nurseries. "We think this must have been an oversight, or in some way inadvertent, for you have covered yourself with glory by introducing so many new things that you cannot covet the introduction of our one ewe lamb." Kelsey rather gently replied, "May I ask in what year you introduced this Rhododendron and to whom?" Very shortly he got a detailed letter citing a long litany of events and dates from 1914 to 1922 supporting their claim. "We began to offer R.C. album in our own pricelists as our own introduction as soon as the Arboretum verified it. We sold it to Westbury, New England and some other nurseries in 1920." Thinking this to be iron-clad, they must have been jolted when they received Kelsey's reply. "It is a plant that I had introduced in the Fall of 1895 when my nursery was at Pomona, North Carolina, under the name of Rhododendron punctatum album. As possibly you know, the Rhododendron punctatum and its variety album were later renamed Rhododendron carolinianum. I had a small stock at that time and most of the plants were sent to England. ... Not only did we introduce them in 1895 but we were the first to discover this plant on the western slopes of the Roan Mountain where we were collecting the Rhododendron carolinianum."

Kelsey's reputation for plant introductions was widely recognized. The September 1, 1932, issue of the *National Nurseryman* carried the following: "Speaking of titles and distinctions, do all of you know that Ed Welch is the only nurseryman in the bunch who has had a college to confer an honorary degree on him? Fact. Next time, just remember to say 'Doctor' Welch. I have often wondered how it is that some others have been overlooked: Harlan Kelsey, for example, who has done more to introduce and popularize beautiful native plants than any man I know. One of these days some University is going to grab the opportunity to gain new distinction for itself by dubbing Harlan, Dr. Kelsey." Kelsey's September 19 response to the author, John Watson, was, "My son Harlan, Jr. ... showed me with amusement your kind reference to me in the National Nurseryman. However, it was mighty good of you to think of it and I admit it would be a pleasant thing to happen though I hardly believe that any college would slip up in such a manner."

Why Not a White Mountains National Park

Ever since Kelsey's work for the Appalachian Mountain Club in creating national forests in the east, he had harbored a dream for the White Mountains of New Hampshire as a national park. This intensified in the early 1920s with his service as president of the AMC, where he was active in enhancing the hut system throughout the area, particularly in the Presidential Range. Of course the White Mountain National Forest already existed, covering almost the whole area in question. Kelsey's problem with this was that the forest service mission was primarily sustained forestry and only secondarily for recreation by the public. As he said to Horace Albright, it "has been one of my pet hobbies for so many years." In letter after letter he reiterated that the White Mountains were "one hundred percent national park material." He felt that the economic return in administering the area as a national forest could never begin to be anything like what the state of New Hampshire got in the way of summer visitors, which would be markedly increased by the presence of a national park. "This area should be left in its natural state and not copsed of its trees, which destroys a great portion of its natural flora as well as its natural beauty."

He did allow that the forest service had taken care of this area in unusually fine shape. "You see very little sign of forestry work along the roadways and from the thousands of views on higher land as you climb the mountains; the general feeling is of unbroken forest. ... The White Mountains are absolutely unique—there is nothing like them anywhere I know of. While many of the slopes have been cut off for pulp-wood material and again where the forest service is actually doing its job of economic forestry, there is sufficient stand of the larger growth so that a few years would wipe out the apparent destruction caused by man."[137]

He explained that he had not yelled louder about it because the forest service, through the funding of the Weeks Act, was in a position to make the purchases and actually acquire the property, whereas the National Park Service was not. He also explained that it was necessary to keep any overtures concerning national park aspirations out of the public notice. The forest service was still purchasing many of the inside land tracts needed to finally complete their acquisitions. The addition of national park interest by the Department of Interior could increase prices to the government. So Kelsey's hands were tied when it came to whipping up public interest and lobbying. There was also the political issue of avoiding any struggle, sibling rivalry, between the Departments of Interior and Agriculture over control and staffing.

Cammerer advised Kelsey that he and Albright had discussed the White Mountains idea often in the past and agreed it had merits, but also drawbacks. He did allow that it should be further investigated. "Couldn't you get the City Club, or the Northeastern Appalachian Mountain Club, or some other club to ask us to investigate the possibilities of it? That would give us a little bit stronger reason to go on than the request of an individual who is a nut on parks anyway."[138]

Kelsey's greatest obstacle lay within the ranks of his friends in New England. He said, "Philip W. Ayres, Allen Chamberlain and others of our group here I know are not now nor never have been with me in this proposition but the increasing use of this area for recreation purposes is proving my contention that the area should be a national park and not a national forest." Chamberlain had been his early mentor in the AMC working on the Weeks Act. Ayres was the leader of the Society for Protection of New Hampshire Forests. Their arguments were quite forceful, insisting that the forest service was doing a splendid job of administering the recreational uses of the forest. They cited that the two million people yearly that used it, many of which were hikers and climbers, critical of any infringement of the wild, had no complaints whatsoever. No cutting at all had been made in the six large scenic areas, aggregating sixty-five thousand acres, designated by Mr. Chamberlain and others at the beginning of the land purchases by the forest service. Beyond that they offered a list of six items where conservation ends had been initiated or vastly improved over the years since inception. These concerned wildlife protection, scientific set-asides, scenic preservation along roads and trails, new trails, and extended protection for forests on the high slopes. To summarize, any conservation or recreational threats, past, present, or future were figments of Kelsey's imagination. Everything was fine as it stood.[139]

Kelsey's counter strategy was to get Albright and Cammerer to come up to New Hampshire and see for themselves what great national park material lay in the White Mountains. They admitted they should and would get up there, but just not now. There is no evidence they ever did. It appears the opposing arguments were simply too strong, and the political risks just too great. In a January 2, 1933, letter from Albright to Kelsey, he said, "I appreciated very much your letters about the White Mountains. I agree with you absolutely, but the formal letters I wrote were what we thought best for the record at this time. You and I think alike on almost everything, and we are certainly together on the idea of a park in the White Mountains, if not now, then ultimately. Again thanks and best regards."

Tension in the Parks

Roads in the Shenandoah Park were pretty well settled with the go-ahead on the Skyline Drive. But roads in the Smokies Park were far from settled. There was some muted resistance to the Tennessee road up to Newfound Gap being extended, crossing over and descending into North Carolina. That was going to happen, resistance or not. The real issue was how to get the public up to the east-west line of mountain crests so they could enjoy the same magnificent views seen by the rugged hikers and horseback riders. Should it be another "Skyline Highway" along the top of the Great Smokies from Newfound Gap to

Deal's Gap at the western end? Such a road was under consideration and Director Albright was getting hammered by resistance from wilderness advocates. Such objecting voices included H. W. Tyler, secretary of the American Association of University Professors, and Lorne W. Barclay, director of the National Parks Association. Kelsey chimed right in with "There are plenty of national parks and state parks where the herd instinct can be fully satisfied but for God's sake let's keep our national parks, so far as we can, in a truly wild state. I know the pressure for 'improvements' is almost irresistible. You are resisting that pressure magnificently and if this policy is continued, the future generation will rise up and call you blessed."

Perhaps more telling on Albright were the objections of Robert Lindsay Mason, a local "mountain man" in the Smokies. He was the author of *The Lure of the Great Smokies* and would soon be publishing a novel covering the known primitive history of the Smokies under the title, *Lonesome Gal*. He had bypassed Director Albright, written directly to Secretary Wilber at the Department of Interior, and poured out his soul:

> The Proposed highway has its sensation, of course, but it is purely an extravagant idea which will hurt the whole project more than it will help it. There is bound to follow a whole culmination and accumulating effect of destruction of vast spaces which shall not have any protection of wilderness characteristics which this area west of Newfound Gap has now. The idea was first merely a road to Clingman's Dome which is the highest point in the Smokies, then it grew to take in the whole range down to the Little Tennessee on the western boundary.
>
> Le Conte, as inaccessible as it is to hikers alone, has suffered mightily from vandalism of all sorts already. One could readily imagine what would happen with hundreds of automobilists daily running through the Skyline Highway area. It would take a regiment of soldiers to protect it properly …

> The mountains are beautiful now. They remind me of a vast canvas; a living painting vibrating with the mystery of color blending that is only possible at this time of year. When one climbs the hills and gazes off high prominences into swimming color that is breathless, it is impossible to describe the feeling of awe and infinitesimal atom that man is when he stands alone in the big universe that stretches out below in a panorama that appalls in its bigness.
>
> I have been against this proposed highway that would be open only a few months in the year owing to ice, fog, and hard freezing. ... In building the motor path we would destroy the very thing we came to see.

Secretary Wilber never saw the letter. In his absence it was passed on to Albright, who replied and took him to task for not coming to him directly. "I am quite surprised that, with all the good things you have had to say about the Park Service in the past and the confidence you have had in our efforts to save the Smokies, you would be one of the first to feel that we were not saving its essential scenic and primitive values." He then pulled no punches and cited the success of the parkway in the Shenandoah Park. "It is so located that it opens up the wonderful vista in every direction from the crest of the Blue Ridge, with wilderness areas of many square miles left for the hiker and saddle horse devotee. The reaction that we have had from our guests, both orally and in writing clearly indicates that our policy of opening to all—children and old people the infirm and crippled included—not only views of the lowlands and valleys, but a part of the high spectacular country as well, is sound. It affords them in the only way attainable the same inspiring reactions you so eloquently tell about. ...

"The gorgeous wilderness areas along the main crest in the eastern half of the park I have already gone on record as saying must be kept free from roads. That eastern half contains the most important wilderness area and is unexcelled anywhere in rugged primitive mountain scenery, except where scarred by fire. If it were from a fire protection standpoint alone, which is incidental, a road in the western section would justify itself, for anyone who has seen the burning over during the past few years of the beautiful azalea-covered flanks of Gregory Bald, or the burning of the rhododendron and myrtle-covered top of Le Conte, all caused by careless hikers, will be grateful for some quick means of access to fires that threaten such beauty spots in that area. ... I have high hopes ... of enrolling you, after you have read this letter, among the large number of those who have the greatest confidence in the work of the National Park Service and its plans for this road."

It was a chastened Lindsay Mason who wrote back November 14, 1932. "After considering from all angles my objections to the 'skyline highway' along the top of the Smokies from the Newfound Gap highway to Deal's Gap, I am willing to admit that the benefits obtained as stated by your letter of recent date, far outweigh the deteriorating effects." Three days later Albright again replied, "I am primarily a trail man. I never ride on an automobile road if I can help it. I am determined that very large areas in every national park shall never be opened up by roads so long as I have a position of authority in the National Park Service. I sympathize entirely with you in your expressions of discouragement and disgust at the way the ordinary run of visitors treat a beautiful piece of wild country. I remember how horrified I was when I rode out into the open place on Mt. Le Conte and beheld that mess of stumps. On the other hand, all of us have to reconcile ourselves to the viewpoint that everyone should have a chance to see and enjoy parts of these great national parks. ... I shall look forward to your new book about the Smokies. I know it will be good."

Kelsey immediately fell in line behind Lindsay Mason. November 30: "Your letter of November twenty-fourth enclosing copies of letters between you and Mr. Robert Lindsay Mason is received. Mr. Mason in his letter to Dr. Wilbur describes my own feelings with regard to the Great Smoky Mountains National Park as well as other National Parks far better than

I have at my command, and in his later letters to you, he also grants your arguments in favor of the proposed roads, just as I do."

Later events in history favored Robert Lindsay Mason and Kelsey. When it was finally built, it went only from Newfound Gap to Clingman's Dome, where it terminates today. There almost any visitor can stand atop the highest point in the Smokies and in season view the spectacular spring masses of flame azalea and gorgeous fall leaf color.

In November 1932 Franklin D. Roosevelt defeated Herbert Hoover for president of the United States. Suddenly the park service was confronted with a potential wave of new uncertainties.

Kelsey wasted no time in sharing his pleasure with others. On November 12, 1932, he wrote George T. Wofford in Johnson City, Tennessee, "I suppose you are very happy over the result of the election and you may be interested to know that I am too. I'm glad to say we had five votes in my family for Roosevelt. The superb arrogance of Hoover and the Republicans in claiming all the virtues of civilization and all the disaster and feeblemindedness to the Democrats got a sudden, swift kick. Probably Hoover's prediction that grass would be growing on the streets of our principal cities next year may be true but if so, then we'll be then able to get some new national parks."

That same day, he wrote Miss Harlean James, executive secretary, American Civic Association. "I do remember your frantic appeal to Mr. Delano and me to save the country by voting for Hoover. Well, I just couldn't see it that way … I think that Mr. Roosevelt's past record shows a lively understanding interest in our national conservation problems and I look for a sympathetic and active administration in both our departments of agriculture and interior."

On December 20 he wrote to Dr. Fredrick V. Coville, "May the shades of Hoover not linger with you too seriously but may the levity of a progressive democratic administration possess your soul as well as a little part of your time."

The following February J. Horace MacFarland wrote Kelsey, "It may be assumed, if one can divest himself, momentarily at least, of partisanship, that Franklin D. Roosevelt is an example of a young man of means and ability who has gone into politics for the good of politics." Kelsey responded March 7, 1933, three days after Roosevelt's inauguration, "As a Roosevelt supporter I appreciate most fully what you say in your second paragraph, coming as I know it does from an arch-Republican. If Roosevelt is not what you say he is, then certainly we are in a bad way. To return to Congress, I do know this—there are bound to be enough senators and representatives if properly approached and cultivated to be of infinite value in the future to our national parks. Of course, we must have the strong support of laymen's groups but it does not take the place of strong friends in Congress. … No one knows what the attitude of the new Secretary of the Interior will be on National Parks. I sincerely hope we will have Horace Albright at the helm for many years to come."

Unlike today's practice, in the 1930s there was more time between the election and the incoming president's inauguration. Roosevelt didn't take office until March 4, 1933. That left almost three months for the lame duck Hoover administration to continue their prior programs, or at least create an atmosphere of speculation regarding how the Roosevelt administration would react to them. Hoover's drive to cut federal expenditures included a proposal to reorganize and consolidate some functions of the Departments of Interior and Agriculture. President Hoover's proposal was to bring together the conservation activities of the two departments under one roof at the Department of Interior. It was clear that the forest service and its forestry friends would not permit this without a vigorous fight. The same would have been true if the consolidation had gone the other way to the Department of Agriculture. Given the entrenched opposition on both sides it was doubtful that the reorganization program would go through in the lame duck session of Congress prior to Roosevelt's inauguration.

In his January 2, 1933, letter to Kelsey, Director Albright confided, "The National Park Service is facing trouble these days. I wish I could talk with you a little. I am assuming, of course, that nothing will happen to us on March 4th, but there is nothing sure about our status. Our friends will do well to keep their eyes on us. Our financial problems are serious too. Finally, reorganization has some dangers. Our forest friends are bent on getting us into the Department of Agriculture, and we understand that the new Administration may favor this move. In my opinion, the parks cannot survive under the domination of Agriculture because it will be a domination of Western sheep and cattle and irrigation interests. Would it not be well to get some word to the Mountain clubs of the country, and to the landscape organizations, etc.?" Pinchot's utilitarian legacy was still in place.

Kelsey responded January 13, "It happens that I appear to be again slated to become a member of the Trustees of Real Estate of the Appalachian Mountain Club. Bearing in mind what you said, I will sound out some of the leading Appalachians and get their views on the consolidation of bureaus. I thought someone had suggested a Department of Conservation which would take in both the Forest Service and the National Park Service so that they would be more closely coordinated. At any rate, if there is any change, that would be my idea of the best thing to do. If there is serious or even possible danger of putting the National Park Service under the Department of Agriculture, then the park people all over the country should get together and really outline a campaign of action. I cannot believe that any administration could not be persuaded into seeing that the Department of Agriculture is almost exclusively devoted to utilitarian projects and that the National Park Service does not belong there in any sense of the word."

For the new President Roosevelt, this reorganization issue must have seemed subordinate amidst the terrible issues facing him. It was the most desperate time of the Great Depression. His inauguration speech coined the famous words, "the only thing we have to fear is fear itself." Four days later Roosevelt declared the bank holiday to stop the wholesale "runs on the banks," following passage of the Emergency Banking Bill by both houses of Congress and signed by Roosevelt only eight hours after its introduction. On the following Sunday evening, he explained to the American public how the banking system worked, on the first of his legendary "fireside chats." By this time fifty million Americans had radios in their homes. He promised immediate federal inspection of the banks and that only sound banks would be reopened; the public could depend on the safety of their deposits. The next morning, Monday, deposits exceeded withdrawals in the banks that were reopened, and stock prices surged 15 percent, the largest one-day rise in history to that time. The special session of Congress lasted exactly one hundred days and adopted a series of other measures at the president's request or on its own initiative. These collectively were lumped under the moniker "New Deal" and primarily were stimulus programs designed to jump-start economic recovery.[140]

Surprisingly, Roosevelt almost immediately started plans to reorganize and streamline the executive branch of the government. For some years the National Park Service had been quietly campaigning to unify administration of all national parks and monuments. Director Albright wasn't sure that, with the new administration coming in, he would be retained and able to continue these efforts. Harold L. Ickes, Roosevelt's choice as secretary of the Interior, asked Albright to stay on, however, and within a short time he emerged as a close and influential advisor to the "irascible" secretary of the Interior. We are indebted to the historians at the National Park Service for their portrayal of what happened next.[141]

> Albright lost no time, once it was clear his job was secure, in approaching Ickes regarding transfer of the military parks. Within days after Ickes had taken office and begun to settle in his new job, Albright had won his approval of the proposal. In the first hectic week of the New Deal, moreover, Albright had

met with and secured the approbation of George Dern, the new Secretary of War.

… On April 9, 1933, Albright was among the invited guests on an excursion to former President Hoover's camp on the Rapidan River in nearby Virginia. As they prepared to return to Washington, Roosevelt asked Albright to ride along in his touring car. Never one to be reticent, or to miss an opportunity, Albright used a discussion of Civil War battles to press his case for transfer of the War Department parks. … In what must have almost been an anticlimax to some sixteen years of effort, Roosevelt asked no questions, but merely agreed that it should be done, and told Albright to present the proper material to Lewis Douglas, chief of staff for reorganization activities.

Over the next two months, rumors swirled that the National Park Service would be merged into the Department of Agriculture. Gifford Pinchot, a longtime acquaintance of Roosevelt, had revived efforts in that regard. Had Albright misinterpreted the president in their April 9 discussion? Lewis Douglas reassured Albright, however, and the NPS director promptly submitted his proposals for transfer of the War Department parks and monuments. The proposals were modest, and he was not prepared for the scope of the proclamation that emerged. Executive Order 6166, issued on June 10, 1933, and effective sixty days later, dealt with a wide range of agencies and functions. Section 2 spoke directly to the National Park Service. Some years later, Horace Albright said that when he first saw a draft of order 6166 he "was stunned by its scope."[142]

Not only would the National Park Service inherit the War Department parks and monuments as Albright had proposed, but also all national monuments and cemeteries within the continental United States, the national monuments administered by the US Forest Service, the parks, monuments, and public buildings in the District of Columbia, and some elsewhere in the country, the Fine Arts Commission and the

National Capital Park and Planning Commission. Excluded was any public building or reservation which was chiefly employed as a facility in the work of a particular agency. This entire consolidation would be administered within the Department of Interior, under the NPS, renamed as the Office of National Parks, Buildings, and Reservations.

This name change was especially galling to park service employees, but it was not until March 10, 1934, that the old name was restored. On July 28, 1933, largely as a result of Albright's well-orchestrated campaign, President Roosevelt issued Executive Order 6228, which clarified Section 2 of order 6166, "postponing until further order" transfer of Arlington and other cemeteries still open for burial, while leaving the cemeteries associated with historical areas in the new NPS organization. In addition, Albright was able to secure separation of the National Capital Park and Planning Commission and Fine Arts Commission.

"Whatever the feelings of NPS employees, it is clear that no event in NPS history, save passage of the enabling act itself, had a more profound impact on the National Park System and the bureau that administers it. In terms of size alone, the number of units more than doubled—67 to 137. The number of natural areas increased from forty-seven to fifty-eight while the number of historical areas nearly quadrupled, increasing from twenty to seventy-seven. Important as it was in terms of numbers, the impact of Executive Order 6166 cannot be discussed in terms of size alone, for the location and diversity of the areas was just as important. Inclusion of the National Capital Parks brought the National Park Service into metropolitan urban parks. George Washington Memorial Parkway represented a new type of unit in the National Park System, one which was predominantly neither historical nor natural, but recreational."

Horace Albright wrote in 1971 that the order [6166] made the National Park Service a truly national bureau, with a national constituency. The service became the primary federal entity responsible for the administration of historical and archeological sites and structures, and he might have added, the leader in the field of historic preservation. Executive Order 6166 was almost a declaration of independence for the National Park Service. The service became a strong bureau that would never again be threatened by consolidation with another.[143]

With the success of his efforts to consolidate administrative control of national military parks and battlefields and national monuments, Horace Albright decided it was time to step aside as director of the National Park Service and accept one of the several offers he had received from the private sector. On July 5, 1933, he tendered his resignation to Secretary Ickes and became vice president, and later, president of the United States Potash Company.

On July 17, 1933, Ickes wrote the following:

My Dear Mr. Kelsey:

I have received your letter of July 11 and I am glad to have an expression of your good opinion of Mr. Cammerer. We have every confidence that he will maintain the high standards of the National Park Service.

I am sure that you know how much I appreciate your willingness to be of service and your unselfish interest in the success of the Nation Park Service.

Sincerely yours, Harold L. Ickes Secretary of the Interior.

Albright was replaced as director by Arno B. Cammerer, who had served as assistant director, then associate director since 1919. It would be up to the quiet, hardworking Cammerer to deal with the far-ranging impact of Executive Order 6166.

With all this effort on the Washington front, one might think Kelsey had given up the nursery business. Far from it. He had his hands full defending it as demand fell during the Depression, and competition increased. One source of competition was the state of Massachusetts itself as they started operating an extensive nursery to grow material for the use of roadside beautification. On January 13, 1933, Kelsey wrote Harris Reynolds of the Massachusetts Forestry Association, asking what the attitude of the Association was on the matter of states entering into competition with an industry which had all it could do to keep on its legs at that time. He argued that the state could actually buy their material cheaper than they could grow it. That is, what they did not collect from the wilds. And it would also be much more suitable material. He pointed to the state spending over $60,000 on its nursery out in Sudbury in a location which was really unfit to grow nursery stock. The state argued that the products of the state nurseries were not being sent out for ornamental purposes but strictly for forestry purposes. Kelsey's rejoinder went to the logic of the state's position, as he saw it:

> If this is to be the policy of the state then, there is no more reason why they shouldn't put up factories to manufacture clothing of all kinds and shoes for the use of every state employee and every dependent upon the state. They should go into road building in the same way and let out no more contracts to contractors—in other words, the state should cease purchasing any material whatever and go into the business of making everything that is used by the state for anyone in connection with the work of the state or who may be dependent on the state.

There is a trace of irony in Kelsey's distress. Here was a case of government intervention into the realm of private enterprise. Kelsey had no concern over such intervention when it was done for the good of the National Park Service. That was to benefit the public good. But here the state of Massachusetts felt that putting people to work for the state was in the public interest. It all depended on "whose ox was being gored."

The year 1933 marked the beginning of Roosevelt's New Deal. Wherever the private sector appeared ineffective in getting the economy moving again, a new government organization was quickly formed to put the government in charge of affairs—intervention on a grand scale. We can't possibly enumerate all of these new efforts of big government to solve the problems. Nor is it our purpose to examine their effectiveness. We will only look into those which had some effect on Kelsey and the areas of his interest. Each case individually was huge compared to the scope of the Massachusetts nursery intervention Kelsey was complaining about.

One of the first new federal organizations was within Secretary Ickes's Department of Interior. The Public Works Administration (PWA) left in its wake a great legacy of public structures, listed here in no particular order:

- Key West Causeway
- Grand Coulee, Boulder, and Bonneville Dams
- Triborough Bridge
- 70 percent of all new educational buildings in the US built in 1933–39
- Municipal buildings, sewage systems, port facilities, and hospitals

A scenic highway connecting the Shenandoah National Park to the Great Smoky National Park had been under discussion for years before the New Deal came along. Now, to the delight of the highway advocates, came Secretary Ickes's November 1933 decision to adopt the Blue Ridge Parkway as a PWA project.[144] Kelsey had little, if anything, to do with the early design and construction work on the parkway. It was later, during the late 1930s and '40s, when Kelsey entered the picture with his efforts to link the parkway to his proposed federal acquisition of Grandfather Mountain for National Park Service purposes. These efforts will be covered in great detail later where they fit into the chronology of the narrative.

As a PWA project, the parkway provided one good example of the New Deal preempting private enterprise, using the federal payroll to hire workers, and letting contracts to private contractors only under strict federal work relief rules. The Civilian Conservation Corps (CCC) had previously built early parts of the Skyline Drive in Virginia and was employed on several of the parkway's recreation and camping areas. The CCC boys earned one dollar a day and worked out of camps under "military-like" regimentation.[145]

"The CCC programs meant that funds were available in unprecedented amounts, so much of the parks development envisioned in master plans prepared during the Mather and Albright years were implemented in Cammerer's tenure. By one estimate, the NPS was able to advance park development as much as two decades beyond where it would have been without the New Deal emergency relief programs."[146]

As of 1935 PWA projects had "directly employed more that 2 million people while indirectly providing jobs for many others by stimulating demand for equipment and materials. Ickes estimated the total number of people benefiting from PWA expenditures by that time to have been nearly 10 million."[147] Kelsey's distress over the state of Massachusetts's venture into the nurseryman's realm appears as a fly-speck when contrasted with the government interventions that were unfolding under the New Deal.

National Parkways

Quoting NPS historians:

> The modern parkway idea, as it is understood in the United States today, had its origins in county and municipal undertakings such as Westchester County Parkway in New York built between 1913 and 1930. ... The increasing population of the country and its needs for outdoor travel made construction of scenic

highways or parkways highly desirable. While the Westchester County parkways were being constructed, Congress began to apply the "parkway" idea locally in the District of Columbia. Congress authorized its first parkway project in 1913—the four-mile Rock Creek and Potomac Parkway. ... Fifteen years later, May 23, 1928, Congress authorized construction of the Mount Vernon Memorial Highway (later renamed the George Washington Memorial Parkway) that would link the District of Columbia with Mount Vernon. ... The first Parkway to be built and administered by the Park Service and the first parkway to be authorized by Congress beyond the District of Columbia vicinity was the Colonial Parkway in Colonial National Monument.

A new era for national parkways began with Congressional authorization of the Blue Ridge and Natchez Trace parkways in the 1930s. Both parkways began as public works projects during the New Deal and were later transformed into units of the National Park System. ... NPS considered them as 'pioneers' in their respective fields of national recreational and historical motor travel. ... According to a Park Service pamphlet the national parkways were a new type of development in the park system consisting of an elongated park area devoted to recreation, which features a pleasure vehicle road through its entire length and is kept free of commercialism. ... The parkway was a road constructed in a manner that would protect, yet make available for public enjoyment the outstanding scenic and historic points of interest along the route. A particular aim of the parkways was to prevent the erection of billboards, signs, and other works that might mar or detract from the natural beauty along the roadway.[148]

While the Blue Ridge and Natchez Trace Parkways started construction, five other parkways proposals were surveyed and studied by the park service, while four others were recommended to the park service for consideration. One of the first five was the Green Mountain Parkway in Vermont, where $50,000 was granted for the investigation.

The Green Mountain Parkway is a great case study in how well-intended protagonists can be thwarted by clever distortions of the truth and stalling, in the self interest of antagonists. In this instance, the protagonists were Governor Wilson and the Chamber of Commerce of the State of Vermont who requested the reconnaissance survey, the National Park Service who provided the funding and oversight, and selected the engineers and landscape architects for the project, and Harlan P. Kelsey who served as the Appalachian Mountain Club's representative in the investigation. The antagonists were the Green Mountain Club (custodians of the Long Trail traversing the crests of the Green Mountains) and a dispersed group of individuals in New England who rallied to the support of the Green Mountain Club.

Our story starts with Kelsey's letter of March 7, 1934, to Arno Cammerer, director of the National Park Service. "As Chairman of the Legislative Committee of the Appalachian Mountain Club, I am getting a great many protests against the proposed Skyline Drive in the Green Mountains, in Vermont." He asked about the status of the survey work and whether they were making it a skyline road or going along the foothills as he hoped would be the case. "Should the government permit a skyline road along the crest of the Green Mountains or the Presidential Range in New Hampshire, an extremely loud roar will come from hundreds of nature lovers in New England."

In his April 2 reply, Cammerer tried to assuage Kelsey's concerns. "Two men eminent in this work and thoroughly familiar with the planning activities in the vicinity, have been appointed by this Service to study the situation. I refer to Mr. John Nolen of Cambridge, Massachusetts, selected as Consulting Landscape Architect, and Professor Laure D. Cox, of Syracuse University, as Resident Landscape Architect for the project. I can assure you that every consideration will be given to each possible route for the parkway."

When the parkway proposal had originally been disclosed, the Green Mountain Club was bombarded by the erroneous assumptions of alarmists. On June 14, 1934, W. M. Fay wrote to Secretary Ickes at the Interior Department to express the attitude of the Green Mountain Club in connection with the parkway. He pointed out that originally the club had entirely opposed the project on the grounds that the proposed route would, they were informed, "either obliterate the Long Trail or be so near to it that the Trail would lose its whole value as a unique and isolated mountain retreat." They feared a "discordant array of hot-dog stands, gasoline pumps cheap tourist camps and a trail of litter and rubbish that would desecrate some of the finest parts of the State."

However, since being informed that the parkway would be under the control of the National Park Service, they were assured such desecration would not be permitted. The highway surroundings would be protected and preserved in their natural state. The letter went on to say that the Long Trail could be relocated where the parkway impinged on it and "the Green Mountain Club is ready to plan such a relocation if the parkway is built here. We have been convinced that the construction of a Parkway will be for the best interests of the people of Vermont—temporarily for the relief of unemployment and permanently as a source of recreational attraction for the State. ... In any event our attitude is entirely co-operative. While we hope sincerely that the Parkway location will be changed, we are ready to take such steps as may be necessary to preserve the Trail for its original purposes wherever the road may be built. We also stand ready to consult with your engineers or other representatives wherever and whenever our counsel can be of any value."

The crux of the reconnaissance survey came down to an inspection trip sponsored by the engineers and landscape architects, July 18–21. They wanted all interested parties to actually witness on the ground the route and the scenic impact of the parkway. Cammerer made sure that W. M. Fay, president of the Green Mountain Club and Harlan Kelsey representing the Appalachian Mountain Club as potential antagonists, were both present. Cammerer had made it clear to John Nolan that without the support of these outdoorsmen it was unlikely the park service would go ahead with the project. He had too many other pressing demands to allow the service to get bogged down where there was not overwhelming support. Nolan had written Kelsey July 6 citing his pleasure at the prospect of having Kelsey come up to Vermont to go over the ground with them. "Nothing is settled, of course, and everyone connected with it wants to do the best thing, but as Walter Lippmann says in his column this morning, the wise settlement of nearly all problems consists in 'remembering several things at once.' The trouble about policies in a democracy comes from the fact that many people have in mind just one thing. You are not of that sort, and that's the reason I place high value upon your interest in this project."

On his return from the trip, Kelsey reported back to Dean Peabody, AMC president, July 24, 1934.

> "We had a strenuous trip of over 600 miles crossing back and forth through every gap in the Green Mountains and making side trips on roads of all types that would give us a complete picture of the Green Mountains from Massachusetts to above Mount Mansfield. I will send you a report in detail so soon as I can get a statement from Mr. Fay, from Mr. Nolan and from Governor Wilson of Vermont with whom we had an extended conference.
>
> I got a clear picture of the proposed plan and was surprised to find that my viewpoint which was very antagonistic, has entirely changed. I believe it is not only desirable for our club to not fight the project but we should heartily endorse it as it is the only way to make the Green Mountains really available for great numbers of people, and the wild areas are entirely protected. I will go into this in detail in my report."

The *New York Times*, August 2, 1934, headlined an article, "VERMONT SKYWAY WINS NEW FRIENDS. Opponents Who Feared for Mountains Are Given Assurance. Federal aid is sought. Survey Being Made and State Chamber Favors Its Construction." Buried within the article the newspaper countermanded its own skyway headline. "Mistakenly it was called at one time a plan for 'a skyline motor highway,' which it is not designed to be. The peaks of the Green Mountains would remain untouched and not 'desecrated.' It is intended to be for a part of its course a 'high highway,' running along the sides of many mountains and hills, perhaps alternating between their sunrise and sunset sides as opportunity offers, but dipping also into the valleys and taking advantage of scenic possibilities wherever they may appear, without impairing the solitude of many sites which Vermonters would not care to see disturbed."

It now seemed that the alarmists' reports had been put to rest and the parkway project could be judged on its merits. These merits were ably demonstrated in Kelsey's five-page report to the AMC dated September 24, 1934.

> The Parkway would in no way resemble the "skyline" route topping the crests of the mountains as found in the Shenandoah National Park. Rather it would be a "flank-line" route that for almost the entire distance would extend through forests and almost never, if at all be seen from the surrounding country. It would follow the foot-hills from which glorious views of the higher mountains and the lower terrain would be had, "as fine scenery in many respects as I have ever seen."
>
> Much of the wilderness of Vermont remained almost unused and was difficult of access, but this unfortunate condition would be entirely changed with the construction of the parkway. The mountains would become really accessible for recreation to the citizens of the state and the country at large without spoiling

them, making possible the use of this beautiful wilderness to thousands instead of to hundreds.

The greater part of the opposition to the Parkway was on account of the alleged spoiling of a portion of the Long Trail. Study of the route showed this to have little or no basis, but would really be of great value to the Trail providing many reasonable points of access which it did not then have. There were very few points where the Parkway clashed with the Trail and where this was so, a relocation of the Trail would be of advantage to it. The State had agreed to rebuild the Trail on approved routes in those few instances.

The Parkway would protect the wilderness from fire and provide a beautifully maintained park strip under National Park standards almost the entire length of the State. More than 25,000 acres or approximately 40 square miles of National Park would be saved from the lumberman's axe.

It was true that with this Parkway more people would use the wilderness but the true lover of the wilderness must not be too selfish and had a real duty to perform in both bringing the wilderness to the people and the people to the wilderness, if that same wilderness could be fully protected in its wildness as he believed it would be.

In his conclusion Kelsey pointed out that the parkway would become a forerunner of similar national parkways throughout the country. They must keep in mind not only the rights but the needs of the great masses of people who were coming more and more to enjoy nature and help to introduce them to a higher type of outdoor recreation. The AMC had a duty to perform in not taking merely a negative position but should actively advocate the construction of the proposed national parkway. Opposition by the AMC and the Green Mountain Club would undoubtedly kill the project while strong work in favor of it might bring about its construction. At least if anyone took a position in opposition they should only do so after a careful investigation directly on the ground.

On September 25 John Nolan wrote Kelsey, "You have rendered a public service, and you have done it clearly and gracefully ... This report of yours, I believe, will become a classic in the discussion of the parkway idea, which is one of the big new park ideas for future understanding and application." On October 6 Arno Cammerer wrote, "Dear Kel, ... It is a marvelous report, and don't see how it could be bettered. What more can I say."

On September 18, while Kelsey was putting the finishing touches on his report, he received a letter from W. M. Fay, Green Mountain Club president. "You may have already seen from the newspaper reports that the Green Mountain Club trustees voted not to reconsider their original motion of 'unalterable opposition' against the Green Mountain Parkway." He hoped the Appalachian Mountain Club would do likewise. He advised Kelsey that the trustees were working on a counterplan to present to the state planning board, "It is one which we believe has none of the disadvantages and many of the advantages of the Parkway." As soon as it was done they would provide the details of it. No target date was given.

In Kelsey's September 26 cover letter for his report, he remarked to Governor Wilson, "The vacillating policy of the Green Mountain Club is something I cannot understand. This National Parkway is truly a matter of national importance far transcending state or local implications. I am disappointed that the Green Mountain Club has taken such a strong stand in opposition, particularly as Mr. Fay clearly indicated to me that he was heartily in favor of it, after we had made this inspection trip together. However, anyone has a right to change their opinion."

Now began a flurry of letters between Kelsey and a Mr. Fred H. Tucker, of Newton, Massachusetts. Tucker wrote as though he was either a trustee or, if not, at least an appointed emissary for the Green Mountain Club. In his September 25 letter, Tucker said, "At one time the proponents of the scheme [note: it's now called a scheme] almost convinced the trustees that such a highway would not harm either the state or the Long Trail, but the more we looked into the matter, the more we became convinced that it would be a great misfortune to the state of Vermont and to the Long Trail as well if this project were put through in any of the forms proposed. … Personally I feel that it would be a crime to put this Parkway through the state of Vermont as it would spoil the unique beauty and wholesome atmosphere we all love."

Kelsey responded with, "The time has come when we must perhaps give up a little of our excessive zeal and special privileges and be willing to share with others and teach others to share with us, these things we love so much." He enclosed a copy of his report to the AMC. Tucker to Kelsey, "You have placed before me many facts that I am interested to know and I shall watch with interest the ultimate conclusion of this question." Kelsey to Tucker, "When it comes to a show-down, those in opposition, as well as those for the project, must have their arguments and evidence clear-cut and unassailable. Is the Green Mountain Club in a position to do this without viewing the matter from a rather narrow, selfish standpoint?" Finally Tucker to Kelsey, October 3, "We are opposed to it much more because we believe that it will injure the state as a whole, than because it would injure the Long Trail."

In reviewing all of the many letters from Fay and Tucker, there is never a concrete piece of evidence ever offered to support their opposition. They always spoke in glittering generalities, such as "injure the state as a whole." In the September issue of the *Long Trail News*, the club included the following under the title, "A Compliment":

At the trustees' meeting a letter from Gov. Wilson, an ardent partisan of the parkway, was read, in reply to an invitation to him to attend the meeting. In this he said that he could see no good reason for his attendance, that if the Green Mountain Club was determined to wreck the parkway project he did not desire to be present at the wrecking. This acknowledgment that the Club has the power to wreck this plan, coming from such a source, is indeed a compliment. The Club has the disposition to accomplish this wrecking, and to make a complete and thorough job of it, and if it also has the power, there is no question as to the result.

Another item in the *Long Trail News* was titled, "Opinions on the Parkway," with extracts from some of the letters received from club members. Following are two representative excerpts that were published, showing the broad strokes used to demonize the parkway.

"I am against this proposed Parkway. Vermont is one of the few and ever fewer places where one may get away from the hellbent tourist menace. This Parkway will 'sophisticate' the natural charm and beauty and splendid isolation of our mountains, and provide just another picture postcard for empty headed sightseers, who sightsee at sixty miles an hour in closed cars."

"Vermont has a great future as a residence region ... I mean a place of residence for high-grade well-to-do people ... There is no other place for them in this part of the world. The White Mountains and the Adirondacks have both been vulgarized and spoiled. The high valleys of Vermont are the last refuge. ... The Parkway would pierce these valleys, even in the most idealized representation of its plans, with the honking of automobile horns and the roar of the through traffic to Canada. It is inconceivable that this move, if carried out, should do other than practically knock in the head this great source of building up Vermont."

On reviewing all eighteen members' comments included in the *Trail News*, it is evident that the members were totally unacquainted with the facts concerning the parkway. The trustees had done nothing to provide those facts; in fact it appears the members were being used in a propaganda effort. The Green Mountain Parkway plans were not dissimilar to the Blue Ridge Parkway in terms of the roadbed (not route). Anyone who has traveled the Blue Ridge Parkway would laugh at the depiction of "honking of automobile horns and the roar of through traffic."

Not explicitly stated above, but underlying the negative attitudes, were some broad general feelings. One was that businesses in small local communities might suffer if the parkway drained business northward, bypassing them. Another was the thought of a wide national park dividing the state along the Green Mountains from Massachusetts to Canada, not under state control. This didn't sit well with a wide range of Vermonters.

Another telling move by the trustees (clever strategy?) was to declare they were working on a counterplan, with no time horizon set on its release. AMC president Dean Peabody wrote to Governor Wilson on October 15. "In accordance with my promise of October 3, I am writing you of the action of the Council of the Appalachian Mountain Club in regard to the proposed Green Mountain National Parkway. Mr. Kelsey's report to us was very full and well received by the Council. Included in it was a letter from Mr. W. M. Fay, President of the Green Mountain Club, mentioning a counterplan to be submitted by this club. Our Council is very anxious to obtain maps showing in detail the layout proposed for the Parkway so that relative merits of the plans can be studied. Until these are received the Council withholds any action."

On October 26 Kelsey wrote to Cammerer, "I want you to understand that the Council of the Appalachian Mountain Club is hard to convince and apparently most of them had made their minds up against the parkway. My report came as a sort of bombshell and I really believe that in the end they will decide in favor."

On November 10 Kelsey wrote to Dean Peabody at the AMC. "By this time you have received the special map made for us by the National Park Service showing practically the entire flagged line of the Green Mountain Parkway together with the extension for which a reconnaissance has been made almost the entire distance of the proposed parkway. This will demonstrate the reasons which I gave for my viewpoint. ... It is now a long time since President Fay promised to submit an alternative proposition but I have had no word from him."

On November 16 the AMC advised Kelsey that the NPS map clearly demonstrated that Kelsey was right in describing the parkway as a "flank-line," not "skyline" road, but now they wanted further information about the northern end of the parkway and, in particular, its direction in the region of Mount Mansfield. This was beginning to look endless. The fact that the AMC Council didn't rely on Kelsey's conclusions might have been honest due diligence but could also suggest some collusive delay along with the GMC.

Kelsey to Fay, November 10. "The alternative proposal to the Green Mountain Parkway which you said would be forthcoming many weeks ago has failed to put in an appearance." Fay to Kelsey November 14. "The seeming delay has been caused by the necessity of making several trips around the state to study certain parts of the proposal and of course, these trips have had to be worked in when it was convenient and possible for the committee to make them. We had not ourselves felt that this was a delay as we did not intend to present the proposal to the Vermont State Planning Board and to the public until the very last of the year; in other words, just previous to the exit of the present state administration. You will or course, realize the reason for this." Whether intentional or not, the delay of the counterproposal was taking on the appearance of "stonewalling" the issue. Perhaps to gain more time to cultivate a broader opposition to the parkway?

On November 22 Fay sent a draft of the counterproposal to Kelsey asking that he keep it confidential, except for discussions within the AMC. "This as you will see is not the final proposal. It needs considerably more study and elaboration." More delay?

The proposal was titled, "Vermont Hillside Highways." In the opening paragraph it said it was "a plan for all-Vermont progress." The plan itself was essentially a proposal to promote more summer home development. It would do this by improving old highways that reach into upland regions and by building new, short, dead-end roads, with much of the actual construction to be done as home sites were sold. The vast bulk of the plan was taken with flowery descriptions of the benefits, and why it would avoid all the evils that might threaten the unique charm, beauty and simplicity of Vermont. Who would pay? Let the federal authorities allocate the money under the National Recovery Act. It had all the earmarks of a complete red herring.

Governor Wilson had asked for copies of Kelsey's report for wide circulation in Vermont, but was refused by the Appalachian Mountain Club until they had reached a conclusion on their recommendation. Accordingly the best instrument available to the proponents for public information was denied them. Meanwhile Kelsey began getting letters from some of the AMC's most notable members expressing their concerns over the Parkway. One came from Allen Chamberlain, his old mentor of the Weeks Act days. Also one from Robert L. M. Underhill, the American who pioneered technical mountain climbing techniques in the United States.

As the new year dawned, both Governor Wilson and President Peabody of the AMC were being replaced by their successors. On January 19, 1935, Kelsey wrote to John B. May, the new AMC president. "We must not let the Green Mountain Club, which is a very small club numerically, determine our attitude in this matter. If the people of Vermont view the matter differently, it should have due weight. Also once Governor Wilson was strongly in favor of the Green Mountain Parkway. Moreover, despite the pronouncement of the Green Mountain Club Trustees, it is a national and not a local matter. These trustees are assuming somewhat the attitude of some of the western states, which have occasionally protested the establishment of a national park, because it took away some local grazing, water right, or other feature which they claimed belonged to the state. Broadly, if any project is of intense use to the nation at large, a state should not be allowed to block it. Similarly if a state wants to put across a project for the whole state, a county or town has no right to block it."

The whole affair finally went beyond the parochial interests of the local mountaineers and the park people. It evolved into a statewide referendum by 1936. First, on December 14, 1935, Act 17 of the 1935 Special Session approved a national park known as the Green Mountain Parkway, established jurisdiction over the park and appropriated money to begin the project. Next, on March 3, 1936, voters statewide were asked to choose between effective dates of April 1, 1936 (a yes vote), or April 1, 1941 (a no vote). After a particularly emotional public debate the voters, by an 11,421 margin, voted no, 42,318 to 30,897. Since the voters had selected the later effective date, the 1937 legislature, through Act 243 (passed February 5, 1937), repealed the Green Mountain Parkway Act. The voters statewide had spoken.[149] In the end, Kelsey would certainly have approved the process, even if not the result.

While the parkway died in 1937, the myth lives on that hearty Vermonters rejected the dreaded Skyline Highway across the very peaks of the Green Mountains that would have wiped out the Long Trail. Any rational discourse on the facts totally blows away the myth. But the myth lives on to support more recent causes that have a similarity to the parkway issue. The *Burlington Free Press*, February 24, 2005, reads:

Vermont – For one state lawmaker, the debate about wind turbines on Vermont's ridgelines is reminiscent of a Depression-era scheme to build a highway along the spine of the state's highest peaks, The Green Mountain Parkway, which was defeated in a statewide referendum in 1936 would have stretched 260 miles from Massachusetts to the Canadian border—*and ruined our ridgelines.* [Italics added for emphasis.]

Returning to the actual case, we see the fulfillment of a change that had been taking place in Harlan P. Kelsey's stance as a preservationist. Early on he had come down firmly on preserving the natural primeval forest and rejecting incursions such as roads. Foot paths, even horse trails, yes. Roads and automobiles, assuredly no. It was Horace Albright who challenged him on the issue of ridgeline roads in the Smokies, abandoning a hardy elite few of the people, to provide for large masses of people who would otherwise miss Robert Lindsay Mason's "vast canvas; a living painting vibrating with the mystery of color blending" from the summits. Kelsey's legacy was now fully formed in his statement, "The time has come when we must perhaps give up a little of our excessive zeal and special privileges and be willing to share with others and teach others to share with us, these things we love so much." There was a real duty to perform in both bringing the wilderness to the people and the people to the wilderness, if that same wilderness could be fully protected in its wildness as Kelsey believed it would be.

Presidential Range Skyline Road

Superimposed on the Green Mountain activity was another "dust-up" over in New Hampshire's White Mountains. While independent, it was the personification of the myth that so distorted the evaluation of the Green Mountain Parkway. As such it may have rattled the judgment of the AMC Council as they considered the Vermont proposition. As for Kelsey, his position in New Hampshire was properly the exact opposite of his stance in Vermont.

On August 25, 1934, the Randolph Mountain Club's President, R. Ammi Cutter, wrote to John G. Winant, governor of New Hampshire. The following excerpt from his letter gives a precise description of what was going on:

> The club unanimously voted to oppose the project advanced by Colonel Barron, operator of the Crawford House, for a so-called "sky line" highway from the Crawford House over the peaks of the Mt. Washington Range to the Ravine House in Randolph.
>
> As you, of course, know, a survey of a route for the proposed highway has been in progress during the past two months under the direction of Mr. Bowker of the State Highway Department. A line has been marked upon the mountains starting at Crawford's, circling up Mt. Clinton to Mizpah Spring, then following the Crawford Path over or near the summits of Mt. Franklin, Mt. Pleasant and Mt. Monroe, past the Lakes of the Clouds to the west side of the cone of Mt. Washington; thence running along or near the present Gulfside Trail over the Northern Peaks to Star Lake near the Madison Huts; thence continuing around the cone of Mt. Madison and down to the Ravine House in Randolph, in part following the routes of two of the principal footpaths up the northern slopes of Mt. Madison and Mt. Adams. The route thus tentatively outlined will necessarily displace two of the principal trails through the mountains and will involve the introduction of motor cars into the spots now most sought by trampers.
>
> ... We would appreciate greatly an opportunity to examine well in advance of any public hearing copies of all reports submitted by the engineers with respect to the project. We have no doubt that the United States Forest Service, the New England Trail Conference, the Society for the Protection of the

New Hampshire Forests, and the Appalachian Mountain Club would like to have the same opportunity.

On September 13 Kelsey, as chairman for the Committee on Legislation AMC, joined the fray, with his own letter to Governor Winant:

> On behalf of the Appalachian Mountain Club, I wish to get the fullest information on the present status of a proposed sky-line route to be built across the Presidential Range. ... The proposed National Parkway in the Green Mountains is an entirely different type of proposition. For the most part it will follow the foot-hills and where it is on higher levels it will be concealed in woods and will cause no disfigurement of the Green Mountains as seen from near at hand or at a distance.
>
> If I understand the route proposed for the White Mountain sky-line highway, it would cause an irremediable gash along the mountain sides above sky-line [he meant tree-line] which would be impossible to so camouflage as to make it even reasonably permissible from any standpoint. It is probable that 99% of the membership of our Club of about 4,500 members—many of whom are citizens of New Hampshire—will be unalterably opposed to such a highway. I can think of nothing that would damage so much, the future prospects for New Hampshire as a desirable summer resort, as the construction of such a highway which would be inexcusable from any standpoint whatsoever.

R. Ammi Cutter wrote Kelsey September 27, "I am very much obliged to you for the copy of your letter to Governor Winant dated September 13th. Placing the Appalachian Mountain Club on record so firmly as opposed to the Sky Line Highway will be exceedingly helpful. ... There is to be a discussion of the plan before the New Hampshire State Development Commission at Peckett's Coppermine Camp on Mt. Cannon on October 6th. Mr. Ayres and I hope to attend (if invited) and we shall appreciate having the benefit of your advice and suggestions prior to the meeting."

By October the opposition forces were being mobilized. The October 27 the *Plymouth Record* newspaper carried a long article by R. Ammi Cutter, headlined "Some Objectons to the Sky Line Highway." It was well organized, thorough, and fact filled. Its organization followed the following subtitles:

1) The Route Surveyed
2) Damage to the Area above Timberline
3) Tourists Can Reach the Area above Timberline by the Existing Carriage Road and Railway
4) An Economic Asset of Northern New Hampshire Threatened
5) The Opposition
6) The Need of Careful Planning and Study

State Highway Commissioner Everett submitted to the governor and council a preliminary report indicating that the project would cost $2,500,000. He also estimated an annual expenditure of $1,000 per mile for each of the twenty-five miles. Meteorological observations indicated that during the four months from June to October the use of the road would be limited to an average of eighteen and a half days per month. The whole matter had been referred by the governor and council to the new administration which would take office on January 3, 1935. Kelsey wrote Philip W. Ayres of the Society for Protection of New Hampshire Forests, "This report would seem to show up the project as a crazy undertaking, entirely outside of its objectionable features as a skyline road. For the original cost with the cost of maintenance and comparatively little use would seem to make it not worth a candle."

By March 4, 1935, a thorough twenty-one-page report was submitted to the Planning Board of the state of New Hampshire on behalf of the Randolph Mountain Club and the Appalachian Mountain Club. It closed with the statement, "It cannot be emphasized too strongly that any concession to the proponents of the scheme which involves road construction on the main range is a sacrifice of the public interest in the National Forest. It is to be hoped that neither any portion of the route surveyed in the summer of 1934 nor any alternative will be constructed on the Mt. Washington Range itself."

Nothing much seemed to happen after that. The National Forest Service had been silent all during the period the issue was under study and discussion. Without their approval, of course, nothing could be done within the boundaries of the White Mountain National Forest, including the Mount Washington range. Let us just assume they quietly informed the state officers their approval would not be forthcoming. The whole matter quietly receded and died.

Old Derby Wharf

We noted earlier that in the mid-1920s, Kelsey must have been suffering from "temporary insanity." He had allowed himself to become involved in four intense activities at once. On top of operating a business he simultaneously spearheaded the publishing of *Standardized Plant Names*, served two terms as president of the American Nurserymen's Association, and worked intensely as a member of the Southern Appalachian National Park Commission. Each and every endeavor was a tribute to his vision and energy. Ten years later, in the mid-1930s, he did it again. We have just seen him struggling with his nursery business in the most trying of times, working to achieve a "classic in the discussion of the parkway idea" in promoting the Green Mountain Parkway, and battling efforts to desecrate the high peaks of the White Mountains with an ill-advised summit road. All this was jammed together in 1934–36. Now, concurrently he undertook an even more demanding project—saving old Derby Wharf in Salem. While the other endeavors involved other major players, Derby Wharf was all Kelsey; there were no other driving forces, only Kelsey.

It was a hugely successful venture, and Kelsey was extremely grateful to people who responded to his efforts. Nothing shows his gratitude and intense feelings about the project better than this letter to Mrs. Benjamin D. Shreve, of Salem, June 20, 1936:

> Dear Kate: As a principal contributor to Derby Wharf Fund, you will be glad to know that last Tuesday Governor Curley signed the Derby Wharf Bill, providing for the cooperation of the State in purchasing the surrounding property as required by the National Park Service, thus assuring the project.
>
> When everything looked so discouraging and practically all hope fled of saving Derby Wharf, it was you who subscribed so handsomely, giving me such encouragement that together with all of our friends, we have gone through and made the project a success.
>
> You should feel very proud of the part you have played in Derby Wharf and now I am writing to cordially thank you for what you did in the hour of greatest need. Sometime before too long I hope that the list of donors (which is a very small one) will be published and that some appropriate record will be made of those whose cooperation and liberality made Derby Wharf possible for Salem and the State of Massachusetts as well as for the whole country at large.
>
> Certainly it might well be said that "you did it" for if you had not encouraged me that evening with your wonderful offer I certainly would not have had the courage to go on with this project. So, my dear Kate, you should always have great satisfaction in the knowledge that you were so largely responsible in putting across the finest historic project we have in Salem. Tell Ben I also appreciate his—what shall I call it—his hearty acquiescence. With much love to you both.

Yours sincerely,   Harlan P. Kelsey

What was Old Derby Wharf? Perhaps the description by James Duncan Phillips, in his January 28, 1936, letter to the chairman of the Committee on Harbors & Public Lands, is as concise and apt as one will find:

> There is no more historic spot connected with American commerce than Derby Wharf. When Salem was the chief port for the trade with India and China, this wharf was owned by Elias Haskett Derby, who when he died in 1800 was the richest man in the United States except George Washington. Mr. Derby was a man of most exceptional ability. As a stern patriot, he equipped and sent out many of the privateers which enabled this people to win the war of the Revolution. Almost one third of the Massachusetts privateers sailed from Salem, and Massachusetts sent out about as many as all the other colonies combined.
>
> As soon as the war closed, Mr. Derby reached right out for the trade of the world. Six months after the treaty of peace his bark "Light Horse" displayed the first American flag in the Baltic and began American trade with St. Petersburg. In 1785 his ship "Grand Turk" rounded the Cape of Good Hope and steered away for Batavia and Canton. She opened American trade with China so that in 1789 there were fifteen American vessels in Canton, of which five came from Salem and four belonged to Mr. Derby. In 1788 his ship "Atlantic" carried the American flag for the first time into Surat, Bombay and Calcutta. A few years later his ship "Astrea" began American trade with Manila. This was a wonderful record for one merchant, and many of these famous ships have tied up at Derby Wharf.
>
> For nearly half a century the old warehouses on Derby Wharf were filled with teas and silk, pepper and spices, ivory and all the other choice rare products of the Orient. The wharf reeked

with the odor of sandal wood and the strong pungent spices of the Far East. Shy Indian boys in turbans and China boys with pigtails serving as stewards on the merchant ships would be seen running about. Derby Wharf is more typical of the India and China trade than any spot in America.

Near the head of the Wharf stands the famous custom house, a beautiful example of America's most beautiful architectural period. There Hawthorne wrote 'The Scarlet Letter'. A few yards east of it stands the lovely little brick house that Captain Richard Derby built for Elias Haskett Derby when he was married. It is a rare and beautiful little home of colonial days—in external appearance a miniature of Massachusetts Hall at Harvard.

Taken all in all, there could be no fuller memorial of the wonderful commercial expansion of the early days of the republic than Derby Wharf and its surroundings.

Derby Wharf extended as a long finger 1,850 feet into the harbor (six football fields laid end to end). Central Wharf ran parallel to Derby Wharf but was only a third as long. Because of total neglect and the absence of any substantial shipping since a century earlier, the sea walls of Derby Wharf had been severely damaged by tidal action and therefore would require extensive rebuilding. The highest grade at the time was 12.5 feet above mean low tide. In places the pier was constructed of cribbing, and in many of these places it had washed out to a grade of approximately 7 or 8 feet. Central Wharf, lined on both sides with wooden planks supported by fender piles and filled in the center with earth, had been badly washed and would have to be completely reconstructed.

In early 1934 Kelsey was promoting a plan for the rehabilitation of Derby Street and the environs of Derby Wharf. The April 6, 1934, Salem Evening *News* called it a "waterfront park and recreation area. ...

Acquisition of Derby Wharf would mean preservation of historic landmark and needed recreation spot in crowded area." The project would fill numerous needs of the city including a municipal landing, nautical and aquatic activities, general recreation, fishing, and preservation of Salem's most prominent historical landmark in maritime history. It would relieve the strain on the Common, which was a constant social problem, and it would provide a practical and diversified recreation area for the most congested district of the city.

Hearings had been held, and J. A. Pitman of the State Teachers College at Salem advised Kelsey, "Notwithstanding our favorable impression of the hearing, the Mayor expresses the opinion that nothing will come of it. He says 'He knows the crowd.' I wonder whether his personal attitude toward the project has colored his views." Kelsey replied, "I am not surprised at your last paragraph. Political expediency after all is the guiding motive in improvements in Salem, as well as probably all other American communities. I might tell you frankly, however, that I am intensely disappointed in both your attitude and that of the planning board as regards Derby Wharf. That is distinctly a matter which should not be left to an individual to put across. If the people of Salem don't want it, I am perfectly ready to drop the matter. I have already spent more time and energy on it than I could well afford. A live planning board could put this thing across. Also, if there was a live Chamber of Commerce, a Rotary Club, and a Kiwanis Club that would join in saving the most priceless thing in Salem, it would have been completed by this time; I have my doubts if any one of the organizations named would have a majority to vote in favor of it. ... I might devote the rest of my life forcing a camel through a needle's eye, but certainly it isn't worth the effort." There also was a bill which was reported favorably in the Massachusetts legislature to take Derby Wharf as a state park, but Kelsey saw little likelihood of its getting by the Ways and Means Committee.

By early 1935 Kelsey came up with a different plan, not dependent on Salem's political class. On March 16, 1935, he wrote Arno Cammerer at the National Park Service, "What I am writing about is something I wrote you about before, namely, Derby Wharf in Salem. I can hardly wait to get your reaction to my proposition, and now I want to add to it that there is an opportunity of buying up some contiguous land and old docks at a very low price and making a real park out of it, and then having the old Salem Custom House added to the picture and come under your jurisdiction. A wonderful museum could be made out of it devoted to Hawthorne, early Custom House affairs in Salem, and a complete collection of the shipping paraphernalia of the older times when Derby Wharf was the chief landing place of American shipping. ... Remember that I have an option on the property and the money to buy it and give it to whoever will preserve it. It can be restored for fifty or sixty thousand dollars. That is the minimum for saving it from destruction and making it available."

The option to buy was from the trustees of the Massachusetts Street Railway Company, who extended it month after month pending the payment of $7,500 for sale of Derby Wharf to the City of Salem Public Property Department. By June 22, 1935, the sum of $300 had actually been paid. Kelsey was gradually raising the funds by subscription among interested residents and descendants of Salem families to secure the purchase of the Wharf. These were the donors Kelsey was referring to in his letter to Kate Shreve, quoted earlier.

The Salem Custom House was owned by the US Treasury Service, as it had been since the government first started levying customs taxes on imported goods coming through Salem. Its acquisition could be arranged on an interagency transfer, but someone would have to get that started. Another key building at the foot of the wharf was the old Derby House. An architectural gem, it was owned by the Society for the Preservation of New England Antiquities (SPNEA). They would have to be convinced that their preservation efforts would be fulfilled appropriately by the National Park Service and be willing to give up the old building. Directly on the waterfront was another key building that housed the very active Home for Aged Women. Would they sell? Where would they go? Beyond these key houses were perhaps fifteen or more buildings that would lie within the bounds of any historic park area. Who would acquire these for use or removal? Finally there were all the political jurisdictions that would be involved in authorizing and funding the acquisition of all needed properties and granting them outright to the National Park Service. Only then would the NPS be able to start work to restore the site.

There was no one but Kelsey to get the ball rolling and see all this through to completion. It was his vision and now it would be his responsibility. Before he started, Kelsey had to be sure that the park service was willing and able to accept a grant and create the historic site. Kelsey knew that within the park service, the climate was excellent for such an event. Since the day discussions had begun about creating the National Park Service in 1915, Horace Albright had favored the transfer of historic sites from the War Department to the NPS. It took eighteen years before Executive Order 6166 accomplished it. That was eighteen years for Albright to perfect his interest in preserving historic sites. Around 1930 Albright had employed Dr. Verne E. Chatelain as the first historian at the NPS, for historical research, interpretation, and report writing. If there was to be a problem it would lie within the US Congress's approval process. But even that was moving Kelsey's way. There was a bill before Congress authorizing the National Park Service to make an investigation throughout the country and save the matters of national historical interest and develop them as national historical parks. It only needed to pass.

In early April 1935 Verne Chatelain did come to Salem for a thorough review of the Derby Wharf site. On April 25 Cammerer wrote Kelsey, "Our historical study and Mr. Chatelain's field investigation indicated that Derby Wharf has definite national historical interest and that the area could be suitably developed." Chatelain did recommend that NPS wait until the pending legislation, S. 2073 and H.R. 6670, was passed and signed into law. Kelsey also made sure that A. Piatt Andrew, Salem's elected congressman to the US House of Representatives, was on board with everything and was favorably disposed. On the federal level things were well in order, leaving only the state and local authorities to provide resources for acquisition of the properties. At all levels Kelsey knew he would need persuasive evidence. This he started to accumulate, working with historian James Duncan Phillips of the Houghton Mifflin Company and Mr. Howard Corning of Salem's Essex Institute.

In early May, Congressman Andrew asked Kelsey about activity in the Massachusetts Legislature for a competing bill to "restore Derby Wharf to future service as a memorial park and playground under state jurisdiction." Kelsey answered saying, it "did pass the committee on the Harbors and Lands, mainly I think as a matter of courtesy to [the Salem legislator]. There isn't one chance in a thousand I understand of its passing the Ways and Means Committee. Nobody in Salem takes the bill seriously except the single proponent. I am working to secure other wharves as well as the Old Derby House to put into the project. The main thing so far as I am concerned is to get the Derby Wharf property itself purchased and deeded to the National Government. I always fear something coming in to intervene and as you know I have my option renewed only from month to month. Have you any idea when the bills now pending in Congress will be acted upon?"

By the spring of 1935, Kelsey was so deep into the Derby Wharf project that he couldn't back out. Yet it was becoming clear that the tangled web of so many different items to be resolved, and so many interested parties, would be almost overwhelming. It was a "chicken and egg" situation. Who would commit first? After you, Alphonse. Perhaps it may help to list them:

Items	Parties
1. Federal Legislation	1. US Congress
2. Derby Wharf	2. Massachusetts Street Railway Company
3. Custom House	3. US Treasury Department
4. Old Derby House	4. SPNEA
5. Home for Aged Women	5. Board of Directors—H. A. W.
6. State $50,000	6. Massachusetts Legislature
7. Other Waterfront Properties	7. Mayor Bates

Some of the parties were beyond Kelsey's reach, such as Congress and the Treasury Department. They were best left in the hands of his friends at the park service. Massachusetts Street Railway was dependent on Kelsey's private contributors who were dependent on assurance of the state funding. SPNEA was dependent on their board and resolving the liabilities burdening their Derby House title. Winning the HAW Board was dependent on their confidence that their wharf and view directly in front of their building would be protected by the park service. Mayor Barnes couldn't move without the state's $50,000 and the appraisals or negotiations of all the properties within the minimum boundaries of the historical site. The Massachusetts Legislature was dependent on reports from the underlying legislative committees. Finally there was the torturous path of the deeds flowing from the various parties to the city of Salem and thence to the Department of Interior. Kelsey had to keep all of these balls in the air and hope that none of them dropped.

First, the Congress. Approved, August 21, 1935. *"Be it enacted by the Senate and House of Representatives of the United States of America in Congress assembled,* That it is hereby declared that it is a national policy to preserve for public use historic sites, buildings and objects of national significance for the inspiration and benefit of the people of the United States. … The Secretary of the Interior (hereinafter referred to as the Secretary), through the National Park Service, for the purpose of effectuating the policy expressed in section 1 hereof, shall have the following powers and perform the following duties and functions: ..." Thus the NPS and Director Cammerer were now free to act, without additional acts of Congress, to identify and create National Historic Sites, with the Salem Maritime National Historic Site being the very first such site under the new law. Verne Chatelain wrote Kelsey December 11, 1936, "I wish to advise you that the Secretary of the Interior approved on December 9, the plan for the proposed Derby Wharf National Historic Site project."

Next, the Treasury Department. It appears Congress would also have to approve this detail for transferring the Custom House from Treasury to Interior. The actual bill was initiated by A. Piatt Andrews, Salem's congressman (H.R. 10934). It fell to him to nurse the bill through all the various committee approvals and obtain approval from all the different Treasury officials. On March 10, 1936, Andrews wrote Kelsey, "Some of these officials have been rather hesitant to release their hold upon the public building until they can be sure that space can be found to house the obviously minor activities now carried on in the old building." Kelsey replied March 13, "I have visited the collector of customs there a number of times and all the business of the Department could be done in one or two rooms at most." On April 10 the Treasury reported that if suitable space was provided in the post office building for the accommodation of the customs service, the Treasury Department had no objection to the bill. On April 22 Andrews advised Kelsey the House Committee on Public Buildings and Grounds voted to favorably report the bill, and that a companion bill had been introduced in the Senate. On May 4 the bill passed the House. On June 4 Kelsey advised Cammerer the Senate had passed it. By the end of June the bill became law and the Custom House matter was settled.

Next, the Old Derby House and SPNEA. In early summer 1935 Kelsey had approached William C. Endicott, president of SPNEA with the proposition of turning over to NPS the Old Derby House and its land. Kelsey fully briefed him on the many fiscal and property donations being made by others on behalf of the project. On August 5 Endicott replied that the trustees were unanimously in favor of the transfer as "the proper thing to do." He closed his letter with, "I am very much excited at this prospect and I congratulate you very much upon the possibility of having your dream realized." There was a sticking point, however. There was a $5,000 mortgage on the house with the house as collateral. If the house were given to the federal government, Naumkeag Trust would immediately call the note for full payment, and SPNEA didn't have the needed funds in hand. A lesser problem was that SPNEA didn't trust the government as custodian and expected to continue in that role.

For the remainder of the year it seemed like each party was waiting for the other to relax its position. In a series of letters Kelsey vouched for the NPS as the very best custodian anyone could wish for (not the case with other bureaus). He pointed out that under the law, NPS could not accept any encumbered property and that the Derby House would have to be transferred free and clear. SPNEA then tried to get Kelsey to generate funding from the state and city of Salem to retire the mortgage for them. By year end they were proposing that their Boston congressman might submit a bill through Congress to legally allow the government to retire the mortgage. None of these "wiggles" went anywhere. Finally SPNEA blinked. On January 8, 1936, the trustees voted to transfer title outright, and authorized the treasurer of the society to pay off the full mortgage "using his discretion as to the manner in which it shall be paid."

SPNEA finally initiated a funds drive of their own but continued to grumble about why the government should treat a charitable organization more favorably than they had. On February 26 Kelsey wrote Arno Cammerer, "In the enclosed copy of my reply to Mr. Appleton, I have tried to disabuse his mind of some of his preconceived notions of government. This Yankee type is very amusing. They are in constant communication with God and only occasionally deign to communicate with the hoipolloi who exist out of the inner circle of the elect in Boston. Naturally this letter is for your eyes alone." On April 6 Mr.

Appleton advised Kelsey that they had raised $2,555, leaving $2,445 to go, without yet having started to solicit in Salem. On July 1 Kelsey wrote Mr. Appleton, "Thank you for your letter of June 29 and I am very glad that it is arranged to have the deed properly made out to the Government for the Old Derby House." He then advised him that because of the nuances of wording in the congressional act, the deed would have to be routed first to Salem and then passed from Salem to the NPS, whose Boston representative would soon be in touch with the details. Now the Derby House was resolved.

Next, the Home for Aged Women. The main HAW building lay just outside of the maximum boundary required by the Park Service. Their waterfront land and wharf, however, was the necessary connection through to Central Wharf, and vital to the overall project. The HAW Board's concern was to protect the view out over the harbor afforded to the HAW residents. The Board wanted deed restrictions for assuring such protection. J. Asbury Pitman, president of the State Teachers College at Salem, was Kelsey's contact on the HAW Board. Pitman wrote Kelsey August 28, 1935, as follows:

> Your letter of the 23rd has reached me here. I expect to return to Salem next Friday. Possibly we may have an opportunity to discuss the present situation in regard to the proposed Derby Wharf project before the next meeting of the Board of Managers of the Home for Aged Women. What their attitude will be is somewhat problematical, but I feel confident that the comprehensive plan that you and Director Cammerer have developed will ultimately appeal to them favorably. Joe Gifford, Harry Batchelder, Christian Lantz and Chapple are all influential members of the Board and men with whom it would be well for you to present the plan when you can see them. Possibly it may be practicable for you and Cammerer if he can be in Salem at some time when I can get the Board together, to present your arguments in favor of the project.

Pitman was suggesting Kelsey see four separate individuals, plus get the director of the National Park Service to come to Salem and act as salesman before their board. And all for a small stub wharf that could otherwise be taken by eminent domain. Kelsey's business was fighting a losing battle with the Depression and he had all the other parties to deal with on the project. Cammerer was buried under a mountain of administration in getting the whole nation's War Department historical sites transferred to the park service. Derby Wharf was not the top thing on his priority list. Was he to take the night train to Boston, another to Salem, spend an entire day in Salem, and another night back to Washington? Why couldn't Pitman take on some of the work of persuasion? It all seems a bit insensitive. In any event, we have no record of Kelsey or Cammerer responding to Pitman's suggestion for these many visits.

But there was some contact over the following year through Pitman. On July 1, 1936, Kelsey wrote to him, referencing earlier letters, that the regulations of the federal government were such that it was not possible to include restrictions in any deed of gift. He continued: "The Home for Aged Women need never fear that the Government will not properly protect the wharf in every possible way. The Society for the Preservation of New England Antiquities also wants to put in a restriction but have agreed to give the Government a clear title without any restrictions, as that is the only possible way that such a transfer can be made. ... Now that we have everything to close this matter up, I do hope that the Home for Aged Women will put no obstacle in the way of a very speedy consummation of the project." Kelsey's only weapon was persuasion, and all through this period he would simply say to the various parties something like "If someone as astute and knowledgeable as SPNEA is willing to trust the Park Service with something as historically valuable as the Old Derby House, surely you can trust them also." Kelsey promised that Cammerer would write Pitman with the details for transferring the deed to the Federal Government, which eventually they did, unconditionally, as an outright gift.

Next, the Massachusetts Legislature. On November 7, 1935, Kelsey began to address the major problem of funds to buy or condemn all the needed buildings and land adjacent to the key wharfs and buildings within the site. He wrote a letter to Samuel A. York, commissioner of Conservation for the State.

> As of course you may know, Derby Wharf is the most conspicuous example perhaps of its kind as the site where American shipping started and therefore is most important from a national historical standpoint. Its significance is by no means local and the State and the National Government are quite as much interested in it, or should be, as the City of Salem. To make of Derby Wharf a really adequate and suitable historic monument, it is quite necessary to secure considerable adjoining property including a few other wharves and this will mean the outlay of considerable money. It seems to me quite fitting that the State of Massachusetts should enter into the proposition and do its share towards preserving this unique historic site.
>
> Among other things I sincerely hope you will include in your recommendations and have a bill prepared for the appropriation by the State of a sum not less than fifty thousand nor more than one hundred thousand dollars to help in securing these necessary additions to the site, as this Commonwealth's fair share of the total costs of securing and rebuilding Derby Wharf. ... Quite a number of buildings owned privately must be secured and wiped out, but of course we are keeping all this very confidential for obvious real estate reasons.

On November 26, 1935, Kelsey wrote a detailed five-page letter with six attachments to Mr. York with all the information he might need for his report to the legislature. On November 29 York submitted his report which was organized differently, but its contents were almost verbatim from the Kelsey letter. York had wasted no time. Kelsey had received a letter from Mayor Bates stating that Salem would undertake the cost of all acquisitions if the State would contribute $50,000, so naturally that was the sum York requested and it became cast in concrete for the legislation. The city of Salem was on the hook for any balance above that.

The Act, House—No. 142, contained some naming problems that eventually were cleaned up. Its preamble called the site a "national monument," which of course it was not. Similarly in the draft bill it was to be "known as Salem Memorial Maritime Park." On December 14 Cammerer pointed this out to Kelsey reminding him that under federal law it was not a national monument, but a national historic site. As we know today the official name became the Salem Maritime National Historic Site.

In mid-November Cammerer had cautioned Kelsey there might not be authority under existing Massachusetts law for the alienation of the properties to the United States if and when they were accepted. He suggested the state have an act passed permitting the alienation of any such properties in the future under the new Federal Historic Sites Act. Kelsey put the question to William Dorman, counsel to the Senate in the Legislature. Dorman quickly replied that the federal act did not aim at political sovereignty over lands acquired under the act. On studying old cases on the subject, "it would appear that no formal cession is required of a state unless the federal government seeks to extend its political sovereignty over the territory acquired." However, he wasn't totally sure of his interpretation, and it might be well for the state to include an alienation provision in its act.

Cammerer's mid-November letter also dealt with the alienation question. He felt the taxation question was moot because federal property was not taxable by state or municipal governments. Moreover the titles transferred would have to be free from any encumbrances. "For these reasons, we do not believe that it is necessary to take special action to cede the right of the property to the United States and we regard the draft as submitted sufficient for the purpose of effecting the transfer." We include these seemingly minor details only to show that Kelsey had managed to become the middleman in just about everything that went on. Most likely he wanted to be sure that no minor points held up the project. In February 1936, he said to James Duncan Phillips "You haven't the time to do 'lobbying' and neither have I, and when I get rid of this affair I'll never take up another one by the tail, it's devilishly hard to let go."

The legislative hearing was held January 30, 1936. Kelsey took no chances. He put together a list of forty-seven influential people he knew to be favorable to the project. To each he sent a notice of the coming hearing, enclosing attachments. "May we count on your valued presence and approval of the bill which means so much for the City of Salem the State of Massachusetts and the Nation at large? Also, will you kindly secure the presence of others who will take an active interest in this bill?" Even though Cammerer was forced to remain in Washington, he did send Verne Chatelain as acting assistant director of NPS.

On February 1 Kelsey wrote A. J. Boardman of the Eastern Massachusetts Street Railway Company, "The hearing on House Bill #142 ... was a great success and was reported out favorably and we may get early action from the Ways and Means Committee where it now has been sent. ... Derby Wharf is fast being batted to pieces and I am hoping that we can put it across very soon so that something may be done temporarily to stop this terrible erosion."

The Ways and Means Committee didn't hold its hearing until May 8, 1936. Kelsey sent out the same notice he had before to the forty-seven individuals asking for their presence and support. On June 13 Elizabeth Morrison of the National Park Service wrote Kelsey, "The Hearing before the Massachusetts House Ways and Means Committee was certainly magnificently staged and you should be congratulated on its success. ... After examination by the Solicitor's Office, these deeds will be held by the National Park Service, until all are received and submitted at one time for the Secretary's signature. As I understand it, W.P.A. funds cannot be allotted for property which is not under State, Local or Federal ownership. ... W.P.A. projects, of course, have to be initiated locally." While the red tape was gradually being removed, Derby Wharf was continuing to be battered by erosion with possibly another winter season passing before corrective work could be started.

On June 19, 1936, Kelsey wrote to A. J. Boardman, "As you have perhaps heard, last Tuesday Governor Curley signed the bill providing for the State of Massachusetts contributing $50,000 in cooperation with the City of Salem, in purchasing the property surrounding Derby Wharf. ... Yesterday, I gave full particulars to your agent, Mr. W. S. Felton, Salem regarding the preparation of a deed to Derby Wharf so that it may be submitted to the Federal Government for their approval and duly executed in course of time."

Finally, Salem and Mayor Bates had to come through with the purchases and takings of all the properties within the minimum boundaries set by the Park Service. On August 26, 1936, Henry Adams Tybure, Democratic candidate for Congress, penned a handwritten letter to Kelsey:

> Dear Mr. Kelsey, Have noticed many statements made by our mayor Geo. Bates in regards to the Derby Wharf project. What is this Republican ballyhoo, or a campaign issue on the part of the mayor? Why fool around with the land owners, why not take over this property by eminent domain.
> Although I have noticed that the unreasonable property owners are all good friends of the mayor and supposed to be Republicans, there is one, who happens to be Joseph Kohn, property assessed for $7,500, and is asking $35,000. This fellow has raved about what a good friend he is of the mayor.
> Now Mr. Bates is threatening abandoning the project after you gentlemen worked so hard to push it through. Am afraid we will have to throw this failure right in our mayor's lap.

My father happens to be one of the property owners and one of the most reasonable in his figure and is anxious to cooperate to the fullest extent.

With kind regards, I am ...

On October 16 Kelsey wrote to Director Cammerer with his letter headlined PERSONAL:

It seems to be very important that you write Hon. George J. Bates, Mayor of Salem, a serious letter regarding the closing up of the Derby Wharf Project. ... The fact of the matter is that this would have all been done had not the Mayor been interested in his campaign for Representative to Congress from this district; his mind is more on that than it is on local affairs. The way to make him take action is to have pressure from all sides brought to bear on the issue. ... The Mayor will answer that he is just holding off to bring some of the land owners to terms but, at this late hour, that is in my opinion an excuse and not a reason. I have followed the matter very closely with the Mayor and his Committee on Adjustment and am well acquainted with the actual details. ... In writing him, it would be well to call attention to the fact that funds for the improvement of Derby Wharf cannot be even put in a budget until the title is actually vested in the Federal Government. ... Please be assured that I am very serious when I say that whatever you do should not be delayed and if you think wise, I would be glad to see a copy of your letter to the Mayor which will also be held confidential, if you say so. Yours truly, ...

The December 1938 issue of *Planning and Civic Comment of the American Planning and Civic Association* carried an article titled, "A National Historic Site at Salem Massachusetts," by Edwin W. Small, acting superintendent, Salem, Massachusetts:

The Nation's first national historic site has been established in the old seaport city of Salem, Massachusetts, ... as *Salem Maritime National Historic Site*. The creation of this site marks the beginning of a new line of activity of the National Park Service ... Through a grant of $110,000 from the Public Works Administration, work has already well progressed on the reconstruction of Derby Wharf. ... Establishment of the site brings to a successful conclusion more than four years of activity on the part of Harlan P. Kelsey, who first envisioned the possibilities of the location and has worked most determinedly to secure the cooperation of the City, the State, various organizations and individuals in meeting the property requirements prescribed by the National Park Service. ...

Recently, three-quarters of a century later, your author went to see the Salem Maritime Visitor Center. Who was the individual given greatest credit in their photographic displays? Kelsey? Of course it wasn't. It was the same Mayor George J. Bates cited above as putting the historical site on hold while he campaigned for Congress. Kelsey was nowhere in sight. Sad.

This closed the chapter on Old Derby Wharf and reminds us of Kelsey's oath, "When I get rid of this affair I'll never take up another one by the tail, it's devilishly hard to let go." This well-intentioned resolve was to be proven short-lived, as we shall see.

Another chapter that was closed in 1936 was the Shenandoah National Park. On May 29, 1936, Kelsey heard from Cammerer, "You are shortly going to receive an invitation to be on the speakers' stand at the time of the dedication of Shenandoah National Park on July 3; that will be on a Friday. Why not plan to drive down here, you and the Missus, and make it a pleasant stay on the 3rd, 4th, and 5th. There are a number of us planning for the same kind of an outing at Skyland, including the Director of the Budget, J. Edgar Hoover, some Interior Department officials, Assistant Surgeon General of the Public Health Service and others. As long as you are going to be here for the one day there should be no reason why you could not make the other two days as well. What do you think about it?"

In mid-July Kelsey had reason to write to Colonel Benchoff, who had been so instrumental in the Virginia activities behind the Shenandoah Park. "While the exercises dedicating the Shenandoah National Park were interesting and picturesque, still it is to be regretted that the few minutes time it would have taken to do it, was not devoted to giving public recognition to those who did so much to put this project across—in fact, the ones who really did the job were almost completely ignored. After all, it is just the way that things happen in this world and good deeds must generally be rewarded by the satisfaction one gets in accomplishing really worthwhile things for humanity. Someday the principal actors in this great event will get their public recognition, of that I am sure."[150]

Bankruptcy

Lurking behind all of Kelsey's notable public service during the years 1934, 1935, and 1936 was the dark cloud of the Depression economy. All the efforts of the New Deal had spotty results, benefiting some but leaving the general population in a difficult state. Total hours worked per adult in 1939 remained 21 percent below their 1929 level, compared to a decline of 27 percent in 1933, when the New Deal was started. Per capita consumption did not recover at all, remaining 25 percent below its trend level throughout the New Deal.[151] Ornamental horticulture was rarely above the bottom of the list for most Americans. Government projects and the ultrarich comprised the only strong segments of the market. Food and clothing always trumped plants.

April, 1935. IN THE UNITED STATES DISTRICT COURT FOR THE DISTRICT OF MASSACHUSETTS. In the Matter of Harlan P. Kelsey Inc., Debtor; in Proceedings for the Reorganization of a

Corporation. No. 57217. ... pursuant to Section 77B of Chapter VII of the Acts of Congress relating to bankruptcy continuing the Debtor in possession of its estate and authorizing it to operate its business, notice is hereby given of a hearing ...

Thomas A. McBeth was a longtime acquaintance of Kelsey in the nursery business. On April 7, 1935, he wrote, "I was grieved to hear of your unfortunate turn in business. I assure you that you have my sympathy. I was inclined to say I was surprised, but nothing surprises us now days. The only surprise is so many are holding out. I often think of the delightful days visit I had at your home in Salem several years ago, one of the bright spots of my travels. ... I hope you will get straightened out and see your way to continue in the nursery business. ... I think there will be a revolution in the nursery business. The days of 'mass production' are gone. We will get off our 'high horse' and quit speaking in units of carloads and millions. We may have to return to some of the primitive methods that they used in my early connection with the trade 50–60 years ago. ... I am enclosing a receipt in full for your debt, hoping it may help to cut down your liabilities." The receipt was for $38 "in full of all accounts to date."

The court's Plan of Reorganization was entered on October 18, 1935. In its basic provisions, Kelsey was obligated to pay claims in equal annual installments of ten percent (10 percent) of each claim. As an alternative, each claimant could receive full payment in nursery stock valued at wholesale prices, at any time prior to October 1, 1936.

At year end 1935, the nursery's total current liabilities were $86,140.11. Their current assets were $47,495.32, of which $40,000 was nursery stock. That left a mere $7,495.32 of liquid assets to cover over $86,000 in claims—an ugly picture indeed.

Kelsey's distress is clearly evident in his July 8, 1936, letter to his twin brother Harry:

Please read the enclosed letter—I am up against it—haven't a chance to raise this premium payment here. You know we are operating under what is called 77B—that is we are really in the bankruptcy court under a plan to pay off 10% of the company's indebtedness each year. The season was a very short one—a month shorter than usual and it is necessary for me to raise $10,000 to $15,000 by quick sales and I have hoped of doing this—but that is in the business and all we are allowed is a very small salary.

It would be terrible to lose a half million dollar plant and I am not going to if possible—but it has been a long heart breaking struggle. The prospects for fall are better than ever before on account of large government contracts and for bids, and much stock is short with rising prices. But it doesn't help me save my life insurance, which is all Florence has left if anything happens to me. There are three policies—two for $10,000 each and one for $5,000. Of course I have borrowed on them but there is still 40% equity or $10,000 still to the good. Now if there is any way you can help me on this I will make one of the $10,000 policies payable to you with $4,000 equity value. So you are perfectly safe and I should insist that you receive 6% interest. It may be that if business does prove good I could take this up another year—but in any event you are protected.

As this comes due on the 15th—the last possible date—please write me by return mail—and send back the N.Y. Life letter. ... Love to all.   Bop.

P.S. Tomorrow we are 64(?). How I wish we could be together on our birthdays at least.

Kelsey wrote to Harry again July 15, 1936:

You certainly lifted a burden off my mind and now that the premium is paid it will carry for a year for the loan value is increased in December as the agent wrote.

I have sent one of the policies in to the Company for endorsement to you as beneficiary and will mail it to you when it is returned. In case of my death you will deduct any amount you have paid with 6% interest and the balance you can pay to Florence. Ordinary death the policy would now pay $4,000 or by accident $8,000.

All my love and a thousand thanks.   Your brother,   Bop.

On August 21, 1936, auctioneers Samuel T. Freeman and Company conducted an absolute auction of fifty thousand evergreens at the nursery. Total cash collected was $12,092.11. Some of the cash was available immediately. On August 31 the auctioneers mailed Kelsey a check for $5,469.67 as the "balance of the proceeds from the sale of the surplus stock of the Kelsey Highlands Nursery." Auction sales of nursery stock, coupled with nursery stock in lieu of cash, coupled with creditors' cash installments paid from nursery revenues, were gradually reducing Kelsey's overhanging liabilities.

During these Depression years, it gradually became apparent that the ever-decreasing revenues of the nursery could not support all three Kelsey men. From 1934–37 the eldest son, HPK Jr., served as executive director of the New England Nursery Association, while still employed at the nursery. This may well have had some modest compensation for the executive time spent. By 1937 HPK Jr. had to leave the nursery and went to work for his uncle at Daniel Low & Company in Salem. There he worked in the mail order department through 1938, selling jewelry, silverware, and gifts by direct mail throughout the world. HPK Jr. was the logical one of the brothers to leave the nursery, since Seth Kelsey was a botany graduate, while HPK Jr. was a student in civil engineering and business administration.

Economist Raymond DeVoe Jr. offers us a bit of comic relief amidst the pervasive gloom of the nation:

> After eight years of a rotten economy and five years after hitting bottom the county's collective nerves were frayed. ... On Halloween 1938 The Mercury Theatre on the Air did a broadcast on CBS radio of H.G. Wells "War of the Worlds" from their studio in lower Manhattan, New York City. However, Director Orson Welles chose to play a Halloween prank and did not broadcast it as a drama. Instead, he did it as a simulated news broadcast of Martians landing in giant space ships across the United States.
>
> ... It was cleverly done, chilling—and believable. Telephones began ringing across the county as people called friends and relatives to tell them that "The Martians have landed." The tone of the broadcaster got more ominous as further "details" became available. His growing fear is apparent in his voice as he described from the top of the CBS Building 'Five great machines coming across the Hudson River towards Manhattan, poison smoke drifting across the city and people diving into the Hudson River while others are falling like flies.' The news reporter falls as well and goes off the air. The last thing heard on the broadcast is a haunting Ham radio operator calling '2X2L calling CQ—Isn't there anyone—?' Then silence.
>
> The result was absolute panic across the country. Families loaded into cars and headed for the hills or anywhere they thought might be safe. Others huddled in their cellars awaiting a knock on the door. There were dozens of traffic accidents since no one paid attention to traffic lights in their panic to escape. But there were other radio stations broadcasting, so that The Mercury Theatre's dead-air silence could be offset with other news broadcasts.[152]

The nursery business improved in both 1938 and 1939 but still showed a net loss after depreciation. By 1939 HPK Jr. was back working at the nursery. For 1940 their projections were for a profit of over $22,000. It now looked as though "the ship would stay afloat."

Horticultural Matters

As we have seen, 1936 was a year of financial trial for Kelsey. But it was also a year of recognition and some satisfaction. E. I. Farrington, editor of *Horticulture Magazine*, wrote in the August 1941 issue of *Parks & Recreation*, "Harlan P. Kelsey—A Tribute":

> It is safe to say, I think, that no other nurseryman knows so many people in so many different walks of life as Harlan P. Kelsey. In business Mr. Kelsey is a nurseryman, but his contacts have led him into many other fields, although for the most part, fields which have a kinship with horticulture. The Massachusetts Horticultural Society has … recognized Mr. Kelsey's ability and accomplishments by awarding him the *George Robert White Medal of Honor*, the most important horticultural award in this country. *This award was made in 1936* on recommendation of a committee of which Professor Oakes Ames was chairman … [Italics added for emphasis]

In 1947 Kelsey's son Seth listed all of his father's accomplishments for Robert Walcott, president of the trustees of Public Reservations, and included the 1936 George Robert White Medal. Seth explained why Kelsey had been selected for this signal honor. It was "principally for his pioneering work in the introduction and conservation of native American plants."[153] This honor came some forty-two years after Harlan Kelsey's seminal paper (1894) to the American Nurserymen that they should shift their focus away from exotic imports and promote native plants. To his dying day, Kelsey never wavered from this theme in horticulture—hardy American plants.

One of the local Boston groups to take advantage of New Deal spending projects was the Emergency Planning & Research Bureau, Inc. It was sponsored jointly by the Boston Society of Architects and the Engineering Societies of Boston, Inc. One of their projects was for planting of the islands in Boston Harbor—ERAM Project #XS-A1-U1. The idea of the project was to improve the attractiveness of the islands for visitors both on land and especially from the water by passing boats. Mr. John H. Harding was the administrator of the project, but more important was Warren H. Manning, the landscape architect directing the preparation of plans and probable supervisor for the execution of the plans.

Manning (1860–1938) was an icon among the notables of the landscape architecture profession in the United States. After spending eight years working under Frederick Law Olmsted Sr. in Boston, he started his own practice on Tremont Street in 1896. This is interestingly the same year young Kelsey had started his practice as a landscape architect on Tremont Street. Manning had been among the founders of the American Civic Association and among the charter members of the 1899 American Society of Landscape Architects (president in 1914). Manning, like Kelsey, had an extensive knowledge of plant materials and was known, like Kelsey, for his sprawling natural design, using native plants.[154] All this notwithstanding, Kelsey found himself in seeming warfare with Manning through his front man, Harding. There is no evidence that Kelsey and Manning ever did meet face-to-face to work out their differences. Of course Manning knew of Kelsey's formidable credentials and perhaps maintained better control by simply avoiding direct contact.

The problem concerned how "natural" the plant material and the landscape arrangement would be. Harding had approached the Massachusetts Nurserymen's Association through W. H. Thurlow, asking help in obtaining plant material from local nurserymen. This was done with a December 20, 1934, letter that inlcuded a list of 399 plant species that were either growing on the island or were recommended by Manning to be planted. In a January 14, 1935, letter to Thurlow, he opened by saying, "We very much appreciate the action of your organization in approving the planting of the Harbor Islands, in which you strongly recommend the use of native plant material." Harding acknowledged that the text of his letter had been written by Manning, and the letter continued for two pages giving details of landscape problems and the ideas Manning had for addressing them. Presumably the letter was also for distribution to interested nurserymen.

One day after Harding's letter (January 15), Kelsey was in Harding's office discussing the issues. On January 16 Harding wrote Kelsey concerning later discussions with Manning about Kelsey's ideas with more about their intentions and rationale. On January 17 Kelsey wrote Harding, "Confirming the conversation I had with you and Mr. Strickland in your office, I will be very glad to write specifically on the subject of the plantings proposed on the islands of Boston Harbor." He probably did not endear himself by closing with a comment on the plant list, "I would suggest that it be carefully type-read for there are a number of typographical errors, and on the lists submitted to me there are several other errors in names, such as Silver Linden which is correctly Tilia tomentosa." But worse was yet to come.

On January 18 Kelsey wrote Harding with a response so caustic it amounted to a declaration of war on Manning's proposals. Had Kelsey not been held in such high esteem by the Boston Horticultural Club and the Massachusetts Horticultural Society, his letter might have appeared impudent when addressing plans by the revered Warren H. Manning:

> Replying to your letter of January 16, I am frank in stating that I do not believe the nature lovers of Massachusetts and those who love the wonderful effects produced along our coastline and islands by the native plant cover will ever submit to turning our islands into artificial gardens, nor to the planting on these

> islands of exotic material, which would destroy this wonderful, naturalistic effect of which there is nothing more beautiful anywhere. Here is an instance where we cannot improve upon nature, but should try to restore it as it was originally.
>
> It is inconceivable that we should try to produce effects which belong properly in parks, gardens and sophisticated plantings in general. Brilliant floral effects are not necessary, but even so there is plenty of native, New England plant material to bring this about with the possible use only of those exotics which have the appearance of being native and therefore do not clash with the native material.

Kelsey continues with a full page of comments on the list of plants, native substitutes, and landscape design issues.

> The measure of what you propose planting seems to be controlled more or less by the question of cost of material. I can think of nothing that might lead to more disastrous results than such a standard. ... You can see from the trend of my letter that my belief is that the islands should be planted nearly 100% with absolutely native material, and so far as possible with material that is either indigenous or once was on the islands themselves. We have large quantities of exotic plants we would dearly like to sell, but I cannot view with equanimity the ruination of our native landscape effects by making exotic parks out of them. ... If you will send the final list which is decided upon, we will be very glad to quote lowest possible prices on such material as we can supply.

After blasting Manning in this manner, one would suspect Kelsey had no illusions of receiving any orders for plants, except as a last resort by Manning, if he could find no other supplier.

The same day he wrote Harding, Kelsey shot off a letter to John May, president of the Appalachian Mountain Club:

> You have no doubt received from Winthrop Packard, Secretary and Treasurer of the Massachusetts Audubon Society, a vote which was passed at the last meeting of the trustees relative to the proposal to plant the islands in Boston Harbor under an ERA project. Here is a matter which I do believe the club should consider for immediate action and pass a similar vote … The Appalachian Mountain Club has always stood for keeping our New England landscape unspoiled by the hand of man so far as possible. You were at the meeting of the Audubon trustees and know the situation, but I will only say that it seems to me inconceivable that the Appalachian Mountain Club would not take official action against planting our beautiful Boston harbor islands as proposed. To me it is inconceivable that any citizen could stand the planting of these islands, and on each island have a special floral display for example, 'Forsythia island, Lilac island, Japanese Quince island, etc.' as proposed. Please give this your consideration.

On February 26 Kelsey did submit bids for a three-page, single-spaced list of plants. Half of them he simply labeled "cannot supply." On March 22 he asked Harding about the status, having heard nothing. On April 4 he made a supplementary quotation on a one-page list, all of which he could supply. On April 5 he quoted on a half-page list. On April 10 he submitted his last quotation for now only eleven trees. It is doubtful he ever did any business for the project, which probably died when Warren H. Manning died, in 1938, of a heart attack at age seventy-eight.

Today, the Boston Harbor Islands are described on the website of the Massachusetts Department of Conservation and Recreation. "The 17-island state park is part of the 34-island Boston Harbor Islands National Park Area. They are a wonderful natural resource, only 45 minutes by ferry from downtown Boston. Seventeen of the islands are managed by the Department of Conservation and Recreation (DCR). Six of the 17 islands … are staffed and open for public use daily during the summer and weekends in the spring and fall. Visitors to the park enjoy shell and slate beaches, easy hiking paths, old hay fields gone wild with bayberry, raspberry and elderberry, and old roadways to historic foundations and forts." One suspects Kelsey wouldn't object to that.

By 1934 it had become apparent that the American Association of Nurserymen was about to go bankrupt, both in money and members. The $10,000 reserve fund had been spent, the balance in the treasury had been reduced to $5,447.46, and the 1934 membership had dropped to 275 active members.[155] The year 1937 saw the AAN still struggling for members as continuing economic pressures saw member after member drop out to save cash rather than pay the dues. This also applied to the regional and state organizations. Another reason for drop-outs was the sporadic delivery of the services members expected from these organizations. Since 1916 there had been numerous proposals for reorganization, none of them successful. By 1937 it seemed imperative, and the national leaders had devoted all of their time to perfect a "vertical" structure in which state associations were embodied into six proposed chapters, whose delegates served on the national board of governors. The contentious dues issues were ironed out and the plan adopted at the July 1937 convention.[156]

There was a move afoot to create a new group called the Council of Eastern Nurserymen to combine New England with the various Mid-Atlantic States. The theory was that this would provide better services, being closer to the member nurserymen than the national association. This was considered more of a "horizontal" organization, because various regions (like New England) would report sideways to the Eastern Council; the council in turn would be considered the chapter with representation on the National Executive Committee. Robert Pyle, a long-standing friend of Kelsey's from West Grove, Pennsylvania, had been trying to enlist Kelsey in the organization efforts. Kelsey responded October 28, 1937, "I'm sick and tired of trying to pull in a lot of lazy and selfish nurserymen into any movement. They expect a few warhorses to do all the work and won't even pay their dues promptly, and yet expect to get all the benefit that accrues from concerted action."

Pyle to Kelsey, October 29, 1937: "I hope you will carefully reconsider your suggestion that New England will probably apply for a charter. New England will be able to get help from a Council of Eastern Nurserymen, and a Council of Eastern Nurserymen can function better, if it is in a position of one section of the National organization. With six or eight months more of good hard work, I believe we can have a set-up that is most promising. … We will soon be past the heaviest of the fall season, and you will want some eleemosynary opportunity and this is it. I hope you will not weaken now that the chances are growing better."

Kelsey to Pyle, November 29, 1937: "I am just a little bit surprised that you don't quite understand the situation. When you realize that I am and will have to give weeks of solid time towards the big eleemosynary job of the new edition of *Standardized Plant Names*, and that I have been actively working on it for the last year, I cannot understand how you think I ought to take on new duties of a public nature, and that is not all; I am leaving tonight for Washington on National Park matters at the call of the National Park Service on one dollar a year putting over a half million dollar proposition in the Derby Wharf National Historic Monument, and then some others besides. I am easy, but I hope I am not another fool. These other New England Nurserymen have got to do their job and they are all in office and I am not. For our own nursery interest, of course, I am going to do what I can, but you had better forget trying to put that AAN job on me."

Yes, Kelsey was easy, and always the warhorse to put any good idea over the top. Those in the business had watched him for some forty years. He simply couldn't stand to see others pulling things in the "wrong" direction. A new super-regional Council of Eastern Nurserymen was, in Kelsey's eyes, the wrong direction. The right direction was to get a New England chapter established in support of the AAN. On December 9, 1937, he wrote Pyle, "It seems New England is, so far as we can find out, practically 100% for having a New England Chapter of the AAN. ... I know you will be disappointed that we have taken this stand but our nurserymen here will not consent to belong to four organizations which would be the case if we went in as an Eastern Chapter, in other words, the State, the New England, the Chapter, and the American. It is unnecessarily complicated."

On December 13 Kelsey unloaded his views wholesale on Chet Marshall, AAN Vice President:

> We believe there is opportunity to get all of the leading nurserymen in New England to become members of the AAN, but in the discussions of the Executive Committee of the New England Nurserymen's Association the vertical plan is believed to be, by far, the best plan of membership. In other words, the nurserymen will be required to join the State organization, the Chapter and finally the AAN, by one payment of dues which is allocated so that the AAN gets their dollar per thousand on the gross business of the firm during the preceding fiscal year. We fully realize that this may leave out many of the smaller nurserymen, yet the time has come to organize on a truly business basis and the modest dues that are required to belong to all three organizations is worth infinitely more to even the smallest nurserymen, than his cost of membership. ...
>
> A letter from Robert Pyle received today, makes me think that the Executive Committee of the AAN believes in direct membership rather than in the vertical membership. My objection to this is that it splits up the nurserymen of a State or Region, into two or more groups, is entirely unnecessary and

cumbersome and the argument that a great many nurserymen will not join the National Association or the Chapters, but will join a local group, is quite true.

My point is that the time has come to use sledgehammer methods, which are perfectly fair and legitimate, and compel those nurserymen who want to reap the benefits of the right kind of organization to take the whole program from start to finish. Where there are no State Organizations the nurserymen can join the Chapter and the AAN. Yet with increasing State legislation applying to the nursery industry it seems inconceivable that any State would not have a State Organization to look after their State affairs. Both our State and New England Nurserymen's Associations are to have their annual meetings in January. All necessary information should be on hand and a definite program outlined in advance, if we are to make the most of this situation, and back up the AAN 100%.

Kelsey agitated for activity by the national organization to create a uniform constitution and set of by-laws for the new chapters, since they would legally be dropping their prior incorporated association status. In his December 18 letter to Pyle, he ranted, "I also take it that you already have considered the draft of a Charter for the Eastern Council, if so, why in the Sam Hill doesn't Osman or somebody else send us copies of this proposed draft of constitution and by-laws for our consideration. ... Holy mackerel! If the National and parent organization which is supposed to correlate the different States and Regional groups with the National Organization and collaborate with them for this result, namely; a smooth working organization from bottom to top, and then simply leave the Regions flopping around without each one knowing what the other fellow is doing, it is just too bad."

On December 21 he again complained to Robert Pyle, "This morning I received from Chet Marshall, a copy or their proposed constitution and by-laws for Chapters. I was simply amazed to find that apparently all that is expected of Chapters is to make a loose organization and its only duties will be to get together and name delegates. If that is the case, and letters from you and others, make me feel that you have this also in mind, it looks to me like a great big flop. If we decide to have a New England chapter under such conditions you may be sure we wouldn't give up our New England Association. I will try and make up a statement of the conditions as I see them to-date, and will distribute them generally."

Bit by bit, piece by piece, Kelsey was getting sucked back into playing a leadership role in the AAN—the very thing he had so disavowed as his wish only a month earlier with Pyle. By December 29 Kelsey had issued a three page circular letter to all of the New England members of the AAN. In it he reiterated all the reasoning for an independent New England chapter. Then he outlined all of the steps that should be taken to bring the new chapter organization into being. Finally he took the bull by the horns, stepping beyond the mild documents suggested by Chet Marshall at the national level, and attached a whole, full-text, four-page proposal for the New England Chapter Constitution and By-Laws. In them he put "teeth," adopting all the objectives and operating rules currently enjoyed by the association that they would be legally giving up, while promoting allegiance with the objectives of the national organization. He left nothing that could be called a reason to postpone action now. Then he asked all the recipients to sign, stating that they had read the constitution and by-laws and subscribed to the formation of the New England chapter on that basis. Kelsey stopped arguing and simply sat down and "did it." If they couldn't get consensus now it would have to be because someone had a better idea for action now. But action was what he wanted. Concurrently, he submitted the document to E. L. Baker, AAN president, for review and acceptance.

Within a month, Pyle's Pennsylvanians voted themselves out of the Eastern Council, following New England's lead. For them there would now be only three levels—the state, the region, and the national executive committee comprised of a representative from each of the six regions. By the time of the national convention in July 1938, that pattern was established for everyone.

The Eastern Region would be Region #1. The others would be #2 Southern, #3 Central, #4 Western, #5 Southwestern, and #6 Pacific Coast. That left the question of who would be the representative for the Eastern Region?

It started with H. G. Seyler, president of the Pennsylvanians, sending a February 21, 1938, circular letter to all the key New England men. "Pennsylvania and eastern New York will back whatever man New England agrees upon for membership to the Executive Committee of the AAN. This assures his election if he has any support at all from western New York and New Jersey." On March 12 Kelsey wrote Seyler, "Last week in Philadelphia, I saw Mr. Pyle and told him that if there was any possible way out of it, I did not want to be elected as the executive committeeman from the Eastern Region, and would only permit my name to be used in case it was impossible to agree upon another candidate."

Then Pyle weighed in on Kelsey March 11, "In the face of this situation, I don't know any nurseryman in America who has the background and equipment of yourself, who for two years was President of the National Association; for many years was a member of the Executive Committee; who has a relationship with the National Government where he is known and well-known for what he stands for, and who has the high respect on the part of men in his own industry. I tell you that times like these call for just such men. And beyond that, you have a way of 'speaking out in meetings', which is just what is needed to stiffen the backbone of the fellows that wobble, and won't know just where to stand or what to think. Now, if in the Executive Committee of the National Association we can inject a member of your type and caliber, the influence over the entire nation may exceed anything you at present imagine. When I think of the contrast between yourself and one, L.L., I shudder for what might occur if you do not accept as nominee for the Executive Committee of the AAN."

On April 1 Kelsey wiggled again, writing Pyle, "Referring back to the question of who is to be the member of the executive committee from the Eastern Region of the AAN, if my name is to be actively brought up, I would be greatly pleased if my son, Seth, could be substituted for me. He is young, ambitious, and really has the right ideas, and I believe would represent the Eastern Group efficiently and fairly. This is only a private suggestion to you to use as you think best." But Pyle wasn't buying. On April 4 he wrote Kelsey, "I think I know Seth well enough to believe that he would make a good member of the Executive Committee. I doubt if many people, however, do know him, and your strength lies in the fact that you are not only known, but it's well-known how you stand. ... I believe you would carry the field." That put Seth out of the picture for AAN, for then. But his father must have been heartened by Seth L. Kelsey's 1940 selection, two years later, as president of the New England Nursery Association. At least in New England Seth was well known.

On July 11, Kelsey heard from Cornelius P. van Tol, writing as secretary for the Eastern Region, "I am enclosing a copy of last Friday's meeting of the delegates from the Eastern Region at New York. As you already know, you were unanimously nominated as our member for the Executive Committee of the AAN."

With the die cast, Kelsey briskly moved forward, writing Pyle August 19, "From now on, believe me that I am not interested in local differences of opinion and misunderstanding, and my one object is to make the Eastern Region a fine active body of nurserymen which will go places and do things, and I wish it were possible to double our membership."

Destruction

The first signs of the storm were traced back to a wind shift noted by French observers at Bilma Oasis in the Sahara Desert on September 4, 1938. As this disturbance passed off the West African coast, it developed into a tropical storm near the Cape Verde Islands, probably about September 10. With the storm picking up speed, about twelve and a half miles per hour, moving westward across the Atlantic Ocean, it reached category 5 status. The Jacksonville office of the US Weather Bureau issued warnings for Florida on September 16. At nine in the morning on Wednesday, September 21, the storm was reported off the coast of Cape Hatteras, North Carolina. The rate of speed was advanced to thirty-two miles per hour, continuing to pick up speed, something unusual. The rapid speed allowed the hurricane to travel far to the north before it had a chance to weaken over cooler waters to category 3.

Weather Bureau observers then expected the hurricane to either swing to the west over the Virginia and Delaware Capes, possibly continuing into New Jersey and Pennsylvania, or swing into the East and vanish out to sea, the usual with such storms. It was unable to swing westward because of a high-pressure area that had developed over the Middle Atlantic states, nor eastward since another high-pressure area had developed over the Atlantic. Between those two areas was a valley of low pressure. A "Valley of Death that was a dagger" pointed into the heart of New England. Into that valley or trough went the hurricane, now sweeping along at more than 60 mph, at least twice as fast as normal.

Except for Charlie Pierce, a junior forecaster in the US Weather Bureau who predicted the storm but was overruled by the chief forecaster, the Weather Bureau experts and the general public never saw it coming. Later that day at three thirty in the afternoon, the greatest weather disaster ever to hit Long Island, New York, and New England struck in the form of a category 3 hurricane. The fifty-mile-wide eye first came ashore at Bayport, Long Island. The tide was astronomically high at the autumnal equinox—when both the sun and the moon's gravity tug at the sea level. When the hurricane and its accompanying tidal surge and surf hit Long Island, the impact registered on seismographs in Alaska. The seismograph of Fordham University recorded the smash of the tide hitting the New England shore as if it were a major earthquake. A cinema at Westhampton was lifted out to sea; around twenty people at a matinee and the theater—projectionist and all—landed two miles into the Atlantic and drowned. This example represents only the tiniest fraction of the havoc that ensued. Long Island somewhat buffered the western Connecticut coast but the storm surge was especially violent along the Rhode Island shore. As the surge drove northward through Narragansett Bay, it was restricted by the bay's funnel shape, and rose to a level of nearly sixteen feet above normal spring tides, resulting in more than thirteen feet of water in some areas of downtown Providence. Destruction at the head of Buzzards Bay might have reached immense proportions had not the Cape Cod Canal been able to take the push of the storm and carry the flood tide through and out into Cape Cod Bay.

From then on the due northward path of the hurricane eye up the Connecticut River inflicted primarily wind damage, the rain accumulation being limited by the rapid pace of the eye northward. The Blue Hill Observatory in Milton, Massachusetts, just south of Boston, recorded a gust of wind out of the south at 186 mph with a sustained wind of 121 mph. Only one anemometer survived those winds, which still remain the third highest winds ever recorded on earth. Of greatest interest to Kelsey, twenty-five miles north of Boston, was the tree damage. The hurricane devastated the forests of the Northeast, knocking down an estimated 2 billion trees in New York and New England. I won't burden the reader with the litany of damages to homes and other structures.[157]

Cornelius P. Van Tol, president of the New England chapter of the AAN, sent a September 28 circular letter to the membership, attempting a survey. He was writing from Falmouth, Massachusetts, on the Atlantic side of Cape Cod:

> The Hurricane, Tidal Wave, and Floods of the past week have left in their wake a trail of damage and destruction as never before in the history of New England.
>
> Our own Community suffered severely, and the loss to property runs into the millions of dollars. Luckily our nurseries escaped without any appreciable damage or loss. I sincerely hope that the same is true in your case. I fear, however, that a great many nurserymen did not fare so well and that the loss to our Industry is quite considerable.
>
> 1. How much damage … at your establishment?
> 2. How much damage … at other nurseries?
> 3. Conditions in general in your community?
>
> … Hoping that your answer will be an encouraging one, I am. Sincerely yours, C.P. Van Tol.

Kelsey responded October 3:

> Your letter of September 28th asking about hurricane damage finds me feeling much better than just after the disaster. Many of our customers on large estates have had terrific losses. This is going to help the industry and already we have seen a great pick-up on this account. Tree surgeons will have enough work for the next two years.
>
> Our damage was entirely from wind. We lost perhaps two hundred saleable trees in the nursery, running from 8 to 33 feet in height, and possibly two hundred large Pines, Oaks, and other trees on our property in the woodlands. I haven't the

faintest idea what damage was done in other nurseries around here at the present moment.

The nursery business is picking up rapidly. Yours truly, ...
HPK

By February 1, 1939, nursery superintendent Jim Ferronetti gave the following assessment:

Pine lumber down 38,120 bd. ft. @ $10.00 per 1000.
Cord wood – about 40 cords of Pine wood @ $2.00 to $3.00 per cord.
About 25 acres to clean up.
To clean up nursery stock that is down it would take 5 men one week to ten days.

Kelsey lost no time in exploiting the situation. The November 1, 1938, issue of *Horticulture* carried his advertisement: "Kelsey Highlands Nursery. Great Autumn Surplus Sale of the finest Trees, Shrubs and Perennials at 25 to 50 percent reduction." He then listed the stock available, closing with the following:

STORM DAMAGE

Now is the time to make replacement for Hurricane Losses. We supply and move safely large specimens up to 30 ft. with our modern tree-moving equipment. For example Koster Blue Spruce 18 to 25 ft. delivered, planted and properly guyed for $75.00 to $150.00 including Insurance for one year against death from natural causes. Also large Pines, Firs, Red Cedars, Arborvitae, etc., for immediate effect $12.00 and up.

In Kelsey's October 3 response to Cornelius P. Van Tol, he had noted, "The nursery business is picking up rapidly." The revenues for 1938 were up to $74,888, with expenses also up to $76,422, showing a net loss of -$1,534 after a $3,220 charge for depreciation. This indicated positive cash flow, a good sign. The revenues for 1939 continued to grow, but expenses grew even faster, increasing the loss after depreciation to -$5,651. Finally, 1940 looked like the first really good and profitable year in the nursery's forecasts since the Depression began. "Prospects for 1940 are encouraging. Sales can be materially increased ... Sentiment in the trade shows that prices will be generally higher by 20-30% in 1940, which indicates that business will be more profitable. It is believed that even without any increase of gross volume the Company will show a net profit of approximately $10,000 and that with the expected increase in sales a minimum profit of approximately $23,000 will result." The heat was off. Kelsey was going to survive.

Only one month after the hurricane, Kelsey was back to his conservation work. He wrote Arno Cammerer October 20, 1938, "It is going to be hard to get away, but Shenandoah National Park is so dear to my heart that I cannot refuse ... I will meet you, arriving Washington about 8:00 o'clock on Federal express. ... I want to talk over with you ... the roadside planting on the Skyline Road. ... The proper selection of native material which belongs to each zone should be most carefully considered. ... You have some good landscape men who are doing good work but they simply cannot apparently divest their minds of the importance of exotic material and other material which has been ordinarily used in landscape work for so many years. If we are to preserve and restore our National Parks to the ecological conditions before the destruction of much of the natural fauna and flora, we must stick closely to the plants which will do the job correctly." Forty-four years had elapsed since Kelsey's first publication initiating the drive for native plants for Americans. Nursery catalogs were now filled with native species, as opposed to virtually none a half century earlier. Most landscape architects were beginning to wave the banner, but the battle between native and exotic species continued with Kelsey an unrelenting spokesman.

Recognition

By 1940 the Great Depression was behind them, though business was a far cry from the buoyant times of the 1920s. Both the industry and the Kelsey Highlands Nursery had survived, just barely. It was time for a well-deserved sigh of relief. Even the American Association of Nurserymen could turn to lighter pursuits than the survival of itself and its members.

The *American Nurseryman* reported (paraphrased): The banquet of the AAN in New York, July 25, was in honor of the past presidents of the association. The menu card carried the names of those who had served the association as president from 1876 up to the present time. Of the twenty surviving past presidents, just one-half sat at the speakers' table. The local arrangements committee had prepared for each of them a lapel button carrying the seal of the association, beneath which was a bar denoting the office held. ... On this occasion one of the past presidents was signally honored: Harlan P. Kelsey, who was presented with a scroll in honor of his service to horticulture, signed by the presidents of seven organizations. The prizes for long-distance attendance were presented. An excellent floor show followed, and the music for dancing continued till an early hour.

Kelsey's scroll was illuminated and exquisitely lettered with the seals of the seven organizations distributed around the periphery.

> To Harlan Page Kelsey
> As a tribute to his outstanding accomplishments in the fields of Horticulture, Landscape Architecture, Forestry and Conservation; his pioneering work in city planning; his devotion to honest public service; his unselfish sacrifices in the fields of National, State and Municipal Park Development and Plant Nomenclature; his enrichment of American gardens through his many introductions of new plants.

Throughout a full and busy career, this public benefactor has freely given of his time, energy and resources, that the public welfare be served. Horticulture and all related fields will forever be indebted to him for his contributions to their advancement.

May this testimonial serve as a public acknowledgement of these accomplishments and of the high regard of those who have been privileged to know and work with him.

American Association of Nurserymen   Amer. Society of Landscape Architects
American Forestry Association   Amer. Institute of Park Executives
Massachusetts Horticultural Society   National Association of Gardeners
Horticultural Club of Boston

Executive Secretary Richard P. White wrote Kelsey August 6, "I look back upon the New York Convention with a great deal of satisfaction on many things which went on there, but I can truthfully say that I believe one of the best things that the Association has ever done took place at the Past Presidents Banquet when the ten past presidents in attendance received a slight token of the appreciation of their fellow men and you received an additional recognition of the great work which you have done for horticulture over your entire span of life. To me, this was the outstanding feature and it is the one occasion which I believe most of us will remember in years to come. I hope the scroll got back to Boxford without getting broken."

On October 9, two months later, Kelsey wrote to Theodore Wirth, Superintendent Emeritus of the Park Commissioners in Minneapolis. "Of course it was a wonderful occasion for me when they bestowed that scroll at the meeting in New York, and I was particularly pleased that the Park officials were represented by your son, Walter, who made a wonderful speech, but saying much more than I possibly could have deserved. I was pretty hard hit, for I didn't have the slightest inkling that such an affair was coming off."

Testimonial. Seven organizations. 1940.

Chapter 7

Unfinished Business

As the new decade of the 1940s emerged, Harlan Kelsey was sixty-eight years of age. He had made enormous contributions to his horticultural and conservation causes. He had achieved broad recognition; one might even say he was revered. At his age, most men would think of retiring while they were ahead of the game. The thought certainly did cross his mind. On November 25, 1941, he wrote to a Mr. Beaudry in Chicago, "Many thanks for your very courteous and thoughtful letter … to tell me you appreciate some of the eleemosynary work I have done over the past 25 or 30 years. I don't take myself too seriously and have decided to stop saving the world in so many different ways. The joke is on me!" But this attitude was quickly swamped by bigger issues he couldn't shake off. They were like his "ticks in hunting quail in the autumn with a woolen suit on and harder to get rid of than nettles."

Standardized Plant Names

By the early 1940s almost twenty years had passed since *Standardized Plant Names* was published. The joint committee knew it would be out of date soon after publishing and had promised new editions about every ten years. They also knew that many thousands of plant species had been ignored because they were out of the mainstream of ornamental horticulture. Failure to act on these problems was beginning to render obsolete all their prior work. This was unacceptable. Kelsey had to act, but it was easier said than done.

Coville and Kelsey had attempted a revision in the early 1930s and sought to address the problems experienced with the first edition. They had been desperate to ease McFarland out of the picture, replacing him with Olmsted as chairman of the joint committee. But Olmsted didn't respond to their entreaties, probably because of health issues. Nor had they been able to find a reasonable substitute for McFarland in funding and printing the significantly larger new edition. Then the Depression deepened. The joint committee's collaborators began to evaporate. Kelsey's allies at the AAN were unable to serve on the Nomenclature Committee because their time was totally committed to saving their businesses. The obstacles overwhelmed Kelsey and Coville. All bets were off. Only the gradual accumulation of new nomenclature material was informally continued by these two men in anticipation of the future second edition.

Then, on January 9, 1937, Frederick V. Coville died. With him gone and Frederick Law Olmsted faded to the background, the editorial committee was reduced to only Kelsey as the survivor. A less dedicated man would no doubt have quit. Only his peeve, McFarland, remained as a named responsible participant, through his chairmanship of the joint committee. This would stand since Olmsted accepted no part in any political moves to replace McFarland. But Kelsey could not quit the cause. In Kelsey's eyes, it was the biggest and most important problem besetting horticulture. He had to rebuild.

To understand the depth of Kelsey's feeling on *SPN*, it is helpful to quote a letter he wrote to the editor of *Horticulture* magazine:

> What's in a name? Quite often something which is not! Careless but homesick Europeans coming to America tacked easy

vernacular names of old world plants to the trees and plants they found in the new world, usually ignoring any botanical considerations, if only the leaves, or perhaps the buds or flowers, carried some real or fancied resemblance to the "old home" plants.

Thus "Hemlock," an umbelliferous herbaceous perennial, decidedly "sedative," was bestowed on a large conifer, perhaps our most beautiful American forest tree, *Tsuga canadensis*, probably because the foliage somewhat resembled the above herb of Socrates' fame.

Our glorious ericaceous Kalmia latifolia was dubbed "Laurel" because of leaf resemblance to a Lauraceae. This "bull" we feebly mitigate now by titling it Mountainlaurel. But why not use the common name Kalmia—surely as pleasing and euphonious a name as Laurel?

Similar ridiculous examples by the hundreds, ad nauseam, could be cited to illustrate the sloppy mental habits and limited imagination of our respected and respective forefathers. Postmaster General Farley and his assistants are every day having their tribulations with the many Bostons, Salems and even Berlins, that feeble-mindedness and mawkish sentimentality have inflicted on our different states as post offices. But today with 60,000 or more different species and varieties of plants already in American horticulture, and approximately 3,000 varieties being imported or originating in this country each year, the problem of correct and intelligent "common" plant naming is a serious matter of major importance.

Hence the fixed rule adopted by the American Joint Committee on Horticultural Nomenclature (similar to the International Botanical Rule with respect to botanical names) "that no two plants have the same common name," we believe to be truly sound in principle and capable of fulfillment.

This is an inevitable conclusion, for otherwise plant identity is lost, to the confusion and loss of the horticulturist and gardener, and to the great benefit of the plant name pirate and the unscrupulous plant tradesman, whose skullduggery is greatly enhanced thereby.

And as we now come to the particular subject of this letter—what are Geraniums and what are Pelargoniums? Because these two genera are nearly related, they need not confuse us. The botanist says they are distinct and we must accept his dictum. In both these genera the common and botanical names are, pleasingly enough, the same. Yet a certain group of true Pelargoniums have until now almost universally been called in greenhouse, window box, and graveyard parlance "Geraniums." So what to do?

In the new revision of *Standardized Plant Names* there will be listed approximately 65 true Geranium species and natural varieties, and some 18 true Pelargonium species and 44 horticultural varieties, the latter being what are commonly or vulgarly known as "Geraniums." Must we believe that to give up a cherished misnomer and call a real Geranium a Geranium and a real Pelargonium a Pelargonium, is too great a strain on the intelligence and mentality of our American people? If so, then Professor Hooton's conclusions as to the natural sequence of "Apes, Men and Morons" would seem to be amply justified.[158]

As 1937 unfolded, nothing new materialized as to organizations that would sponsor and fund the *SPN* second edition. The American Association of Nurserymen was the logical party, but the proposal never got beyond their executive committee stage. Kelsey was thus inextricably linked with McFarland, who again assumed his role as chairman of the joint committee and manager of all publishing issues. Kelsey again assumed his duties as secretary and treasurer of the joint committee, and also now became chairman of the editorial committee, a committee of one. Obviously he immediately had to get editorial help. For this, he turned to the two organizations where he had strong connections beyond the nurserymen—Coville's US Department of Agriculture and Harvard's Arnold Arboretum.

The task facing them was immense. Beyond the listings in the first edition were all the horticultural additions and suggested changes that had accumulated since it was published in 1923. Then came the addition of all the categories not covered in 1923—drug plants for pharmaceuticals, economic plants ("Important Plants and Plant Products Useful in Industry, Medicine, and for Food and Beverage Purposes"), western browse and range plants, lumber trade names, cacti and succulents, herbs and simples, and many other special lists all brought up to date. Much needed to be done to update and add to tropical plants in North America. Before they were through, there were more than ninety thousand standard common and scientific names. This was over twice the entries in the first edition. They added also the accepted pronunciation of all plant names. Ultimately, to accommodate this in a single volume, they had to go to a three-column page layout on 675 pages.

A tentative agreement was worked out with Dr. E. D. Merrill, head of the Arnold Arboretum, that they would formally endorse the gathering and editing of the scientific "botanical" names as part of their work. Dr. Alfred Rehder, internationally known and respected, took over this workload. Kelsey and Rehder had always been on the best of terms. Merrill also assigned Dr. Donald Wyman, horticulturalist on the Arboretum staff, as a member of the *SPN* editorial committee. Wyman was also named as assistant secretary of the American Joint Committee to take some of that load off Kelsey. This gave Wyman responsibility for working on the common name problem.

By February 1939 the compilation of the scientific names and their alignment with the new international standard was completed. Rehder had wasted no time. Kelsey reported, "The only thing undone is the completion of the common name list. On this, consultation has been had with the Chief of the Forest Service in Washington, Mr. F. A. Silcox; with the Acting Chief of the Bureau of Plant Industry, Dr. M. A. McCall, and with Secretary Wallace's assistant, Mr. J. D. LeCron. All these have agreed to the importance of the work and to the desirability of aiding in getting common names assigned, because these names are believed to be extremely useful in the outside work of these bureaus of the Department of Agriculture." While common names are often repugnant to botanists, scientific names were viewed by the western ranchers and farmers as highbrow nonsense; they wanted nothing to do with them. Of course these were the people of greatest interest to the US Department of Agriculture.

On March 8, 1939, Kelsey wrote to Silcox advising him that McCall was rapidly completing arrangements for William A. Dayton of the forest service to have suitable office space and assistants in the Bureau of Plant Industry for work on *SPN*. Dayton had taken the place of Olmsted. "We are about to print some new letterheads and I would like to have your formal approval that his name appear on it as a member of our Editorial Committee. I understand that Mr. Dayton is agreeable to this being done. He should have this formal recognition and we feel it will add great prestige to our Committee to have his name appear in this way." Dayton had already been at work on *SPN*, assembling the list of western browse and range plants, his forest service specialty. This completed the rebuilding of the editorial committee to full strength, with Kelsey (as chairman), Dayton, and Wyman.

Almost immediately Dayton galvanized the Washington troops into action. Even before his assignment to the editorial committee, he had established a Tree Name Committee. They had identified seventy-one names that should be different from the original *SPN* list; this because of long-standing practice in the trades, especially the lumber trade. Kelsey accepted all but thirteen of them where he wanted to try convincing them to accept his reasoning. The ball was now rolling.

Meanwhile, McFarland had been busy. By mid-March he had completed final arrangements for publication by the Macmillan Company in New York. He had arranged for a fifty-cents-per-volume royalty that would accrue to the joint committee. Of this amount, $1,500 was to be available before publication. McFarland, of course, immediately asked for a schedule. Was this to be a rerun of the trials between McFarland and the editorial committee, experienced back in 1922–23? Kelsey first noted that Dr. McCall, the man designated to put across the project in Washington, assured him that the set-up would be made and that there would be immediate action. But he pointed out to McCall, "there seems to be an inevitable sequence of red-tape occurrences that gum up the works." Not what McFarland wanted to hear—he wanted a schedule now. Kelsey replied, "This all depends on how quickly and efficiently we can get Dr. Dayton set up in his office. Until that is done and we can go over the material with him in detail, it will be impossible for me to make an estimate as to the probable number of pages." Kelsey continued, "I have noted carefully your estimates and tentative arrangements with Macmillan which look all right to me. Regarding set-up and the possibility of getting complete copy to you for a beginning, this is going to be extremely difficult for I don't see how we are going to begin to start setting type until the entire copy is ready and cross-indexed. We cannot cross-index common names under the Latin Z, going way back to A, until Z is finished, so far as common names are concerned."

Kelsey continued with McFarland, introducing another serious problem facing him on the editorial committee. "It is not wise for you to address him [Wyman] on the editorial policy, but to let me handle that part of it. In Washington, by grape-vine route, I heard of an extraordinarily indiscreet letter which Wyman wrote to B. Y. Morrison which placed the Joint Committee in a very unfavorable light and might quite well have sabotaged everything had it not come to my attention. As you will remember, this is not the first time he has done such a thing, and Dr. Merrill had to call him to account in no uncertain way. ... D. W. is a very capable and efficient man, but a single-team worker, or in other words an individual rather than a team worker, and my guess is that he is sore that the whole thing was not turned over to him and the credit passed on to him accordingly. ... You must also remember that notwithstanding his more recent pronouncements, he very clearly and distinctly stated at one of the earlier meetings that he was not interested in the common name problem. ... In all probability Dr. Wyman will be of comparatively little use in the Washington conferences on common names ... Pardon this long letter, but it did seem to be necessary. You will understand this is also very confidential."[159]

This situation effectively placed all the editorial committee work on the shoulders of Kelsey and Dayton. This would first be the thousands of decisions needed to filter out duplications of names and botanical absurdities as they became apparent. Later would come the tiresome proofreading and cross-referencing both before and after the galleys were set. Dayton's assistants would do much of this, but only if they were sufficiently schooled to do error-free work. That was yet to be proven. On the first edition Olmsted could always be counted on to help, giving them a true three-man team. Now it looked more and more like they would operate as a two-man team.

Often much time was spent on policy decisions that might seem inconsequential but involved differing viewpoints by noted authorities and had to be dealt with. One such decision was whether to spell "clone" with an "e" or without it, as "clon." In *SPN*, "A clon (pronounced klone) is a group of plants propagated only by vegetative and asexual means, all members of which have been derived by repeated propagation from a single individual." Back in 1923 this wasn't an issue, but in the intervening years propagators had produced and named thousands of such plants. Now they needed to be listed; they were noted by placing the symbol CL with the L slashing down through the C as in the engineering symbol for centerline. For one, the New York Botanical Garden had decided to use the correct English language spelling with the final "e." In his April 23, 1940, letter to Dayton, A. B. Stout, curator of Education and Laboratories, argued for the spelling "clone." "This change was not merely mine—it was already being used by reputable scientists etc. This spelling will be in my article soon to appear. It will be too bad for such a disagreement in your publication."

Dayton quickly answered on April 25:

> With regard to the spelling of clon(e): I fully agree with you that "It will be too bad for such a disagreement." ... The ultimate decision of how clon(e) will be spelled in the new edition of *SPN* must rest with the majority of our Editorial Committee ... Frankly, my own strong personal preference (which may be worth precisely $0.000) is for *clon*, because: (1) It is shorter; (2) It is far better etymologically; and (3) Most important of all, in my judgment, *it accords with the original spelling* by Webber & Cook. In systematic botany we cannot change the original spelling of a plant name unless we can demonstrate that it is a typographical error or otherwise distinctly erroneous, and the evidence must be overwhelming. Even then many excellent botanists refuse to correct the original spelling.

> It may be argued that the final (e) is necessary, in the English language, to show that the preceding vowel (o) is long. But we have exceptions even to that rule. ... I think it is a true general statement that, in the evolution of the English orthography, where two spellings of the same word occur, the shorter one invariably wins out in the long run.

> You have heard the old story of the farmer and his ram? A railroad track traversed the farm and the ram, a bellicose old

critter "skeered of nothing", attacked the locomotive one day without hurting the locomotive any. The farmer, viewing a winter supply of mutton, remarked: "I admire y'r pluck, but d—n y'r judgment." Your sentiments may harmonize with those of the agriculturist mentioned, as you view my temerity in challenging the expressed opinion of the International Committee of Horticultural Nomenclature and that of a professional horticulturist and of the eminence of yourself. I've stuck my neck out, so here's a fine chance to climb all over my frame and tell me very distinctly where to get "off at!"

On April 26 Kelsey came to the aid of his fellow committeeman and wrote Stout, "Your arguments are very good, and they move me very much, because you have done so much to emphasize the importance of the clon in horticulture, but very frankly, I don't think it makes much difference if we spell it 'clon' and you spell it 'clone,' because I think before very long everybody else will be spelling it our way. However, I am very glad to leave this to the decision of Dr. Wyman, Dr. Rehder, and Dr. Merrill. Let the votes count, including your own and mine."

As it turned out Kelsey couldn't have been more wrong. While *SPN* did adopt the spelling "clon," a half century later the English language convention of recognizing the long vowel *o* with the terminal *e* is universally used for clone by horticulturalists. Hereafter this text will use the spelling with the terminal *e*, except in direct quotations.

All this time spent discussing clones relates directly to the work of the editorial committee. It had been agreed that the *SPN*, second edition, would include the names of the hundreds of clones that had come on the market since the first edition. Since Dr. Wyman had expressed no interest in plant common names or the work to establish them; he had been asked to assemble and verify the list of all the new names that were clones and should bear the clone mark in the text. This was not inconsequential and would relieve the committee of one important task. However, as time passed, even this assignment was in doubt:

> McFarland to Kelsey, April 12, 1940: "Yours of April 10 comes after I had already written you transmitting a wail or a howl or a hope that we would get service, and not scrap, in the relation to Wyman. ... As I see it at this moment, the matter of primary importance is to get Wyman going on the clon list."
>
> Kelsey to McFarland, April 17: "Regarding Dr. Wyman, it is a closed incident to me, and no requests of any sort will go to him from this office regarding *SPN*, though I shall continue to send to him all vital carbons with regard to *SPN* matters."
>
> McFarland to Kelsey, April 19: "I don't quite understand the Wyman status, unless it is now implied that he is to produce the clon marks. Is that the idea?"
>
> Kelsey to McFarland, April 22: "My understanding is that Dr. Wyman has definitely refused to have anything to do with the clon marks. I had a letter from him on this subject, and I note that he sent you a copy, so unless you have had some word from him since that time, it is all off so far as he is concerned. I shall hesitate to ask him to do anything further on *SPN* under all the circumstances. He will get copies of vital correspondence, and that is as far as I am going."

With McFarland's commitment to the Macmillan Company looming larger on the horizon every day, he could not resist assuming his accustomed role as "expediter-in-chief." This promised a replay of the troubles he created pushing the editorial committee back in 1922. Dayton took it all in stride. In his April 17 letter, McFarland had proposed sending Miss Meikle, one of his employees, down to Washington to help on the workload. Dayton applauded but could not resist also writing the following: "I note your proviso that I write (you) promptly. It's hard for dear old Uncle to do his work promptly. For example, Mail addressed to me has to go to the Department Mail Room, then it is sorted out and goes to the Forest Service mail room, where it is again sorted out and goes (when a messenger is available) to Room 401. If 'wim, wigor and witality' are wanted, 'let George do it' instead of Sam!"

When it came to Dayton's sense of humor, Kelsey loved it. In his April 17, 1940, letter to Dayton, he concludes with the following: "Dayton, I want you to know that your letters with their both acute and droll comments supply my inspiration for every day, because I get them every day, and I'm glad I do." When it came to Dayton's technical capability and judgment, Kelsey had total confidence in him. McFarland seemed to think Dayton was reluctant to move on anything without Kelsey's explicit approval. In this regard, Kelsey wrote McFarland May 4, saying, "He is one of the most lovable men in the world, and is always very careful about hurting anybody's feelings, or assuming prerogatives that he is not absolutely certain are justified. Really, sometimes I think that red tape and officialdom in Washington has got his goat. I am extraordinarily fond of him and have a profound respect for his extraordinary abilities, so I didn't know just how to write him a letter transferring such authority as I may have in this matter, but did the best I could."

On May 4 McFarland wrote Kelsey one of his expediting letters in which he said, "Mr. Dayton is doing more than any one man ought to do and the sound, sane thing for us to do is to get two men to help him from the outside, not subject to interference from the complicated mechanism of the Departmental organization. ... Now here is a sour suggestion which you can at least think about. It would be to ask Don Wyman to go to Washington and help finish the job." Kelsey replied May 6, "Regarding suggestion about Don Wyman. From our past experience and knowing what his cooperative standards are, it would be just about the worst thing we could do to have him enter the picture any more than he is at present. It not only wouldn't get us anything, but would do just the opposite, and I guess you will find that W.A.D. thinks just as I do about it. Unpleasant as it may sound, my best suggestion is to add two months onto the program. We will get an infinitely better job and it will give me an opportunity to put in several weeks' time in Washington after the spring season is over and help on the common names problem, which I am best fitted to do; and I can assure you this suggestion is just as bitter to me as it could be to anybody else, but I do think it is the right one to make."

Wyman wrote Kelsey May 9, "I have just received several carbons from you, Mr. Dayton, and Dr. McFarland, showing that there is an undercurrent of trouble about which I know nothing. If your various difficulties could be lightened by my resignation from the Committee, you have it at once. I did my part of the work in the best way I knew how with a minimum of conferences here at the Arboretum, on which I counted so heavily. During the past year criticism has been heaped on the preliminary work I did, even though I have shown by our corrections to the galleys that we did not consider the original cards final by any manner of means. Consequently, if you would prefer to accept my resignation and make no mention of me at all in the final book, this is perfectly satisfactory."

Kelsey replied May 11. "I think none of us are interested in what has happened in the past, but just how we can get out of what apparently seems to be a crisis and get our job finished with credit to all concerned."

A year and many months later, October 28, 1941, Wyman wrote to Kelsey, "After due consideration, I would like to ask you to remove my name from the title page of the forthcoming edition of *Standardized Plant Names*. I have just read the rewritten introduction and my name appears on the title page together with the names of the other committee members. *Standardized Plant Names* in its final form is actually the result of your generous and indefatigable effort. Because of the years of major effort you have spent at this task, you should be given the major credit for the completed volume. That is why I believe the fewer names on the title page, the better for all concerned." Kelsey quietly responded October 29, "Thanks for your letter of October 28th, and we will comply with your final decision to have your name removed from the title page." The Wyman affair was now a closed book.

Beyond Wyman, May 1940 was explosive for all concerned with the *SPN* workload. It was marked with a cascading of obstacles, frustrations, and unconstrained emotions. There were two major events facing the editorial committee that caused all the anxiety: One was the commitment to the Macmillan Company that had been solely negotiated by McFarland. The other was the terminal date for Dayton's tour of service agreed to with the forest service.

The revised contract with Macmillan signed February 9, 1940, changed the size of the book so as to get it into one volume and included this proviso: "The manufacturers agree to deliver the said flat sheets and jackets not later than July 31, 1940." By now it was quite clear this provision would be breached and the committee would be liable to return the $1,000 advance already received from Macmillan. This would be sticky, given that $500 of it had already been dispensed to the Arnold Arboretum for Rehder's work on the scientific names. Kelsey had repeatedly urged McFarland to approach Macmillan for a two-month extension, allowing him to clear the mandatory spring nursery work and then go to Washington full-time to work with Dayton. McFarland couldn't comprehend what was mandatory about the nursery business; to him the *SPN* work was mandatory. He never revealed why he wouldn't approach Macmillan. Was it pride as a fellow publisher? His alternative was to bludgeon Kelsey into accelerated effort in the hope that the deadline could be met. This was a mistake.

Bill Dayton's May 3 letter to Kelsey provides a capsule of what a "mess" things were in, physically and emotionally:

Partly as a result of my solicitation, Dr. McFarland sent down two people from his office on April 30 so that he could get a first-hand knowledge of the status of things. Dr. McFarland signed contracts for turning over this job, it seems to me, not having a clear picture of the status of the work or of the volume and type of personnel and cooperation that were <u>essential</u> to getting the work done on schedule time. I appreciate very much his sending Miss Meikle and Mr. Rowe to spend the day with us. It set back our work temporarily, of course, but it has given Dr. McFarland a clear picture for the first time of what we are up against here. Dr. McFarland called me long distance May 1st and intimated that he might call a conference of the Committee together to decide what should be done. He asked me (out of a clear sky) if I would be "author" of the book and take full charge of it. I told him that was impossible without the *heartiest* approval and endorsement on your part. I told him that *SPN* is your "baby," that it never would have existed if it had not been for your farsighted and unselfish devotion to it, and that, moreover, there is no one in this country to take your place on it. …

Needless to say, I did not have any conception, when I took over the job, of what my difficulties were going to be. For one thing, I had no conception of the tremendous personnel turnover we were going to have. Just yesterday, for example, we lost one girl and got another. People are continually going and coming, and there is a lot of waste motion in this sort of thing. Another thing I did not anticipate was the difficulty of cooperation—the struggle to get lists from people in anything like adequate shape. Still another feature is the time that is necessary for me to spend on overhead. For example, it took me practically all day yesterday to get (almost by main force) two letters of the alphabet on one list from one of our staff here. This is not by way of criticism, because all our people are giving everything they have to the job and I have to restrain them from putting in overtime. It is just "one of those things." But everything put together tends to reduce my efficiency, and things are approaching a show-down. ... I will have to get more technical assistance and get it quickly or else I am going to be very distinctly "on the spot," as I am distinctly in the "goat" role in this job and if the book isn't done on time, I am going to get the blame.

Two letters McFarland wrote May 13 inflamed Kelsey. McFarland scolded Kelsey for seemingly mismanaging things as chairman of the editorial committee. If only ... Why didn't you ... If you had raised the red flag at the beginning ... "I do hope you will see that your commitments to your friends and associates warrant the disturbance of your business relations required to have a day's visit in Washington which may at least start toward conclusive effort."

Kelsey roared back May 15, "Two letters from you ... are received this morning, and I can answer both of them in very few words. Your impudent, gratuitous, and uncalled for directions as to how I should spend my time and run my business must cease. Should I get another letter carrying the implications of your latest letter to me, I will after that return all of your letters unopened. Your amazing discovery that I am the goat because the printing of the galley sheets from the cards were not as effective as everyone concerned thought they might be is nothing short of silliness." Kelsey went on rebutting McFarland's assertions for many more paragraphs before closing with, "Now, Dr. McFarland, in closing I want to again warn you that the insinuating, meddling tone of your letters as to my business and my movements must cease from now on if you expect to have me correspond with you further. I could very easily write a letter which would show where a muddling of this whole proposition really originated and what it is all about, but that would not get us anywhere, and unless I am driven to it, I will not do so. So again let me tell you that all I am now interested in is to forget the past and see what we can do best for the future. If you want to go on that basis, O.K. If not, it is easy to say so."

McFarland's May 17 reply closed with, "I am returning your letter of May 15, which I do not want in my files for your sake or for mine, and I can only regret that it was written in a moment of ill temper."

The second huge obstacle was the terminal date for Dayton's tour of service agreed to with the forest service—July 1, 1940. This was just six weeks away. Up to this time Kelsey and McFarland had been playing an unyielding game of "chicken." McFarland labored under the delusion that if he asserted himself as president of the joint committee, his title and elder status would force Kelsey to submit to his wishes. He wanted Kelsey to find some people from the outside to help Dayton, even if it meant Wyman. (Why Kelsey? Why not McFarland?) He insisted on a joint meeting in Washington. Somehow a one-day meeting would magically finish the editorial work and produce a satisfactory set of materials for the Macmillan Company by July 31. Kelsey, knowing there was no magic in a meeting, would not budge from his position that he would not sacrifice his nursery's spring business, which needed every day he could give to it. He kept urging McFarland to just get a two-month extension from Macmillan to create a reasonable time for completion by September 30. But now that game was submerged by the nearer deadline of losing Dr. Dayton.

There finally was a meeting in Washington May 31 with Kelsey, Dayton, McFarland, and Mr. Foley of the Department of Agriculture. Two things were accomplished: One was that the whole process was streamlined by giving Dayton final authority on everything remaining so he wouldn't need approval by Kelsey; by no longer waiting on the D of A's Committee on Plant Names for any more input; and by side-stepping any further input from the forest service's Tree Name Committee, or any of the contributing organizations under the joint committee. The second and more important accomplishment was to put Mr. Foley to work in the Department of Agriculture on getting an extension for Dr. Dayton's continuing work with Kelsey. It is not clear how he did this, but there seemed to be no more anxiety after that over Dayton's being able to finish his job.

Kelsey agreed to spend every available day he could muster to be in Washington to work with Dayton for the remainder of the summer. McFarland agreed to get an extension from the Macmillan Company until September 1. The "game of chicken" was ended. Both parties had swerved. But Dayton's effort was not totally clear as to the help he could get from D of A staff. On June 12, Dayton reported to Kelsey, "I have had numerous telephone conversations lately with Messrs. McCall, Chapline, and Raw but nothing definite has happened as yet [concerning staff], outside of the following:

1. The Government has refused to renew the lease on the Atlantic Building after July 1st. We, therefore, will have to move but, at this writing, it is not certain where <u>we</u> will go. The occupants of the Atlantic Building are supposed to go (outside of the Forest Service library) into the Columbian Building on 5th Street, between D and E Streets. At last reports they are unwilling either to furnish us temporary (2 months') headquarters in either the Columbian or Atlantic Building, so we may have to work on the sidewalk! ...
2. Mrs. Jackman has left us, permanently. This is a big loss.
3. Miss Grady (stenographer-checker), lent us by SCS, cannot be returned to us after July 1 as she does not have Civil Service status and drastic cuts in that Bureau's appropriations have made it necessary for them to drop many of their employees.

More later!"

Poor old Dayton's bureaucratic obstacles never seemed to end. Nor was there a quick end of Kelsey's efforts to finish the lists, as the summer came and went. On October 9, 1940, he wrote E. H. Costich of the Hicks Nurseries in New York, "I am just back from the job of completing copy for the new edition. It is now in the printer's hands, and I think that you may expect it to be actually available the first of the coming year. It has been a terrible job and my last one for the horticultural public. I have had to neglect the family and business, forget vacation and everything else, and have plugged day and night to get it done. Let us hope that the results will be worth what it cost, for it sure did come pretty high."

One full year later (one year!), October 17, 1941, Kelsey wrote to Dayton, "As you know, we have been requested to relieve certain contributors and certain other individuals from all responsibility of the editorial and other content of the 1941 edition of *SPN*. I suggest the following change. Please rearrange or change as you think best and let me have it when you return the copy for Preface which I left with you.

EDITORIAL RESPONSIBILITY.
>The responsibility for all editorial and other contents of this 1941 Edition of *Standardized Plant Names*, other than attaches to collaborators for specific and acknowledged contributions, is fully assumed by the Editors, Harlan P. Kelsey and William A. Dayton.

I will let you know as quickly as possible the conclusions of Attorney MacDonald re. the contract with J. H. McFarland Company. ... I sincerely hope you people will write a strong letter to McFarland regarding the editorial content being left absolutely unchanged and that it is not subject to the whims of McFarland. Found his letter here regarding the Glossary, and it's the 'bunk'. I am sorry you don't class along with the great botanists he names, although I don't know one of them who has ever really written a Glossary as you have done for the National Forestry Service."

That same day, October 17, Attorney MacDonald had written a memo to Kelsey. "At the outset you pointed out that both you and Dr. McFarland are only interested in a contract that will properly protect the company on the one hand and the members of the committee on the other. I am confident that this can be done." The contract had to protect all the members of the joint committee, appointed representatives of various associations or societies, all serving gratuitously, holding them harmless from any actions that might affect their personal liabilities and/or bind their estates. At the same time such persons had to be willing to authorize the publisher to produce the work and to provide for proper compensation from the proceeds of sales by the publisher to cover his costs.

What had happened during the intervening year, 1941? Kelsey had told E. H. Costich, October 9, 1940, "I am just back from the job of completing copy for the new edition. It is now in the printer's hands." Failure to meet the copy deadlines had apparently resulted in the withdrawal of the Macmillan Company as publisher. The only alternative was for McFarland to put forth his Mount Pleasant Press as publisher, and to assume all the publishing expense up front. He would again have to be repaid out of sales, as he was with the first edition back in 1923. Interestingly, after all the effort of the last twenty years to divorce the editorial committee from McFarland's influence, and McFarland from the financial risk as the publisher, events had conspired to bring them all right back to the arrangements they so disliked in the publishing of the first edition. A full year had been consumed in making this adjustment.

The book was put through to publication on January 15, 1942, a mere thirty-nine days after the December 7, 1941, Japanese attack on Pearl Harbor. They had beaten the rigors of war mobilization by the skin of their teeth, with its stringent rationing of personnel for any nonessential purposes. Dr. Dayton's temporary assignment to *SPN* would certainly have been in jeopardy.

The year 1942 was a replay of 1923. As the book reached the nursery industry, *SPN* immediately brought forth praise. They had been waiting for it for years; now the nurserymen had it in their hands. The year 1943 was also a replay of 1924. The critical botanists, academics, and entrenched Kelsey enemies had been sharpening their knives for a year and began their assault. These, of course, were the people who didn't face the consequences of nomenclatural chaos in their daily business. Early 1942 went something like this:

Edwin J. Stark, President American Association of Nurserymen—"I do not know of any individual who has contributed more to the nursery industry than you in editing the edition of *Standardized Plant Names*, which will be a monument to the services you have rendered the association for many generations."[160]

Resolution offered to the AAN Convention—"RESOLVED, that recognizing the unselfish devotion and long continued and still continuing contribution of Mr. Kelsey's time without whose zeal and energetic promotion, we are assured, this book would never have been published, we hereby recommend that the Treasurer of our Association be directed to present to Mr. Harlan P. Kelsey as a token of our appreciation for what he has done, an honorarium of an amount to be determined by the executive Committee."[161]

Richard P. White, Executive Secretary, AAN—"I will do as you ask in expressing to President La Bar and the other members of the Executive Committee your thanks for their contribution towards your personal expenses and efforts which, as we realize, have been tremendous. I know you and I both feel the same toward such things. One's highest reward is good will, and I can assure you there is nobody in the nursery industry I have ever seen or talked to who does not hold you in the highest respect. Such expressions as I have received from men, concerning you and your contribution, could not be bought."[162]

Kelsey to Dayton—"You refer to the times when you and I were both over tired and a little bit peevish but forget it. No one could have sacrificed themselves more nor worked more honestly than you did on this job. You have nothing to regret and everything to be proud of and it has been one of the greatest joys of my life to have been associated with you on this job. ... I just want to reiterate what I have said before that the bright star in the firmament in this whole matter is yourself. I hope and believe that time will come when you will get adequate acknowledgement of the part you have played in it."[163]

By the end of 1942, the criticism started from the "academics":

Dayton to Kelsey—"It seems odd you don't remember P. L. Ricker. He used to be an assistant to Dr. Coville, and you must have met him during the old days. He is president of the Wildflower Protective Association and is a professional systematic botanist. He is ordinarily mild-mannered enough, as a wildflower person might be expected to be, but vitriol seems to ooze from his pores every time *SPN* or Dr. Coville is mentioned. I don't quite understand how he gets that way. C. R. Ball, the willow man, is another exhibit of this type of Homo sapiens. It's too bad your pal, Doc Hutton, never started studying botanists; man, they're funny guys!"[164]

E. H. McClelland, Carnegie Library of Pittsburgh, wrote a "letter to the editor" of the *Journal of Forestry*: "There does not come to mind any other set of standards in one specific field on which as much labor has been lavished as on the new edition of *Standardized Plant Names* but this extensive reference work loses something in value through disregard of the medium in which it is presented—the English language." McClelland then went on to criticize the book under six main areas:

1. Failure of the American Joint Committee ... to appoint on their Editorial Committee somebody "with a good grasp of, and an adequate feeling for, English."

2. Failure of the Editorial Committee to follow the *Century, Standard,* and *Oxford* dictionaries, and such floras as those of Gray, Britton & Brown, Small, and Jepson for English plant names.
3. Faults of omission and commission in hyphenation, solidification, apostrophic deletion, etc.
4. Criticism of coined English plant names.
5. Insufficient cross-referencing.
6. Criticism of alphabetization.

Bill Dayton was moved to respond, at the editor's request, with a four-page treatise that utterly destroyed McClelland's arguments in each of the six areas. He used a combination of humor and logic to rebut or marginalize McClelland's complaints, point by point. It would take an entire subchapter to recite them all, so just two examples will have to suffice:

1. For item one, which categorically stated that the editors had no feeling for English, there was nothing concrete to rebut. So Dayton resorted to humor to marginalize the near insult: "We will award this round without argument to Bro. McClelland. It would have been bully if the A.J.C.H.N. could have appointed an authority on the English language to the Editorial Committee, but apparently they failed to do so—'tis true 'tis pity, and pity 'tis 'tis true. Mr. Kelsey and I 'no spikka da Ingleesh good!' 'S too bad!"
2. However, in most cases McClelland had ventured specific objections that could be rebutted, such as in item 3. It will suffice to show only one rebuttal in Dayton's own tongue-lashing form: "Mr. McClelland indicates that boxelder should be spelled with a hyphen. Does he spell color and labor with a 'u,' because that is the *Oxford* Dictionary form and perpetuates the Norman

origin and pronunciation? Mr. McClelland takes us to task for not following Gray's, Jepson's and Britton & Brown's manuals and floras more sedulously. But these three works write boxelder as *two words* (and the plant is not an elder!). Besides, there might someday be a true box elder, just as there is a desert willow and desertwillows. Incidentally, it is boxelder (solid; one word) not only in *SPN*, but in Sudworth's *Check List* (published in 1927; official standard of the U.S. Forest Service), in Sudworth's *Forest Trees of the Pacific Slope* (1908), the Forest Service's *Range Plant Handbook* (1937), Van Dersal's *Native Woody Plants of the United States* (1938), Wyman's *Hedges, Screens and Windbreaks* (1938), Deam's *Flora of Indiana* (1940), as scholarly a flora as any listed by Mr. McClelland, with fully as much—and I think more—attention devoted to the English names, Kearney & Peebles' *Flowering Plants and Ferns of Arizona* (1942; a scholarly work if there ever was one)—but why go on? Mr. McClelland will find it boxelder in the G.P.O. *Style Manual* and many other places. Frankly I'm 'from Missouri'; Mr. McClelland should demonstrate to his readers more convincingly why box-elder (with an antiquated, space-wasting, and unlovely hyphen) is superior typographically or in any other way to boxelder."[165]

Very few negative comments emerged from the working, nonacademic, nonbotanist community. One, of course, had to be offered by P. J. van Melle, the nurseryman from Poughkeepsie, New York. There was never anything done by Kelsey that didn't elicit something scathing from Van Melle:

> I cannot help expressing my amazement at the relative distribution of polybrid and clonal signs in the new Edition of

SPN. [This was followed by five erudite paragraphs of detailed denunciation of *SPN*'s technical merit.] ... One dreads to contemplate the implications of your dispositions in practice. You have deprived a multitude of hybrid-names of the only significance and trading value they possess, and thrown them wide-open to miss-use for non-descript mongrels. A little more rope for your Committee, and it will hang itself.

At first, Kelsey would respond to the critics with long, detailed explanations as to why the editorial committee made the choices it had to make. It didn't take long however, before Kelsey simply referred critics to the preface of the book, where everything was explained in great detail.

Mount Cammerer

There is yet another reason for Kelsey's seeming absence from *SPN* matters during the full year 1941, following his October 9, 1940, completion of copy for the new edition. Arno Cammerer died April 30, 1941. Kelsey had lost his dearest friend, short of his twin brother, Harry. For the remainder of 1941 and early 1942, Kelsey was devoted to the cause of memorializing his friend, "Cam."

Cammerer became the third person in the NPS's founding triumvirate—hard-working, intelligent, amiable and even-tempered, with a great sense of humor and an optimistic, businesslike devotion to duty. In Albright's view, Cammerer evolved "into one of the best administrators in Washington, and in his quiet, unassuming way saw to it that things got done. He was also the person most responsible for getting private funding," which was so crucial to the NPS's early acquisition efforts. These words are from a biographical sketch attending the Cornelius Amory Pugsley Gold Medal Award, won by Cammerer in 1938. The sketch closed with, "The frenzied pace of development in the parks spurred by the availability of CCC labor in Cammerer's tenure as director led to him taking less than two weeks leave in five years. This workload and pressures from the disdain with which he was treated by Secretary Ickes, resulted in a heart attack in 1940. At that point, he asked Ickes to reassign him to become regional director in Richmond and he died from another heart attack a year later in 1941."[166] This is an inadequate description of Cammerer's contributions to the national parks, but must suffice for now.

Backtracking chronologically, two people had been recognized by the National Geographic Board for their contributions to the Great Smoky Mountains National Park. Mount Chapman was named for Colonel Dave Chapman's work leading the Tennessee Great Smoky Mountains National Park Committee. Mount Kephart was similarly named for Horace Kephart's well-known early work as an exponent of the Carolina mountains, authoring books and letters. Kelsey was unimpressed with the virtue of isolating this praise to only two individuals. Quoting from his letter to Cammerer of October 31, 1939:

> Dear Cam: … Many thanks for the book. I have just glanced through it and I know I will enjoy it, but it does seem as though it was written for the special benefit of Dave Chapman, while many others who were quite as active in the movement have been extremely soft-pedaled.
>
> The North Carolina group may be noticed, if so I will find it but I can't understand why the National Geographic Board would ever fall for naming a mountain peak except posthumously. I thought it was a fixed rule. Kephart was a great exponent of the Carolina Mountains but there are many other good writers starting with Rebecca Harding Davis and to be perfectly honest "Cammerer Mountain" would have been infinitely more appropriate and justified.
>
> Thank God I had the nerve to fight the Tennesseans who wanted to name a peak after the members of the Commission. As you

know there were two members who highly favored it and I think they felt very sore with me for taking such an active part in killing the proposition.

One month after Cammerer's death, Newton B. Drury wrote to Kelsey, "In recognition of the esteem and respect in which we hold the memory of our late Director, Arno B. Cammerer, the National Park Service feels that some important geological feature should bear his name. ... With the approval of the Secretary of the Interior, I am requesting that you, together with Mr. Will E. Carson, Director of the Virginia Conservation Commission during the establishment of Shenandoah National Park; Colonel David Chapman, Chairman of the Tennessee Great Smoky Mountains National Park Committee; Mr. Ross Eakin, Superintendent of Great Smoky Mountains National Park; and Mr. Conrad L. Wirth of my staff, serve as a committee to present a recommendation to be submitted to the Department of Interior for approval."

Kelsey to Drury, telegram, June 6, 1941: "Appreciate honor and accept on Cammerer Memorial Committee. Heartily approve other names."

Kelsey to Drury, telegram, June 7: "If possible, suggest North Carolina be represented on Cammerer Committee stop Colonel Webb, Editor Asheville Citizen, great admirer of Cammerer."

Wirth to Kelsey, letter, June 24.: "Director Drury appreciates and concurs in your suggestion that Colonel Charles A. Webb be added to the committee."

Kelsey to Wirth, letter, July 1: "At Gatlinburg I saw Ross Eakin and was rather flabbergasted, when I spoke about the committee, to hear him say, 'Well, Colonel Chapman and I have about settled the matter, and I'll show you the correspondence.' I asked him why all the haste, and whether the committee had been functioning at all, but he said as there was no money to have the committee meet, it would probably be just a matter of correspondence anyway. Also he said he was very anxious to have the matter settled at once, because he didn't know how long he was going to be Superintendent of Great Smoky Mountains National Park, a very commendable wish, but I can't see why that is germane to an orderly and careful consideration if the subject matter the committee is supposed to handle." The letter continued for two more pages outlining the many considerations that might be deliberated and the administrative procedures for a proper committee deliberation.

Wirth to Kelsey, letter, July 8: "We have heard from several members of the committee selected to choose a memorial to Cam regarding their choice for the chairman of that committee. You have suggested Will Carson. Colonel Chapman writes that 'it would probably be best not to have anyone from the Smokies or Shenandoah for chairman.' Will Carson has proposed me for the honor. However, my acceptance is out of the question because Director Drury has expressed the wish that someone not connected with this Service act as chairman. How about you acting as chairman? You are the logical choice for that position, because of your close and long association with Cam and your interest in geographic nomenclature."

Kelsey to Wirth, letter, July 11: "Replying to your letter July 8th, if you and the rest of the committee really want me to act as chairman on the Cammerer Memorial Committee, of course, I would consider it a great honor and accept. As soon as this point is actually confirmed, I should be very glad to take up the matter with you in detail for action."

Wirth to Kelsey, letter, July 29: "I have deferred replying to your letter of July 11 until I could learn from the members of the 'Cammerer Committee' with reference to the selection of a chairman. You are their choice."

Wirth to each of the committee members, letter, August 26: "Harlan Kelsey has asked me to write all of you regarding a meeting of the

'Cammerer Committee' which we hope to hold at the Great Smoky Mountains National Park Headquarters at Gatlinburg at 10:30 a.m., Friday September 5."

Kelsey was now in charge. He had one long standing bias against renaming mountains that complicated the affair. Kelsey to Wirth, July 1: "There is another thing that worries me no end, and that is the eliminating of old names to mountains and giving them new names. If this generation can do it, so can the next, and our work might easily be undone unless we use the greatest skill and judgment in the matter. ... You will see that I am going to be a very contemplative member of this committee." Conrad Wirth replied July 8, "I agree with you, as I am sure all the other members of the committee do, that we do not want to change any well-established names. However, I would not be adverse to giving Cam's name to some outstanding feature, which at present is known by several names, or which should be changed for reasons of good nomenclature."

Connie Wirth was well aware of the work of the nomenclature committees of both the North Carolina and Tennessee booster organizations, immediately following Cam's death. Most of the work had been done by the Tennessee group and then endorsed by North Carolina. Their recommendation neatly fit within Wirth's suggestions, above, to Kelsey. The Tennessee nomenclature committee's report to Colonel Chapman June 6 read in part as follows:

> After considering three or four points in the Great Smokies the committee recommends that White Rock be designated as Mount Cammerer, or Cammerer Point—preferably the latter. The feature that has recently been known as White Rock is really more of a point or an end of a mountain than a separate peak, hence the preference for Cammerer Point. Since this point is on the Tennessee-North Carolina state line, it should be acceptable to North Carolinians as well as Tennesseeans who are interested in the park.

White Rock is available for this purpose because this name has never been generally accepted—although it was officially so designated some eight or ten years ago. Most old maps show no name for this point. Those that did have a name used Sharp Top. There was another Sharp Top in the Park (on the North Carolina side) so the original Nomenclature Committee recommended the name White Rock. This name was selected because many people in the vicinity of Newport had been in the habit of referring to the point as White Rock because at certain times and in certain light the rocks appeared to be white. The rocks really are not white, however, and for that reason that name is not considered appropriate.

The elevation at White Rock is 5,025 feet. Although there are many peaks in the Smokies considerably higher than this, there are very few that are as spectacular or conspicuous. The point provides a 360 degree view with a very spectacular or dramatic foreground. A beautiful stone tower, used as a fire tower, now adorns the spot.

Members of the committee are unanimous in the belief that this is the most logical spot in or out of the Great Smokies to be used in paying a tribute to Cam.

By September a complication had arisen. Colonel Webb, committee member from Asheville, North Carolina, had changed his mind. While in June, as a member of the North Carolina nomenclature committee, Webb had joined the majority in favor of White Rock, he now wanted to make a strong case for renaming the Chimney Tops, on the North Carolina side, as Cammerer Peaks. On September 10 he wrote Kelsey, laying out his case:

> I regretted more than I can tell that I was unable to accompany you and the others of the committee to view White Rock last

Friday ... I knew the trip would be too hard for me ... As I came home and passed the Chimney Tops—in my opinion the outstanding feature in the Great Smoky Mountain National Park—I felt more strongly than ever that the very best thing would be to accept my suggestion and give these Tops the name of Cammerer Peaks.

Mr. Cammerer towers far ahead of any of us in the final establishment of the park, and as it is the intention of all of us to honor him, it does seem to me that it would not be the right thing to name a mountain of only 5,000 feet elevation and one that is way off in a far corner of the park where few people would see it, after him, when there are other higher mountains—notably Mount Kephart and Mount Chapman—named in honor of other people.

Personally I could never see any sense in naming a mountain after Kephart. He had less to do in establishing the park than anyone who had anything at all to do with it. It is true that his book, The Southern Highlands, had a great deal to do with attracting people to the peaks in the Smokies, but as to actual work, Kephart had very little to do with it. However, that is the way of the world.

I presume Mr. Wirth will write me as to the decision of the committee, but if White Rock is finally decided on I am unwilling to sign the report.

On September 22 Kelsey replied to Colonel Webb. As editor of the *Asheville Citizen-Times*, Webb was a man of considerable import. Kelsey wanted him on board and worked hard to persuade Webb in favor of White Rock:

I wish it had been possible for you to go with Colonel Chapman and myself to the top of White Rock. I was enormously impressed with the mountain, and have changed my views very considerably, particularly after viewing that mountain and then going back and taking another view of the Chimneys, which, I understand, do not constitute the rather limited range of mountains in which they occur, but just the two peaks that are very close to each other. Another thing that impressed me was the fact that the Great Smoky Mts. Broke off abruptly at White Rock Mountain, and it is the culmination of the Great Smoky Mountains National Park to the north.

Mount Chapman, for instance, while higher, is relatively unimportant from the standpoint of the valleys below, and some day the northern end of the park will be very much more used than it is today, and White Rock stands out as the northern rampart of the park. The view from White Rock is one of the finest I have seen anywhere in the eastern mountains—or the western mountains for that fact—owing to the fact that the northwestern slopes are so extremely precipitous. …

You could readily make the top of White Rock and back from Asheville in a day, and I know that Major Eakin will be glad to arrange to have horses there for you to make the trip over a very fine bridle trail which entails very little fatigue—in fact, I couldn't tell I had been on a horse after I got back, and I really believe, Colonel Webb, that you will not do yourself justice in voting on this matter unless you have personally gone to the top of White Rock Mountain. I only wish it were possible for every other member of the committee to make the trip if they have not already done so.

On October 4 Connie Wirth weighed in with his views. He appreciated Colonel Webb's view that the mountain or any other object chosen to honor "Cam" should be one of the park's outstanding features. But he reemphasized that the selection could not run counter to the geographic board's principle that well-known names should not be changed. It would be embarrassing to suggest that an exception be made in the case of the well-known Chimney Tops. White Rock in his view was in a different class, given the chaotic history of its name. He enhanced the case by suggesting that Mount Cammerer apply to the entire stretch of mountain extending for some six miles from east of White Rock to Low Gap. This would make "Mount Cammerer" the outstanding feature and most conspicuous name in that side of the park. This long span ascending the crest of the range from Low Gap to the mountain top, and then plunging two and a half miles down to the valley of Pigeon River, could be named concurrently as "Cammerer Ridge."

While efforts in the Smokies were unfolding, Will Corson, former director of the Virginia Conservation Commission during the establishment of the Shenandoah National Park, was surveying memorial possibilities in that park. The peaks and outcrops of note all held long established and accepted names. The only thing really new and notable involved the construction of the Skyline Drive. The committee observed that the tunnel, now nameless, through Mary's Rock near Panorama, could be named "Cammerer Tunnel." This seven-hundred-foot tunnel, which had been bored through solid granite, was one of the outstanding engineering accomplishments in the construction of the Skyline Drive.

Thus, by the end of December, a round-robin final report to Director Drury was circulated for signature to all the committee members. Colonel Webb had graciously withdrawn his objections, so the report could be unanimous. On January 15, 1942, the report was in Director Drury's hands. Drury imposed his authority to eliminate "Cammerer Tunnel" from the picture, on the grounds that the tunnel was a man-made product emphasizing engineering skill and was insufficient recognition of the extent and nature of Cam's contributions to the park. He placed in abeyance the question of perpetuating his memory in Shenandoah Park until some other time. Mount Cammerer and Cammerer Ridge were accepted and forwarded to the US Board on

View from Mount Cammerer. Northern terminus of the Great Smokies.

Geographical Names for approval. The approval was rendered and announced February 25, 1942. The Department of Interior press release, which cited each of the committee's members, included "Harlan P. Kelsey, National Park Consultant, who had collaborated with Mr. Cammerer in locating the sites of the Shenandoah and Great Smoky Mountain National Parks."

Thus, February 1942 marked two significant achievements for Kelsey. His best friend had been appropriately memorialized, and his lifelong efforts in plant nomenclature were rewarded with the publishing of *Standardized Plant Names*, second edition. Both occurred in the same month.

While all this conservation and horticultural recognition was culminating in the East, the carping criticism in the West over the quality of the "new" inferior eastern parks was simmering. Robert Sterling Yard, as editor of the National Parks Association bulletin, had used the name "primeval parks" to separate the great western geological wonders from the lesser wonders of the newer eastern parks. To him a towering granite spire was a primeval wonder while a secluded Appalachian cove with towering horticultural wonders was, well, just a secluded Appalachian cove. Why enthuse over an eight-foot-diameter tulip tree when one could gaze upon the giant sequoias of California? Who cares if a hundred square miles contains more species of trees than all of Europe? Yard was a writer, and these biases infused his articles. His March 1942 article, titled "The Great Smoky Wilderness" in the *Living Wilderness* magazine was no exception.

On March 30, 1942, a peeved Harlan Kelsey was moved to complain to Newton Drury, now director of the National Park Service. "To my mind Mr. Yard is the best writer on National Parks that we have in this country, and his paper is by far the best thing I have seen on the Great Smoky Mountains National Park until he gets to the end where he takes up the matter of the history of its genesis and accomplishment."

Kelsey's commentary on Yard's historical perspective, or lack of historical perspective, provides an insider's recounting of the true sequence of events and appropriate credits, unlikely to be found elsewhere in the literature. Accordingly it deserves to be reported in its entirety:

> As a matter of historical accuracy, however, I should like to call your official attention to a statement made by him at the end of the article, which is totally unjustified as to fact and essentially unfair to all those who had so much to do with the establishing of the Great Smoky Mountains National Park. This [Yard's] statement reads as follows:
>
>> The actual achievement of Great Smoky Mountains National Park may fairly be attributed to Colonel David C. Chapman, who devoted years to the work. In turn, Chairman of the Association, Chairman of the Tennessee State Commission, and Chairman of the Joint State Commission, to his executive ability, vision, personal sacrifice and devotion the people of the country owe more than can be repaid.
>
> Meager credit is given to Mark Squire and the other members of the North Carolina Commission, and in the whole article the members of the Southern Appalachian National Park Commission are not even mentioned by name. Mr. Yard always bitterly resented the fact that he was not chosen on this Parks Commission and from the beginning has criticized severely the work of this Commission. In the article I am discussing, he says, regarding this Committee (afterwards Commission):
>
>> To keep the political risks of such an experiment outside of the Department, he appointed none but laymen, and these, under the pressure of local demand, picked three

locations instead of one. Of these only Great Smoky met the standard of the National Park System. Nevertheless the others, Shenandoah and Mammoth Cave, were swept into the system in the excitement of sectional promotion, as conditional, however, on purchase of the land for presentation to the National Government.

Hundreds of our best National Park people in this country have declared over and over again that Shenandoah National Park area did meet National Park conditions, Mammoth Cave probably not, but the facts are, and which are clearly in the records, that the whole movement would have been killed unless at a certain time unanimous consent would be given by Congress to approve Great Smoky and Shenandoah areas, and the representative from Kentucky would not give this unanimous consent unless Mammoth Cave came into the picture. Now, should the Commission have stuck to their guns, or did they do right in accepting Mammoth Cave for a National Park? The whole movement would have been killed otherwise, and while Mammoth Cave may not be entitled to the title "National Park", it certainly ought to be in the custody and management of the National Park Service.

But my chief astonishment in Mr. Yard's "History of the Movement" is his utterly ignoring of the part Arno B. Cammerer played in the securing of these Parks. May I say now that I do not take one jot or tittle away from all due honor that should go to Colonel Chapman for the fine work he did as Chairman of the Tennessee State Commission, but I do say that he fell far short of what members of the Southern Appalachian National Park Commission did, and that the North Carolina State Commission should get full and equal credit. As you may know, I was in the battle for these parks from the very beginning until the present time and was very close with the officials of the National

Park Service throughout the entire period of acquisition and development. I therefore make the following statement:

> The actual achievement of Great Smoky Mountains National Park may be almost entirely attributed to Arno B. Cammerer, Director of the National Park Service. It was Mr. Cammerer who coordinated all Park efforts in North Carolina and Tennessee, as well as in Virginia, who saved the situation dozens of times when the success of the movement hung by a thread, and who personally succeeded in inducing Mr. Rockefeller to put up the funds without which neither the Great Smoky Mountains National Park nor the Shenandoah National Park would have been acquired. It was almost entirely to Mr. Cammerer's executive ability, vision, personal sacrifice and devotion that the people of this country owe for their now having these two Parks.

I have gladly stuck my neck out and might just as well finish for your personal record. The naming of mountain peaks or the changing of names of mountain peaks, excepting posthumously, is a dangerous practice and I believe totally unwarranted by the National Geographic Board. Changing the name of one of the major peaks in the Great Smoky Mountains and giving it to Colonel Chapman, who is still living, comes under this category. If my statement above is correct, this had no warrant either in naming it while the recipient was living, nor even posthumously. It was done, however, through exceptionally strong local pressure in Tennessee, and no member of the Tennessee Commission should have had a peak named after him any more than should one from the North Carolina Commission.

What in my opinion had developed into a disgraceful situation was partly remedied by the changing of White Rock to Mount

Cammerer, but in all sincerity, and with perhaps as clear a knowledge of all the facts connected with this matter under discussion, I believe that the National Park Service itself should challenge that statement of Bob Yard's by giving a clear-cut historical statement of the facts in a future publication of the Great Smoky Mountains National Park. The fact that in this article of Mr. Yard's the one man who more than all others was responsible for the American people now having possession of not only the Great Smoky Mountains but the Shenandoah National Parks was not even mentioned, although the author of the article knows full well the truth of this statement I have made, seems to me to justify the friends of Mr. Cammerer demanding that a clear record of the facts be made and disseminated, and I think, personally, it should be done by the National Park Service itself.

You will realize that the writing of this letter has been a disagreeable duty so far as the debunking part is concerned, the glad part, however, is in calling your direct attention to the inaccuracy of this historical record as written by Mr. Yard and his astonishing remissness in giving credit to a member of the State Commission which should have gone to one man, and one man only, and that is Arno B. Cammerer.

Not once did Kelsey mention his personal contribution to the parks, nor did he want to. But think about it. After the Southern Appalachian National Park Commission had finished their work, the park service—Cammerer—had to make it all happen. He needed Kelsey. Kelsey was the horticulturalist and the one best able to support Cammerer in judging the quality of the lands to be acquired by the states and accepted by the secretary of the Interior. Cammerer asked for—no, more like pleaded—for Kelsey's guidance, which he got all during the year 1927.

Here was the problem facing Cammerer: April 5–8, 1926, the commission finally reported on the recommended boundaries for each of the three parks. They described the metes and bounds, much as a surveyor would, starting at point A and ending up back at point A again. Shenandoah contained 521,000 acres. The Smokies contained 704,000 acres. Mammoth Cave contained 70,618 acres.

The Temple Legislation included, for the first time, a minimum acreage required for each park, before the National Park Service would initiate administrative and protective services—250,000 acres for the Shenandoah Park, and 150,000 acres for the Smokies Park. Moreover, no general development of either park could be undertaken until a major portion of the remainder in each area had been accepted by the secretary of the Interior.

But the states didn't want to spend their funds on lands that might be rejected by the secretary. Nor could they take land by condemnation without the express assurance in the courts that the land would become park land once it was acquired. Nor did they want to evict the mountain people from their homes, only to say later that it was a mistake. In the final analysis, only the National Park Service could give assurance, in advance, that any lands would be accepted by the secretary.

In early 1927 Secretary Work wrote the governors of North Carolina and Tennessee, committing the National Park Service to an investigation in the Smokies to begin on the ground just as soon as weather conditions permitted and that the work would probably be completed about June 1, 1927. He would then designate the acceptable 150,000 acres, the minimum required to initiate administration and protection by the park service. Moreover, he would designate the "major portion" of the area of 704,000 acres without which "no general development" could be undertaken, as set forth by the act. All this "designation" fell to Cammerer. How was he to do it?

Cammerer to Kelsey, March 15, 1927. "Could you start on Smoky Mountain inspection trip with me and other members ... This will take three to four weeks and I consider your presence particularly important. Do what you can."

Cammerer to Kelsey, April 18, 1927. "You must be sure to make the Great Smokies trip about the 22 of May, because we could not do without you."

Cammerer to Kelsey, April 20, 1927. "I leave for the Shenandoah Sunday until I complete the job. I should have you, and if you possibly can make it I hope you'll join me ... You ought to go, or decide not to kick me in the pants if I do the best I can with those birds and the circumstances, you old son of a gun."

Later in the year the governor of Virginia asked Secretary Work to make an inspection of the proposed Shenandoah National Park area, similar to the earlier Great Smokies inspection. Cammerer wrote Kelsey, "I'll need you. First of all, the nights are cold and I need a bedfellow, and secondly I need your advice on some of the holdings. Drop me a line when you can spare the time to meet me. I also feel that if and when you are along I needn't worry about not being able to find a bit of moonshine as well as sunshine."

On October 31, 1927, Cammerer wrote, "Dear Kel, Am sitting in Zerkel's office in Luray to get this line to you. Am about half done in my survey of the Shenandoah area, and it is evident that I won't find more than one-half of the original 521,000 acres. Glenn Smith is with me. It is important that you come down at the earliest possible date to go over some of these things with me on the ground."

By the end of November they had finished their survey, and in December 1927 Cammerer submitted his extensive report to Secretary Work. Cammerer explained that he, Smith, and Kelsey had set the metes and bounds for a new boundary line "aimed only at the inclusion of desirable or necessary park lands, both from a scenic and an administrative standpoint, with such a topographically outlined boundary as would, all things considered, meet those requirements." The entire boundary line had been carefully inspected either by motor, or in some instances on horseback and on foot, and with a few interruptions due to inclement weather when roads were not passable and streams leading from the hills were unfordable. Cammerer's report then detailed the reasoning and logic for their selections. This was important because he had to preempt the inevitable critics.

So there is the evidence of Kelsey's strong hand behind Cammerer in only one year, 1927. That hand was there whenever Cammerer needed it, until the end, posthumously, in 1942.

Wartime

For the United States, WWI was relatively brief and essentially "over there." While it started in 1914, the United States didn't declare war until April 6, 1917, and by November 11, 1918, it was over. Kelsey's participation in building the Cantonments and war housing for shore support personnel was devoted to getting men and materials over to Europe to aid the British and French.

WWII started with the 1939 German invasion of Poland and in short order had spread throughout Europe, North Africa, the Balkans, and Scandinavia, to mention many of the principal areas of conflict. For the United States it was the storied "Battle of Britain" that drew us into the conflict in 1940, long before Pearl Harbor, December 7, 1941. Hitler's fateful decision to invade Russia in winter drew German resources away to the Eastern Front and possibly saved England. Roosevelt had agreed with Churchill to fund the build-up of US war materials with the Lend-Lease Program and transporting the material became our first involvement.

Germany countered with a massive build-up of their U-boat (submarine) fleet to interdict the shipping convoys that made their way across the North Atlantic. U-boat strength was reckoned at 65 vessels in July 1941, growing to 198 in September 1941, and to 230 by the war's end. Starting with individual U-boats torpedoing isolated merchant vessels, the threat grew into large "wolf pack" fleets to rip into huge convoys of allied shipping all across the North Atlantic. By the time war was formally declared shortly after Pearl Harbor, German U-boat sightings were frequent off the eastern US coast, especially close off New England and Canada's Maritime Provinces. U-boats carried on-deck armament as well as torpedoes, so our shoreline installations were always vulnerable, even in shallow waters. German aircraft carriers were not an imminent threat, but of course that could change. The war was no longer "over there." It was now quite possibly "over here." Camouflage became a desirable protection for any shoreline installation.

On October 30, 1941, during the lull in Mount Cammerer deliberations, Kelsey boarded a US destroyer in Boston's Charlestown Navy Yard bound for the naval air base at Argentia, Newfoundland. He had been brought by the Bureau of Yards and Docks to study the landscape and recreational developments of the naval base, as well as the landscaping, etc., of 375 housing units. Peat bog stabilization was one of the tasks. "After having been involved for several weeks with the strenuous activities of national self defense and the amazing preparations that are being made ... And after a terribly stormy trip home in which I got banged up quite a bit, it is a great pleasure to come into almost spring-like weather here with the sun shining every day and an absence of the fog and low flying clouds, which seems to be the normal condition of Newfoundland a large part of the time."[167]

Eight months later Kelsey wrote, "I am just back from a six weeks' trip ... I feel a little bunged up after six weeks of from 12 to 16 hours a day on the job, and would like to get off somewhere with a fishing pole, sleeping 20 hours and fishing four hours a day. I have been doing some pretty strenuous work in camouflage planting, and partly on account of the enormous amount of dust I absorbed at the Dow Air Field, Bangor, Maine, so the doctor says, I was taken down with a very severe summer cold and am just getting around at the present time. ... Certainly, with my experience with both the army and navy recently at different airports, the subject of camouflage and its relation to the nurserymen is a most important one."[168]

"I have only just now returned to the bosom of my business, having engaged in planting a thousand trees to camouflage an army airport, these trees ranging from 18 to 50 feet in height."[169]

On January 8, 1943, Kelsey wrote "There is considerable camouflage planting being done on a pretty big scale, and there is going to be more of it, I believe, whether the war ends soon or ends later. We have not only been connected with Navy and Army camouflage of airports, but have also done quite a lot of camouflage planting for war housing. I believe the net result is going to be a far clearer understanding by engineers, architects, and the public in general on the absolute necessity for planting all homes, factories and other places where people live or do their daily work. ... Our nursery did about four acres of victory planting last year, and we'll probably do eight or ten acres this year."[170] Conversations with Kelsey's grandchildren reveal that Kelsey also operated a makeshift lumber mill on the property, taking logs trucked in and sawing them into lumber for the war effort.

June 9, 1944: "I know the terrific handicaps of business today, for labor here is practically nonexistent while at the same time we are overwhelmed with orders which we are physically unable to fill."[171] During the dark days of the Depression, Kelsey's nursery enjoyed a plethora of labor and a paucity of orders. Only a few years later, as WWII stretched on, the business enjoyed a plethora of orders and a paucity of labor to fill it. These two body blows to the nursery's fabulous growth and condition in the Roaring Twenties, was something from which the business never fully recovered.

In 1945, a year later, the war ended with VE Day (May 8) and then VJ Day (September 2).

The four war years since the memorializing of Arno Cammerer were stressful for the nursery business and personally stressful because of the rigors of camouflage construction for Kelsey. He was ready for a break, but that would have to wait. Perhaps time and activity had muted Kelsey's remorse from the death of his close friend Cammerer; perhaps not. He was about to get another serious blow with the death of his twin brother, Harry, in March 1946. They had been very close, the only sibling Kelsey had ever turned to when in trouble. The twins were the stars of STK's family. Harry was a celebrated orthodontist and professor at Johns Hopkins Hospital in Baltimore. Like Harlan, Harry had served as president of numerous orthodontists organizations reminiscent of Kelsey's presidencies of nursery organizations. Much as Kelsey's achievements had inspired the 1940 New York dinner of the AAN in his honor, twin Harry was feted in 1928 by the Baltimore City Dental Society on the occasion of the Meeting of the Southern Society of Orthodontists.

About a month (April 11) after Harry's death, his wife, Polly, wrote a poignant letter to Kelsey: "Here I come bothering you again, this time about the marking on the stone. That old question about age. Which shall I put on the stone, 1872 or 1873? I have ordered a simple foot marker like at Daddy and Mother Kelsey's. ..." This clears up the question of where Katie Kelsey, who died at her daughter's in Las Cruces, New Mexico, was buried. It appears Harry had her brought back for interment in Baltimore, and also makes sense out of STK's being brought down to Baltimore from Salem for interment on his death. They were buried together.

Grandfather Mountain

At 5,938 feet altitude, Grandfather Mountain is the tallest peak in the Blue Ridge. While not as high as Mount Mitchell in the Black Range, Grandfather achieves a majestic solitary splendor denied the former due to its proximity to other peaks. Grandfather stands alone and is an eyeful of a mountain from all approaches. "Soft landscapes in contrast to the startling ruggedness of the Western and Canadian mountains. Grandfather Mountain has both to some degree."[172] It is located just off the Blue Ridge Parkway, which crosses its lower eastern flanks immediately north of Linville, North Carolina. To the southeast is smaller Grandmother Mountain, helping to cradle the village of Linville.

In 1999 Miles Tager of Boone, North Carolina, wrote a book, a brief but compelling book that deserves reading, simply titled *Grandfather Mountain—A Profile*. In his preface Tager effuses, "No question; it is here in the High Country of North Carolina, not the Alps or the Rockies, that we have hiked the most stunning mountain trail of our lives." A few paragraphs later, Tager says, "Thanks then ... to Harlan Kelsey, the Grandfather's greatest advocate, who lost the ultimate battle to completely preserve his most beloved place, but never lost his integrity or will."[173]

Kelsey wrote *Grandfather Mountain, Shall It be Saved?* in April 1944 to promote his efforts for public ownership of the mountain. The opening two paragraphs give us a concise summary of the mountain's attributes:

> In the morning of the world a mighty convulsion heaved heavenward the Appalachian System—first-born of earth's mountain ranges. Some geologists say 140 million years ago, while others claim not less than 200 million years' antiquity; and so Grandfather Mountain, most rugged, picturesque and highest peak in the entire Blue Ridge Range was born.

Grandfather Mountain towers above the surrounding Blue Ridge peaks and affords from its several summits vast panoramas in every direction. It lies along the Blue Ridge Parkway, which connects the Shenandoah and Great Smoky Mountains National Parks about halfway from Asheville and the Virginia–North Carolina state line at Cumberland Knob Park.

Grandfather Mountain.

Flora of Grandfather Mountain.

Today this venerable landmark is clothed with an exquisite virgin mantle of rare forest trees and flowers; cold tumbling brooks cascade down its steep slopes under dense canopies of white and purple rhododendrons and mountain laurel of almost unbelievable size and luxuriance; in May and June on more open ridges the flame azalea, most gorgeous of American shrubs, flashes fire; while charming alpine-like plants in a hundred varieties fill every nook and crevice on its craggy summits.[174]

To appreciate Grandfather Mountain it may help to repeat an anecdote telling of John Muir's conversation with Charles Sprague Sargent on the summit of the Grandfather, September 1898. The two had "trudged up slope after slope, Muir impatiently leading the way. When they reached the bald top, he fell into poetic raptures over the view, while Sargent stood aloof clothed in his 'frosty, inherited dignity.'"[175]

I couldn't hold in, and began to jump about and sing and glory in it all. Then I happened to look around and catch sight of Sargent, standing there as cool as a rock, with a half-amused look on his face at me, but never saying a word.

"Why don't you let yourself out at a sight like that?" I asked.

"I don't wear my heart upon my sleeve," he retorted.

"Who cares where you wear your little heart, mon," I cried.

"There you stand in the face of all Heaven come down to earth, like a critic of the universe, as if to say 'Come Nature, bring on the best you have. I'm from Boston!'"[176]

On January 20, 1925, Kelsey had written a letter to Dr. Joseph Pratt of Western North Carolina, Inc., explaining his position and the logic of the Southern Appalachian National Park Commission in recommending to Congress exclusively the Shenandoah National Park, holding in abeyance the Great Smoky Mountain National Park. Kelsey closed his letter with a one-sentence paragraph: "Personally I shall never be satisfied until we have a great national Park in the Great Smokies and either a National Park or a State Park in the Grandfather area." Kelsey meant it then and he never forgot it. Of course months later Congress approved not only the Shenandoah, but also the Great Smokies and even Mammoth Cave in a single act.

Kelsey's Grandfather Mountain story evolved in two parts. First, the Hugh MacRae years unfolded; second, the Hugh Morton (MacRae's grandson) years that closed the book. MacRae displayed a consistent application of private enterprise, where the optimal generation of revenues dominated everything in favor of the shareholders—nothing wrong with that in general. Of course MacRae was effectively the sole shareholder. Morton started out in his grandfather's footsteps, and after gaining control, quickly launched into a pattern of accelerating opportunism to gain his ends. This is not the impression held by today's general public in North Carolina. Throughout most of the post–WWII years, Morton was the dominant voice as he rewrote history to burnish his family's reputation as conservationists and conservators of Grandfather Mountain. One of the last acts of his life was the publishing of his book, *Hugh Morton's North Carolina*. It is primarily a book of his photographs but includes in the preface (viii.) the following statement:

> Most North Carolinians know that Hugh Morton owns Grandfather Mountain. Being the strong environmentalist and conservationist that he is, Hugh has led major efforts to clean the air, purify the water, protect animals, and preserve the magnificent wildflower and forest legacy so rich and important to each of us.

It would be worthwhile to test this viewpoint against the litany of evidence that exists as to the facts that actually unfolded with Morton and his family before him.

Grandfather Mountain—The MacRae Years

Ever since 1896, when MacRae bought out Mr. Ravenel, the entire Grandfather Mountain/Linville block of land had been in the total control of Hugh MacRae. He walked a tightrope between stripping the land of its timber resources on one hand, and preserving it for attracting tourists to his exclusive Eseeola Inn on the other hand. By the time this story starts in 1939, MacRae had been walking the tightrope for over forty years. Most of the time he fell off on the side of lumbering. In the flats and flanking mountain slopes, primeval old-growth timber had been stripped for pulp and an occasional golf course. More commonly, second growth had begun to erase the lumbering scars. The initial phase of the second growth was first lumbering slash, then tangles of wild berries, then forest fires, and finally a mix of young deciduous and evergreen forest trees. All this was guided by the Linville Improvement Company, later shortened to just the Linville Company. By 1920 MacRae had stripped the area around Linville to the point where the town earned the nickname "Stumptown."[177] It is highly likely that Stumptown is why Kelsey's father, STK, left Linville in 1910, never to return again. To him it was a reprise of the lumbering devastation that had driven him as a young man from western New York state through Illinois and out to the plains of Kansas.

MacRae's headquarters were in Wilmington, North Carolina, under the letterhead "Hugh MacRae & Co.—Real Estate—Residential Properties—Agricultural Lands—Colonization—Timber Resources—Coal Properties—Resort Properties—Tourist Hotels." In today's terms, he was a cross between an investment banker, a commercial real estate broker, and a private equity firm. His Linville Company also was headquartered in Wilmington, with the letterhead showing son Nelson MacRae as president, and son-in-law J. W. Morton as vice president. It was strictly a family affair.

As the Depression later deepened, the Linville Company struggled and its revenues sagged. In 1936 the main lodge building of the Eseeola Inn had burned and was replaced on a smaller scale. MacRae sold timber rights to more and more of the mountain's acreage. Years later MacRae's grandson would extol the family's wonderful history of conservation and love of the mountain. The actual history was a half century of opportunism and disregard for any part of the mountain that interfered with the generation of revenue. Some incidental money was earned from a one-lane dirt toll road they had cut, up an old horseback trail to a wooden platform on Grandfather's Cliffside overlook. There tourists could get a striking view of the Blue Ridge terrain for miles around. But even that was apparently done in a slapdash manner. On June 9, 1939, Kelsey received a letter from his friend, Boston attorney Robert Walcott, who had just returned from a tour of the southern Appalachians. "Grandfather Mountain at present seems to me to have a rather second rate development and a very poor road into its base. Its sale-booths and posters suggest Revere Beach!" [Revere Beach was Boston's seedy answer to New York's Coney Island.]

The idea that the sale of Grandfather Mountain would give the Linville Company a revenue boost was not lost on MacRae. The ravages of the Depression had not abated even into the early 1940s—until WWII began. MacRae disclosed in one letter to Kelsey, "Developing [Linville] to the extent that has been achieved, has not only been unprofitable, but the net cost has been great; handicapped and even threatened the destruction of our other interests."[178] One can only speculate on what "net cost" caused this "threatened destruction of other interests." Possibly it was the burning of the Eseeola Inn. More likely it was some tangled web of interlocking debt covenants between the Linville Company and MacRae's many other real estate interests. We only need to know that it was revenue that drove MacRae's early discussions with Harlan Kelsey, not preservation of the mountain.

The first initiatives from the Linville Company were focused on possible revenue from the Blue Ridge Parkway that was nearing Linville from both north and south. Nelson MacRae had written Kelsey February 16, 1940, regarding sale of land for a parkway camp site to serve the parkway drivers. Kelsey responded February 27, "I have had two conferences with the National Park Service in Washington, the last one as late as last Friday, with reference to the Grandfather-Grandmother Mountain Camp Site Project which is desired to be set up as a part of the National Blue Ridge Parkway. ... Mr. Cammerer tells me that at the present time there is no money available for the purchase of park lands anywhere nor with the program of retrenchment going on in Washington is it very likely there will be for years to come. However, I pointed out the strategic value of the Grandfather-Grandmother area, it lying about half-way between Shenandoah and Great Smoky Mountains National Parks, and being by all odds the most scenic feature along the route, and the place where a major camp should be made by the National Park Service."

Kelsey continued by reassuring Nelson MacRae that he needn't be concerned about competition for the Eseeola Inn because "Mr. Cammerer told me that under no consideration would the National Park Service erect a hotel on the site, nor in fact on any of the other camp areas on the Blue Ridge Parkway." Kelsey then went into considerable detail on what prices had been paid for various types of lands elsewhere along the Parkway route. "But, Mr. Cammerer keeps warning that the price of the land would have to be extremely reasonable, otherwise they would make their major developments elsewhere, much as they would like to get the Grandfather-Grandmother area." Kelsey closed, asking for a property map of the Linville Company holdings for use by the park service, and promised to try to get Cammerer down to Linville in the near future to personally view the property on the ground. Of course Cammerer's resignation and subsequent death prevented that.

Almost a year later, January 5, 1942, Nelson MacRae tried again, writing to Kelsey in a somewhat more assertive tone. Noting that almost the entire parkway would soon be open, shouldn't the park service start acquisition of the needed land planned for the Linville section? "While we wish to cooperate with the Park Service in enabling them to secure from the Linville Company what may be needed ... we cannot be expected to hold the matter open indefinitely, as we think the Park Service officials should reach some definite decision about the matter at an early date." How much land do they want? Can we start price negotiations? Kelsey's January 8 response was simply, "from my recent talk with the National Park Service people, they are so tied up with the war that I feel quite sure we cannot get them much further interested in recreational areas on the Blue Ridge Parkway until the war is over ... I feel it is hardly worthwhile to try to push them too hard at this time."

MacRae, January 13. He agreed it is not a good time to push but wonders if the planning can't be done now. Can't the NPS define the acreage they would want? Can't the price be negotiated? "If they then did not have the funds to proceed with the purchase it could be held in abeyance until the program ... was resumed."

Kelsey, January 16. He agreed to pass on MacRae's view to Newton Drury, the new National Park Service director.

Drury to Kelsey, February 16. Drury sent two copies of a map "showing the Service recommendation for the proposed Grandfather Mountain Park adjoining Section 2-H of the Blue Ridge Parkway in the vicinity of Linville ... The principal purpose of the federal ownership of the area would be the preservation and protection of Grandfather Mountain, one of the finest single mountains in the east." He continues outlining the steps to assure that protection. Limited numbers of parking areas for hikes, horseback rides, nature study, trips, or picnics. Only buildings necessary for emergency motor vehicle service and comfort stations and perhaps picnic shelters. No hotels, dining service, or overnight accommodations. "Until 1936 the Grandfather Mountain area was among those proposed for acquisition and development as part of the recreation plan for the Blue Ridge Parkway. Since that date, however, this Service has more or less 'given up' mainly because the high price asked the Forest Service for the 2,000 acres above the 5,000-foot contour level was beyond consideration."

Kelsey to MacRae, February 20. He passed on Drury's letter, including Drury's suggestion that a citizens committee of some kind be established to get subscriptions to help defray the land cost. "At the same time, you will readily see that an excessive price for the land would kill the project before it even got started, so I feel it is very important for you and the Linville Company to carefully consider the outstanding advantages this Park will give to Linville and return on as low acreage basis as is possible to do under all the circumstances."

Then suddenly Hugh MacRae, Nelson's father, reentered the picture. On February 24 he wrote to Kelsey, "Your letter of February 20th to Nelson has been received. You will join us in distress in the fact of Nelson's death, resulting from the strain of many problems—mainly the fire, the flood, and infantile paralysis at Linville. He had to face and bear the results of the burdens." On February 10, 1942,[179] Nelson MacRae had committed suicide.[180]

Without missing a beat, Hugh MacRae's letter showed he was taking over the pursuit of revenues from his properties. The consummate salesman, his style was different from the measured style of his deceased son. First came a bit of the old soft soap. "Your proposal in regard to the Grandfather Mountain Park is highly interesting and would be a culmination of the dream which your Father, Mr. S. T. Kelsey and the writer had fifty years ago when it was decided to develop the Grandfather-Linville area as a pleasure resort." Let the reader go back to the earlier Linville chapter and note that it was Mr. Ravanel who wanted a pleasure resort, not MacRae nor S. T. Kelsey. Ravenel sold out rather than fight MacRae over this issue—a resort vs. a railroad for timber resources. MacRae then moved on to polish his product, with a towering description of the unique and beautiful Grandfather Mountain. It was almost as though he felt Kelsey didn't fully appreciate the glory of the mountain.

Next MacRae's letter proceeded to the plans he had, if the park service did not buy the mountain. Given the persistent claims in later years that the MacRaes were conservation-minded conservators of the mountain, it is worth quoting old Hugh MacRae in detail for the tone as his letter continued:

> The Company's only chance to justify the large investment made during the past fifty years would seem to be to improve and extend the present toll road to the top of the mountain and count on that income as an important factor. In this connection our friends at Chimney Rock have written that in their opinion the Grandfather Mountain will attract a greater number of visitors than Chimney Rock, which we understand has an income from tourists of more the $50,000.00 a year. It was Nelson's purpose to extend the toll road to the top of the mountain. This past summer he initiated the plan with an attractive stone toll house and entrance gate.

> My reason for going into the above detail is that I doubt if the Park Service realizes what the Grandfather Mountain means to the Linville Company, and what the Company believes it will mean in the near future. ... The average person who might subscribe could not properly appraise the value of the Grandfather Mountain and on that account would hardly subscribe an amount which would with other subscription prove adequate.

My thought would be to handle this situation step by step, first having the Park Service take the Grandmother Mountain, which is easily accessible and has great scenic value, and from this build up an interest in the Grandfather Mountain.

We would not wish to take advantage of the values so built up and it might therefore be advisable to agree in advance as to the amount which the Park Service would pay for the Grandfather and which we could afford to accept. The payments would not have to be immediate. I think we could agree to having them spread over a period of five or ten years.

One day later, February 25, MacRae continued in another letter:

Since writing you on yesterday I have given further careful thought to your proposal ... the matter of price cannot be approached successfully on an acreage basis. We know the difference between the value of carbon by the ton as coal and by the karat as a diamond. The Grandfather being the outstanding feature on the great National Blue Ridge Parkway has an intrinsic value as a unit. ... Now as to the price there will be no use in making a move unless we can agree on a figure which is fair and mutually satisfactory. ... An official of the Park Service once asked Mr. Nelson MacRae if we would accept a million dollars for the Grandfather. I do not recall that he made a definite reply but my reply now is that we would. The next question is would we accept less than one million dollars? My reply to that is that the Linville Company would. Now the next step would be for Mr. Drury representing the National Park Service to indicate the figure at which he would recommend a purchase.

Kelsey could never get MacRae to name his price. Nor could MacRae get the park service to name a price. MacRae's letter continued with a veiled threat, seeking to pry loose some action:

> I am greatly impressed with the possibilities of a Parkway higher up on the East side of the Grandfather Mountain ... and think eventually a similar parkway should be built along the West side of the mountain with an entrance from the crest of the Blue Ridge at the head of the Linville Valley and connecting with the highway which it is proposed to extend up the Linville River and down the Watagua and on to Boone. Because streams flow in every direction from the Grandfather it will be logical eventually to build a wonderful system of approaches to the proposed Parkway if extended around the mountain. ...

Note carefully MacRae's endorsement of "a Parkway higher up on the East side." Years later Hugh Morton would castigate the park service for proposing a *high route* for the parkway, which they did not, and totally ignore his grandfather's endorsement of such a route. Kelsey's response to MacRae was immediate, on March 2, and pulled no punches. It also deserves detailed coverage of certain excerpts:

> Regarding the Grandfather Mountain Park project, I hardly know how to answer your letters. From your two letters, however, I am convinced that the attitude of the Linville Company is so at variance with that of the National Park Service that unless there is a decided change in the Linville Company's viewpoints that further negotiations with the National Park Service would accomplish little, if anything.
>
> Everyone concerned agrees, I am sure, that Grandfather Mountain is the most outstanding peak in the Blue Ridge range, but if a road is extended to the main peak and down around the other side, in my opinion, as a National Park item

the mountain will be ruined. In fact, the short toll road and the platform and little building at its terminus on the first peak of Grandfather, in my opinion, has done very much to spoil the beauty of the mountain as a natural park. Blowing Rock is an outstanding example of a natural attraction which has been exploited and utterly ruined in a most disgraceful manner. Hasn't the day for exploiting these great natural wonders of our country for the benefit of private interests gone by, and shouldn't they be dedicated to the use of our future generations? ...

Personally, I am extremely disappointed that the outlook is so remote of the Linville Company and the National Park Service getting together on a basis that would be satisfactory to both. There is little use discussing the means for buying the property until the fundamentals are settled satisfactorily. As you say, it was a dream of yourself and my father that the Linville region would become a great playground center, but I think both you and he had in mind more the exploiting of the mountain for the purpose of making money for the Linville Company rather than dedicating the mountain itself as a beautiful natural object for the enjoyment of it, unspoiled, by all the people of this country for the future. If I am not mistaken in this viewpoint, then you will see that the whole approach to the problem by the Linville Company and the National Park Service and myself is at total variance.

For nearly 25 years at a most unusual sacrifice to my business I have been working to get National Parks in the east, and as a culmination of my efforts had hoped to see Grandfather and Grandmother Mountains put into the National Park picture with the beautiful resort of Linville at its base and enjoying the prosperity that surely such a park would give. A really liberal attitude on the part of the Linville Company might very well react more favorably in a financial way than to cling too closely to getting paid for a theoretical value of the mountain itself.

Newton Drury's response to all this flurry of correspondence between Kelsey and MacRae was firm and consistent with the park service's view from the beginning. To Kelsey he wrote March 12, "You know that I appreciate your interest in furthering the movement to make the Grandfather Mountain area one of the park enlargements of the Blue Ridge Parkway. I feel, however, that at this time no Government Bureau could advance a request for funds for land acquisition. ... I hope the owners do not undertake a development program such as Mr. MacRae outlines. I understand the spruce has already been cut off. This has damaged considerably the natural beauty of the area. If the additional roads and buildings were to be constructed, I doubt that the area would then have any value for Park purposes." Kelsey to MacRae, March 30, "From what Mr. Drury told me personally about a week ago, I doubt if the National Park Service will care to take up the matter again until a definite and reasonable proposition is made by the Linville Company." Both Drury and Kelsey were tired of skirting around the main issue. What was the price for the mountain?

MacRae in the meantime had been in contact with R. Bruce Etheridge, director of the Department of Conservation and Development for the state of North Carolina. Would the state be interested in buying him out? Perhaps he could generate some competition for the mountain. In an April 6, 1944, letter to Kelsey from J. W. Morton, MacRae's son-in-law, Morton, added more detail about the overtures with the state. "About a year ago when the North Carolina Legislature was in session, Mr. MacRae put on quite a campaign and tried to get a bill passed, authorizing the Department of Conservation and Development to purchase the Grandfather for park purposes. A good deal of support was gotten for this project from a great many influential people throughout the state until the price was mentioned and confidentially they all turned against it and it is my belief that this killed the project, although after a great deal of arguing with Mr. MacRae, he advised our Representative in the Legislature to put in another bill which would not stipulate a price as far as we were concerned, but would leave it to the Department of Conservation to put a price on it and make us an offer. This came after the other bill could not pass and most of the support had cooled off and also the type of bill was not particularly attractive to the Legislators, therefore it was never passed."

On May 7, 1942, Drury wrote Etheridge, "It would be unfortunate if Mr. MacRae carried out his threat to cut the remaining timber as it would greatly injure the property in the event that it could finally be secured for park purposes. Your offer of cooperation in preventing despoliation of the area is greatly appreciated, but there appears to be nothing that either the Service or your Department can do in the event Mr. MacRae carries out his threat."

With no offers from the state, MacRae took a new tack. On May 7 he wrote Kelsey, "From our correspondence it is my understanding that Mr. Drury ... is not in a position to complete the purchase. For this reason I believe it will be advisable to undertake to negotiate a sale through other channels ... In this case it may be necessary for us to pay commissions to certain parties who will prove advantageous in bringing the negotiations to a conclusion ... Please advise me as to your views in regard to this and whether it would be agreeable to you." Kelsey replied June 17, "While I do not know what the cooperative effort is that you refer to with regard to the Grandfather-Grandmother area, unquestionably if others come in and help put this across, they are entitled to a part of the commission. ... Of course the war comes first." It is puzzling why MacRae felt that Kelsey needed some financial motivation, when Kelsey was clearly doing all he could without it. Money was not the issue to him. Perhaps it was to enlist Kelsey in pushing for as high a price as possible with the park service; the higher the price, the higher would be a percentage commission. On July 24 Kelsey wrote to MacRae to forget the park service—the war had intervened. But if MacRae would set a reasonably low fixed price, Kelsey might try to find an angel to produce the money.

Hugh MacRae agreed to the park service's definition of the site but still was not forthcoming in naming a price. Nevertheless by mid-1943 Kelsey had contacted Horace Albright in New York to enlist his aid in finding an angel. Albright agreed to "dig further into the matter as he got a chance." On September 18, 1943, Kelsey wrote Albright with "a tip on a possible benefactor who might be the answer, if it is put up to him properly as you certainly could do." His name was Stillman, the New York banker, whom Kelsey's informant at Harvard University had suggested. Nothing came of it.

On October 22 Kelsey wrote Albright that MacRae had definitely asked him to represent them in the sale of the property for a commission. Kelsey's acceptance was only if it was understood that his "first interest was with the Park Service and always would be." The most serious hitch was that he was still unable to get MacRae to name a price. Then he reviewed the case with Drury, who approved of his going ahead, but suggested Kelsey resign as a collaborator of the NPS. On November 5, 1943, Newton Drury "regretfully" accepted the resignation but added, "I hope that when the Grandfather Mountain project is completed, we will be able to work out an arrangement whereby you will again be officially associated with the Service. We should not lose permanently the official connection of one who has contributed so much to the National Park System, and who will have much to contribute in the future."

If money was not a motivation for Kelsey's effort in getting the mountain into the park service's hands, then why did he agree to a commission? We can only surmise that it was for the same reason that MacRae granted it. With the war on, business had slowed to a trickle.

If Kelsey was to divert considerable time to fund-raising, it would further damage the nursery's prospects. If the commission was just sitting there, Kelsey was certainly going to accept it, after eliminating all conflicts of interest.

Finally there was a break in the impasse at the Linville Company. By November 1943, Hugh MacRae had bowed out as president and given that responsibility to Julian W. Morton, his son-in-law. Almost immediately there was a newspaper report that the company had sold three thousand acres of its property, including the town site of Linville. On November 29 Kelsey wrote Morton, asking for details that might affect the boundaries needed by the park service. Also he reiterated his plea for price, without which he could make no headway. On December 13 Drury wrote Kelsey, "Thank you for your letter of December 9 enclosing copies of the letter of December 3 from Mr. J. W. Morton indicating that the Linville Company would sell 12,000 acres of their Grandfather Mountain property for $200,000. I congratulate you on your progress and sincerely hope that you can bring about the public acquisition of this area."

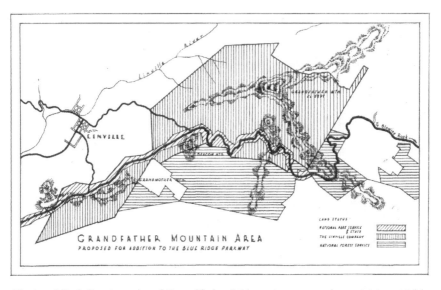

National Park Service map of Grandfather Mountain proposed acquisition. 1944.

Now all Kelsey needed was a little philanthropy to come his way. Instead, he was reined in a bit by Newton Drury. December 28, 1943: "We note that you refer to the Grandfather Mountain area as a 'national park objective.' We are not seeking to establish a new national park at Grandfather Mountain but rather as a natural unit of the Blue Ridge Parkway. I would not favor this area as a 'national park'." Not a problem, according to Kelsey's response. "I used the term in a generic sense just as for instance the Blue Ridge Parkway is a part of the National Park system. You may recall our Southern Appalachian National Park Commission made a study of this area and definitely turned it down as not being adequate in size for a national park, and I have not changed my views since."

On March 7 Kelsey gave Drury sort of a status report:

> I am hoping to get the 'Grandfather Mountain Park Association' a going organization this spring, and Mr. Wharton, Pres. Of the National Park Association is willing to serve on its Board. Beyond that I shall try to make up the rest of the small membership from North Carolina.
>
> It will probably be wise to try for a fund large enough to purchase the much needed land to the North and West of the Linville Company property, and my ambition far exceeds the boundary proposed as shown on the maps you have sent me. However it is going to take the devil of campaigns to put the project across, still it has got to be done. ... Why not have the G.M.P. Assn. go after a half million dollars and do the job right.
>
> Now you can't hurt my feelings, so please give me your advice and criticisms ad lib. ... I am sure it will be much nearer 40,000 acres than 20,000 acres. ... If such a program is approved, there is no reason why we should not tackle the N.C. Legislature

for a substantial share of the funds, and I believe the N.C. Conservation Com. will back us up. Am I a NUT?

On March 12 Kelsey sounded out Drury with yet another twist. Wharton of the National Parks Association had advised Kelsey he thought it should be called some *kind* of a park and suggested the word "memorial." Would Drury be agreeable to campaigning for funds using the slogan, "Grandfather Mountain Memorial Park"? No immediate comment was forthcoming from Drury. Then he tried the name out on Horace Albright, March 18. "You asked me to draft a letter for you to send to Mr. George A. Ball [Mason fruit jars], and I shall be glad to do so … The idea of a memorial Park might appeal to him, and possibly others." Finally March 22 Drury gave his reaction. He didn't like the idea, not at all, and gave a number of reasons. Further, he continued, "I also notice that you refer to the 'Grandfather Mountain Park.' The term 'park' we like to preserve as a distinct name for the Great Smokies and other areas of that caliber. We have always looked at the Grandfather Mountain as a part of the Parkway, similar to Blowing Rock, Peaks of Otter, and other areas along the Parkway. All of these so-called bulges are referred to as 'areas' along the Parkway. In other words, they are outstanding natural areas located along and connected by the Parkway, none of which would be included in the National Park System if it were not part of the Parkway. Here, again, I realize that perhaps the word 'park' would be a better selling word than just 'area.' However, officially, when and if the area is turned over to us, it will be known as the Grandfather Mountain Area of the Blue Ridge Parkway."

Drury's reaction set off a flurry of letters from March to May debating the naming issue. Kelsey argued that existing Blue Ridge Parkway maps used the word "park" (not "area") to delineate points of interest along the way, and Grandfather was by far the most important of all of them. Further, "If the total area is secured which it seems to me should certainly be included, it will comprise a park area at least 1/3 larger than Acadia National Park, and it is certainly more primeval than the latter, or Shenendoah or Mammoth Cave National Parks." Even further the name "area" would be demeaning when soliciting for donors. Finally Drury relented; "park" would be okay, but only if it was made clear that it was part of the Blue Ridge Parkway. "When we have an opportunity to study the whole matter we shall make a decision that will, we hope, clarify and unify all of the names along the parkway. All of the areas along the parkway that are similar in character, such as Grandfather Mountain, Blowing Rock, and others, will be known by similar designations, be it 'park', 'area', or 'what-not'."

Just as Kelsey was getting up a head of steam, with a genuine proposal in hand to promote, he got a jolt from J. W. Morton. For the first time Morton acted like his father-in-law, implying a veiled threat, looking to motivate Kelsey. Kelsey was already energized; what the threat did was to give Kelsey a new, stronger talking-point in the search for donors. Lumbering was back in the mix. Morton's March 22, 1944, letter included the following:

> We are now cutting some of the merchantable timber but not on the Grandfather Mountain, nor are we cutting it close. … If the sale of the property as a whole is not made within the next year we will most probably start timbering much closer on other parts of the property. I do not know where Mr. Wharton got the idea that there was no danger of lumbering on the property. We are going to continue to cut timber and also are going to sell either the timber or the land as a whole to the first purchaser that will pay us a satisfactory price.

There are two parts to this situation. First is the actual lumbering by the Linville Company. Second is the intention to sell the "timber or the land" to the first purchaser to come along. This second factor is perhaps the greater threat, since a new owner might have no compunction to prevent a quick stripping of all merchantable timber on the mountain for quick gain. Kelsey's declaration of this threat in his promotional material was wholly justified by this letter alone—regardless of future disclaimers by the MacRae family that they loved the mountain and would never threaten it.

Kelsey passed on a copy of Morton's letter to Albright with the following comment:

> As you will see from a copy of letter I received from the President of the Linville Company, the whole area is in danger of destruction, not only because the owners cannot carry its liabilities much longer, but also the war shortage of lumber products has made it possible to negotiate timber sales more advantageously than ever before, probably in the history of our country.

Kelsey had firsthand knowledge of the lumber shortage. While he never cut timber on his Boxford property, he did set up a saw mill to supply lumber from imported logs. This was to help the war effort and also to help take up some of the slack the war imposed on nursery revenues.[181]

Kelsey wrote an article for the April-June 1944 issue of the *National Parks* magazine. He titled it, "Shall Grandfather Mountain Be Saved?" It started with the importance of the mountain property to the Blue Ridge Parkway and its superlative natural beauty. Then he gave a status report on efforts to buy from the Linville Company. Finally he closed, describing why it needed saving. The closing paragraph read as follows:

> Is the natural beauty of Grandfather Mountain to be lost forever by becoming the victim of commercialism as have other gems in the Carolina mountains? That is a question that must be answered without delay by those who would save in its natural beauty the remnants of a glorious mountain region. Outstanding, unimpaired scenic and wildlife areas remaining in the eastern

United States that may yet be saved to serve the spiritual and recreational needs of present and future generations are few. Postwar demands for jobs and the development of resources soon may put in jeopardy those areas that have escaped destruction. Grandfather Mountain must be saved!

"To be lost forever by becoming the victim of commercialism" was the only possible phrase that later could be considered offensive to the Morton/MacRae family.

Almost three times as long and detailed as the *National Parks* magazine article, was the similar one published in the April 1944 *Planning and Civil Comment* publication of the American Planning and Civic Association. Kelsey reversed the position of the word *shall* in the title so it read, "Grandfather Mountain, Shall it Be Saved?" It was notable for the more flowery and compelling descriptions of the mountain, such as: "In the morning of the world a mighty convulsion heaved heavenward the Appalachian System—first born of earth's mountain ranges." Or "This is the 'Land of the Sky', where the snowbird nests, and where on the heights in summer cool breezes are born, which forever sweeping downward temper the hot valleys and plains far below to the east, south and west." Again, "under dense canopies of white and purple rhododendrons and mountain laurel of almost unbelievable size and luxuriance; in May and June on more open ridges the flame azalea, most gorgeous of American shrubs, flashes fire; while charming alpine-like plants in a hundred varieties fill every nook and crevice on its craggy summits."

"It is yet to be acquired and today is threatened with immediate calamitous destruction of its virgin glories by lumbering operation and other commercial exploitation" was the phrase in the text that later could be considered offensive to the Morton/MacRae family. The following also occured in a subnote to a map illustrating the area: "This property is in immediate danger of irreparable despoilment by lumbering and other disastrous exploitation. ... Is it conceivable that this incomparable heritage of wildlife and recreation shall be lost forever to future generations?"

Kelsey enlisted the help of North Carolina Representative Joe W. Ervin to bring the matter to the attention of the US Congress. Both of the above articles were appended into the Congressional Record by Ervin in his remarks to the House of Representatives March 20, 1945. Ervin stated his case as follows:

> Mr. Speaker, I believe it is my duty to call to the attention of our Nation, and particularly, to the people of North Carolina, the fact that Grandfather Mountain, the most rugged peak in the Blue Ridge Range, which is said to be geologically the most ancient of any mountain on the American Continent, is about to be subjected to commercial exploitation. There are no Federal funds available at this time with which to purchase this property, and, in view of the size of the public debt after the war, we cannot rely upon any expectation that Federal Funds will be available for this purpose after the war. Therefore, it is my hope that the people of North Carolina, by private subscription, may see fit, without delay, to acquire this property and preserve it in its natural beauty. ... Under leave to extend my remarks in the Appendix of the Record, I include therein two articles by Mr. Harlan P. Kelsey, who is one of our foremost advocates of preserving the beauties of our mountains for future generations.

Kelsey did get the break he had been seeking from the Linville Company in J. W. Morton's letter of January 22, 1945—a definitive and reasonable price. "Referring to our conference this morning in regard to the sale of the Grandfather Mountain; and the Grandmother Mountain and such areas and acreage lying East of the lines of the Blue Ridge Parkway, we beg to say that we will accept One Hundred Sixty-five Thousand ($165,000.00) Dollars for the area which is described as follows: ..."

What followed was a detailed metes and bounds description, which also referenced the National Park Service's Grandfather Mountain Area Acquisition Map, dated May 4, 1944. At the end of the letter was, "The Linville Company will pay you a commission of 10% of the cash received. This offer of sale and commission will hold good for twelve (12) months from this date, but if the sale is not made within the specified twelve months it will be our disposition, if we believe enough progress has been made, to extend this time." Gone was the ethereal and elusive probing of old Hugh MacRae with his million-dollar estimate; it took his son-in-law to bring things back to earth, so progress could be made. One snag, however, was that the proposal was for only 5,555 acres, as calculated by the park service. The mountains were included, but much of the original 12,000 acres had been retained by the company.

On March 26 Kelsey wrote Morton, "Again I want to call attention to a situation that has made it extremely hard to interest many who are anxious to see Grandfather Mt. become a part of the park system; and that is the exclusion of the Linville River valley from your last offer of sale."

Just as the good news of the price breakthrough sank in, a new development of serious proportions occurred. Kelsey reported to Newton Drury on April 12 "that Mr. Morton, President of the Linville Co. had dropped dead a short time ago." It was a fatal heart attack. "Can't tell what effect this will have on MacRae but I am in hopes that he will now be willing to include all the Linville Co. land as originally agreed upon. But it is not safe to predict anything that Hugh MacRae might do. He is almost completely self-interested, and has that reputation generally throughout N.C., and it has been the biggest snag I have run up against." R. M. Sheppard, secretary-treasurer of the Linville Company, took over as acting president.

Kelsey didn't have long to wait. On May 4 MacRae wrote him, "Please do not expect me to make any change from the proposal which Mr. Morton and I made to you in connection with the Grandfather

Mountain. I can assure you that during my life time there will be no change and this is fully concurred in by Hugh Morton, who is expected to represent our interests which relate to the Grandfather region as soon as he is definitely relieved of his military duties, which we hope will be in the near future. Hugh is, we believe, the greatest living admirer of the Grandfather Mountain, and has selected a home site at the foot of the mountain on the head waters of Grandfather Creek."

It is noteworthy that on April 12, 1945, President Roosevelt suffered a massive cerebral hemorrhage and died, closing the book on his strong support of conservation and the national parks. Also noteworthy, May 8 was declared VE Day. Four months later, September 2 was declared VJ Day. The war was over.

This effectively closes part one of the Grandfather Mountain story—the Hugh MacRae years, 1896–1945.

Grandfather Mountain—The Hugh Morton Years

We should open part two with a brief introduction to Hugh Morton, MacRae's grandson. The quickest way is to quote William Friday's foreword to Morton's book, *Hugh Morton's North Carolina*. "Hugh's love of photography began when he was a boy at summer camp. Later, as a staffer for the *Daily Tar Heel* at the University of North Carolina, his subjects ranged far and wide, including his famous photo of university president Dr. Frank Graham pitching horseshoes. He experienced, and he filmed, the violence of World War II as a combat cameraman of distinction, and he captured life behind the lines, traveling with Bob Hope and his show and covering General MacArthur in the South Pacific. When Hugh came home from the war, he determined, like so many of his generation, that he would spend the rest of his productive years making a difference in the growth and development of the state he loved."[182] Growth and development aptly describe his approach to Grandfather Mountain. Development, not conservation, ruled his activities, as we shall see, contrary to common lore in North Carolina. He was constantly photographing notables in the state and giving them pictures of themselves, a grand way to gather his stable of contacts and supporters.

On July 12 MacRae wrote Kelsey, "Thank you for sending me a copy of 'Improving Marion, S. C.' I shall read this with much interest as I am sure it is a sample of the best city planning. Hugh Morton has received his discharge from the Army in order to take an active interest in our agricultural and other developments, and has recently returned from Linville where he reports that there is much activity and an excellent outlook." Note two things. First, MacRae's word "agricultural" really meant lumbering. Second, Marion, South Carolina, had hired Kelsey for his first city-planning contract in many years. Taking each in turn, first we turn to lumbering.

On June 24 Kelsey heard from Robert F. Cope of Stanley, North Carolina. "I think your idea of preserving the Grandfather is a grand one, but it is a late hour to try to save the virgin woodlands of that region. I spent several summers in Avery near Linville a few years ago, and while there I saw many train loads of pulp wood leave Linville. I imagine it is shipped by truck now as the railroad has been taken up. … Writing on the above subject, Mr. Dugger in the third edition of the Balsam Groves (pages 216–17) says: 'But it is doubtful how long our description will hold good, for the destroying agents are fast at work. The citizens who could save, and ought to save, a part of their forest in its natural beauty are right into it with fire and smoke, and it does seem to me that if they could use brimstone without stifling their own selves to death they would certainly order a few train loads in exchange for tan-bark and lumber.'"

On July 2 Kelsey responded to Cope, "Dugger was right, and we are living in an age of selfish capitalistic individualism, where natural resources are turned over for personal exploitation, raping and destruction, and the inheritance of all the people given over to a few special-privileged 'free enterprisers' and the people can go to hell. Still more, those we place in authority are in the main controlled by this buccaneer group of bankers, lawyers and exploiters, all merrily giving quid pro quo. Is it any wonder Grandfather Mountain and a hundred other priceless heritages are despoiled? And those who lift up their voices in protest are 'anarchists, socialists and un-American!' If only a few more Jeffersons and Tom Paines were with us, the emancipation of the countless millions of suffering humanity might come about sooner. Well I guess I must be an anarchist!" These emotional private words from Kelsey certainly display the intense anxiety he felt at the time and the urgency of the situation he saw confronting him.

Second turn to Marion, South Carolina. In 1904, forty years earlier, Kelsey had completed one of his first city planning jobs—"Planting a Plan of Public Square" for the Civic Improvement League of Marion. Apparently it was remembered favorably. The city council engaged him to return for an intensive survey of the entire city, from January 13 through 18, 1945. His May 20 report to the Mayor and City Council was simply titled "Improving Marion, South Carolina."

It was a vintage Kelsey city plan, starting with Marion's problems, in common with most American cities, large and small, that had never been comprehensively planned: increasing traffic congestion; dead-end streets and other factors that tended to "blight" some districts; the need for zoning and housing standards; the need for more parks and playgrounds; tree improvement; advice for Marion's planning board; and forward-looking needs, such as building a municipal airport. Kelsey was very specific in identifying the blocks, streets, highways, and large outlying areas that could use his suggestions for betterment.

His conclusion was quite practical. "It should not be expected that all, or even a major part of the improvements recommended can be undertaken or carried out at once; but concrete plans should be completed and approved, and a definite program of accomplishment agreed upon, with the most vital needs given first consideration."

Why did he diverge from the primary task of saving the Grandfather? The consulting fee was very important at this particular time for the nursery's business. War times had been tough. On June 26, 1945, Kelsey confided to Devereux Butcher, editor of the *National Parks* magazine, "My energies of necessity have been devoted entirely to my business here, on account of a terrible shortage of labor due to war conditions." It is small wonder that Kelsey jumped at the prospect of an unexpected city planning job from Marion. While fortuitous, it was to be his last such job.

The Hugh Morton years began as favorably as could be expected. The months before Morton's discharge were spent establishing contacts at the state level and among private individuals Kelsey knew throughout the East. All contacts yielded favorable receptions and included Governor Cherry, who approved of the idea but emphasized that no state funds were available. He agreed to discuss the matter with officials of the North Carolina Conservation and Development Commission.[183]

By July, Hugh Morton was discharged from the army and back in North Carolina. He immediately got up to speed by reviewing all the correspondence that his father, uncle, and grandfather had with Kelsey about Grandfather Mountain. In a July 11 letter to Kelsey he proposed that they coordinate their efforts, and it was clear they were both "on the same page" and seeking the same ends. He said, "I have always been interested in seeing it be made a park, but at the present time am uncertain as to which way to turn." He had recently taken some photographs of the mountain and distributed them to people and organizations who might publish them. "Have you need for more pictures? If so, let me know and I will supply them as soon as possible." Kelsey's July 21 response outlined the three ways he saw to go about the job. First was to form a state organization to collect funds. Second was to get the governor and legislature to appropriate the money. Third was to seek one or more large donors to put up the money.

For the next year and a half, that was the pattern, with Kelsey following his three-part plan, and Morton providing pictures as needed. Morton was not passive. He sent copies of his prints to Bill Sharpe of the state of North Carolina News Bureau of the Department of Conservation and Development, and also a set to Carl Goerch, publisher of the *State* magazine. "I'm pleased to report that Mr. Goerch has already run two of them full page each, along with some very favorable comments about the mountain." Morton's efforts were naturally channeled toward the North Carolina press establishments, given his background in journalism.

Kelsey's efforts were centered on beautifully written articles for the various publications promoting conservation and the national parks. The hope was that by broadcasting the need, the volunteers would materialize. Kelsey's friend Laurence Fletcher, secretary of the Trustees of Public Reservations, wrote him April 18, 1946, "I think the *National Parks* magazine is one of the most attractive that is published, and I read with great interest the *Flora of Grandfather Mountain*. I never saw more beautiful reproductions of photographs. I congratulate you on your photography for I have never seen anything more beautifully reproduced than the Catawba Rhododendron. I have followed you pretty closely in your dogged determination to secure Grandfather Mountain and to add to your long list of accomplishments. I certainly salute you."

Kelsey's efforts were hampered by his remote residence in Massachusetts. He had ample contacts there and in Washington, DC, the National Park Service, and the Cosmos Club. But most of his North Carolina contacts were necessarily secondhand. He had no network. "Your name has been mentioned as one who might be willing to join the movement to acquire Grandfather Mountain" was a typical "cold calling" start. A typical finish was that from Mr. John M. Morehead, November 12, 1946, "I have looked this over with great interest, and thank you for sending it to me. I regret to say, however, that I am not in position to make any considerable contribution to this very worthy project. As a matter of fact, I have given the North Carolina University a Building and a Planetarium, which is taking up all of my income tax deductions for the present and for the next 2 or 3 years, and in any further donations I might make the net and the gross would be the same."

Kelsey often complained about the many millionaires in North Carolina that could easily afford to single-handedly fund the acquisition but never materialized. The times were certainly different from the Roaring Twenties, when the contributions poured in from an array of wealthy men in Tennessee, North Carolina, and Virginia, pushing for the Smokies and Shenandoah Parks. Each of the three states had commissions focused on the fund-raising efforts. The Great Depression and the war seemed to have taken the spirit out of them. Everyone stayed on the sidelines, cheering but not participating. They already had their national parks. The Grandfather simply couldn't rise to the stature of those earlier efforts. Time was dragging on, without results.

Kelsey sought to form a Grandfather Mountain Park Association. Back on February 16, 1944, he obtained a draft of the articles in good legal form from A. E. Demaray of the National Park Service. He then sought to man the association with the kind of driving leaders he had observed in the 1924 state national park associations. A number of candidates for directors materialized, but he needed a president and officers. As late as November 25, 1946, he approached Alexander James Jr. of Charlotte, North Carolina. "As more Charlotte people are interested in the Grandfather Mountain region than elsewhere, it would seem proper to have the Association organized there and have a Charlotte bank be the depository for donations. It would please me exceedingly if you would act as President, and advise as to the other officers." On November 26 he made another attempt to persuade Newton Drury to let him portray the Grandfather as a true national park. He pointed out that with the addition of forest service lands, it would fully qualify under NPS park standards. "To call it simply Grandfather Mountain, or a Monument, or any designation other than some kind of 'Park' will kill donations and endanger the success of our campaign." We have no record of Drury's response, one way or another.

On November 28 Alexander James turned him down. Health, three recent operations, necessary long trips, and absence from Charlotte were all reasons. But, "With every good wish for the success of your patriotic effort to 'Save the Grandfather', I am Sincerely Yours, A.L. James Jr." On November 29 Kelsey replied with an almost desperate tone. Could he suggest officers? Could he suggest someone else for president? Would he be willing to let his name appear as a vice president without duties? "The hard work I expect to do myself, but without well-known *sponsors* it will be a very uphill road to climb."

On December 3 the hammer fell, or at least began to fall, on Kelsey. He had sent Morton an approval copy of a circular for use by the future association. Morton's letter complained about the "last nine lines on page 3." They were "not an accurate presentation of the facts. The Linville Company is decidedly opposed to your presenting the points contained in those nine lines in that light. ... We think that we have done a good job, deserve some credit for what we have done, and are absolutely opposed to statements of the nature which have appeared in the press recently, which you now propose to include in your folder. I say again most emphatically, we have no plans whatsoever for abuse of Grandfather should we continue to own that mountain. We are unanimously agreed on this point, and there are members of my family who are more wrought up about the trend of your recent propaganda than I am." This was an abrupt reversal of the position Morton and MacRae had taken to the similar text in all his many earlier articles on saving the Grandfather, wherein they had expressed approval.

An amazed Kelsey responded December 10:

> I have read for the first time the article by Burke Davis in the November 23 Charlotte News, and have had several others read

it. All are agreed that in no place does it refer to the Linville Company directly or indirectly as "villainous woodsmen" or as having caused destruction in the past or as intending to do so in the future. In no place it seems to me is there the slightest intimation justifying your statement "I think it is a bit unfair to paint our intentions as being so dishonorable." This is the conclusion of Mr. Davis himself where he interpolates in your "rebuttal" quote, *"Mr. Kelsey, in fact sees danger to Grandfather Mountain only in the future, figuring that so long as the tract is under any private ownership, it may some day be cut over, as have so many other invaluable lands."*

It appears the light had suddenly dawned on Hugh Morton. The potential value of the mountain's lumber assets was going to be less than the potential value of developing the tourist facilities. The lumbering activities would gradually dissipate the mountain's value. A growing postwar tourist volume would gradually increase the revenue potential of the mountain. Aha—a "no-brainer." Thus began the half-century-long effort to rewrite history to show the MacRae family as conservators of the mountain. That was Morton's first strategic move, so evident in the December 3 letter. The second was to develop the tourist facility to increase the daily take from the toll road and revenue-producing activities once the tourists reached the terminus of the road. Some would call this a "tourist trap." More on this later.

Kelsey's December 10 letter was met by Morton's December 13 response. "Frankly, The Linville Company's position is this. When we made our agreement with you in regard to the sale of the mountain a few years ago, we were in sad financial condition, and could have used the money from its sale … This is not the situation today, and for that matter, our agreement with you expired almost a year ago. Yet we want to be as fair as possible, and will continue to mark time until April 1, in order to permit you to determine the successfulness of your campaign." Morton was using their "fairness" to establish the family credentials, while reasonably assured that nothing had a chance of happening before April 1, anyway—a sure bet.

Morton's letter continued with two diatribes. First, against Kelsey: A long paragraph started thus, "We object to statements or implications that we may abuse Grandfather unless the mountain is 'saved.' Say what you like, your releases have not gone out of the way at all times to pay tribute to the integrity of The Linville Company." Morton refused to acknowledge Kelsey's insistence that the threat was from future owners; he just continued from this point on to insist that Kelsey was impugning the MacRae family reputation. The historical record was clear on MacRae's lumbering of the mountain's flanks plus Julian Morton's threats to continue it; Kelsey had ignored that in his articles. Morton was asking Kelsey's help in erasing history. Recall J. W. Morton's March 22, 1944, statement:

> We are now cutting some of the merchantable timber but not on the Grandfather Mountain, nor are we cutting it close. … If the sale of the property as a whole is not made within the next year we will most probably start timbering much closer on other parts of the property. I do not know where Mr. Wharton got the idea that there was no danger of lumbering on the property. We are going to continue to cut timber and also are going to sell either the timber or the land as a whole to the first purchaser that will pay us a satisfactory price.

Morton's second diatribe targeted the National Park Service itself. "Their general policy seems to be that of non-cooperation with the tourist industry. As an example, last January I began negotiations for the erection of one small directional sign reading 'Grandfather Mountain 1', to be placed at the Beacon Heights intersection of the Parkway and U.S. 221. Not only would this sign have been quite helpful to the tourists who traveled the Parkway to see such leading attractions as Grandfather Mountain, it would have increased our business at least $5,000 last season. The negotiations took us into a tedious hair-splitting wrangle about Grandfather Mountain being 'commercial', we did not get the sign." Morton never forgave the park service for this "noncooperation," even years later. His letter continued with the claim, punctuated by identifying his numerous contacts within the North Carolina tourist industry and the journalistic community, that all of these people and institutions also felt that the park service was noncooperative with tourism. Morton didn't want to acknowledge that even one sign for one commercial interest could cascade into cries for equal treatment for hundreds of businesses bordering the Blue Ridge Parkway.

Finally Morton outlined what he suddenly perceived about the economics of the situation. "The Government will certainly be doing us no favor by taking the mountain over at the ridiculously low price at which it is offered to you. We know that we could make that much out of it in seven years, and still have the mountain. As you may know, Chimney Rock reportedly makes $50,000 a year, and it seems reasonable that Grandfather Mountain, a far greater attraction, could do half of that, if it were handled properly. By not harming Grandfather in the least, we could straighten our toll road and pave it, improve our observation platform facilities, put on an intensive advertising campaign, and take in $25,000 per year." To Morton, development—blasting, straightening, paving—was not harmful in any way. He simply didn't grasp, or want to grasp, the concept of people wanting to observe nature in its unaltered way, according to National Park Service standards. Why force visitors to climb a forested natural path to the summit, when you could haul them by the toll-paying carloads to your hamburger and hotdog stand (the little "Swiss" refreshment building[184]) at the observation platform? While Kelsey was not willing to accept it yet, the hammer had conclusively fallen on his aspirations for the Grandfather.

One quip Kelsey was fond of using noted that "he was born a Jayhawker, raised a Tar Heel, and adopted as a Yankee." And a Yankee he was to Morton and his journalist friends in Charlotte and Wilmington, North

Carolina. He was just a botanist from Massachusetts and a "front man" for the National Park Service.[185] This, notwithstanding his unrelenting efforts on behalf of conservation in the South. These efforts were not lost on his fellow Yankees in the North. A month after Morton's decisive negative letter, Kelsey received "the Conservation Award for 1946 for distinguished service in Conservation" from the Massachusetts Trustees of Public Reservations. It was announced and awarded January 29, 1947. Now often dubbed TTOR, the organization dropped the word "Public" from its name in 1954 to avoid confusion with government-owned land. Its national stature, and coveted Conservation Award, stem from its being the oldest regional land trust in the world, with one hundred thousand dues-paying members today, owning one hundred properties in Massachusetts. It was founded in the spring of 1891 by the Massachusetts Legislature.

This affirmation was sorely needed at the time to keep Kelsey going in his efforts to save the Grandfather. Concurrently he received discouraging news from Horace Albright, January 16, 1947. "I hope you are getting some encouragement on Grandfather Mountain. Of course I have no idea that there will be any money forthcoming for the purchase of land by the Park Service. There is likely to be an economy drive which the Park Service would be one of the bureaus to fall afoul of. Believe me, I say this with plenty of regret but out of an abundance of experience." An undaunted Kelsey replied February 5, "This project is coming along and I am starting a Grandfather Mountain Park Association, with headquarters in Charlotte, N. C. and now have a fine group of sponsors including four N. C. Congressmen. As the option for Grandfather Mt. expires April 1st, I must do some tall hustling."

Kelsey's emotions were being dragged up and down like a yo-yo. A month later Kelsey confided in Albright, "While widespread interest has been developed, it has become clear to me that with the time limit so close, I could not possibly raise the $165,000 by general subscriptions to acquire the Linville Company property before the option expired.

Therefore, unless some speedy way is found to do so, I fear the project is dead. Undoubtedly Grandfather Mountain will then become the victim of commercial exploitation in one form or another and a superb park lost to the people of America forever. Horace, that alternative is almost unthinkable! Posterity will find no excuse for such a failure on our part." The letter continued with apologies for the time he was taking from Albright, but he was "up against it" and did not know where else to go. Was there a possibility of finding someone to supply the money?

On March 12, Albright wrote Kelsey, "I shall try to do something on this project within the next few days. I am in no position to offer the slightest word of encouragement … Nevertheless, I shall make one good, strong effort with the material you have given me." On March 25 Albright's secretary wrote, "He did ask me to write you and tell you that it looks as though Mr. John D. Rockefeller, Jr. will see the papers on the Grandfather Mountain project." On March 24 Kelsey had written Morton, "Will you grant me a six months extension on the Linville Company's Grandfather Mountain option? I have several very encouraging leads, but cannot get decisions until after April 1." An undated telegram, Kelsey to Albright, read "Owners of Grandfather Mountain absolutely refused to renew option, but stated a new agreement might be made in the Fall but at higher price, probably about $180,000. They might accept this price now. Union National Bank Charlotte agreed to act as depository while transfer papers were being executed."

> The Asheville Citizen, dateline April 1 (AP)—Private development of the Grandfather Mountain area … seemed assured today with expiration of an option to purchase the site for a public park. Hugh Morton of Wilmington, president of Linville Company which owns the tract, said his organization will develop the site as a camping area and cut some timber. … Morton said there is a strong feeling in the western part of the State that the National Park Service should concentrate on

completing the Blue Ridge Parkway and the Smoky Mountain National Park. "We want a chance to prove that we will not abuse the natural beauty of the mountain."

Cut some timber? Not abuse the natural beauty? Oxymoron? This had all the earmarks of a press release from Morton, just waiting for the critical April 1 date for release. With it began the drumbeat that would last for decades. Repetition. Repetition. Repetition. No matter what they chose to do to the mountain to meet their revenue goals, *it did not constitute abuse to the natural beauty of the mountain.* Sam Weems, Blue Ridge Parkway superintendant, wrote Kelsey April 2, "I hardly know what comment to make about the attached copy of a news item from the *Asheville Citizen* of April 2. This came as a great surprise to me as I never thought Morton would pass up any chance to realize some ready cash for Grandfather. I need not tell you how shocked I am about the possibilities of this grand old mountain being exploited, especially by Hugh Morton."

After a flurry of telegrams and letters during April 1947, the following letter came to Kelsey from Horace Albright, May 3. Dear Mr. Kelsey:

> I have received your telegram reading as follows:
>
>> "Re your telegram. Option not renewable at $165,000 but probably new option at approximately $180,000 can be secured. Can you get guarantee of one half the amount raised accordingly. Such a pledge is of greatest value both in securing new option and raising balance of amount."
>
> I am glad to tell you that I have assurance, in fact a firm pledge, that if you can secure an option that is good for at least a year on the Grandfather and Grandmother Mountain properties

for their purchase at a price not exceeding $180,000, one half of that sum will be available when an equal amount has been obtained from other sources in good and responsible pledges.

I hope that the assurances of this letter will enable you not only to obtain the option but will also facilitate securing the additional funds to the end that this project may be completed in the early future.

With kindest regards, ... Horace M. Albright

On May 13 Hugh Morton wrote Kelsey on new Linville Company letterhead showing Morton as president and in the upper right a picture of the mountain, with observation platform and the name Grandfather Mountain overlaying some fluffy clouds. Just below the picture read "Carolina's 'Top' Scenic Attraction." The letter enclosed a season pass on the toll road for Kelsey and any number of friends who "will enjoy driving up to the majestic peaks that make Grandfather the outstanding mountain of Southern Appalachians." Ouch! That must have smarted a bit.

Kelsey to Albright, July 16: "The MacRaes interests who own Grandfather Mountain refused to consider a renewal of an option until this Fall when I am to take the matter up with them again. Hugh MacRae is a very obstinate Scotchman, is very old, and tells me his 'memory is nearly gone.' Hugh Morton his grandson ... inherits his grandfather's obstinacy and 'feels his oats'. He is about 26 years old and the sudden death of his father landed him in his present job. He wants to show the world what he can do and is exploiting the road up to the first peak of Grandfather this summer. My belief is they are after a bigger price. So all I can do is to wait till the 'Linville season' is over and then tackle the job again to a finish."

While Kelsey was waiting, as the summer waned, he heard from his old compatriot, Representative H. W. Temple, chairman of the old

Southern Appalachian National Park Commission. Temple had been defeated in his congressional race of 1932 and was immediately hired to teach at his old college where he had started as a professor in 1898. At age eighty-three he was still teaching. Kelsey was by then seventy-five years old and wrote back August 8, "It was indeed a great pleasure and satisfaction to hear from you again. At the dedication of Mammoth Cave National Park I was the only member present of our old S.A.N.P. Commission. In fact all had passed on but you and me. I missed you greatly and questioned Demaray but he nor any other could give me an answer why you were not there." Of the five commissioners, Kelsey was "the only one left standing" in active work for the park service.

Kelsey to Morton, November 20. Reminded Morton of promise to consider a renewal of option in the fall. Confirmed the $90,000 pledge based on a "not to exceed $180,000 price." Offered to cut to 7 percent his commission for covering campaign expenses, increasing the Linville Company's net gain.

Morton to Kelsey, November 28. "It is the wish of the majority of the stockholders ... to advise you that after due consideration we are not interested in selling Grandfather Mountain at this time." He then listed four contributing factors: (1) the 1947 season had been quite profitable, despite the toll road fee being lower than admission charges at nine tenths of the South's other leading privately-owned tourist attractions; (2) after commissions and taxes, the price was insufficient to overcome the mountain's long-run investment potential; (3) the park service should be concentrating on its existing commitments on the Blue Ridge Parkway and the Smokies. "In the meantime, Grandfather Mountain will serve as a far greater asset to North Carolina's tourist industry if preserved and developed as a tourist attraction by the Linville Company"; and (4) "Reported mineral resources on Grandfather Mountain have not been fully investigated."

First lumbering. Next blasting the road up the mountain. Now possible mineral extraction. But *no abuse to the natural beauty of the mountain.* Then, quoting, "We hope that as a businessman you will be sympathetic with our present position." When it came to *natural beauty* and *abuse* Hugh Morton was either in denial, or just didn't get it (in today's vernacular), or got it but didn't care. When it came to roads, park service standards were very different. The minimal roads in the Great Smokies were a good example.

Recall Robert Lindsay Mason's plea to Secretary of the Interior Wilber in prior years; should there be another Skyline Highway along the top of the Great Smokies from Newfound Gap to Deal's Gap at the western end? Mason implored, "The mountains are beautiful now. They remind me of a vast canvas; a living painting vibrating with the mystery of color blending that is only possible at this time of year. When one climbs the hills and gazes off high prominences into swimming color that is breathless, it is impossible to describe the feeling of awe and infinitesimal atom that man is when he stands alone in the big universe that stretches out below in a panorama that appalls in its bigness. ... In building the motor path we would destroy the very thing we came to see."

At the time, Kelsey had chimed in to Albright, "There are plenty of national parks and state parks where the herd instinct can be fully satisfied but for God's sake let's keep our national parks, so far as we can, in a truly wild state. I know the pressure for 'improvements' is almost irresistible. You are resisting that pressure magnificently and if this policy is continued, the future generation will rise up and call you blessed."

Ultimately a lesser road was built only to Clingman's Dome from Newfound Gap, roughly seven miles. It was out of sight, well below the summit crest-line and the Appalachian Trail, ending with a hiking trail to the summit. Ultimately Kelsey reversed his stand and supported the limited lesser road.

Hugh Morton's third contributing factor represented his hostility toward the park service. "The Park Service should be concentrating on its existing commitments on the Blue Ridge Parkway and the Smokies." The park service wanted to keep the Blue Ridge Parkway an experience with nature for its travelers. Morton and his friends in the North Carolina tourist industry wanted it to be a feeder road with signs leading the traveler to their particular business enterprises and more exits nearer to their attractions. As for the Smokies, the park had been dedicated before the war, and was fully developed according to park service standards for an encounter with primeval horticulture. What more did Morton want? More and wider roads? Restaurants inside the park? Morton never clarified his objections.

For Kelsey, the hammer had come down on him conclusively with Morton's November 28 letter. On December 12, 1947, he wrote to Albright:

> I only wish it were possible for me to continue the campaign in a vigorous way and bring it to a conclusion. But as I have pointed out before, I cannot continue the burden of expenses alone. In all the years I have worked for the advancement of the National Parks I have never asked or received a nickel in pay for my time and never will, and would not accept it if offered. It has been a labor of love and a civic duty. But I would hate to estimate what it has cost me in expenses and I am quite sure I have not been quite fair in this respect to my family or business. You have shown yourself to be most understanding and so I am telling you the facts so you will see it is not lack of fervent interest in this project that compels me to discontinue my efforts at this time, when it seems so near fruition.

Much like John Muir in 1913, Kelsey had to accept defeat. Muir poured his last energies into resisting plans to dam Yosemite National Park's wild Hetch Hetchy Valley. The city of San Francisco wanted the water this dam and reservoir would provide to them. Muir's Sierra Club and an army of conservationists pleaded for saving the valley but lost in the face of stronger political forces in San Francisco.[186] Kelsey had lost in the face of malaise on the part of North Carolina's prominent wealthy citizens; lost in the face of lackluster will on the part of the park service; lost in the face of commercial opportunism on the part of the MacRae/Morton family.

From this point on Kelsey stayed clear of direct involvement, even though efforts at the state level continued, as did efforts by Sam Weems of the Blue Ridge Parkway. These battles with Morton continued well into the 1960s. Most had to do with the route of the parkway across Morton's land east of the mountain. At times the exchanges became shrill. Morton claimed a leadership role for the tourist industry, and continued to claim his development of the mountain was not harmful. This grew into new claims that he was in fact the "protector" of the mountain. The new claims reached a climax when the Parkway wanted to direct the route above the twisting path of US 221 to smooth the road.

The route recommended by the park service on average was 300–400 feet higher than US 221, but still on average about 1,600 feet below the summit at Calloway Peak. It was a full 1,075 feet below Morton's Mile High Swinging Bridge built in 1952. Morton claimed it would interfere with his "attraction" because of its proximity. He claimed the highway "went over the top of the mountain." It was like "taking a switchblade to the Mona Lisa." As outrageous as these claims were, they were encouraged by some press reporting and widely believed. Morton held out that he was the savior of the mountain, protecting it from the deprivations of the park service. Ultimately the parkway was built about halfway between the High route and US 221. We will resist filling out the detail of the next twenty years following Kelsey's exit from the scene. This is a narrative about Harlan P. Kelsey, not Hugh Morton. The reader is strongly urged to read Anne Mitchell Whisnant's book *Super-Scenic Motorway: A Blue Ridge Parkway History*. The forty pages of detail on the battles between Morton and the park service are found from page 285 to page 325 of this excellent work.[187] Let the reader be the judge.

Earlier it was suggested that Morton's expansion of the toll road and facilities at the observation platform was the start of creating a tourist trap. What is a tourist trap? Not finding the label in any authoritative work, your author asked his friends how they would define it. For most it was puzzling at first but evolved to the following: it was an establishment that in a splashy way offered more than it delivered. But once inside, after paying to get in, even the disappointed tourist would probably buy whatever merchandise was offered—food, souvenirs, postcards—just to make the stop worthwhile. It usually contained man-made elements that sought to embellish whatever natural "wonder" it advertised. It was almost always advertised on the highway by billboards, and more billboards, extolling its virtues.

In the spring of 2004, your author visited Grandfather Mountain for an interview with Hugh Morton. If the facility was a tourist trap, it was certainly the most polished one you might ever see. The observation platform was replaced by the much enlarged "nature museum." The parking lots were properly tiered to nestle into the slope and divided by shrubbery. The road continued toward the summit but stopped far short of it at the "visitor center." We stopped at a road pull-out and were dazzled by the spring bloom of the pinkshell azaleas at roadside. Inside the nature museum was high, open architecture, with a bookstore on the left, a cafeteria straight ahead to the left, and a hallway to the right leading to a substantial auditorium. Featured that day was an excellent lecture on the mountain's geology by Loren A. Raymond, PhD, from Appalachian State in nearby Boone, North Carolina. Lining the hallway to the auditorium was a display of delicate glass flower blooms simulating the various rhododendron and kalmias of the region. Up the road at the visitor center there was another restaurant and a room full of local wood carvers practicing their craft before your very eyes.

So far everything was in good taste, clean, and attractive. But there was nothing, repeat *nothing*, that couldn't have been built outside the toll booth on US 221, with exactly the same effect. Once it was put up on the side of the mountain it was all pure artifice. Then outside the visitors center was the Mile High Swinging Bridge (dedicated in 1952) that was extolled in all the billboards as we had approached Linville. Business cards, letterhead, and the billboards all showed it as a very long suspension bridge spanning a deep valley (a "chasm") on the side of the mountain. Unlike everything else, it *had* to be high on the mountain at roughly five thousand feet elevation. Otherwise it couldn't be touted as the Mile High Bridge. That was the hook that certainly qualified the mountain as a tourist trap. It was grossly misrepresented. As he stood on the bridge, your author noted that it spanned a shallow gully (hardly a "chasm") to reach a better viewing outlook, easily reached (if they had wished to do that) by making a trail around the end of the gulley. It was half or less the length pictured on billboards and ads. The footer at the bottom of the letterhead contains the deceptive artwork with the title "Nature on a Whole Different Level," evidently referring to its mile-high elevation. A naturalist might, however, interpret it as man's attempt to improve on nature. For a photograph, see page 2 of the company's brochure, *Grandfather Mountain: Discovering Nature On A Whole Different Level,* © 1993, 2002. The bridge was not only a disappointment but clearly helped diminish the mountain's natural beauty while you were in sight of it.

Once the tourist infrastructure was in place, there was no more that Morton could effectively do to increase the traffic and revenue potential. He could only try to polish the image of the mountain. This he did by turning most of the undeveloped portion of the mountain over to the Nature Conservancy, a respected national conservation organization. He also got a United Nations organization to designate the mountain as a biosphere reserve. All this was to the good and is to be lauded, as your author did in his May 26, 2004, thank-you letter to Hugh Morton. But again, it could have been done without the distraction of the tourist facility.

Today's Grandfather Mountain meets all of the criteria of the tourist trap defined earlier. If you are ever there, try to imagine the whole thing as a national park facility, with rustic materials, placed not to use the mountain, but to enhance it—being greeted by a ranger with the traditional flat-brimmed hat and all the right answers. No swinging bridge. The road narrowed back to a horse trail. The exceptional flora viewed in season on a narrow hiking trail, not glass flowers in an artificially lit hallway. Or look at the Great Smoky Mountains National Park and imagine that subdued natural approach on the Grandfather. What could have been but now will never be. Old Hugh MacRae died in the early 1950s. His grandson, Hugh MacRae Morton, died in 2006. Today his children continue the MacRae/Morton dynasty.

Moving On

On December 14, 1947, Horace Albright expressed his sorrow to Kelsey over the Grandfather affair but hoped that Kelsey might somehow get "another chance at it." "John D. R. Jr. told me the other day in the elevator that he wanted to see me this coming week. He will surely take up this North Carolina project. I'll tell him all about it from your letters and enclosures you sent me. He is terribly broken up about the Acadia fire which just about ruined the national park as you probably know. If he and others should go in for quick restoration which would involve much planting, you ought to get in on that, and I'll keep you posted. Mr. Bartholomew whom you know has been retained on the planning end, and I'll be seeing him soon."

Kelsey's immediate response on December 18 passed quickly beyond the Grandfather, to the fire. "The Acadia National Park disaster is really a tragedy." He then cited his long observation of inadequate reforestation after the logging and fire devastation in the Shenandoah and Great Smoky Mountains National Parks. "The problem is to reforest and replant to restore so far as feasible the *original primeval* growth and landscape." He then launched into a tutorial on proper reforestation.

Paraphrasing: First control the "weed" trees such as pin cherry, gray birch, poplars, and certain pines that are first to seed in naturally. Mesh this with a program to reintroduce the *original* species. The "weed" trees should then be largely eliminated from season to season, until a *biotic balance* has been reestablished, and nature takes over. "Yet I want to point out that ... even without this scientific treatment, nature has done so well in many areas, that the layman would hardly be aware that the new forest cover was not a primeval one. And each year shows added improvement." He lauded Mr. Bartholomew as an able planner but questioned whether Congress would appropriate sufficient funds to allow an adequate planting program. "The National Park Service has a splendid corps of men, but it will need more than good wishes to enable it to promptly and adequately do the job as it should be done."

As the year 1948 started, Kelsey's nursery was again asleep for the winter. There was no current active collaboration with the park service. However, his service on the Advisory Council of the National Arboretum in Washington, DC, had been a continuous part of his life for almost twenty-five years. It remained so now as a constant background activity. We have deliberately bypassed this work previously in the narrative, giving priority to his more focused projects.

The National Arboretum, first conceived with a formal study in 1901, did not become a reality until March 4, 1927, with a congressional bill signed into law delineating the location alongside the Anacostia River in northeastern Washington, DC. The law authorized $300,000 to be expended under the authority of the secretary of agriculture for acquisition of lands. There was to be an advisory council to include representatives of national organizations interested in the work of the arboretum, comprised of fifteen members. Harlan P. Kelsey was one of those first fifteen; he remained continuously on the council until his resignation in April 1954 at age eighty-two. By 1950 only two of the first fifteen were still serving—Kelsey and his old sidekick from the American Association of Nurserymen, Robert Pyle. Kelsey's associate author of

Standardized Plant Names, Dr. Frederick V. Coville, was named the first director, with the task of acquiring the land for the arboretum.[188]

The next director after Dr. Coville was Mr. B. Y. Morrison. Morrison and Kelsey locked horns for over twenty years, until Morrison's resignation in 1951. Morrison was consumed with the view that the American public and scientific community should be most interested in the many exotic plants not found normally in the United States. Kelsey was consumed with exactly the opposite view, stressing native plants. Morrison, being the director, and being very tenacious, always won the day. One of the arboretum's early featured masses was of azaleas, some native Appalachian species, but many others mostly Japanese evergreen large-bloom azaleas. Morrison felt that scientific exploration might best be directed toward adapting the exotics to American use. While Morrison's view won the day then in the National Arboretum, Kelsey's view has prevailed elsewhere, until today American gardeners need an excuse to plant exotics.

Kelsey thought that not only should the emphasis be on native plants, but also the National Arboretum should have branch locations disbursed around the United States, each of which would feature the native plants indigenous to that area. This was because of the widely varying climatic conditions in those areas. The notion of disbursed locations to bring horticultural education to people in various locations was the beginning of a thread that would trace to a number of future Kelsey proposals.

The next such proposal for disbursed horticulture was to place an arboretum along the Blue Ridge Parkway. Travelers could pull off the parkway and enjoy a self-guided tour through the flora of the arboretum for both relaxation and education. Kelsey wrote to Park Service Director Drury September 27, 1946. "Re Southern Appalachian National Arboretum. Mr. Demaray wrote me his approval of this project, and I sincerely hope you will officially sanction it so that action will follow at an early date. I shall try to see you in person soon and present the whole matter, and its extreme importance scientifically and as a very desirable and attractive feature to add to the Blue Ridge Parkway. This matter has been broached to a great many influential people, and their unanimous reaction is favorable and even enthusiastic. Many sites for a possible 2,000 to 3,000 acre Arboretum along the Blue Ridge Parkway already have been examined by Superintendent Weems, Resident Landscape Architect Abbott and me, and I think I am correct in saying that an entirely satisfactory tract may readily be determined if authority is given by you to proceed." Unfortunately, such authority was never forthcoming.

Unknown to Kelsey in 1948, were the stirrings among his many friends in Massachusetts. Quietly taking shape was that old honor, out of his reach, about which he had often joked.

> "The Board of Trustees of the UNIVERSITY of MASSACHUSETTS. To all persons to whom these presents may come, greeting: Be it known that we hereby confer upon Harlan Page Kelsey, in recognition of his distinguished attainments, the Honorary Degree of Doctor of Science, with all the rights privileges and dignities pertaining to that degree. Given at Amherst June 7, 1948."

Dr. Kelsey had arrived on the scene.

Roadside Horticulture

Even at age seventy-six, he wasn't about to quit, and a seed began to germinate in his mind as the next proposal for disbursed public exposure to horticulture. The seed had been planted years before as Kelsey began to "beat the drum" for better roadside development, especially for better landscaping and plant materials. The explosion of automobile travel in the 1930s had overtaxed the old road system, and while massive efforts were being made to unclog things, the treatment of roadsides lagged, with a low priority in funding. "We must sadly admit that

Honorary Doctor of Science. University of Massachusetts. 1948.

much of our present so-called roadside improvement is little more than a landscape hair-cut or perhaps a horticultural manicure." This was an opening line in Kelsey's address, delivered at the Annual Meeting of the Massachusetts Forest and Park Association, Boston, February 6, 1936.

He cited narrow restricted rights-of-way as the biggest obstacle to an "adequate and successful road and roadside development program." The ancient forty- or fifty-foot right-of-way for country roads was an intolerable hindrance.

> The two and three-lane roadways must be abolished, at least on our main highways, both as a matter of safety and to ease congestion, and be replaced by two traveled ways each direction with an island strip between, properly treated to eliminate the menace of glaring headlights. The roadways for opposing streams of traffic also need not be on the same levels, and they may be located at varying distances apart to conform to the natural contours of the terrain, usually at a material saving of construction costs, and adding greatly to landscape possibilities.

He called for trained landscape staff to be better integrated with trained engineers. With expanded rights-of-way, picnic grounds and small parks should replace hotdog stands; they would allow protection of unusual natural features such as shady groves or groups of trees, ponds, brooks, boulders, historic sites or objects, fine vistas and distant views, perhaps a waterfall or glen, or bold rocky cliffs and the like.

Native plants vs. exotics. "It is established that low-growing native shrubs, vines and other ground covers should constitute the bulk of roadside plantings, and yet, we see thousands of state-grown Norway Spruce, Red, Scotch and Austrian Pines planted closely together on cuts and banks along our highways with our beautiful native Hemlock and White Pine largely neglected." Avoid spotty planting in favor of large masses better suited to viewing from a speeding automobile and lower cost maintenance. These are only a few of his suggestions, but the most important ones. He closed the address with an appended specific list "of our beautiful and appropriate native plants that should constitute the bulk of roadside plantings."

Kelsey's roadside development ideas and initiatives may seem obvious today but were clearly ahead of their time in the mid-1930s. In mid-1949 Kelsey came up with a more grandiose disbursal theme. On September 27 he wrote to a Mr. Ovid Butler, "Enclosed is my paper *Arborways for America* in redrafted form. You were good enough to say you would find out if American Forests would use it in an early edition of that magazine. I could have it published in several other periodicals, but I much prefer American Forests. At any rate an early decision would be greatly appreciated by me." *American Forests* was the magazine of the American Forestry Association, Washington, DC.

He didn't have long to wait. His paper appeared in the December 1949 issue as the lead article. "The proposal is made here that we establish a network of arborways along the major highways of the country—national arborways and interstate arborways, state arborways and even county arborways. Eventually, perhaps, Canada and Mexico will undertake a similar program, linking their highways with ours. Indeed every nation in the world should have a comparable system of arborways." A full-page map followed the lead paragraphs showing a highway system spanning all of North and South America. As an example, an early photograph of the Merritt Parkway in New York was superimposed in the upper right corner. The map looked like today's simplified maps of the US Interstate Highway System.

"The location of each arborway must necessarily be scientifically studied as to rights-of-way, soils, landscape features and possibilities for wayside parks, camp sites and recreational areas. Above all, it must qualify for the establishment of adequate group, orchard and forest plantations of native and exotic trees and plants for experimental, educational and ornamental purposes." The arborways should be of sufficient length to span most of the ten US Climatic Zones, so that cross-country travelers could appreciate how the flora changed, zone by zone. (It included a half-page zone map.) He then went on to cite numerous hypothetical examples, such as Route 1 from Maine to Florida. "Except where 'civilization' has made too bold an incursion on the original plant cover, plantings should be of native material exclusively, as is already the laudable National Park Service practice on the Blue Ridge Parkway, but where as yet only a comparatively limited number of the extraordinary wealth of species and varieties indigenous to the Southern Appalachian region have been used. ... At suitable intervals in each climatic zone, adequate sections should be designated and used for the planting and testing of the greatest possible variety of ornamental and economic exotic plants. Other sections should be devoted to test plantations of fast-growing hybrid trees, to native and exotic fruits and nuts, and to all other types of economic plants, even drug plants and grasses. It is highly important that a correct ecological balance be maintained, not only by correct plant combinations, but by restoration and protection of native wildlife including useful insects."

Kelsey ordered 750 reprint copies at his own expense to distribute among his friends and anyone else who might influence highway roadside policy.

His overall plan was excessive, but it was not lost on Kelsey that land acquisition was the major cost of new horticultural plantations and arboretums. Why not strike while the iron was hot and funds were forthcoming anyway for highways? Adequate rights-of-way could make millions of acres available for roadside horticultural development, at little incremental cost under funds appropriation bills. Kelsey was no doubt aware of the Federal-Aid Highway Acts of 1938 and 1944, which sought a network of superhighways. Neither act authorized funding for construction. It took the Eisenhower administration to get Congress to enact the Federal-Aid Highway Acts of 1954 (authorizing $175 million) and 1956 (authorizing $25 billion), finally funding the Interstate Highway System. The construction standards under these acts mandated many of Kelsey's ideas, like divided highways with at least two lanes in each direction and wide median strips often at different grade levels, with periodic rest areas. However, horticultural standards for roadsides were notably absent. Today the American Association of State Highway and Transportation Officials—AASHTO—dictates practices. Of their fourteen technical committee titles, not one of them speaks to ornamental horticulture. On the plus side, the concept of "limited access" legislates against the billboards and hotdog stands that were anathema to Kelsey. The rural sections of today's interstate highways are by and large nicely planted and attractive.

Mississippi River Parkway Survey

Of course the interstate highway system came later. The only specific interstate highway project in 1949 was the Mississippi Valley Parkway proposition, running from its northern headwaters to the Gulf of Mexico. On November 29, 1949, Kelsey wrote Director Drury of the National Park Service, expressing his interest in the project. Since April 1949 Kelsey had held an appointment as consultant, GS-15, on a "when actually employed" basis. He told Drury about his forthcoming Arborways article in *American Forests* magazine and its relationship to the impending survey for the Mississippi Parkway. "I am very much interested in being assigned by the National Park Service to this survey, and would like to discuss with you at an early date the scope of the undertaking as I see it, and especially as to the flora, fauna, land use and protection, flood control and scenic implications."

Only a month passed before Kelsey had his answer. On January 3, 1950, he heard from Conrad Wirth, assistant director. "Let me start the New Year off right by dropping you a note and complimenting you on a very fine article in the *American Forests* of December 1949, entitled 'Arborways for America.' I think it is an excellent job and a very fine idea. As a matter of fact, you know now that Greensfelder has written in regarding the possibility of the arborway idea of yours being used in connection with the Mississippi Parkway. ... Our plans are not all set yet, but Stan Abbott is working on the parkway and, as you know from Mr. Greensfelder, there will be a meeting in Mississippi, at which we would like you to be present. We would like to have you go down there as our consultant and we would pay your per diem and travel expenses there and back." Connie Wirth cautioned Kelsey to hold his Arborway enthusiasm in check. "In this stage of the preparation of the study, we will not want to go into the details of such an Arborway, and perhaps would not want to do so until Congress has definitely authorized the construction of the parkway."

Stan Abbott was an old friend of Kelsey's dating back to the Blue Ridge Parkway days where he acted as landscape architect for the park service. Now he carried the title supervising landscape architect, Mississippi River Parkway Survey. Mr. A. P. Greensfelder of St. Louis was the head of the Mississippi River Parkway Planning Commission, composed of one hundred members, ten from each of the ten river states. Instead of the title president, Greensfelder was called "pilot," taken from the person in charge of navigating river boats among tricky shoal obstacles along the river course. In like fashion, he had two copilots (North and South) as assistants from among the members, instead of vice presidents.

The MRPS had its roots in Law 770-1/2 passed by Congress June 23, 1936. It authorized the secretary of the Interior to cooperate with the various states in the preparation of a nationwide park, parkway, and recreation plan and program for America. Among the states energized by the law, Missouri was the first to produce such a plan in 1937. Perhaps this is why Greensfelder, from St. Louis, emerged as the leader of the MRPS proposition. The five states along the western shore of the river organized a parkway planning committee in 1938. Interior Secretary

Ickes suggested they add the five eastern-shore states to form a ten-state group, which the Interior Department would support for a study of a midcontinent national parkway from the source of the river to the sea. The ten-state group introduced bills in both the House and the Senate in 1939 that were still in committee when the emerging pressures of WWII pushed the effort into the background.

It wasn't until 1949 that the ten-state group named a one-hundred-member delegation, comprised of five diversified state government officials, coupled with five prominent interested citizens from each state. They introduced a new bill in Congress, which passed, authorizing $250,000 to be used by the National Park Service and the Bureau of Public Roads to make a joint survey of a route for the parkway, now named the Mississippi River Parkway. The ten-state group was named the MRP Commission. The two federal departments would spearhead the survey with Stan Abbott as supervising landscape architect, working with now consultant Dr. Harlan P. Kelsey. The federal group took the name Mississippi River Parkway Survey, with offices in Arlington, Virginia. They also took responsibility for publishing a periodic newsletter, reporting events and progress of the survey.

After a St. Louis breakfast meeting of the MRP Commission in February, the federal group began a series of inspection trips to sections of the River in various specific states. In his January 17, 1950, letter to Connie Wirth, Kelsey had suggested, "Reconnaissance trips are a vital necessity and should be made before the meeting in Mississippi. ... Frankly I would like to go over the entire area with you and Abbott, and it should be done by blimp as was done so successfully over the Florida Everglades." But then Kelsey took off February 3 for a twenty-four-day trip to Guatemala, missing the federal group's early March inspection trip. The March 20 newsletter reported that they started by train from Chicago: "The meetings we had en route left no doubt in our minds of the local interest in the parkway. St. Paul officials started us off confidently. Down through Minnesota, Iowa, Illinois, and Missouri, the highway and other state officials, and the press, stood unmistakably ready to help."

On April 17, 1950, Connie Wirth wrote Kelsey, "By the time you receive this I hope you have bid the Salem Hospital adieu and are swiftly recuperating from your sojourn there. ... Take care of yourself, Kel, and do not come to Washington ... before you have recovered fully from the operation." Kelsey to Wirth, May 3, "Your letter of April 17 was received when I was in durance vile and incommunicado, with wild Doctors brandishing different kinds of instruments of torture over and into my unprotected body, and shrieking for my life's blood—which they extracted in copious quantities—and injected almost all of Materia Medica into my veins, my tummy and my fanny. But Lo, I survived and am beginning to feel ornery and a rarin' to go. So if the N.P.S. Dictators so determine, I shall probably be in Washington next week and sincerely hope to see you."

Next came the first full meeting of the MRP Commission, in Jackson, Mississippi. From the July 6 newsletter, "May 26 'dawned clear' as the pilot's log used to read—and made a fine day for some 60 Commissioners to see a national parkway [Natchez Trace Parkway] under development. ... The business sessions and the banquet under the chairmanship of Pilot Greensfelder and Co-Chairmen White and Brooks provided a long list of interesting speakers who developed some of the very many sides to the Mississippi River parkway. Pilot Greensfelder, back from extensive travels abroad, described the great roads of Europe and the Mediterranean countries. Dr. Harlan P. Kelsey, eminent horticulturist and conservationist, presented his view of the Mississippi River Parkway as a great arborway, and Mr. William T. Pryor, Highway Engineer of the Bureau of Public Roads, reported on the progress of the Survey."

This was Kelsey's best chance, right at the beginning of the survey, to establish his arborway philosophy—to sell the commissioners. If he could get them to exchange the name "Arborway" for the already established "Parkway," his emphasis on horticultural education might have a chance. Thus he titled his paper "An Arborway Proposal for the Mississippi River Parkway." He focused on three themes: (1) education that plant life is the most important natural resource, upon which all other resources depend; (2) education on the breadth of plant life across the climate zones from subarctic zone 2 in northern Minnesota, to subtropical zone 9 in Louisiana; and (3) education on the importance of native plant material for major plantings along rights-of-way and landscape effects. Brief excerpts from the paper show his reasoning and call to action.

> 1. All animal life in this world including man, is dependent for existence on plant life in one form or another. Carnivora, the flesh-eating animals, live off of other animals which in small part may be weaker carnivore, but are principally vegetarians. … And so with man … The original source of his food, and for that matter most of his raiment, originates from some form of plant life. This vital fact has been recklessly ignored by all peoples and all nations since the beginning of time, so far as we can ascertain. Frightful and selfish exploitation of plant life for private gain, and in fact of all natural resources by each successive generation has been and for the greater part of the world still is the ruling incentive and procedure. … If we are to restore to the world a reasonable normal productive capacity for the benefit of all mankind and keep it so, it can be done only by educating all of the people to a clear knowledge of all natural resources, both expendable and renewable; and the greatest and most important renewable resource is plant life.

> 2. Travelling from zone to zone, the display of the different native plants of each region will excite increasing interest as the traveler goes South or North from plant zone to plant zone, as the trip may happen to be planned. Proper informational

bulletin boards will be a chief educational feature, telling what the plants are and their uses, the labeling always to give correct botanical and common names. In the upper Mississippi basin in zone 2 is found an almost sub-arctic flora, and going Southward we first meet with forests of white, Norway and jack pine, whitecedar, larch, spruce, birches, white and other poplars, willows and a vast variety of other trees, shrubs, and plants that are acclimated to the intense cold of Minnesota winters. On the other extreme when we reach Southern Louisiana and approach the delta region in zone 9, what an amazing contrast we find in the glorious live oaks draped with tillandsia, often called Spanish moss and everywhere the parasitic mistletoe of Yuletide fame. Here are forests of sweetgum, tupelo and the lovely wax-flowered evergreen Southern magnolia, and the smaller scented sweetbay magnolia, bursts of flowering dogwood and silverbell and dark groves of longleaf and slash pines. ... In each of the 10 States involved the best possible site along this Parkway-Arborway should be selected for a 'Combination Park' large enough to provide ample space for a complete demonstration and exhibition of each State's resources and activities, and should include the following: 1. Park Headquarters and Museum housing historical ... other exhibits and Staff Offices. 2. *An Arboretum and Botanical Garden exhibiting the complete flora of the State.* [italics added] 3. A Forestry section ... 4. Recreational and Camp areas ... 5. Fish ponds and Zoological exhibit of native fauna.

3. I recommend that in each plant zone and in each of the ten States involved, strictly indigenous plant material only should be used for major plantings along rights-of-way and for landscape effects. ... Each State might reasonable exploit its State tree and flower at proper intervals, but again let the stress that outside of the very desirable test plantations above referred to, **exotic plants have no legitimate place along the**

major stretches of the Arborway through the countryside. It can truthfully be said that a really comprehensive Arborway is a great educational institution, both as to imparting definite plant knowledge and demonstrating proper uses and combinations of all types of native plant material, while at the same time restoring and preserving beautiful natural landscapes that have for so long been thoughtlessly and ruthlessly despoiled. ... **Let me urge that along the entire Mississippi River Parkway where primeval growth may still be found, such areas be set aside and dedicated as wildlife sanctuaries for native plant and animal life, and permanently protected from any type of encroachment. ... A fully developed Arborway for the Mississippi River basin, scientifically planned and planted, might well become the yardstick for Arborways throughout the Nation.** [Bold print is used above exactly as Kelsey used it in his paper.]

Passion. One can see passion written all over Kelsey's speech (and paper). At age seventy-eight, Kelsey no doubt saw this as the last chance, in his so fruitful lifetime, to make a positive difference for horticulture. The excerpts above were selected to lay out his case in a clear clinical way. Many of the elements not excerpted showed his passion. For example, "A world without abundant plant life would be an uninhabited desert, a wind-swept howling wilderness." Kelsey's, and his father's, lifelong battle with the lumberman, oozed out of his conservation rhetoric. "In America nearly all of our once glorious forests have been laid waste, our waving prairies torn up and exposed to blighting winds, our rivers, streams and shores polluted,—all this resulting in forest fires, drouths [sic], floods, soil erosion, a dangerous lowering of precious water tables and many other evils. Nature has been grossly violated and it will take intelligent, universal, and heroic measures to restore our land to a normal condition of **sustained productiveness** and fair landscapes."

To Kelsey the Mississippi River Parkway was a means to his primary end—elevating plant life and conservation to a higher conscious level, through public education. To his park service friends, and to the one hundred commissioners, horticulture was only one of many means to their primary end—getting their precious parkway approved by Congress, funded, and ultimately built. Educating the public on the history of past events along the river was more popular than botanical education. This because to the average citizen, human events were vastly more interesting than botany; unless, of course, it was botany in their own backyard garden. John A. Hussey, historian retained by the park service, provided a revealing anecdote. "I once heard someone ask an eminent professor of history, 'What good is an historian, anyway?' The answer surprised me. 'Well,' he said, 'I suppose the historian has about the same function as the artist, the novelist, or the actor—he sometimes inspires people, but mostly he entertains them. People are curious about the world and about life, past and present; and the historian helps to satisfy that curiosity.' The professor, I believe, was having his little joke, but there was enough truth in what he said to make it sound entirely plausible at the time."

Kelsey's idea of a "combination park" was well received by Abbott, who wrote June 14, "No, we haven't so far stressed the possibility of a museum along the Parkway in each of the ten States. Your suggestion to house historical, archeological, and scientific things of interest in a botanical setting is quite new as such and we ought to talk about it at the first chance. … It has struck me that there ought to be a good deal of thought given to the marriage of these various categories of educational or interpretive nature." It was subtle, and probably unconscious on Abbott's part, to include botany as a "setting," not a feature such as "historical, archeological, and scientific things of interest."

Kelsey went further with the "combination park" idea by urging adequate land taking at a very early stage. He wanted hundreds of acres at each park to accommodate all the elements in the combination. Abbott's reaction in a June 23 letter was mixed. He said, on the plus side, "I think, as apparently you do, that our job as planners of the integrated parkway plan would be to see that initial acquisition of rights-of-way provide appropriate lands on which this and other developments might take place through the years as the parkway grows. In nearly every instance of failure in highway and park planning, insufficiency of initial land taking is at the root of the problems." On the minus side he said, "It is good, too, to have your un-frightened advice in these various matters because I confess, for one, to a certain rueful doubt as to how much we can load our conception of a proper project without having it fall of its weight. Perhaps this is because I am daily in touch with the mounting estimates of costs."

Starting back before Christmas 1949, a group of park service people and commissioners took a maiden trip for reconnaissance of the river from St. Paul to St. Louis. These trips were routinely taken every month or two in a different location, with whichever group of commissioners was available to discuss road routing and features for the survey report. The newsletter would report the findings and commentary to the full population of commissioners so that everyone could see things evolving over time. By August 22, 1950, a group of over a hundred people met for a two-day session at Lake Itasca, Clearwater, Minnesota—this being the headwaters location for the river. There is a sign reading, "Here 1,475 ft. above the ocean the mighty Mississippi begins to flow on its winding way 2,552 miles to the Gulf of Mexico."

The newsletter declared, "Discussions ... may turn out to be historic. We say this because Federal officials saw fit for the first time to set forth a preliminary specification for a Mississippi River Interstate Parkway and their proposal pioneers a new field in planning. Principal statements were made by Associate Director A. E. Demaray of the National Park Service and Division Engineer Harold J. Spelman of the Bureau of Public Roads." Demaray's statement was where the ten-point "master plan" was offered forth. He opened with a discourse on the justification for the parkway, and then moved on to the plan. "For purposes of discussion during our forum tomorrow we would like to project at this time a tentative picture which might be called an 'Interstate Parkway' or 'Tourway' as suggested by Pilot Greensfelder." This was an ominous threat for Kelsey's explicit push to adopt the name "Arborway."

Demaray continued, "Such a facility would start from a system of marked existing highways which would be improved and joined by sections of construction on new locations where the scenic or historic or other considerations indicate a new section would be more attractive and useful. The program would be carried out according to a 'master plan' by stage-construction through the years. This master plan could and should be a vital and growing plan—not a static plan. Here are some of the elements which would be included in the program of improvement and development as we visualize it: ... "

> Items (1)–(4). These were all *acquisition* elements. Acquisition of historic sites, scenic/recreational areas ... rights-of-way for road structural improvements ... rights-of-way for connecting links around towns and cities ... purchase or condemnation of the highway development rights of abutting property owners ...
>
> Items (5), (6), and (8). These were all *structural highway* elements. Improvement of parallel roads for trucks ... elimination of grade crossings ... Elimination of unsightly existing roadside structures ...
>
> Item (7). Fee simple control of key lands for uniform development of tourist facilities.
>
> Item (9). "*More than usual attention to landscape planting along the lines of Dr. Harlan Kelsey's Arborway proposal.*" [Italics added for emphasis.]

Item (10). "Federal consultation and supervision over the integrated plan, and, what is equally new, discretionary and proportional financial assistance to the States in accomplishing the plan. Development and operation of the facility would remain with the State highway Departments."

The park service felt obligated to respect old friend Kelsey's Arborway proposal (item 9), but it was always Dr. Kelsey's proposal, never the park service's proposal. To the park service, it represented a menu from which the states could pick and choose, could accept or reject, as their individual situations warranted.

The December 15, 1950, newsletter summarized a series of reconnaissance trips following the Lake Itasca meeting: Tri-City area, Dubuque, Davenport, Burlington, Hannibal, St. Louis. Kelsey was absent from all of these, finally joining the group in Memphis. From the newsletter, "Out of Memphis we cruised upstream in a Corps of Engineers craft, and we got to watery places that have eluded us before. We put ashore in the Shelby Forest and tramped a good piece of this large public holding. Dr. Harlan P. Kelsey of Boston, our Consulting Horticulturist, was along on his first inspection, and we know now how rough are the edges of our botany."

Kelsey was not taking the hints Abbott dropped about his overreaching with his arborway proposal. He wanted more land for planting primeval forests and more federal control rather than letting the individual states develop their portions as they saw fit; he wanted to solve, overnight, all of the potential problems he had experienced in past work with the park service. Finally, January 24, 1951, Abbott called a halt to the overreaching. "You are good for us when you ask, as you did in your letter of January 16, these searching questions that shake us down to our foundations and make us begin thinking again. When you challenge our good sense in suggesting the acquisition of *easements* for much of the Mississippi job rather than *outright purchase of the land*, you are challenging the very cornerstone of the conception we've drawn of a proper parkway for that Valley. ... Let me present a tentative rebuttal to your several numbered points." Abbott laid it on pretty thick—forcefully and eloquently—in his four-page, single-spaced letter. We will condense, but not too much. The park service's carefully structured plan needs to be fully appreciated.

1. Abbott agreed with Kelsey about the need for *limited access*, but gradually "through limited access highway laws which would be applied as we widened existing narrow rights-of-way or purchase new ones to the standard basic width of 220 feet. ... Admittedly, 220 feet of fee simple ownership is only sufficient to accommodate adequately the pavement or pavements, the shoulders, slopes, guard rails, etc.—that is, the physical features of the motor road proper. That is why ... we felt the need for additional controls over and beyond this basic construction width. This is part 2 of a two-part story, if you will. It might be titled, 'Adding Parkway Aspects to the Limited Access Highway,' and the latter is all we have at the close of part 1.

    New characters enter, and they are the conservation family, including natural beauty, the Grant Wood landscapes, wildlife, and history. They are worked into our manuscript in various ways. First, the states buy various scenes of history and natural beauty ... Secondly, we reach out and purchase, also in fee simple, such lands as are best in public ownership along the parkway because they are sub-marginal, of a greater potential beauty and usefulness as park land. These would include the wildwoods, the bluff faces, swamp lands, islands, and the superfluous woodlots of farmers. Thirdly, and lastly, but not least important in our noble trinity (because the Grant Wood landscape is so large a part of the Mississippi Valley), we propose to control by *easements* the vast mileages of open farm field ... I cannot imagine a parkway through the length of the

Mississippi Valley as being anything but terribly monotonous if it were allowed to go to second growth forest thickets lining both sides of the road. Gone, the comforting look of fallow field and ripening wheat; the big red barn and the silo. No pastoral left!

Yet, surely, this is precisely what will happen if we seek our roadside control through the *outright* purchase of the farmer's land. One cannot conceive of public budgets which would provide adequately for the maintenance of these lands which, since man must live, seem fittingly to be farmed? And if one could think of highway forces maintaining an open character, they would only do so 'less naturally' than the farmer does it himself. Even then, we all know the sad plight of the reduced budget such as we know it today even in the great national parks.

No, Kel, I for one am convinced that the plan *falls* without the versatile 'easement' which is one of our best tools. The kit, mind you, has other tools as well.

2. Industry or private enterprise would be blots on the landscape and waterscape *in any case* under your paragraph two. I think we have to take a broader point of view and a more realistic one, for we are considering no Yellowstone, no Blue Ridge Parkway. … Let's make use of everything we can to sustain the interest of the Parkway, including these factories, this farming, the oil structures and the waterworks. They will be only occasionally on the stage, after all, and Shakespeare foiled his most noble characters with the fool.

3. On this there is no contest between us, but the state authorities will likely have a contest with that big family of the public known as sportsmen and who often pose, a little hypocritically,

as conservationists. There should indeed be much more wildlife *preservation*. ...

4. I agree, but it's easy to have an understanding fall apart when we have to depend on such categorical phrases as 'urban.' It seems to me that a good many towns and cities through the Valley must be thought of as tourist objectives in themselves. We should not be too smug when we 'by-pass.' We must have feeder roads?

Now as to the rest of your letter, ..."

"I think your allusion to the Mississippi River Parkway setting standards for parkways all over the country may be a key to making my position clear to you. I do not believe that this project should set a standard for *parkways* all over the country. In the first place, I do not think the Nation can afford parkways all over the country though, heaven knows, I wish we could, for I could make a life work of it and be very happy. I think, in fact, that there will be very few national parkways like the Blue Ridge which can measure up to a standard of beauty and conservation that you and I would like to see. And this reasoning is exactly why I am enamored of this new formula which we are bringing out for the Mississippi River 10-State parkway.

It is a more practical plan, because less costly, which could spread, conceivably, to a good many of the important *highways* in America, transmuting them by adding <u>some</u> of the parkway aspects I believe to be thoroughly sound but also know to be too costly *in their entirety*. If you will, then, I see this Mississippi River job as a compromise from the high standards which were set on the Blue Ridge Parkway. We have dreamed too long and it seems to me that *the things* of which our dreams are fabricated, the beauty spots and history in America, *are disappearing while we dream.* If we can devise a way to save something if not all of what is left along the American highway we will have accomplished a tremendous thing. It is not a matter of a half loaf as against the whole. It's nearer to a half loaf or none at all.

If this sounds like a preachment, so it is, but you asked for it and I am glad you did for, perhaps, I have stated things more clearly for myself than I have before. I hope it is somewhat clearer to you."

The remainder of 1951 was devoted to the writing of the survey report by the people responsible for its various elements. It was written in two parts. Volume 1 was a readable, heavily illustrated, general report to be easily absorbed by all the Congressmen—synopsis, the river, the project, the recommended plan. Volume 2 was the technical report with all the details—history, engineering, recreation, horticulture, and cost.

In Volume 1 Kelsey suggested a paragraph in the letter of transmittal that emphasized the alarming and accelerating increase in traffic—thus the need for adequate relief through road planning and rights-of-way, before it was too late. Abbott responded November 13, "Your suggestion of September 24 was reviewed, incorporated in drafts, and then the whole works thrown out of the final copy in favor of a very simple and non-committal Letter of Transmittal for signature of the two Secretaries. The opinion of Wirth, Vint, Spelman, and others, seemed to be that we avoid in any of the printed report any statements that might be taken by Congressmen or others to be promotional in character. The main body of the report, however, is not too much changed from our joint version, and I think you and I can be pleased about that."

The plan for joint state and federal control of the parkway was troubling to Kelsey. He asked Abbott, "Who maintains this Highway after completion and will profits from concessions be used to cover upkeep and improvements? Will minimum standards be agreed upon and enforcement be provided for? Will parks and forests that may be established be under State or Federal control?" Abbott responded simply, "I want to take time … to explain how I think a State project for the Mississippi would operate in actual practice, because I think I might be able to mitigate some of your fears that things will get out of hand." Kelsey had to be satisfied with that.

Volume I—Parkway for the Mississippi—was issued over the signatures of the Secretaries of Interior and Commerce on November 28, 1951. Kelsey's portion was included under the section titled "Natural Interest," with the subtitle, "Woodlands":

> The wildwoods along the parkway offer a large opportunity in two important directions. First, public control would permit conservation of plant and animal life which now exists there and would protect these wooded lands from commercial cutting, fire, and vandalism. It would afford added protection and permit better management of the fish and wildlife resources of the valley.
>
> Second, the wildwoods provide the proper places in which to bring back to their favorite habitats a host of trees, shrubs, and flowers which have all but disappeared in each of the natural plant associations, once a glory of the valley's eight climatic zones. Scientific introduction of the now rare but once common species would result in a self-maintaining natural landscape of significant value to popular education. This part of the proposed landscape program might be dovetailed with the arborway proposal of Dr. Harlan P. Kelsey. A statement in the second volume of this report by Dr. Kelsey, noted horticulturist of Boston, Massachusetts, and consultant to this survey, describes how, in its broadest

aspects, a Mississippi River Parkway might grow toward the ideal of a great midcontinent botanical museum.

Volume II contained the much longer treatises by all the various contributors. It mirrored the ten-point master plan put forth by Demaray at the Lake Itaska meeting the prior summer. Kelsey's submittal carried his own title—the Mississippi River National Arborway Proposal. He opened with a general overview: an Arborway definition, then the "unique and unsurpassed opportunity for constructing the first such informative, pleasurable, highly scenic and indispensable travel route," then its broad general natural attributes and benefits. He then went on to his specific topics of interest:

- Rights-of-Way—His usual plea for adequacy, while there was still time. Excessive initially, but barely adequate in the future.
- Resources and Recreation Exposition Centers—His "combination parks." One in each state. Showplace for each state's total native resources and attractions. Central building to house museum and administrative functions. Outdoor area (five hundred acres minimum) including botanical and zoological gardens exhibiting native flora and fauna of the state, demonstration forest, and recreation facilities.
- The Bountiful Flora of the Mississippi River Valley—Treatise on the supreme importance of plant life. The eight climate zones and each state's exposure to them. Examples of specific species across the various zones.
- The Mississippi Flyway—Greatest in the World (Circ. 16, Fish & Wildlife Service)—Description of the flyway and the teeming wildfowl population. Description of the supporting food in the form of fruits, seeds, buds, twigs, leaves, bark and roots; from both woody and aquatic plants.
- Notable Trees, Shrubs and Other Plants of the Mississippi River Valley—The profusion of natives (exotics not needed). Plants of the Upper Region and of the Lower Region. Deciduous trees,

conifers, shrubs, groundcovers, and vines. Specific listing of common and scientific names for plants in each category. Total list of 154 species. All available for use in restoring natural landscapes along the arborway.

Kelsey to Abbott, December 3, 1951, "Enclosed you will find three copies of my final contribution to the Survey Report just off the typewriter. Be as gentle as you can with it, though no doubt there is much room for improvement. The technical parts have not been easy owing to the unbelievably mixed-up jargon of local alleged 'Floras' of the 'Sovereign States'. Please tell me how to make out my bill to Uncle Sam for my 'blood, sweat and tears'."

Abbott to Kelsey, December 6, 1951, "We have your summation for Volume II, and all here have read it with great delight. We all think it everything that it should be, and the emphasis on the 'Flyway' is a fine addition. The discussion on plants only you could write with such feeling. You have well earned your emolument."

While Kelsey's official work was over, his emotional arborway attachment was still in full bloom. When Congress acted on the survey's recommendations, the individual states would be in charge of implementation. He knew that if the commissioners and future state authorities were not sold on his horticultural ideas, the arborway theme would die a slow, lingering death. His only remaining tool was the name of the road, acting as a continuous reminder to revisit his horticultural suggestions. On December 11 he wrote Abbott, "How does *Mississippi River National Parkway—Arborway* appeal to you as a compromise title, if the recalcitrants insist on retaining the inadequate 'Parkway' designation?" Getting no response, he turned from the Park Service to the Commissioners via Pilot Greensfelder, who responded to him November 5. "We will give every consideration to your suggestions but phrase our wording in legislation so it will be encompassed by the ordinary wording of State and Federal legislation, e.g., I just received this morning a copy of the Mississippi State Act just passed in which they have slipped in the word 'parkway' in the midst of roadways, etc., so you see we have to make haste slowly. However, we will certainly keep your suggestions definitely before us."

Kelsey to Greensfelder, "Thank you for your good letter of Nov. 5 … If my 'Arborway' proposal is not mentioned in the Bill to be offered in Congress in January, I fear it will be difficult to introduce it later. I shall 'hang on' to the end in my efforts." No response. Kelsey tried again a year later, January 15, 1953. "Thank you for your very interesting and thoughtful 'latest report on our proposed Great River Road,' … May I make a few comments? Adopting the title 'Arborway' will give great distinctiveness and publicity to the project, 'parkways' usually having but local or at most state significance." The name had started out back in 1938 as a "parkway," but this didn't really fit the now proposed route of mostly existing local, state and federal numbered highways. Arborways was too foreign to the ear of most Congressmen. So the name retreated to merely "road"—*The Great River Road*. Thus it remains to this current day.

There is a long tortuous history of planning and funding of the Great River Road. In 1976, the Federal Highway Administration issued program guidelines setting criteria for the Great River Road. The states then set up their own procedures for selecting the route of the road within their state boundaries. The original Mississippi River Parkway Commission still exists as a "multi-state organization to work collectively to preserve, promote, and enhance the scenic, historic, and recreational resources of the Mississippi River." Interestingly no mention of horticulture, landscape, or plants is mentioned other than within the broad category of "scenic."

A parallel highway movement was grinding forward at the same time as the Great River Road. It was, of course the US Interstate Highway System, following the Federal-Aid Highway Act of 1954. Basically it is a series of parkway-like highways traversing the nation, both east-west and north-south, similar to Kelsey's National Arborways. It embodies many of Kelsey's specifications: Ample rights-of-way, limited access, often landscaped center strips, periodic "combination" service areas, naturalistic side views (often beautifully landscaped), no offending commercial intrusions. Not bad, but there is one major difference. The interstates are designed for rapidly moving all of our traffic, cars and trucks alike, with high minimum design speeds. They are designed to get there fast. Kelsey's arborways were designed to get there easily, but slowly, in order to soak in the rich horticultural environment through which the motorist passed. In this author's view, the interstate's landscape treatment is usually excellent for someone passing through at 70 mph, stopping only when absolutely necessary. Who can say if Kelsey's ideas were consciously invoked by those who drafted the Interstate specifications? Ordinary common sense is much more likely to have been the driving force.

<u>Final Strokes</u>

As the world came off of hold at the end of WWII, the issues surrounding plant nomenclature also resurfaced. Four years had passed since the second edition of *Standardized Plant Names* was published. Nearly 2,500 copies had been sold during the war period and distributed in various parts of the world. McFarland's publishing company was still $30,000 in the red.[189] The immediate postpublishing critics and cheerleaders also resurfaced, alongside all those who simply ignored the problems of incorrect nomenclature.

Kelsey wrote to J. F. Styer of the AAN's Plant Nomenclature Committee June 19, 1945, "The facts are that among seedsmen, nurserymen, laymen, horticulturists, etc., each one is a law unto himself, and so chaos reigns supreme. To conduct honest business in the plant world it is just as important and necessary to have national laws compelling 'true' names as in the realm of foods and drugs. 'Fair competition' is impossible without it. ... I consider the settling of this question the most important matter in the plant world today."

Kelsey was corresponding with Robert W. Hess of the Yale School of Forestry on plant names for use in the magazine *Tropical Woods*. Hess wrote, "The need and also the magnitude of the problem are very clear to me. With a catalog file of over 25,000 common names, not to mention the additional thousands readily available in literature, I cannot very well escape dealing with it. ... Your challenge of Dr. Dadswell's article opens a vast field for missionary work in plant name standardization. Dr. Dadswell, as you know, is an Australian. A casual perusal of the timbers of Australia will reveal various kinds of Walnut, Rosewood, Sassafrass, Ash, Oak, Alder, Mahogany, [and on and on]. To further complicate the situation they use as adjectives such names as Laurel, Hickory, Yellowwood, Walnut, Hazelwood, Maple, Honeysuckle, etc. Needless to say none of these are even related to genera bearing similar common names in this country or Europe." Kelsey's reply included "You speak of 'sales value.' Lumber dealers realize this to such an extent that no one really knows what he is getting when he buys alleged 'mahoganies,' which are not even distantly related to *Swietenia*. But the name 'mahogany' has 'sales value' and crooked lumber dealers deliberately rob the public under such false pretenses. ... You gave quite an imposing list of Australian misnomers, most of them so obviously wrong that the most ignorant dealer should blush to use them, and fool the customers. Maybe you are right, standardization may not be possible until *ethics* are standardized!"[190]

An article titled, "What's in a Name?" appeared in the May–June 1945 issue of *Green Thumb*. "What is the reason for the nurseryman's apathy? It was the nurserymen and the ornamental growers who organized the American Joint Committee on Horticultural Nomenclature thirty years ago to 'make buying easier' by bringing about, so far as practicable, the consistent use of a single standardized scientific name and a single standardized common name for every tree, shrub and plant 22 years ago ... Yet today ninety nine nursery catalogs out of a hundred 'make buying difficult' by failing to utilize the text which the nurserymen themselves made possible. ... Of course there are many plant names that many botanists disagree with. That is the very reason why the text is necessary. So we have this anomalous situation; the botanists agree that for over a hundred years chaos has existed in plant nomenclature; the botanists have never provided a registration mechanism, or even a standard work of nomenclature, [y]et when the American Joint Committee, the Department of Agriculture, and a staff of the most eminent scholars in the country do the botanist's job—and do it well—they stubbornly refuse to accept it. Nurserymen, come to life and use our text!"

Kelsey responded to the situation by publishing a long detailed article in the *American Nurseryman*, November 1, 1945. It once again outlined the general problem of "Most nurserymen seem to be in favor of standardization as a general proposition (especially for the other fellows), yet curiously enough feel justified in clinging to their own pet exceptions, usually of provincial significance only, however misleading, malaprop and equivocal such names may be." He continued with a seemingly endless display of erroneous and often ludicrous practices to show how pervasive the problem was. He ended with a speech on why the nursery industry should act now to end the folly.

By September 26, 1947, 3,462 copies of *SPN* had been sold.[191] The prior April 10 Kelsey wrote Bill Dayton, "Yes, McF was in Wash.—a very lame old sleepy brokendown man, but still of good courage. He was almost maudlin in his extravagant praise of *SPN*—'the most authoritative work of nomenclature in existence.' How different a view from the olden days!" On October 6, 1948, Dayton wrote a note to Kelsey, "I attended the McFarland funeral yesterday, but did not go to the cemetery. I suppose you have seen the write-ups in the Harrisburg press. He really was an unusual man and the help seem to have been devoted to him, so he apparently had his good points." Kelsey replied, "McFarland had his faults like everyone else, yet he was a *great* man and his civic accomplishments have earned a Nation's gratitude. He was a civic pioneer."

With McFarland gone, Kelsey was the only remaining member of the American Joint Committee on Horticultural Nomenclature. Coville died in the 1930s; Frederick Law Olmsted Jr. had resigned in the 1930s; Dayton had never been a member. That left Kelsey as the sole living "owner" of the copyright on *Standardized Plant Names*. The naysayers had taken their shots and the sentiment had begun to change. The second edition was approaching ten years of age and needed revision to keep up with horticultural progress. All eyes turned to Kelsey; what was he going to do about it?

On September 28, 1949, Frank F. Styer of the American Horticultural Council wrote Kelsey, "I am frequently asked whether steps are being taken to bring *Standardized Plant Names* up to date and get out a new edition. ... To be frank, we cannot go forward ... if we do not have the benefit of your ideas on this." On September 30 Kelsey replied, "You must know that the 1942 edition of *SPN* was produced thru, 'blood, sweat and tears.' It took the greater part of my personal time for several years and large personal expense for which I received no compensation. Mr. Dayton my co-editor who was assigned by the Forrest Service to this job gave so much overtime, often far into the night as to really injure his health. ... Therefore, if and when a new edition of *SPN* is undertaken, to get adequate results the following program is necessary if not compulsory in my opinion." Kelsey then cited five necessary ingredients: (1) a fund of not less than $50,000; (2) a chief editor with a salary of not less than $10,000 per year plus all expenses; (3) the editor having complete authority to select assistants; (4) sponsorship by leading organizations not only interested in *SPN* but also in the creating and establishing of a national and international code for selecting suitable and exclusive common names for plants; and (5) an advisory council of one only from each sponsoring organization.

This significantly raised the ante. For decades Kelsey had taken the lead. Now suddenly the industry was confronted with who could replace him and who would be serious enough to accept the responsibility? No takers. On January 7, 1952, Kelsey replied to Edwin A. Mason, "There has been no new edition of *Standardized Plant Names* since 1942. No new edition is planned for at the present time and it is doubtful if there will be one, but if so it would not be edited by me."

On February 10, 1953, Dayton closed his letter to Kelsey with, "You are still and always have been the Papa of *SPN* and someday I hope that some of these meatheads will appreciate the services you have rendered."

On June 10, 1953, Dayton to Kelsey, "To put it mildly I am much perturbed about your last note, with its report that you are hors de combat, with a cracked cervical vertebra, and your neck girt about with a modified horse collar. I did not realize that bathing could be so vicious a habit and have so disastrous consequences. I trust your particular Aesculapius has the proper skills and got everything back in the right place and with the right controls. You will have to sit in a swivel chair for a while to watch a tennis match and ease up on 'sidelong glances' and the like. At least be thankful you ain't a giraffe."

On December 22, 1954, Kelsey wrote to the Copyright Office, Patent Department, Department of Commerce, as follows: "Dear Sirs: This is to advise you that on behalf of the American Joint Committee on Horticultural Nomenclature, I hereby release the copyright of *Standardized Plant Names* to the American Association of Nurserymen. I will appreciate your advising me in turn that your office in turn acted accordingly. ... Harlan P. Kelsey, Secretary-Treasurer." With that, Kelsey terminated his responsibility. The transfer was approved and recorded by the Copyright Office on January 18, 1955.

In his history of the AAN, Richard P. White closed out the story: "Consideration was being given to another revision and up-dating by the association at this time. Estimated costs were to run in the vicinity of $50,000 and a grant of funds from outside sources was being considered. When this possibility became known to the publishers of *Hortus*, who had another revision of *Hortus* underway, the wisdom of having two publications on the same subject was seriously questioned. Publishers of *Hortus* reported that the revised issue would include common names as well as scientific, making it more like *SPN* and that their revision would be available in about two years. This was less than the minimum time it would take to up-date *SPN*, so the association abandoned its efforts."[192]

Even today, over a half century later, nothing has appeared to rival *Standardized Plant Names*. Even today it is extraordinarily useful to those who have the now-out-of-print 1942 second edition. Even today Harlan P. Kelsey stands as the giant in the realm of solving the problems of plant nomenclature for the public. In the seventy years since *SPN*, human nature has reasserted itself and many plants have more than one common name. Today, Michael A. Dirr's monumental *Manual of Woody Landscape Plants* simply lists multiple common names where they exist. One species picked at random is *Robinia pseudoacacia*. *SPN* says it has one common name, "Black Locust." Dirr cites its common name as "Black Locust, also Common Locust, or Yellow Locust, or White Locust." That's nice, it can be either black or white, take your pick. As time goes on, the proliferation of common names, and confusion, will only intensify.

Today, the confusion is illustrated in the fall 2012 newsletter of the Gardens of the Blue Ridge:

> We know many of you get a bit frustrated when looking through our catalog or on our website because we list everything by the Botanical Name. The reason we do this is because there are so many different common names for each plant and also one common name may apply to several different plants. So to

eliminate the possibility of you getting the wrong plant we must go by the Botanical Name. For instance you may call and tell us you want a Bear Grass; well many plants are called this, such as Yucca, Spiderwort, Turkey's Beard just to name a few. So unless we know the Botanical Name, you could receive any one of these plants. Also common names vary depending on which part of the country you live in. Many locals around here refer to the Flame Azalea as Orange Honeysuckle; of course it is not a Honeysuckle. Also our Mountain Laurel is locally called Ivy, and then Rhododendron is called Laurel by locals. See the possibility for confusion? So bone up on your Botanical Names to make sure you get the plant you are looking for.

Without Kelsey, things have lapsed back to exactly where they were one hundred years ago when *Standardized Plant Names* first aimed to "make buying easier."

John Muir lived only one year after the waters poured into the Hetch Hetchy Valley. Harlan Kelsey's downward spiral took longer. In the final ten years of his life, he first suffered the loss of Grandfather Mountain to commercial interests. Then his aspirations for the Mississippi River Parkway as a model for his "Arborways for America" were gradually eroded. Finally, only three years before his death, *SPN* was abandoned by the American Association of Nurserymen.

Chapter 8

Legacy

<u>Obligation</u>

To really put Kelsey in perspective, we must dwell on the award given at the 1940 AAN banquet in New York, and Executive Secretary Richard White's August 6, 1940, follow-up letter to Kelsey. White spoke of "the great work you have done for *horticulture* over your entire span of life." He also could have said, "For *forestry* over your entire span of life." He also could have said, "For *parks* over your entire span of life." Or how about *city planning*? Or *landscape architecture*? The combined *breadth* and *time span* of Kelsey's public service is mind-boggling.

So how does one deal with this? Use an analogy. In the film industry we have Oscars for individual actors and films; we also have Oscars as lifetime achievement awards. That's where Kelsey appears to fit. That's also why Kelsey is a forgotten hero. How many people remember even one recipient of a lifetime achievement Oscar? Typically, by the next day, no one remembers. But—the Oscar-winning actress? Everyone remembers for weeks, if not years, because attention is focused on a single deed, not disbursed over many deeds and years.

Now move to *landscape architecture* or *conservation*. And the winner is ... Frederick Law Olmsted for New York's Central Park. And the winner is ... John Muir for Yosemite National Park and the Sierra Club, which protects it. Their achievements were focused, not disbursed. They were first—initial forces in their field. Kelsey was everyone's great public servant in 1950. Fifty years later: Kelsey? Who was *he*? What did *he* do? To change this, let's add some focus to the picture.

A hundred years ago he was *first* and for a half century the *leader* in pioneering *native plants for the American landscape.* The aristocrats of today's gardens are the ericaceous beauties he promoted from the high southern Appalachian Mountains. Think rhododendron or azalea. He brought the flora first to New England and very quickly his wholesaling spread it to wherever its hardiness zones would allow. As the twentieth century started, exotics were the most sought after in gardens. Native plants were weeds. Today, over a hundred years later, exotic flora is commonly shunned, except in special cases.

Continuing: eighty years ago he was the *de facto leader in bringing all of America to the native plants* in their finest setting. This he did by helping make the Great Smoky Mountains National Park a reality—the zenith of horticultural biomass and diversity—the beautiful land of the sky. He wrote, "If you miss the Azalea calendulacea varieties on Gregory Bald and the Rhododendron carolinianum varieties on Mt. LeConte you are missing one of the greatest flower shows in America."[193] That work pioneered the creation of national parks east of the Mississippi. True, Arno Cammerer got the crucial Rockefeller donation, but when it came to grinding out all the massive work in the background, Cammerer depended on Kelsey and continuously told him so. Kelsey wrote, "I spent weeks going over the Smoky Mountains area, and the actual metes and bounds were drawn by myself. To aid in this we had aerial surveys on a large scale, and the possibilities of the entire area between the Blue Ridge watershed on the east and the Tennessee Valley on the west were most carefully studied and considered."[194]

As for the Southern Appalachian National Park Commission, Horace Albright noted, "It is no disparagement of the work of the other four committee members to say that Mr. Kelsey's knowledge of the eastern mountains *made him the natural leader* of the search for areas possessing features so outstanding as to make them worthy of national park status." [Italics added for emphasis.]

Therefore—the envelope please. For *native plants in America*, the winner is ... *Harlan P. Kelsey. He brought the plants to Americans—and Americans to the plants.*

So what's the big deal about native plants? Well, it's a very big deal—changing the culture of an entire nation of gardeners over a period of fifty years. To make this case one is required to contrast it with other big deals—stars, champions, overlapping contemporaries. We of course mean Frederick Law Olmsted in horticulture and John Muir in preservation. Why not Robert Marshall for wilderness? We have to stop somewhere.

First, take Olmsted. Parks, parks, parks. Big ones in big cities. There, hundreds of thousands of people enjoying the artistry of his landscape architecture—each in large settings commissioned by local governments or wealthy individuals. Contrast that with millions upon millions of people enjoying their own artistry using Kelsey's native plants in their own gardens, day after day after day. The horticultural settings for Kelsey's national parks were few, but massive in size when compared with Olmsted's. And, they were commissioned by Congress, the biggest client of all.

Next: Muir's Yosemite and the Sierra Club, vs. Kelsey's Smokies and Appalachian Mountain Club. Nine million people a year visit the Smokies' often intimate horticultural wonders in the land of the sky vs. only three million a year visiting Yosemite's massive geological wonders in their Sierra valley (e.g., El Capitan, Yosemite Falls, and

Half Dome). However, in the public mind, Muir is the icon. Wikipedia connects Muir's name to the locales, institutions, and noteworthy accomplishments listed in the provocation at the beginning of this biography. All we can do here is to lay their accomplishments side by side as best we can.

At the end of part 1 we listed nine of these parallels, occurring during the first quarter of the twentieth century. It's time to continue the list.

10. Muir's national park work focused on California's central Sierra vicinity, culminating with the Yosemite Act of 1890. Subsequently the Sequoia and Kings Canyon areas were included. Mount Rainier was added as a national park in Washington's Cascades in 1899. Full federal control of the California parks was achieved by 1906. Kelsey didn't begin his park journey until his 1913 letter to McFarland laid out some of his early ideas on broadening national park coverage. He later lobbied Mather and Albright but wasn't involved full scale until he was established on the Southern Appalachian National Park Committee. Muir was long since dead.

11. Professor Nash labels Muir as the "publicizer" of the wilderness movement. Here we have *the key to Muir's dominant iconic stature.* He was a writer, and a prolific one. Wikipedia cites seventeen books, and twenty-two essays online. Every time he took a trip his journal was weighing in his pack. Each time he returned, the journal was the raw material for a book or essay. Every piece he wrote put his name indelibly in the minds of his readers—the public at large. It was a substantial and growing segment of the population. Professor Nash writes, "The prime of John Muir's life coincided with the advent of national concern over conservation." Robert Underwood Johnson of *Century Magazine*, the nation's leading literary monthly, pursued Muir in 1889 and assured him of a large and broad

audience for his emotional messages to appreciate and preserve the wilderness—estimated at over 200,000 per issue.[195] This restarted Muir's prolific writing of the 1870s, published in the *New York Tribune* and *San Francisco Bulletin*. He had become "the leading contributor" to *Overland Monthly*, where in April 1873 he had fifteen articles in preparation.

12. Kelsey wrote also, but for a narrow audience, small in number, primarily in the nursery trade. Less than 3,500 copies of *Standardized Plant Names* were sold, because of its confined audience. Magazine articles were also tightly focused (e.g., "Arborways for America" appeared in *American Forests* magazine, the journal for the American Forestry Association, Washington DC).

13. When it comes to the founding of national parks, Muir can be assigned Yosemite, Kings Canyon, Sequoia, and Rainier. Kelsey can be assigned the Smokies, Shenandoah, Mammoth Caves, and Isle Royale. Muir helped promote other wilderness causes, such as the Petrified Forest National Monument. Kelsey had a heavy hand in promoting the Everglades National Park and single-handedly created the nation's first national historic site—Salem Maritime.

14. In the twilight of their lives, both Muir and Kelsey had to admit defeat in their final battles for wilderness preservation. Muir saw his precious Hetch Hetchy Valley submerged forever under mountains of water. Kelsey saw his once pristine Grandfather Mountain scarred by roads, parking lots, and buildings for the autobound tourist trade. Beyond the Hetch Hetchy Reservoir, and the Grandfather's tourist infrastructure, lies the remaining wilderness of Yosemite National Park and the belatedly protected portions of the Grandfather. Both are grand, but as wilderness, must "go through life with a slight limp."

Leaving the list of parallels, we come to one major difference between Muir and Kelsey—geology vs. horticulture. Having rock climbed there, your author stands in awe of the big walls of Yosemite. People come from all over the world to climb them. Anyone gazing up at them has to be stunned in wonderment at their majesty. Ah, but the Smokies, totally different, equally stunning. It's time to repeat the comments of the early proponents of the Great Smoky Mountains National Park, quoted previously.

> Their supreme beauty is their mantle of shimmering verdure—practically all that remains of the original American forest. ... Comparatively few lovers of woods in this generation have ever seen, to recognize or study it, even so much as an acre of the original deciduous forest which was once the glory of America. ... The Great Smokies will introduce into the picture gallery of our National Park system a new and exquisite type of mountains.

> The Smokies have other titles to distinction beside the glowing beauty of their forests. The climax of a broad scenic region, this is the most massive uplift anywhere in the East, with eighteen peaks towering 6,000 feet above sea level, while few western mountains equal them in elevation above their own base levels. [This may be true for the Rockies, but certainly not for the Pacific Crest and Alaska where 12,000- to 14,000-foot vertical rises from base to summit are common, e.g., Whitney (east side), Rainier, Denali.] Then, too, the Smokies are among the most ancient mountains on earth. They were old when the Rockies were young. Moreover, they are softly veiled with a delicate, exquisite, dreamy blue haze that gives them a loveliness and an endearing charm which the Rockies lack.

> But always it is the dim, cool, cathedral-like forest of the Smokies that most enchants the visitor—a forest densely tangled with laurel and rhododendron and fragrant with azalea.[196]

The National Park Service Official Map and Guide describes this 520,976-acre forest as follows:

> No place this size in a temperate climate can match Great Smoky Mountains National Park's variety of plant and animal species. Here are more tree species than in northern Europe, 1,500 flowering plants, dozens of native fish, and more than 200 species of birds and 60 of mammals. International Biosphere Reserve and World Heritage Site designations have recognized this remarkable biological diversity and the cultures humans wrested from its abundance. The National Park Service mission is to preserve this natural and cultural heritage unimpaired for this and future generations. Most of the park is now managed as wilderness.

This is not to say that Sequoia National Park and Redwoods National Park are not wondrous for their horticulture. But you are dealing with a massive display of only two species—*Sequoia gigantea and Sequoia sempervirens* (redwoods). They are most notable for their size and age. Sprinkled around generously underneath was the sugar pine *Pinus lambertiana*, which Muir "loved above all other trees," but not as the name for a national park.

One dictionary's[197] second definition of *myth* is "A real or fictional story, recurring theme, or character type that appeals to the consciousness of a people by embodying its cultural ideals or by giving expression to deep commonly held emotions." The same dictionary's primary definition of *tradition* is "transmittal of elements of a culture from one generation to another." Its primary definition of *truth* is "conformity to fact or actuality." Today's material portraying the Great Smoky Mountains National Park is often accompanied by calls to remember the individuals who were instrumental in its establishment. Such remembrances are subject to intermixing of myth, tradition, and truth. If sufficient time passes, truth and mistruth may be transformed into tradition, and ultimately myth. At this stage, it is exceptionally difficult to extract the truth in pure form.

Two contemporary video pieces emphasize the role of Horace Kephart in bringing the park into being. *The National Parks—America's Best Idea,* the film by Ken Burns, is one. The official National Park Service film shown at the Sugarlands Visitor Center, Great Smoky Mountains National Park[198] is another. The NPS film DVD cover displays the following caption: "Those who fought for the creation of the Park have handed down a never-ending legacy of caring for this land. It is a responsibility now in the hands of all who are touched by its gifts of peace, beauty, and recreation." Who are those who fought?

Kephart did write books and letters which displayed the merits of the park to the American public at just the right time to encourage dollar contributions for the park's acquisition. These video pieces emphasize Kephart's role by elevating him at the expense of other meritorious individuals, left unmentioned, that made equal or greater contributions to the Park's founding. Kephart has been romanticized by his personal history as a discomfited mid-American man. He worked out his problems by camping out in the deep forest of the Smokies for a number of years, only to emerge as a renewed figure fighting the good fight for the forests' preservation. As a mythical figure Kephart certainly qualifies as "giving expression to deep commonly held emotions" of many.

Yet consider also Robert Lindsay Mason, a local mountain man in the Smokies, author of *The Lure of the Smokies,* and his novel covering the known primitive history of the Smokies under the title *Lonesome Gal.* He fought for the prevention of roads on the crest of the Smokies and ultimately prevailed. Whose work was more important?

Mount Kephart lies in the center of the park as a tribute to the man. Yet we refer to Colonel Charles A. Webb, editor of the *Asheville Citizen,* who wrote to Kelsey, September 10, 1941: "Personally I could never see any sense in naming a mountain after Kephart. He had less to do in establishing the park than anyone who had anything at all to do with it. It is true that his book, The Southern Highlands, had a great deal to do with attracting people to the peaks in the Smokies, but as to actual work, Kephart had very little to do with it. However, that is the way of the world."

Mount Chapman is located on the ridge crest of the Smokies, very near to Mount Kephart. Here lies another intermixing of myth, tradition, and truth. Robert Sterling Yard's March 1942 article, titled "The Great Smoky Wilderness," in the *Living Wilderness* magazine gave high and almost exclusive credit to Colonel Chapman for the Park: "The actual achievement of Great Smoky Mountains National Park may fairly be attributed to Colonel David C. Chapman, who devoted years to the work … to his executive ability, vision, personal sacrifice and devotion the people of the country owe more than can be repaid." Kelsey complained to Director Drury, March 30, 1942: "Meager credit is given to Mark Squire and the other members of the North Carolina Commission, and in the whole article the members of the Southern Appalachian National Park Commission are not even mentioned by name. Mr. Yard always bitterly resented the fact that he was not chosen on this Parks Commission and from the beginning has criticized severely the work of this Commission."

Kelsey continues in his March 30 letter to Drury: "As you may know, I was in the battle for these parks from the very beginning until the present time and was very close with the officials of the National Park Service throughout the entire period of acquisition and development. I therefore make the following statement:

> The actual achievement of Great Smoky Mountains National Park may be almost entirely attributed to Arno B. Cammerer, Director of the National Park Service. It was Mr. Cammerer who coordinated all Park efforts in North Carolina and Tennessee,

as well as in Virginia, who saved the situation dozens of times when the success of the movement hung by a thread, and who personally succeeded in inducing Mr. Rockefeller to put up the funds without which neither the Great Smoky Mountains National Park nor the Shenandoah National Park would have been acquired. It was almost entirely to Mr. Cammerer's executive ability, vision, personal sacrifice and devotion that the people of this country owe for their now having these two Parks."

Of course, partly through Kelsey's efforts, there is today a Mount Cammerer at the northern end of the Smokies' crest line.

There were actually three phases in the creation of the Smokies and Shenandoah Parks. Phase I was the approval by Congress of the commission's report. Phase II was the boundary delineation and accumulation of the land titles where both the commission and Cammerer played key roles, along with the Tennessee, North Carolina, and Virginia state organizations. Phase III was the actual development of the parks and their infrastructure. This was Cammerer's with his able management of the CCC boys in the southern Appalachians and throughout the entire national parks structure in the 1930s—leading to the parks' final dedications by President Roosevelt. One man was devoted to the effort through all three phases. He was Harlan P. Kelsey.

Among the great explorers and crusaders for preservation, Kelsey stands out as the preservation hero of the East. The point of all this is that Kelsey deserves his own pedestal, equal to that of Muir. Neither larger nor smaller. Equal.

The rationale for this pedestal lies in the long list of credits, from so many sources, during Kelsey's lifetime. They all impinge on the thesis that the public should be *forever indebted* to him. In no particular order they are:

- Horticulture and all related fields will forever be indebted to him for his contributions to their advancement. (AAN, July 25, 1940)
- ... your services over a period of years in connection with the establishment of the eastern national parks ... saving, while they still could be saved, such great primitive areas ... The fact that we could rely on your ripe experience, judgment and enthusiastic interest at such critical points has contributed more to their success than you probably will realize. (Sec. Wilber, January 27, 1932)
- Those who fought for the creation of the Park have handed down a never-ending legacy ... it is a responsibility now in the hands of all who are touched by its gifts ... (NPS Smokies film DVD cover, 1999)
- I am sure that you know how much I appreciate your willingness to be of service and your unselfish interest in the success of the National Park Service. (Sec. Ickes, July 17, 1933)
- Mr. Harlan P. Kelsey, who is one of our foremost advocates of preserving the beauties of our mountains for future generations. (Congressmen Joe Ervin before Congress, March 20, 1945)
- Conservation Medal for 1946 of the Trustees of Public Reservations. "In making the presentation as President, I emphasized that although previous Conservation Medals have been given to many of the outstanding figures in the field of conservation, we feel that nobody deserved the Medal more than he." (Robert Walcott, Massachusetts, 1947)
- George Robert White Medal of Honor ... principally for his pioneering work in the introduction and conservation of native American plants. The most important horticultural award in this country. (Massachusetts Horticultural Society, 1936)
- The nation's first national historic site has been established in the old seaport city of Salem, Massachusetts ... as *Salem Maritime National Historic Site*. ... Establishment of the site brings to a successful conclusion more than four years of activity on the

part of Harlan P. Kelsey. (NPS Acting Superintendent Edwin Small, December 1938)
- … confer upon Harlan Page Kelsey, in recognition of his distinguished attainments, the Honorary Degree of Doctor of Science. (University of Massachusetts, June 07, 1948)

In February 1959, former director of the National Park Service, Horace Marsden Albright, eulogized Harlan Kelsey in *National Parks* magazine.

> A great conservationist died on July 28, 1958 at his New England home. He was Harlan Page Kelsey of Boxford, Massachusetts. Head of one of the largest nursery enterprises in the country, his interests extended far beyond the boundaries of his business. He was an outstanding horticulturist, a writer on natural history topics, a talented landscape architect, a planner of national parks, a mountaineer, a worker in the conservation of natural resources, and a far-sighted leader in protection of historic sites.
>
> He was a big man physically and possessed of civic interest, unselfish devotion to causes in which he believed, enthusiasm and vitality to carry out his projects regardless of obstacles, and wisdom to guide aright his energies and those of his associates. Add to all these fine qualities a delightful personality with great capacity for abiding friendship, and we have the man to match the mountains east and west that he loved.[199]

Remedy

It has been this author's contention that Harlan P. Kelsey is John Muir's forgotten eastern counterpart. Why has history treated John Muir so favorably and Kelsey with so little recognition today? My thesis is that Muir was the dramatic "publicizer" of the wilderness movement before there was a National Park Service; reaching millions of mesmerized

The American Horticultural Council

through the Board of Directors

presents this

Citation

to

Harlan P. Kelsey,

East Boxford, Massachusetts,

for a lifetime devoted to the

Nursery Industry and Conservation.

For more than 50 years you have given unselfish and unstinted service in behalf of the American nursery industry, and have been a leader in the conservation of our natural resources. As Dean of American nurserymen, this Council accords you highest acclamation.

October 28, 1954

Carl F. Wedell, PRESIDENT

George H. M. Lawrence, SECRETARY

Citation. Dean of American Nurserymen. American Horticultural Council. 1954.

Horticultural Award

to

Harlan Page Kelsey

by the

College of Agriculture
University of Massachusetts

Distinguished horticulturist, landscape architect, city planner and past director of the Council on National Parks, Forests and Wildlife; already recipient of many honors and awards for your contributions to plant introduction, conservation, park development, plant nomenclature and civic progress; yours has been a life of outstanding service to mankind, especially enriching horticulture through introduction and distribution of choice ornamental plant materials, and through your activities in preparing and editing that monumental work, "Standardized Plant Names."

J. Paul Mather
President

Dale H. Sieling

Horticultural Award. University of Massachusetts College of Agriculture. 1956.

readers from the public at large, with his numerous books (seventeen), essays (twenty-two),[200] and articles in mass circulation magazines. He reached his iconic status in the West, long before there were wilderness parks in the East. Kelsey was the serious "collaborator," dealing mostly with the newly established National Park Service and other serious-minded men of note; when he wrote, it was for the decision makers, reaching a few thousand at best, but with telling results. The same for horticulture—he dealt with the few hundred nurserymen of the time and they were the ones who contacted the public at large pushing native plants. The answer lies in the audience—Muir's was huge and Kelsey's miniscule.

So what's the remedy for this injustice? There must be a remedy.

The preceding section closed with a long list of credits from notable persons and organizations celebrating Kelsey's enormous contributions to preservation and horticulture. Why weren't these enough to assure that Kelsey would remain in the forefront of the public's memory, as someone to whom they are "forever indebted"? Perhaps it is because these credits, after over a half century, now reside in archives, and the people who extended them are now gone. In contrast, Muir's credits are emblazoned on solid geographical features as names that are always in view to any visitor, and likely to remain there—mountains, glaciers, schools, sites, and locales. The remedy for the Kelsey injustice may simply be to place Kelsey's name on the enduring visible geographical features, where he played a dominant role in their preservation.

Why is there no Mount Kelsey or Commission Peak in the Great Smoky Mountains National Park? There would have been, were it not for Kelsey himself successfully fighting to prevent it. Recall from our earlier narrative, Kelsey's 1939 letter to Cammerer, complaining about the naming of Mounts Chapman and Kephart while the two men were still living: "I can't understand why the National Geographic Board would ever fall for naming a mountain peak except posthumously. I thought it was a fixed rule. Thank God I had the nerve to fight the Tennesseans who wanted to name a peak after the members of the Commission. As you know there were two members who highly favored it and I think they felt very sore with me for taking such an active part in killing the proposition."

Such a move today would be a posthumous honor. Certainly there must be a notable promontory high on a well-traveled trail in the Smokies that could be named Kelsey Point or Kelsey Peak.

That portion of the AT that lies within the park could be assigned the name "Kelsey Ridgeline Trail," or such. After all, it was Kelsey who was most influential in convincing Benton MacKaye to bring the trail through the Smokies, rather than terminate it at Mount Mitchell off the Blue Ridge. He was the one who introduced MacKaye to Paul Fink, the man who showed MacKaye how to route the trail from the Blue Ridge over the Cross Ranges to the Smokies. He was the one most influential in helping Arno Cammerer define the metes and bounds of the park.

There is precedence, since the northern terminus of the AT is named the Hunt Trail, ascending Mount Katahdin. Why couldn't the southern terminus carry Kelsey's name? There is further precedence. The National Park Service points out that "Because the John Muir Trail overlaps the Pacific Crest Trail for most of its length, the Pacific Crest Trail Association also provides details about the John Muir Trail." John Muir's name adorns three mountains and three trails, one even in Tennessee. Why shouldn't the National Park Service finally reward Kelsey with at least one trail, for the original establishment of the park?

Alternatively, deep within the primeval woods of the Smokies there must be a well-traveled foot path that could be renamed the Kelsey Trail. This in honor of his enormous contribution, bringing the native flora of the Smokies into prominence with American gardeners across the nation. Or could there be a Kelsey Cove or the Kelsey Woods?

Alternatively, somewhere along the Blue Ridge Parkway there must be a strip of sufficient length to establish the Harlan P. Kelsey Blue Ridge Arboretum. Kelsey proposed such in his March 29, 1946, letter to his friends, Sam Weems, superintendent, and Stan Abbot, supervising landscape architect, of the Blue Ridge Parkway:

> The Blue Ridge Parkway offers an unparalleled opportunity permanently to exhibit in perfect naturalistic settings, the unique and remarkable flora of the Southern Alleghany's. The Rhododendrons, Azaleas, Kalmias, Hemlocks etc. obviously will play a major part in developing the landscape, as your fine plantings along the Parkway have already demonstrated. However, there are hundreds of rare and very beautiful trees, shrubs, and herbaceous perennials which may be overlooked unless special effort is made to secure them, in sufficient quantities which will not be easy ... My hope is that the Parkway will become throughout its length a glorified arboretum and botanical garden, naturalistically planted yet having adequate plantations in suitable locations and combinations of every plant native to the 500 mile region through which the Parkway runs. Never before has such an opportunity been presented permanently to preserve and display this wonderful flora.

Kelsey attached a list of forty candidate species for starters. This could at last be a microcosm of Kelsey's 1949 *Arborways for America*.

Today the parkway does have Craggy Gardens north of Asheville. Where did the name Craggy come from? Couldn't the USGS rename it Kelsey Gardens? It would be more meaningful, both horticulturally and historically.

Quoted earlier from the December 1938 issue of *Planning and Civic Comment*, Acting Superintendant Edwin Small announced:

> The Nation's first national historic site has been established in the old seaport city of Salem, Massachusetts, ... as *Salem Maritime National Historic Site*. ... Establishment of the site brings to a successful conclusion more than four years of activity on the part of Harlan P. Kelsey, who first envisioned the possibilities of the location and has worked most determinedly to secure the cooperation of the City, the State, various organizations and individuals in meeting the property requirements prescribed by the National Park Service.

Today there is no recognition of Kelsey in the site's Visitor Center. Would it not be appropriate to place the above citation, with a picture, in some prominent place?

Collectively, the foregoing could be called a "wish list" of suggestions to place Kelsey's name on enduring visible geographical features. Of the six suggestions only one would involve big dollar expenditures in the NPS budget—Kelsey's 1946 proposal for an arboretum along the length of the Blue Ridge Parkway to permanently preserve and display native flora of the region. The others involve only the establishment of names for trails or areas. Someone would have to be assigned the role of coordinator in selection, approvals, administration, and fulfillment of the naming process. This presumably would be within the National Park Service, with contact elsewhere, such as with the Appalachian Trail Conservancy, and the US Geological Survey. Who knows what other organizations would have an interest? AMC?

If this is viewed as a daunting task layered onto some existing person's already overloaded task list, nothing is apt to happen. If, on the other hand, this is viewed as an opportunity for some person, or group of people, to gain satisfaction in seeing an obligation satisfied, indebtedness repaid, it stands a good chance of success. The items on the "wish list," taken one at a time, are not really that imposing. Nor is the list exclusive of other great ideas that could surface as the NPS seeks to honor "one of their own." Kelsey, the reliable collaborator, was truly one of their own. *John Muir's forgotten eastern counterpart.*

Speaking of other great ideas, the grandest idea of all is the prospect of establishing the Harlan P. Kelsey National Historic Site. John Muir's Historic Site, lauding his western achievements, is located on the West Coast near Martinez, California, just east of Oakland. Kelsey's prospective site would balance it on the East Coast just north of Boston, lauding his eastern achievements. Muir's site centers on the Strentzel house and fruit orchard surrounding it. Kelsey's site could center on the nursery office building and arboretum surrounding it. That building (now a three-unit condominium) would be ideal for archiving and display of Kelsey's documents and drawings now dispersed in other locations. There is more than adequate acreage for adjacent parking without disturbing the beauty of the arboretum. Acquisition costs would be under $1 million, quite manageable for donation to the National Park Service.

Epilogue

Changing Times

In the mid-1950s the Kelseys made some notable changes. They had moved the nursery headquarters about a mile away to the area of the packing sheds. It suited the business better. Next, they got the town to rezone the now-empty office building as a three-family dwelling. The sales floor became two smallish mirror-image apartments, renting east and west. Kelsey's private office on the second floor was remodeled into a large apartment for Harlan and Florence Kelsey. Their son, Seth, and his wife, Penel, had then moved into the now-vacant Spofford Barnes House next door.

After Harlan's death, with Florence alone in the big apartment, she decided to return to her roots back in Salem. There she found accommodations atop the Hawthorne Hotel, nicely situated in a parklike setting in downtown Salem, which was also comfortably close to longtime Salem friends. Florence finally died December 9, 1963, after a brief illness, while visiting her daughter Katherine Kelsey Sawyer in Dalton, Massachusetts. She was buried next to Harlan in the Low/Kelsey Plot at the Salem Cemetery.

The Spofford Barnes House was really too large for Seth and Penel, with both of their boys married and in their own homes. So they decided to move next door into Florence's second-floor apartment. Now the house would soon be empty and available for sale. With their first child on the way, Sally and Loren Wood were actively looking for an old house to buy, and the historic Spofford Barnes House was a compelling purchase. They moved in late November 1961, only weeks before daughter Sarah was born.

At the real estate closing for the house, it became apparent Seth and the nursery were facing some financial pressure. The proceeds of the sale were carved into segments for various creditors awaiting payment. Changes in the nursery business after WWII gradually took their toll on the Kelsey Highlands Nursery. The wholesale business had been shifting to massive supernurseries in areas with cheap land, large-scale fertilization, and plentiful water. Oregon and western Tennessee are examples. The Kelsey nursery had to constantly import new soil to replace that taken with large earth balls as the now-mature nursery stock was sold. With the wholesale business declining, the retail business assumed new importance. But that too was now shifting to the "garden centers" on or near the commuter routes, where people could quickly duck in to pick up a desired plant on the way home from work. It took extra effort to drive all the way out to Boxford for the same transaction. It was a gradual process of erosion on all fronts.

Landscape architecture was one remaining area where Seth Kelsey's reputation gave him a competitive advantage. Throughout the 1930s, '40s, and '50s, the Kelsey Highlands Nursery received top awards at the annual flower show of the Massachusetts Horticultural Society in Boston. The large estates around Boston were all planted. These big jobs were now gone. Residential landscaping had shifted dramatically to subdivisions within the spread of suburban post–WWII America. Here the builder simply bought the cheapest stock available and plunked it in as foundation planting. Landscape design was still needed, but the market was shrinking.

In the 1950s the American Association of Nurserymen promoted industrial landscaping and beautification, culminating in an annual Plant America Award. Kelsey Highlands Nursery was the national winner in 1955 for its design and installation of the grounds of the CBS Hytron Manufacturing Plant in Danvers, Massachusetts. Again in 1956 it was the winner for the Northeastern University Campus in Boston. The 1956 nursery catalog used two full pages to declare these awards, pointing out that industrial, institutional, and public landscaping was a specialty of Kelsey Highlands Nursery. The text read:

> Good landscaping is good business. Manufacturers and business men in all lines have found that beautiful surroundings increase worker efficiency, reduce employee turnover, and make for better relations between labor, management and the community at large. At educational institutions, offices, service establishments and at all levels of government is found each year, greater recognition of the unique contribution of good landscaping to the American way of life. We are proud of the part we have played in this movement, which has been greatly stimulated by the 'Plant America' program of the American Association of Nurserymen.

On the facing page was a long list of institutions where Kelsey carried out extensive plantings, including (1) Massachusetts Institute of Technology, (2) Phillips Exeter Academy, (3) Haverhill Park Department, (4) Boston Edison Company, (5) Sylvania Electric Products Corp., and eight other well-recognized customers. Each of these jobs was comparable to the landscape design and installation for a large estate's grounds on Boston's North Shore of old. In a sense, things had come full circle. In 1896 Harlan Kelsey had come to Boston as a landscape architect to promote his expanding nursery operations back in North Carolina. Fifty years later his son, Seth, began to lean on landscape architecture to prop up his declining nursery operations in Boxford.

End Times

Hidden within the success of Seth's institutional landscaping was a fatal seed leading to failure. The jobs were getting bigger and the volume of plant material needed also grew—well in excess of the nursery's available stock. Material had to be bought in the open market and the nursery's accounts payable grew and grew. This was all right, so long as the accounts receivable could quickly be used to liquidate the payables. In 1963 the nursery won the bid on a big office park job in Washington, DC. This placed a new strain on nursery cash being funded with short-term debt from Naumkeag Trust in Salem, with the nursery pledged as collateral. Normally this had been simply rolled over by the bank to the next year. When Seth sought payment from the prime contractor in Washington, he was informed that until the prime recovered funds from the office park developers, none of the subcontractors (like Seth) would be paid anything. Seth had already paid all his plant material sources, leaving his cash position in perilous shape. Now he was dependent on the bank expanding the loan into the new year.[201] Instead, the bank foreclosed. In the fall of 1964, the Kelsey Highlands Nursery "closed its doors."

Seth, with no other options, offered to sell the entire remaining nursery to the town for recreation or any other town purposes. At a noisy special town meeting, the proposed purchase was defeated. Worried over the possibilities of adverse development, Seth did obtain from the planning board an approved thirteen-lot subdivision he felt was appropriate. This was to be available to any future buyer of the property. Naumkeag Trust filed notice that the entire property would be sold at public auction March 5, 1965, at 10:00 a.m.[202] After spirited bidding, with about sixty-five people present, the real estate developers had all dropped out, leaving only two bidders, unknown to most of those present. The ultimate winner was Dr. Simeon Locke, an abutting resident, well known in the Boston medical community. Locke said he considered the purchase a "long-term investment" and had voiced concern to friends and neighbors about what might happen to the property, which faced his own. One newspaper reported that abutters they interviewed were without hesitation "delighted."[203]

For Seth Kelsey, now what? He could still live in the apartments that were independent of the foreclosed nursery. He was still active in Boston horticultural activities, including the Board of Overseers Visiting Committee of Harvard's Arnold Arboretum. Dr. Richard Howard, director of the Arnold, provided the path forward for Seth. It was in far northern Delaware, at the estate of Lammot du Pont Copeland, president and CEO of the giant E. I. du Pont Chemical Company. The estate was dubbed Mount Cuba and was surrounded by 630 acres of land on Barley Mill Road in Greenville, Delaware, just northwest of Wilmington. The colonial revival house had been built in 1937 and formally landscaped by successive noted landscape architects. Now the Copelands wanted to expand the gardens down the slopes in a naturalistic manner to feature native trees, shrubs and native wildflowers. Dr. Howard sent a letter to Copeland's people, alerting them to Kelsey's availability and bestowing him with high recommendations. The match was made, and in the late summer of 1965, Seth and Penel departed Boxford for residence in Kennett Square, Pennsylvania, just northwest of Mount Cuba.

On his departure, Seth put the apartment building up for sale, and the Woods had to buy it to keep the Kelsey compound intact (house/apartments/arboretum) and to prevent its falling into the hands of some absentee landlord. The closing of the sale was March 25, 1966. Wood quietly operated the apartments for the next thirty years until after his retirement.

Mount Cuba was perfect for Seth. He was given a staff of two and worked smoothly with Lammot Copeland. Pamela Copeland was a somewhat different story and her diary showed numerous incidents where she had different ideas from her husband and Seth. But the work continued apace for the next five years. In the spring of 1970, adverse financial events developed within the Copeland family. Lammot stood behind these family members and the cash drain siphoned funds away from the landscape program; it was now effectively dead. "On January 23, 1971, [Seth] Kelsey was summoned to speak to Pamela and Lammot. Clearly Kelsey was given his notice at this time as Pamela's diary stated that he 'was shattered by our news,' and that 'it was a hard meeting for all.' Soon after meeting with the Copelands, the shocked Kelsey shared the news with his staff members ... and provided them with one month's notice. He asked them to clean up and organize the office so that it could be closed up until it would again be needed."[204]

Seth's horticultural reputation again helped him land on his feet. On July 1, 1971, he was employed by the University of Connecticut as research professor in plant science and as a horticulturist at the university's Bartlett Arboretum in Stamford, Connecticut. Only a year and a half later, December 4, 1972, the university sent a brief notice to key horticultural organizations:

> Dear Sirs: Regrettably I must advise that Mr. Seth Kelsey died on Saturday, December 2, 1972. His passing represents a tremendous loss to the field of horticulture and to horticulturalists everywhere.

One year later, November 7, 1973, the university announced:

> Dear Sirs: Since the death of Seth L. Kelsey last December, we have received a number of requests regarding appropriate ways of honoring his memory, particularly from those who recognize Seth's outstanding contributions to horticulture and related fields. We are delighted to announce that a section of the ericaceous plant area now under development at the Arboretum has been designated to become the *Seth Low Kelsey Rhododendron and Azalea Species Garden*.

Seth had carried forward his grandfather STK's and his father Harlan's legacy, but now the three-generation dynasty was ended.

Fast forward to current times. For thirty years after Seth's death, Wood shared his time for career and family with time for maintaining the arboretum. By the turn of the century, with retirement behind him, what then? One option was for Wood to sell the house, sell the apartments, and move back to his birthplace in Tucson, Arizona. The uncertainty for the apartments' future appearance under an absentee landlord, and the near certainty that the maintenance-intensive arboretum would be lost to deterioration over time, made that most unattractive—both to the Woods and to the town. The ultimate solution was to found the Horticultural Society of Boxford to act as grantee for the Conservation Restriction on the Arboretum, including all the land outside the apartment building's foundation structure. The society also agreed to act as grantee for the Preservation Restriction placed on the historic Spofford Barnes House next door, before it was sold. The final measure was to eliminate the danger of a future absentee landlord. The building's interior was rebuilt substantially into three condominium units, assuring permanent owner occupancy.

Also at the turn of the century, Dr. Locke finally implemented the approved subdivision of the nursery land. Here, too, he acted to preserve the Kelsey legacy. The subdivision was named Kelsey Highlands, and the streets were appropriately named Carolina Road, Azalea Way, and Rose Lane. Those who purchased lots were obligated to build houses in conformance with a portfolio of designs that were of quality North Carolina character.

All that remains of Harlan Kelsey's own touch is the Harlan P. Kelsey Arboretum, established by him in 1929, and today open to the public, dawn to dusk, seven days a week. Its tiny two-and-a-half-acre area is surrounded by a deer fence to defend the understory plants. One hundred and fifty plant labels help identify over forty different genera and over eighty species. The canopy is massive; after walking through, a friend wrote "it gives the feeling of being in another time and place." A small Board of Directors for the Horticultural Society of Boxford volunteers time for the restoration and maintenance of the arboretum, and to raising funds to meet expenses. There is not a botanist, nor a landscape designer among the lot of them, but they do their best. Gracious townspeople pay modest dues to assist. They need a staff. They need a visitor center to display the Kelsey story and house his records, with someone in attendance to serve public visitors. They need an endowment. They need an "angel," or better yet, a national historic site.

Of course the "Land of the Sky" still stands high and beautiful over the western North Carolina mountains. And the Great Smoky Mountains National Park still stands as the zenith of the horticulture that makes the Land of the Sky what it is. But one man, Harlan P. Kelsey, pioneered the move to native plants and worked relentlessly over time to bring that horticulture to the American gardener. That same man was "the natural leader"[205] of the Southern Appalachian National Park Commission that selected and successfully promoted the Smokies and Shenandoah Parks through Congress. Thus he brought all of America to the primary source of our native flora—the Beautiful Land of the Sky.

Author's Note

This biography was born over ten years ago when a local acquaintance of the author's, Linda Laderoute, received a class assignment for her Harvard-Radcliffe landscape architecture course. She was to pick a noted figure in the field and prepare a term paper on the person. Linda picked Kelsey, even though she knew even less than I did at the time. He was just an obscure figure from local history that had a big nursery and landscape architecture business. Well, when she did her research, the story unfolded for her. Her term paper got an A and was read widely in the local area. Linda didn't continue the work; she and her family moved to a new life in St. Joseph, Missouri. I was left with her source material and cautiously began the search for answers to the endless remaining questions.

The search led me to Linville, North Carolina, where I met Katy Fletcher, granddaughter of Harlan Kelsey's right-hand man, E. C. Robbins. She opened all her family records for me, and I quickly learned there was more to the Kelsey story than I had ever expected. When I continued down to Highlands, North Carolina, the historical society directed me to Ran Shaffner, local bookstore owner and historian. He showed me key parts of the town and later sent me his newly minted book on the history of Highlands. All this was immensely helpful, but after the late 1890s, Kelsey had moved to Boston, where the North Carolina material didn't apply. I needed new sources.

The local Boxford Historic Document Center learned of a Kelsey collection held by the Massachusetts Nurserymen's Association, in Hopkinton, Massachusetts (thanks to Martha Clark and Lou Gould). When Seth Kelsey left Boxford, he had offered his father's archives to the Arnold Arboretum, who accepted them. But after years of storage, with space at a premium, they passed them on to Massachusetts Nurserymen's for storage at the Weston Nurseries in Hopkinton, Massachusetts. Your author and others were graciously invited by historian Richard Bemis to make occasional trips to Hopkinton to sample the collection. It proved to be a "gold mine"; it was so extensive we hardly knew where to start. Estimated at fifty thousand items, it was mostly tissue carbons of all Kelsey's letters. The balance was magazines, bulletins, and brochures of interest to Kelsey.

Eventually the collection was moved to a barn loft at a sod farm in Northfield, Massachusetts—dusty and randomly heated. Thanks to new historian Phillip Boucher and Rina Sumner, executive secretary of Massachusetts Nurserymen's, permission was gained to bring all of the collection to the author's home in Boxford for study and processing. Each of the boxes was replaced with acid-free archival boxes, and each file folder with an acid-free replacement. Acidic newspaper clippings were isolated to avoid contamination. No attempts were made to catalog or change the order of the collection. The association even helped defray the high cost of materials for preservation before they retook possession (twenty-four tightly packed archival boxes).

The final event in the research saga came from Susannah Haney, the librarian at Tower Hill Botanic Garden, in Boylston, Massachusetts. She had taken possession, from Craig Anthony, of numerous boxes of Kelsey records formerly at the Worcester County Horticultural Society. Again, she had no room for them but contacted the Horticultural Society of Boxford. Would we take possession? The next day we were at Tower Hill loading them into my station wagon. It turns out they were all part of the original collection but had been split off when the Arnold

Arboretum originally divested them. After processing they comprised ten acid-free tightly packed archival boxes now in possession of the Horticultural Society of Boxford. This brought the total number of boxes to thirty-four.

Your author personally read each Kelsey letter, beginning to end, copying those needed for the biography. Hellishly time consuming, but compensated by the joy of discovery. The same applies to the many brochures, catalogs, and other memorabilia, but selectively, not beginning to end. Such a large body of primary source material led to inclusion of numerous quotations and anecdotes not necessarily needed to tell Kelsey's story. However, their inclusion serves to "bring them out of hiding" to join the visible body of historical material surrounding people and events of importance.

Neighbor Clarke Haywood provided the urging to visit the AMC library in Boston and provided the cover photo for the book. The book's first gratuitous editing was by Tom Holbrook, owner of River Run Bookstore in Portsmouth, New Hampshire. He inspired me to search for ways to make a flat biography read more like a climactic novel. Sister-in-law Frannie Hall's boundless enthusiasm for the manuscript was a treasure. Erin Perry's copyediting exposed the many hundreds of errors in the original manuscript, and her comments on her emotional reactions were priceless. Deborah McGill, likewise, offered editing expertise. Then there is Nancy Bender, my insurance agent. She patiently listened to my ranting over the injustice of Muir vs. the forgotten Kelsey. "Well, Loren, all you have to do is tell them," she replied. And so we have.

Then there is my immediate family: I am grateful to daughter Laura, who early on convinced me to stick to a chronological narrative and abandon the organization by subject groupings; daughter Sarah, whose technical expertise on digital matters made life a breeze communicating with my publisher; and wife Sally, soul mate, who kept pace reading the manuscript and redirected my efforts toward simplification. Sal also constantly saw the bright side of things, as I would berate myself for various shortcomings.

We cannot overlook Nancy Merrill, whose steadfast attention as president of the Horticultural Society of Boxford has preserved and maintained the Kelsey Arboretum for the public's benefit.

Finally I want to acknowledge Margaret Mowvy Ricksecker, Harlan's grandmother, out in Kansas in 1883. Her letter to her daughter Katie, in Highlands, during that terrible cold winter, "Soup Meagre after all was pretty comfortable fare. Especially when the Holy Word chimed in and said 'Be content with such things as ye have.'" This powerful faith infused the family and worked its way down the generations to Harlan. He spoke little of it, but it showed mightily in his role as a servant to mankind.

Loren M. Wood earned an engineering degree from the University of Arizona and an MBA from Harvard. He is a retired chartered financial analyst. Wood lives with his wife, Sally, in Boxford, Massachusetts. They have three married daughters.

Selected Bibliography

The following books are those used by the author for information about peoples, places, and times spanning Kelsey's lifetime. Where specific quotations are used from books, they are cited in the source notes. Bulletins, articles, press releases, magazines, and other loose materials are cited in the source notes.

Albright, Horace M., and Robert Cahn. *The Birth of the National Park Service: The Founding Years, 1913–33.* Salt Lake City, UT: Howe Brothers, 1985.

Connor, Sheila. *New England Natives.* Cambridge, MA: Harvard University Press, 1998.

Dupree, A. Hunter. *Asa Gray 1810–1888.* Cambridge, MA: The Belknap Press of Harvard University Press, 1959.

Ferrell, Mallory Hope. *Tweetsie Country, The East Tennessee & Western North Carolina Railroad.* Johnson City, TN: The Overmountain Press, 1991.

Garland, Joseph E. *The North Shore.* Beverly, MA: Commonwealth Editions, 1998.

Kelsey, Harlan P., and William A. Dayton. *Standardized Plant Names*, 2nd ed. Harrisburg, PA: J. Horace McFarland Company, 1942.

McElvaine, Robert S. *The Great Depression*. New York: Times Books, 1993.

McIntosh, Gertrude Vogt. *Highlands, North Carolina: A Walk into the Past*. Birmingham, AL: Birmingham Printing and Publishing Company, 1983.

Morton, Hugh. *Hugh Morton's North Carolina*. Chapel Hill, NC: The University of North Carolina Press, 2003.

Nash, Roderick Frazier. *Wilderness and the American Mind*, 4th ed. New Haven, CT: Yale University Press, 2001.

Rybczynski, Witold. *A Clearing in the Distance: Frederick Law Olmsted and America in the 19th Century*. New York: Touchstone, 1999.

Shaffner, Randolph P. *Heart of the Blue Ridge: Highlands, North Carolina*. Highlands, NC: Faraway Publishing, 2001.

Sutton, S. B. *Charles Sprague Sargent and the Arnold Arboretum*. Cambridge, MA: Harvard University Press, 1970.

Tager, Miles. *Grandfather Mountain—A Profile*. Boone, NC: Parkway Publishers, Inc., 1999.

Waterman, Laura and Guy. *Forest and Crag*. Boston: Appalachian Mountain Club, 1989.

Whisnant, Anne Mitchell. *Super-Scenic Motorway: A Blue Ridge Parkway History*. Chapel Hill: The University of North Carolina Press, 2006.

White, Richard P. *A Century of Service: A History of the Nursery Industry Associations of the United States.* Washington, DC: The American Association of Nurserymen, 1975.

Wolfe, Linnie Marsh. *Son of the Wilderness: The Life of John Muir.* Madison, WI: The University of Wisconsin Press, 1973.

References

Many of the source notes cite letters and other forms from the Kelsey files held by the Massachusetts Nurserymen's Association and the Horticultural Society of Boxford. Far more letters are simply cited in the text as *from* and *to* and *date*. They are so numerous that for simplicity the reader is to assume they are from the Kelsey files. All other sources are cited specifically in the References.

Chapter 1: Even as a Child

1. Harlan P. Kelsey, "President's Address" (American Association of Nurserymen, June 25, 1925).
2. Randolph P. Shaffner, *Heart of the Blue Ridge: Highlands, North Carolina* (Highlands, NC: Faraway Publishing, 2001). Most of the account above is excerpted from this source.
3. City of Hutchinson. Website covering early history of the city founding (last update January 9, 2001).
4. Harlan P. Kelsey, "The Carolina Mountains" (paper delivered to the "Club," most likely the Appalachian Mountain Club. Assumed to have been delivered 1920–21, when Kelsey was president of the club. Draft copy found in his files), 12.
5. Gert McIntosh, *Highlands, North Carolina: A Walk into the Past* (Birmingham, AL: Birmingham Printing and Publishing Company, 1983).
6. The original diary is in two ledger books held in the archival materials at the Gardens of the Blue Ridge, Pinola, North Carolina.
7. Shaffner, *Heart of the Blue Ridge*, 56.
8. Harlan P. Kelsey, "President's Address" (American Association of Nurserymen, June 25, 1925).

9. Ibid.
10. Colman, with a lifelong passion for agriculture, was appointed the first secretary of agriculture by President Cleveland. Deman, in 1886–87, was pomologist for the US Department of Agriculture.
11. McIntosh, *Highlands, North Carolina*.
12. Ibid., 41.
13. Ibid., 61.
14. Ibid., 64.
15. McIntosh, *Highlands, North Carolina*, 35.
16. Shaffner, *Heart of the Blue Ridge*, 152.
17. Harlan P. Kelsey, "The Carolina Mountains," 10.
18. Ibid.
19. Letter from the Robbins family archives at the Gardens of the Blue Ridge. Pineola, North Carolina.
20. John Parris, *Highlands—A Town with a History*. Clipping from an unidentified newspaper, 1980.
21. Blake Spurney, "Native Tribes Came and Went at White Man's Whims," *Ottawa Herald*, March 9, 2001.
22. Dr. Thomas Grant Harbison. *Journal of the Elisha Mitchell Scientific Society* 52 (1936): 140, 145.
23. Ibid.
24. Randolph P. Shaffner, *Good Reading Material, Mostly Bound and New: The Hudson Library 1884–1994* (Highlands, NC: The Hudson Library of Highlands, North Carolina, 1994).
25. McIntosh, *Highlands, North Carolina*.
26. Dr. Thomas Grant Harbison. *Journal of the Elisha Mitchell Scientific Society* 52 (1936): 140, 145.
27. Letter from the Robbins family archives at the Gardens of the Blue Ridge. Pineola, North Carolina.
28. Shaffner, *Heart of the Blue Ridge*, 95.
29. Ibid., 52.
30. Dr. Harry E. Kelsey to E. C. Robbins, December 13, 1941, Linville, North Carolina.
31. Obituary, *Midland Journal*, March 8, 1946.

Chapter 2: Emerging Entrepreneur

32. Mallory Hope Ferrell, *Tweetsie Country: The East Tennessee & Western North Carolina Railroad* (Johnson City, TN: The Overmountain Press, 1991), 1.
33. Ibid.

34. McIntosh, *Highlands, North Carolina*, 34.
35. John Preston Arthur, *History of Western North Carolina*. Raleigh, NC., Edwards & Broughton Printing Co., 1914.
36. Ibid.
37. Ferrell, *Tweetsie Country*, 25.
38. Randolph P. Shaffner, *Heart of the Blue Ridge*, 85.
39. Shepherd H. Dugger (historian for Avery County), *Brief History of Avery County*.
40. Ibid.
41. S. B. Sutton, *Charles Sprague Sargent and the Arnold Arboretum* (Cambridge, MA: Harvard University Press, 1970).
42. Letter by S. T. Kelsey, "To the good citizens of Pomona," *Pomona Republican*, August 10, 1916. Replying to a request for an account of his connection with the inception and early history of the Pomona enterprise.
43. Ferrell, *Tweetsie Country*, 25.
44. All Biltmore material from Bill Alexander, Landscape and Forest Historian, at today's Biltmore Estate.
45. Harlan P. Kelsey, "The Highlands Nursery, Whose Motto is 'American Plants for American Planters,'" *The National Nurseryman* 18, no. 2 (February 1910).
46. From a customer flier furnished by Gardens of the Blue Ridge, Pineola, North Carolina.
47. Ferrell, *Tweetsie Country*, 25–26.
48. Letter by S. T. Kelsey, "To the good citizens of Pomona," *Pomona Republican*, August 10, 1916. Replying to a request for an account of his connection with the inception and early history of the Pomona enterprise.

Chapter 3: Broadening Scope

49. Highlands Nursery Catalog, 1898–99, 8.
50. Richard P. White, *A Century of Service: A History of the Nursery Industry Associations of the United States* (Washington, DC: The American Association of Nurserymen,1975), 199.
51. Joseph E. Garland, *The North Shore* (Beverly, MA: Commonwealth Editions, 1998), 118.
52. Based on drawings in his drafting loft surveyed by the author.
53. John P. Gerber, AMC Librarian, *The AMC and the Creation of the White Mountain National Forest*. A paper given to the author by Mr. Gerber in 1997.
54. Ibid.
55. Ibid.

56. Garland, *The North Shore*, 175.
57. National Park Service. Salem Maritime National Historic Site brochure.
58. Garland, *The North Shore*. For all the descriptive material regarding the North Shore activities, we are indebted to Joe Garland's work.
59. Selected, scanned, edited, provided with headnotes, and formatted as a web document by John W. Reps, Professor Emeritus, Department of City and Regional Planning, Cornell University, Ithaca, New York.
60. Marion County—Marion Points of Interest, February 28, 1999, http://www.co.marion.us/poi.html.
61. Gerber, *The AMC and the Creation of the White Mountain National Forest*.
62. Proceeding of the club taken from various issues of Appalachia, AMC annual bulletin.
63. Martha Carlson, "Private Lands—Public Forest: The Story of the Weeks Act," *Forest Notes* (Summer 1986): 8.
64. Fredrick W. Kilbourne, *Chronicles of the White Mountains* (New York: Houghton Mifflin, 1916; repr., Hampton, NH: Heritage Books, 1978).
65. Roderick Frazier Nash, *Wilderness and the American Mind*, 4th ed. (New Haven, CT: Yale University Press, 2001).
66. Carlson, *Private Lands—Public Forest,* 9.
67. White, *A Century of Service*, 32.
68. 1903 Highlands Nursery Catalog, Kawana, Mitchell County, North Carolina.
69. 1908 Highlands Nursery Catalog, Salem, Essex County, Massachusetts.
70. 1911 Salem Nurseries Catalog.
71. White, *A Century of Service,* 165.
72. Internet resume of Marsden Jaseal Perry. Redwoodlibrary.org.
73. Taken from numerous letters between Kelsey and Sheldon, January 9, 1912 to April 2, 1908. Kelsey Files held by the New England Nurserymen's and Landscape Architects Association.
74. *Salem Evening News*, February 4, 1911.

Chapter 4: Gaining Stature

75. Library of the Arnold Arboretum, Harvard University, The Arborway, Jamaica Plain, MA.
76. Ibid.
77. Tabulation from Kelsey Files held by the New England Nurserymen's and Landscape Architects Association.
78. A Guide to the Biltmore Estate (Asheville, NC: The Biltmore Company, 2003), 17.

79. Arthur B. Jones, *The Salem Fire*, 1914. Online Version. (Retrieved from http://en.wikipedia.org/wiki/Great_Salem_Fire_of_1914).
80. The Mattamuskeet Foundation, 4377 Lewis Lane Road, Ayden, NC 28513.
81. Archives of the Boxford Historical Document Center, Boxford, MA.
82. This paragraph from an East Carolina University website. Ecu.edu.
83. The Mattamuskeet Foundation, 4377 Lewis Lane Road, Ayden, NC 28513.
84. Ibid.
85. 1932 Kelsey catalog.
86. Kelsey activities with army and US Housing Corporation taken from letters and contracts in the Kelsey Files held by the New England Nurserymen's and Landscape Architects Association.
87. Data on World War I taken from *Encyclopedia Britannica*, Volume 23, 1972. Data on nursery activities taken from White, *A Century of Service*.
88. Wolfe, *Son of the Wilderness*.
89. R. M. Sheppard to Harlan P. Kelsey, February 3, 1922, Kelsey Files, New England Nurserymen's and Landscape Architects Association.
90. *Standardized Plant Names: A Catalogue of Approved Scientific and Common Names of Plants in American Commerce* (American Joint Committee on Horticultural Nomenclature, 1923), v.
91. Ibid., ix.
92. Ibid., vi.
93. Ibid., x.
94. *1920 Prospectus of the Official Catalogue of Plant Names* (American Joint Committee on Horticultural Nomenclature), 3, item 3.
95. Olmsted to McFarland, April 14, 1924. This letter clearly identifies Kelsey as Manager and Secretary of the Sub-Committee during the business phase following publishing of the finished book. Nothing has been found explicitly naming him as Manager during the creation phase of the book, but it appears likely, given the sole address of the Sub-Committee being Kelsey's Salem office. He is clearly named as Secretary of the Joint Committee in the book, and Treasurer of the Sub-Committee.
96. Kelsey to McFarland, March 14, 1927. Kelsey identifies himself as Treasurer of the Joint Committee.
97. McFarland to Olmsted, June 27, 1924.
98. Ibid., p. 3, item 4.
99. McFarland to Kelsey, July 1, 1924.
100. Kelsey to DeLaMare Company, June 30, 1924.
101. Harlan P. Kelsey, "President's Address."
102. Richard P. White, *A Century of Service*.

Chapter 5: National Stage

103. Roderick Frazier Nash, *Wilderness and the American Mind*, 4th ed. (New Haven, CT: Yale University Press, 2001).
104. Charles W. Blood, "In Memoriam." Appalachia, December 1958.
105. President's Annual Address, AMC Bulletin, March 1921.
106. Ibid.
107. Laura and Guy Waterman, *Forest and Crag*. (Boston, MA: Appalachian Mountain Club, 1989), 493.
108. Ibid., 486.
109. Ibid., 486, 488–91.
110. From the Myron Avery Collection at Harpers Ferry (Appalachian Trail Conference) and the McClury Historical Collection in Knoxville.
111. Boston is often, even today, referred to as "the Hub."
112. The two spellings, Smokies and/or Smokys, are equally acceptable and in broad use.
113. *Save Our Mountains* (brochure issued in 1923 by The Great Smoky Mountains, Asheville, NC, and the Great Smoky Mountains Conservation Association, Knoxville, TN), 1–4.
114. All the material for this section, including many verbatim passages, taken from Harlan D. Unrau and G. Frank Williss, *Administrative History: Expansion of the National Park Service in the 1930s* (Denver: National Park Service, Denver Service Center, September 1983), chapter 1, sections A and B, http://www.cr.nps.gov/history.
115. Reed L. Engle, Cultural Resource Specialist in the Division of Natural and Cultural Resources, *Shenandoah National Park: A Historical Overview* (Shenandoah National Park. CRM No. 1—1998).
116. Chase P. Ambler, "Our Mountain Forests," *Country Life in America* 2, no. 1 (May 1902).
117. *History of the Great Smoky Mountains National Park*, Internet piece from Smokiesweb.com , 1997–2002.
118. *Guide to the Great Smoky Mountains National Park. Gatlinburg Supplement* (Gatlinburg News, 1939).
119. Reed L. Engle, Cultural Resource Specialist in the Division of Natural and Cultural Resources, *Shenandoah National Park: A Historical Overview* (Shenandoah National Park. CRM No. 1—1998).
120. *Three Eastern National Parks Authorized by Congress* (Civic Comment. American Civic Association. Washington, DC, July 19, 1926), 6.

121. *Final Report of the Southern Appalachian National Park Commission to the Secretary of the Interior. Draft.* Harlan P. Kelsey personal files held in the custody of The Massachusetts Nurserymen and Landscape Architects Association.
122. *Three Eastern National Parks Authorized by Congress* (Civic Comment. American Civic Association. Washington, DC, July 19, 1926), 5.
123. *Final Report of the Southern Appalachian National Park Commission to the Secretary of the Interior. Draft.* Harlan P. Kelsey personal files held in the custody of the Massachusetts Nurserymen's and Landscape Architects Association.
124. Bulletin Potomac Appalachian Trail Club, October 1937, pp. 102–6; January 1938, pp. 15–17.
125. Reed L. Engle, Cultural Resource Specialist in the Division of Natural and Cultural Resources, *Shenandoah National Park: A Historical Overview* (Shenandoah National Park. CRM No. 1—1998).
126. William Gregg to Col. Glenn Smith, March 26, 1931, with corrections to Commission Draft Final Report, p. 22, ln. 22, on p. 2 of letter.
127. Representative H. W. Temple to Harlan P. Kelsey, June 18, 1927.

Chapter 6: Trials and Triumphs

128. All quotations above are from the 2006 web pages of the Cosmos Club: www.acosmos-club.org.
129. "Weekly Economic Report," *ISI International Strategy and Investment* (October 13, 2008): 11.
130. Stock market description from Robert S. McElvaine, *The Great Depression* (New York: Times Books, 1984, 1993), 47–48.
131. Harold C. Jordahl Jr., *A Unique Collection of Islands* (Department of Urban and Regional Planning, University of Wisconsin-Extension, 1994), 179–86.
132. Data taken from the US Forest Service website for the Superior National Forest, 2008.
133. Description of Pigeon River from Wikipedia..org/wiki/Pigeon_River.
134. Always keep in mind the value of a dollar was hugely greater in 1930 than a dollar is today.
135. Sheila Connor, *New England Natives* (Cambridge, MA: Harvard University Press, 1994), 111.
136. Economic description from Robert S. McElvaine, *The Great Depression.*
137. Kelsey to Horace M. Albright, November 1, 12, and 23, 1932.
138. Arno Cammerer to Kelsey, November 22, 1932.
139. Philip W. Ayres to Harlan P. Kelsey, November 21, 1932.
140. Robert S. McElvaine, *The Great Depression.*

141. Expansion of the National Park Service in the 1930s: Administrative History. Chapter Two: Reorganization of Park Administration. C. Reorganization of 1933. National Park Service. www.nps.gov.
142. Ibid.
143. Ibid.
144. Anne Mitchell Whisnant, *Super-Scenic Motorway: A Blue Ridge Parkway History* (Chapel Hill, NC: University of North Carolina Press, 2006), 53.
145. Ibid., 45.
146. *Arno B. Cammerer*. Cornelius Amory Pugsley Gold Medal Award, 1938. www.rpts.tamu.edu.
147. Whisnant, *Super-Scenic Motorway*, 35.
148. Expansion of the National Park Service in the 1930s: Administrative History. Chapter Four: New Initiatives in the Field of Recreation and Recreational Area Development. J. National Parkways. National Park Service. www.nps.gov.
149. Office of the Vermont Secretary of State. Vermont State Archives, www.vermont-archives.org, accessed June 7, 2006.
150. Kelsey to Colonel H. J. Benchoff, July 16, 1936, Woodstock, VA.
151. Professor Harold L. Cole and Professor Lee E. Ohanian, "How Government Prolonged the Depression," *Wall Street Journal*, February 2, 2009.
152. *The DeVoe Report* 30, no. 24 (November 7, 2008).
153. Seth L. Kelsey to Hon. Robert Wolcott, January 21, 1947.
154. "Warren H. Manning," Wikipedia.org, accessed February 11, 2009.
155. White, *A Century of Service*, 50–55.
156. Ibid.
157. Hurricane data selected from three Internet sources: (Wikipedia.org; pbs.org/wgbh/amex; southstation.org.)

Chapter 7: Unfinished Business

158. Letter to E. I. Farrington, Editor, *Horticulture*, April 19, 1940.
159. Letter to J. Horace McFarland, February 24, 1939. Marked "Confidential."
160. Edwin J. Stark to Harlan P. Kelsey, July 17, 1942.
161. Robert Pyle to Harlan P. Kelsey, July 29, 1942, attaching a proposed resolution by Mike Cashman at the AAN convention at Kansas City, July 23, 1942.
162. Richard P. White to Harlan P. Kelsey, September 14, 1942.
163. Harlan P. Kelsey to W. A. Dayton, March 1943.
164. W. A. Dayton to Harlan P. Kelsey, December 30, 1942.
165. W. A. Dayton, Letter to the Editor, *Journal of Forestry* 40, no. 11 (November 1942).

166. Texas A&M University website. http://www.rpts.tamu.edu/Pugsley/Cammerer.htm.
167. Kelsey to Frederick A. Delano, November 21, 1941, and to Robert Pyle, November 25, 1941.
168. Kelsey to Arno H. Nehrling, June 16, 1942, and to Edwin J. Stark, July 15, 1942.
169. Kelsey to C. Russell Mason, December 23, 1942.
170. Kelsey to J. Horace McFarland, January 8, 1943.
171. Kelsey to J. Horace McFarland, June 9, 1944.
172. Pencil note from Kelsey files in H. P. Kelsey's hand.
173. Miles Tager, *Grandfather Mountain—A Profile* (Boone, NC: Parkway Publishers, 1999), viii.
174. Harlan P. Kelsey, *Grandfather Mountain, Shall It be Saved?* (Planning and Civic Comment, April 1944), 59.
175. Wolfe, *Son of the Wilderness*, 277.
176. Melville B. Anderson, "The Conversation of John Muir," *American Museum Journal* 15 (March 1915): 116–21.
177. Ibid., 89.
178. Hugh MacRae to Kelsey, March 6, 1942.
179. Hugh MacRae to Kelsey, March 2, 1942.
180. Whisnant, *Super-Scenic Motorway*, 280.
181. Based on comments made to the author by Kelsey's grandchildren.
182. Hugh Morton, *Hugh Morton's North Carolina* (Chapel Hill, NC: University of North Carolina Press, 2003), vii.
183. R. Gregg Cherry, Governor, to Kelsey, April 16, 1945.
184. Kelsey to Albright, August 1, 1947.
185. Hugh Morton and Edward L. Rankin, *Making a Difference in North Carolina*, 1988.
186. Roderick Frazier Nash, *Wilderness and the American Mind*, 4th ed. (New Haven, CT: Yale University Press, 2001), 139.
187. Whisnant, *Super-Scenic Motorway*, 285–325.
188. Charles A. Goodrum, Library of Congress History and General Research Section. *The History and Development of the National Arboretum* (reprint from the Proceedings of the 75th Annual Convention of the American Association of Nurserymen, 1950).
189. J. Horace McFarland to J. F. Styer, Chairman AAN Plant Nomenclature Committee, May 15, 1945.
190. Robert W. Hess to Harlan P. Kelsey, June 25, 1946; H. P. Kelsey to Robert W. Hess, July 8, 1946.
191. J. Horace McFarland to H. P. Kelsey, September 30, 1947.
192. White, *A Century of Service*, 127.

Chapter 8: Legacy

193. Kelsey to Frederic P. Lee, July 1, 1948.
194. Kelsey to Edward P. Moses, February 25, 1935, Chapel Hill, NC.
195. Nash, *Wilderness and the American Mind*, 129–31.
196. *Save Our Mountains*, 1–4.
197. *Webster's II New College Dictionary*, 3rd ed. (Boston: Houghton Mifflin, 2005.)
198. *Friends of Great Smoky Mountains National Park* (a production of Great Divide Pictures, 1999).
199. Horace Marden Albright, Harlan Page Kelsey (1872–1958) Obituary, *National Parks* (February 1959). "Mr. Albright was a trustee of the National Parks Association. His twenty years of national park administration—including ten years as superintendent of Yellowstone National Park—eminently qualify him to tell of Mr. Kelsey's contributions to the field."
200. "John Muir," summations are from lists in *Wikipedia*, http://en.wikipedia.org/wiki/John_Muir (accessed April 7, 2012).

Epilogue

201. The 1965 narrative is based on the author's recollection of conversations with Seth Kelsey at the time of the events described.
202. Clipping from the *Salem Evening News*, Salem, MA, February 4, 1965.
203. Clipping from the *Lawrence Eagle Tribune*, Lawrence, MA, undated.
204. Jody E. Cross and Nedda E. Moqtaderi, *A Landscape History of Mt. Cuba*. (unpublished manuscript, January 2004), 108.
205. Horace M. Albright, second director of the National Park Service, "Harlan Page Kelsey (1872–1958)," *National Parks* (February 1959), 12.

Index

A

AAN. *See* American Association of Nurserymen
AASHTO. *See* American Association of State Highway and Transportation Officials
Abbott, Stan, 528, 537–41, 569
Act 243 (1937), 380
An Act to Establish a National Park Service (1916), 229
Adventures in the Wilderness: or, Camp-Life in the Adirondacks (Murray), 131
Albright, Horace M., 217, 229, 317, 323–24, 343–44, 345–46, 352, 355, 360, 490, 493, 509, 511–12, 515, 564
AMC. *See* Appalachian Mountain Club
American Alpine Club, 215
American Association of Nurserymen (AAN), 21–22, 194–205, 208, 349, 416, 432–33
  1925 address to, 27
  advertising, 196
  Certificate of Appreciation to Harlan Kelsey, 205
American Association of State Highway and Transportation Officials (AASHTO), 527
American Board of Orthodontics, 27
American Civic Association, 227, 348, 358, 410
American Forests, 525, 528, 557
American Horticultural Council, 565
American Joint Committee on Horticultural Nomenclature, 181, 183, 431–32, 547–48
  1923 edition, 93
American Nurseryman, 346–47, 426, 548
American Pomological Society, 18
American Society of Landscape Architects, 317–18
"America's Greatest Garden," 24
Andrews, A. Piatt, 394
Animals, plants and, 531
"Annual Handbook of Native American Plants," 80
Anthony, Craig, 582
Apostle Islands National Park Committee, 323
Appalachian Mountain Club (AMC), 96, 360
  establishment of, 105–8
  national parks and, 213–17
  report from Harlan Kelsey in 1934, 372–74
Appalachian National Parks Association, Inc., 261
Appalachian Trail, 217–26
Appleton, Mr., 395–96
Arborways, 522–46
Arnold Arboretum, 337, 433
  description of, 148
  founding of, 23–24
  Harvard University and, 24

letters from Harlan Kelsey, 147–48
proposed letter from C. S. Sargent to Harlan Kelsey, 99–100
Arthur, John Preston, 67
Asheville Citizen-Times, 459, 560–61
Associated Charities of Salem, Mass, 120
Avery, Myron, 219–22
Ayres, Philip W., 107, 128, 353–54, 384
Azalea, 85, 92

B
Bailey, L. H., 183, 185
Bald, Gregory, 357
Ball, George A., 493
Barclay, Lorne W., 355
Barnes, Phineas, 297
Bartholomew, Mr., 520
Bascom, H. M., 28, 48, 59
Batchelder, Harry, 396
Batchelder, Samuel F., 336–37
Bates, Mayor George J., 398–99, 401–2
Bell, Thomas M., 236
Benchoff, Colonel, 404
Bennett, J. L., 167
Benschoff, Co., 269
Berckmans, P. J., 23
Better Homes and Gardens, 332
Beyond the Hundredth Meridian (Stegner), 291
Biltmore Estate, 81, 150
Bird, Governor, 260
Black Tuesday, 313–14
Blood, Charles, 213–14
Blue Ridge Enterprise, 57
The Blue Ridge Highlands of Western North Carolina, 29
Boardman, A. J., 400, 401
Board of Aldermen, 119
Bobbink, L. C., 350
Bonsall, Marshall K., 34–35
Bop. *See* Kelsey, Harlan Page
Boston Directory, 101
Boston Evening Record, 160

Boston Evening Transcript, 107, 109, 337
Boston Globe, 337
Botany, achievements of Dr. Thomas Grant Harbison in, 55
Boucher, Phillip, 582
Boundary Waters Canoe Area Wilderness (BWCAW), 330–31
Bowers, Dr. C. G., 347
Boxford Literary Society, 144–46
Boxford Nursery, 144–50
  1912–13 catalogs, 146
  in the 1920s, 299, 310–11
  photograph of installation, 304
Boxford Village, 143–44
Boynton, Charlie, 89
Boynton, C. W., 48
Boynton, Frank E., 88–89
Boy Scouts of America, 104
Brooks, Katherine, 160–61
Brown-tail moth, 137
Brundage, H. W., 63
Bureau of Forestry, creation in 1901, 133
Burlington Free Press, 380–81
Burns, Ken, 560
Butcher, Devereux, 502
Butler, Ovid, 525
BWCAW. *See* Boundary Waters Canoe Area Wilderness
Byrd, Governor, 269

C
Cambridge Tribune, 336–37
Cammerer, Arno B., 267, 270, 273, 276, 279–80, 315, 318–19, 325–27, 353, 364, 390, 425, 453–70, 466, 561–62. *See also* Mount Cammerer
  death of, 455
  relationship with Harlan Kelsey, 470
Camp brothers, 94
Cannon, Joseph, 130
Carolina hemlock, 86, 100–101
Carr, Professor and Mrs. Ezra Slocum, 207

Carson, Will E., 455
CCC. *See* Civilian Conservation Corps
Century Magazine, 556
Chamberlain, Allen, 107–8, 128–34, 213, 353–54, 379
Chapman, Col. David C., 231, 237, 251, 455, 464, 561
Charivari, 41
Chatelain, Dr. Verne E., 391–92, 394
Cherokee Indians, 3
Civic Improvement League of Marion, 123
Civic League of Salem, 118
Civilian Conservation Corps (CCC), 367
Civil War, 9–10, 30–31, 62, 69
Clark, Albert, 57
Cleaveland, W. B., 49
Cleveland, President Grover, 72–73, 208
Clingman, General, 12
Clon, 436–37
Cobb, Jessamine, 55
Cobb, John, 55
Coe, Ernest F., 318–20
Collins, Charles J., 154
Colman, Norman J., 23
Committee on Community Planning—AIA, 218–19
Conservation, 128–34, 292–95
Conservation Award, 509
Cope, Robert F., 500
Copeland, Lammot, 577
Copeland, Pamela, 577
Cornelius Amory Pugsley Gold Medal Award, 453
Corning, Howard, 392
Cosmos Club, 224–25, 291–92
Costich, E. H., 446–48
Council on National Parks, Forests, and Wild Life, 233
Country Life in America, 230–31
Coville, Dr. Frederick V., 186, 275, 347–48, 348–49, 358, 430, 521
  death in 1937, 430
Cox, Professor Laure D., 369

Coxey's Army, 73
Crampton-Vanderberg Bill, 328–29
Cranberry, 61–63
Cranberry Iron & Coal Company, 62
Crane, Richard T., Jr., 115
Curley, Governor, 401
Cutter, R. Ammi, 382–84

D

Dadswell, Dr., 547
Daniel Low & Co., 108–9
Darwin, Charles, 71–72
Daughters of the American Revolution, 297
Davidge, Miss, 38
Davis, Burke, 505–6
Davis, Franklin, 23
Davis, Mr. and Mrs. Willis P., 231
Davis, Rebecca Harding, 36–46, 454
Davis, Richard Harding, 28
Davis, W. P., 237, 269, 286, 322
Dawson, Jackson, 336
Dayton, William A., 434–35, 451, 548–49
DCR. *See* Department of Conservation and Recreation
Debs, Eugene, 73
DE&F. *See* Department of Exploration and Forestry
Deforestation, 94–95
DeLaMare, 192–93
Demaray, A. E., 504, 521–22, 535–38
Department of Conservation and Recreation (DCR), 414
Department of Exploration and Forestry (DE&F), 128
Derby, Captain Richard, 388
Derby, Elias, 114, 388
Detwiler, S. B., 292–93
Devils Tower, 227
DeVoe, Raymond, Jr., 408
Dictionary of Plant Names (Van Wijk), 182
Dirr, Michael A., 551

Distilleries, moonshine wars and, 36–46
Douglas, Robert, 23
Downing, A. J., 23, 347
Downing, Charles, 23
Drury, Newton B., 455, 463–64, 488, 527, 561
"Dry Falls," 8
Dugger, Shepherd H., 69, 94–95, 500
Dutton, Clarence, 291

E

"Eagle Rock," 116
Eakin, Ross, 455
East Tennessee & Western North Carolina Railroad, 62
Edmunds, J. Rayner, 107
E. H. Camp & Company, 73
Eisenhower, President Dwight, 526–27
Elisha Mitchell Scientific Society, 51
Endicott, Gov. John, 143
Endicott, William C., 394–95
Engle, Reed L., 230, 253
ERAM Project #XS-A1-U1, 410
Ervin, Joe W., 497
Esch Bill, 217
Etheridge, R. Bruce, 488–89
Executive Order 6166, 363–64
Exotic plants versus native plants, 524–25
E. Y. & John C. Teas, 23

F

Faben, E. J., 156
Farrington, E. J., 89, 409
Fay, Charles, 106
Fay, W. M., 370–71, 374, 377
Faye, Professor Charles E., 215
FDR. *See* Roosevelt, President Franklin Delano
Federal-Aid Highways Acts
  1938, 526–27
  1944, 526–27
  1954, 545–46
Federal Highway Administration, 545
Federal Plant Quarantine Act (1912), 199
Federal Water Power Act (1920), 217
Federation of Women's Clubs, 231–32
Felton, W. S., 401
Fernald, Senator Bert, 174–75
Fink, Paul M., 221
Fisher, Walter L., 227
Fitzgerald, W. T., 288
Fletcher, Katy Robbins, 78, 178, 581
Fletcher, Laurence, 503
Florists Exchange, 333
Ford, Tom, 44
F. P. Moore & Co., 64
Frick, Henry Clay, 115–16
Friday, William, 499

G

Galax leaves, 90, 91
The Gardening World, 82–83
Garland, Joseph E., 102–3, 116
Garside, Frank T., 340
Geological Survey, 233
George Robert White Medal, 409
Gerber, John P., 106, 128–34
Gifford, Joe, 396
Gilbert, Dr., 340–41
Girl Scouts of America, 104
Gleason, Herbert, 288
Goerch, Carl, 503
"Gold Coast," 114–20
"Gold Panic" of 1869, 10, 76
Grandfather Mountain, 474–519
  during the Hugh Morton years, 499–519
  during the MacRae years, 479–99
  map of, 491
  Park Association, 492–93
  photographs, 475–76
Grandfather Mountain, Shall It be Saved (H. Kelsey), 474, 477
Grandfather Mountain—A Profile (Tager), 474

Grant, President Ulysses S., 226
Graves, Douglas Nelson, 162, 332
Gray, Asa, 71–72, 87, 88
"The Greatest Health and Pleasure Resort in the United States. The Most Perfect Climatic Sanitarium in the World," 58
Great Smoky Mountains Conservation Association, 322
Great Smoky Mountains National Park, 225–26, 454–57, 466, 558–59
Greensfelder, Mr., 528
Green Thumb, 547–48
Greenville, South Carolina, 150
  proposal from Harlan Kelsey, 124–26
Gregg, William C., 233, 255–56, 279, 290, 314, 316
  photograph, vi
Guild, Irving T., 117–20
Gypsy moth, 137

H
Hahn, Wallace, 63
Hall, Frannie, 583
Haney, Susannah, 582
Harbison, Dr. Thomas Grant, 50–56, 120
  photograph, 52
  scientific achievements of, 55
  Shaffner on, 53
  thousand mile walk, 52
Harding, John H., 410
Hardy American Rhododendrons, Kalmias, Azaleas and Other Rare Ericiceae (H. Kelsey), 114
Harris, Senator, 236
Harrison, President, 132
Harvard Magazine, 87
Harvard University
  Arnold Arboretum and, 24
  herbarium, 72
Hatfield, T. D., 336
HAW. *See* Home for Aged Women
Haywood, Clarke, 583

H.B. 142, 399–401
Heinz, H. J., 115
Herrick, Mary Abby, 144
Hess, Robert W., 547
Hetch Hetchy, 132–34, 208, 278, 515–16, 557
Higginson, Major Henry Lee, 102–3, 104
Highlands
  arrival of city folk, 47–50
  chamber music in, 49
  description in 1883, 46–47
  first piano in, 49
  founding in 1875, 42–46
  war with the Moccasins, 42–46
Highlands, North Carolina: A Walk into the Past (McIntosh), 11–12
Highlands Academy, 54
Highlands Directory, 58
Highlands Library, 50
Highlands Nursery, 178–79
  1902 catalog of plants, 89–92
  1925 catalog, 92
  1930 catalog, 93
  1932 catalog, 305
  advertisement for, 26–27
  article about, 80
  bankruptcy, 404–9
  business, 134–38
  establishment of, 69
  expansion, 69–72
  map, 309
  move in 1897–98, 97
  promotions, 80
  staff photo montage (1931), 308
Hillborn, Mr., 350
Hillenmeyer, W. W., 298
Hodges, Colonel, 260
Hodges, Mrs. J. Clarence, 59
Holbrook, Tom, 583
Home for Aged Women (HAW), 396–99
Homer, A. F., 10
Hoopes Bros., 22
Hoover, J. Edgar, 403–4

Hoover, President Herbert, 313–14, 341, 358, 359–60
Hope, Bob, 499
Horticulture
  during the 1930s, 404–20
  during the 1940s, 426–28
  arborways, 522–27
  boxed trees ready to ship, 307
  business of, 404–9
  hurricane and, 421–25
  large specimen trees, 306
  roadside, 522–27
Horticulture Magazine, 89, 409, 424, 430–32
Hortus, 551
House Beautiful, 194
House Committee on Public Lands, 328
Houses and Happenings on a Boxford Plain (F. Kelsey), 144–45
Houston, John, 28
Hovey, Charles M., 23
H.R. 6670, 392
H.R. 10934, 394
Huber, W. L., 278
Hugh Morton's North Carolina (Morton), 478, 499
Hurricane, 421–25
Hussey, J. Fred, 293
Hussey, John A., 534
Hutchinson, Clinton Carter, 12–13, 20, 77
  in 1875, 7–9
Hutchinson, Kansas, founding in 1875, 11

I
Ickes, Harold L., 361–62, 364, 528–29
Isle Royale Protective Association, 328

J
Jack, J. G., 337
Jackson, Mr., 16
Jail, 39–40

James, Alexander, Jr., 504, 505
James, Harlean, 358
James and Samuel C. Moon, 22
James Veitch & Sons, Ltd., 149
Jenks, Charlie, in 1875, 7–9
J. Horace McFarland Company, 190–91
John Schroeder Lumber Company, 324
Johnson, Robert Underwood, 213, 556–57
Jones, Arthur B., 154
Jones Bill, 217
Judd, William, 339

K
Kansas State Horticultural Society, 18
Kelsey, Florence, 144–46
Kelsey, Harlan Page
  in 1875, 8
  1894 speech, 83–85
  in 1925, 21–22
  in the 1940s, 429–552
  on army cantonments, 172–73
  award from AAN in 1940, 553
  bankruptcy and, 404–9
  business strategy in Boston, 101–5
  Certificate of Appreciation from the American Association of Nurserymen, 205
  as chairman of the "Committee of 100," 158
  on childhood and horticulture, 19–27
  childhood of, 21–27
  citation from the American Horticultural Council (1954), 565
  conservation activities, 128–34
  Conservation Medal (1946), 563
  eulogy by Horace Marsden Albright, 564
  family environment, 46–47
  on fishing, 273–74
  formal and horticultural education of, 25–26
  George Robert White Medal of Honor, 563

on Highlands Nursery, 70–71
honorary doctorate of science (1948), 523, 564
horticultural award from the University of Massachusetts (1956), 566
involvement with Old Derby Wharf project, 385–404
on irrigation and water issues, 216–17
landscape architecture, 138–41
as leader in national park development, 2
as leader in native plants for American landscape, 554–55
lifetime credits of, 562–64
Linville and, 69
map of compound—house/office/arboretum, 310
marriage to Florence Low, 113–14
on membership in the Appalachian Mountain Club, 214–15
on mountain folk, 34–35
nursery business, 134–38
parallels to John Muir, 207–9, 556–64
photographs of, vi, 49, 103, 127
posthumous honors, 568–71
as preservationist, 381
as President of the American Association of Nurserymen, 194–95
as President of the Appalachian Mountain Club, 213–17
as President of the New England Nurserymen's Association, 165–70
Professor Harbison and, 50–56
proposal to City of Greenville, South Carolina, 124–26
proposed letter from C. S. Sargent to, 99–100
recognition during the 1940s, 426–28
relationship with Arno Cammerer, 470
report to Appalachian Mountain Club in 1934, 372–74
reputation for plant introductions, 351–52

role in horticulture business bankruptcy, 404–9
role in national parkways, 367–81
as secretary of the American Joint Committee on Horticultural Nomenclature, 184–94
testimonial, 428
tribute to, 409
as Trustee of the Massachusetts Horticultural Society, 332
during World War II, 471–73
Kelsey, Harlan Page, Jr., 117, 312
Kelsey, Harry, 27, 141
career in orthodontics, 59
death of, 473
letters from Harlan Kelsey in 1936, 405–7
Kelsey, Harry E., 89
Kelsey, Jane, 117
Kelsey, Katherine, 117
Kelsey, Katy, 7, 20
letter from her parents in 1883, 46–47
Kelsey, Polly, 473
Kelsey, Reno, 14
Kelsey, Samuel Truman (STK), 105, 162, 176–77
in 1875, 7–9
advertisement for Highlands Nursery by, 26–27
childhood and horticulture, 19–27
death of, 176–77
diary entries
  1875, 12–14, 16–18
  1876, 29–31
  1879, 18
household of, 20
on Linville, 63–66
memorial tablet, 312–13
obituary, 59
photograph, 15
similarities to Muir, 20
Kelsey, Seth Low, 117, 312, 409, 575–80, 582
Kelsey, Truman, 30, 59, 141

605

Kelsey Airport, 306
Kelsey and Guild, formation of, 117–20
Kelsey Highlands Nursery, 77–82
  Plant America Award (1955), 574–75
Kephart, Horace, 454, 560
Killam, Chester, 292, 297
King, Edward, 8

L

Laderoute, Linda, 581
Lamora, 323
Landscape architecture, 138–41, 574–75
Laney, C. C., 350
Lantz, Christian, 396
Law 770-1/2 (1936), 528–29
LeCron, J. D., 434
Leduc, Mrs. Polly, 37
Legislation
  Act 243 (1937), 380
  An Act to Establish a National Park Service (1916), 229
  for conservation, 128–34
  conveyance of Kentucky land to the National Park Service, 314–15
  Crampton-Vanderberg Bill, 328–29
  Esch Bill, 217
  Executive Order 6166, 363–64
  Federal-Aid Highways Acts (1938; 1944; 1954), 526–27, 545–46
  Federal Plant Quarantine Act (1912), 199
  Federal Water Power Act (1920), 217
  H.B. 142, 399–401
  H.R. 6670, 392
  H.R. 10934, 394
  Jones Bill, 217
  Law 770-1/2 (1936), 528–29
  Mississippi State Act, 545
  for pests and plant diseases, 136–38
  Public Bill No. 437, 252–53
  Revenue Act of 1932, 341
  S. 2073, 392

  Selective Service Act (1917), 171
  Shenandoah Bill (1928), 284–85
  on shipping plant material, 199–204
  Smoot-Hawley Tariff Act, 321–22
  Temple Bill, 254, 255
  Weeks Act (1911), 106, 129–30, 133, 256, 353
  Yosemite Act of 1890, 556
Lend-Lease Program, 470
Lenoir, Col. W. W., 64, 65, 66
Lenoir, T. B., 67
Leucothoe Sprays, 90, 91
Lincoln, President Abraham, 226–27
Linville, 63–72
  founding, 63–66
  industrial center, 68
  Linville: A Mountain Home for 100 Years, 62–63
Linville Company, 481–99
Linville Improvement Company, 64, 73–75, 179
Linville Land, Manufacturing and Mining Company, 67
Linville Litigation, 66–70
Literary Society, 49
Living Wilderness, 463, 561
Locke, Dr., 579
Long Trail News, 375–76
Lovin Brothers, 64
Low, Daniel, 108, 141–42
Low, Dr. Harry, 142
Low, Florence, 108–14
  letters from Harlan Kelsey, 109–10
  marriage to Harlan Kelsey, 113–14
  photograph of, 112
Low, Seth F., 142
Low, S. Fred, 142
Lumber industry, 255–87, 334, 494–95
  railroads and, 93–96
The Lure of the Great Smokies (Mason), 355

M

MacArthur, General, 499
Macdonald, M. Q., 201, 275
MacKaye, Benton, 218, 223–24
MacRae, Donald, 65–66, 479–99
MacRae, Hugh, 483–84
MacRae, Nelson, 481–82
Magee, E. E., 51
Mammoth Cave National Park, 231–32, 264–67, 314–15
Manning, Jacob W., 22
Manning, Warren H., 410, 411–12
Manual of Woody Landscape Plants (Dirr), 551
Maps
 of Grandfather Mountain, 491
 of Kelsey compound—house/office/arboretum, 310
 of Kelsey-Highlands Nursery, 1929, 309
 Nantahala National Forest, 32
Marlatt, Dr. C. L., 199
Marshall, Chet, 416–17
Marshall, Robert, 229
Mason, Robert Lindsay, 355, 357–58, 381, 514, 560
Massachusetts Horticultural Society, 332, 333
Mather, Stephen T., 217, 229, 232–33, 270, 290
Matthes, Francois, 225
May, John B., 379–80, 413
McBeth, Thomas A., 405
McCall, F. A. A., 434–35
McClelland, E. H., 450
McDonald, Andrew H., 170
McDowell, Colonel Silas, 12, 22
McFarland, John Horace, 120–23, 181, 184–85, 227–28, 261, 329–30, 333, 348, 359, 430
McGill, Deborah, 583
McGinley, Mrs. Holden, 334–35
McIntosh, Gertrude Vogt, 11–12, 30
 on arrival of city folk in Highlands, 47–50
 on Linville, 65

McKinney, A. D., 25–26
McKinney, John "Dock," 28
McMillan, James, 115
Meikle, Miss, 439–40, 443
"Menominee Indian Project," 330
Merrill, Dr. E. D., 433
Merrill, Nancy, 584
"Message to Salem Citizens," 118
Messer, Richard, 172
Michaux, Andre, 88
Mile High Swinging Bridge, 518
Mississippi River National Parkway—Arborway
 Volume I, 541–43
 Volume II, 543–44
Mississippi River Parkway Survey (MRPS), 527–46
Mississippi State Act, 545
Mitchell, Henry, 142
Mitchell Society, 55
Moccasin, war with the Highlands, 42–46
Moonshine wars, 36–46
Moore, Barrington, 233
Moore, William H., 16, 115
Morehead, John M., 503
Morganton Herald, 63
Morley, Margaret W., 33–34
Morrison, B. Y., 435–36, 521
Morton, Hugh, 498, 499–519
Morton, Julian W., 488–89, 491, 494
Mountain folk, 32–35
Mount Cammerer, 453–70. *See also* Cammerer, Arno B.
 photograph, 462
Mount Chapman, 459–60
MRP Commission, 529–30
MRPS. *See* Mississippi River Parkway Survey
Muir, John, 176, 180–81, 477, 515–16, 552, 554
 awards, 1
 conservation and, 131–32
 death in 1914, 228

as founder of national parks in the East, 1–2
parallels to Harlan Kelsey, 207–9, 556–64
similarities to Kelsey, 20
Mulloney, D. H., 320–21
Munson, T. V., 23
Murray, William H. H., 131
Myopia Hunt Club, 115

N

Nantahala National Forest map, 32
National Arboretum (Washington, DC), 520–21
National Nurseryman, 83–85, 135–36
National parks, 226–32
  effects of politics on, 354–67
  entrances to, 316–17
  financing, 276–78, 281–82, 286–87
  irrigation and water issues, 216–17
  requirements for Congress to consider, 247–48
The National Parks—America's Best Idea (Burns), 560
National Park Service, 217, 317–31
  during the 1930s, 360–67
  conveyance of Kentucky land to, 314–15
  guidelines, 267–69
National Parks magazine, 230, 495–96, 502
National parkways, 367–81
National Register of Historic Places, 297
Native Americans, 330–31
Native plants, 134–38, 531–33
  versus exotics, 524–25
  introductions to, 85–93
  promotion, 82–85
  quarantine issues, 137–38
Nature, 106
Naylor, Hugh, 241–42
New Deal, 361–62, 366–67, 404
New England Nurserymen's Association, 165–70

New Holland, North Carolina, 161–65
New Holland Farms, Inc., 162, 163–65
New York Times, 28, 138–39, 263, 372
New York Tribune, 557
Niles, William, 106
Nolan, John, 369, 371, 374
North Carolina Conservation and Development Commission, 502
North Carolina Farms Company, 163–65
North Carolina Park Commission, 314–17
North Shore, 108–14

O

Oakes, Helen Hart, 194
Oastler, Dr. Frank R., 328
Oberholtzer, Ernest C., 323
O'Brien, Dan, 156
Ochs, Adolph S., 263
Office of National Parks, Buildings, and Reservations, 363
The Official Code of Standardized Plant Names, 185–86
Ogden, Mrs. Ansel R., 59
O'Gorman, V., 87
Old Derby Wharf, 385–404
Olmsted, Frederick Law, 81, 216, 234, 288, 317, 430, 554
  creation of nursery, 81–82
Olmsted, Frederick Law, Jr., 171
Ottawa Indians, 9
Ottawa University, 9
Overland Monthly, 557

P

Packard, Winthrop, 413
Palisades Interstate Park Commission, 233
Pardee, Ario, 62
Parelle, Haliard De La, 203–4
Parker, Thomas F., 63, 66, 75

Parks & Recreation, 409
Parkways, 367–81
Parris, John, 42–46
Partridge, William, 48
Peabody, Dean, 371
Pearl Harbor, 471
Peavey, Congressman, 324
Penland, Mrs., 79
Perkins, Arthur, 219–20
Perkins, Ben, 61–62
Perkins, Jake, 61–62
Perkins, Joshua, 61–62
Perry, Erin, 583
Perry, Marsden, 138
Petersburg Cantonment, 172–73
Phillips, James Duncan, 387–88, 392, 400
Phillips, Rev. Mr., 143
Pickering, Edward, 213
Pierce, Charlie, 421–22
Pinchot, Gifford, 132, 133–34, 207–8
Pineola nursery, 79–80
 photograph, 79
Pinkshell azalea, 86
Pitman, J. A., 389, 397
Planning and Civil Commitment, 496, 570
Plants. *See also Standardized Plant Names: A Catalogue of Approved Scientific and Common Names of Plants in American Commerce*
 animals and, 531
 biotic balance of, 520
 climate and, 102
 clon, 436–37
 common names of, 93, 433–35
 legislation on shipping plant material, 199–204
 nomenclature, 546–52
 pests and plant diseases, 136–38
 preservation of, 208
 scientific names of, 93
 sustained productiveness, 533
Plymouth Record, 384

Pollock, George Freeman, 239, 241, 242–46, 342
Pomona Project, 10, 76
Powell, John Wesley, 291
Pratt, Colonel, 236
Pratt, Dr. Joseph, 250–52, 477–78
Pricip, Gavrilo, 171
Prince, Fredrick H., 115
Prince, William, 23
Pritchard, Senator, 230–31
Pryor, William T., 530
Public Bill No. 437, 252–53
Public Works Administration (PWA), 366–67, 403
PWA. *See* Public Works Administration
Pyle, Robert, 414–15, 417–18, 420, 520

Q
Quetico Superior Project, 330, 331

R
Railroads, 67–68
 lumber industry and, 93–96
Ravenel, S. P., 48, 63, 65, 479
Ravenel, Marguerite A., 312–13
Raymond, Loren A., 517
Red cedars, 140–41
Rehder, Dr. Alfred, 433
Reps, Professor Emeritus John W., 120
Revenue Act of 1932, 341
Reynolds, Harris, 340, 365
R. Harris & Co., 109
Rhoades, Verne, 334
Ricksecker, Katy, 9
Ricksecker, Margaret Mowvy, 584
Ritter, William T., 94
Robb, Gordon, 298–99
Robbins, Edward Culby, 77–79, 135, 141, 145, 177–78, 581
 photograph, 78
Robbins, Edward Page, 77–78, 178

Rockefeller, John D., Jr., 115, 234, 286, 510
Roosevelt, President Franklin Delano (FDR), 342, 358, 359, 360–61, 499, 562
Roosevelt, President Theodore, 133, 227
Rouse, Henry C., 115
Rowe, Mr., 443

S

S. 2073, 392
Salem, Massachusetts
  city planning, 120–27, 150–53
  Civic League of, 118
  "Committee of 100," 158, 159
  fire in 1914, 153–58
  history of, 114–15
  housing, 152–53
  neighborhood committee, 159–60
  nursery business, 292–95
  Planning Board establishment, 154
  rebuilding after the fire, 158–61
  shipping industry and, 114–15
Salem Evening News, 108–9, 141–42, 333, 388–89
The Salem Fire (Jones), 154
Salem Maritime National Historic Site, 403, 563–64
Salkovich, Reuben, 154–55
Samuel Parsons, 22–23
Samuel T. Freeman and Company, 407
San Francisco Bulletin, 557
SANPC. *See* Southern Appalachian National Park Commission
Sargent, Charles Sprague, 24–25, 72, 88, 132, 165–66, 477
  1925, 22–25
  as founder of Arnold Arboretum, 23–24
  proposed letter to Harlan Kelsey, 99–100
Sawyer, Mary Barnes, 299
Scanlon, Mayor, 157

Schmeckebier, L. F., 225
Scribner's Monthly, 8
Selective Service Act (1917), 171
Senger, Professor J. H., 213
Seyler, H. G., 419
Shade Trees, 119
Shaffner, Randolph P., 28, 53, 581
Sharpe, Bill, 88–89
Shenandoah Bill (1928), 284–85
Shenandoah National Park, 403–4
Shepard, Harvey N., 164–65
Sheppard, R. M., 179, 498
Sheridan, Charles M., 323
Sherman, David M., 221
Shipping industry, 114–15
Shreve, Mrs. Benjamin D., 386–87
Sierra Club, 208, 213, 554
  founding in 1892, 131–32
Silcox, F. A., 434
Sizemore, Charles, 196–97
Skinner, I. M., 48
Small, Edwin, W., 402–3, 564, 570
Smith, Col. Glen S., 233, 246–47, 258, 315
  photograph, vi
Smith, J. J., 48
Smoot-Hawley Tariff Act, 321–22
Society for the Preservation of New Hampshire Forests (SPNHF), 107, 128, 390–91
Society of American Florists and Ornamental Horticulturalists, 346
Sorrs & Harrison, 23
Southern Appalachian National Park Commission (SANPC), 258–59, 318
Southern Appalachian National Park Committee
  establishment of, 232–55
  photograph, vi
Southern Land Reclamation Company, 162
Southland magazine, 34–35
Spelman, Harold J., 535–36

SPN. *See Standardized Plant Names: A Catalogue of Approved Scientific and Common Names of Plants in American Commerce (SPN)*
SPNHF. *See* Society for the Preservation of New Hampshire Forests
Spofford, Benjamin, 297–98
Spofford, Lydia Warren Barnard Wood, 297
Spofford, Sally, 207
Spofford Barnes House, 297–314
  on National Register of Historic Places, 297–98
  photograph of complex—house/office/arboretum, 303
  photographs of barn, 300, 301
  photographs of house, 300, 302
Squire, Senator Mark, 257–58, 285, 464–65
Standard Cyclopedia of Horticulture (Bailey), 183, 185
Standardized Plant Names: A Catalogue of Approved Scientific and Common Names of Plants in American Commerce (SPN), 93, 181–94, 557. *See also* Plants
  1941 revision, 429–53
  copyright issue, 549–50
  proposed revision in the 1930s, 346–52, 415
  sales flyer, 189
  title page, 188
Stannard, F. H., 23
Stark, Edwin J., 449
State magazine, 503
Stegner, Wallace, 291–92
Stein, Clarence S., 218–19
Stewart, Henry, 28
S. T. Kelsey & Son, 30
Storrow, James J., 104
Stout, A. B., 437–38
Strickland, Mr., 411
Styer, J. F., 546–47

Super-Scenic Motorway: A Blue Ridge Parkway History (Whisnant), 516–17
Sutton, S. B., 24–25
Swift, Edwin Carleton, 115
"Swiftmoore," 115

T

Tager, Miles, 474
Teague, John, 16
"Temperance City," 10
Temple, Henry W., 233, 246–47, 258–59, 262–63, 315, 512–13
  photograph, vi
Temple Bill, 254
  wording of, 255
Thomas, Ellwanger & Barry, 22
Thomas C. Thurlow, 23
Thomas Meehan, 22
Thurlow, W. H., 410–11
Tree Name Committee, 445
Tropical Woods, 547
Tropic Everglades Park Association, 318
Tucker, Fred H., 375
Twentieth Century Club, 105
Tyler, H. W., 355

U

U-boats, 471
Underhill, Robert L. M., 379
"A Unique Collection—the Highland Nursery," 80
United States
  Congress, 132–33, 247–48, 359, 368, 393–94, 497
  depression of 1893–96, 72
  depression of 1929, 164, 331–45, 404–9
  economy in the 1930s, 331–45, 404–9
  election of 1892, 72–73
  New Deal, 361–62, 366–67, 404
  post–World War I recession, 175–76
  World War I, 171–76, 470
  World War II, 448, 470–71, 470–73

US Department of Agriculture, 349, 433
US Interstate Highway System, 545–46
US Juniata, 322–23

V

Van Deman, H. E., 23
Vanderbilt, George, 81, 150
Van Melle, P. J., 346–47
Van Tol, Cornelius P., 420, 422–23
Van Wijk, Gerty, 182

W

Walcott, Robert, 409
Walker, Governor, 236
Walsh, Governor, 157
War of 1812, 114–15
Washburn Times, 323
Watauga Valley News, 80, 81, 83
Watson, John, 351–52
Webb, Colonel Charles A., 455, 560–61
Weeks Act (1911), 106, 129–30, 133, 256, 353
Weems, Sam, 511, 569
Welch, Ed, 351
Welch, Maj. W. A., 225, 233
Welsh, photograph, vi
Wentworth, Franklin H., 154
Wharton, Mr., 494–95
Whetstone, John H., 10, 76
Whisnant, Anne Mitchell, 516–17
Whitaker, Charles Harris, 218–19
White, Richard P., 102, 427, 449, 550–51, 553
White, T. Baxter, 28, 48
White, Elias, 25–26
White Mountain National Forest, 106–7, 381–85
White Mountains National Park, 352–54
White Rock, 457–58
Wilber, Secretary of the Interior, 355–56, 514

Wilbur, Ray Lyman, 2, 344–46
Wilder, Marshall P., 23
Wilderness Society, 323
Wilson, Governor, 379–80
Wilson, President Woodrow, 132, 157, 171, 229
Winant, John G., 382
Winthrop, John, 143
Wirth, Conrad L., 455–57, 527–28
Wirth, Theodore, 427
Wofford, George T., 358
Wood, Aaron, 297–98, 578–79
Wood, Laura, 583
Woods, Mrs. C. A., 123
Work, Hubert, 232–33, 234–35, 266, 284, 468–70
Works Progress Administration (WPA), 400–401
World's Fair (Chicago, 1893), 72–73
World War I, 171–76, 470
World War II, 448, 470–73
  Lend-Lease Program, 470
  Pearl Harbor, 471
  U-boats, 471
  VE Day, 473
WPA. *See* Works Progress Administration
Wyman, Dr. Donald, 433, 438–39

Y

Yard, Robert Sterling, 279, 464–65, 561
Yellowstone National Park, 216–17
  creation of, 226–27
  protection of, 229–30, 287–90
York, Samuel A., 398–404
Yosemite Act of 1890, 556
Young, John, 167–69
Young, Robert C., 166–67, 169–70
Youngken, Dr. Heber W., 349

Z

Zoellner, Louis, 48

Made in United States
North Haven, CT
15 October 2021